SIXTY SUMMERS

PETER COX

Published by Labatie Books
www.sixtysummers.co.uk

Project management and editing by the Cambridge Editorial Partnership
Design by Paul Barrett Book Production, Cambridge
Printed by Piggott Black Bear, Cambridge

ISBN   0-9551877-0-2
       978-0-9551877-0-4

To the woman whose left-arm fast bowling terrorised her younger
brothers, and to the man who 20 years later upbraided me with
these words: 'Peter, I didn't bring you all this way so you could sit
in the tent and read Wisden.'

Acknowledgements

I would like to thank those willing friends who read the manuscript as it
evolved and offered such constructive criticism: John Cooper, Greg Howard,
Patrick McNeill, Mike McHugh, Roger Riddell and Sheelagh Alabaster. Ros
Horton and Sally Simmons of the Cambridge Editorial Partnership, and
designer Paul Barrett, have been equally helpful, as well as painstaking and
long-suffering, and any remaining infelicities of style and convention are
entirely mine. To Stephen Chalke, who blazed a self-publishing trail, I owe a
debt of gratitude for his early and continuing encouragement, as I do to Raman
Subba Row. Of those I have consulted I'd like to mention in particular Tony
Borrington, Donald Carr, John Carr, Vanburn Holder, Roger Mann, Peter
Wright and Peter Wynne-Thomas; David Paton of Nottingham University for
his work on recent county attendances; and Peter Cameron for his and his
team's website expertise. Finally, Trevor Jones at the Oval library was assiduous
in his support over many months.

Contents

Tables and graphs

Test Series and World Cups

England v Australia
1946–7, 17–18
1948, 21–4
1950–1, 29–30
1953, 38–41
1954–5, 43–6
1956, 49–52
1958–9, 59–60
1961, 68–70
1962–3, 72–3
1964, 83–4
1965–6, 87
1968, 92–3
1970–1, 113–5
1972, 117–9
1974–5, 130–1
1975, 140–1
1976–7 144–5
1977, 153–4
1978–9, 158–9
1979–80, 161–2
1980, 164
1981, 165–8
1982–3, 178–80
1985, 197–8
1986–7, 201–3
1987–8, 207
1989, 209–11
1990–1, 222–4
1993, 248–50
1994–5, 254–6
1997, 272–5
1998–9, 278–9
2001, 296–7
2002–3, 301–3
2005, 334–40

England v Bangladesh
2003–4, 316–7
2005, 334

England v India
1946, 17
1951–2, 36–7
1952, 37–8
1959, 65–6
1961–2, 70–1
1963–4, 82–3
1967, 89
1971, 116–7
1972–3, 125–6
1974, 129
1976–7, 143–4
1979, 160–1

1979–80, 162
1981–2, 175
1982, 176–7
1984–5, 196–7
1986, 200
1990, 221–2
1992–3, 247
1996, 269
2001–2, 298
2002, 300–1

England v New Zealand
1946–7, 18
1949, 25–6
1950–1, 30
1954–5, 46
1958, 54–5
1958–9, 65
1962–3, 72–3
1965, 85
1969, 110–1
1970–1, 115
1973, 126
1974–5, 132
1977–8, 155–6
1978, 157
1983, 181–2
1983–4, 182–3
1986, 200–1
1987–8, 207
1990, 220–1
1991–2, 226–7
1994, 252–3
1996–7, 271–2
1999, 281–2
2001–2, 298–9
2004, 320–1

England v Pakistan
1954, 43
1961–2, 70–1
1962, 71
1967, 89–90
1968–9, 109
1971, 115–6
1972–3, 125–6
1974, 129–30
1977–8, 154–5
1978, 156–7
1982, 177–8
1983–4, 183–4
1987, 203–4
1987–8, 205–7

1992, 229–31
1996, 270
2000–1, 294
2001, 295–6

England v Rest of the World
1970, 111–3

England v South Africa
1947, 19–20
1948–9, 24–5
1951, 36
1955, 48–9
1956–7, 52–3
1960, 67–8
1964–5, 84–5
1965, 85–7
1994, 253–4
1995–6, 258–60
1998, 276–7
1999–2000, 290–1
2003, 315–6
2004–5, 323–6

England v Sri Lanka
1981–2, 176
1984, 185
1988, 209
1991, 226
1992–3, 247–8
1998, 278
2000–1, 294–5
2002, 300
2003–4, 317–8

England v West Indies
1947–8, 20–1
1950, 26–9
1953–4, 41–3
1957, 53–4
1959–60, 66–7
1963, 81–2
1966, 87–9
1967–8, 90–2
1969, 109–10
1973, 126–7
1973–4, 127–9
1976, 141–3
1980, 163–4
1980–1, 164–5
1984, 184–5

1985–6, 199
1988, 207–9
1989–90, 219–220
1991, 224–6
1993–4, 250–2
1995, 256–8
1997–8, 275–6
2000, 292–3
2003–4, 318–20
2004, 321–3

England v Zimbabwe
1996–7, 270–1
2000, 291–2
2003, 314–5

World Cup Finals
1975, 139–40
1979, 159–60
1983, 180–1
1987, 204–5
1992, 227–9
1996, 260–2
1999, 280–1
2003, 312–4

Preface

A policeman tries helplessly to stem the tide as spectators rush across the ground after England's Ashes victory at the Oval in August 1953.

'Cricket is a wonderfully civilised act of warfare.'

HAROLD PINTER

Imagine a time-travelling spectator, plucked from post-war England to watch a day-night match 60 years later. He would happen on a strange scene, and it would take him a while to get orientated. While the grass is still green, the familiar cricket colours have been transformed into some negative image. Dark-clad umpires walk out onto a field where the pitch, still – blessed relief – 22 yards, is book-ended by black stumps, framed by black sightscreens, and surrounded by a circle of white dots. Fielders trot on in coloured clothing with names and numbers on their backs, followed by helmeted and much-padded batsmen, their height their only differentiator. The bowlers use a white ball: disconcerting at first, but gratifyingly easier to see than the old dark red one. The bowling at least is familiar. Despite the preponderance of faster bowlers, each side will usually play one or two slower bowlers, even though none is a wrist-spinner. Everything is hustle. The batting is audacious, the ball aloft more often than it ever used to be. The running between the wickets seems frenetic, while the fielding – diving, sliding, stopping, catching, throwing – is breathtaking. With luck, the same sun shines, but is augmented even in mid-afternoon by floodlights that take over as night falls on a gripping climax. Bemused, our spectator walks home in moonlight.

Take a spectator who has seen England, backs to the wall, grind out a slow defensive series against Australia in 1953, and eventually regain the Ashes at a packed Oval for the first time for nearly 20 years. Tell him that over 50 years later, at an even more animated Oval, an England team will be battling to save a game to regain those Ashes after another gap of nearly 20 years. Tell him that a cricketer, wearing a diamond ear stud and with hair like a skunk's, will save his (adopted) country with a maiden Test century, an innings containing more sixes than anyone has hit for England against Australia before. He will think you're mad. Tell him that England scored nearly twice as many runs an over as their predecessors had in 1953, and he will know you are.

The idea for this book came as I watched a live day-night match for the first time, at Hove in 2003. What would someone like my grandfather, who played his first cricket in the Edwardian era, and watched his last in the post-war years, make of that game and the great Oval climax of 2005? How could I explain it to him, explain how the bat v ball balance has shifted to and fro like a kind of arms race? How, after the war, bowlers went from the pre-war classic off-side attack over to the leg-side, then, thwarted by fielding restrictions, and encouraged by change to the lbw law, progressively reverted to the off? How some fast bowlers threw and dragged until changes in the law prevented them, then directed their attack at the batsmen's head? How leg-spinners in England became a vanished species, while off-spinners and slow left-armers have now dwindled in turn? Why? Wickets before the war were supposedly too good, when they weren't spiteful after rain. After the war pitches were allowed, even encouraged, to deteriorate. Now they're fully covered and arguably too good again. Batsmen, once suspicious and crabby, awoken by the demands of the new one-day cricket, invented the first new strokes to appear since Ranji's 'heathen' leg glance. They hit 'on the up', with bats up to a pound heavier. Fast bowlers swing the ball mystifyingly the 'wrong' way, and spinners turn apparent off-breaks from the leg, the first such invention since Bosanquet's bamboozling googly of a century earlier. Fielding has improved immensely, largely under one-day cricket's influence. Field-placing has become more 'scientific'. Fields are changed more often, and fielding sides under the cosh take longer and longer to bowl their overs. Twenty overs an hour in first-class pre-war cricket dropped to 15 and below, despite exhortation and fines, and now cricketing days start earlier and end later to compensate. Has the longer reflective game been pushed off the road by the one-day bandwagon? Has one-day cricket surfeit led to obesity? We now have Twenty20, a game little longer than a football match. Whatever next?

I looked for answers in the bookshops. I found many books that told me some of the answers, but none told me all of them. Moreover, while there were histories of every other nation's cricket, there was a curious gap in England's case. While several histories had been written over the years, none was in print, and none was quite what I wanted. So I decided to write the book that I wanted to read. It would tell the story of the England team since the war. It would describe those first stumbling years after 1946, when fast bowlers could not be found for love nor money; the great renaissance of the next decade up to its controversial ending; the long years since then of increasingly isolated peaks amid a succession of troughs; and the ultimate great revival of 2004–5. At intervals I would break off from this narrative to explore the game's changes as they emerged.

I chose the period after the war because it covers the lifetime of my oldest readers. The title, *Sixty Summers*, refers to the number of summers of cricket in England since the end of World War 2, and I chose it not least because 2005 would be my own six-tieth summer. I could not have asked for a better summer to finish with, as the book-shops have since loudly proclaimed. So here it is. I end it after the Ashes series is over; you will read it after a hard winter on the subcontinent when England's resurgence has been seriously tested – nothing stands still.

While looking at intervals at how the domestic game in England develops, the book concentrates largely on the performance of the England Test team and its place in world cricket. And although I look at every World Cup, the innumerable one-day series I leave to another writer. In Henry Blofeld's words: 'We can all remember what happened in the Test matches, but, my dear old thing, who on earth can remember what went on in all those one-dayers?'

I begin by going back to the last week of 1939, before Test and county cricket was abruptly ended for seven years by the war. Late that August, a West Indies team that included George Headley and Learie Constantine was about to take the boat home across an increasingly dangerous Atlantic, and Len Hutton's and Hedley Verity's Yorkshire was pushing for its third county title in a row. Now read on …

Peter Cox
London
January 2006

CHAPTER 1

Prologue – Cricketers at War

Early portents of war – outside Lord's before the MCC v West Indies game, May 1939.

I shall always remember that match. It seemed like a strange dream.
There were the big elms throwing grave shadows on the English grass,
the wild roses in the hedges, the lazy caw of a rook passing overhead, the
old village in the distance, and the quiet sound of bat on ball; then came a
sudden vision, as real as the other, of a 5000 ton ship heeling over with
pathetic black figures scrambling up her tilting deck.

BILL EDRICH

August 1939

In 2005 the Ashes series ended on 12 September, although the county cricketer laboured on for another fortnight. The England team had played seven Test matches, ten one-day matches and an inaugural Twenty20. Their predecessors in 1939 had only to play in three Tests of three days each. Their opponents were the West Indies, whom they beat 1–0, despite the efforts of the great George Headley, known as the 'Black Bradman', who had made two separate hundreds at Lord's in a losing cause. Their chief attraction though was the effervescent Learie Constantine, the ultimate combination of hostile fast bowler, thrilling hitter and electrifying fielder. At the Oval on the morning of 22 August, the last day of the series, Constantine thrashed the England opening attack for 79 in 50 minutes, the ball flying chaotically to all parts. At one stage on the previous day, eccentrically, Len Hutton and Denis Compton were bowling, and 'it was as if all the long hops and full tosses in the world were being simultaneously released'. Thus wrote the delightful R. C. Robertson Glasgow in the 1940 Wisden, published in the eighth month of World War 2, to console a populace starved of its cricket.

In the previous August, the coming war had been presaged for long enough for Constantine to write that his team left the Oval 'with newspapers in our hands and the match already forgotten, and the great silver balloons catching the last sunlit rays as the world beneath darkened steadily into chaos and war'. Here in England we would be confronting bombing raids, but the tourists had to get back to the Caribbean across an Atlantic likely to be infested with U-boats. They made hurried arrangements and left on a nerve-racking journey from Glasgow to Montreal, and thence down through the US home.

Their final matches had been cancelled. For the West Indians there was no Guinness-sampling tour of Ireland to enjoy, no festival matches at Scarborough or Hastings, where their opponents could relax in front of holiday crowds and try to complete their season's 1000 runs, or 100 wickets, or both. The county season was due to end in the last week of August, after a treadmill of up to 32 three-day games, Saturday to Tuesday with Sunday off, then Wednesday to Friday. Back then, some of the professionals at the end of the season would be displaced by amateurs, often schoolmasters, coming in to play for the county in their August holidays.

The last week

As August drew to its close, the news from Downing Street became progressively more disturbing, but the last week of county cricket went on, with England players well to the fore. Yorkshire needed to win their last two games to make sure of their third successive championship, and only Middlesex could stop them. On Saturday 26 August their England left-arm spinner Hedley Verity bowled Hampshire on their way to defeat with 6–22, while at Lord's against Surrey the young Bill Edrich and Jack Robertson scored hundreds, as they would again next match. But Middlesex couldn't force a win over Surrey, and so ceded the title. On that Saturday, Gloucester's England captain Wally Hammond made a typically masterly 153, and the Glamorgan secretary-captain Maurice Turnbull an ebullient 156. They were old hands, but the crisis proffered chances for newcomers. The Kent keeper Hopper Levett had been called up for the Territorial Army, so at Dover a cheeky 17-year-old apprentice car mechanic called Godfrey Evans was called in to deputise, and 'kept wicket especially well' that day to the awkward quick leg-spinner Doug Wright.

The writing was visible on the wall of the barrage-ballooned Oval when it was requisitioned, so Surrey's last home game with Lancashire on Wednesday 30 August was switched to Old Trafford. But that last set of games did go ahead. Down at Hove the prospect of cancellation would have disturbed one Sussex man – Jim Parks, father of the England post-war wicketkeeper-batsman, who had chosen this last home match with Yorkshire for his Benefit. After two future England captains, Len Hutton and Norman Yardley, had made centuries, the match was evenly poised after two days. But during the night of 31 August Germany invaded Poland, Chamberlain had issued his hapless warning, and the inexorable countdown to war had begun.

In view of the crisis the games at Old Trafford and elsewhere were abandoned, but play at Hove went into its last day, 1 September. There, on a wicket made spiteful by overnight rain, Verity bowled out Sussex for 33 in under 12 overs, with the startling figures of 7–9. No relaxation from Yorkshiremen then, no beneficiary's single to get off the mark: Verity had poor Parks lbw for nought. (Perhaps to be charitable he was given one in the first innings – he made just two.) Verity was as devastating that morning as when he had destroyed Australia so famously on a wet wicket at Lord's in 1934. He had dismissed Don Bradman twice, taking 14 wickets in a day, just a year after he had taken an amazing 17 in a day at Leyton. Clearly England's best spinner in the 1930s, he already had 144 wickets from 40 Tests. When that first day in September he bowled Sussex's Billy Griffith, the future MCC Secretary, he had taken his 1965th first-class wicket in just 10 years. Griffith's wicket would be his last.

In that Yorkshire side was Bill Bowes, tall and bespectacled. England were as chronically short of good pace bowlers in the late 1930s as they would prove to be after the war, but the best pairing was Bowes and Ken Farnes. Even taller than Bowes, Farnes was able to extract awkward lift from a good length in the way Joel Garner and Curtly Ambrose were to do for the great post-war West Indies teams. Farnes was now a full-time schoolmaster, so he could turn out for Essex only as an amateur in the school holidays. In that last week he took 6–47 at Clacton, one of those seaside grounds now lost to the county scene. He and Bowes would not bowl together again.

War was declared by Chamberlain on the following Sunday, 3 September, and all further games were abandoned. In England cricket bags were packed, bats oiled and put away. Lord's excepted, many of the major grounds were requisitioned. Although the Oval was never actually used as intended as a prisoner of war camp, it did contain anti-aircraft batteries, and was in a terrible mess when the groundsman Bert Lock started sorting it out late in 1945, importing 45 000 turves from Hoo Marshes. Old

Trafford was taken over by the Army and was later bombed. So that they couldn't be used for enemy landings, all the grounds had to be littered with obstacles, only removed before a rare wartime game.

To war

Cricketers of course were able-bodied young men and almost all would work directly for the war effort in some form or another, as flyers and soldiers and seamen, firewatchers and wardens and miners. Although most of the more than 300 first-class cricketers pitched up in the Forces, it was a minority who saw action. In many cases the military used professional sportsmen as PT instructors, which kept them fit, away from the front, and playing as much friendly cricket as they could. For some reason it was largely the batsmen, like Cyril Washbrook, Willie Watson and Len Hutton, who spent their time in the gym. Hutton was unlucky, on the face of it. Scorer of that monumental 364 at the Oval in 1938, he was actually undergoing commando training in March 1941, when a mat slipped from under him. As his group later went on the disastrous Dieppe Raid of the following year, this was probably a blessing in disguise. A very good disguise, though: he fractured his left forearm badly and dislocated the ulna, had successive bone grafts patched in from both legs, sealed with 45 stitches, and he wouldn't play again until April 1943. With his left arm now over two inches shorter than his right, he would have to completely remodel his technique. After the war he rarely hooked. But you could say that at least his courage, and the fierce determination that had brought him the world Test record 364 in 1938, was not lost but reinforced.

Of the young players who would go on to play for England after the war, Alec Bedser, together with his identical twin Eric, joined the RAF police and went to France. In those fraught early days they were lucky to escape being hit by the tracer bullets that whistled between them at the airfield at Merville in Belgium. Probably that was the only thing that did come between them in the war years. Though they had only played a few games for Surrey in 1939, their unmistakeable physique and looks enabled them to be spotted and picked up by a Surrey member as they trudged back towards Boulogne in 1940 with the Germans hard behind. Another Surrey man would be evacuated later, at Dunkirk. Major Douglas Jardine, reviled by Australians everywhere for his steely resolve in introducing and refusing to abandon bodyline bowling in 1932–3, came back on HMS *Verity*. Did he smile and think of Hedley? Later, in Italy on 12 March 1944, the Bedsers found themselves visiting Pompeii at the moment Vesuvius erupted for the first time since 1906, and subsequently they described evacuating local people as a 25–30 foot wall of red earth advanced on them. In due course both were recommended for promotion to Warrant Officer. Had they both accepted they would have been split up, so they tossed for it. Eric won, Alec declined his promotion, and they shared the pay increase as they shared everything, and as they still do. One of the little incidental stories that emerge from war, oddly affecting.

Bill Edrich

War was most dangerous for the flyers. Two pilots who survived the war – on the same side until the Victory series of 1945 – were Bill Edrich and the young Australian Keith Miller. Miller arrived in England in 1942 and flew Mosquitoes with the RAF. He survived intact until the end of the war, when the starboard engine of a plane he had taken up for a spin caught fire. He cut the engine and doused the fire, but the landing was somewhat untidy. He took a nagging back injury with him as he limped away, but it didn't stop him arriving like a meteor on the cricket scene in the Victory Tests.

The Middlesex all-rounder Bill Edrich joined up as soon as he could and piloted bombers. Like most flyers who survived he led a charmed life. On one occasion his rear gunner had run out of ammunition with a Messerschmitt on his tail. But so too had the attacking pilot, who in exasperation flew round Edrich's plane, shrugged, gave him a thumbs up, waved and departed. In one crucial raid in August 1941, Edrich as acting squadron leader led a section of the 54 bombers that attacked power stations near Cologne. It was one of the first major daylight raids into Germany, and won him the Distinguished Flying Cross. Flying as ever in his tattered England sweater, Edrich and his crew hedge-hopped their bomber across Europe and back, finding as much danger in the flocks of geese and ducks in the Scheldt estuary as in the anti-aircraft fire. Twelve of the 54 aircraft weren't so lucky, and failed to return.

Most of their activity was against enemy shipping in the channel. Edrich described these low-level raids as being carried at about 250mph at mast level. They flew a mere 10 to 20 feet above the waves straight at the target ship, before climbing steeply to project their bombs at its side. He was based at Little Massingham in Norfolk, home county of the prolific run-getting Edrich clan. One such raid happened on the morning of a cricket match due to take place in the grounds of Massingham Hall: Edrich had promised to turn out for the local squire if he could. On the way back from the raid their section of three was chased by Messerschmitts, and one of his fellow bombers was shot down into the sea. Nonetheless Edrich made it to the match, rattled up a rapid 80, and retired to the long grass to muse.

> 'I shall always remember that match. It seemed like a strange dream. There were the big elms throwing grave shadows on the English grass, the wild roses in the hedges, the lazy caw of a rook passing overhead, the old village in the distance, and the quiet sound of bat on ball; then came a sudden vision, as real as the other, of a 5000 ton ship heeling over with pathetic black figures scrambling up her tilting deck. Every now and then would come the old, accustomed cry – 'Owzat?!' – and then my mind would flicker off to the morning's briefing and to joking to a pal whose broken body was now washing in the long, cold tides...'

Think of that next time you play in a rural village on a Sunday afternoon. Of all the cricketers whose careers bracketed the war, and who wrote memoirs, few voiced any deep feelings about what they had seen and done, preferring a few laconic words in passing from under a stiff upper lip. Edrich's lyrical piece is pretty much the closest we get.

Cricket in England was run by the Marylebone Cricket Club, the MCC, then as now a private club. They didn't do as much as the football authorities to keep the sport going during the war – it took a while for a viewpoint of 'we shouldn't be seen playing cricket when our young men are playing a Greater Game' to be replaced by one that encouraged games to cheer wartime spirit. Still, there were a few matches at Lord's each summer. In one game there in 1941, Edrich walked to the wicket to a standing ovation because the crowd knew he had just been awarded his DFC. Soon he was back to the same applause after being caught brilliantly in the deep by his Middlesex mate Denis Compton, of all people. After the war the two would become nearly as inseparable as the Bedsers.

Denis Compton

Actually Compton saw no action, but plenty of cricket. Moreover, he was a brilliant footballer as well. Naturally – indeed only – left-footed, he was a dribbling left-winger of the old school, at his best like Stanley Matthews on the right. He and Matthews were on the wings when England destroyed Scotland at Maine Road in 1944, laying on five of the goals in an 8–0 win, in a game containing players who would become some of the great post-war managers. Stan Cullis was England captain and centre-half, and Tommy Lawton was centre-forward. Compton wasn't as pinpoint a crosser as Matthews – this was the match in which Lawton (think of Shearer) is famously supposed to have asked Matthews politely, after one bullet header had found the net, to deliver his crosses with the ball's laces facing away from him. In those days centre-forwards looked rugged with good reason. You might suppose that Scotland must have had a poor side out that day, but the half-backs were Bill Shankly and Matt Busby of blessed memory, and I can't imagine they took many prisoners.

Compton was a good enough footballer to score the equaliser in the wartime Cup Final of 1941 for Arsenal against Preston North End at Wembley, to win a first division championship medal with Arsenal in 1948 to go with his Middlesex championship the previous summer, and to play in the 1950 Cup Final against Liverpool with his wicketkeeping big brother. Les was a tall and uncomplicated centre-half in the Jack Charlton mould. Recalled for the 1950 semi-final against Chelsea at White Hart Lane, with 13 minutes to go and Arsenal behind, Denis forced a corner and called his brother up from the back. Captain Joe Mercer waved him back angrily, but they both ignored him, and Les duly scored with a header. Arsenal won the replay, and Compton played in the final even though by his own admission he was nearer 14 stone than his summer 12, and far from fit – at half time he said he was 'blowing like a stranded whale'. No subs back then, of course, but Alex James, legend of Arsenal legends, slipped him a glass of brandy and he lasted the game, doubtless celebrating in his usual fashion way into the night.

Compton stories are legion. You might wonder why you're reading about wartime football in a book about post-war cricket, but it illustrates that playing both games at the top level was entirely possible back then if you were good enough. Compton had joined the Lord's ground staff at 14, played his first games for Arsenal and Middlesex at 18, and cricket for England at 19. He joined the army and saw the world, if no action. Promoted sergeant major in 1943, he was in pre-partition India at the end of the war training their officers (including General Zia, later ruler of Pakistan). There, bizarrely, he played in the Ranji trophy final for Holkar against Bombay, where he ran out of partners with his score 249 in the fourth innings, chasing a mere 863 to win.

Compton found himself playing for East Zone at the end of 1945 against an Australian Services team that included Keith Miller, and his not-out hundred in the second innings was instrumental in the Australians' two-wicket defeat. Against a background of fierce campaigning for Indian independence, the atmosphere was incendiary, and at one point when Compton was batting rioters invaded the pitch. (Miller to Compton: 'There's only one Pom in the ground and you start a bloody riot.') One beflagged rioter came up to Compton and said, 'You very good man Mr Compton but you must go.' This later became a refrain for Miller, spoken in a Peter Sellers' Indian accent whenever he decided Compton had been at the crease too long. There can have been no more intense rivalry and friendship in cricket than theirs. I wrote these lines a few weeks after Miller's death. At Compton's funeral he had said: 'Denis and I were like brothers... no, we weren't, we were soulmates.' They drank, bet, played cards, and generally raised hell together. They used hand signals to communicate racing results from balcony to field in Tests, and they were the core of the Anglo-Australian card school that included Edrich, Evans and Ray Lindwall.

Some did not return

Bill Edrich managed to survive his tour of duty, and retired to train younger pilots. Other cricketing pilots weren't so lucky. Ken Farnes trained to be a night-flyer but misjudged a landing during his training and died in the wreckage. Peter Eckersley was an MP and a pre-war Lancashire captain, restless and reckless, who sometimes flew to county matches in his own plane. He died in another wartime flying accident. George Macaulay, the much loved Yorkshire bowler who played eight Tests and took over 1800 wickets, and who had been in the artillery in World War 1, volunteered for the RAF at the age of 43 in 1940. He never came back from a bombing raid. Squadron Leaders Winlaw and Ashton died on the same mission late in 1942; Charles Ashton of Essex had been a triple blue at Cambridge and an amateur football international. A few months later Squadron Leader F. G. H. Chalk of Kent died, a rear gunner who had retrained to fly Spitfires. His county captain G. B. Legge, who had made 196 in a Test in New Zealand, died at sea. Maurice Turnbull, Glamorgan's inspirational captain, had been one of the great all-rounders – he played cricket for England, rugby and hockey for Wales, and became South Wales squash rackets champion on his days off. They don't make them like that any more. He had taken Glamorgan by the scruff of the neck in the 1930s, and transformed their shambolic cricket on the field, and their even more shambolic finances off it. A major in the Welsh Guards, he was killed by a marksman's bullet in Normandy two months after D-Day.

In World War 1 the death most greatly mourned had been that of Colin Blythe, the legendary and much-loved genius of a left-arm spinner, as highly strung as the violin he played at the day's end, who died in France in 1917. The poignant equivalent in World War 2 would be Hedley Verity, another classical slow left-armer. Not many cricketers took an active interest in the science of war before its outbreak, but it seems Verity saw his future, and read army manuals on the long voyage down to Cape Town to the winter series in South Africa in 1938–9. The image we now have of him is of a tall, thin-moustached man smoking a pipe, not in cricket whites but in an army greatcoat.

Verity, like Norman Yardley, was in North Africa and then in Italy, where Yardley was wounded but survived. On 20 July 1943 Verity's Green Howards mounted a night attack on the Hermann Goering division at Catania in Sicily. He and his men were wriggling through a field of summer corn, under attack from a farmhouse to their left. The corn started to blaze as he led one platoon towards the house, while another attempted to give covering fire. He was hit in the chest – 'Get the Germans out of the farmhouse and me into it' – but was captured. A German military doctor gave him an emergency operation in a farm stable before he was moved with other wounded prisoners in open trucks to the coast, and then across the Straits of Messina. After a painful journey of five days he arrived at Naples on 26 July. The German hospital there was already overflowing with German and Allied wounded, so he was sent to the Italian hospital at Caserta. The hospital's Italian director did his best with a further operation under local anaesthetic to relieve the pressure of a broken rib on his lung. But the attempt was in vain, and Verity died on 31 July. Later, his fellow Yorkshire cricketer Ken Smailes erected a gravestone, and his grave became a place of impromptu pilgrimage for cricketers serving in Italy, such as the Bedsers, before he was moved to a Commonwealth war cemetery.

Prisoners of war

Other cricketers taking part in the invasion of Italy evaded capture. The young Surrey wicketkeeper Arthur McIntyre, hit by shrapnel at the Anzio beachhead, trekked across country to find his mates the Bedsers, and caught up with them in Bari. 'Mac' became a PT instructor at a convalescent camp near Salerno, where he met and played with Jim Parks's Sussex brother Harry, and with Tom Dollery. Dollery would become the first professional captain of Warwickshire and steer them to a famous championship win in 1951. Other cricketers were already in Italy, but their cricket was rather more restricted. Bill Bowes, who had joined up with Verity, was captured in Tobruk in June 1942. Among 20 000 others held in North Africa was Surrey's Freddie Brown, who had won the MBE helping in the dangerous evacuation of Crete. The two of them proceeded on a prison camp tour of Italy, where the weather and camp cricket were distinctly better than in the German camps in which these once-brawny men finished the war, Bowes three stone and Brown over four stone lighter. Norman Yardley was in Italy at the same time, where he had been wounded at the beginning of 1944.

While the Allies were fighting their way up through Italy, and prisoners were creating ersatz cricket in the German and Italian camps, the same thing was going on in the Far East. Among the prisoners there were Wilf Wooller, another Welsh rugby international, who would become the fiercely partisan post-war Glamorgan cricket captain, and a Middlesex man who later played for him, Sergeant Len Muncer. Both would help complete Turnbull's work in Glamorgan's unlikely first championship win in 1948. The South African Test cricketers Catterall, Wade and Mann were also in Japanese camps, as were the Australians Ben Barnett and D. K. Carmody, after whom the famous Australian post-war array of slip-fielders was named. Many were in the infamous camps on the Burma railroad.

One minor cricketer there, who had turned out for Middlesex as an amateur a few times before the war and would later turn his hand to writing, was E. W. Swanton, forever Jim. Organising entertainment was tougher under the notoriously brutal regimen of the Japanese camps, but there was a bowdlerised form of cricket played. In the first post-war Wisden, Swanton described matches at Wampo on Christmas Day 1942 and at the hospital camp of Nakom Patom on New Year's Day 1945. There an Australia v England match was played on a patch of concrete pitched lengthways 60 yards by 30 – small, but not inappropriate for their debilitated state. No runs could be scored behind the wicket, where the eager spectators massed and pressed, the batsman standing in front of five thin bamboo stumps with a three pound wooden bat and facing a tight-bound cloth ball. Over the fence was not six and out, but nought and out. Balls were in short supply.

The Japanese war came to an abrupt end, amazingly so to the prisoners in the Far East. Seven days later Swanton, another prisoner who found himself over four stone lighter, was taking his first walk as a free man, with him the much-patched 1940 Wisden that had been his companion in the camps. He came upon Thai villagers listening to a radio from which English voices emerged. He was astonished to realise that the radio was playing a commentary on the last of the 1945 Victory Tests, hastily organised when the German war was over. Entranced, he heard of an Australian called Cristofani belting the English bowling round Lord's. Cristofani was soon to disappear from sight, but not from memory. And Swanton would soon be back to see how cricket, and England, had changed.

CHAPTER 2

Starting Again but not Afresh

Before a war-damaged Lord's pavilion for England v the Dominions in August 1943 are three post-war England greats: Denis Compton shaking hands, Alec Bedser two to his right, Trevor Bailey second from the end.

The powers-that-were condemned without hesitation all proposals to tamper with the fundamentals of the game, pronounced themselves firmly in favour of three-day matches and against one-day, placing their faith irrevocably in a sound psychological approach to the game, led by captains willing to animate their sides into enterprise.

E.W. SWANTON

Counity cricketers returning after the war might have been aged and altered, but they returned to a familiar round. The only real changes were the abandonment of 1939's one-year experiment of eight-ball overs, and the arrival of a new ball at 55 overs instead of 75. This latter was designed to encourage the missing fast bowlers but in hindsight it seems madness: it only had the effect of allowing Miller and his opening partner Ray Lindwall to come at England relentlessly in the three post-war Ashes series in 1946–7, 1948 and 1950–1, remorselessly and without retaliation in kind. Alec Bedser was stout-hearted, but he swung and cut the ball at a lesser pace and until Trevor Bailey arrived in 1950–1 he was incapable of defending the pass alone.

The boring '30s?

It seems a little puzzling today that many of the ideas that emerged in wartime, when for example much exuberant one-day cricket was played, were promptly shelved when the cricket authorities got together again. The 1930s, in retrospect studded every couple of years with gripping, close-fought, sometimes acrimonious battles for the Ashes – Larwood and Voce, Tate and Verity against Woodfull and Ponsford, Bradman and McCabe; Grimmett and O'Reilly against Hammond and Hutton – were not at the time regarded as halcyon days. The big worry was that the bat v ball balance was tipping inexorably in the batsman's favour. Having prompted a new lbw law, the repercussions of which would still be felt long after the war, this also provoked a grumbling against 'doped' pitches, heavily loamed, which sapped fast bowlers of the will to live. Following England's extraordinary 903–7 in the last Test of the drawn 1938 series against Australia, scene of Len Hutton's immense 364, this reached its nadir in the notorious timeless-yet-unfinished Test in Durban in early 1939.

With both sides stronger in batting than bowling, the final Test was extended to try to ensure a result. When the tenth day began England, after two long days' batting in the fourth innings, were 496–3 in pursuit of a hitherto impossible 696 to win. But rain threatened, and they had reached 654–5 when the heavens opened. However 'timeless' doesn't mean what it says when there's a boat to catch, a long wait until the next one, and the then daunting alternative of several days of flights up the length of Africa. So the game was abandoned as a draw. When I first read of this as a boy I was incredulous, and not a little annoyed, that the chance of such an extraordinary record had been passed up just to catch a wretched boat. I thought, if the scores were level and someone had hit a six, they would have made 700. But the players were mighty weary, and many were barely standing. Robertson-Glasgow again:

> 'The pitches, plumb but without pace, had so far overstepped perfection as to be of little use to the bowler and to impose some inexplicable narcotic on the batsmen. That 30 runs an hour crawl, that grand climacteric of the ten-day Test when the home-bound ship foreclosed on the battle between eight and a half whole Englishmen and seven and three-quarters South Africans still erect upon their legs.'

But 1939 revived his jaded palate. In the 1940 Wisden he wrote that 'the poisonous vapours of dullness and dunce-like inaction... were at last dispersing'. Perhaps Headley and Constantine had helped, and the privations of war had begun to lend enchantment to pre-war cricket. That was before any wartime cricket had begun. It eventually started, slowly, with a few one-day games. The wartime Wisdens provide a scattering of peculiar fixtures. Who knows, for instance, John Betjeman's friendly bombs having spared it, that Slough beat the British Empire on 13 May 1945? Most were one-day, and Lord's in particular drew large crowds. You'd think that someone might have recognised the germ of an idea here.

One such game was between the Army and the RAF in 1944, played on a dull day with thick low cloud. At one point Flying Officer Bob Wyatt was about to bowl to Lieutenant Jack Robertson – another who had been at Dunkirk, now a battle school instructor – when they heard the sound of an engine approaching. The noise intensified, then cut out, a V1 rocket still invisible in the cloud until it emerged in a shallow dive, flying over Lord's and exploding 200 yards away, shattering the pavilion windows. The players had hit the ground, as the famous photograph confirms, but Wyatt and Robertson, bat and ball still in their hands, dusted themselves down and calmly continued where they left off. Robertson promptly pulled the next ball for six.

Could anything better justify the view of the German Institute for Foreign Policy Research, which in 1940 published a series of booklets on the theme 'The British Empire in World Politics'? This was their mystified take on cricket: 'Cricket embraces a thousand attributes which a wretched foreigner neither understands, possesses, nor may aspire to. If the Americans had kept cricket as a national game, the English would not have regarded them as semi-savages.' One of the few untapped speculations on the theme of 'what would have happened had the Germans invaded' is how they would have taken to cricket. Perhaps we just have to be grateful that neither the Third Reich nor the Land of the Free ever seriously adopted it.

Victory games

As the war drew to its close more three-day games were hastily arranged. The climax was the impromptu series arranged after VE day between an English team and one from the Australian Forces. Each side had several men who had played or would play for their countries, with ex-Wing Commander Hammond captaining England, and Warrant Officer Hassett – an NCO, note – captaining Australia. The matches were a huge success, played with a will to win in a friendly, chaffing spirit in front of huge crowds. Fifty thousand came to the second match at Sheffield over three days, 90 000 to Lord's over the four days of the fourth. At Old Trafford, hastily reassembled and redecorated by masses of German POWs paid three-farthings an hour, England won the final match to draw the series 2–2, to everyone's satisfaction, on the day E. W. Swanton heard of Cristofani's hundred in that tiny Thai village.

The scene was set for the final flourish, a game between England and the Dominions, a now archaic expression from the fast-fading twilight of the British

Empire, captained in Hassett's absence – an imaginative gesture by the players themselves – by Learie Constantine. War preparations notwithstanding, in the last week of August in perfect weather 1241 runs were scored in three days for all 40 wickets in 379 overs. Wally Hammond scored two centuries, but Keith Miller upstaged even him with a savage innings of 185. He hit seven sixes, one clattering around the guttering by the broadcasting box. He and the anarchic Constantine added 117 in 45 minutes, and England were to die gloriously in the chase, losing by 41 with eight minutes left, an electrifying run out by Constantine turning the game. In the final innings the Dominions bowled over 100 overs in under four and a half hours, a rate of 23 an hour. The crowd, starved of cricket, was thrilled – none more ecstatic than the doyen of Lord's, Pelham Warner: 'feats of brilliant strokeplay… cricket *in excelsis…* a *joie de vivre* in the batting sparkled through the game'.

Lessons

What lessons were learnt by cricket's administrators? As early as 1940 Sir Home Gordon, a shrewd observer writing in *The Cricketer*, reflected on experiences after World War 1. Then England had rushed into an ill-fated two-day county cricket experiment in 1919, promptly jettisoned in 1920, and its cricketers would be horribly beaten twice by the Australians in eight excruciating months in 1920 and 1921. Gordon accurately predicted that there would be a boom in enthusiasm for cricket once the war was over, but that it would decline, and the training of county colts would have been neglected, a shortfall sapping the strength of the county elevens. Australia would be all-conquering. He even contemplated Sunday play, which would not come for a generation.

In the event the crucial meeting of the Advisory County Cricket Committee (ACCC) came down decisively in favour of a return to three-day county cricket, adulterated only by a possible knockout tournament. This was tried and abandoned in mid-flight in 1946 after a game on a dangerous pitch at Lord's. But it wasn't to be composed of one-day games as we know them, the idea of overs restrictions was not raised, and quite understandably they couldn't think of a satisfactory way of resolving rain-affected games. But their collective heart wasn't in it anyway. They decisively rejected one-day cricket, which suited Robertson-Glasgow: 'The clockwork monkey in the nursery delights for a few hours, but… first-class cricket is a three-act play, not a slapstick turn.' Perhaps it's as well that he is no longer here, now the nursery is overrun by a tribe of clockwork monkeys.

As Swanton put it: 'The powers-that-were condemned without hesitation all proposals to tamper with the fundamentals of the game, pronounced themselves firmly in favour of three-day matches and against one-day, placing their faith irrevocably in a sound psychological approach to the game, led by captains willing to animate their sides into enterprise.' There was a child-like conviction that somehow, in the hands of the right buccaneering amateur, a county side would play what became known as brighter cricket, and constantly risk defeat to gain a glorious victory. Many Wisden

Almanacks in the years after the war contained articles or editorial comment seeking ways to bring back the amateur. But for every Freddie Brown and Wilf Wooller and Stuart Surridge (Surrey's inspirational leader) there were many who wouldn't or couldn't animate a side of professionals whose end-of-season average was all too closely linked in their eyes with the prospect of re-engagement. The game's leaders were all ex-amateur Romantics, who felt that if only the *attitude* was right then the game could still be the same one they had loved when they played it. Much of English cricket's next 30 years could be seen as a struggle between Romance and Reality. Sadly, the two could rarely be reconciled.

The cricketing landscape of 1946

So what was the cricketing landscape that the 300-odd professionals returned to after their eventual demob? Little had changed. The 17 counties played three-day matches that started each Saturday and Wednesday, beginning on 4 May and ending on 3 September – only the resorts of Hastings and Scarborough saw play any later. In contrast, the 2005 season began as early as 8 April and ended on 25 September. The counties played 26 each, at least regularising the pre-war position when sides could play as many matches as they liked, and the result would be decided by percentages. Thus in 1939 Yorkshire had played 30 and the runners-up Middlesex only 25. But that still meant that each county played 10 others twice and six once. The Indian tourists played just three three-day tests against England, 20 county and six other first-class matches. Unless the Australians were here, Test matches were of much lesser import than they are now.

The big occasions at Lord's were more games that harked back to an Edwardian past – Eton v Harrow, Oxford v Cambridge – 15 000 seeing play on the Saturday – and Gentlemen v Players, some 10 000. This last was an attractive fixture when the amateurs were strong, and took on the nature of a Test trial. It often produced exciting matches, and it is one of the few things to miss about the demise of the amateur/professional distinction. Also at Lord's, Tonbridge School beat Clifton by two runs in their traditional two-day game. At 13, the youngest player ever to appear at Lord's made 75 and 44 in a low scoring game, and took 3–58 and 5–59 with leg breaks, getting three successive batsmen stumped in the second innings. As every schoolboy was to learn, Michael Colin Cowdrey had been given the initials 'MCC' by a cricket enthusiast father. Cowdrey did rather better than a 15-year-old had done the previous year, one P. B. H. May, who came to play in the representative Schools games at Lord's with an average of 55 at Charterhouse and a growing reputation, but managed only 0, 0 and 1. Thus was the next generation of amateurs beginning to flex its muscles.

Amateur captains

It's surprising perhaps in retrospect that the amateur cricketer survived so long after World War 2, when class barriers were much less sturdy than they had been a generation earlier, and a war that ended with a Labour election landslide. Post-war England continued with the democratising effects of rationing, a time when – in theory at least – money and privilege could not buy you extra eggs or a length of dress fabric. Indeed, one American commentator described immediate post-war Britain by comparing it with Soviet Russia: drably-clothed people waiting patiently in long queues. Was there still a place for the man with a private income, or generous employers happy to see him swan off for four months playing county cricket?

Well, yes, there was. The end of the cricketing amateur had been predicted during the war, but he survived until 1963. In 1946 every county but Leicestershire – who couldn't find one good enough until the following year – was captained by an amateur, and as late as 1953, Coronation year, only Jack Crapp of Gloucestershire and Tom Dollery of Warwickshire were professional captains. Dollery declined his county's request to change in a room away from his team-mates, as though he were an amateur. In 1946, with wondrous ineptitude, Surrey even managed to invite the wrong Bennett to be captain. Turning up at the Oval in the spring to see if there might be any 2nd XI games that year, Nigel Bennett was amazed to be asked to be 1st XI captain: it was a Leo Bennett whom Surrey had intended to appoint. Bennett was not a success. Wisden recorded with orotund circumlocution that 'his want of knowledge of county cricket presented an unconquerable hindrance to the satisfactory accomplishment of arduous duties'. Probably he was not alone.

The conviction that county captains should be amateurs, almost irrespective of ability, continued long after the war. In 1962, the year before the distinction was abolished, there were still 13 amateur captains, four of whom wouldn't have commanded a place in the side had they not been captain. Three of them were their county's secretary as well as captain, so were paid. Later, professionals came to realise that at least an amateur captain had been more able to protect them from an interfering county committee. At the time, the best argument for their retention was perhaps that, financially independent, they were better placed to represent the players' views to the county authorities. But in 1962 Yorkshire, under a professional (Vic Wilson) beat Worcestershire, led by another (Don Kenyon) into second place at the last gasp. At Kenyon's side was Tom Graveney, a professional who two years earlier had left Gloucestershire after being replaced as captain by the Old Etonian Tom Pugh (batting average 16) and having to spend the Ashes year of 1961 effectively banned from first-class cricket, so difficult was it to leave a county in those days. It was not until 1963 that the position of initials on scorecards lost their arcane meaning: no more would be heard in the land the classic and by no means apocryphal announcement 'on your scorecards F. J. Titmus should read Titmus F. J.'. Initials in front signified an amateur.

But that was a long way off as 1946 began. What would English cricket bring to a weary, rationed populace eager to see cricket again?

CHAPTER 3

The Post-war Struggle 1946–50

Denis Compton hit during his innings of 145* for England v Australia, Old Trafford, July 1948. He had earlier retired hurt after edging a Ray Lindwall no-ball onto his head.

In a period still sore and shabby and rationed, Compton spread his happy favours everywhere. The crowd sat in the sun, liberated from anxiety and privation. The strain of long years of affliction fell from all shoulders as Compton set the ball rolling or speeding or rippling right and left, as he danced forwards or danced backwards, hair tousled beyond the pacifying power of any cream or unguent whatsoever.

NEVILLE CARDUS

1946 India

The lack of organised cricket during the war, of county structure, and of proper training for youngsters coming through, meant that county sides wore a geriatric look in 1946. The average age of the England team that took the field for the first post-war Test was 33. Wally Hammond, the captain, had just turned 43, no longer the colossus he had been, the youngest was Alec Bedser, a fortnight short of his 28th birthday. Bedser, a tireless, broad-shouldered bowler with huge hands, was the find of the season. Too young to make an impact in 1939, now his strength, accuracy and movement gave him 24 wickets in the three-match series, one more than the rest of the England bowling put together. His opening bowling partners included the veterans Bill Bowes, Bill Voce and Alf Gover, all 37 or 38. There was dust and rust: literally at the county grounds and figuratively on their cricketers. But, for all 1946 was a wet summer, crowds were eager to see cricket again. In all not far short of two million people paid to see cricket in England that year. England duly beat weak opposition 1–0 and Yorkshire retained the championship. Superficially little had changed.

India	200 & 275	**England**	428 & 48–0
England	294 & 153–5d	India	170 & 152–9
India	331	England	95–3

With the Tests of only three days' duration – a rather severe reaction to the timeless 1938–9 fiasco – England only had time for one victory, set up at Lord's by a double century from Joe Hardstaff, the elegant Nottinghamshire batsman who had played his first Test in 1935, and Bedser's 11 wickets in his first Test. Another 11 for him at Old Trafford were not enough to force a win in the final three hours available. The rain-ruined third was notable only for Vijay Merchant's innings of 128, and for its end, run out from mid-on by Compton of Arsenal, who kicked the ball onto the stumps.

1946–7 Australia

Despite the precedent of 1920–1, when a debilitated England had been persuaded to tour Australia and lost 5–0, virtually the same thing happened now. The Australians pressed England to tour in 1946–7 and MCC acquiesced, albeit with misgivings. Although Australia had suffered from the war too, with their own prisoners of war coming back from the Japanese front – Lindwall carrying a legacy of dengue fever – they had kept four-day cricket going at home, so they had more young cricketers coming through. For the first Test at Brisbane, where England were slaughtered in stifling heat by an innings and 332, the average age of England's attack was 32 to Australia's 27. In the first two Tests Australia topped 600 and they were only twice bowled out for under 480. Five Australians had better batting averages than the best

Englishman, Hutton, and six bowlers better bowling averages than Yardley, the medium-paced all-rounder who was England's best.

Australia	645	England	141 & 172
England	255 & 371	Australia	659–8d
Australia	365 & 536	England	351 & 310–7
England	460 & 340–8d	Australia	487 & 215–1
England	280 & 186	Australia	253 & 214–5

New Zealand	345–9d	England	265–7

In the first Test no Englishman reached 40, and although Edrich battled in the second with 71 and 119, it wasn't until the third that their batsmen achieved parity, Hutton's opening partner Cyril Washbrook batting most of the last day for 112 to save the game. Washbrook was a small man, a staunch Lancastrian, cap set at a jaunty angle, a great hooker and puller. In the fourth match he and Hutton opened with a century stand in each innings, and Compton made two hundreds. That second Compton century saved the match in company with Evans who, in an unlikely feat of self-denial for a natural attacker, batted 95 minutes before scoring. A win in the last Test would have restored English self-esteem, and England deserved it, but after a courageous 122* on the first day, Hutton came down with tonsillitis and took no further part in the match. Despite magnificent leg-spin bowling by Doug Wright (7–103) a Huttonless England – and with no other bowlers worthy of the name apart from Bedser – couldn't set a stiff enough target in the final innings. A crucial dropped catch when Bradman was only on 2 was England's last chance.

The series was not without controversy. There was no love lost between Hammond, the supreme English batsman of his generation, and his junior by five years, Don Bradman, who since he burst on the scene had eclipsed Hammond in all except the Bodyline tour of 1932–3. The tetchiness between them set the tone for the tour and it didn't help that most of the contentious umpiring decisions, by common consent, went Australia's way. Jack Ikin's celebrated disallowed slip catch early in the first Test (Hammond to Bradman: 'A fine way to start a series') had allowed the Australian captain to escape to 187, which he followed with 234 in the second at Sydney.

Bradman scored 680 runs and Hammond just 168, before fibrositis kept him out of the last Test. Hutton, Compton, Edrich and Cyril Washbrook at least consolidated their reputations, Washbrook establishing himself as Hutton's opening partner, a cross-Pennine alliance that would lead England out for the next five years. But the bowling was woeful – Wright's 23 wickets cost over 40 runs each, and Bedser's 16 over 50, and from this tour on Bedser would continue to be over-bowled. The only real plus was the emergence of Evans behind the stumps. He was a livewire, on and off the field. Quite apart from his brilliant catches, the bowlers said that his endless energy and optimism kept their spirits up long after they had begun to fade.

1947 South Africa

Big crowds had turned up to cricket in Australia to see the English beaten, and when the team returned to face South Africa in 1947, a season of fine weather brought out the English spectators too, even more than in 1946. Over 2.3 million paid for admission to all first-class matches, a figure that did not include members, whose numbers also rocketed. Despite their county suffering its worst season since 1910, Yorkshire's supporters paid to watch over 278 000 times, an average of nearly 7000 a day. Kent's 182 000 was a record, up 57 000 from 1946.

But it was Middlesex who profited most, and above all Compton and Edrich. In an astonishing season of batting records, each broke Tom Hayward's 1906 record of 3518 runs in a season. Compton had already broken it when Middlesex came to the Oval as champion county to play the Rest of England, but made 246 nonetheless. Edrich needed 170 and beat it by 10. Against South Africa, Compton and Edrich scored over 2000 runs between them in all matches, astonishing as it sounds. In retrospect the season was characterised entirely by the pair's delectable batting, always seemingly on long summer days in their contrasting styles: partnerships of 370 in the second Test, 228 in the third, 287 against Surrey, 277 against Leicestershire, 223 against Sussex, 211 against Northants, 210 against the Rest. Moreover they had enough energy to take 140 wickets between them. Of their cricket that year Robertson-Glasgow said:

> 'Compton and Edrich are the mirror of hope and freedom and gaiety... of that happy philosophy which keeps failure in place by laughter, like boys who fall on an ice-slide and rush back to try it again. They seem to be playing not only in front of us and for us, but almost literally with us. We are almost out of breath at the end of an over by Edrich. We scratch our heads perplexedly at a googly from Compton which refuses to work. We smile with something near to self-satisfaction when, with easy vehemence, he persuades a length-ball from the leg stump to the extra cover boundary... Compton uses cover point as a game within a game, tantalises him with delayed direction and vexes him with variety... Compton is poetry, Edrich is prose, robust and clear.'

And Neville Cardus, referring to the Brylcreem Boy, the first advertisers' sporting idol:

> 'In a period still sore and shabby and rationed, Compton spread his happy favours everywhere. The crowd sat in the sun, liberated from anxiety and privation. The strain of long years of affliction fell from all shoulders as Compton set the ball rolling or speeding or rippling right and left, as he danced forwards or danced backwards, hair tousled beyond the pacifying power of any cream or unguent whatsoever.'

England won the series of five four-day Tests 3–0. Only once were they bowled out for under 400, in the first Test at Trent Bridge, but they put it right by scoring 551 to save the match, Compton's 163 and a last wicket stand of 51 putting the game out of South Africa's reach. At Lord's came Compton and Edrich's 370 stand, in 2005 still an England third-wicket record, and Wright won the match with five wickets in each innings. Another 228 together followed at Old Trafford, Edrich augmenting his 213 runs in the match with eight wickets. Headingley was the only place where South Africa's batting really failed, with the Nottinghamshire opening bowler Harold Butler having match figures of 52–24–66–7 in his first Test. Playing for pride at the Oval 3–0 down, South Africa batted magnificently on the last day in pursuing 451 in six and a half hours, which translated then into an amazing 141 overs, more than 21 an hour. Bruce Mitchell added 189* to his first innings 120, but they couldn't quite get there.

South Africa	533 & 166–1	England	208 & 551
England	554–8d & 26–0	South Africa	327 &252
South Africa	339 & 267	**England**	478 & 130–3
South Africa	175 & 184	**England**	317–7d & 470
England	427 & 325–6d	South Africa	302 & 423-7

From today's perspective this series looks like a last throwback to the summer idylls of the 1930s. More than 2400 overs were bowled at nearly 23 an hour, over 600 more than in the comparable South Africa series in 2003, which had a day longer for each Test. Edrich made 552 runs at an average of 110, Compton 753 at 94; next came Washbrook at 49. The indefatigable Edrich, a small man with a muscular, slingy action who had missed the last Test, wound up opening the bowling, and was surprisingly successful with 16 wickets at 23. With Alec Bedser out of sorts, the search for supporting bowlers unearthed Butler and Ken Cranston of Lancashire. In a high-scoring series Cranston took 11 wickets at 17. Were things looking up on the opening bowling front? Spin was largely in the hands of the leg-spinners, Doug Wright taking 19 wickets, and again the bowling was strengthened immeasurably by the cheerful aggression of Godfrey Evans behind the stumps – and moreover his pugnacious batting came at an average of over 40.

1947–8 West Indies

The South Africans weren't strong, but they were always combative, so there was a sense at the end of the season that England were now better prepared to take on the Australians in 1948. But that optimism faded as the winter tour to the West Indies went on. In those days it wasn't mandatory to tour, especially to the then minor countries, and few amateurs could afford to, despite the expenses available. It wasn't just the amateurs though, for – as well as Edrich and Yardley – the professionals Compton, Hutton, Washbrook, Wright and Bedser didn't go, though Hutton answered an urgent summons in mid-tour. So the four top run makers and the two top wicket takers from the 1947 series were missing. Bedser was absent because Surrey – his employer – felt that he needed a rest, an ironic reversal of the current position. It was a severely weakened team, with the 45-year-old Gubby Allen as captain. Moreover Allen, bizarrely, pulled a leg muscle while skipping on deck on the trip out: achieving fitness was a matter of individual taste. Another pulled leg muscle followed by a bout of malaria limited Butler to one Test, his second and last, and there was a rash of other injuries.

West Indies	296 & 351–9d	England	253 & 86–4
England	362 & 275	West Indies	497 & 72–3
West Indies	297–8d & 78–3	England	111 & 263
England	227 & 336	**West Indies**	490 & 76–0

England were saved in the first Test at Bridgetown by the Middlesex opener Jack Robertson, and rain on the last day, and by Robertson and Billy Griffith in the second at Port-of-Spain. It was injuries that propelled Griffith, the reserve wicketkeeper, into his first Test as emergency opener, and he responded with his first century in any form of cricket. Robertson's second innings 133 saved that game but, despite the arrival of Hutton, the batting couldn't cope in the last two matches after centuries from Worrell and Weekes. The sole successes were Robertson, averaging 55, and the young off-spinner Jim Laker, whose 19 wickets included an impressive 7–103 on debut. Had it not been for the war Laker would have played for his native Yorkshire, but at its end he was billeted in Catford and Surrey snapped him up. Tall, with strong fingers that could turn the ball on virtually any wicket, like most spinners he took time to acquire control and variation, and it would be a long time before he became a regular for England. On this tour he often bowled in pain from damaged stomach muscles: his and the other injuries made it a sorry crew that arrived back in England in April nursing a 2–0 defeat.

1948 Australia

The Australians had warmed up for 1948 with a comprehensive dismantling of India at home. Hassett averaged 110 and Bradman a cool 178: four centuries in six innings, and only once out under 100. The man was in his 40th year – was he immortal as well as indestructible? Worse in prospect for England was the performance of the bowlers, for Lindwall, Toshack, Johnston and Johnson all averaged under 20. How would England fare?

The tourists arrived for their first game at Worcester in 1948 in the last week of April, as all touring sides used to do. A comparison between 1948 and 2005 is instructive. Then Australia played 34 matches, 31 of them first class, including five Tests in a 10-week span from mid-June. Between each pair of Tests there were games against the counties. In fact they played every county at least once, and three of them twice. The counties saw them as big attractions – indeed Cyril Washbrook used the second Old Trafford game as his benefit match, a phenomenal success whose takings stood as a record until the inflationary 1970s. In the 2005 season, after a month of one-day cricket, the Australians played their five Tests in seven and a half weeks, with just four other first-class matches against the counties. Moreover their opponents were unknown until the domestic one-day competitions unfolded, and there was never a chance they would play Surrey, Yorkshire or Lancashire, games that attracted massive crowds in 1948. Thus in 2005 they were distinctly unprepared for the longer game, having to adjust, among other things, to a red ball. That didn't matter, of course, because most of the contracted England players had played no first-class cricket for six weeks.

The counties back then, too, made sure they put out their strongest sides. Little did it avail them: from first to last it was a procession. Against Worcester, traditionally every touring team's first match, Bradman failed with a mere 107: in each of his three pre-war tours he had taken a double hundred off Worcester. They won by an innings nevertheless. Of 26 first-class games outside the Tests they won 19, all but four by an innings, two by ten wickets and one by nine, and lost none. Most of the seven draws were rain-affected. That Australian side has been called the best ever, and although they were never really tested between 1946 and 1952, when they swept all before them, it's a conclusion hard to contest until Steve Waugh's team (1999–2004), which had tougher and more varied opposition. Bradman, who turned 40 during his last appearance at Lord's at the end of August against the Gentlemen – Australia 610–5, Bradman 150 and Hassett a double century – was by now a master tactician. The batting was immensely strong, with Morris, Barnes, Bradman and the new young left-hander Neil Harvey averaging over 60 in the Tests, Hassett 44.

But it was the bowling that would dominate England, the pernicious 55-over new ball rule allowing Lindwall (27 wickets at 19) and Miller (13 at 23) a new-ball burst every three hours. The smooth and menacing Lindwall, an echo of Harold Larwood, was perhaps at his peak in this series. In the period between their attacks England were held in thrall by Johnston (27 at 23) and Toshack (11 at 33), who kept the chains tight by yielding only two runs an over. The battles between these four and Hutton and Washbrook, Edrich and Compton at the top of the English order were gripping in their intensity. By contrast for England only the leg-spinner Eric Hollies took five wickets in an innings, a reluctant Test player in his sole Test of the series. Bedser bowled 275 overs for 18 wickets at 38; no one else managed 10.

England	165 & 441	**Australia**	509 & 98–2
Australia	350 & 460–7d	England	213 & 186
England	363 & 174–3d	**Australia**	221 & 92–1
England	496 & 365–8d	**Australia**	458 & 404–3
England	52 & 188	**Australia**	389

England began the first Test appallingly, losing eight wickets for 74 to Miller and Johnston before Laker hit 63. Hundreds by Bradman and Hassett gave Australia a lead of 344, but Hutton and Compton led a fightback by adding 84 in the last 70 minutes of the Saturday against a bouncer barrage from Miller, five in eight balls to Hutton, which led to some booing from the crowd. Compton's batting in this series, when he averaged 62 against the best attack in the world, was thrilling. His season was a tale of two innings, and each gave us an image burned on the retina. On this occasion he battled on through a Monday plagued by a thunderstorm and awful light (Wisden – 'rarely can a Test match have been played under such appalling conditions') and was not out when play resumed on the final day. He and Evans nudged England ahead until Miller induced him to hook, the 'fastest ball he bowled on tour', according to wicketkeeper Don Tallon. He changed his mind mid-stroke, lost his balance on the muddy turf, and fell on his wicket after making 184 in just under seven hours. His was the last resistance.

At Lord's England lost comprehensively, making just 401 in the two innings despite Miller being unfit to bowl. Nor could he bowl in the first innings at Old Trafford, where Compton played his second memorable innings after one of those selection decisions that boggles the mind from this distance: Hutton was dropped. Coming in after both openers had gone cheaply, Compton early on hooked at a Lindwall no-ball and edged it into his forehead. He 'staggered around' – the second famous image – and was led off to get stitched up. He would have come back at the fall of the next wicket if he'd had his way, but was persuaded to wait till 119–5, soon 141–6. 'At once he introduced an air of confidence into the batting' and forged partnerships with Evans and Bedser, who each reached the thirties. When England were all out for 363 he was 145* and 'nothing earned more admiration than the manner in which he withstood some lightning overs of extreme hostility by Lindwall'. Inspired by Compton, the English bowlers, led by Bedser and the Lancastrian Dick Pollard, bowled Australia out for 221, and by the end of Saturday England were 316 ahead with seven wickets and two days left. With the opener Sid Barnes doubtful, after Pollard the batsman hit him a sickening blow in the ribs at short leg, England had an opportunity to force a win. But then the weather broke and with it any chance they had.

Tragedy at Headingley

Although the tide was so strong that it was unlikely to turn, if England had gone into the Headingley Test only 2–1 down it would have put a different complexion on an already fascinating match, the best of the series. Astonishingly England passed 400 with two wickets down, Washbrook and a restored Hutton adding 168, Washbrook and Edrich 100, and Edrich with the nightwatchman Bedser a further 155. Australia replied to England's 496 with 458, Neil Harvey 112 in his first innings against England, who then batted consistently to set them 404 to win in 345 minutes. Yardley declared five minutes into the last day, to enable him to deploy the heavy roller to help break up the wicket. The rest of the last day was pure tragedy for England.

For anything like it for dashed hopes in recent times you have only to recall Gordon Greenidge's last day double hundred in 1984. The ball was turning, and to support Laker was Denis Compton – his Middlesex colleague Jack Young had been left out on the morning of the game – who often enjoyed success with his left-arm chinamen and googlies. He deceived Hassett and caught him brilliantly off his own bowling, but should have had Morris stumped at 32. Worse, in the course of a beautiful early over to Bradman, he had him missed at first slip by Jack Crapp, the unfortunate Gloucestershire batsman who is now remembered for it. Had these chances been taken, thought the old Australian opener Jack Fingleton, the game would have been all over by tea. But Compton couldn't sustain the effort, Laker was out of sorts, a display that would put his England career largely on hold for four years, and Morris and Bradman added 301 to win by seven wickets with 15 minutes to spare. This was an extraordinary achievement on the last day, despite the impoverished attack which included, weirdly, four overs of bad leg breaks from Hutton, who only bowled seven for Yorkshire all summer, as the desperate Yardley would have known. 'It was wretched stuff', said Fingleton. Incidentally, had the game been played under modern rules of engagement England would have bowled 86 overs at Australia. As it was England bowled 114 overs in five and a half hours, a rate of 21 an hour.

The final Test, Bradman's last, was horrible for England. Fingleton thought it England's worst batting in living memory. In a humid atmosphere Lindwall's 6–20 bowled England out for just 52, Hutton 30, which Barnes and Morris had more than doubled by the time Bradman walked in to a standing ovation and three cheers from the England players. 'Evidently deeply touched', wrote Wisden, he was bowled second ball by Hollies' googly, whereupon he was applauded back in with even more enthusiasm. It's pretty hard to believe that Bradman was 'blinded by tears' as some commentators suggested. A patriotic youngster doing his sums 10 years later, even I was sad that Bradman couldn't have made just the four he needed to make his Test average exactly 100 instead of 99.94. What a testament to his perfection and dominance that would have been. An era ended, Morris went on to carry his bat for 196, and England folded again, Hutton showing his class by top scoring a second time. So it finished 4–0. By no means a sour or partisan commentator, Fingleton thought, for all Australia's strength, that England's team was the poorest to have represented it in the twentieth century, 'both in the quality and spirit of its cricket'. He saw 'an obvious apathy' in English cricket that year, compared to Australia's 'zeal and zest' – something that English supporters in the 1990s would recognise all too well. The county bowling he had seen was so poor he wasn't surprised by the record breaking of Compton and Edrich the year before.

1948–9 South Africa

The 1949 season would offer a respite from Australian hostility and dominance. During the winter, spirits had been lifted by a tour victory over South Africa, 2–0 in a five-match, four-day series, led by the Middlesex captain F. G. Mann. Exactly 10 years on from the unfinished Durban Test, this was a series settled by two unprecedentedly close finishes. Both sides were strong in batting and South Africa had the better bowlers – Tufty Mann and the 19-year-old tearaway Cuan McCarthy took their wickets at well under 30 apiece, something no English bowler could manage.

South Africa	161 & 219	**England**	253 & 128–8
England	608	South Africa	315 & 270–2
England	308 & 276–3d	South Africa	356 & 142–4
England	379 & 253–7d	South Africa	257–9d & 194–4
South Africa	379 & 187–3d	**England**	395 & 174–7

The series hinged on the low-scoring first Test, when England had to score 128 in 135 minutes to win. Despite heroic bowling by McCarthy, England came to the sixth ball of the last (eight-ball) over at 127–8, with all four results possible. Bedser and the Derbyshire in-swing bowler Cliff Gladwin scrambled a leg-bye off the last ball to win, the first and only Test to achieve a positive result off the last possible ball. Three draws followed on good pitches for which four days were not enough. Hutton and Washbrook opened with 359 in the second (still the record England opening stand in 2005); Hutton and the Glamorgan all-rounder Alan Watkins made hundreds in the fourth. In the fifth, England were given a narrow lead by a fighting century from Mann. Until this point South Africa had taken no risks whatsoever to try to force a win, so they were obliged to do so now, setting England 172 in 95 minutes. Gratifyingly, there was no attempt to draw and seal a 1–0 victory. Hutton and Washbrook cracked off with 58 in under half an hour, but wickets fell readily to the spinners, the seventh at 153. In the end Crapp ended the match with 10 from three balls, the win coming off the seventh ball of what may have been the last over. Hutton and Washbrook both made over 500 runs at 60 plus; Compton made 400 at 50; the amateur Edrich was missing. Although the Worcestershire leg spinner Roly Jenkins proved an able deputy for Hollies, he and Watkins were the only finds from the tour. But when the New Zealanders came in 1949 these two were to play only one Test between them, and England's bowling was still woefully short of penetration.

1949 New Zealand

England	372 & 267–4d	New Zealand	341 & 195–2
England	313–9d & 306–5d	New Zealand	469–7d
New Zealand	293 & 348–7	England	440–9d
New Zealand	345 & 308–9	England	482

The New Zealanders, for whom cricket was even further behind rugby in popularity then than it is now, were not expected to give England much trouble. In consequence, in a move perhaps prompted by wistful nostalgia but soon to be regretted – 'give them less time and they'll play in the right spirit' – the four Tests were reduced to three days in length. In a fine summer the New Zealand batting was strong and stubborn, and in none of the four drawn Tests did England ever look like winning in the three days allowed. Six England batsmen scored centuries, including Jack Robertson standing in for an injured Washbrook. Robertson, who in retrospect should perhaps have played more Tests, was promptly dropped for the third, and while it was under way he hit 331* for Middlesex, seeming to underline our batting depth against all but the best. So immovable was the England top order that Robertson never played a Test in England again.

Although otherwise unsatisfactory, 1949 did bring in four new players who would prove important for England in the next few years. The oldest, and hardly new, was the leg-spinning all-rounder Freddie Brown, who when at Surrey in the 1930s had played six Tests in four different series, the last 12 years earlier. Back after his prisoner-of-war experience, and up to his substantial fighting weight, he was now captaining Northamptonshire at the age of 38, helping to shore up the English middle order. Two other new all-rounders did the same. Young Trevor Bailey of Essex played in all four Tests, took more wickets than anyone else, six in an innings twice, and averaged over 70 with the bat. Opening support for Bedser at last? Even younger was Brian Close, who would do the double for Yorkshire at only 18. In 1949 he played once for England, starting a chequered Test career that, amazingly in this day and age, would span 27 years. The last of the four was the elegant free-scoring Nottinghamshire amateur Reg Simpson, who in his two innings made 103 – the second 50 in 27 minutes – and 68.

One of the opening bowlers tried, for a single Test in which he took 3–72 in 39 overs, was Les Jackson, whose career I watched intently because I was born in the same Derbyshire mining village as he was. Biased as I was, I was not alone in thinking that one Test in 1949 and one in 1961, in a famous England victory, was a puzzling reflection on an outstanding county cricket career (check the averages on pages 368–71). Perhaps successive selectors' reticence was due to something as mundane as his slinging, low-armed action, in the days when Trueman-classical was the epitome of the fast bowler, and to the influence of Gubby Allen.

1950 West Indies

There had been no winter tour by England, so their leading players were refreshed for the visit of the West Indies, who would play four five-day Tests. Although the West Indies were hard to beat at home, England had never yet sent anything like a full-strength side out there, and they had never even managed to win a single Test in England. Everyone was keen to see their by now famous batsmen, the Three Ws – Clyde Walcott, a burly back-foot destroyer, Everton Weekes, short and strong-wristedly savage, and Frank Worrell, slim and elegantly languid. But the attack was not expected to be formidable. Their opening bowlers were bound to be fast but erratic, and only the captain and off-spinner John Goddard was of proven Test calibre. And he was a stock bowler rather than a big spinner: the West Indies simply didn't produce spinners. So everyone anticipated a high-scoring series, and many imagined that the tourists would be hard-pressed to win a Test. England were in for a ghastly shock.

The early matches provided little to dispel English confidence. After a narrow win in a low-scoring game against Yorkshire, the West Indies batsmen did start to produce. Weekes 132, Worrell 228 against Surrey. Then came an astounding game of records on a perfect wicket at Fenners, the University of Cambridge ground. Cambridge made 594–4 – John Dewes 183 and the freshman David Sheppard 227 in an opening stand of 343 in 280 minutes. That was amazing enough, but West Indies topped it with a staggering 730–3 – Christiani 111, Stollmeyer 83, Worrell 160, Weekes 304* in 325 minutes. The West Indies' two young unknown spinners Sonny Ramadhin and Alf Valentine, who had arrived with just two first-class appearances between them, took 0 for 183, and, although Valentine took 5 in the next game v MCC, the tourists were outplayed. Ramadhin however took 5, 6 and 5 in successive innings in the next two matches, and Valentine 13–67 against Lancashire, so both were included in the team for the first Test at Old Trafford.

England	312 & 288	West Indies	215 & 183
West Indies	326 & 425–6d	England	151 & 274
England	223 & 436	**West Indies**	558 & 103–0
West Indies	503	England	344 & 103

Wisden's report began by saying that the game 'will be remembered chiefly for the arguments aroused by the remarkable nature of the pitch'. Half the matches at Old Trafford the previous season had been drawn, so in order to prepare fewer batsman-friendly pitches 'the Lancashire ground committee ordered that less use should be made of the heavy roller and watering in pitch preparation'. The outcome was that the ball turned from the start, and the left-arm spinner Valentine reduced England to 88–5 on the first morning. Hutton had retired hurt as well, but the ebullient Evans rattled up 104, his first first-class century in England, Trevor Bailey eked out a more circumspect 82, and the pair turned the game. On his Test debut Valentine took the first eight wickets to fall, 8–103 in all. But 312 on a pitch with almost too much turn was enough, and eight wickets for Hollies and nine in his first Test for the Lancashire left-arm spinner Bob Berry gave England a 202 run win. The Three Ws made just 118 between them in their six innings.

That was all right, then. The West Indies batting had failed at the top level, and an England batting side even without the injured Washbrook and Compton had made enough runs against an attack dependent on two promising but raw young spinners. What followed was captivating for the first few West Indian immigrants in this country, fascinating for the neutral, and an absolute disaster for England. At Lord's England were beaten by 326 runs. Centuries by the opener Allan Rae and by Walcott saw off an England attack including three spinners, and the English batsmen were mesmerised into strokeless inactivity by Ramadhin (115–70–152–11) and Valentine (116–75–127–7). By contrast Jenkins' nine wickets came from 94 overs at a cost of 290. It was a nadir of English batsmanship, relieved only by 114 from Washbrook in the second innings. Compton was desperately missed.

At Nottingham after a horrible collapse to 25–4 in the first innings against the West Indies' barely-used opening bowlers, England's batsmen at least recovered some pride in the second when Simpson and Washbrook opened with 220 (Hutton was missing with lumbago). But it failed to stave off a defeat by 10 wickets, because Worrell with a majestic 261 and Weekes with 129 had added 283 in three and a half hours of pulverising batting. In England's second innings Valentine bowled 92 overs and Ramadhin 81. To anyone inured to watching the awesome West Indian pace bowlers of the later 20th century, not a spinner in sight, this is an astounding statistic. At the Oval, centuries from Rae and Worrell once more enabled the West Indies to top 500. Hutton was back and so was Compton at last, and they added 109 for the third wicket, with Compton showing increasing confidence after taking some time 'to fathom the wiles of Ramadhin and Valentine', whom he had never yet faced. But a stop-start run-out ended his innings at 44, and the rest was a procession on the way to another humiliating innings defeat, with no other batsman reaching 30 in the match apart from Hutton, who carried his bat for 202 out of 344. 'Nobody who saw his effort of concentration and perfect stroke play will forget the great attempt he made to save his country.'

Injuries didn't help, but the English selectors got themselves into a terrible tangle, selecting 25 people for four Tests. Not one played in all four. Hutton and Washbrook averaged over 60, but the nine other specialist batsmen chosen averaged 23. The bowling was in as much disarray: 14 bowlers were picked, seven of them spinners, and none took more than 11 wickets. The West Indies used just 12 players. As well as their Three Ws they found an excellent opening pair in Rae and Stollmeyer, had six batsmen averaging over 40, while Valentine and Ramadhin in an extraordinary 800 overs took their 59 wickets at under 22 each, and at just 1.6 runs an over. Can there be any greater praise, or stronger indictment of England's supine batting, than that? Their faster bowlers took only 12 wickets in eight innings.

Never before or since have two young spinners come from nowhere to wreak such havoc. Born within two days of each other in the spring of 1930, they thus had their 20th birthdays during the first week of the tour. It was a pretty cold and wet spring and early summer too, not one of dry, crumbling wickets. Tall and somewhat ungainly, the Jamaican left-arm spinner Valentine looked more like a clerk than a cricketer, his new NHS glasses – procured for him mid-tour when his team-mates were tickled to discover he couldn't read the scoreboard – stuck to his forehead with pink sticking plaster to stop them slipping. He was an orthodox left-arm spinner who seemed simply to amble up to the wicket and turn his arm over. He came on the tour with first-class figures of 2–190.

Two days younger than Valentine, Ramadhin was from Trinidad, an orphan of Indian parentage. Like Valentine, he too had played just two first-class games before the tour in West Indian heat, and he was so slight that John Goddard said, only half-joking, that he couldn't put him on in a high wind. That his third first-class game was in the damp chill and poor light of Worcester didn't seem to bother him, and he stayed behind after the tour to play with great success in the Lancashire League. Just 5 ft 4 ins and weighing nine stone, with sleeves buttoned to the wrist, he had a fast arm action that made him particularly difficult to pick. A self-taught rarity, who hardly bowled until he was 17, he bowled off-breaks, leg-breaks, and the one that goes straight on, with no perceptible change of action, spinning off the middle finger. Twelve of his 26 Test wickets were bowled: only Hutton played him with any confidence. Adding to the impression of paralysis, no Englishman dared use their feet to either spinner – in Hutton's words they came too fast through the air.

1950–1 Australia and New Zealand

Thus England, who had perhaps viewed the West Indian summer as a useful warm-up and trial ground for the following winter's tour against an Australian team undefeated since the war, were left with a battlefield littered with the dead and shell-shocked. Twelve of England's 25 players of that summer played just six Tests between them after 1951. In Australia they would rely on a 40-year-old captain, the larger-than-life Freddie Brown, whose driving seemed to Ray Robinson 'to be full of red corpuscles, like the ruddy face above the kerchief knotted at his neck'. But Ramadhin and Valentine were hardly the ideal preparation for the next dose of Lindwall and Miller, and Australia too had a mystery spinner. Jack Iverson was 35, and in fooling with a table tennis ball during the war he had perfected a freakish grip that only a man with huge hands could manage, releasing the ball from between thumb and bent-back middle finger, cocked like a trigger. He topped the bowling averages with 21 wickets.

Australia	228 & 32–7d	England	68–7d & 122
Australia	194 & 181	England	197 & 150
England	290 & 123	**Australia**	426
Australia	371 & 403–8d	England	272 & 228
Australia	217 & 197	**England**	320 & 95–2

England were desperately unlucky at Brisbane. The weird declarations reveal the classic Brisbane 'sticky dog', where a fierce downpour on an uncovered pitch would leave it acting viciously for a couple of hours. Bedser and Bailey had done wonderfully well to bowl Australia out on the opening day, before the weather made it a lottery. They gave England a winning opportunity once again at Melbourne, but jittery batsmen couldn't make 179 to win. Those Tests were close, but the next two weren't, only Hutton carrying his bat with an unbeaten 156 delaying the end in the fourth. A 5–0 whitewash would have been ill-deserved, but it was avoided when everything clicked at last. Fighting bowling from Bedser and Brown, who had bowled his new medium-pace skifully all tour, brought Australia back from 111–1 to 217 all out. Hutton and Simpson took England to 171–1 with the best batting of the tour, but the new ball scythed through the middle order. Simpson hung on, and was 92 when the young off-spinner Roy Tattersall joined him at 246–9, the lead only 29. Tattersall survived for an hour, while Simpson 'flayed fast and slow bowling to all parts of the field' in reaching 156*. Bedser promptly disposed of both openers, and went on to take a second set of five to set up the win. So England lost 4–1, which was about what the realists had predicted, although two of the defeats were narrower than expected in surprisingly low-scoring games.

| New Zealand | 417–8d & 46–3 | England | 550 |
| New Zealand | 126 & 189 | **England** | 227 & 91–4 |

England salvaged more pride in the final game of the New Zealand series when Wright and Roy Tattersall spun them to victory. The previous match had been a laboured draw distinguished only by a maiden Test century from Bailey. So ended a tour in which he was one of the few pluses for England.

Yes, Freddie Brown proved time and again an inspirational captain, leading from the front with 210 runs and 18 wickets. Yes, Bedser (30 at 16) and Bailey (14 at 14 in three Tests) bowled so outstandingly well with the new ball that their records were better than Lindwall and Miller. Yes, Hutton with 533 runs at 88 was by far the outstanding batsman of the series – the highest Australian average was 43 – and his performance must be a strong candidate in the circumstances for the best English batting of all time. Only Simpson and Brown, 38 and 26, had averages even above 20. But without his brilliant 156* in the final Test Simpson would have averaged 21, and all the others with pretentions to batsmanship together scored 418 runs in 35 innings at an average of 13. Horrible. Compton's comeback after a knee operation was particularly wretched: 53 runs at 7.

So, after two humiliating series, it was back to the drawing board. Where could England find cricketers to take on Australia? And, especially, how could they find fast bowlers to challenge Lindwall and Miller? It seemed their batsmen couldn't play either pace or spin, and their bowlers couldn't bowl it. As one letter writer to *The Times* had put it in 1948, it was 'bren guns v water pistols'. Why was England's Test team so poor? Where was the next generation of Test cricketers?

Specialist batsmen and opening bowlers used from 1946 to 1950–1					
Batsman	**runs**	**average**	**Bowler**	**wkts**	**average**
Hutton	3423	56.11	Bedser	132	29.97
Compton	2879	52.35	Bailey (from 1949)	40	25.75
Edrich W. J.	1793	49.81			
Washbrook	2448	43.71			
Other specialist batsmen (18)	3369	26.53	Other opening bowlers (11)	56	41.95

CHAPTER 4

The Talent Gap

The young Peter May in watchful defence against Australia at the Oval, August 1953.

Fast bowlers – none at all.
Slow left-armers – none of true Test class.
Slow off-spinners – J. C. Clay born 1898, Tom Goddard born 1900.
Leg-break and googly – one of true Test class.
Medium-fast right-handers – dozens, nearly all willing,
nearly all misdirected.

R. C. ROBERTSON-GLASGOW QUOTED BY JACK FINGLETON

R obertson-Glasgow's view of the state of English bowling came at the end of 1947. Three years later it seemed little better. At the start of 1951 there appeared few reasons for hope on any front in the English game. After a barren spell Bedser was at last achieving his potential, and in particular beginning to acquire a crucial ascendancy over the dangerous Australian left-handed opener, Arthur Morris. Evans in Australia had been quite brilliant behind the stumps, catching some spectacular catches and missing none. Hutton was head, shoulders and most of his body above the other batsmen, for Compton and Washbrook had wretched Australian tours, and Edrich had been unavailable. And they were ageing: of these only Evans was under 33 in the summer of 1951. Although there was supposed to be a crop of young batsmen – Dewes, Sheppard, Doggart, Insole, Parkhouse – they had all failed comprehensively so far at Test level. Bailey had really begun to improve as a bowler, but although he was England's fastest bowler of any quality he couldn't compare for controlled hostility with Lindwall and Miller. Moreover, in the previous two series nine spinners had been tried but none had cemented a place. Captain Freddie Brown epitomised the bluff British bulldog spirit, especially to Australian crowds to whom he became an unlikely hero, but, although his stamina on that tour was quite amazing, he was now 40 and wouldn't be around much longer.

So England needed a new captain, two fast bowlers, a good pair of spinners, and – unless the old guard recovered to rally round Hutton – about four new batsmen. Not a lot to ask… Australia seemed to find new players with ease. Although Bradman was irreplaceable, Harvey and Burke (opening in place of Barnes) had both averaged 40 in the low-scoring 1950–1 series, and Jack Iverson had come from nowhere – almost literally – to top their bowling averages. Why, with England's widespread county system, was it still so difficult to unearth new talent over five years after the end of the war? The war had disrupted England's game, to be sure, but they had not won a home series since 1947, and their record against Australia since the war was won one, lost 11, drawn three.

Where was all the talent?

The war had reverberations that lasted longer than anyone expected. The counties had virtually closed down for six years, and their colts' training systems were perfunctory at best. They couldn't start properly after the war either: the Control of Engagement recruitment order favoured specific key occupations, and young players were difficult to recruit. Full post-war employment, too, led to higher wages, and made alternative careers attractive for young cricketers who hadn't already been hooked by a county, as they might have been before the war. Wages weren't moving in line: according to Fingleton, professionals felt that 'their calling has not been made more attractive'. Moreover, not only had cricketers not played competitive top-class cricket for six years, but war service had delayed university careers for some, and national service for virtually everyone able to play cricket (unless you worked in the mines, or had peculiar feet that exempted you, as they did Colin Cowdrey). So, although forces cricket was competitive, and the Combined Services team strong enough in the post-war years to beat several counties, there was a two-year development lag automatically built into the system. For those who went to university too, of course, that delay was five years. In the desperate search for younger cricketers at the end of the 1940s, and seeing the strength of Oxford and Cambridge building up, the selectors quite understandably thrust young batsmen into the breach before they were ready, and some never were.

The figures are telling. There were only 65 men who would subsequently play county cricket born in the five years 1924–8: in other comparable five-year periods typically more than twice as many did. Fifteen of those got to Test level: Tom Graveney played 79 Tests and the other 14 just 72 between them. But eventually a backlog of class cricketers started to come through. In 1947 Peter May, still only 17, announced himself with 148 in a total of 270 for Southern Schools v the Rest, then 146 out of 239 for the Public Schools v Combined Services: he had already made 183* for Charterhouse against Eton and another hundred against Harrow. In the Cambridge side of that year were the Essex pair of Trevor Bailey and Doug Insole. In 1948 they were joined by John Dewes and Hubert Doggart. Dewes batted impressively for the Gentlemen at Lords, and Doggart made a double hundred against a strong Lancashire attack on his first-class debut, so you can see why the selectors were eager to push them on.

That year the young Surrey left-arm spinner Tony Lock took 6–43 to help Combined Services beat Glamorgan, who would become the county champions. In 1949 the Cambridge trio of Dewes, Doggart and Bailey made the Gentlemen team at Lords (as did two future Test captains from Oxford, Kardar and van Ryneveld). That was May's breakthrough year. He had chosen to go into the Navy before Cambridge, and that year came third in the first-class averages behind Hardstaff and Hutton with 695 runs at 63, scored entirely in Services games, before he had played a single game for Surrey. In the win over Worcester he made 97 and 175, more than half the runs in each innings. For the Navy he hit 162* and 58* v the RAF, although he failed against the Army – bowled by Frank Tyson for five. Tyson, fast but erratic, didn't make the Combined Services team against the Schools, where May was caught and bowled by Cowdrey for 12: Cowdrey and Micky Stewart played for the Schools.

In 1950, the year Cambridge rattled up 594–4 against Ramadhin and Valentine (a misguided justification for playing Dewes and Doggart in the Tests), Dewes, Doggart, Sheppard and May headed their batting, and John Warr opened the bowling. Warr was the only Test bowler produced by Oxbridge, and he played for England only twice. It seemed that the public schoolboys would do the batting and those from humbler backgrounds the bowling. In the Oxbridge sides of 1948–52 were Dewes, Doggart, Insole, Bailey, Sheppard, May, Cowdrey and Raman Subba Row. In the Combined Services sides from 1948–53, as well as May, were Lock and Close, Frank Tyson, Alan Moss, Fred Titmus, Ray Illingworth, John Mortimore and Fred Trueman, and the three wicketkeepers Jim Parks, Keith Andrew and Roy Swetman. A side

Test team of Oxbridge and Services players, 1948–52				
Player	Tests	Batting runs–av	Bowling wkts–av	Fielding ct–st
Sheppard	22	1172–37		
Subba Row	13	984–46		
May	66	4537–46		42
Cowdrey	114	7624–44		120
Parks (wk)	46	1962–32		103–11
Bailey	61	2290–29	132–29	32
Close	22	887–25	18–29	24
Illingworth	61	1836–23	122–31	45
Lock	49	742–13	174–25	59
Trueman	67	981–13	307–21	64

selected from those proving grounds in that brief period would be pretty tough to beat.

There are five future Test captains in this list, a balanced attack headed by opening bowlers of fearsome pace; brilliant close fieldsmen; three top-class all-rounders; an opening pair of batsmen whose commitments, spiritual and temporal, prevented them playing as many Tests as they should; followed by two of the top five England batsmen of the last 60 years. A glaring absentee is Brian Statham, who never played Services representative cricket while he was in the RAF. Omitted too is Keith Andrew, arguably the best keeper in England in the 1950s, Evans included.

It seems logical to conclude that the post-war recovery was delayed while a substantial repository of talent was building up in universities, barracks, ships and airfields. When they emerged to join and ultimately take over from Hutton and Washbrook, Compton and Edrich, Bedser and Evans, they would form an England team whose record would not be bettered for the rest of the century. But to start with they had to find a new captain. To make the right choice the selectors would have to overcome years of prejudice – the presumption that England had to have an amateur as captain. After much hovering on the edge, casting about among amateurs of little distinction or insufficient experience, they took the plunge. And so the ghost of the Yorkshire grandee Lord Hawke – 'pray God a professional never captains England' – was finally put to rest. Hawke claimed to be taken out of context, for he was referring to his worry about the shortage of good enough amateurs as much as the competence of professionals. But it was a line that stuck in the minds of cricket's administrators, and in the craw of many professionals.

The next chapter belongs to Len Hutton.

CHAPTER 5

On Top of the World

Frank Tyson tended after being concussed by a ball from Ray Lindwall at Sydney, December 1954.

We watched horrified as he went down like felled timber and lay inert and still... When he came out of his concussed state I swear there was a new light in his eyes as if a spark had been kindled deep down inside him... The blow seemed to trigger off something, perhaps a new willpower... His pace at Sydney that decisive and extraordinary day was nothing short of frightening. After one ball Evans and the slips exchanged significant glances and moved back several paces. I never saw Evans so far back.

LEN HUTTON

1951 South Africa

The South Africans came in 1951, and Freddie Brown stayed for one more season. After the first Test the portents were ominous. Despite first innings centuries by Simpson and Compton (back to form, to England supporters' relief) in the second they capitulated again to spin, this time purveyed by Mann and Athol Rowan, accurate but hardly in the Ramadhin and Valentine class. But after that defeat England rallied. In the second Test the lanky Lancastrian off-spinner Roy Tattersall took 12 wickets on a pitch affected by rain to level the series at 1−1, and in the third it was Bedser who took 12. Hutton, sensing the chance of his hundredth first-class century, steered England home in that match under a thunderous sky with a brilliant 98*. If he had won the match with a six instead of a lofted four he would have reached the target that day. At the Oval the following week 15 000 people suspended their county loyalties and cheered the trademark cover drive that took him to his hundredth hundred, in just his ninth full season. No man deserved it more. Imagine what he would have achieved had the war not intervened.

South Africa	483−9d & 121	England	419−9d & 114
England	311 & 16−0	South Africa	115 & 211
South Africa	158 & 191	**England**	211 & 142−1
South Africa	538 & 87−0	England	505
South Africa	202 & 154	**England**	194 & 164−6

It was 2−1 then, as England came to the fourth Test. There a bland high-scoring draw was enlivened for English eyes by the first Test innings of Peter May. With 1286 runs at 71 for Cambridge, and an immaculate century against a strong Players attack a month earlier, he had staked a claim that the selectors couldn't ignore, despite their experiences in 1950. Tall and slim but extremely strong, a classical driver with a watchful defence, he batted 'with equanimity and a sound technique that stamped him as a player well above the ordinary' (Wisden sticking its neck out) and made 138. England came to the Oval still at 2−1, and there won a tense low-scoring contest by four wickets. At a tricky moment, it needed a bold 40 from Brown to settle the issue in his last innings as captain. A potential 2−2 draw became a 3−1 win, and England had at last won a home series for the first time since 1947. Perhaps things were looking up. Apart from May the batting had been strengthened by the stylish Yorkshire left-hander Willie Watson, a footballer with Huddersfield Town, who was one of the last of the double internationals. Hutton and Compton averaged 50. Bedser took 30 wickets, and the off-spinners Laker and Tattersall 14 and 21 respectively.

1951−2 India

A winter tour of the Indian subcontinent in 1951−2 gave the leading English players a rest. Watson might have cemented his place but he went back to football. In fact it was virtually a 2nd XI that went, under the less than suitable young Lancastrian amateur Nigel Howard.

England	203 & 368–6d	India	418–6d
India	485–9d & 208	England	456 & 55–2
England	352 & 252–5d	India	344 & 103–0
India	121 & 157	**England**	203 & 74–2
England	266 & 183	**India**	457–9d

Of the team at the Oval only Tattersall toured, and he took another 21 wickets, at 28 each. On easy pitches the first three matches were all draws, distinguished for England only by centuries for Watkins and Graveney. The last two helped the spinners of both sides, with the Lancastrians Tattersall and Malcolm Hilton successful in the fourth at Kanpur, Vinoo Mankad in the fifth. In the 1–1 draw two new batsmen stood out. Alan Watkins of Glamorgan and Tom Graveney of Gloucestershire both averaged over 60. Watkins, a predatory close catcher, would play only three more Tests, but this was the beginning of a stop-start Test career stretching nearly 20 years for the elegant and enigmatic Graveney. Enigmatic in the early part of his career, anyway, for he would have difficulty putting a run of scores together in Tests, and for a long time the expression 'suspect temperament' hung about him. Unfairly perhaps, for despite the coming dominance of May and Cowdrey he would achieve a place in the public affection hitherto reserved only for Compton. Born in 1927 and so older than the Oxbridge batsmen, he had done National Service at the end of the war and had been in the Gloucestershire side for the last four seasons. On this first tour not only did he make 175 against India in Bombay, but he scored centuries in both matches against the newly-formed Pakistan, as yet a year away from Test status, and in the one against Sri Lanka, then still called Ceylon.

1952 India

1952 brought the Indians back to England. At home England were expected to win in comfort. Of more interest was the question of who should captain England after Freddie Brown's retirement. In the end the selectors plumped for Len Hutton, soon to be 36 but towering increasingly over England's other batsmen. Wisden's editor was in favour: the selection committee 'made a vital decision in the interests of England', but nevertheless he hoped that soon we would have an amateur in charge again 'if May and Sheppard continue to improve'. This equivocation found a ration-ale in the oft-repeated assertion that a professional captain would find it 'onerous if disciplinary action was necessary against a fellow professional'. That was perhaps understandable on the county scene, but seems a little far-fetched in Tests when the MCC, who in those days picked the selectors who picked the team, didn't actually employ the players.

India	293 & 165	**England**	334 & 128–3
India	235 & 378	**England**	537 & 79–2
England	347–9d	India	58 & 82
England	326–9d	India	98

India indeed proved no match for England, largely because in a wet summer they at last found a new young fast bowler to partner Bedser, the explosive Freddie Trueman, scowling, blunt-speaking, black-haired and beetle-browed. Trueman set his stamp on the series in the first Test. After a close contest for a first innings lead the game came to life when India lost their first four wickets of the second innings before a run was on the board. England duly won by seven wickets, and although Hutton failed twice with the bat his adroit handling of the bowlers, and particularly his nursing of his county colleague Trueman, won potential critics over. Hutton's batting didn't fail often, and 150 in the second Test, complemented by a hectic 104 from Evans, led to an easy victory despite the all-round heroics of Vinoo Mankad: 72 and 184 sandwiching his 73 overs of left-arm spin. Hutton was nevertheless criticised for his caution on the fourth evening, when he failed to press for victory. Never mind that the weather forecast was good and the bowling taxing – commentators had conveniently forgotten the travails of the past three years, and wanted a cavalier end to the match (and a day off). Some were never satisfied.

They couldn't complain much about the last two Tests, though. Another hundred from Hutton in the third Test was upstaged by the violent destruction that followed. In little more than three hours India were swept away for 58 and 82, the only time a Test side had been bowled out twice the same day until the same thing happened to the lamentable Zimbabwe team of 2005. India were unmanned and humiliated by Trueman's terrifying bowling in the first innings, 8–31, while Bedser, and Tony Lock on his debut, did the damage in the second. Lock, the Surrey 'slow' left-armer, had an on-field presence to match that of Trueman, and was also a brilliant close fielder whose spectacular catch at short leg had started the first innings rout. The Indians were spared total disaster in the fourth and last Test by vile weather, after David Sheppard had returned with a cultured 119. That he, May and Graveney (who averaged 47) had finally arrived was great encouragement for England, especially as Compton, Edrich and Washbrook had all lost form and missed the Tests, and Watson had only made it to the Oval. Trueman and Bedser profited with 29 and 20 wickets respectively, each at just 13.

1953 Australia

There was no tour that winter, so England awaited with trepidation the arrival of the Australians in 1953, Coronation year. There was a little more hope than usual, but Australia only lacked Iverson from the 1950–51 series, replacing him with the leg-spinners Doug Ring and the young Richie Benaud, promising but raw. So they would still be formidable, especially as a new opening bat, Colin McDonald, had emerged in the recent winter series against South Africa. The good news for England was that despite fantastic batting by Harvey – 834 runs at 92 – Australia had failed to win a series for the first time since 1938. A 2–2 draw came about because, unusually on Australian wickets, an off-spinner was successful, the young Hugh Tayfield taking 30 wickets at 28. But the last Test victory, when South Africa chased 295 and won, was achieved when both Lindwall and Miller were missing injured, and most commentators felt that if everyone could keep fit they would still be practically impossible to beat.

For the first time since 1926 the Australians took the field at Worcester without Bradman, but they still scored over 500 – Miller an unbeaten double century. Harvey did likewise in the next match, the first of four they won by an innings, including Surrey and Yorkshire, first and second the previous season. In these games – in the long warm-up that used to precede the Tests in an English summer – Hutton was bowled Lindwall 0, and May made only 0 and 1, which did nothing for England's confidence. Moreover the new young bowlers, Benaud and the fast-medium Ron Archer, were instrumental in the demolition. Things got worse at Lord's, when the MCC put out an England batting line-up missing only Hutton. This was the first match I ever saw, at the age of seven, and I can recall vividly the iron grip the Australian bowlers exerted as they disposed of the cream of England's batting for a mere 80, the top score just 16. The England batsmen seemed barely able to hit the ball off the square.

Australia	249 & 123	England	144 & 120–1
Australia	346 & 368	England	372 & 282–7
Australia	318 & 35–8	England	276
England	167 & 275	Australia	266 & 147–4
Australia	275 & 162	**England**	306 & 132–2

And so to Trent Bridge for the first Test. For three days the cricket was taut and enthralling. England went in with only four bowlers, though Alec Bedser would have been enough if he could have bowled from both ends. On the second day, after Morris, Hassett and Miller had taken Australia to 237–3 between showers, the last seven wickets fell for just 12. Then, after England struggled to 144, Bedser took the first five second-innings wickets to fall. Seven in each innings gave him 14–99 from 55.4 overs, a monumental achievement. England had 229 to win, which was a doubtful proposition in view of their first innings, but so well did Hutton bat that at the end of Saturday they were 120–1, Hutton not out 60. Everyone held their breath. But the rain bucketed down for the last two days – Monday and Tuesday (play didn't take place on the Sunday of a Test until 1991) – and so sadly ended the first of the summer's might-have-beens.

The Lord's Test is one that deserves a chapter to itself. For three and a half days the sides wrestled for advantage. Both captains made hundreds, Hassett's 104 out of a first innings score of 346 matched by Hutton's 145 out of 372. The batting of Hutton and Graveney, who added 168 for the second wicket, brought a rare eulogy from Wisden: 'The sight of England batsmen giving full rein to their strokes brought undisguised delight to many who had bemoaned the lack of spectacle in so much Test cricket. The spectacle was glorious to behold.' Unfortunately for England fans it was matched by Morris and Miller on the fourth day. Taking Australia to 368, they left England seven hours to make 343. In the last hour of Tuesday England lost their top three, including the first innings' heroes Hutton and Graveney. On the last day Compton left at 73 to a ball that kept wickedly low. This brought in Bailey, the last recognised batsman, to join the imperturbable Willie Watson, sandy-haired and slight of build. Having rather surprisingly displaced May from the first match, Watson had failed in the first innings. This was his hour. With the Australian bowlers trying everything they knew, Watson and Bailey lasted out, seeing off a fierce spell from Lindwall and Miller with the new ball in mid-afternoon, until half an hour from the close. If England had lost then, they would have needed to win two out of the last three to regain the Ashes. So the teams went to Old Trafford still at 0–0.

No England v Australia match in Manchester had produced a result since 1905, and 1953 would not do so either. Little more than the two first innings would be possible – England 276, Australia 318 – but the little that did remain was quite bizarre. With the game dead Australia finished 35–8 – four wickets for the Yorkshire left-arm spinner Johnny Wardle, and two stumpings for Evans. That brought the series to Headingley, and another backs-to-the-wall job for England. It was a grind. Lindwall at his best was instrumental in bowling England out for 167 in 110 overs. Australia passed that total with three wickets down, but Bedser held them to 266. With the weather interfering, England battled to 177–5 at the end of the fourth day, 78 ahead. Compton had reached 60, but a blow on the hand he sustained avoiding a Lindwall bouncer prevented him batting when the last day began, and though he resumed after lunch he could only defend.

It was left to Bailey and the tail, led unexpectedly by Laker. Australia would need 177 in 115 minutes when Bailey was last out, after a painstaking 38 in over four hours, to end an innings of 275 in 178 overs. Bailey wasn't finished yet. Australia went off like a train and were 111–2 after 70 minutes, needing 66 in 45 minutes to retain the Ashes. At this point Harvey was lbw, and Bailey persuaded a despairing Hutton to bring him on to bowl outside leg stump with no slip. Once Graveney had held a vital catch high above his head on the square leg boundary to dismiss Hole, Australia found it so hard to score that they finished 30 short. As Wisden remarked, leg theory saved England, and an over rate that meant they 'bowled only 12 overs in the last 45 minutes', an over rate quite unremarkable today.

To the Oval

So to the Oval, still 0–0. The new queen had been crowned, the highest mountain in the world had been climbed, could England climb another? In those days the Oval pitch at the end of the season would always turn sooner or later, and Lock and Laker had no counterparts in the Australian side, for unaccountably Australia didn't replace the injured Johnston with a spinner. Trueman, who was on National Service and had not bowled well for Yorkshire when he could turn out, returned for England, and a hostile spell in the middle of the first afternoon helped limit Australia to 275. Led by Hutton's 82, and with another crucial contribution from Bailey, England eked out a narrow 31 lead at little over two an over. Hutton's astuteness was now crucial. England had faced no genuine spinner, but after five overs he had Lock and Laker operating in tandem, and they took nine between them. England had 132 to win, and although they lost only two wickets they were made to fight every inch of the way until Morris bowled the last over, the 64th, and fittingly Compton and Edrich sealed a lifetime of battling against odds to bring the Ashes back home after 20 years' absence, in front of a rapturous crowd. The Australians were no killjoys, and helped the celebrations go on long into the night. Miller said, 'We were drowning our sorrows but were happy for the England boys. One of the flying champagne bottles struck the dressing room clock which stopped at a historic time for English cricket.' He didn't say so, but he was the clock-stopper.

Thus England won back the Ashes they were perilously close to losing in the second and fourth Tests. Their giants were Hutton, Bedser and Bailey. Though critics would always cavil at what they saw as defensive captaincy, Hutton marshalled his resources shrewdly, and his batting was unaffected. He made 443 runs at 55 each in a series when no other batsman on either side averaged over 40. Bedser, apparently tireless, took 39 wickets at 17 in 265 overs, figures approached only by the ever-threatening Lindwall, 26 at 18. Bailey's figures don't compare, but Hutton regarded him as 'every captain's ideal: responsive, perceptive, guaranteed to be a tactical move ahead of his shrewdest opponent, and never overawed or intimidated'. His accuracy saved the side at Headingley, and the Australians must have been sick of the sight of him with the bat. In the two Tests saved from defeat he batted five hours for 71 and over four hours for 38. Not pretty, but essential. England ground out their runs at two an over, and it was the consumption of time as much as anything that held defeat at bay until the Oval.

1953–4 West Indies

So in the last three seasons England had beaten South Africa, India and Australia. That winter they would go to the West Indies, a further test of their resilience and a chance to revenge the humiliation of 1950. England had never won a Test series there, and its billing as a world championship decider heightened anticipation and excitement. That feeling spilled over into crowd riot and cricket rancour early in the tour, marring a series of much drama and heroics. The English players felt the umpires were intimidated by the crowd's hostility and, said Wisden, 'being human, the less phlegmatic did not always hide their annoyance and displeasure. In some instances only someone with the forbearance of the most highly-trained diplomat could have been expected to preserve absolute *sang-froid*.' Frank Worrell would later call them the most unpopular team to tour the Caribbean. At that time the West Indian islands were still colonies of Britain – they wouldn't achieve independence until 1962 – and there was still some tension between the white community and the majority. The umpires were drawn from each home island, and they were a very mixed bag, but neutral umpires wouldn't come for over 40 years. England were careful to complain not about bias but of incompetence.

West Indies	417 & 209–6d	England	170 & 316
West Indies	383 & 292–2d	England	181 & 313
England	435 & 75–1	West Indies	251 & 256
West Indies	681–8d & 212–4d	England	537 & 98–3
West Indies	139 & 346	**England**	414 & 72–1

After his exertions in the summer, Bedser took a break, so England were without their most formidable bowler. They lost the first two Tests in Jamaica and Barbados with ominous ease and in similar circumstances, batting second in both and scoring 170 and 316, then 181 and 313. In each first innings they were mastered by Ramadhin and Valentine, then recovered in the second before collapsing, the last seven wickets mustering just 54 and 55. On the third day of the second Test, a day redolent of the worst of 1950, their batsmen could only muster 128 from 114 overs. So it was a terrible start, and 2–0 down with three to play. Not until Hutton won the toss in British Guiana (now Guyana) did England start to compete. Hutton's 169 gave his bowlers a platform, West Indies never recovered from Brian Statham's brilliant new-ball burst, and England retained their grip after enforcing the follow-on. This was the match when a first innings recovery, ended by a clear run-out after a stand of 99, led to a bottle-throwing riot, doubtless fuelled by alcohol and impromptu betting on the partnership reaching 100. Compton described the crowd as one where 'Keith Miller would have been very much at home'. Advised to leave the field, Hutton adamantly refused: 'I want a couple of wickets before the close tonight.' He got them, and England went on to win.

After a high-scoring draw in Trinidad, where May and Compton made hundreds and Graveney 92, England returned to Kingston for the final Test. The groundsman, talking to Hutton before the game, said that the side batting first should make 700. So Hutton was dismayed when the West Indies won the toss for, 2–1 up, they simply had to bat for as long as they could to win the series. Moreover Statham was injured, so Bailey had to open the bowling. The outcome? Bailey was inspired – his first day figures were 16–7–34–7 – and the West Indies' collapse for 139 'bordered on the incredible'. Bailey then opened the batting with Hutton, whose 205 was a masterpiece of concentration and control against an attack whose best bowler was a 17-year-old left-arm spinner called Gary Sobers, playing in his first Test and batting at No. 9. A lead of 275 was enough to consign West Indies to their first ever defeat at Sabina Park. So the series finished 2–2.

Hutton was magnificent in the West Indies. It was a tough enough tour for a captain when, as he said, 'cricket was caught up in Caribbean politics and other emotive matters'. He personally hauled the side back from 2–0 down – his innings were 24 and 56, 72 and 77, 169, 44 and 30*, 205. In all, 678 runs at 96, at the age of 38. But the tour left him, in his own words, 'physically and emotionally drained, and I am in no doubt that my playing career was foreshortened maybe by two years as a result'. He was never again a force as a Test batsman. In support Compton and May averaged in the forties, while Statham, Bailey and Laker took 44 wickets between them at around 30 each. Statham, a lithe and loose-limbed Lancastrian, was altogether more reliable than was Trueman at this stage of his career, both on and off the field. It's notable that Hutton, regarded subsequently as a champion of fast bowling almost to a fault, went into the two winning Tests with three spinners – Laker, Wardle and Lock – while playing only one of his openers, Trueman or Statham.

1954 Pakistan

Hutton played only in the first and last Tests of 1954, the year of Pakistan's first visit. In that damp summer England were overwhelmingly superior, but rain would keep them to a lead of 1–0 when they came to the fourth and last match.

Pakistan	87 & 121–3	England	117–9d
Pakistan	157 & 272	**England**	558–6d
England	359–8d	Pakistan	90 & 25–4
Pakistan	133 & 164	England	130 & 143

After a rain-ruined first Test, the young David Sheppard took over as captain from the injured Hutton for the second, and saw Compton make an exquisitely brilliant 278 in 290 minutes, of which 165 came in a stand of 192 with Bailey in just 105 minutes. Earlier Yorkshire's Bob Appleyard, who mixed seam and spin and who had missed two years of cricket stricken with tuberculosis, had taken 4–6 in his first 26 balls in Test cricket. Pakistan were close to another innings defeat in the 11 hours' play possible in the third Test. Then, of all things, England contrived to lose the fourth. First, to test out new players, they omitted Bedser and Bailey, on a pitch as ideal for them as it turned out to be for Fazal Mahmood, an accurate in-ducking seamer with a bowling arm even lower than Jackson's. Then, after Wardle's 7–56 had left them with 168 to win, England collapsed after May and Compton were coasting at 109–2, pressing carelessly for the expected victory before the end of the fourth day. Fazal took six in each innings, including twice getting May and Compton, and even a startled Hutton to a newly-learnt away swinger.

1954–5 Australia

To lose their first Test at home for three years to a Pakistan side whose highest innings was 69 and highest batting average 22 was almost farcical, and especially galling with an Australian tour beckoning. Although the side for Australia looked strong enough on paper, from the bowling attack that won back the Ashes at the Oval a year before three big names were missing – Trueman, Lock and Laker. This seems odd now, especially as they all finished the 1954 season with bowling averages between 15 and 16. But Trueman's unreliability after some incidents during the West Indies tour saw him replaced (after much debate by the selectors) by the promise of Frank Tyson's raw pace. Lock hadn't played a Test after his West Indies experience, and was displaced by Wardle, whose 20 wickets against Pakistan had come at under 10 apiece. Laker was replaced by Bob Appleyard, the man in possession. Laker's exclusion would have been more understandable had they not included the Glamorgan off-spinner Jim McConnon, who would prove a peripheral figure on tour, before and after injury.

Australia	601–8d	England	190 & 257
England	154 & 296	Australia	228 & 184
England	191 & 279	Australia	231 & 111
Australia	323 & 111	England	341 & 97–5
England	371–7d	Australia	221 & 118–6

It all began disastrously. Hutton was relying on pace. So with plenty of justifiable precedent at Brisbane he put Australia in to bat. Two days and a dozen missed catches later he would be opening a batting side without Compton, chasing 601. Compton had fractured a bone on his hand on the boundary railings, and England lost ignominiously by an innings and a lot. Tyson took 1–160 in 29 (eight-ball) overs. Back then Hutton complained that they only had three matches to sort things out before the second Test, two of which were up-country (compare that with 2004–5, a series of five Tests in six weeks in South Africa with no meaningful cricket between the Tests). They had time enough, however, for Tyson to cut down his immense run-up, particularly wearing in the heat, and gain accuracy. The fear was, though, that Tyson would lose pace, but he clean bowled five in the first innings of Victoria at Melbourne before they moved off to Sydney. Here, Hutton made the unenviable decision to drop his heroic mainstay, Alec Bedser, who had been ill with shingles, came back too soon, and had been innocuous at Brisbane. At Sydney, England, put in by Morris, plummeted to 111–9 on the first afternoon. England's prospects for the series looked very grim at that moment.

The last pair, Wardle and Statham, then added 43, which may have seemed important only psychologically at the time, but was crucial in retrospect. Bailey and Tyson, with four wickets each, kept the Australian lead down to 74, but England lost three wickets before they had inched ahead. May's 104 kept England in the game, but they led by just 176 before 46 from Appleyard and Statham (again) for the last wicket left Australia 223 to win. At the close they were 72–2, the game in the balance.

Frank Tyson

Hutton dates England's revival to the moment Tyson, batting at the head of a long tail in that second innings, was knocked unconscious by a bouncer from Lindwall.

> 'We watched horrified as he went down like felled timber and lay inert and still. There was a hush around the ground, and it took quite a time to get him on to his feet and back to the dressing room. When he came out of his concussed state I swear there was a new light in his eyes as if a spark had been kindled deep down inside him. I am not given to fanciful imagination, and the fact is that when he resumed bowling the next day he was a yard, perhaps a yard and a half, faster than before... The blow seemed to trigger off something, perhaps a new willpower... His pace at Sydney that decisive and extraordinary day was nothing short of frightening. After one ball Evans and the slips exchanged significant glances and moved back several paces. I never saw Evans so far back.'

The next morning Tyson, the wind at his back, bowled four batsmen, and caught a fifth off the mean and metronomic Statham, who toiled into the wind and closed the other end. Harvey batted brilliantly for 92*, but Tyson ended another defiant and nerve-racking last wicket stand, of 39, and England had won by 38 runs. For May, years later, 'the joy and relief of it come surging back as I think of it now'. He is not alone.

After May had rescued England at Sydney, Colin Cowdrey did the same at Melbourne. Still at Oxford, and an unexpected choice for the tour, he batted unflinchingly against Lindwall and Miller at their best in making 102 in a total of 191. Statham's 5–60 kept the Australian lead to 40, and May's 91 left them 240 to win. At the end of the fourth day they were 79–2 with Harvey again not out, echoing the Sydney position. This time the last day began with a sensational leg-side catch by Evans off Tyson from an authentic leg-glance by Harvey in the first over, and in 80 minutes Australia were all out for 111. Tyson, 7–27, 'blazed through them like a bush fire', said Wisden, abandoning its customary restraint. May said he 'fielded in the slips to him... and Frank's pace was such that I would not have backed myself to hang on to anything snicked to me'.

One up, two to play. At Adelaide Australia's 323 was matched by England's 341, Hutton 80 despite a heavy cold, Cowdrey 79. At this point Hutton, who had relied on Tyson and Statham in the previous two Tests when some commentators felt that Appleyard would be the most dangerous, now startled everyone by bringing him on after just two overs from Statham, who had damaged a big toe. Six overs later Appleyard had 3–6 and Australia closed the day at 69–3. Then next morning Hutton fooled everyone again by starting with Tyson and Statham, who bowled with a hole cut in his boot to relieve the bloodied toe. They took three quick wickets each and Australia were once again shot out for 111. As Hutton was to stress, they didn't bowl a single bouncer – they didn't need to. England had just 94 to win, but a blistering spell from Miller in Lindwall's absence had them 18–3, Hutton out and his nerves shredded. There are various versions of the conversation as Compton was getting ready to bat. The gist of it was: Hutton – 'It's Miller. The so-and-so has done us again.' Compton – 'Steady on, Len, there's still me.' At 40 Miller caught May brilliantly but controversially in the covers, rolling over and losing the ball: May walked without a backward glance. But Compton and Bailey steadied things, and Evans, who as he came in bet Compton a fiver that he'd make the winning hit, did just that.

Rain reduced the last Test to 13 hours, and saved Australia, 221 and 118–6 to England's 371–7, from the indignity of losing four successive Tests. Graveney made an exquisite century in a delightful stand with May of 182 in 160 minutes, including four successive fours off Miller, who with his characteristic generosity of spirit applauded them all. The usual New Zealand leg that followed gave England two easy wins, the second including a demolition of the home side by an innings after heading them by only 42 on first innings. New Zealand were all out for 26.

New Zealand	125 & 132	**England**	209–8d & 49–2
New Zealand	200 & 26	**England**	246

Given the strength of their bowling as Australia disintegrated, England's batsmen did just enough. Hutton may have averaged only 24 but, after Brisbane, Graveney, Compton, May, Cowdrey and Bailey all played crucial innings when they were needed. Adding in the New Zealand leg, Tyson and Statham took 69 wickets between them at 18 apiece, Appleyard and Wardle 35 at 19. The England attack in the winter of 1954–5 must rank as one of the best ever – Tyson, Statham, Bailey, Appleyard, Wardle – and even then it was missing Laker, Lock, Trueman and the unfortunate Bedser. In the six Tests after Brisbane, Tyson took 38 wickets at 14, Statham 28 at 17, Appleyard 20 at 15, Wardle 15 at 23. Hutton, writing in 1984, reckoned Tyson was for three Tests as fast as any bowler in the history of cricket, before or since. Few who saw him disagreed. The best ever attack? Let's put it this way. The England captain in 1953–6 had such an armoury of bowling talent available that he could cope with virtually any amount of injury or loss of form. Would anyone then have guessed that in the next Ashes series, only 18 months later, 80 per cent of the wickets would be taken by bowlers who weren't even picked for this tour?

England were on top of the world.

CHAPTER 6

Unbeatable

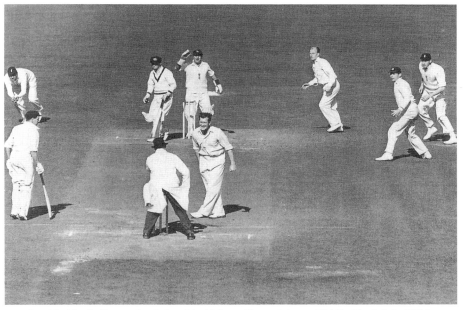

Len Maddocks lbw to Jim Laker, his 19th and last wicket at Old Trafford, July 1956,
and England have won with an hour to spare after nearly two days lost to rain.
Laker took 9–37 and 10–53.

On the way back to London I stopped at a pub in Lichfield. It was packed
out. I stood at the bar with a sandwich and a pint, saw about eight of my
wickets on the television news and listened to the bar chatter about this
bloke Laker. I took my time swallowing my pint and walked out.
Nobody recognised me.

JIM LAKER

1955 South Africa

Although England's bowling seemed incredibly strong, the batting, while adequate on paper, was paper thin, with no reserves competing strongly enough for a place. This became marked in 1955, when Hutton pulled out with lumbago, signalling his retirement. Peter May took over for the South African visit.

England	334	South Africa	181 & 148
England	133 & 353	South Africa	304 & 111
England	284 & 381	**South Africa**	521–8d & 145–7
South Africa	171 & 500	England	191 & 256
England	151 & 204	South Africa	112 & 151

The new captain, 582 runs at an average of 72, and a revived Compton, 492 at 54, were on good enough form. But in a summer of fine weather in which all five Tests with South Africa brought a result, from the nine other batsmen chosen there were only three other fifties, and a next best average of 24. Perhaps England became complacent, because they won the first two Tests, completing a run of seven wins and a near-miss from their last eight. Tyson produced another fulminating second innings spell to bowl four of his 6–28 at Trent Bridge, while at Lord's it was Statham's devastating 7–39 (in yet another innings of 111) that enabled England to capitalise on a fighting recovery, May 112, after a big first innings deficit. In Tyson's absence, the apparently tireless Statham actually bowled 29 overs unchanged in that innings. Although he was freshened by occasional breaks for rain, his was a stupendous effort of sustained hostility and accuracy.

The third Test at Old Trafford, blessed for once with clear skies, provided a tremendous match, which South Africa won by three wickets in the penultimate over, chasing 145 in 135 minutes against Tyson and Bedser, who would be playing in his last Test in Statham's absence. May (34 and 117) and Compton (158 and 71) again received little support. Compton's dashing performance had its comical side. At lunchtime the day before the game began he was 'enjoying a pint in the Bull in Gerrards Cross' when someone casually inquired whether he wasn't due at Manchester by now for the following day's Test. Compton, famously off-hand about time and kit, found a friend with a private aircraft who flew him as far as Derby, when bad weather forced him down and onto the train. That he missed the nets didn't seem to bother anyone – Denis was Denis – and the only one perturbed was his young county colleague Fred Titmus, who in his second Test was obliged to lend him a bat. Compton made 158 with it, Titmus nought with one he'd had to borrow. In his second innings, which Compton rated as one of his best, interestingly, he hit the impressive off-spinner Tayfield for six fours in one over, all to different parts of the ground. Tayfield's bemused applause at the end of the over summed it up – in his other 51 overs he went for just 78.

South Africa were becoming formidable, and England now had a fight on their hands. The attack was led by an increasingly hostile opening pair, Adcock and Heine, with Tayfield and the accurate in-swinger Trevor Goddard to follow. They were, too, the best fielding side to have been seen in England. And their batting, settling down on dry wickets, was strong enough to have the wicketkeeper-batsman John Waite at No. 7, and a big hitter at No. 8, Peter Winslow. Winslow had made a booming century in the third Test; now Russell Endean did it at number eight in the next. England lost comfortably despite May's second innings 97. All square to the Oval. No problem in those days – call up Laker and Lock. They took 15 wickets between them, Tayfield and Goddard 14, in a low-scoring game. The series was in effect decided by the second innings battle between May – 'as hard an innings as I have ever played' – and Tayfield (53.4–29–60–5).

In the four England second innings of the 1955 series in which May batted he made 112, 117, 97 and 89*. The England selectors, however, were not at all happy with the rest of the batting, and injuries forced them to tinker so much that they tried 25 players, 13 of whom played a single Test. Wardle, Tyson, Statham and Lock all took between 10 and 20 wickets, but South Africa twice made 500. With no winter tour, England would have some sorting out to do before the Australians returned in 1956, with the opening batsmen a particular worry. Moreover, after their traumatising Ashes defeat the previous winter, Australia had bounced back by beating comfortably the same West Indies side that England had been unable to defeat the previous winter, winning 3–0 despite 827 runs and five centuries from Walcott. The Australian batting was so strong that the top 10 in the order all averaged over 35. (Remember that statistic for a couple of pages.)

1956 Australia

Australia came from the blazing heat and bright light of the Caribbean to England, and the wettest of all summers in memory, which was certainly to England's advantage. They started with a new opening pair. Cowdrey, in and out of the RAF and then injured, had been able to play only one Test the previous summer, but was persuaded to open the innings. He didn't like the idea much but buckled to, and took in with him the young Worcestershire captain Peter Richardson, a tough left-hander who had made an impressive century in the tourists' traditional opener.

England	217–8d & 188–3	Australia	148 & 120–3
Australia	285 & 257	England	171 & 186
England	325	Australia	143 & 140
England	459	Australia	84 & 205
England	247 & 182–3d	Australia	202 & 27–5

My first daffodil Wisden, now broken-backed and mud-coloured, carries a graphic photograph. It records the moment early in the game when a horrible mix-up could have led to the run-out of either batsman – indeed both, if that were allowed. It seems impossible, with the ball already in the keeper's hands, for either batsman to escape. But Langley and Miller made a mess of it, and Cowdrey said later that he 'learnt more Australian dialect in the next minute than he would ordinarily have learnt in a year'. It was a critical moment, and they survived to make hugely encouraging stands of 53 and 151 against Lindwall and Miller, Davidson and Archer. In the circumstances of a low-scoring game against that opposition, Richardson's 81 and 73 must rank as one of England's best Test debuts ever. Australia looked shaky against Laker and Lock, who took 10 of the 12 wickets to fall, but there was never a chance of a result.

So to Lord's, where English optimism was shattered. Once McDonald and Burke had opened with 137 England were on the defensive and lost by 185 runs. May made two fifties but the next highest score was 32. In the absence of Lindwall and the young left-armer Alan Davidson, they were bowled out by Ron Archer, increasingly dangerous as the summer progressed, and the magnificent Miller, now 36, who took 10–152. When the Australian second innings wavered, the promising all-rounder Richie Benaud, who had already taken a stupendous catch in the gully to hold a rocket from Cowdrey, snatched back the initiative with a brilliant 97 in 143 minutes, an innings entirely against the grain of the game. We would hear more of Benaud, but not in this series.

Selectors have to take a lot of criticism. But what followed in the last three Tests was the stuff of their dreams. With Graveney and Watson badly out of form, for the Headingley Test they decided to recall one of their own number, Cyril Washbrook, out of Test cricket for six years and now 41. The press thought it madness and May himself voted against it. Nevertheless they had all recanted by the end of the first day when Washbrook's doughty battle with May, after Archer had reduced England to 17–3, arguably saved the series. Lindwall was back but Miller, crucially, could bat but not bowl. Washbrook made 98, May 101, and when the ball started to turn on the second day the Australians were in serious trouble. Although rain hampered England, their opposition subsided meekly to 143 and 140, Laker 11–113 in 70.3 overs, Lock 7–81 in 67.1.

Laker's match

Working in Islington as a curate that summer was the Reverend David Sheppard. Now 27, he had not played regularly for Sussex since captaining them brilliantly to second place in the county championship in 1953. Apart from occasional outings for the London Clergy, he had only played three matches in 1956, but in one he had scored an impressive 97 against Lindwall. For Old Trafford, his was the surprise name the selectors pulled out of their hat. England won a vital toss on a shaven wicket, and rollicked along to 459 – Richardson and Cowdrey another 180 together, Sheppard a chanceless 113, Evans 47 in half an hour. Johnson and Benaud, the Australian spinners, took 6–274 between them, but Laker was a different proposition. His accuracy and sharp off-spin, supported by a predatory leg-trap, turned 48–0 into 84 all out. His 9–37 were the best figures for England in the 20th century, a record that seemed likely to stand for a long time. It stood for a single innings.

By the end of Friday Australia were 51–1, following on. Then three days of violent weather ensued. Only 105 minutes' play was possible before the last day, for which heavy bails were used because of the strength of the wind. Under an overcast sky and on a damp pitch, Colin McDonald led Australia grimly to 112–2 at lunch. There was very little turn in the morning – on wet wickets in those days it was the drying action of the sun that made them spiteful. Now the sun came out for a spell after lunch, and the ball started to turn again. Australian captain Ian Johnson blamed divine intervention, in particular Sheppard – 'It's not fair! You've got a professional on your side.' McDonald battled on until he was seventh out for 89, but Laker steadily worked through the rest until, with half an hour to spare, he had Maddocks lbw, phlegmatically slung his sweater over his shoulder, and ambled off. No high-five histrionics back then.

Laker had taken 9–37 and 10–53, 19–90 from 68 overs. May reckoned he bowled just six bad-length balls in the match. That Lock, attacking fiercely, should take only one wicket in 69 overs at the other end seems scarcely credible. Laker's success was a feat unmatched, perhaps unmatchable, before or since. The Australians were quite justified in complaining bitterly about the pitch, which, with too much marl applied, was manifestly not of Test standard. Whether it was deliberately fixed to help the English spinners, no one could tell, but most think it unlikely, and of course if the toss had gone the other way it could have been very different. The groundsman Bert Flack took some, well, flak, but after such a historic win the newspapers didn't belabour the point for long.

The Ashes had been retained, but such was English ascendancy that the Oval would give them a good chance of a 3–1 win. Now it was Compton who completed the selectors' triumph, recalled after another operation that this time removed a kneecap. He made 94, dominating a partnership of 156 with May – 'I always enjoyed batting with him… It was a joy to watch from close quarters the one-kneed genius at work, or, in his case, at play.' Australia replied to England's 247 with 202, but, although the game fizzled out, after further rain in that endlessly vile summer, a humiliated Australia contrived to lose five second innings wickets for 27 in 38 overs after tea, Laker 4–8.

In a five-Test series Laker had taken 46 wickets at 9.6, figures from the Victorian era. Moreover, his hold over the Australians was such that he took 10 of their wickets in an innings *twice* that summer, his 10–88 – on the opening day, on a good pitch – enabling Surrey to inflict the first defeat by a county on the Australians since 1912, a figure that attests to an amazing run of Australian resilience. Only McDonald, who made 89 in that match too, could fathom him, and Laker for Surrey and England took 63 wickets against the tourists, almost unimaginable today. Laker and Lock took 65 of the 87 Test wickets to fall to bowlers, and in this series no Australian batsman even averaged more than 30. For England Richardson in his first season made a vital 364 runs at 45, while May was again imperious in such a low-scoring series. In scoring 453 runs at 90 his innings were 73, 63, 53, 101, 43, 83* and 37*. It's extraordinary that only once since the Ashes triumph at the Oval in 1953 (when he made 37) had May been out for under 50 in the second innings of a Test, usually batting at a critical stage.

1956–7 South Africa

May was by some margin the best batsman in the world in August 1956. But when he returned from South Africa in the spring of 1957 things would look very different.

England	268 & 150	South Africa	215 & 72
England	369 & 220–6d	South Africa	205 & 72
England	218 & 254	South Africa	283 & 142–6
South Africa	340 & 142	England	251 & 214
South Africa	164 & 134	England	110 & 130

This was a series of accurate bowling on sluggish pitches, with batsmen unable or unwilling to break the shackles. No batsman on either side averaged 40, and England's problem was exemplified by the averages of Compton and May, 24 and 15 respectively. For the hobbling Compton it was one tour too far. For the captain it was an unprecedented and unaccountable calamity, for outside the Tests May averaged nearly 90. Only Insole, Richardson and Cowdrey, and Goddard and McLean for the South Africans, averaged over 30. The average completed innings by a side in the series was 204, and runs were scored at a rate of only 30 per 100 balls, the equivalent of 1.8 per six-ball over (South Africa had eight-ball overs at that time). For England Bailey took 19 wickets at 12 each, while Johnny Wardle was the surprising spinning success, often switching to his rare chinaman style, his 26 wickets at 13 keeping Lock out for all but one Test. The tour was a major disappointment for Laker, the star of 1956, who took only 11 wickets, especially as the South African off-spinner Tayfield ended with 37 at 13.

It all sounds a desperate trial for the spectators, but despite the terrible scoring rate the series was gripping because it was so close. It was a mirror image of the West Indies tour three winters earlier, in that South Africa fought back to draw after being two down with three to play. Centuries by Richardson (in eight hours) and Cowdrey gave England a grip on the first two matches that they never lost. South Africa were bowled out for just 72 in each of their second innings, Bailey 5–20 in the first, Wardle 7–36 (12 in the match), in the second. In the third Doug Insole's battling maiden (and only) Test century rescued England from the grip of Tayfield, who at one stage reduced the labouring Compton to 13 in two and a half hours. What a telling contrast from 18 months earlier. The critical match was the fourth, which England needed only to draw in order to win the series. Set 232, they were at one stage 186–5, but they slithered to a 17-run defeat, the redoubtable Tayfield taking

9–113. The last Test was played on a truly awful relaid pitch, with the batsmen 'receiving more shooters that would normally be seen in a season'. Although Tyson was back for England with 6–40 in the second innings, the match scores had a 19th-century ring about them: South Africa 164 and 134, England 110 and 130.

Although England hadn't lost the series, their batting and lack of ambition were shown up again. Two days' play sum it up. On the first day of the first Test, England reached 157–3, Richardson batting all day for 69. Bailey beat that by two on the first day of the third Test, albeit shortened a bit, when England made 184–4. The Wisden correspondent concluded: 'I hope never again to watch a series in which so many batsmen were so frightened to make forcing strokes, and mere occupation of the crease was the prime consideration of nearly everyone'. At the end of the tour England looked weary, playing 17 matches outside the Tests, 15 of them first class. Of course in the 2004–5 South Africa tour England played no first-class matches outside the Tests at all, which left them in real difficulty when form deserted Vaughan and Harmison, among others. One feels that somewhere, even today, when the international schedules are congested and money holds sway, there is a happy medium to be found between those two extremes.

1957 West Indies

England returned to battle in the summer of 1957, against the West Indies team with whom they'd drawn in the controversial Caribbean tour three winters earlier. Ramadhin and Valentine were comfortably the right side of 30, the Three Ws were still going strong, and they were strengthened by two exciting young all-rounders in Gary Sobers and Collie Smith. It looked a tough prospect.

England	186 & 583–4d	West Indies	474 & 72–7
West Indies	127 & 261	**England**	424
England	619–6d & 64–1	West Indies	372 & 367
West Indies	142 & 132	**England**	279
England	412	West Indies	89 & 86

The opening Test was the first to take place at Edgbaston since 1929, and at the end of the third day England were in a terrible mess. First, Ramadhin had taken 7–49 to bowl them out for 186. Then Collie Smith's carefree 161 had pulled West Indies round from 197–5 to 474. England reached Saturday's close at 102–2. Sunday's break gave May time to reflect, and he decided that Ramadhin, so difficult to pick, had to be played as an off-spinner, and off the front foot. It worked. After the third wicket had fallen at 113 May and Cowdrey added 411 in 500 minutes. At my school in those days the prefects would post the score outside their sanctum every half-hour or so. On the fourth day, hours after my under-12 nets had finished, unwilling to tear myself away, I left for home at 6.35, hugging a score of 378–3 to myself.

Rarely can a series have been swung so decisively by a single partnership. In those days, and with an lbw law that prevented dismissal from a ball hitting the batsman outside the line of off-stump, a spinner was unlikely to get a decision if he made a long stride forward and played the ball with his front pad. Umpires are less reluctant to give a batsman out these days, for reasons that may have everything to do with seeing countless television replays. Ramadhin, with Valentine not playing, and first Worrell and then Gilchrist unable to bowl, was dumbfounded by countless failed appeals during his 98-over marathon. Johnny Wardle, England's 12th man, watched the whole innings. 'I could have cried for Sonny... I reckon a good proportion [of his appeals] were absolutely plumb.' So May made 285* – more than he'd made in the entire winter series, exorcising his lost form – and Cowdrey 154; England 583–4. A traumatised West Indies stumbled to 72–7 against Laker and Lock.

The rest of the series went decisively England's way. Another brilliant piece of opening-day bowling by Bailey, 7–44, dismissed West Indies for 127 at Lord's, and a second successive 150 from Cowdrey took England to 424 and an innings victory. At Trent Bridge Richardson and May scored centuries, but it was a masterly 258 from Graveney, back in favour at last, that completed the destruction of Ramadhin. Despite captain Frank Worrell's 191, carrying his bat, West Indies were obliged to follow on and were struggling at 89–5 before a superb 168 from Collie Smith saved them from defeat. He couldn't do the same at Leeds – after he had been bowled by Trueman from the last ball of an over, Peter Loader of Surrey, an even stringier version of the Statham he was deputising for, took the last three wickets with the next three balls, only the second hat trick by an Englishman in a home Test. Tragically, Collie Smith was to die in a car crash two years later. England's 279 was enough to win by an innings. It would have been in the Oval Test too, for, after hundreds by Richardson and Graveney in a total of 412, West Indies perished for just 89 and 86. The young Sobers, who had celebrated his 21st birthday only a month before, battled with 39 and 42, but on a turning wicket the rest capitulated against Lock, who took 11–48.

So England had won 3–0 to restore their self-esteem. The batting, untested by pace, had seen off poor Ramadhin, who after his 7–49 at Edgbaston took only another seven wickets in over 230 overs. The only lbw decision in his favour was his last wicket, England's last man at the Oval, and it's worth noting that West Indies gained only four lbw decisions in the Tests – not something remarked on at the time. Imagine the journalists' headlines if that had happened to England on a West Indies tour with local umpires. Graveney averaged 118, May 97, Cowdrey 72 and Richardson 58. Trueman, like Graveney left out of the South African tour, came back with 22 wickets, and Loader, Lock, Bailey, Laker and Statham each took between 10 and 20 cheaply.

1958 New Zealand

1957 had been largely a pleasant summer, but the 1958 weather was dismal. So was the opposition, for New Zealand was at its lowest ebb.

England	221 & 215–6d	New Zealand	94 & 137
England	269	New Zealand	47 & 74
New Zealand	67 & 129	England	267–2d
New Zealand	267 & 85	England	365–9d
New Zealand	161 & 91–3	England	219–9d

New Zealand's batting was appalling, five times failing to reach 100 and averaging 124 an innings overall, and in five Tests no batsman could muster more than 66. The England bowling figures look extraordinary. Lock took 34 wickets at 7 each, and Laker, Bailey, Trueman, Statham and Loader all averaged under 20. The batting was still a bit thin, but at least May kept his form, in a summer when he topped the first-class averages with 63 (next highest only 46). He hit three of the five English hundreds. Richardson hit the fourth and Arthur Milton, like Watson a double international, the fifth on his Test debut. That's as much description as the series merits.

As preparation for a tour of Australia, the 1958 series was inconsequential at best. England still had severe doubts about the batting and were far too dependent on the captain, as the South African series had emphasised. The bowling, although Tyson had shot his bolt, still seemed wonderfully strong and varied. In the last four series, 20 Tests, the opposition had passed 300 only four times, and averaged just 177 per innings. Look at this list.

Test sides bowled out by England for under 100 from 1956–8

1956	Headingley	Australia	84
1956–7	Johannesburg	South Africa	72
1956–7	Cape Town	South Africa	72
1957	The Oval	West Indies	89 & 86
1958	Edgbaston	New Zealand	94
1958	Lord's	New Zealand	47 & 74
1958	Headingley	New Zealand	67
1958	Old Trafford	New Zealand	85

It had been the bowling, and determined innings by batsmen at crucial moments, that had taken England from 1950–1 to 1958, the best part of eight years, without losing a series. That hadn't happened to England since the 1880s, the dawn of Test cricket, when Australia were the only opponents until a weak South Africa arrived. The 12-series undefeated run was unprecedented for England. It was that record that made England hot favourites to retain the Ashes when they steamed out of Tilbury in October 1958. But there was a shock in store, as well as something very nasty Down Under, and it would take five years for the demons lurking there to be laid to rest.

CHAPTER 7

Throwing and Dragging

Geoff Griffin of South Africa, left, bowling in 1960, when he was called for throwing, and Gordon Rorke of Australia, right, in 1959, when he was called neither for throwing nor dragging.

It is the most complex question I have known in cricket, because it is not a matter of fact but of opinion and interpretation; it is so involved that two men of good will and sincerity can hold opposite views.

DON BRADMAN

Batsmen and bowlers will always seek to exploit the Laws if they allow them any leeway. Bowlers are constrained to bowl from within a width of four feet at a batsman standing between 20 and 21 yards away. The pitch length itself has been 22 yards, the chain that defined the width of a mediaeval farmer's strip, since the Laws were first codified in 1744, and for as long before that as anyone could remember. The same 22 yards served for bowlers delivering underarm to unprotected batsmen in top hats in the early 19th century, just as it does now for those bowling at over 90 miles an hour to batsmen helmeted and padded. That 22-yard length has been inviolate. Oddly, while everything else has been up for grabs, only Ted Dexter has seriously suggested lengthening the pitch.

Fast bowlers, especially when the ball is swinging or directed at the body, prosper because the batsman has very little time to react. Bowlers can minimise that time further in two ways that press the borders of legitimacy: by bowling faster, or by releasing the ball closer to the batsman. Every bowler straightens his arm a little at the moment of delivery. To be legitimate the ball must be 'bowled, not thrown or jerked', the original wording, still expressed that simply in the Laws in the 1950s. Just a fraction more leverage can sometimes make a real difference in pace, and if it pushes at the confines of what defines a throw, well, it's hard to spot, especially if the bowler does it only occasionally. Moreover the no-ball law in place in the 1950s, also unchanged since the Laws began, required only that the bowler's back foot be grounded fractionally behind the crease at 'the moment of delivery'. Now, for a bowler of pace, the umpire had little enough time to check on where the back foot had landed before switching his focus to the batsman, and certainly had no chance of identifying exactly when the ball had been released. Consequently the bowler could get away with 'dragging' his back foot over the line before he released the ball. Both throw and drag had been intermittent worries since the war, but never to the explosive combined effect they had in 1959. Nothing like it had been seen for 60 years.

In the 1890s James Phillips was one of only a few professional umpires. He was so well regarded that he was paid to umpire in both English and Australian seasons. Concerned about the increased frequency of what he felt were dubious bowling actions in the game, and unlike local umpires beholden to no one, he began to call the main suspects for throwing. This caused a furore, but he stuck to his guns, and once he had the forthright support of the respected editor of Wisden, Sydney Pardon, the English authorities took notice. In 1900 six bowlers were named as illegal, including the highly successful Lancastrian Arthur Mold, who had played three Tests in 1893, and the ultimate all-rounder C. B. Fry, who played 26 Tests but not as a bowler. That act of umpiring courage stamped throwing out, apart from very rare occurrences, and no one thereafter fussed much about what constituted a throw. You kind of knew it when you saw it...

The umpires' problem

By the 1950s, when dubious actions once more emerged, umpires had a problem. It was they who were responsible for calling a bowler for throwing from the square-leg viewpoint, which is only one of many: recent suspect bowlers have been filmed from 27 different camera angles. Moreover, by the time a bowler has arrived in first-class cricket any doubt about his action should really have been sorted out. So an umpire has to deal with a bowler established in the first-class game, and in England that means almost certainly – for most amateurs were batsmen – a fellow professional in danger of losing his livelihood. Furthermore, unless he's dealing with the extreme rarity whom he thinks throws every ball, he's watching for a throw that occurs perhaps once every few overs. Thus he has to watch the bowler intently before he's confident enough to spot the throw in time to call it. And assuming he's confident of *that*, he has then got to feel sure that the authorities (who pay him) will support him, because if not his own future is on the line. It was largely that fear of lack of support that deterred umpires, despite the fact that – as the editor of Wisden never tired of pointing out – the law requires that he should call a no-ball if 'he be not *entirely* satisfied of the *absolute* fairness of the delivery' (my italics).

In 1951 its editor Hubert Preston commented that in Australia the MCC tourists had encountered three bowlers whose actions were dubious. In 1952 the South African fast bowler Cuan McCarthy, who had already played his 15 Tests and was now leading the attack for the great Cambridge side of that year, was no-balled for throwing at Worcester by umpire Corrall in a protracted last over of the morning. A year earlier the doyen of Test umpires, the one-armed Frank Chester, had watched McCarthy intently from square-leg in the Trent Bridge Test. At lunch he asked 'two senior men on the MCC Committee' if they'd support him if he were to call McCarthy. They declined in forthright terms – 'If you do, it will be the last time you umpire a Test match' – so he chose not to take the risk. That's what umpires faced.

Tony Lock

Later in 1952 the Oval crowd was incensed when Tony Lock's quicker ball was called by umpire Fred Price when Surrey played India. This was 10 days after Lock had played his first Test, and three weeks since the England captain had been able to watch him at length in the Yorkshire match. After delivering a typically graceful speech following Australia's surrender of the Ashes at the Oval in 1953, their captain Lindsay Hassett had been congratulated by Walter Robins. 'Yes, I thought it was pretty good, considering Lockie threw us out.' Lock's quicker ball had been a problem waiting to happen. Originally he had bowled a flighted slow left arm, with very little spin. But, impressed by Laker's powers of spin when he first came into the Surrey side, he asked his advice. Lock took it, and spent the winter practising in the indoor nets at Allders department store in Croydon. The top net there was low, and to avoid the ball hitting it, Lock, a tall man, developed a bent-arm action. At Surrey, said Laker later, gully would go back a yard when Lock replaced Alec Bedser in the attack. Exaggerated or not, it's a telling comment.

The authorities everywhere seem not to have been so attuned to the throwing threat at that stage. It wasn't until much later in his career that Lock would be forced to remodel his action completely, rather than tinker with it. This is despite the fact that in Barbados in January 1954 he was called twice in three balls by Harold Walcott, uncle of the great Clyde, and someone presumably less likely to be intimidated (especially if he was built on the massive scale of his nephew). Hutton later described Lock bowling the 44-year-old hero of 1939, George Headley, in the first 1953–4 Test: 'his stumps spreadeagled by Lock's fast ball which, not surprisingly, he did not see. A faster ball from an alleged slow bowler would be hard to imagine.' Once he had been called, Lock was told by Hutton to drop his quicker ball forthwith, and his nine wickets in the four Tests thereafter in the series were to come at a cost of 67.

Clearly, then, strong action by umpires could have an effect, but it was short-lived if it was not followed up by the authorities. By the time of the 1956 Ashes series Lock's quicker ball was back. It's not as though English players thought him innocent. Several Surrey players, let alone their opponents, had privately expressed misgivings. Doug Insole, later Secretary of MCC, when bowled by Lock's quicker ball in a Rest v Surrey match at the end of 1955, turned to the square-leg umpire to inquire innocently whether he had been bowled or run out. But the ingrained propensity of Lord's to prefer peace and a quiet life to public controversy would rebound on them. If they had publicly dealt with Lock early on there is at least some chance that the 1958–9 problem would not have occurred.

Australia 1958–9

So we come to that series. This chapter is prefaced by a stunning, if poor quality, photograph from the 1960 Wisden which shows Gordon Rorke, just before he has delivered the ball with a suspiciously bent arm, and his back foot already over the popping (batsman's) crease. Thus were the twin evils of throw and drag dramatically combined. England had arrived unbeaten in a series since 1950–1 having won the last three Ashes encounters, with batting headed by May, Cowdrey and Graveney all at their peak, and with the mouth-watering opening attack of Trueman, Tyson and Statham, Bailey in reserve, with Lock and Laker to follow. They lost 4–0.

England	134 & 198	**Australia**	186 & 147–2
England	259 & 87	**Australia**	308 & 42–2
England	219 & 287–7d	Australia	357 & 54–2
Australia	476 & 36–0	England	240 & 270
England	205 & 214	**Australia**	351 & 69–1

The scene was set for the series on a dreadful first day for England at Brisbane, when no batsman reached 30 in an innings of 134. That they did better in the second innings was down to a long vigil by Bailey, but his 68 took seven and a half hours, and England lost to a brilliant 71* out of 89 from the debutant Norman O'Neill. Until that innings it was a Test of unalleviated slowness, with 142, 148, 142 and 106 scored on each of the first four days. Never again in the series did England's vaunted attack bowl Australia out for under 300. May made 113 in the second Test after Davidson had taken three wickets in his second over, Statham took 7–57 but was defied by Harvey with 167, and Meckiff finished England off. May and Cowdrey saved the third Test with a second innings stand of 182 to give some hope, but McDonald's 170 won the fourth – the only time Statham, Trueman and Tyson had ever played together – and his 133 the fifth.

Commentators were certain England would have lost anyway, outplayed by Benaud's aggressive out-cricket, his and Davidson's entirely fair bowling – 55 wickets between them out of 94 – and Australia's more solid batting. The sober Hubert Preston, soon to succeed his father as editor of Wisden, put it like this: 'The umpires ... should have called for throwing on many occasions Burke, Meckiff, Rorke and Slater, of the Test bowlers, and several other men of lesser reputation'. That included two Victorians named Trethewey and Hitchcox, known thereafter to the tourists as Trethrowey and Pitchcox. Not one bowler was called for throwing in the entire tour, despite the misgivings of many Australians. Ray Lindwall called himself the last of the Australian straight-arm bowlers. Their former Test player H. L. Hendry said it was 'well known that some Australian bowlers chucked, and that to argue otherwise was sheer hypocrisy'. Jack Fingleton and Keith Miller agreed. Several England players wanted an official complaint at the outset, but the England management vacillated, then felt they couldn't complain once behind in the series. The Australian Board were certain enough that they had no problem, however, and trenchantly denied the existence of throwers in their side. They pointed to Lock, cutting the moral high ground from under English feet, and his Surrey colleague Peter Loader, too, was suspect. They even, bizarrely, accused Laker of throwing at one point.

The aftermath

The Australian Board continued to deny the existence of throwing – until they had regained the Ashes, that is. Both countries were galvanised into action in 1959, largely by Don Bradman in Australia and Gubby Allen in England. In England the MCC revealed that in early 1958 they had urged umpires to 'do their duty' and call bowlers with dubious actions. No umpire did. But at the end of the season the umpires themselves proposed compiling a list of suspects. In March 1959 they were 'assured of the fullest support of MCC, the counties and county captains', umpires having gone so far as to assert that they didn't think the law needed changing. That year Syd Buller called Pearson and Aldridge of Worcestershire, and Paul Gibb called Tony Lock when he slipped back into his old ways. Lock had mended them after the New Zealand leg of the tour, when he saw himself on film and, as Dexter recalled, 'We could see the bend of his arm at the point of delivery, and several gasped out loud. When the lights went up, there was Locky sitting white-faced and silent.' In Australia, though, umpires did feel the Laws needed rewording, and as an experiment the Australians removed the words 'or jerked'. From this distance it's hard to see how that improved things. Meanwhile, to combat drag, an existing problem hitherto ignored, as film of Lindwall himself in 1946 showed, Australian umpires were empowered to place a white disc behind the bowling crease behind which they felt a dragger's foot should land. That was all right up to a point, but left the umpire having to guess the distance, and then look down and behind him to check it.

The South Africans joined in, the President of their Board affirming that they must 'make sure that their touring teams do not contain a suspect bowler'. This is ironic considering what was to follow. In fact, no South African tour would be without controversy of some sort thereafter, to the point where there would be no tours at all. In 1960 they included Geoff Griffin, a pace bowler of just 20 who immediately attracted concern. His first game passed off without incident, or at least any incident involving him, for it was the young Derbyshire fast bowler Harold Rhodes who was called by umpire Gibb. At the wrong end to scrutinise Griffin's action, he instead called him three times for dragging. But four different umpires then called Griffin in successive matches, and he went off to Alf Gover's school in Mitcham to try to fix it. Griffin had a very open, chest-on, bowling action, a tell-tale sign of a potential thrower, and he worked up a fair pace even with little follow through. He got through Glamorgan and the first Test safely, but Jim Parks senior and Charlie Elliott called him at Southampton, followed crucially by Elliott once again in the Lord's Test. England won that so quickly that an exhibition match was arranged for the fourth afternoon. Buller promptly no-balled him again, then when in desperation he switched to underarm Elliott no-balled him for failing to notify him of the change. The poor lad, 21 on the Sunday of the first Test, was humiliated. He didn't bowl again on the tour, and his brief Test career was over.

Benaud and Meckiff

Next summer, 1961, the Australians were due and alarm bells were jangling. Fearing trouble, an edgy MCC instituted a five-week moratorium on calling dubious bowlers at the start of the season. In the event they needn't have worried. Of the usual suspects, Slater hadn't played again for Australia. Nor had Burke, though he was an opening bat and only an occasional off-spinner. Rorke played little part in two Tests in India in 1959–60, and food poisoning there ended his Test career. That left the left-arm opening bowler Ian Meckiff, who played the full 1959–60 series but with only limited success. He went on to play in two Tests in the wonderful West Indies tour of Australia in 1960–1, the series that began with the first ever Test match tie when Meckiff was run out in the last over. But his bowling, with a modified action that rarely produced real pace, was taken apart by Gary Sobers in his prime. To everyone's relief, Meckiff's form allowed him to be omitted from the touring team to

England. It improved dramatically in 1962–3 when he headed the season's bowling averages by some distance, reverting to his old action, but he didn't appear against England that year. Were the selectors avoiding any risk? What might have happened in those two gripping Ashes series had he played was illustrated by the events of Meckiff's last appearance, in the first Test against South Africa in December 1963.

That was Richie Benaud's last Test as Australian captain, for he broke a finger shortly afterwards and decided not to return. Benaud seems to have undergone a conversion in the five years between 1958–9 and 1963–4. His own writing suggests that originally he saw nothing wrong with his bowlers in the England series. Indeed after the second Test in 1958–9 he issued a statement saying he had watched Meckiff from square-leg and was certain his action conformed to the Laws. Don Bradman, equally unconcerned to start with, became increasingly perturbed, and rightly described it as 'the most complex question I have known in cricket, because it is not a matter of fact but of opinion and interpretation; it is so involved that two men of goodwill and sincerity can hold opposite views'. It was his diligent pursuit of the problem and its resolution that was largely responsible for gaining agreement to a new definition of throwing. It was a film show of Bradman's, in which he showed many doubtful bowlers in action, including Harold Larwood switched to make him appear a left-armer, that convinced Benaud that the problem was really serious, and he thereupon decided that any bowler called for throwing when he was captain would not bowl again in that match.

The great Alan Davidson had retired, and since Meckiff had been in good early form for Victoria he was picked to play in that first 1963–4 Test. In his first and only over Colin Egar called him four times. Benaud promptly took Meckiff off and didn't bowl him again, even though an incensed crowd wanted him put on at the other end (where Benaud asserts Lou Rowan would also have no-balled him). Egar was roundly booed and Meckiff was carried shoulder high by the crowd at the close, so high was popular feeling running: indeed extra police patrolled the ground on later days in case Benaud and the selectors were targets for the crowd's disapproval. It would be Meckiff's last over in first-class cricket. Australian conspiracy theorists have long suspected that their Board had instructed Egan to no-ball him, which seems a novel way to penalise your side at the start of a key series.

Charlie Griffith

That dealt with the South African and Australian problems. But a new issue had arisen in England in 1963. Wes Hall, the first of the great West Indian fast bowlers of the post-war era, had been joined by Charlie Griffith, who had played a single Test against England in 1959–60 but hadn't appeared since. Griffith had been no-balled once, by Cortez Jordan, playing for Barbados against the Indians in 1962. His bouncer appeared particularly difficult to pick up: the Indian opener Nari Contractor fractured his skull ducking into one and was close to death for a week. West Indies captain Frank Worrell visited him in hospital and gave blood, a typical gesture. Clearly

Griffith was quick, and in 1963 he was deadly, taking 32 wickets at 16 each, twice as many as Hall. He had a bouncer and yorker that were disconcertingly quicker than his stock ball, and both Ted Dexter and Ken Barrington were quite certain that he threw them on occasion. So was Benaud, watching him then and against Australia the following year.

In July, there was a rumour in the press that 'an influential member of the MCC' had advised umpires not to call Griffith. It was officially denied, but, nonetheless, it seemed strange that even the robust Syd Buller never called Griffith for throwing in 1963, and he only intervened – one of the few umpires to do so – when Griffith in his view bowled too many bouncers. It was only recently that Fred Trueman revealed that, while in the bath at Lord's that year, he had heard Walter Robins telling umpires Buller and Phillipson not to no-ball Griffith. The trenchant Australian umpire Cec Pepper wanted to call him in a one-day exhibition match in Birmingham, but Trevor Bailey persuaded him not to. No one at Lord's was prepared to risk the possible political fall-out. Three years later in 1966, with a modified action, Griffith was no-balled early on by Arthur Fagg against Lancashire, and warned but not called by Charlie Elliott in the Headingley Test, during which he hit the debutant Derek Underwood in the mouth. Test umpires thereafter that summer would constantly and ostentatiously switch from square-leg to point to make it clear they were scrutinising his action. Although Griffith was never called in the Tests, Elliott warned him at Headingley after a nasty bouncer bowled at Tom Graveney. Griffith seems as a consequence to have toned down his quicker ball, and was not as effective, with his 14 wickets costing 31. When he played England on the 1967–8 tour of the Caribbean he had lost his edge, and with it his place on the side.

A new law

A sad and messy period ended with new definitions of both throwing and dragging. Bradman's industry had borne fruit. By the end of the 1960s, after much trialling to and fro, the law read:

> 'For a delivery to be fair, the ball must be bowled, not thrown... A ball shall be deemed to be thrown if... the process of straightening the bowling arm, whether it be partial or complete, takes place during that part of the delivery swing which directly precedes the ball leaving the hand. This definition shall not debar a bowler from the use of the wrist in the delivery swing.'

That was joined by a new front foot no-ball law to end dragging, a law that many pace bowlers of the time detested, Fred Trueman as vociferously as any. But it has stood the test of time, and they were hardly rendered an impotent force. Thus was the illegal delivery question put to rest, resurfacing only occasionally, until the great Muralitheran debate of the present day. In the meantime it wasn't how and from where fast bowlers bowled that became the issue, but where they pitched it. That became a problem that wouldn't be solved so quickly, as I explore in Chapter 16.

CHAPTER 8

The Trueman
and Statham Years

Fred Trueman, left, and Brian Statham, right, bowling in their prime.

On Trueman:

He was a cocked trigger, left arm pointed high, head steady, eyes glaring at the batsman as that great stride widened, the arm slashed down, and as the ball was fired down the pitch, the body was thrown hungrily after it…

On Statham:

After the long loping acceleration of his run, the final delivery swing is high, his right hand sweeping through after the delivery until his knuckles almost scrape the ground.

JOHN ARLOTT

1958–9 New Zealand

Not surprisingly after their battering, England's batsmen left Australia trailing pretty dire averages behind them. May and Cowdrey managed 43 and 40, Graveney 31, no one else above 20. Moreover only Laker with 15 and Statham with 12 managed 10 wickets. Some balm was poured on the wounds in New Zealand.

| England | 374 | New Zealand | 142 & 123 |
| New Zealand | 181 | **England** | 311–7 |

The confident young Cambridge Blue Ted Dexter had been out of his depth in Australia after being flown out in mid-tour, but made a refreshing 141 batting at No. 6 in the first Test. Lock took over where he had left off against New Zealand the previous summer, taking 11–84 to bring his tally against them to 45 wickets at under 8 apiece, an almost ludicrous average. Then he saw that film of his bowling action, which made him blanch, modify his action, and relaunch his career. Rain ruined the second match after 100 not out from May.

1959 India

After that pretty meaningless interlude, England came back severely chastened. But, in a summer as warm and dry as 1958's had been foul, they beat a poor India side 5–0. This was an ideal setting for new batsmen to come through to replace those traumatised in Australia.

England	422	India	206 & 157
India	168 & 165	**England**	226 & 108–2
India	161 & 149	**England**	483–8d
England	490 & 265–8d	India	208 & 376
India	140 & 194	**England**	361

India's batting couldn't cope with Trueman and Statham, or any of the other nine bowlers used for that matter: only in the second innings of the fourth Test at Old Trafford, when Cowdrey decided not to enforce the follow-on to avoid another early finish, did they do more than scrape past 200. Then Polly Umrigar and the young Oxford blue Abbas Ali Baig scored their only centuries, Baig's a brave wristy affair in his first Test after being felled by a bouncer from Harold Rhodes of Derbyshire, not yet under a throwing interdict. England's centuries came from May in the first match, Cowdrey in the third, Pullar and Smith in the fourth.

The batting averages were headed by three batsmen who hadn't been on the Australian tour. Geoff Pullar of Lancashire was a solid left-handed opening bat; the

Warwickshire captain M. J. K. Smith, the last man to have played both rugby and cricket for England, was a forceful batsman with a strong legside bias; Surrey's Ken Barrington was an adhesive, battling accumulator. They all took their chance and averaged over 50. A further bonus, after a struggle to find a settled opening pair, was the arrival of the Northamptonshire captain Raman Subba Row, another gutsy left-hander, who had made 94 in the last Test. With Peter May suffering from a debilitating abdominal complaint and needing an operation that kept him out of the last three Tests, this was all heartening news, despite the weakness of the opposition. Trueman and Statham led the bowling with 41 wickets between them, supported by a new leg-spinner, which set old romantic hearts aflutter. Unfortunately Tommy Greenhough, 14 wickets at 18 each, who was in truth largely a googly bowler, ran into problems – literally – later in the series. After a curious arms-extended run-up, oddly similar to Jonny Wilkinson preparing to take a kick, he had a habit of following through on the pitch, which he had much difficulty remedying. When he did he was, sadly, never as effective. From a position of strength England experimented with new players, using 21 in all, including two future England captains: Ray Illingworth and Ted Dexter.

1959–60 West Indies

England spent the winter of 1959–60 in the West Indies. Despite wonderful batting that brought Gary Sobers over 700 runs, England won the toss and batted first in every game, and that gave them the edge in a high-scoring series.

England	482 & 71–0	West Indies	563–8d
England	382 & 230–9d	West Indies	112 & 244
England	277 & 305	West Indies	353 & 175–6
England	295 & 334–8d	West Indies	402–8d
England	393 & 350–7d	West Indies	338–8d & 209–5

Centuries by Barrington and Dexter, and a nine-and-a-half hour stand of 399 by Sobers and Worrell, ground the first Test to death, and it was the second and third Tests that were crucial. After centuries from Barrington and Smith, superb bowling by Trueman and Statham at Port of Spain bowled West Indies out cheaply, and England won by 256 runs in a game marred by another bottle-throwing riot. The third Test was a classic. It began with courageous batting from a battered Cowdrey, who held at bay the unflagging menace and aggression of Wes Hall, 7–69. The West Indies batsmen took control but, 22 ahead at 299–2 with Sobers in command, West Indies collapsed while trying to up the scoring rate. Cowdrey added 97 to his first innings 114 in a stand of 177 with Pullar, but nine wickets fell for another 103. If the last wicket had gone then, West Indies would have needed 205 in around 75 overs. As it was, a second vital last wicket stand by Statham and Allen, the young Gloucestershire off-spinner, made the target 230 from 63. After a hectic start

Trueman pegged them back, Sobers was run out, and when Kanhai left for 57 at 152–6 West Indies called it a day.

No other game came close to a result, although England were in trouble in the fifth until Smith and Jim Parks, the Sussex wicketkeeper-batsman flown out as a replacement, added a match-saving 197 for the seventh wicket. It had been a hotly-contested series in which both sides attracted criticism – West Indies for excessive use of bouncers, and England for slowing the over rate down after going 1–0 ahead. But frankly these were just faint foretastes of what was to come. England's batting was impressive, especially as May's illness contributed to a loss of form, and once more Cowdrey took over the captaincy. Ted Dexter had been threatening to break through for some time, and he topped the averages with 526 runs at 65. Dexter was a batsman who had rheumy old eyes at Lord's sighing for the dashing greats of the Edwardian era: tall, unruffled, dismissive in the classic superiority of his strokeplay, and a useful fast medium change bowler with a touch – only a touch, alas – of Keith Miller about him. With an exotic Italian upbringing, he was a brilliant amateur golfer, and had an aristocratic bearing that quickly earned him the soubriquet Lord Ted. That winter there were nine centuries in all: two each for Cowdrey, Dexter and Barrington, one each for Smith, Subba Row and Parks. Pullar made a top score of only 66, but so consistent was he that he still averaged 42. With Statham missing two Tests, Trueman carried the bowling with 21 wickets at 26 each.

1960 South Africa

England's dominance of all but Australia continued in the summer of 1960. South Africa were thought to be competitive after two well-fought recent series, but they didn't exhibit any real fight until the last Test. Remarkably, for the second successive series, England won the toss and batted first every time.

England	292 & 203	South Africa	186 & 209
England	362–8d	South Africa	152 & 137
England	287 & 49–2	South Africa	88 & 247
England	260 & 153–7d	South Africa	229 & 46–0
England	155 & 479–9d	South Africa	419 & 97–4

South Africa's batting was no match for Statham and Trueman at their absolute peak, 52 wickets at 19 between them. In the first three Tests they took 12, 13 and 14 wickets, and the other bowlers simply mopped up behind them. England batted first and led on first innings in every Test, South Africa failing to reach 250 until the final match. Then, after bowling England out for 155 and taking a lead of 264, they were obliged to watch Cowdrey and Pullar, 155 and 175, erase the deficit without being parted, in a stand of 290. They were the only English centuries of the summer, and it wasn't an easy series for batsmen all round. Despite being deprived of Griffin by the throwing debacle, Neil Adcock was a formidable opening bowler in the Trueman/Statham class, taking 26 wickets. In fact England passed 300 just once before that last Test, and only the consistent Pullar and Subba Row averaged over 50, with Barrington next on 37.

In the winter of 1960–1 there was no England tour. The Australians on the other hand had warmed up for their next Ashes visit with an outstanding series of brilliant cricket against the West Indies that seesawed this way and that, a series that can (still, despite 2005) lay claim to being the best ever, set up by the first ever Test match tie at Brisbane. That match's dramatic, madcap ending was followed by two others that were in doubt until the last ball. Frank Worrell and Richie Benaud set the tone for their teams' thrilling cricket, and Benaud cemented his reputation as the greatest Test captain. He was a shrewd diplomat too, and the England series would need one. The throwing controversy still rankled, and although Meckiff and Rorke were out of form and favour and did not tour – to general relief – the two countries agreed a throwing truce, so that suspect bowlers were reported and not called. In the event only England's Rhodes went on the list, and off for remedial treatment.

1961 Australia

The 1961 series turned out to be a gripping one between two evenly-matched sides, and hinged on a single day's play, at the end of the fourth Test. Benaud made it plain from the outset that his team would aim to play attractive cricket, and he stuck to his word even when the going was tough. Both Benaud and May would miss a Test through injury, but both were back and on form for that crucial last Manchester afternoon.

England	195 & 401–4	Australia	516–9
England	206 & 202	**Australia**	340 & 71–5
Australia	237 & 120	**England**	299 & 62–2
Australia	190 & 432	England	367 & 201
England	256 & 370–8	Australia	494

Australia dominated the first Test before England were rescued by contrasting centuries from the stubborn Subba Row and the flamboyant Dexter, whose increasingly imperious 180 lit up the last day. Australia took the lead by winning the second Test at Lord's, as England struggled to reach 200 in each innings against Davidson and McKenzie, particularly at the Nursery End where the infamous Ridge appeared to be causing unusual lift. Ridge or not, a grimly determined 130 by the lean and imperturbable opener Bill Lawry, helped by 102 for the last two wickets, put Australia in command, and they won by five wickets despite being reduced to 19–4 by Trueman and Statham. This was the last of 12 successive tosses won by England, and the first time in that sequence that they had lost a match.

England had to get back into the series quickly, and at Headingley they did, despite the absence of Statham. For a game played on a treacherous two-paced pitch, England replaced him, to general amazement, with Derbyshire's Les Jackson, now 40 and with his bowling arm lower than ever, 12 years after his only other Test. He bowled admirably in the match, 4–83 in 44 overs, but England's match-winner was Trueman. On the first day, bowling at full pace with the second new ball, he took five of the last eight wickets that fell as Australia slipped from 187–2 to 237 all out. England too slumped, from 190–2 to 299, Cowdrey 93, and the game was exquisitely poised when Australia reached 98–2, 36 ahead. At this point Trueman dismissed Harvey, after his second 50 of the match, with a ball that stopped and lobbed to cover. Trueman promptly told May he would bowl off-cutters off a short run, and did so to such effect that he took six for five in 47 balls, and England won by eight wickets.

Old Trafford

To Old Trafford all square. Statham returned, but unfortunately Cowdrey developed a throat infection, and was replaced by Close. England dominated for the first two days. At that point, after a rain-affected first day, England were 187–3 in reply to Australia's 190, Statham 5–53. The May–Benaud duel had been won decisively by the England captain, who was back at his best with a masterly 90*. Although he added only five next morning, England eventually led by 177. But Lawry's grindingly patient 102 led a fight back, helped by three missed slip catches that underlined a crucial aspect of Cowdrey's absence: his catching there was so reliable. When the last day began Australia were 331–6, 154 ahead. A quarter of an hour later Allen's off-spin had reduced them to 334–9, and Australia were staring at defeat when McKenzie, with no batting reputation, joined Davidson. Davidson clearly felt that he had to seize the moment, and launched himself at Allen, whose figures at that point were outstanding: 37–25–38–4. He went for 20 in an over, and May, feeling that he didn't want to chase more than 200 on that last day pitch, reverted to his quicker bowlers. This fateful decision, understandable but hotly debated, took the pressure off and the pair added 98 for the last wicket.

May felt that 256 in 230 minutes was too stiff a target, but events changed all that. With Subba Row anchoring one end, Dexter played a savagely brilliant innings of 76 out of 110 in 85 minutes, putting Benaud to the sword. England were 150–1 and coasting to victory. I had been at Old Trafford for the second day and was glued to the television set for the whole of that final day. I can still feel the exhilaration of that batting, and the anguish that followed it, when Benaud in desperation went round the wicket to bowl into Trueman's footmarks. Dexter was caught behind cutting, May unaccountably and uncharacteristically swept at his second ball and was bowled behind his legs, Close was caught behind square, sweeping at everything, and Subba Row bowled by the last ball before tea. 150–1 had become 163–5. After tea it seemed a set of mesmerised English batsmen all pushed forward to leg-breaks to be caught at slip, and England lost by 54 with 20 minutes left when Davidson bowled Statham. England hadn't had a serious target to chase for five years, and they seemed to lose the plot. Benaud defied the pain of his injured shoulder to take 6–70. He may have taken only nine other wickets in the series at 47 each, but he won the Ashes that afternoon. His decision to bowl round the wicket into the footmarks, debated with the watching Ray Lindwall overnight, was the vital innovation. Everyone does it now, but few did then.

The final Test was a high-scoring draw, with England rescued by a long stand between Barrington and Subba Row on the last day, Subba Row battling on to 137 with a groin strain, with Dexter as a runner. Subba Row, Barrington and Dexter averaged over 40 for England, May 38 and Pullar 31. This, incidentally, was the year in which Tom Graveney, who you will recall left Gloucestershire after being replaced as captain, was not allowed to play for his new county, so he took no part in the series. In another of those decisions that seem strange in retrospect Trueman was left out of the last Test; despite that he took 20 wickets at 26. Allen took 13 at 27, Statham 17 at 29. Australia were perhaps just the better side, but it was only that last day at Old Trafford that prevented England regaining the Ashes. If it hadn't been for Davidson and McKenzie, the luckless David Allen, who had bowled exquisitely, might have been the bowling hero who regained England the Ashes. As it is, he now merely merits a passing mention in Wisden, in a sentence that begins 'After Allen had taken three quick wickets on the final morning…'.

1961–2 Pakistan and India

Statham, Trueman, May and Cowdrey didn't take part in the strenuous winter tour of the subcontinent in 1961–2. Subba Row had decided to retire at the end of the season while still only 29 – thus scoring a century in both his first and last Ashes Tests – and May, recovering slowly from illness and injury, chose to call it a day at the end of the year when not yet 32. For 10 years May had been the outstanding English batsman. All five would be missed that winter, but, though the Indian wickets were far more conducive to spin than to pace, the loss of Trueman and Statham was the most severe. Moreover England's luck with the toss had deserted them, for Dexter lost seven out of eight.

Pakistan	387–9d & 200	**England**	380 & 209–5
England	500–8 & 184–5d	India	390 & 180–5
India	467–8d	England	244 & 497–5
India	466	England	256–3
India	380 & 252	England	212 & 233
India	428 & 190	England	281 & 209
Pakistan	393–7d & 216	England	439 & 38–0
Pakistan	253 & 404–8	England	507

In eight Tests against India and Pakistan the replacement opening bowlers for Trueman and Statham could only manage 24 wickets between them. Spin was in the hands of Allen and a reformed, remodelled Tony Lock, his boundless energy undiminished. They took 66 wickets between them. But they came at a cost of nearly 30 each, and at the crucial moment in India they were out-bowled by the left-arm spinner Salim Durani. The only victory came against Pakistan in the first Test of the tour, when England, set 208 in 250 minutes after Bob Barber and Allen had spun them a victory chance, were struggling at 108–5 before Barber and the new captain Dexter added 101 in 85 minutes to see them home. Barber was a promising leg-spinning all-rounder from Lancashire, batting left and bowling right. Three high-scoring draws in India followed, with Barrington scoring a hundred in each game, but at Calcutta and Madras India won crucial tosses and the series. With Durani taking 18 wickets, the series was lost 2–0. Apart from those two matches, England's batting was so powerful – in all the Tests Barrington scored 821 at 92, the captain Dexter 712 at 71, and Pullar 570 at 71 – that the defeats were all the more frustrating, and the Pakistan pitches at the end of the tour didn't allow a remedial victory.

1962 Pakistan

But Pakistan came to English pitches in 1962, for the first time since 1954, and like every other team except Australia since 1956 were outplayed by a side with Trueman and Statham back in harness.

England	544–5d	Pakistan	246 & 274
Pakistan	100 & 355	England	370 & 86–1
England	428	Pakistan	131 & 180
England	428–5d	Pakistan	219 & 216–6
England	480–5d & 27–0	Pakistan	183 & 323

That England's lowest score of 370 was greater than Pakistan's highest tells its own story, and the summer's tale was one of easy victories everywhere except Trent Bridge, where most of two days were lost to rain. Pakistan's bowling was so poor that in a five-match series none of their bowlers totalled more than six wickets. Graveney returned with two hundreds, Cowdrey made two over 150, Dexter one, and the tenacious young Middlesex left hander Peter Parfitt, blooded in the winter, plundered the weak attack with three. All four averaged over 80 with the bat, and only Barrington had a poor series. Statham and Trueman took another 38 wickets between them at 18, supported by the Worcestershire seamer Len Coldwell, 13 at 17, and the immensely tall David Larter, who took nine wickets in the last Test, his first. A competent performance by England, but not very exacting a test before another tour of Australia.

1962–3 Australia and New Zealand

In 1962 Dexter and Cowdrey had shuffled the captaincy between them. For the 1962–3 tour of Australia it went to Dexter, who, with over 1100 Test runs at 76 in the last calendar year, was a batsman at the top of his game.

Australia	404 & 362–4d	England	389 & 278–6
Australia	316 & 248	**England**	331 & 237–3
England	279 & 104	**Australia**	319 & 67–2
Australia	393 & 293	England	331 & 223–4
England	321 & 268–8d	Australia	349 & 152–4

As the scores attest, it was a close-fought series throughout. After a high-scoring draw at Brisbane, Dexter illuminating the last day with a blistering 99, the teams moved to Melbourne for the traditional New Year game. After Australia had made 316 and England 331, collapsing from 254–3 after Dexter and Cowdrey had added 175, Australia were bowled out for 248, unsettled by Trueman's constant hostility. England needed 234 in a day and a bit and had lost Pullar overnight, with Benaud threatening to repeat Old Trafford 1961. But, to the happy astonishment of England supporters huddled round their cold pre-dawn radios, supported by further fifties from Dexter and Cowdrey, the Reverend David Sheppard led England to a seven-wicket victory with an immaculate 113. It was an amazing achievement to return again to Test cricket over six years since his 1956 comeback, with only 25 games for Sussex in that period.

After that high point the series went downhill. England lost the third at Sydney comprehensively, bowled out for 104 in the second innings by Davidson at his best. Gallingly, that was the only time in the series that the batting failed, and both sides approached the last two Tests too cautiously to break an increasingly dreary dead-lock. Australia had no need to press to retain the Ashes – that little urn has a lot to answer for, often prompting defensive cricket from the holders, because a drawn series would allow them to retain it – but England also batted too slowly. Barrington was England's mainstay at the end, making 63 and 132*, 101 and 94 – but England needed the stroke-players to make runs, not just the sheet anchor. The indefatigable Trueman once more headed the averages, with 20 wickets at 26, though Statham seemed to be losing his zip. Fred Titmus was the England bowling revelation, a teasing off-spinner with a flat-footed amble to the wicket. He took 21 wickets at 29 and even averaged 36 with the bat, his superb 7–79 in a lost cause at Sydney deserving a better reward. By now his subtle variations made him the best off-spinner in the world on a flat pitch.

England	562–7d	New Zealand	258 & 89
New Zealand	194 & 187	**England**	428–8d
New Zealand	266 & 159	**England**	253 & 173–3

After Australia the team went to New Zealand as usual and won each of the three Tests with ease, Titmus and Trueman taking their winter tally to 34 wickets each. Barrington took his to 876 at 79, Cowdrey 686 at 62. Late stands were the highlight of the New Zealand leg. After yet another Barrington hundred at Auckland, the Chaucerian partnership of Parfitt and Knight added 240 for the sixth wicket. A ninth wicket Test record at Wellington followed, a finger-damaged Cowdrey coming in at No. 8 to add 163 with Alan Smith, the Warwickshire wicketkeeper. So poor was the New Zealand batting still that at Christchurch John Reid made their first century against England since 1949, 100 out of a total of just 142.

In that match Trueman edged ahead of Statham to reach 250 Test wickets, taking 7–78 in the first innings. Trueman remained an inspiring spearhead, Statham an immaculate support, but, at 33 and 32, how long could they stay at the top? In 1963 the West Indies were returning, and in those days fast bowlers were expected to play for their counties all season, yet turn up fit, fresh and in form for the Tests. Trueman would in fact play 16 county games that year and Statham 21, a sharp contrast with their 21st-century counterparts. Moreover, there would be another tournament for them to participate in for the first time. In 1963 England was to see its first ever one-day knockout tournament. How had that come about?

Bowling records of Trueman and Statham from 1958–9 to 1962–3

Test series		Tests	Trueman wkts	average	Tests	Statham wkts	average
1958–9	Aus/NZ	5	14	27.21	4	12	23.83
1959	Ind	5	24	16.71	3	17	13.11
1959–60	WI	5	21	26.14	3	10	28.60
1960	SA	5	25	20.32	5	27	18.19
1961	Aus	4	20	26.45	5	17	29.47
1962	Pak	4	22	19.95	3	16	17.38
1962–3	Aus/NZ	7	34	20.15	5	13	44.62
Test record		**35**	**160**	**21.82**	**28**	**112**	**23.62**
Domestic summer							
1959			140	19.50		139	15.01
1960			175	13.98		135	12.31
1961			155	19.35		104	20.25
1962			153	17.75		102	21.63
Domestic record 1959–62			**623**	**17.49**		**480**	**16.76**

CHAPTER 9

County Cricket – a Suitable Case for Treatment

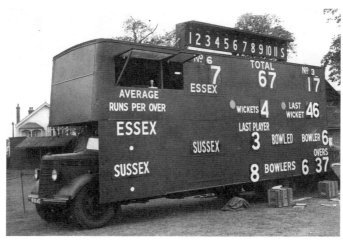

The Essex travelling scoring van at Ilford in May 1962. It was employed at the seven Essex county grounds used that year.

We can't possibly disassociate its future from the cold hard facts of finance. Nor can we blind ourselves to the fact that cricket (except possibly Tests) is losing support or losing ground versus other forms of entertainment.

DON BRADMAN

We were the cheated generation. We had been brought up on Hutton and Compton, we queued up to watch the 1948 Australians, clamoured into county grounds with thousands of others, and when we ourselves made the grade there was no one watching.

TONY LEWIS

Bradman, as usual well ahead of his time, wrote this in Wisden in 1939. He was referring to all cricket everywhere, rather than county cricket. But the cap fitted just as well. As we have seen, when the war ended the overwhelming feeling among the administrators of domestic cricket in England was that they should leave well alone. There was no need to tamper. For a few years that caution seemed justified. The county championship was pretty exciting: between 1946 and 1952 no side won it in successive years. In the years 1949 and 1950 the title was shared, by four different counties, while in 1948 and 1951 it was won by unfashionable ones – Glamorgan for the first time in 1948, Warwickshire for their second title in 40 years in 1951. This was a refreshing change from the period between the wars, when Yorkshire had won the title 12 times in 21 years, and the only feature in an otherwise predictable landscape was Derbyshire's unlikely win in 1936.

For a while the public seemed happy. In the 1930s, attendance at county matches had steadily diminished. In Yorkshire, for example, the total gate slipped below 200 000 a year to an average of 188 000 during 1935–9. In 1947, that high-water mark of county cricket in England, it had leapt to 278 000, and it was the same elsewhere: the total gate in England was 2.3 million, nearly double the figure from 10 years earlier. These figures are notoriously tricky, because they exclude members, but are tolerable for purposes of comparison.

After 1947

But 1947 was followed by a slump, an accentuation of the pre-war decline. From that 2.3 million it fell to 1.8 million in 1951, dipped below a million in the wet summer of 1958, recovered to 1.37 million in the long hot summer of 1959 when Surrey were at last vanquished after seven consecutive victories, but the inexorable slide continued so that in 1963 it had fallen to 720 000, below a third of the 1947 figure. This effect was dampened by the stability of county memberships – 135 000 in 1966 – but while members still paid their subs, fewer and fewer actually went and watched. We had become, as we still are, a nation of avid cricket followers, who emerge from hibernation in times of excitement like 1981 and 2005, but one of increasingly occasional spectators. The early 1960s threatened a fatal loss of lifeblood: the state of the patient was critical.

Why did this happen? As usual there is no simple answer, but a barrage of contributing factors. The war had stimulated the increasing advance of competing forms of entertainment that Bradman had envisaged after the 1938 season. There were more cinemas and a wider variety of films, the BBC had increased its radio output threefold during the war, and a baby boom meant fewer households were able to spare the time for a man's day out. Cricket took up seven hours, whereas football and the cinema occupied only two. Football, too, while a far greater live attraction than cricket, then as now, suffered in the same way. And an increasingly important factor was television. Before 1953 television output was small and available for only a few who could afford it. But the Queen's Coronation spurred a buying boom, and the arrival of ITV in 1954, plus the stimulus it had on a complacent BBC to get its act together, led to a vast increase and improvement in output. By the late 1960s TV ownership had increased from 10 per cent of households to nearly 90 per cent. There were then no video recorders to compensate for missing a favourite programme while you were at the cricket. And of course the BBC showed Test matches live. The forecast's iffy, it might rain. So why bother to go?

And what of the cricket? Well, cricketers and their masters didn't help matters. County cricket reverted to being less competitive: in the 12 years from 1952 to 1963 only Hampshire (1961) won the title apart from Surrey and Yorkshire. Play grew slower and slower, and matches were less and less likely to be finished inside three days – in 1946 and 1947, 70 per cent of championship matches were finished; in 1962 and 1963 the figures were 54 per cent and 52 per cent. Even then, the most popular day was the first, when a finish wasn't possible. Football or a film at least guaranteed a denouement. Watching county cricket became increasingly confined to aficionados, usually the retired man and the schoolboy, dreaming of past or future glory. Test cricket became steadily more attritional, with more scientific field-placing restricting defensive-minded batsmen, and that attitude inevitably spread. Largely conservative batsmen were taught a safety-first approach. The MCC coaching manual I was given in 1952 included a photograph of a mass drill, with a 100 schoolboys practising their forward defensive stroke. A defence is essential, of course, but significantly that was the photograph chosen as an illustration. Bowlers bowled a good length either at or outside off-stump, where the batsman could leave the ball alone or use the latitude of the then lbw law to deploy his pads; or he aimed, spun or swung the ball towards the legs, where the batsman could play it only into a leg-side, then composed of a close-set leg-trap and an unlimited number of fielders beyond it.

Then as now, if their side wasn't in with a chance of the title (ruling out most spectators) crowds wanted to see top-class cricketers, especially great attacking batsmen or thrilling fast bowlers. They had few. The days when Denis Compton could fill a ground, as he regularly did at the benefit matches of fellow professionals, were over by the mid-1950s. The real attacking batsmen could be counted on the fingers of one hand – Roy Marshall of Hampshire, Harold Gimblett of Somerset, Maurice Tompkin of Leicestershire, Jim Parks of Sussex. There were a few exciting fast bowlers – Trueman and Statham, Tyson and Loader. But such was the nature of three-day cricket, that for the most popular day, Saturday, at the point you left home you had little more than a 50-50 chance that you would actually see your hero in action – your Hutton or May or Graveney, your Bedser or Wardle or Evans. By contrast, you were sure to see Matthews and Mortensen, Gable and Monroe...

And did you get your money's worth? In the 1981 Wisden, Gubby Allen came up with a comparison of the Lord's Tests of 1930 and 1980, 50 years apart. Spectators at the four-day 1930 match saw 1601 runs in just over 23 hours of play. Those at the rain-affected five-day match 50 years later saw 1021 runs in just under 22 hours of actual play. That's 69 v 48 runs per hour. But the 1930 match had 260 overs of pace and 245 overs of spin, bowled at 21.5 overs per hour. Fifty years later the figures were

210 and 122, at 15.8 overs per hour. So the scoring rates per 100 balls were actually very much the same: 53 *v* 51, just over three runs an over. Healthy enough in both cases, but in 1980 you spent more of your time watching captains pondering changes to their field placing, and fast bowlers ambling back to a distant mark. Not just the pace men: it reached its nadir in India in 1981–2, when Wisden described the slow bowlers' over rate as 'abominable'.

A defensive mindset

In print, there was no shortage of fulmination against the insidious creeping dullness. In the 1954 Wisden Freddie Brown, a selector drafted in to one of the 1953 Tests, said that his own leg-breaks now needed a deep fielder behind him only for Gimblett and Tompkin, so few were the batsmen willing to hit over the top. That series saw England score at 33 runs per 100 balls (two an over, Australia at 44). In the 1956 edition Lord Cobham wrote 'I do not think people will follow cricket much longer unless the game is reborn… Can we get rid of those awful bores who prod doubtfully at half-volleys and let every long hop pass by? They are the ones who are emptying our cricket grounds.' The editor of Wisden remarked in 1966: 'One can scarcely tell one county from another – just a succession of seam bowlers against numerous batsmen static on their feet, ready to use their pads as the main line of defence against the ball not directed at the stumps.' The year before there had been just three spinners in the top 20 of the national averages. These were the 'willing workhorses' Basil Easterbrook wrote about in 1975, quoting the well-known lines:

> 'To do my best with bat and ball
> From twelve o'clock till evenfall
> Maintain a length, avoid a blob
> Is what I call an English job.'

From spectators to football pools

Gate money drained away. In 1946, for example, over 90 per cent of Surrey's income came directly from match attendance and members' subs. In 1948 it was under 80 per cent. By 1960 it had dropped below 60 per cent. Between 1947 and 1953 its income from match receipts never dropped below £20 000. In 1960 it dipped under £10 000. The difference was made up from its share of Test income, broadcasting rights, and a football pools scheme. Surrey were slower than many to find other ways of raising income. In the 1950s Worcestershire and Warwickshire pioneered the search for alternative sources of income, Warwickshire spurred on by its determination to restore Edgbaston as a Test match ground (which it achieved with the extraordinary first Test of 1957). It's no coincidence that Worcestershire won their first two championship titles in 1964–5, and Warwickshire won the Gillette Cup in 1966 and 1968. In that period Essex were reduced to a playing staff of 12. Foremost in the battle to keep county clubs afloat were supporters' clubs. In 1956 a select committee headed by Harry Altham produced a report which included in its preamble, 'But for supporters' clubs, the Championship as we know it would be standing today with at least one foot on the scaffold.' A few years later its head was in the noose.

Altham's report was the first of several to try to galvanise county cricket. It was limited to an experimental restriction on leg-side fielders of five, with a maximum of two behind square; to standardising boundaries at 75 yards to encourage batsmen to try to hit sixes, both changes that would unwittingly help to discourage spinners; and to adding (only) two bonus points for faster scoring on first innings. It declined to change the lbw law to penalise the padders, weakly citing the umpires' difficulty in discerning intent to play a stroke. It allowed the umpires to caution the fielding captain for timewasting, but do nothing more than exhort. And it postponed all thought of a one-day competition until at least 1959. The Altham committee came up with a blinkered approach to knock-out cricket, suggesting matches lasting two days, of two 54-over innings each, with drawn matches decided by first innings lead. No wonder that plan won few adherents. The prospect of a knock-out split the administrators, but most cricket followers could see no reason for delay, nor could they fathom why county cricket wasn't played on a Sunday (as a 1964 *Daily Express* poll confirmed) – something the committee didn't appear to consider. The Altham prescription kept the patient alive, but could not stem his steadily deteriorating health. Eventually, after much vacillation, and, spurred by successful one-day charity matches, a one-day county knock-out tournament was begun in 1963.

1963 – That was the year that was

1963 was the year the Beatles first topped the hit parade, the year satire became a staple of British television with *That Was the Week That Was*, the year of the Profumo scandal, and arguably the year the Sixties began in earnest. The Gillette Cup was a one-day tournament of 65 overs, with no special fielding restrictions, but with bowlers limited to 15 overs each. Thus England began the cricket world's prototype one-day tournament, with its innate bias in favour of batsmen, allowed to bat through the innings if they had the energy and skill. Tactics took a while to change, and Ted Dexter's calculated defensive approach was certainly not to everyone's taste. When Dexter decided to move every fielder into a run-saving position and bowled 65 overs of seam, the opposing captain Peter Richardson was moved to say, 'If this is the way you play it you can stuff this knock-out cricket'. Not surprisingly there was soon a groundswell of anxiety about the demise of the spinner, but, crucially, the paying spectator loved the Gillette Cup. Its inaugural 1963 final, won by Dexter's Sussex, was the first all-ticket match to be a sell-out in advance. One-day cricket was an instant success: gate receipts were soon substantially larger than for the three-day county championship, just as the Twenty20 games encouraged huge crowds when they arrived 40 years later, in 2003.

Other things were changing too. In November 1962, after decisively rejecting such a move as recently as 1958, an MCC committee had voted after much vacillation to abolish the distinction between amateur and professional. So an outmoded relic was swept away, though with it naturally went the Gentleman v Players fixture, an attractive pseudo-Test trial: the MCC didn't have the gumption to replace it with something as useful. As a further crack in the country's class structure, by the time the first Gillette Cup final was played the Peerage Act had been passed, allowing Lord Dunglass and Viscount Stansgate (Alec Douglas-Home and Tony Benn) to renounce their current and future peerages. Sir Alec Douglas-Home (he was knighted after giving up his hereditary title) became Prime Minister in 1963, not surprisingly the only premier to have made 50 at Lords, for Eton v Harrow 41 years earlier. He would have a minor but crucial part to play in an unhappy cricketing issue at the end of the decade, explained in Chapter 12.

I shall return to the county championship in Chapter 27. As a measure both of how the bat v ball balance has shifted, and how attendances have inexorably declined, look at this table, which shows 2001–05 for comparison.

County championship 1946-65

Year span	runs per wicket	runs per 100 balls	% results	Annual paying attendance (millions)
1946–50	26.21	46.04	64	2.0
1951-5	25.55	44.52	59	1.6
1956–60	23.44	44.19	62	1.1
1961–5	24.24	43.53	57	0.8
2001–5	34.23	57.43	58	0.5*

* Total attendance

But now let's return to the Test scene in 1963. The West Indies were coming, and Lord's would see its most dramatic ever Test match climax.

CHAPTER 10

Wind from the Windies

Ted Dexter defends against Wes Hall, left, and Charlie Griffith in his follow-through, right.

No more popular side has ever toured the old country, and with so many
thousands of the coloured population from the Caribbean having
emigrated to the big cities of Great Britain they received plenty of
support from their own people. They flocked to the grounds, and their
good humour and incessant banter helped to keep the game alive...
By their sparkling batting, bowling and fielding they caused the whole
nation to follow the progress of the Tests.

WISDEN 1964

1963 West Indies

1963 brought the West Indies back for the first time since their humiliation in 1957. Since then Frank Worrell's side had acquired a real spearhead in Wes Hall, a genuine off-spinner in Lance Gibbs, and their batting was led by the exciting stroke players Rohan Kanhai and Gary Sobers, still only 21 back in 1957. Their wonderful series against Australia in 1960–1 made them an attractive proposition, and they let no one down. The words with which Wisden prefaced its report of the tour have an old colonial ring, but the sentiment was genuine. The country buzzed with excitement, and cricket grounds resounded with more than polite applause.

West Indies	501–6d & 1–0	England	205 & 296
West Indies	301 & 229	England	297 & 228–9
England	216 & 278–9d	West Indies	186 & 91
West Indies	397 & 229	England	174 & 231
England	275 & 223	West Indies	246 & 253–2

West Indies won the first Test with ease. The opener Conrad Hunte made 182, a calm stabiliser at the top of the order ahead of the stroke players who followed, and the off-spinner Lance Gibbs took 11 wickets. It was the second Test at Lord's that set pulses racing. West Indies made 301, Trueman 6–100. Charlie Griffith promptly shot out the new all-Surrey opening pair of Micky Stewart and John Edrich. But Dexter, against Hall and Griffith at their most hostile, changed the direction of the game with a brilliant innings of 70 off 73 balls in just 81 minutes that thrilled the crowd. Barrington, Parks and Titmus then helped England to 297, four behind. Trueman, and Derek Shackleton of Hampshire, helped by immaculate slip catching by Cowdrey, then reduced West Indies to 104–5, but another great counter-attacking innings of 133 by Basil Butcher took them to 229. England needed 234 in the best part of two days, but slumped to 31–3. Another defiant innings by Barrington restored the balance, but in bad light Cowdrey broke his wrist, instinctively protecting his face from a rearing ball from Hall, who was then bowling out of the dark pavilion background. Astounding as it may seem to us now, MCC member power ensured there was no sightscreen at the Pavilion End. That dismal light ended play early with the score at 145–3, only 89 needed by England.

On the last day the weather was foul, and play didn't restart until 2.20 pm. Barrington left for 60, but Close led England grimly to 171–5 at tea, 63 needed in 85 minutes, anybody's game with Hall and Griffith sustaining their hostility at just 14 overs an hour. Close, in the days before helmets and copious body padding, finished with a mass of bruises. His 70 was quite magnificent in the context of the game, taking the fight to Hall and Griffith and even coming down the wicket to them to upset their rhythm. But Griffith got him, and England slipped behind the clock, so that when Hall's last over began Allen and Shackleton needed 8, all four results possible. With 6 needed off the last three balls, Shackleton was run out, outpaced by Worrell, going for a desperate single. Thus Cowdrey came down the pavilion steps with his arm in plaster, to watch from the non-striker's end as Allen kept out two final snorters from Hall.

Well as Hall and Griffith bowled, the bowler of the match was Fred Trueman, with 11 wickets for 152. That couldn't bring victory, but an equally superb performance at Edgbaston from him did. After England had made 228, he cut down his pace and bowled cutters, as he had done at Headingley in 1961. Trueman and Dexter bowled West Indies out for 186, but the outcome was uncertain when England stood 69–4, whereupon a defiant innings of 86* by the stocky Yorkshireman Phil Sharpe in his first Test steered England into a position where they could set West Indies 309 in 280 minutes. They could only muster 91, Trueman 7–44, and 12–119 in the match. It was superbly sustained bowling throughout two Tests against a batting side strong enough to have Worrell at No. 7.

To Headingley at 1–1. There Sobers and Kanhai took West Indies to 397, and after Griffith had torn through England with 6–36 the result was never in doubt. So to the Oval, with West Indies 2–1 ahead, and a close-fought game that was in the balance until the last innings began. England 275 and 228, glued together by Sharpe's 63 and 83, sandwiched West Indies' 246. They thus needed 255. It could have been a repeat of Lord's, with Statham back and in form to support Trueman. But Trueman damaged an ankle on the Saturday morning and couldn't bowl, and 108* from Hunte gave West Indies a deceptively easy-looking eight-wicket victory and a 3–1 triumph.

How different it could all have been had Cowdrey and Trueman not been injured at crucial times: 3–1 could have easily been 2–2. After Lord's Cowdrey played no further part in the series, and, despite that, Graveney was not called on. Against Hall and Griffith the openers all struggled, and in 20 openers' innings only Micky Stewart once passed 50. Sharpe averaged 53, an immensely impressive start against what had become the best bowling attack in the world, as well as successfully replacing Cowdrey as a brilliant slip, but no one else averaged even 35, hard though Dexter, Close and Barrington battled. Trueman took 34 wickets at 17 and was absolutely outstanding, but, although the immensely accurate medium-fast Shackleton took 17 at 34, and always exerted control, they had very little support. It was particularly disappointing that Titmus couldn't repeat his Australian success, as the tall, long-fingered off-spinner Lance Gibbs took 26 wickets at 21. Griffith dominated, with 32 wickets at 16, and, although his career became subsequently somewhat tainted because of the growing certainty that he occasionally threw, he was the key figure in the last two Tests.

1963–4 India

In the February and March of 1964 a below-strength England team led by M. J. K. Smith went on an experimental eight-week tour of India. So many of the team came down with digestive ailments that it became a test of endurance, and so little enterprise did India show in taking advantage of a weakened side that England escaped with each of the five Tests drawn.

India	457–7d & 152–9d	England	317 & 241–5
India	300 & 259–8d	England	233 & 206–3
India	241 & 300–7d	England	267 & 145–2
India	344 & 463–4d	England	451
England	559–8d	India	266 & 347–3

The pace of the first match after the first day can be judged from the fact that, facing a side succumbing to a tummy bug, the left arm spinner Nadkarni bowled 32 overs for only five singles in the first English innings, including 131 successive scoreless balls. So stricken did the English party become that they endured most of the second match with only two specialist batsmen – the third fell ill after day one. The side was completed by two wicketkeepers, four pace bowlers and two spinners, one of whom, Titmus, normally No. 8, saved the first innings with 84* from No. 5. The second was begun by the least likely pair of Yorkshiremen to compile a century opening stand in England's history, Brian Bolus and Jimmy Binks. For the later matches the batsmen recovered health and form, with Cowdrey, Parfitt and the Essex all-rounder Barry Knight making hundreds. Neither side scored at much more than two an over, and only Titmus, back to form and the outstanding bowler of the series with 27 wickets at 27, and the Middlesex opening bowler John Price, with his exaggeratedly curving run-up, really enhanced their reputations.

1964 Australia

The England selectors had little more to go on when the Australians arrived in 1964, under Bobby Simpson following Benaud's retirement. Dexter retained the captaincy.

England	216–8d & 193–9d	Australia	168 & 40–2
Australia	176 & 168–4	England	246
England	268 & 229	**Australia**	389 & 111–3
Australia	656–8d & 4–0	England	611
England	182 & 381–4	Australia	379

It was an exasperating series for England, who were clearly the better side in the first two matches, in both of which rain had the last word. In each they bowled Australia out for under 200 and led on first innings, Edrich's maiden Test century holding the side together at a rain-ruined Lord's. They threatened the same in the third Test at Headingley, but the whole series changed its complexion in a single session. Shortly after tea on the second day Australia were 178–7 in reply to

England's 268, enmeshed after reaching 124–1 in a web beautifully spun by Fred Titmus (4–69 in 50 delightful overs). At 187, controversially, Dexter took the new ball with Peter Burge 38, but so badly did Trueman and Jack Flavell bowl, and so severely were they punished by the burly Burge, whose penchant for the pull they continually fed, that Australia escaped to 389 and subsequently won by seven wickets. England never had a sniff in the last two matches. In the fourth Simpson ensured his side retained the Ashes by making 311 in nearly 13 hours out of a total of 656–8 made in 256 overs against an attack from which Trueman had been banished. He was probably grateful. So immaculate was the wicket, and so good the batting of Dexter (174) and Barrington (256), that England replied with 611 – the first innings being decided in the 29th hour of the match. Rain on the last day ruined the last match, and so England lost 1–0 to a very ordinary Australian side. As in 1961 they had to pay for one bad day – indeed this time it was for just one bad session.

There was some consolation in the arrival of a reliable new opening batsman. Geoffrey Boycott, a studiously spectacled young Yorkshireman, took to Test cricket as though born to it and averaged in the forties in his first series, as did Dexter, Cowdrey and Edrich. Boycott made his first Test century of many at the Oval. The battling Barrington, who had adopted an exaggeratedly two-eyed stance, headed the averages with 531 runs at 75, and was the mainstay, but his career was continuing to be dogged by the feeling that he was a match-saver rather than a match-winner. Trueman, despite his third Test trauma and his omission from the following Test, still finished with 17 wickets at 23 each. This would turn out to be his last major series. In six summers and two winters since the dire 1958–9 tour he had taken 197 wickets in 39 Tests. Only in 1964 did he take fewer than 20 wickets in a major series, an outstanding achievement of sustained aggression, accuracy and fitness for a strike bowler.

1964–5 South Africa

Some muddled planning led to England playing eight Tests against South Africa in nine months, sandwiching a short tour by New Zealand in the first ever twin-tour summer. M. J. K. Smith captained England in South Africa in place of Ted Dexter, who was campaigning for the General Election against the future Chancellor of the Exchequer (and ultimately Prime Minister) Jim Callaghan. Later, Callaghan would play an unexpected role in English cricket. Dexter joined the tour once the election was over.

England	485–5d	South Africa	155 & 226
England	531	South Africa	317 & 336–6
South Africa	501–7d & 346	England	442 & 15–0
South Africa	390–6d & 307–3d	England	384 & 153–6
South Africa	502 & 178–4	England	435 & 29–1

In a pattern that was becoming familiar, one side secured an early victory, and then battened down the hatches on bland pitches against a team unwilling or unable to take the initiative sufficiently to force a win. In this instance it was England in the first Test at Durban, when Allen and Titmus spun them to victory after centuries from Barrington and Parks. It was England's first victory after 12 barren Tests. Thereafter England's batting was far too strong for a South African side in transition, with Colin Bland, Graeme and Peter Pollock, and Eddie Barlow arriving on the scene. Dexter and Barrington made hundreds in the second Test, after Barber had made 97 in the kind of spectacular opening blitz he now sometimes produced. At Cape Town it was Smith, at Johannesburg Parfitt, at Port Elizabeth Boycott. Barrington averaged over 100, Barber over 70, and Dexter, Boycott, Parfitt, Parks and Smith over 40. Their lowest completed innings was 384. Allen and Titmus took 35 wickets between them, but no one else managed 10, and a toothless post-Trueman pace attack averaged nearly 70 between them.

1965 New Zealand and South Africa

New Zealand were still not able to challenge England at home or abroad. England's batting continued to prosper into the summer, and England won all three Tests comfortably under M. J. K. Smith in the first half of the season.

England	435 & 96–1	New Zealand	116 & 413
New Zealand	175 & 347	England	307 & 218–3
England	546–4d	New Zealand	193 & 166

Barrington scored 137 in over seven hours in the first match, including a period of 20 overs when he was on 85 in which he didn't score a run. He was promptly dropped for slow scoring but returned for the third Test to make a decidedly more attractive 169 in little over five and a half hours, adding 369 with Edrich. Edrich went on to make 310^* in 151 overs, an innings of crisp strokes that threatened to pass Hutton's 364 and Sobers' 365^*, until Smith's early declaration. John Edrich was an unflappable left-handed opener, one who 'knew the whereabouts of his off-stump', with a wide range of strokes once set. Apart from the second Test at Lord's, which Boycott and Dexter won in a race against rain and the clock, it was a series with little challenge for England. The genial left-arm opening bowler Fred Rumsey was eased in as Trueman's opening partner, and Titmus was back to his best form. South Africa, though, under a new captain in Peter van der Merwe, would prove a tougher proposition.

This was the beginning of a short-lived period of outstanding dominance for South African cricket, in which they won three successive tours against England and Australia. Apartheid, of course, meant that they couldn't test themselves against the West Indies. England ran them closer in this series than Australia would do, and each of the three games was hard-fought.

South Africa	280 & 248	England	338 & 145–7
South Africa	269 & 289	England	240 & 224
South Africa	208 & 392	England	202 & 308–4

At Lord's England had the edge for most of the game. South Africa recovered from 212–8 to 280, and England took a lead of 58 after Barrington's 91, run out, as Parks would be later in the innings, by a direct hit by Colin Bland, whose brilliant fielding was a major highlight of the summer. Bland's predatory presence in the covers was a constant threat, and he was the first post-war fielder who really caught the public's imagination, making them realise that fielding was a neglected art that needed as much practice to perfect as batting and bowling. South Africa struggled to 248, which left England 191 to win in nearly four hours, in practice 58 overs. At 70–1 they were in with a chance, but Edrich retired after being hit on the head by Peter Pollock, and England slithered to 145–7.

At Trent Bridge, after the naggingly accurate Warwickshire medium-pacer Tom Cartwright had reduced South Africa to 43–4, England met a stupendous innings of 125 out of 160 in 140 minutes by the brilliant free-hitting left-hander Graeme Pollock. His last 91 came out of 102 in 70 minutes after lunch, a breathtaking rate of scoring at that time. South Africa made 269, Cartwright 6–94, but he broke a thumb in the field, didn't bowl again, and batted No. 11. At 220–5, Cowdrey 105, England were in good shape, but the new ball demolished the tail and South Africa were 29 ahead. Despite five wickets for Larter, they were able to set England 319 to win with two days left. Peter Pollock broke through early, and despite a fighting 86 from Parfitt England lost by 94, Cartwright's injury and Edrich's absence clearly crucial. In the match Graeme Pollock made 125 and 59, and his elder brother Peter took 5–53 and 5–34 in a succession of hostile spells. The Oval game was equally tight. The Lancastrians Higgs and Statham – recalled for a last fling at 35 – bowled South Africa out for 208 on the first day, but, after another five for Pollock had kept England to 202, a century from Bland meant England would need 399 in seven hours. This seemed out of the question, but excellent seventies from the Middlesex opener Eric Russell, and from Barrington and Cowdrey, took England to 308–4, 91 needed in the last 70 minutes, perhaps 16 overs. So well was Cowdrey batting, the wicket playing, and Pollock's new ball spell seen off, that an amazing win was on the cards. But then it rained, curse it.

England's batting had been held together that summer by Barrington and Cowdrey, each scoring over 500 runs at 60-plus. The absence through injury of Edrich and Dexter, who had broken his leg, was a major factor in the loss to South Africa, while in the post-Trueman era a pack of different opening bowlers was used. Rumsey, Cartwright and Larter were the most successful, not to mention Statham's final fling, and also tried were Brown, Snow and Higgs. Some of these would have to be England's future spearhead, in Australia and beyond. Rumsey bowled left arm over, Cartwright metronomically accurate in-swingers, Larter from a great height. David

Brown and John Snow were fast but lacked control at this stage, while Ken Higgs bowled fast medium, with a curious action that lacked a high left arm. Who would come through? It was Titmus who was again the best bowler, with 23 wickets at 23.

1965–6 Australia

M. J. K. Smith retained the captaincy for the 1965–6 tour of Australia, with Dexter again missing.

Australia	443–6d	England	280 & 186–3
Australia	358 & 426	England	558 & 5–0
England	488	Australia	221 & 174
England	241 & 266	**Australia**	526
England	485–9d & 69–3	Australia	543–8d

This was again an Australian tour of two crucial Tests. After two draws, one rain-affected, the other high-scoring, England stunned Australia at Sydney with an astonishing and unprecedented period of batting on the first day after winning a crucial toss. They began with 303–1 in under five hours, led by Bob Barber's magnificent innings of 185 from 255 balls. A left-hander who had begun his career with a rather crabbed style, he was now a born-again opener who took the attack to the bowlers from the off. It was a major disappointment that this was his only Test hundred, and that his leg-spin was largely only trusted by his captains on the Indian subcontinent. As the wicket broke up, so Australia capitulated twice to Brown and the off-spinners. But it was the only time in the series they would be out for under 350, and the pattern of 1962–3 was repeated when Australia won the next Test easily, and had no difficulty saving the fifth to retain the Ashes once more, Bob Cowper making 307. So it was another one-all draw. Apart from in the fourth Test England's batting was again strong, with Barrington topping the averages and six other batsmen over 40. But no bowler averaged under 30 on largely benign wickets, and the batting's strength was revealed as a reflection of Australia's weak bowling once the West Indies arrived the next summer.

1966 West Indies

In 1966 the West Indies returned with very much the same side as three years earlier, with Gary Sobers now in charge, and his young cousin David Holford, a leg-spinning all-rounder, adding balance.

M. J. K. Smith's career as an England captain ended after the first Test, lost humiliatingly by England inside three days, when after centuries by Hunte and Sobers they folded twice against Gibbs, 10–106, just as they had in 1963. Lord's brought another might-have-been. After Higgs' 6–91 had bowled out West Indies for 269, nineties from Graveney and Parks, gave England a lead of 86. The crowd had applauded Graveney, back in the fold on his 39th birthday after an absence of three years, all the way to the wicket. With West Indies 95–5, nine runs ahead, England were nearly home, but an unbeaten stand of 274 by the cousins Sobers and Holford made the match safe, and it needed a bludgeoning 126* from the opener Colin Milburn, who had made 94 in the second innings of the lost cause in the first match, to save this one for England. His was 'an amazing display of powerful hitting', said Wisden, and it was a real sadness that his career was cut down by an eye injury. From Northumberland via Northampton, Milburn was larger than life in every sense. His formidable bulk gave the selectors doubts, but he had rapid reactions as a close fielder, he was daunted by no bowler, and he was immensely popular.

West Indies	484	England	167 & 277
West Indies	269 & 369–5d	England	355 & 197–4
West Indies	235 & 482–5d	England	325 & 253
West Indies	500–9d	England	240 & 205
West Indies	268 & 225	**England**	527

Again in the third Test England squandered a first innings lead. Snow and Higgs took four wickets each as West Indies could only manage 235 on the opening day. After a start of 13–3, superb batting by Graveney, Cowdrey and Basil D'Oliveira took England to a lead of 90. D'Oliveira was a South African refugee cricketer in his first series at the age of 34, though then he admitted only to 31 (more about his impact later). But England then dropped Basil Butcher five times as he reached a double hundred, and despite further late defiance from D'Oliveira, Griffith's pace and bounce was too much for England. A more comprehensive defeat occurred at Leeds, when England were bowled out twice after a big stand by Nurse and Sobers, only D'Oliveira resisting with a third successive fifty. Sobers dominated the game: his match figures were 174 runs, 5–41 and 3–39. He was absolutely awesome at this stage of his career, as captain, batsman, fielder and bowler in three distinct styles. The series stood at 3–0 to the West Indies.

Sobers was bested only in the last Test, when for once the tables were turned, and it was England who recovered from a seemingly lost position. England recalled Close for his first Test as captain, and his pugnacious attitude was a marked contrast to the restrained Cowdrey. With England 166–7 in reply to 268 early on the Friday afternoon another humbling defeat was on the cards. But Graveney was joined by another returning prodigal son, the tall Middlesex wicketkeeper John Murray, hitherto kept out of the England side by Jim Parks's superior batting. Murray's riposte was an innings of 112 in an eighth wicket stand of 217 in which he matched even the 'matchless' Tom Graveney, 163, in the elegance of his driving. An unlikely last wicket stand of 128 followed between numbers 10 and 11, Ken Higgs and John Snow, an extraordinary performance against Hall and Griffith, Sobers and Gibbs. A lead of 259 allowed

Close to exert real pressure, exemplified by Sobers' first ball, at 137–5. In a move that summed up the man's attitude and bloody-minded bravery, Close came up close at short leg and told Snow to bowl a bouncer, apparent madness. Sobers duly hooked, and instead of the ball hitting Close between the eyes – and probably rebounding to the cover boundary needing repair – it lobbed to him softly off the glove.

A win at last: too little, too late, for England that year, but a little restorative balm after a dismal summer for English cricket. In the cold light of the following morning, it was instructive that not one of the seven batsmen who had averaged over 40 in Australia could even reach that figure in 1966. Graveney headed the averages with 76, Milburn 52, D'Oliveira 42, and not one of them had been in Australia. Sobers in his pomp scored 722 runs at an average of over 100 and took 21 wickets at 27. He, Gibbs, Hall and Griffith took 73 wickets between them, to once more lay claim to being one of the best – and certainly best-balanced – Test attacks of all time. It's much to Higgs's credit that he took more wickets than anyone on either side, 24 at 25. He was the only Englishman to play in all five Tests, in a summer when the selectors in desperation called on 23 players.

1967 India and Pakistan

There was no series in the winter of 1966–7, and Close retained the captaincy for the twin-series summer against India and Pakistan. Subcontinent cricket was still at a low ebb, and England won five out of six – India 3–0, Pakistan 2–0.

England	550–4d & 126–4	India	164 & 510
India	152 & 110	England	386
England	298 & 203	India	92 & 277

In the first Indian Test, Boycott earned the same opprobrium for slow scoring as had Barrington two years previously, despite scoring 246* in nine and a half hours. This looks rather harsh in retrospect, though Barrington, apparently reformed, outscored him with 93 out of a second wicket stand of just 129 before he was run out. So perhaps the wrist-slapping worked. In the second Test, an immaculate 151 by Graveney was followed by 6–29 by Ray Illingworth, an England spinner for once out-bowling a set of Indian spinners. The pattern continued at Edgbaston, where Illingworth, Close and the new leg-spinner Robin Hobbs took 15 wickets, out-performing the Indian quartet, not yet legendary, of Bedi, Chandrasekhar, Prasanna and Venkataraghavan, the last soon shortened to Venkat to spare untutored English tongues. For once the England pace men took a back seat.

England	369 & 241–9d	Pakistan	354 & 88–3
Pakistan	140 & 114	England	252–9d & 3–0
Pakistan	216 & 255	England	440 & 34–2

Pakistan fared little better that summer. A magnificent innings of 187* by the 'little master' Hanif Mohammad on his last tour – he had played in Pakistan's first Test at the age of 18 – rescued them from 139–7 to earn a draw in the first match at Lord's. In the second, Underwood's first five-wicket haul led to a 10-wicket win. Derek Underwood, a remarkably accurate slow-medium left-armer with a long, plodding, run up, had been threatening to break through in Test cricket since his sensational first season, when he took 100 wickets for Kent in the summer he turned 18. In the final match another ignominious Pakistan defeat was staved off for a while by a wonderful innings of 146 in 190 minutes by Asif Iqbal, batting No. 9 and arriving at 53–7 after the top order had been destroyed by Higgs. Asif, full of smiling charm and wristy improvisation, would be part of the great Kent revival the following summer. In each of the Pakistan matches Barrington had made a century, batting with necessary care on a tricky rain-affected pitch at Trent Bridge, but with much more freedom for his other two. His 750 runs at 93 in the six Tests emphasised his recovery from a battering by the West Indies. Boycott, D'Oliveira and Graveney averaged over 50. Close in truth wasn't seriously challenged as a captain, but took his record to six wins out of seven, and bowled well himself to support his leading bowlers, Illingworth, 23 at 14, and Higgs, 18 at 18. The attack looked good, but was hardly tested. A West Indian winter would do that.

1967–8 West Indies

West Indies were firm favourites for the series of 1967–8, and with good reason. Sobers' side was still intact, and was strengthened by the arrival of Clive Lloyd. Lloyd didn't at first look like a cricketer. A tall, stooping, almost apologetic figure with thick glasses and a moustache, he seemed unathletic off the field. But once on it, he was a predatory cover fielder in the Bland class, and a fearsome batsman who could destroy bowling attacks. The omens were pretty awful, and no one expected England to survive. Before the tour began, the selectors made it clear that they wanted Close to continue as captain, but they were overruled by the MCC, incensed at Close's delaying tactics at the end of a key Yorkshire match at Edgbaston before the last Pakistan Test.

From this distance Close's sacking from the Test captaincy looks draconian. He effectively exploited a loophole in the Laws – the fracas would lead directly to the sensible '20 overs in the last hour' ruling – and paid heavily for it. Times were different then: 30 years later Atherton's dirt-in-the-pocket incident led to a reprimand but he kept the captaincy. It's interesting, if idle, to speculate on how England would have fared under Close's inspiring leadership against the 1968 Australians. Back in 1967, though, M. J. K. Smith had announced his retirement, so Cowdrey was effectively the selectors' third choice when given the West Indies job. He had been sacked as captain after two defeats in 1966, so how likely was he to do any better now?

From the start the series followed an unexpected pattern. England dominated and nearly won the first Test, then dominated and nearly lost the second. After centuries by Barrington and Graveney in a total of 568, West Indies followed on in the first Test

206 behind, and seemed to be coasting to safety until David Brown took three wickets in the final over before tea on the last day, taken at a perilous 180–8. But Hall, dropped immediately after tea, accompanied Sobers to the end. Amazingly enough, West Indies followed on again in the second, stunning bowling by John Snow with 7–49 dismissing them for just 143. Then at 204–5, the West Indies still 29 behind, another Jamaican bottle-throwing riot erupted when Butcher was brilliantly caught by Parks down the leg side. On the eventual resumption, Sobers with a masterly unbeaten century again rescued his side, and on a wicket full of cracks England barely held out when set 159 in two hours, the last 70 minutes of which were added on at the start of an extra day because of the riot.

England	568	West Indies	363 & 243–8
England	376 & 68–8	West Indies	143 & 391–9d
West Indies	349 & 284–6	England	449
West Indies	526–7d & 92–2d	**England**	404 & 215–3
West Indies	414 & 264	England	371 & 206–9

A second successive century from John Edrich and more aggressive bowling from Snow gave England the best of a draw in Barbados, so it was still 0–0 when the teams arrived in Trinidad for the fourth Test. For the first time in the series West Indies took a first innings lead, but they didn't begin their second until the final day. The game was surely destined for a draw, but Sobers to everyone's amazement declared to set England 215 in 165 minutes. True, the unlikely leg breaks of Basil Butcher had removed England's first innings tail, and yes, England were deemed vulnerable and hadn't shown much enterprise in similar fourth innings chases, and nearly lost at Kingston. Cowdrey was in fact dubious about the chase. But... Boycott batted with uncharacteristic verve, Cowdrey made a brilliant 71 in 76 minutes to follow his first innings 148, and England won by seven wickets with eight balls to spare. Sobers' quixotic declaration, made moreover with Charlie Griffith injured, had handed England a priceless 1–0 lead.

The last Test was extended to six days and was a test of English nerve. Sobers, stung by Caribbean condemnation for Trinidad's declaration, batted and bowled like a demon. He and Kanhai both made over 150 in a total of 414. After a Boycott hundred England were rescued from 259–8 by Lock's rapid 89, a good moment for his highest score in a career that had begun 20 years earlier. He had only been called up – from leading Western Australia to their first proper Sheffield Shield title – because of a freak boating accident that had deprived poor Fred Titmus of four toes. On the fourth day 95* from Sobers, against more superb bowling by Snow, 10–142 in the match, set up a sixth-day target of 308 for England. They made a disastrous start against Gibbs, to be 41–5 after 95 minutes. At this point the Kent pair of Cowdrey and Knott came together, not parted until 70 minutes before the end, reminiscent of Bailey and Watson in 1953. There were 13 balls left when Knott was joined by No. 11

Jeff Jones, father of Simon, who somehow scrambled through Gibbs's last over to save the day and the series. Alan Knott was the nimble, puckish, 21-year-old Kent wicketkeeper who had displaced Murray, and his batting was to become increasingly important to England.

Given his experiences against West Indies in the last two series, from a broken arm to the loss of the captaincy, this was an outstanding triumph for Cowdrey, both as captain and batsman. He and Boycott averaged 66 with the bat, with Edrich and Barrington each 42. But England's man of the series had to be John Snow. Always aggressive, with a muscular action that brought him surprising lift, he was now exerting much greater control than before, and his 27 wickets at 18 in four Tests was outstanding. He did it against a batting side including Sobers, who averaged 90, Kanhai, Butcher, Nurse and Lloyd, all at the height of their powers. It was the best performance by an England bowler in the West Indies until Harmison in 2004–5. Indeed the monosyllabic fast-bowling attack of Snow, Brown and Jones, with 55 wickets, consistently out-bowled Hall, Griffith and Sobers, quite a feat. England had some fast bowlers again.

1968 Australia

Not surprisingly, Cowdrey retained the captaincy for the 1968 visit by Australia who, having been well beaten by the South Africans in 1966–7, were not regarded as a strong combination.

Australia	357 & 220	England	165 & 253
England	351–7d	Australia	78 & 127–4
England	409 & 142–3d	Australia	222 & 68–1
Australia	315 & 312	England	302 & 230–4
England	494 & 181	Australia	324 & 125

The toss helped Australia win a first Test in which England went in with an odd attack of Snow, Higgs, D'Oliveira, Pocock and Barber, presumably to strengthen the batting. It didn't: despite a battling 87* by D'Oliveira on the last day, England's only 50, they lost easily. Thereafter rain for the rest of the summer conspired to help Australia escape. Half the playing time was lost at Lord's, where inspired bowling by Brown and Knight and faultless slip-catching bowled Australia out for just 78 in reply to 351–7, Milburn a typically pugnacious 83. The third Test lost its first day and all but 90 minutes of its last, when Australia, deprived of their captain Lawry by a finger broken by Snow, had needed 330 to win. Edrich, Cowdrey and Graveney had put England in a winning position, although Cowdrey batted with a runner because of a pulled leg muscle. The match ended with Graveney and McKenzie acting as captains.

The fourth match at Headingley was virtually rain-free, and was close-fought. England replied to Australia's 315 with 302, before their opponents – needing only a draw to retain the Ashes – ground their way to 312 in 154 overs on a slowly-turning pitch, and England had a target that was just too tough. That brought the teams to the Oval, where England sought consolation for a dismal season. The manner in which they achieved it in the face of a torrential thunderstorm on the last day was quite extraordinary, and deserving of a series-decider, not just a series-saver. For its big opening 494 England were indebted to 164 from Edrich and a masterly and timely 158 from D'Oliveira. Despite his first Test defiance D'Oliveira had been dropped from the side, and was restored only when Roger Prideaux fell ill and dropped out. The repercussions of his return and that innings will be the subject of Chapter 12. By the time the last day began Australia had already lost Lawry and Redpath cheaply in chasing 352, and were struggling at 85–5 when the heavens opened just before lunch.

Within 10 minutes the ground was literally under water, and everyone thought the game was over. But the sun was out again by 2.15 pm, and a spectator army armed with squeegees wrought such a miracle that the game was under way at 4.45 pm. Under way for Underwood, 75 minutes left. At first the pitch was dead, and it took a peach of a ball from D'Oliveira to remove Jarman's off-bail with half an hour to go. Now it began to turn for Underwood, and he took 4–6 in 27 balls, though it was a straight ball, which the equally heroic Inverarity unaccountably let hit his pads with six minutes to go, that clinched England's unlikely victory, Underwood 7–50. This was some consolation for England, although it palled once they realised that after their winter heroics in the West Indies against Hall and Griffith, Sobers and Gibbs, they had failed to regain the Ashes against a side whose top four bowlers were Connolly, Cowper and Gleeson, hardly names to chill the blood, with McKenzie toiling behind them at an average of 45. Edrich stood out with 554 runs at 61, followed by Barrington and Graveney over 40, with D'Oliveira averaging 87 in two Tests. Underwood's final Test allowed him to top the averages with 20 at 15 followed by Illingworth, 13 at 22, but Snow and Brown couldn't match Connolly's 23 at 21.

So, a series to stay in English memories only for Underwood's bowling and D'Oliveira's batting in the last Test. Those with their ears to the ground, though, realised that D'Oliveira's comeback would give the selectors a tricky problem for the winter's South African tour. D'Oliveira had become British, both legally and by enthusiastic adoption by English crowds, but he wouldn't be welcomed back so warmly by apartheid South Africa's white leaders. The face of England and world cricket would look very different in the early 1970s from the way it had in the early 1960s, and the next two chapters explain how that came about. First, 1968 saw the barriers come down to foreign cricketers in English county cricket, and by 1972 they would be playing in four competitions. English domestic cricket would have changed completely in just a decade.

CHAPTER 11

Foreign Invasion and the One-day Explosion

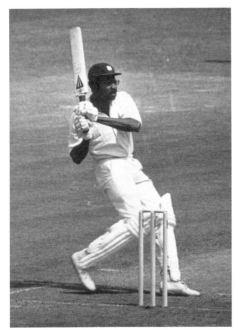

Clive Lloyd pulls during his match-winning innings in the first World Cup final, Lord's, Midsummer Day 1975, left, and Gary Sobers in the delivery stride, right.

Gilmour comes in, bowls, and Lloyd hits him high over mid-wicket for four, the stroke of a man knocking a thistle-top off with a walking stick… Umpire Bird having a wonderful time, signalling everything in the world, including stop to traffic coming on behind… What an innings – 100 off 82 balls.

JOHN ARLOTT commentating on the first World Cup final, 1975

There had been foreigners in English cricket before, and with notable exceptions they had always been viewed with suspicion. In the late 19th century many were dual-qualified Australians born in Britain, such as William Midwinter, from Gloucestershire via Bendigo, who was the occasion of an almost literal tug-of-war between W. G. Grace and the Australian tourists in 1878, and who went on to play for each country against the other – something that even today's rules can't enable. In 1896 the Indian Prince Ranjitsinhji played for England against Australia, after politely ensuring that the opposing captain Harry Trott would have no objection. Trott's younger brother Albert played for Middlesex for many years, a popular Australian, whose gigantic hit in 1899 is still the only shot to have cleared the Lord's pavilion.

But until the 1950s there were few foreign imports. The rules required that they should spend two years' residence before qualifying. That did allow the great Australian fast bowler Ted McDonald to play for Lancashire in 1924, having been a professional in the Lancashire League since 1922. It would have allowed the crowd-captivating West Indian Learie Constantine to play for them, too, had not Lancashire, to their eternal shame, refused to sign him because he was black. He responded with an eloquently expressed rage in his writing, but lived to see some belated wrongs righted, and died only a couple of years after his compatriot Clive Lloyd joined Lancashire. While the number of imports increased after the war – and indeed the championship-winning Warwickshire side of 1951 included the New Zealanders Pritchard, Hitchcock and Taylor – on the whole they were not cricketers of Test class, and they remained few and far between. Indeed, no foreign cricketers played in the Surrey and Yorkshire sides that won the county title in all but three years in the period 1952–68.

The best of the rest of the world

However, the financial threat to cricket led to some creative thinking. The arrival of the one-day knock-out in 1963, and in particular the success of the West Indian tourists, whose financial circumstances made them intrinsically the most keen to play in England, gave progressive counties an idea. In 1966 the rules of engagement ran as follows. A player had to reside in England for two years before he could play for a county, although he could return to his own country to play if the county agreed. No player could play for his country on a tour of England while registered for a county's first team. Only if the player had lived in England for five years would the residency rule be cut to one year. Thus the South African Basil D'Oliveira, designated 'coloured' under the apartheid regime, started in the Lancashire League in 1960, and, although signed by Worcestershire in 1964, had to experience a demeaning year in the 2nd XI before he could play for them in 1965.

In 1966 came the second of two reports into the state of the English game under the aegis of the Kent chairman David Clark. The proposals were far-reaching, and too far ahead of their time for the conservatives, however close the bailiffs were to the gates. The Clark report pointed to the players' negative approach, the decline in over rate, run rate and slow bowling, the game's lack of spectator appeal and too much three-day cricket. The prescription was a championship of just 16 three-day matches (in 1966 counties played 28), augmented by a one-day league of 16 matches played on Sunday, and an approach to sponsors to bring more money into the game. In fact, the situation in 2005 was not at all dissimilar, except that the 18 first-class county games are of four days' duration, and they are not played over a long weekend, as Clark suggested.

For the counties it was too much, too soon, and only four voted in favour: no one-day league, no play on Sundays. But the times they were a-changing. Following rejection of the idea in 1964, a proposal that each county should be allowed to register one overseas player immediately, without a residential qualification, was tabled again in 1967. When this was first proposed early in the year, it met with a clear-cut rejection, but, after much soul-searching, a distinct mood shift led to its being passed at the end of November.

Overseas players – pros and cons

The arguments about overseas players in English cricket were broadly the same then as they are now. Against is the view that overseas cricketers prevent young Englishmen coming into the game, and enable foreign cricketers to hone their skills on English pitches for four solid months a year, an advantage that would strengthen the opposition at England's expense. (Indeed in 1973, five years after the rule change, the entire West Indies team had been playing county cricket the previous season.) In favour, as expressed typically by John Arlott at the time, is the conviction that it would enliven a terminally tedious game, and that they would displace only 16 marginal players from county teams, less than 10 per cent. Seeing the best, day in and day out, would improve England's cricketers: a young spinner then learning his trade, Pat Pocock, said that the foreign players brought new and exacting standards, and the young professionals had to meet them in order to survive. The most promising would still come through, and would benefit from emulating the best that money could buy. The sting in that last comment, of course, was that while the cost of the contract might well be repaid in gate money, there was a risk that more than one player would be laid off to pay for the expensive newcomer, sometimes an unknown quantity who might not deliver as much as promised. In those circumstances his inflated salary could lead to internal dissent among the less well-paid home-grown professionals.

With the game's finances in a parlous state, at the heart of the issue was the question: who is the game for, the paid player or the paying spectator? At the end of the 1960s, the answer was firmly 'the spectator'. (The answer was not quite so simple by 2005, of course.) Gate money and members' subscriptions, while falling, were still more than half the average county's income. It was crucial to revive interest in the game. And Nottinghamshire, who had made the initial proposal, produced the first coup by signing the West Indies captain Gary Sobers for the 1968 season. The immediate result was a revival of the standard of the county's cricket, and increased crowds everywhere to see Sobers play. That year he rewarded them with virtuoso performances, none more so than at Swansea when he became the first batsman to hit six sixes in an over, and at Dover where he hit the fastest century of the season in 77 minutes. Although Sobers couldn't sustain that standard day-to-day amid a busy life as West Indies captain, and his county team-mates remained moderate, he showed what could be done. Inspiring foreign captains have had the same effect down to the present day, as Shane Warne proved at Hampshire from 2002.

Some counties were caught on the hop. Yorkshire reaffirmed their determination to play only Yorkshire-born cricketers, and won the championship in 1967, the year the rule changed. That they would not win it again until 2001, a year in which they did include foreigners, makes its own point. Five other counties didn't recruit anyone that season, slow to see the significance of the rule change, slow to put out feelers, or wary of the sensible stipulation that players must be offered three-year contracts. But 1968 was to see the arrival in county cricket of Rohan Kanhai, Mike Procter, Barry Richards, Farokh Engineer, Asif Iqbal, Majid Khan and Vanburn Holder. Holder was snapped up by Tom Graveney in Barbados for Worcester, the first not to be an established Test player. Clive Lloyd would follow Engineer to Lancashire after a year's qualification – he had spent 1967 playing for Haslingden in the Lancashire League.

The one-day explosion

If 1968 saw many of the barriers to foreign cricketers come down, then 1969 saw the dismantling of another bastion. The Gillette knockout tournament had been immensely popular, but its nature meant that such receipts were necessarily skewed in favour of the most successful. What was needed was a league, where everyone could milk the new cash cow. But when to play it without disrupting the first-class fixture list? Only on Sunday, hitherto a no-go area. But in 1966 the tobacco company Rothmans had begun to sponsor Sunday matches – starting after church services were over – played by an assorted team of stars, known as the International Cavaliers, against the counties, often in support of a local player's Benefit. That they were soon televised was crucial: the authorities saw their appeal and the crowds they attracted, and noted that churches were not abandoned as a consequence. For the 1969 season they said goodbye to Rothmans, and signed up the rival cigarette manufacturer John Player as sponsor of a new 40-over Sunday league. Tobacco companies' sponsorship of sport would be ended, of course, in 2003, but cricket prospered from the sale of cigarettes in the meantime, even if smokers didn't. Drinking cricketers can still profit from sponsorship.

The result was even better than anticipated: a huge surge in interest, with many new spectators, including families. Shrewd acquisitions of foreign players brought counties swift results. In 1969 Majid Khan, Peter Walker and Bryan Davis helped unfancied Glamorgan, languishing 14th in 1967, win the championship. The West Indian Davis had qualified in 1968, and Walker was a long-naturalised Englishman born in South Africa. That year Kanhai and Lance Gibbs, who had qualified in 1968, helped Warwickshire win the Gillette Cup, and Engineer and Lloyd were in the Lancashire team that won the inaugural Sunday League. While some of the foreign imports, notably Sobers and Barry Richards, had difficulty keeping their enthusiasm and concentration on the seven-day treadmill of county cricket, they were typically able to reserve their best for the big occasion. In 1970, some overseas players were missing for the Rest of the World series, but Lancashire won both one-day tournaments, while the engaging and talented Asif Iqbal helped Kent to their first championship title since 1913. The title was being shared around again and, what is more, there were more titles to go round. A single available title in 1962 had expanded to four within 10 years when Benson and Hedges, another cigarette manufacturer – not yet forced to proclaim their product's deadly qualities on each box – was engaged to sponsor a third one-day competition, this time of 55 overs, which began in 1972.

Everyone a potential winner

Now, at the start of each season each county (bar one because, inconveniently, there were 17 counties, not 16) was potentially three matches away from a knockout final. From 1972 all of them were six away from a Benson and Hedges final, making every season one of potential success, however poor the county had been in the previous summer. A judicious signing, a little luck, and their supporters could be on their way to Lord's. That was a far cry from the situation from 1952–68, when only four counties had won titles, some by hugely dispiriting margins. Many players had, from the end of June, been fighting for little more than pride, their averages and next year's contract. Now everyone had something to look forward to. Indeed, in the 10 years after the fourth tournament began, each county barring Yorkshire and Glamorgan (ironically, successive championship winners in 1968 and 1969) won at least one title. Yet that left room for Kent to win nine titles, and both Leicestershire and

Year	Championship	Gillette Cup	Sunday League	B & H Cup
1972	Warwickshire	Lancashire	Kent	Leicestershire
1973	Hampshire	Gloucestershire	Kent	Kent
1974	Worcestershire	Kent	Leicestershire	Surrey
1975	Leicestershire	Lancashire	Hampshire	Leicestershire
1976	Middlesex	Northants	Kent	Kent
1977	Middlesex/Kent	Middlesex	Leicestershire	Gloucestershire
1978	Kent	Sussex	Hampshire	Kent
1979	Essex	Somerset	Somerset	Essex
1980	Middlesex	Middlesex	Warwickshire	Northants
1981	Nottinghamshire	Derbyshire	Essex	Somerset

Middlesex five. While sceptics felt it devalued the currency, tell that to the supporters of Essex and Somerset, who had never before won anything, but swept up all four titles in 1979; to those of Northamptonshire, who had won nothing before the Gillette Cup in 1976; and to those of Derbyshire, despairing of winning anything ever again until they scrambled home with the scores level in the Gillette Cup final of 1981. Even the supporters of Glamorgan and Yorkshire went up to Lord's for a final in that 10-year period. Only those of Hampshire and Nottinghamshire failed to, and they had a championship title to warm them.

Not only had the arrival of one-day cricket spurred competition, but a combination of circumstances had led to a levelling of standards – although whether up or down was a matter of debate. Had the wealthier counties been able to afford the best cricketers and buy as many as they liked, as football teams can now, then the outcome would have been a further skewing of the strength of different sides. But as gate money became less and less important – because the money distributed from Test income only slightly advantaged the counties with Test grounds, and because other centrally distributed money was parcelled out more-or-less equally – it resulted in a democratisation of county cricket. Indeed, the six Test-hosting counties won only nine titles in that period, five fewer than if they had been handed out equally.

Many pundits deplored the descent of cricket into a 'mindless slog' and, while accepting the meteoric rise in fielding standards, felt that it was damaging England's ability to produce spinners and middle-order batsmen (although no more so than in other countries of course, once they too had adopted one-day cricket). But the majority of spectators applauded heartily. Moreover they put their hands together and in their pockets at the grounds rather than from their armchairs. They could go to a match, see both sides bat, see more runs and wickets than in a day of a first-class match – except perhaps on the days of increasingly frequent contrived third-day finishes – see a winner, and very possibly be caught up in a palpitating finish. It wasn't long before receipts from one-dayers exceeded those from three-day matches, and by a huge margin if a county had a cup run or was in with a chance of the Sunday league title.

That was all ahead of us, though, in 1968. Let's return to just one of those foreign visitors, Basil D'Oliveira. He had arrived in a damp and chilly Lancashire in the spring of 1960. Prevented by South Africa's apartheid regime from playing cricket at the level his ability warranted, he had left his friends and family behind and come to try his luck in England. He could hardly have foreseen that eight years later his innings of 158 and a vital wicket would help England square a Test series against Australia, and that he could even contemplate a return to his native land in English colours.

CHAPTER 12

'The Human Race, Of Course'

Basil D'Oliveira drives during his 158 in the final Test at the Oval, August 1968. This was the innings that seemed to have cemented his place for the South African tour.

For two decades after the formal introduction of apartheid the white countries did everything possible to avoid consideration of the ethical questions involved... It was the Home Secretary, James Callaghan who forced the cancellation of the 1970 tour of England. For the next two decades of formal isolation, cricket's attitude was ineffective and half-hearted. The culture of the game was such that no odium attached to players who were so well-rewarded for going on the seven rebel tours.

MATTHEW ENGEL

1948–9 The reality of apartheid

Ten years after the notorious Timeless Test in 1938–9, England returned to tour South Africa. It was a popular tour destination: the sea journey was relaxing but not too long, the country was beautiful and the hospitality generous. With them on that tour went John Arlott, an ex-police constable from Hampshire who was a cricket enthusiast and a bit of a poet. He had managed to get a job at the BBC during the war, putting on programmes of poetry with such luminaries as Dylan Thomas, and afterwards contrived to get himself assigned to covering cricket. With his usual curiosity he was one of the very few who left the designated white areas to travel, and look outside the white man's world.

What he saw there appalled him and made a deep impression: towns of grinding poverty and filth; houses made of tar barrels hammered flat, single-room hovels for entire families; a stream used for drinking and washing at one end of the village and for sewage at the other; a black pedestrian suddenly, randomly, kicked into a gutter by a white man; driving a black cook home in a thunderstorm after a dinner party in a white home, to the consternation of his hosts. In 1948 the moderate Jan Smuts had been narrowly beaten in the general election by the National Party, and as a consequence the pernicious apartheid laws of separate racial development were being rapidly and inexorably strengthened. When filling in the form he was obliged to complete on leaving the country, Arlott left the entry for 'race' blank. Challenged by a police officer to identify his race he replied, 'The human race, of course.'

Apart from Billy Griffith, the future MCC secretary whom Arlott had taken to a black area and who appeared equally horrified, and Mike Brearley, few England tourists ever visited black ghettos or exhibited unease at apartheid. Brearley – future England captain but then a fringe tourist – stayed on after the 1964–5 tour to see the Bantustans and the Transkei, and met several politicians. It was even worse than he had imagined. But the issue remained largely undiscussed in sporting circles, and only the highly principled Reverend David Sheppard, later Bishop of Liverpool, ever declined to play the South Africans. Most cricket lovers in England, to be frank, knew little about apartheid and cared less. That is, until Basil D'Oliveira arrived at Worcester in 1965.

Basil D'Oliveira

That D'Oliveira was the best non-white player in South Africa was probably known to barely a dozen people in England, and hardly any more in white South Africa. They regarded non-white cricket as of poor quality, largely because they knew – and wished to know – nothing about it. D'Oliveira turned up in the Lancashire town of Middleton in 1960, through the good offices of John Arlott and the Manchester journalist Charles Kay, filling in for Wes Hall for the Central Lancashire League side, a league that fostered fiercely competitive cricket. After a damp and miserable start he recovered to head even Gary Sobers at the top of the league batting averages that season. In England, eager to learn, he had decided to rein in the natural attacking style that had enabled him to hit 225 in 70 minutes back home in the 1950s.

In 1965 D'Oliveira scored a century on his debut for Worcestershire, having been persuaded there by Tom Graveney, and the pair helped the county to win the championship: both had added determination from being forced to qualify. D'Oliveira finished sixth in the national batting averages, two behind Graveney, and his subtle variations at medium pace chipped in with key wickets. Next year, with the weight of non-white South African expectation on his shoulders, he was playing for England against the West Indies, and became the only player ever to hit Wes Hall back over his head for six. He did the same to Peter Pollock too, at the Scarborough Festival against a Rest of the World XI, the ball after Pollock had bowled him a beamer. Pollock later disavowed intent, but it took him a long time to apologise. A generation later, in a changed world, Pollock's son Shaun was opening the South African bowling with Makhaya Ntini, once a village boy walking barefoot in the cowpats in winter to keep his feet warm.

In 1961, the year after D'Oliveira arrived in England, South Africa had withdrawn from the Commonwealth, automatically forfeiting its membership of the ICC, then called the Imperial Cricket Conference. In July, though, the South Africans demanded a change in the constitution to allow them to continue to play Tests, a move that was deadlocked when India, West Indies and Pakistan voted against. Tests against South Africa were thereupon designated 'unofficial', a fact that England, Australia and New Zealand – and the editor of Wisden – promptly ignored. So everything continued as before.

The 1968–9 tour

As before, that is, until the summer of 1968. A tour of South Africa was scheduled for the winter of 1968–9, and people in high places were growing nervous. In South Africa, President Vorster was taking a keen interest. He was determined that D'Oliveira must not tour, but wanted to avoid the international incident that an outright ban would cause. Vorster made this clear to Lord Cobham in March, but it was known to only three members of the MCC hierarchy. Meanwhile the recently-ousted Conservative Prime Minister Sir Alec Douglas-Home, back from a visit, gave them the unfortunate advice 'not to press for an answer to hypothetical questions' of the South African government. Top MCC officials were eager for the tour to go ahead. E. W. Swanton and Billy Griffith – the man who had been shown the unpleasant face of South Africa by John Arlott – even tried to persuade D'Oliveira to declare that he wanted to play for South Africa, this after he had already played for England! Of all the curious events of that year, described so lucidly by Peter Oborne in his book *Basil D'Oliveira: Cricket and Conspiracy*, this seems the most bizarre.

For a while it looked as though the tour was in no danger. D'Oliveira had had only a moderate tour of the West Indies that winter, the series won by England 1–0 after Sobers' unexpected last-day declaration. Moreover his hitherto immaculate behaviour was marred by one or two incidents: the man who arrived in England a teetotaller was one no longer. Then in the Australian series of 1968, despite being the only batsman to shine in the lost first Test, with 87* in the second innings, he was omitted for the remaining matches because his was designated the all-rounder's berth, and his bowling wasn't deemed good enough. D'Oliveira returned to county cricket. But just before the Oval Test a South African businessman named Teeni Oosthuizen, with the encouragement of his government, offered D'Oliveira a huge sum of money and a 10-year deal to go back to South Africa and coach, an offer made with the stipulation that he must decide before the touring team was announced. Clearly the South African government was determined D'Oliveira should not tour.

After his omission from the final Test side D'Oliveira was wavering. But the withdrawal of Tom Cartwright through injury, and Roger Prideaux after a minor illness (later exaggerated, by his own admission, so he could avoid a failure at the Oval that would jeopardise his chance of a tour place), led to D'Oliveira's recall. There he made that magisterial century, took a key wicket to unlock the Australian door for Underwood in the last hour of that damp last day, and was once more the popular hero England had taken to their hearts – a wonderful cricketer and a man who was dignified, modest and calm. As the umpire Charlie Elliott said to him in a prophetic aside during the last Test: 'You've set the cat among the pigeons now.' Surely D'Oliveira would have to be in the touring party?

Well, no, he wouldn't. Although Colin Cowdrey, the captain designate, had told MCC secretary Jack Bailey that they couldn't leave him out now, and had assured D'Oliveira he wanted him in the side, he was omitted by the selectors. To be fair, so were others with a strong claim, such as Colin Milburn. But it was the manner of his omission that reeked. The selection committee met until well after midnight, with several extra establishment figures present. The minutes of the meeting ('mislaid' for many years) offered an egregious explanation for D'Oliveira's omission: 'for cricket reasons'. The taint was apparent to the press and several journalists were scathing. D'Oliveira was inconsolable, Graveney disgusted, swearing in protest that he would not take part in the tour, President Vorster delighted. A small group within the MCC, including David Sheppard, called for the tour to be cancelled and John Arlott, writing in the *Guardian*, said it was 'ludicrous to think that anyone of open mind could believe the selectors left out D'Oliveira for valid cricketing reasons'.

Three weeks later Tom Cartwright, selected despite doubt about his fitness, pulled out, and D'Oliveira was picked 'as a bowling replacement', a transparently unlikely explanation for a change of heart. It enraged Vorster, who, in a wonderful illustration of South African attitudes, regarded the MCC, in reality a pillar of the establishment, as a 'subversive leftist group taking its orders from Harold Wilson' (the Labour Prime Minister). He promptly declared that D'Oliveira would not be welcome, and the MCC had no alternative but to cancel the tour. Sheppard, just appointed Bishop of Woolwich, and seconded by Mike Brearley, pressed the MCC to declare that no further tours should take place until progress had been made towards multi-racial sport. They lost an acrimonious public debate of MCC members by just 386 to 314 in the hall, but by a much larger margin outside it.

Early on the Saturday morning of that final Test, the Australian wicketkeeper Barry Jarman had dropped D'Oliveira from a sharp chance when he was 31. Had he caught him, the tour would in all probability have gone ahead. While the sporting ostracism of South Africa would almost certainly have taken place sooner or later, there is no doubt that D'Oliveira's innings, and the chain of events it triggered, was a defining moment in South African history. Although in 1969 their retreating government declared that in future their teams would be 'selected on merit', without fundamental internal change it would be quite impossible for non-white cricketers to catch the eye of selectors, especially selectors liable to be afflicted with a cast.

The 1970 tour

A year later the South Africans, after their unprecedented 4–0 destruction of Australia, were on top of the world. They were due to tour England again in 1970, but opposition to the tour had been steadily building, led by a 19-year-old South African engineering student at Imperial College in London, Peter Hain – 30 years on the Leader of the House of Commons. In September 1969 he set up the Stop the 70 Tour committee, and succeeded in disrupting, but not halting, both the private cricket tour by a team sponsored by Wilfred Isaacs, and the 1969–70 South African rugby tour. The rugby tour was costing an immense amount to police, requiring over 2000 officers at one match in Manchester. Nevertheless the newly-formed TCCB (Test and County Cricket Board) decided to continue the tour, but shortened it to 12 matches. Over 80 per cent of English county cricketers who were polled wanted the tour to go ahead.

In January 1970 the tour's opponents orchestrated a concerted attack on several county grounds. A fund was begun, with a committee including Alec Bedser, Colin Cowdrey and Brian Close, to raise money to pay for the tour's policing. On the same day the Supreme Council for Sport in Africa threatened to withdraw 13 African countries from the Commonwealth Games in Edinburgh that July. The stakes were being raised. David Sheppard chaired a group set up to oppose the tour by non-violent methods, with a peaceful march set for the Saturday of the Lord's Test. Clive Lloyd and Farooq Engineer of Lancashire received anonymous death threats, and the TCCB wrote to players saying that those appearing for England would have their lives insured, an action hardly likely to stiffen resolve. The Sports Council, the Royal Commonwealth Society and The Archbishop of Canterbury wanted the tour cancelled and Buckingham Palace declined to hold the usual reception, taken to be a sign of the Queen's displeasure. On 14 May there was a Commons debate on the subject: although the government wouldn't tell the TCCB what to do, it had decided to lean on them pretty hard. Then by a wonderful accidental piece of timing they called a general election for 18 June, the first day of the Lord's Test.

Just a few days after the Commons debate, South Africa was expelled from the Olympic movement. On 19 May Billy Griffith announced that the tour would continue, citing a massive majority in its favour. Acknowledging the tide of opinion, though, he said that no future tour would take place until cricket in South Africa was played on a multi-racial basis, though the TCCB would continue to pursue a policy of 'contact'. With the general election looming, and unsavoury riots in prospect, on 21 May the Home Secretary James Callaghan invited a TCCB delegation to the Home Office to a meeting, requesting that the tour be cancelled 'on the grounds of broad public policy'. Whether or not they had been shown any instruments of torture, the TCCB bowed to *force majeure* and cancelled the tour the next day.

That was the end of official cricket between England and South Africa for a generation, until 1994. In England, a hastily organised tour by a Rest of the World team – which had the two Pollocks, Richards and Barlow playing with Sobers and his fellow West Indians, against an England team including D'Oliveira – produced some brilliant cricket. The series made people realise, some for the first time, that South Africa had never played with or against the West Indies, or any side from the subcontinent.

Unofficial tours – and the backlash

So official tours of South Africa were to be over until they introduced genuine multi-racial cricket. But there were plenty of unofficial attempts, which had the effect of souring relations with the non-white Test playing nations. English cricketers like Robin Jackman found wintering abroad a useful – and for many a very necessary – way of increasing their earnings in days when cricketers' incomes were lagging behind steeply rising inflation. South Africa were keen to invite them, and many went to play and coach, increasingly often in deprived black townships, and in the tough provincial tournament. Some West Indies players, such as Alvin Kallicharran and Franklyn Stephenson, found their way there too. This led to irritation in the West Indies, which was after all by now a conglomeration of separate countries, with governments of varying shades of opinion, who came together to play cricket. In 1980–1 the government of Guyana refused to play an England side because Jackman was in the party, so England withdrew from the Guyanese leg of the West Indies tour. In 1982 the Indian government of Indira Gandhi threatened to cancel the tour by England because Geoff Boycott and Geoff Cook had been in South Africa, but ultimately relented. In 1984 the West Indian tourists were instructed not to play Yorkshire if Boycott and Arnold Sidebottom were picked.

In 1982 an unofficial team sponsored by a brewing conglomerate toured South Africa and played a series of unofficial Tests. The team was led – initially reluctantly – by Graham Gooch, and 12 of the members had played for England in the previous year. They felt that they should be allowed to ply their trade where they wanted, and many in England agreed with them. However, those who knew what apartheid really meant didn't. In his visceral poem 'I Found South African Breweries Most Hospitable', Kit Wright contrasted what was happening in prisons with the attitude of the tourists:

'Meat smell of blood in locked rooms I cannot smell it,
Screams of the brave in torture loges I never heard nor heard of
Apartheid I wouldn't know how to spell it....

….So spare me your views spare me your homily.
I am a professional cricketer.
My only consideration is my family'.

Ironically, when 20 years later England cricketers were reluctant to tour Zimbabwe, a country in not entirely dissimilar circumstances, the ICC threatened the ECB (the England and Wales Cricket Board, successor to the TCCB) with a huge fine if they did not go. As a consequence of the 1982 rebel tour, in a bid to preserve multi-racial Test cricket, the tourists were banned from playing for England for three years. Feelings were running high: five of them had just toured India, and the Indians were particularly aggrieved. Moreover the elevation of Sri Lanka to Test status in 1981 had shifted the balance – now there were seven Test-playing nations, and if it came to a vote on multi-racial lines the traditional white countries could be outvoted. Though the players were not strictly bound by the so-called Gleneagles Agreement that regulated sporting links with South Africa, they were at best naive if they expected no repercussions. In the event, although there was an attempt to reduce the ban to two years, the West Indies dug in their heels and the ban remained.

Freedom in Sport?

A year later, in 1983, the Freedom in Sport pressure group attempted to persuade the MCC to mount a tour to South Africa. The MCC committee voted to reject the proposal, whereupon the pressure group, headed by the Conservative MP John Carlisle and supported by such bygone stars as Denis Compton and Bill Edrich, forced a special general meeting of the MCC on the night before that summer's first Test against New Zealand. It was just after Margaret Thatcher's government had been resoundingly re-elected in the wake of the Falklands War; Carlisle's majority had gone up from 2000 to 12 000, and that very night the House of Commons was debating a motion to bring back hanging. Such was the mood of the time. An articulate speech by Carlisle, which compared the double standards with which business and sporting links were treated, was supported from the floor by Compton and Brian Johnston. It was opposed by MCC president Hubert Doggart and Colin Cowdrey, this time stressing the realities of a boycott by the non-white Test-playing nations, and by David Sheppard, now Bishop of Liverpool, from the floor. The motion was defeated at the meeting by 535 to 409, and by a 60:40 majority outside. Although lost, it meant that nearly half of MCC members voted for touring, despite the likely effects, and against its own committee.

In 1987, although two players with South African links, Graham Gooch and John Emburey, were in the England team for the World Cup, the Indian government was wary of risking a ban, and let them in. In 1988–9, though, eight English players who had been to South Africa on a rebel tour were denied visas by the Indian government. This time they didn't relent, and the tour was called off. This led to some hard thinking in the white cricketing world. That January the ICC meeting – whose balance had changed crucially with the elevation of Sri Lanka to Test status in 1981 – decided that from 1 April it would ban from Test cricket anyone visiting South Africa in a cricketing capacity, for periods depending on their age. This polarised views in England once again. Those opposed to this move accused them of ignoring what had been happening in the Black townships, and felt that ideals about fostering cricket had been pushed aside. That countries could not now select their best teams was the particular complaint of Jack Bailey, former MCC Secretary. The moral counter argument was that it was the ending of apartheid that was important, not the number of black cricketers under the regime. Anyway, it was clear that England could not select banned players without risking the cancellation of many of their Test series.

Cricketers and supporters in England tended to the view that politics should be kept out of sport. But it wouldn't stay out. Two successive Olympics underlined that. While many in England tend to pronounce the word with a faint air of disgust, when appalling inequalities are wilfully perpetuated, those who wish to remove them will use every means at their disposal. It was heart-warming that English cricketers were coaching black children in Soweto but, as Donald Woods pointed out in an article in the 1992 Wisden, those children were still subject to 317 laws that restricted them on account of their race. Soweto was still a ghetto, Nelson Mandela was still in prison, and the African National Congress (ANC), which represented the vast majority of South Africans, was still a banned organisation. Virtually the only ally the ANC had in its attempt to overthrow apartheid was world opinion, and it was understandably against any attempt to weaken South Africa's sporting isolation. So it would continue to oppose the laudable attempts of people such as Dr Ali Bacher, captain of the great South African team of 1969–70, and MD of the South African Cricket Union (SACU) in 1990, who – as a Lithuanian Jew who had worked in a non-white hospital – was all too aware of the iniquities of the system. He had indeed received death threats in 1970 after advocating changes in the law.

Things came to a head in 1989–90. England were playing the last Test of the 1989 Ashes summer, when Mike Atherton and Angus Fraser saw the names of another rebel team to South Africa flashed up on a TV screen. That was the first they knew of it. Of a team of 15, all but one had played Tests for England, eight of them in the Australian series. Ironically one of them was Chris Cowdrey, son of Colin, putative captain of the cancelled 1968–9 tour and now chairman of the ICC. The captain was Mike Gatting, the manager David Graveney. Fraser turned to Atherton and said: 'Surely playing for your country is meant to mean more than this?'. The rebel players were promptly banned from playing for England for five years. The tour itself lasted barely a month. It started on 26 January amid violent demonstrations, but on 2 February President F. W. de Klerk announced the unbanning of the ANC and on 11 February Nelson Mandela was released after 27 years in prison. The tour was abandoned a fortnight later. Mandela was elected President of South Africa in May 1994. That summer England played South Africa officially for the first time for 29 years.

CHAPTER 13

Illingworth – the Stopgap Captain

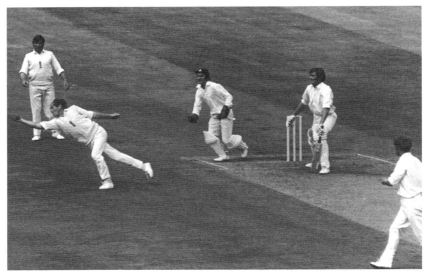

Ray Illingworth catches Paul Sheahan off Derek Underwood at Headingley, July 1972.
Sheahan had batted 29 balls without scoring, as Australia went from 79–1 to 146 all out.

Considering the rather mediocre talent Raymond Illingworth had at his command he served England creditably during his four years as captain… England turned to Illingworth at a time of a dearth of natural leaders and he responded in full with his sound knowledge of the game, his tactical skill and his own ability as a player when crises occurred. With the resources at his disposal, that he should win and then retain the Ashes was a great achievement for someone who for years was regarded as little more than an honest journeyman not quite of Test class.

NORMAN PRESTON

1968–9 Pakistan

After the cancellation of the South African tour in the autumn of 1968, the MCC hastily organised a visit to India, Ceylon and Pakistan, which turned out to be pretty disastrous. For financial reasons the Indian leg never took place, and the Pakistan series was played against a background of violent unrest by students and others calling for the independence of its eastern part. If you had used the words 'Bangladesh' and 'Sri Lanka' to the English tourists that year they wouldn't have known what you meant. Moslem Pakistan had been created after the war in two parts, separated by a huge chunk of India. The poorer eastern section, whose capital Dacca hosted the second Test, was renamed Bangladesh when it gained independence two years later. Ceylon became Sri Lanka – literally and accurately 'resplendent island' – the following year. After a pleasant sojourn there the tourists arrived in a seething Pakistan.

England	306 & 225–9d	Pakistan	209 & 203–5
Pakistan	246 & 195–6d	England	274 & 33–0
England	502–7		

Unusually, the Tests were of four days' duration, which gave little enough time for a result, even without the frequent interruptions from demonstrations. Cowdrey's 100 gave England the edge in the first match at Lahore, but they couldn't bowl Pakistan out on the last day after they were 71–4. At Dacca the game was actually policed by students, which ensured some sort of calm. England were in peril on a baked-mud wicket at 130–7, but D'Oliveira nurtured the tail in a magnificent innings of 114*, on a devious pitch reminiscent of his early South African days. Underwood took five in the second innings, but a home batting side with Hanif at No. 7 was too strong even on that pitch. For the last match at Karachi Colin Milburn flew in from Western Australia, where he had been demolishing attacks for Tony Lock's team. There he had made an amazing 181 between lunch and tea against Queensland. In Karachi he made a brilliant 139. Graveney followed with 105, and Knott was 96* when the team retreated to the pavilion as the last riot of the tour gathered dangerous momentum. In those circumstances three draws were probably inevitable, despite the hard toil of Underwood, 20 wickets at 19, and the intelligent young Hampshire seamer Bob Cottam, 16 at 23.

1969 West Indies and New Zealand

Cowdrey was all set to captain England again until a ruptured achilles tendon at the end of May put him out for the season. England decided to give the captaincy to Ray Illingworth, an interesting and far from obvious choice. Illingworth had just joined Leicestershire as captain from Yorkshire, who were still led by Close despite his being despatched by MCC to the outer darkness two years earlier. An off-spinning all-rounder from Yorkshire's tough training school, Illingworth was not even a certain choice as a player, despite having played 30 Tests on and off over the previous 10 years. Just turned 37, he was facing a West Indies in transition, for Hall, Griffith and Nurse had all gone. He was regarded very much as a stopgap, but he couldn't have timed his start better, despite three crucial retirements – Milburn (eye), Barrington (heart) and Dexter (business).

England	413 & 12–0	West Indies	147 & 275
West Indies	380 & 295–9d	England	344 & 295–7
England	223 & 240	West Indies	161 & 272

England won the first Test easily. A Boycott hundred was followed by a West Indies collapse to Snow and Brown, and no Sobers-led recovery this time after Illingworth, proving a shrewd captain, enforced the follow-on and kept the screws tight. The Lord's match was fascinating. West Indies followed their 380 by taking the first five England wickets for 61. England were rescued by their debutant John Hampshire, an elegant stroke-player from Yorkshire, who added 128 with Knott, and then by Illingworth, whose first Test hundred included a last wicket stand of 83 with Snow. West Indies extended their lead of 36 to 331, and England were set 332 in five hours and 20 overs. Boycott and Sharpe led England's spirited attempt, and at 263–3 they needed just 69 in the last 12 overs, but the loss of both to the new ball left England 295–7 at the close. The game was a triumph for Yorkshiremen – three made centuries and Sharpe only fell short after a brilliant 86 at nearly a run a minute.

The third and last Test at Headingley was equally close all the way. England made only 223 but West Indies managed a mere 167 after Knight had taken the first four wickets. West Indies were now handicapped by the loss of Kent's John Shepherd with a severe back strain, but Sobers bowled absolutely magnificently to take 5–42 in 40 testing overs, and England, with no batsman reaching 40, crawled to 240 in the 132nd over. West Indies wanted 303, the highest score in the match, but so well did Camacho and Butcher bat that they were in sight of victory at 219–3 when Butcher left for 91 to a questionable catch behind off Underwood. Sobers arrived to join Lloyd, so they were still favourites, but Sobers was promptly bowled for 0, an ugly heave at Knight, and England went on to win by 30 on the last morning, the attack again cleverly marshalled by Illingworth. Although England had the rub of the green in the last match, and faced an attack without the unremitting new-ball menace of Hall and Griffith, 2–0 was gratefully welcomed.

The England team had done what they had to, something they repeated against New Zealand.

England	190 & 340	New Zealand	169 & 131
New Zealand	294 & 66–1	England	451–8d
New Zealand	150 & 229	England	242 & 138–2

In a low-scoring first Test, Edrich's 115 in the second innings was twice as much as anyone else could manage, and on a poor pitch Underwood was in his element, 11–80 in 60.3 overs. With nearly two days lost to rain, the Old Trafford Test was drawn, although Edrich helped himself to another century and Sharpe made his first. The last was again dominated by Underwood, with 12–101, and Sharpe and the debutant Mike Denness, from Scotland via Kent, took England to an eight-wicket win. Against batsmen of all but the highest class Underwood could be virtually unplayable on some English wickets. Sadly they didn't make them like that for him abroad, except in New Zealand, whose rainfall could match England's.

So, two series won 2–0 in Illingworth's first campaign as captain. His form didn't suffer either – he averaged 31 with the bat and 24 with the ball. The bowling, headed again by Underwood with 30 wickets at only 10 apiece, and with Ward, Brown, Illingworth, Knight and Snow all taking 10 or more wickets at reasonable expense, was strong enough to compensate for a batting side missing Cowdrey and other familiar names. Tom Graveney's innings of 75 in the first West Indies Test, just before his 42nd birthday, would prove his last. In another run-in with the powers-that-be he had been banned for three Tests for playing on the Sunday of the Test without permission (a promised appearance in his own Benefit match). For a cricketer who had many brushes with authority during his career, he could smile wryly when he became the first ex-professional president of the MCC, presiding benignly over the great Ashes summer of 2005. Worse, though, was Colin Milburn's tragic loss of an eye in a car accident on 23 May, the night after his county had beaten the West Indies, a severe blow for every cricket-watcher, for whom Milburn's arrival at the wicket could stir the blood on the coldest day. Through the summer, only Edrich and Sharpe had averaged over 40, so batting replacements needed to come through quickly.

1970 Rest of the World

As we have seen, the 1970s began with another cancelled tour, so England would not be tested against the best team in the world. But they could be tested against the best players, and five of the South African team who had destroyed Australia 4–0 in the previous winter were available for Gary Sobers' Rest of the World team. Now that so many of the top foreign players were playing for English counties, the newly-formed TCCB made the imaginative late decision, at the end of May, to organise a series between England and a Rest of the World team managed by Freddie Brown. The TCCB had come into being because the MCC, a private and exclusive club, could hardly administer the largesse distributed by Harold Wilson's government to British sporting bodies via its newly established Sports Council.

For the Rest of the World series a lack of any opportunity for advance booking, coupled with the football World Cup in Mexico and the Commonwealth Games in Edinburgh, kept attendances down at first, but after a dreadful start England competed well against a superb team. In the end it turned out a closely contested series with some brilliant performances. Anyway, it took our minds off Mexico, and that West Germany match...

England	127 & 339	**The World**	546
The World	276 & 286	**England**	279 & 284–2
England	294 & 409	**The World**	563–9d & 141–5
England	222 & 376	**The World**	376–9d & 226–8
England	294 & 344	**The World**	355 & 287–6

As it happened, in an unusual reversion of accepted wisdom, every match was won by the side losing the toss and batting second. In the first match at Lord's on 17 June a makeshift England batting line-up, missing Cowdrey, Boycott and Edrich, was wiped out by Sobers' 6–21, despite Illingworth's brave 63 coming in at 23–4. When the Rest rattled up 546 – Barlow 119 and an imperious 183 from Sobers – the series promised to be a horrible mismatch, but fifties from D'Oliveira and Brian Luckhurst, the replacement opening bat from Kent, and a further 94 from Illingworth, salvaged at least a little hope from an innings defeat. That hope was fulfilled at Trent Bridge. On the opening day, despite a century from Lloyd, the England bits-and-pieces bowlers – D'Oliveira and the Sussex South African exile Tony Greig, who each took seven in the match – held the Rest to 276. A slump from 78–0 to 195–9 against Eddie Barlow followed, but that doyen of No. 11s John Snow, helped the tenacious Illingworth – another 97 for him – scramble a narrow lead. A brilliant innings of 142 by Barlow, next highest score 30, left England 284 to win. Against an attack of Procter, Sobers, McKenzie, Intikhab, Gibbs and Barlow this should have been far from easy. But so composed was Luckhurst, who batted through for 113*, and so confidently did Cowdrey and the young Essex batsman Keith Fletcher shape, that England won by eight wickets in 135 absorbing overs. In the catalogue of fourth innings wins by England this chase tends to be forgotten because the matches were denied Test status. Wrongly, in my opinion and that of successive editors of Wisden. That the players chosen to play for England, against the toughest opposition in the world, should have their feats taken away from them seems completely wrong. Alan Jones of Glamorgan lost his only Test appearance as a consequence.

The third match was an uphill struggle for England after they had been bowled out by Sobers and Procter for 294, D'Oliveira 110. Two days later they were batting again, facing a deficit of 269 with D'Oliveira again leading the resistance. But it didn't quite last long enough, and the Rest won by five wickets. The best match was the fourth at Headingley. Eddie Barlow's four wickets in five balls swept away the England lower order after Fletcher and Illingworth had taken them to 209–4. A century by Sobers gave the Rest a lead of 154, but Boycott, Luckhurst and Fletcher saw off the arrears with just two wickets down before Barlow again – 12–142 in the match for an opening bat and change bowler – made the Rest's target 223. Snow and Illingworth bowled superbly, however, so they were 62–5 when Intikhab joined

Sobers in a stand of 115. Three quick wickets then left them 183–8, needing 40. Unfortunately out at No. 10 to join Procter came Barry Richards, down the order courtesy of a damaged back. Bad back or not, he was fit enough to see off Snow's new ball burst and see the Rest home.

The final game was another terrific match. England this time began with 294. Graeme Pollock and Sobers had threatened in a wonderful stand of 165 to put the Rest out of sight, but in one of the best pieces of bowling ever on debut for England, the Lancastrian Peter Lever, fair hair flying, bowled them both on the third morning, and finished with 7–83, restricting the Rest to 355. Led by a magnificent innings of 157 by Boycott, England looked favourites at 289–3, leading by 233 and with the ball starting to turn, but a slump left the Rest to score 284. At 92–3 they had lost their three South Africans, but three West Indians were on better form. Kanhai scored 100, sobering down after a manic start, and fittingly it was Sobers who steered them home by four wickets late on the last day.

It was a superb series played in a splendid spirit, with every match going to a finish in excellent weather. For England to lose by 4–1 was no disgrace, and 3–2 would not have been unreasonable on the balance of play. The alternative of a summer with no representative cricket would have left the selectors scratching their heads for the Ashes tour that was to follow, but now they had Luckhurst averaging 44 despite a pair in the last Test, and Fletcher, another newcomer, joining Boycott, Illingworth and D'Oliveira in averaging over 40. Brian Luckhurst was one of those journeyman batsmen who emerge from time to time from the ranks of consistent county cricketers, and prove to have the temperament and technique for Test cricket. To score over 400 runs in his first four Tests against such an attack was tremendous. The bowlers, against that batting side, headed by Sobers with 588 runs at 73, had a tougher time, but Greig took 11 wickets at 26, Snow 19 at 35, and Peter Lever's arrival at the Oval was another great bonus.

1970–1 Australia and New Zealand

Confidence was therefore higher than it might have been for the tour of Australia. The Australians had been severely traumatised by their catastrophic 4–0 loss in South Africa the previous winter, losing one match by an innings, and two others by over 300 runs. Nobody had scored a century: among the batsmen only Redpath had averaged over 32, and the bowling depended heavily on Connolly. But they were sure to have been stung by that, and England certainly expected a backlash. Illingworth remained as captain, Cowdrey a distinctly reluctant vice-captain. He had secured a decent run at the captaincy at last, forfeited it when his achilles tendon ruptured, and was now supplanted by a successful Illingworth.

The first two Tests showed there was little between the teams. That didn't look the case, though, on the first day of the series when Australia, led by a cavalier 207 from their dashing opener Keith Stackpole, stood 372–2 in fewer than 100 overs. But Snow devastated the tail, and by steady batting not only did England chisel out a lead of 31, but bowled Australia out for 214 on the last day, this time the Lancastrian Ken Shuttleworth doing the damage. There was not enough time to force a win, nor was there in the first ever Test at Perth. Here Luckhurst's century and Snow's new ball burst left Australia 17–3 after England's 397, but they were saved by Redpath and an ominously mature 108 by Greg Chappell in his first Test.

Australia	433 & 214	England	464 & 39–1
England	397 & 287–6d	Australia	440 & 100–3
England	332 & 319–5d	Australia	236 & 116
Australia	493–9d & 169–4d	England	392 & 161–0
England	470 & 233–4d	Australia	235 & 328–3
England	184 & 302	Australia	264 & 160

The traditional New Year Test at Melbourne was then completely washed out, and for what was already a six-Test series England agreed to a replacement Test instead of the return Victoria game, squeezed in after the penultimate Test at Adelaide. In the next Test at Sydney England were on top from the moment Boycott set off uncharacteristically with 77 from 31 overs. He followed it with 142* when England had gained a lead of 96, and Australia capitulated for 116, on a pitch taking spin, to 7–40 from Snow, in a manner not seen in Australia since 1954–5. Tyson had beaten them for pace; Snow did it by sometimes vicious lift from a worn pitch. So England went to Melbourne for the extra Test 1–0 up with three to play, and plenty of time for a turnaround. England made it difficult for themselves when Cowdrey, of all people, dropped four slip catches on the first day alone. Facing 493, England were indebted to centuries by Luckhurst – with a broken finger – and D'Oliveira, and Australia had neither time nor the bowlers to put England to a fourth innings test. At Adelaide a first day hundred from Edrich put England on top, and late on the third day England led by 235. Illingworth chose not to enforce the follow-on, wanting to keep his bowlers fresh. Though it was argued that he should press for a victory while in the ascendant, making the last Test's outcome academic, the wicket was still excellent. The rest of the match proved that – Australia finishing 328–3 chasing 469.

And so back to Sydney for the final Test, with an extra day allowed, a factor very much in the favour of Australia, who needed to win to rescue the Ashes. The match was played at a high pitch of tension throughout. The wicket took spin, as Sydney so often does, but that didn't prevent Australia's new captain, Ian Chappell, putting in an England side missing Boycott with a broken arm, which seemed a crucial handicap, and Cowdrey, who was out of form. Chappell was rewarded by a poor English batting display that enabled them to reach only 184; a long tail was headed by Snow at No. 8. Australia edged ahead with seven wickets down, and the game erupted when Terry Jenner ducked into a ball from Snow and was hit in the face. Umpire Rowan warned Snow for persistent short-pitched bowling, Snow remonstrated, the crowd lobbed missiles in his direction at long-leg, and with beer cans littering the field Illingworth took his side off. The umpires told him they would award the game to Australia if he didn't return, so he did, and the crowd quietened down.

Australia eventually took a lead of 80, and the game came back into balance when Edrich and Luckhurst added 94 for the first wicket. But nobody else could reach 50, and Australia needed 223. In his first over Snow bowled Eastwood, an inadequate replacement for the sacked Lawry, but in the fifth, going to field a hook at long-leg, Snow broke bones in his hand on the perimeter fencing just as Compton had in 1954–5. His loss was a dire handicap, but England worked away assiduously and Illingworth himself took the key wicket when he bowled Stackpole for 67 at 131. The last major resistance ended when he had Greg Chappell stumped by Knott, and England had won a famous victory by 62 runs without their leading batsman and bowler. It had been a tremendous series for England, and a personal triumph for its captain. As E. M. Wellings said in Wisden, 'Illingworth did a magnificent job. Under severe provocation he remained cool off the field and courteously approachable by friend and foe alike.' This is worth remembering, as he subsequently developed a reputation as a rather tetchy authoritarian.

The batting in Australia depended hugely on the three openers Boycott, Edrich and Luckhurst, who averaged 93, 72 and 56 respectively, while Illingworth, D'Oliveira and Knott topped 30. Snow bowled with consistent aggression and accuracy, pounding life out of flat pitches, to take 31 wickets at 22, one of the greatest ever performances by an England bowler in Australia. Underwood, Lever and Illingworth, all got into double figures. So did the young replacement Bob Willis, all spidery legs and flailing arms at this early stage of his career.

| New Zealand | 65 & 254 | **England** | 231 & 89–3 |
| England | 321 & 237 | New Zealand | 313–7d & 40–0 |

After Australia, the team without Boycott and Snow won one New Zealand Test easily and drew another altogether tighter match. Underwood was unplayable at times and took 17 wickets at 12 in three innings, while Knott's 101* and 96 saved any possible embarrassment in the draw.

1971 Pakistan and India

England began 1971 with an enviable record of won 15, lost one in the 33 Tests against other countries since they lost to West Indies at home in 1966. 1971 brought India and Pakistan, and Illingworth was for the first time a unanimous choice as captain. With only Intikhab Alam and Farokh Engineer from the subcontinent having played any part in the Rest of the World series, the opposition wasn't expected to be strong, especially in English conditions. Wrong!

Pakistan	608–7d	England	353 & 229–5
England	241–2d & 117–0	Pakistan	148
England	316 & 264	Pakistan	350 & 205

At the beginning of June the young Zaheer Abbas, batting in rimless glasses with an easy supple-wristed charm, gave England's bowlers a rude awakening with a wonderfully dominant innings of 274 in just over nine hours. So free was he outside the off-stump that he looked somehow like a classic left-hander in reverse. Centuries by Mushtaq and Asif took Pakistan to a massive 608–7. England were 148–6 before they were rescued by D'Oliveira and Knott, but still had to follow on. An unbeaten century by Luckhurst anchored them to a precarious 229–5, still 26 behind, when the fourth day ended, but England were saved by rain that washed out the entire last day. The tall Asif Masood, like some Northwest Frontier warrior with flowing black hair and moustache, took 9–160 in the match.

Rain ruined the second Test, in which Boycott made a hundred, so the series went to a decider at Headingley. In a cracking match, another century from Boycott took England to 316, which consistent Pakistan batting headed by 34. England lurched to 142–5, recovered through a second 70 from D'Oliveira to 248–5, then crumbled to 264, leaving Pakistan 229 to win on the last day. Illingworth reduced them to 65–4, but Sadiq and Asif took the score to 160, just 63 short. But Asif was stumped, Illingworth brought on D'Oliveira in an inspired move to dismiss Sadiq for 91 and his captain Intikhab, and then Lever with the new ball to sweep away the tail. Once more the nerveless Illingworth had wrought a miracle when England had stared defeat in the face. England had won a series they could easily have lost 2–0.

Now for India. Since 1932 India had lost 15 Tests in England without a single win. India were hard to beat at home but had never travelled well. However a 1–0 win in the Caribbean, Sobers and all, led by an astonishing 774 in his first four Tests by their 21-year-old opening prodigy Sunil Gavaskar, had given them the self-belief they had been lacking abroad since they began Test cricket.

England	304 & 191	India	313 & 145–8
England	386 & 245–3d	India	212 & 65–3
England	355 & 101	**India**	284 & 174–6

India showed their mettle in the first Test at Lord's. England recovered from 71–5 to post 304, John Snow, restored after injury, loss of form, and accusations of lack of effort by Sussex, top-scoring with 73. India battled to a lead of nine, and thereafter their spinners exerted such a grip that England expired for 191 on the last morning, leaving India just 183 to win in 260 minutes. Early in the innings Snow appeared to barge Gavaskar over as each chased a quick single: it cost Snow a reprimand, an apology, and a place in the next Test. Gavaskar went on to add 66 with Engineer in 50 minutes, to take India to 87–2, 97 needed. But he was stumped off the Worcester left-arm spinner Norman Gifford, who went on to take 4–43 in an immaculate spell, and India stuttered to 145–8, 38 short, when rain prevented any play after tea. With Bedi in and Chandrasekhar to come, no batsmen, the weather probably saved them in the end, but both sides had flirted with defeat.

At Old Trafford England were on top from the moment Lever joined Illingworth at 187–7. They added 168, and despite Gifford's broken thumb England took a lead of 174, Lever 5–70. A century from Luckhurst allowed Illingworth to set India 410 in seven and a half hours. At the close they had lost 3–65, including Gavaskar, and looked set for defeat. But it rained all the last day, and England had once more to go to the final Test of three to find victory. For the Oval match England were without the injured Boycott, but had Snow back as compensation. England batted in cavalier fashion on the first day, led by Boycott's replacement, John Jameson, an aggressive opener from Warwickshire who recalled Colin Milburn in his approach and – at least to some extent – his build. A collapse was halted by a big stand by Knott and Richard Hutton, the all-rounder son of Len, and England had totalled 355 by the close. Friday was lost to rain, but when England led by 71 on day four they held a significant advantage.

That advantage went up in smoke. The luckless Jameson suffered his third successive run out, this time as non-striker when a drive was deflected onto his stumps. There followed a ghastly collapse against Chandrasekhar, the slightly-built googly bowler with the polio-withered arm, who perplexed everyone and finished with 6–38. He couldn't bat for toffee, but was a marvellous example of how a major childhood disability need prove no bar to sporting success. India had 173 to win: similar to Lord's, but now they had time and they took it. Snow for the second time disposed of Gavaskar for single figures, but this was a pitch for spin, and Illingworth and Underwood wheeled away for 74 overs. At 134–5 England had a chance, but Engineer took charge, and eventually India won their first Test and series in England after 101 tense overs. Illingworth was a magician, but, hard though he fought, for once he couldn't conjure up a miracle, as his luck finally ran out in a series England might have wrapped up before the Oval Test.

Somehow, although their team was somewhat unlucky to lose the series, to Englishmen a generation ago losing to India, perpetual underdogs in England, didn't hurt quite as much as it would have done to a more traditional enemy. Apart from the Rest of the World season, it was Illingworth's first Test defeat as captain, and England's first loss in 23 Tests. In the six Tests of the summer Boycott averaged 70, emphasising how much he was missed at the Oval, but no one else averaged 50. Gifford, Price, D'Oliveira, Lever and Illingworth each took over 10 wickets at less than 30 each, but the winter spearhead of Snow was sorely missed.

1972 Australia

There was no tour that winter, although the Australians took a leaf out of the English book and invited a World XI to replace a rejected South African team. Although several English players went, only the tall, aggressive Greig, first of the white South African imports and confident to the point of arrogance, enhanced his reputation with both bat and ball. The Australians gave a good account of themselves before going down 2–1. The desperado-moustached Denis Lillee, the Victorian Demon Spofforth reincarnated, proved increasingly formidable. With the Chappell brothers in good form Australia threatened to be tougher opposition in 1972 than they had been in their last two tours here.

England	249 & 234	Australia	142 & 252
England	272 & 116	**Australia**	308 & 81–2
Australia	315 & 324–4d	England	189 & 290–4
Australia	146 & 136	**England**	263 & 21–1
England	284 & 356	**Australia**	399 & 242–5

The first Test began on Illingworth's 40th birthday, in his 20th full season (amazingly, he was still playing 11 years later). Winning the toss was the ideal birthday present in a low-scoring match, played in dreary weather and poor light. England won without passing 250 in either innings. Only Greig and Stackpole, each with two fifties, could master the conditions until Rodney Marsh clubbed 91 at the end in a lost cause. Snow, returned to fitness, form and favour, took eight wickets, as did Lillee.

Bob Massie had not played in the first Test, and, although he had appeared in the World series in the winter, the Lord's Test would be his first for Australia against a country. There had never been a debut like it. After two early wickets for Lillee he took the remaining eight as England battled back from a bad start to reach 272. Australia recovered likewise against aggressive bowling from Snow, thanks to Greg Chappell's immaculate 131, and held a slender lead of 36. But it wasn't so slim after all, as half the England side were out before the arrears were cleared. This time there was no recovery, and Massie again swept through the rest. He had phenomenal figures of 8–84 and 8–53, swinging the ball late and both ways with frightening accuracy, and it was extraordinary – and a huge relief for England – that he played only two more Tests after this series. English batsmen were mesmerised at Lord's, with Massie profiting from the new lbw law that allowed batsmen less freedom to use their pads outside off-stump. Lillee was an indispensable foil, getting two of the top three in each innings. Indeed Boycott, Luckhurst and Edrich, the scourge of Australia in 1970–1, made just 38 between them in their six Lord's innings.

At Trent Bridge Illingworth put Australia in, doubtless still bearing the scars from Lord's, and Stackpole profited from poor catching behind the stumps to make a century out of 315. England stumbled their way to 189, and when Ross Edwards had reached 170 Ian Chappell was able to set England 451 in nine and a half hours. Their survival seemed unlikely, but Luckhurst retrieved some form, the wicket eased, and D'Oliveira and Greig were able to bat out the last three hours to end 290–4 in 148 overs. While slow, it was an important innings psychologically, to combat the superiority of Lillee and Massie. And at Headingley their grip over the England batsmen was loosened still further by a pitch, under-prepared after a freak thunderstorm the previous weekend, that favoured spinners from the first morning. Underwood and Illingworth were on before lunch, taken at 79–1, and in the afternoon they bowled Australia out for just 146, six wickets for 69 between them in 52 overs. England fared little better against the tall off-spinner Ashley Mallett, and were 128–7 when Snow joined Illingworth in a stand of 104 that effectively decided the match. Once more Illingworth gathered stubborn resistance around him at a crucial stage. On the third day Australia disintegrated again against Underwood, 10–82 in the match, and England needed only 20 to win.

That fourth Test win enabled England to retain the Ashes on a poor pitch, just as they had done in 1956. The fifth Test would enable Australia to regain some pride, in a seesawing match that was the best fought of the series. England were rescued by 92 from Knott after hostile bowling by Lillee had propelled them to 181–8. A brilliant stand of 201, in which both Chappell brothers scored a century in a long battle with Underwood, gave Australia the edge and a lead of 115. England's reply was led by the stocky Lancastrian debutant Barry Wood, opening with Edrich in the absence of both Luckhurst and the injured Boycott, who fell 10 short of a maiden Test hundred. Despite more jaunty defiance from Knott, ended when he became Lillee's 10th victim in the match, Australia would need 242 in plenty of time in a game allocated six days. As a last innings target, received wisdom says anything around 250 in a Test is tough. But injuries to Snow, Illingworth and D'Oliveira, who bowled only 15 overs between them, made Australia's task simpler, and a stand between Sheahan and Marsh took them from 171–5 to a deserved share of the series. Had England's captain and main strike bowler been on the field it might have been very different.

On figures alone Australia should have won the series. Both sides were dogged by a failure to find an opening pair – the best opening stand out of 20 was just 68 – and England's top average was Greig's 36, with only Illingworth of the others beating 30. That shows how poor the specialist batsmen were against Lillee and Massie. Australia on the other hand had three averaging over 48, headed by Stackpole and Greg Chappell, the outstanding batsmen of the summer. Lillee and Massie took 31 and 23 wickets, each at 23, but had little support, whereas England were led by Underwood, 16 at 16 in two Tests, and the nagging Surrey seamer Geoff Arnold had arrived to give support to the ever-dangerous Snow, who took 24 at 24. So it was some relief for England to retain the Ashes, but there were still severe worries about their batting. Illingworth and D'Oliveira were in their forties, and Edrich, Boycott and Luckhurst well into their thirties, so England's selectors needed to find some new batting blood, and fast. They needed to cope with the pace of Lillee, the swing of Massie, and the spin of the Indians, and they needed to be able to counter that new lbw law too.

CHAPTER 14

Away from the Dark Side
— a New LBW Law

John Inverarity lbw to Derek Underwood at the Oval, August 1968. He took 7–50
as England won with six minutes to spare after the crowd had helped mop up an
inundated ground.

The practice of deliberately defending the wicket with the person
instead of the bat is contrary to the spirit of the game and inconsistent
with strict fairness.

MCC INSTRUCTION, 1888

Three major changes to cricket's fundamental Laws took place between 1900 and 1946. In 1927 the ball was made marginally smaller, in 1931 the stumps an inch higher and wider, and in 1935 the lbw law was changed. Only the third caused any serious repercussions. Until then, a batsman could only be out lbw if hit between wicket and wicket by a ball pitching in line as well. But, as we've seen, in the 1930s there was growing concern that lifeless pitches had tilted the balance too much in the bat's favour, and moreover that top batsmen had become adept at leaving the ball outside the off-stump. Timeless matches were tried from the 1920s, but that started to result in huge scoring, including the only two team innings over 1000, both in Australia. It was partly in reaction to this batting superiority, and more explicitly to the threat of Bradman's dominance, that Douglas Jardine had devised the bodyline strategy that so scarred relations between England and Australia in 1932–3. Harold Larwood, Jardine's greatest weapon, himself felt that a change in the lbw law was necessary to give bowlers their just reward. The MCC, anxious to avoid any recurrence of deliberately hostile bowling, agreed in more than usual haste.

The 1935 lbw law

In late 1934 MCC adopted an experimental law that allowed a batsman to be out even if the ball pitched outside the off-stump, as long as it still hit him in line. Now batsmen could no longer confidently cover the stumps with their pads and leave alone good-length balls pitching outside the off-stump, as Hobbs and Sutcliffe in particular had done to such effect. The new law worked, in that whereas in the 1934 England season 14 batsmen had averaged over 50, in 1935 no one did. Most observers felt initially that there was more off-driving and less pad play, but some already anticipated a switch of bowling attack towards the leg side. Of 1560 lbw decisions that year, 483 were given under the new law, and that was the law in force when cricket ended in 1939. By that time there were seven batsmen with averages over 50: they had been able to adjust their technique, often taking advantage of the umpires' reluctance to give an lbw decision to a ball striking the pad of a batsman on the front foot. The new law wasn't invigorating off-side play, so much as encouraging the skilful pad-pusher.

The new rule had its vociferous opponents from players past and present, articulated in a survey Bill Bowes carried out for Wisden in 1956. Cyril Washbrook said it encouraged a shift of line from off towards leg, a natural bowler's reaction to batsmen thrusting an ugly pad forward to off-stump balls. Bill Edrich said it had killed leg-spin: for although there were still many leg-spinners operating in England in the early 1950s they had learnt the game under the old law. Off-spinners, off-cutters and in-swing bowlers became more common, until the reduction in leg-side fielders behind square began to hamper them. In the 1939 Wisden, however, Don Bradman had applauded the change. He had actually gone on to advocate a further extension, that a batsman could be out to a ball pitching outside the off-stump even if it hit him outside its line, always assuming the umpire could be sure it would have hit the wicket.

Although typically ahead of his time, Bradman was very much out on a limb, as the Bowes survey showed. Hobbs, Sutcliffe, Constantine, Merchant, Wyatt and Leyland preferred to revert to the old law. Robins, Surridge and Wooller wanted the new law retained. Most deplored the switch of bowling attack from off to leg, which they blamed with easy simplicity on the 1935 law. Bowes too was against it, but, recognising that a reversal would not have the desired effect, he preferred Bradman's idea reckoning it would redirect the attack. In this, they were supported by Larwood, Peebles and Gover.

In 1957 a committee rejected the Bradman proposal, on the grounds that umpires would find it too difficult to decide if the ball would certainly hit the wicket. In 1960 they discussed, but took no action on, a refinement to Bradman's proposal that would have a batsman lbw to a ball striking him outside off-stump *only if he had played no stroke*, provided, of course, that it would have hit the wicket – the law in force today. But in 1969–70 a hybrid amendment was trialled by Australia and West Indies, and in 1970 it became an experimental law in England too. For this experiment a batsman could be out to a ball pitching outside the off-stump *only if he was not attempting to play a stroke, even if it hit him in line*. This partially reverted to the pre-1935 position but was an attempt to outlaw the pad-pushers.

Wisden's editor Norman Preston welcomed this change. In the following year's Wisden he felt that it 'gave the batsman more freedom and consequently led to more attractive cricket.' Moreover: 'Only four bowlers took 100 wickets, yet all were spinners, so the new lbw condition did not worry them as much as was suggested.' One was the leg-spinner Robin Hobbs. But the Australians weren't happy. They had found that the number of lbw dismissals in the 20 Sheffield Shield matches had dropped from 46 in 1968–9 to only 25 in the first experimental year of 1969–70, and was making life too easy for batsmen on their plumber wickets. They promptly recommended that the law revert to the pre-1970 position, but retaining the new proviso that a batsman could be out to a ball hitting him outside the line of off-stump if he played no stroke, provided of course that the umpire could be certain that the ball would have hit the wicket and he could be sure of the batsman's intent.

The ICC agreed – as Wisden rather caustically reported 'under pressure from Australia' – and the experimental law was replaced for 1972. Preston lamented that the ICC had again 'tampered', wishing for a longer period of experiment. Thereafter

Year	Law	v	Dismissals	lbw	%lbw
1968	old	Aus	157	20	12.7
1969	old	WI/NZ	196	28	14.3
1970	exp	Rest of World	169	8	4.7
1971	exp	Pak/India	173	5	2.9
1972	new	Aus	166	27	16.3
1973	new	NZ/WI	196	30	15.3
2005		Aus	182	33	18.1

he's silent on the subject: when we look at the figures we can guess why. Not only did Australia's domestic lbw count go up – it was as high as 72 in 1972–3 – but the results in Tests in England were even more startling.

These are pretty dramatic statistics, although they were little remarked on at the time. Thereafter, unusually for cricket, there's virtual silence on the subject. Here is another curious incident of a dog in the night-time. (Note the 2005 increase, by the way. Of the 33 lbw dismissals, 21 were by England, testament to the reverse swing effect, perhaps. Had England's rate been the same as Australia's, the lbw percentage would have been 13.2 per cent, and Australia would have retained the Ashes.)

Changes in laws can have unexpected and pernicious side-effects in all walks of life. So it was with the 1935 law. But the 1972 law, combined with the reduction of fielders behind square on the leg side, seems to have largely balanced things up. It certainly didn't provoke the chorus of disapproval that the 1935 law did. Bowlers who swing, cut or turn the ball both ways force batsmen to play strokes to balls close to the off-stump in case they swing or cut back, so fewer balls are left alone. Bowling variety is rewarded, as Massie discovered at Lord's in 1972. In 1989, Trevor Bailey wrote that batsmen, hitherto used to pushing a long way forward with the bat tucked behind the pad, avoiding the risk of lbw, would have to adapt. Cowdrey was one who was adept at that, and he did adapt, late in his career. Bailey felt the new law helped the away-swing bowler, encouraged front foot play, and, by contributing to a switch to off-side field setting, opened up the leg-side to players like Viv Richards and Mohammad Azharuddin, who learnt to whip the ball to leg off the stumps.

Of course, there is still huge concern over spinners, particularly in England, and especially leg-spinners. At various times there have been suggestions that the lbw law should be changed to help them. Bradman has been one such advocate, but critics felt that it would lead to a disproportionate advantage to left-arm over bowlers, or leg-spinners bowling round the wicket into the rough. To counter this, Jeff Stollmeyer of the West Indies came up with the idea of allowing lbw if the ball pitched outside the leg stump, provided the bowler came to the offside of the umpire, that is right-arm over or left-arm round. (This would reward big spinners like Shane Warne, although England batsmen might well complain that he needed no such assistance.) It was an interesting idea that drew some adherents in the late 1970s, and a trial took place in Australia and New Zealand in 1980–1. Don Oslear, umpiring in New Zealand that winter, gave just two men out under the experimental law, but felt it really worked, preventing batsmen kicking the ball away. But no one was bold enough to take the experiment further, and there has been no law change since.

Concern over the lost spinner remains, though when three of the top five Test wicket takers are spinners, as they were at the end of 2005, then the accusing finger points to the English game and its coaches, rather than the Laws. But spinners are a larger issue, and we will discuss them in a later chapter. Meanwhile, after battling against Lillee and Massie in 1972, England's batsmen had to re-engage with Chandrasekhar, who had bamboozled them in 1971, and his confrères of the Indian spin academy – Bedi, Prasanna and Venkataraghavan.

CHAPTER 15

Heading Downhill

A ball from Dennis Lillee hits Keith Fletcher on the head after being deflected off his glove, Sydney, January 1975. The ball rebounded so far that he was nearly caught at cover.

When Thomson and Lillee were bowling, the atmosphere was more like a soccer ground than a cricket match, especially at Sydney, where England's batsmen must have experienced the same sort of emotions as they waited for the next ball as early Christians felt as they waited in the Colosseum for the lions.

JOHN THICKNESSE

1972–3 India and Pakistan

It was a much weakened side that revisited India and Pakistan after the 2–2 draw with Australia that retained the Ashes in 1972. The Glamorgan captain Tony Lewis took over, with a side missing its spine: Illingworth, Snow, Boycott, Edrich, Luckhurst and D'Oliveira. To win against the India team that had beaten them in 1971 was a tall order, but the series got off to a most unexpected start at New Delhi.

India	173 & 233	**England**	200 & 208–4
India	210 & 155	England	174 & 163
England	242 & 159	**India**	316 & 86–6
India	357 & 186–6	England	397
India	448 & 244–5d	England	480 & 67–2

From the moment Arnold took the first four wickets England were on top. Lewis showed his mettle in a low-scoring match, his 70* steering the tourists to a surprise six-wicket win, set up by excellent bowling by Arnold and Underwood. England in their second innings overcame the menace of Chandrasekhar, 8–79 in the first, when only Greig played him with any certainty. Chandrasekhar took another five in the first innings in the cauldron of Calcutta, where this time Old and Greig set up a victory target of 192. Greig, again, led a recovery from 17–4 to 110–4, but Chandrasekhar and Bedi this time were too strong and England lost by 28 runs in a tense finish. At Madras, where Chandrasekhar took another six in the first innings, a battling 97* by Fletcher took England to 242, but their second innings folded around Denness. Though India wobbled against Pat Pocock, chasing 86 for victory, they took a 2–1 lead by four wickets, and held it through two high-scoring draws on better wickets to secure the series. Lewis, Fletcher and Greig made a hundred each in the last two games, but England had never looked like winning again.

England	355 & 306–7d	Pakistan	422 & 124–3
England	487 & 218–6	Pakistan	569–9d
Pakistan	445–6d & 199	England	386 & 30–1

Nor did they look like winning for most of the three Tests in Pakistan, except for a brief moment on the last day of the final match when the spinners Norman Gifford and Jack Birkenshaw kindled a flicker of hope, soon extinguished. The series of three draws was notable only for hundreds by the Warwickshire opener Dennis Amiss in each of the first two Tests, and for a third Test in which he, Majid and Mushtaq each made 99. So in a long tour England again won only one Test out of eight, but there were at least some good encouraging signs. Greig was dominant with bat and ball, averaging 58 and 29 respectively, and was alone in taking on the Indian spinners. But two younger stroke-players did come through at last: the nimble-footed Keith Fletcher and Dennis Amiss. An opening bat with a sound temperament, Amiss had copied Ken Barrington's exaggerated stance, facing wide mid-on rather than the bowler. Arnold and Yorkshire's Chris Old took 20 and 15 wickets, while as many as four spinners – Gifford, Birkenshaw, Pocock and Underwood – shared 64 wickets at 33. They were outshone by Chadrasekhar and Bedi, though: 60 wickets at 21.

1973 New Zealand and West Indies

1973 was another two-series summer, with the West Indies following New Zealand, and Illingworth soldiering on as captain at 41. By the end of the summer he probably wished he hadn't.

England	250 & 325–8d	New Zealand	97 & 440
England	253 & 463–9	New Zealand	551–9d
New Zealand	276 & 142	**England**	419

For two Tests New Zealand provided much stronger opposition than they had hitherto. In the first at Trent Bridge, second innings centuries by Amiss and Greig set them a stiff target of 479 to win in over two days. At 68–3 it looked all over, but centuries from the captain Congdon and the young Pollard took them steadily to 402–5 as lunch approached on the last day. Could they achieve the impossible, for their first ever Test win over England? No. Greig took the last three wickets to complete another terrific all-round match for him, and New Zealand fell 38 short, to great acclaim. At Lord's their batsmen continued where they had left off. Congdon made 175 to follow his 176 at Trent Bridge, and centuries by Burgess and Pollard gave New Zealand a lead of 298. Despite solid batting at the top of the order, England were staring at defeat when Arnold joined Fletcher at 368–8, 70 ahead with two hours left. Had Arnold not escaped a third-ball chance behind the stumps, New Zealand would probably have secured that first win, but he helped Fletcher, who made an increasingly assured 178, to put off that day for another 10 years. The third Test was the only one-sided match, Snow and Arnold proving too strong for the New Zealand top order on both occasions, and Boycott, not dismissed by a bowler in the series for under 50, making 115.

West Indies	415 & 255	England	257 & 255
West Indies	327 & 302	England	305 & 182–2
West Indies	652–8d	England	233 & 193

Now for a sterner test. England hadn't played the West Indies, since a 2–0 win in the 1969 short tour. England were reasonably confident, although Sobers, now 37 and absent from the side that had lost 2–0 at home to Australia in the winter, made himself available for the Tests while captaining Nottinghamshire. Moreover Camacho and Rowe were injured early on and would play in none of the matches. The opening attack didn't look formidable either. Unusually, the first Test was at the Oval, and a stand of 208 between the little and large left-handers, Kallicharran and Lloyd, took West Indies to 415. Despite Boycott's 97 England lost their way against Sobers and Keith Boyce, a popular all-rounder who had been at Essex since 1965, and late on the fourth day England began a forlorn chase for 414. They didn't get anywhere near it, Boyce finishing with 11 wickets, but the innings did produce a gem of a maiden hundred by the young Lancastrian Frank Hayes, whose back foot strokes illuminated the last day. Sadly, he was a notoriously bad starter at the highest level, was condemned to play all his Tests against West Indies, and wouldn't play any other Test innings of note.

A sign of the change that had swept cricket in England since the mid-1960s was that the West Indies side for Edgbaston was drawn entirely from players at English counties. Kanhai's side generated some unpleasantness on the second day when they subjected the umpire Arthur Fagg to constant criticism after he'd given Boycott not out to a catch behind. Fagg struck a blow for umpires by refusing to stand the next morning until an apology was forthcoming. Roy Fredericks' 150 had retrieved the West Indies cause on day one from 128–5 to 327, and England battled at under two an over to 305, with no batsman reaching 60. After criticism by the umpires of a slow over rate on that Saturday morning, 26 in two hours, Sobers and Gibbs contrived to bowl 24 overs of spin in the hour after lunch! The game petered out on the final day, England not surprisingly unwilling to chase 325 in 230 minutes.

The final match, disrupted by a hoax IRA bomb scare on the Saturday afternoon, was a disaster for England. On the first day Kanhai dominated with 157. On the second it was Sobers and Julien with a seventh wicket stand of 231. On the third Holder and Boyce bowled England out for 233, Fletcher 68*. On the fourth only his fighting 86 delayed the end, and England lost ignominiously by their biggest margin since Brisbane in 1946–7, an innings and 226. Fletcher, Boycott and Amiss had batted well enough, all averaging over 50 for the summer, but they received little support. It was a similar story with the bowling, its weakness found out by the West Indies, although Arnold was consistently impressive in taking 31 wickets at 23, and Old and Snow took their wickets at under 30. It was a sad end to the Illingworth era. It was characterised by the intense concentration of his captaincy, several battling innings in adversity, and by successful bowling spells at crucial moments.

1973–4 West Indies

The quirks of the fixture list sent England straight back to the West Indies in 1973–4, with not much hope, it must be said, under a new captain, Mike Denness of Kent, who had played no part in the summer's two series. By another quirk, he won the toss in every match, as had Cowdrey six years earlier.

England	131 & 392	**West Indies**	392 & 132–3
England	353 & 432–9	West Indies	583–9d
England	395 & 277–7	West Indies	596–8d
England	448	West Indies	198–4
England	267 & 263	West Indies	305 & 199

The first Test in Trinidad continued England's downward slide. They were destroyed on the first day for 131, then saw Kallicharran's 158 take West Indies from 196–6, stumbling against the off-spin of Pat Pocock, to 392. But determined batting from Boycott (93), Amiss (174) and Denness brought England to 315–1 at lunch on the fourth day, 54 ahead and with just a sniff of an unlikely victory. Then Denness was run out, Amiss got a rough lbw decision, Sobers and Gibbs spun the rest out cheaply, and England lost by seven wickets.

On the final morning of the second Test in Jamaica England stood 271–7 in their second innings, just 41 ahead, and a second successive defeat looked a formality. At the wicket still was Dennis Amiss, owing England because he had twice taken on Clive Lloyd at cover-point and seen him hit the stumps on each occasion to run out Hayes and Knott. For the rest of that final day, in the company of a threadbare England tail of Old, Pocock and Willis, Amiss played one of the great escape innings, making 262* against a bouncer barrage from Julien and Boyce, with Sobers and Gibbs to follow. An innings of epic proportions, with a next highest score of 38, and England survived to stay just one down. In that Test West Indies had amassed 583–9, and they followed this in Barbados with 596–8, Lawrence Rowe 302. Greig took 6–164 in this innings, mostly bowling off-breaks, to follow the 148 he had made to rescue England with Knott from 130–5. Another recovery was called for on the last day, which began with England 40–4, still 161 behind. This time it was Fletcher, whose 129*, again with Knott, kept England precariously in the series. Any chance of the series being decided in Guyana was dispelled by rain after centuries from Amiss and Greig had taken England to 448.

So back for the last Test to Trinidad, which England somehow reached still only 1–0 down. There were constant rain interruptions, but the pitch gave bowlers enough assistance to ensure a result. Although Boycott had batted with grim defiance for 99, by lunch on the third day West Indies, with Rowe in command, were 208–2 and only 59 behind. At this point Greig, bowling now entirely in his off-spinning style, changed the game by taking an amazing 8–33 in 19 overs, all caught but one. The West Indies lead was thus limited to 38, and after another marathon effort by Boycott (112), they would need 226 to win in seven hours. At 63–0 they were coasting, but three wickets fell for two runs, including the daft run-out of Fredericks, and Greig was back in business. The once-maligned Fletcher caught three slip catches off him – 12 of his 13 wickets were caught, indicating how much bounce he was extracting from the pitch with his height – and England sneaked home by 26 runs amid great tension.

Rarely had a Test victory been dominated by two men as had that by Boycott and Greig. Somehow England had squared the series, after being kept in the hunt by Amiss and the heroic tail in Jamaica, and by Fletcher, Knott and Greig in Barbados. In the series Amiss was immense, scoring 663 at an average of 82, with Greig, Knott, Boycott and Fletcher averaging in the forties. Greig with 24 wickets at 22 was the only bowler into double figures, so impregnable was the West Indian batting until Trinidad.

1974 India and Pakistan

So England returned to another Indo-Pakistani twin tour with some encouragement after their dogged cussedness against a superior team in the Caribbean, and Denness stayed as captain. Everyone expected the Indian series to be a tough one.

England	328–9d & 213–3d	India	246 & 182
England	629	India	302 & 42
India	165 & 216	England	459–2d

England were on top at Old Trafford, where cold, rainy, early season conditions seemed to dispel the threat of the three Indian spinners, who took only five wickets between them. Centuries from Fletcher and Edrich set up a last day in which India couldn't hold out once Gavaskar, 101 and 58, had departed. At Lord's, the tall Lancashire left-handed opener David Lloyd displaced Boycott, who after a poor run against India had asked not to be considered, and kept him out for the rest of the summer. Centuries from Amiss, Denness and Greig, and a near-miss for Edrich, enabled England to run up 600. After a century opening stand, Old and Mike Hendrick, a miserly, probing opening bowler from Derbyshire, too often dogged by injury, worked through the Indian batting. Once they had followed on they collapsed catastrophically to Old and Arnold, who bowled them out for 42 in 17 overs. At Edgbaston the first day was lost to rain, but it didn't incommode England (fielding an unchanged team, believe it or not, for the first time in over eight years). Arnold and Hendrick bowled out a dispirited India for 179, a double hundred by David Lloyd allowed an early declaration at 459–2, and the England seamers did the rest. It was a chastening turnaround in fortune for India, whose spinners could only take 15 wickets at nearly 70 each between the four of them.

Pakistan	285 & 179	England	183 & 238–6
Pakistan	130–9d & 226	England	270 & 27–0
Pakistan	600–7d & 94–4	England	545

Pakistan were altogether stronger, and indeed went through the entire tour unbeaten. The first match at Headingley was a battle between two sets of seamers –

Arnold, Old and Hendrick for England; Asif Masood, Sarfraz Narwaz, and a young Imran Khan for Pakistan. Sarfraz the batsman took Pakistan from 223–9 to 285, to which England could reply with no more than 183. Pakistan's 179 then left England 282 to win with over two days to go. Edrich revived them after a bad start, and at the end of the fourth day England were 238–6, 44 short with Fletcher 67* and the tail for company. England were favourites, though not by much, but rain throughout the fifth day ended the speculation and the chance of a dramatic finish.

At Lord's, rain and leaky covers brought controversy. Five hours were lost to rain on the first day, but when play restarted Pakistan collapsed catastrophically to Underwood, from 71–0 to 131–9, when Intikhab declared to get England in before the close. Next day England too were in trouble, at 118–6, before Knott organised another rescue act with 81. England led by 140, but Pakistan fared better on a stop-start Saturday and reached 173–3, Mushtaq and the young Wasim Raja having added 96. However, heavy rain on Sunday and into Monday morning penetrated the covers. The Pakistan management were entirely justified in their bitter complaints at this failure at cricket's HQ, and it was no surprise that Underwood should now exploit a damp patch at one end to cut down the Pakistanis and finish with 8–51, 13–71 in all. At the close England, needing 87, were 20–0 but a justice of sorts was done when once more it rained throughout the last day. The last Test, on a slow pitch at the Oval, yielded big totals and hundreds for Amiss and Fletcher after Zaheer's 240, but little else, so the series was left drawn, frustratingly for England, at 0–0.

Taking the two series together, England had five batsmen averaging over 50: Fletcher 99, Amiss and Lloyd over 70, Edrich and Denness in the fifties. Five bowlers too averaged under 30: Underwood, Hendrick, Old and Arnold taking over 20 wickets at averages from 17 to 25. Greig averaged 41 with the bat and 28 with the ball, and with Knott at No. 7 the side for Australia had a well-balanced look about it.

1974–5 Australia and New Zealand

England were about to discover that balance wouldn't be enough. Two factors were crucial. Boycott withdrew a month before the party was due to go because he felt 'he couldn't do justice to himself', a curious observation by someone who was the leading Englishman in the averages in 1974, and whose Test average stood at a shade under 50. The other was the recovery of his fitness by Lillee, the arrival of Max Walker to replace Massie, who had vanished, and the discovery of a pace bowler named Jeff Thomson, whose javelin-like action from a comparatively short run-up somehow brought sharp lift at a frightening pace from a good length. Perhaps Boycott had second sight?

At Brisbane an uneven pitch, hastily prepared after heavy storms by the eccentric Lord Mayor of Brisbane, who had sacked the curator 10 days before the match, didn't help England's cause after Australia won a key toss. A fighting century from Greig kept England's arrears to 44, and England needed to bat through the last day. They were bowled out for 166, Thomson 6–46. This set the tone for the series. Lillee and

Thomson bowled with hostility, allowed by the umpires to pepper the English batsmen with bouncers. According to Amiss, Thomson was warned for 'sending three whistling past my chin in failing light – he didn't take a blind bit of notice and if anything the next four flew even faster past my face. Batting was a complete misery.' Once Thomson and Lillee had got away with ignoring umpires' warnings, it was open season on queasy Poms. At Brisbane 265 and 166 began a sequence of 10 innings in which England failed to reach 300. At Perth 208 and 293, Thomson 5–93: defeat by 10 wickets. At Sydney 295 and 228: defeat by 171. At Adelaide 172 and 241: defeat by 163 despite Knott's defiant 106* at the last.

Australia	309 & 288–5d	England	265 & 166
England	208 & 293	**Australia**	481 & 23–1
England	242 & 244	Australia	241 & 238–8
Australia	405 & 289–4d	England	295 & 228
Australia	304 & 272–5d	England	172 & 241
Australia	152 & 373	**England**	529

Between Perth and Sydney came Melbourne. Here was an almost totally even match, which ended in excitement and puzzlement over Australia's strange tactics. England made 242 and 244, Australia 241 – Willis 5–61 in an attack deprived of Hendrick by a hamstring injury. Australia needed 246 in a day and a bit, but were constantly pegged back by a four-man attack in which Titmus bowled 29 overs with a damaged knee (not to mention a shortage of toes, from which he had made an amazing recovery). When the last hour began, with its 15 mandatory (eight-ball) overs, Australia at 191– 6 needed 55, and Denness declined the new ball. At this point they added just seven runs in seven overs from the spinners, convincing Denness they were going for a draw, so with 48 needed from 64 balls he did give Willis and Greig the new ball. Australia promptly accelerated to the point where they needed 16 from the last three overs, 24 balls. They managed just 8, and finished 238–8, short by just 8 runs.

After the dismal experience of losing four Tests out of five, England went to the sixth and last at Melbourne and discovered what might have happened without Lillee and Thomson to face. Thomson was away injured, while Lillee's bruised foot allowed him to bowl only six overs. Two days after he trudged off the field the scoreboard read Australia 152 (Peter Lever 6–38) England 507–4 (Edrich 70, Denness 188, Fletcher 146, Greig 89), and England went on to win by an innings. Thus began a habit of England winning dead final Tests against Australia, an opportunity that would arise only too often. In those days, a tour of Australia would be followed by the chance to soothe bruised averages with a tour of New Zealand. A rude awakening would be in store eventually, but not yet.

| England | 593–8d | New Zealand | 326 & 184 |
| New Zealand | 342 | England | 272–2 |

This time, Denness and Fletcher followed up their stand of 292 at Melbourne with one of 264 at Auckland. Denness made 181 and Fletcher 216, a sequence of Compton/Edrich 1947 proportions (a far-fetched comparison perhaps, but welcome enough at the time). Greig, bowling his quickish off-spin again, took 10 in the match to give England a comfortable innings win. In the second match rain prevented play on three days, and Dennis Amiss from adding to an undefeated 164.

But the first New Zealand Test match ended with a horrible incident in which Ewen Chatfield, batting 11 in his first Test, had his skull fractured by Peter Lever, who was distraught. Chatfield swallowed his tongue, and was saved – his heart having actually stopped beating for several seconds – only by prompt heart massage and mouth-to-mouth resuscitation from the England physio Bernard Thomas. England, bombarded by Lillee and Thomson with no protection from the umpires, were now dishing out too, and at tail-enders. Something would have to be done. Would it?

CHAPTER 16

Shot and Shell

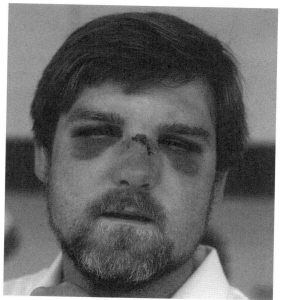

Mike Gatting after his nose had been broken by Malcolm Marshall at Kingston, February 1986, before the first Test. (Just be grateful the photo's not in its original colours.)

The persistent bowling of fast short-pitched balls is unfair if, in the opinion of the umpire at the bowler's end, it constitutes a systematic attempt at intimidation.

THE LAWS OF CRICKET IN FORCE IN 1975

I bowl bouncers for one reason, and that is to hit the batsman and thus intimidate him… I try to hit a batsman in the ribcage when I bowl a purposeful bouncer, and I want it to hurt so much that the batsman doesn't want to face me any more.

DENNIS LILLEE

Bodyline

The term bodyline was applied to bowling deliberately aimed at the batsman's body with a packed leg-side field. It was late on the afternoon of 14 January 1933 that the England tour manager Pelham Warner walked into the Australian dressing room to enquire politely after the health of their captain, Bill Woodfull, after another bodyline pounding from Larwood and Voce, bowling short to a packed leg-side field. 'I don't want to see you, Mr Warner. There are two teams out there; one is trying to play cricket and the other is not.' They might not have expressed it so politely nowadays. With Woodfull staggering after being hit on the heart, and Jardine saying 'Well bowled' to Larwood after he had fractured Bert Oldfield's skull, the third Test at Adelaide was 'the most unpleasant Test ever played'. Telegrams flew; diplomatic relations reached breaking point. Two years later MCC condemned what it chose to call 'direct attack' bowling.

Thereafter every bowler fast enough to intimidate a batsman has done so, with varying frequency and intent. The Laws when cricket restarted in 1946 deemed the 'persistent and systematic' bowling of fast short-pitched balls to be 'unfair', and gave the umpires powers to first caution, then ban, the bowler in question. The vagueness of 'persistent and systematic' made it unlikely that an umpire would caution a bowler unless it was blatant and continuous. Bowlers rarely bowled more than one or two an over, though in 1948 Miller bowled five in eight balls to Hutton, the last ball of the day hitting him on the elbow. Compton too was hit on the elbow, during the innings in which he top-edged the Lindwall no-ball onto his head, before returning to make 145, bandaged like a failed Kamikaze pilot. At Manchester in 1951 McCarthy hit Hutton and Ikin repeatedly, Ikin being 'left black and blue with bruising on his arms and chest', according to Graveney. In the period after the war England simply had no bowlers fast enough to retaliate. Umpires didn't intervene, and the law remained unchanged.

Hall and Griffith

In the 1960s it was Hall and Griffith who led the charge. In 1962, Griffith broke Contractor's skull. A year later at the Oval, umpire Syd Buller, a man of rare determination and courage, warned Hall and Griffith for bowling too many bouncers. To Worrell, their captain, he said, 'Look, this can't go on. You will have to stop it, skipper.' When Griffith said, 'I am allowed two every over', Buller replied, 'No. You are not allowed any.' (A maximum of two seems to have been an unwritten rule.) With more recent captains this might have led to a major incident, but Worrell, the most dignified of men, concurred, echoing the wording of the law at the end of the day's play by saying: 'As far as I am concerned the umpires are the sole judges of fair and unfair play'. In 1966, the next West Indies series, Griffith hit Derek Underwood in the mouth as England battled for a draw. This brought forth 'wholesale condemnation', breaking the unwritten 'not at the incapable' code, and Sobers made Griffith apologise in writing. Underwood was playing in his first Test and batting No. 11. Ray Lindwall, skilful purveyor of the selective bouncer, told Jim Laker that if he had to bowl bouncers at him he would have given up the game.

Lillee and Thomson... and helmets

Things were quiet for a few years until the mid-1970s, when Lillee and Thomson of Australia were matched by Roberts and Holding of the West Indies, and by Willis of England. Now there were no umpires with the strength of Buller. The 1976 Wisden imagined the England batsmen's emotions at Sydney on the 1974–5 tour, facing Lillee and Thomson, as akin to those of early Christians as they awaited the lions in the Colosseum. 'When someone gets hit,' wrote Christopher Martin-Jenkins in 1979, 'you think you are in a bullring. The sight of blood seems to arouse them and they howl for more.' Lillee was frightening enough – Keith Fletcher said 'he exposes every area of your technique' – but Thomson was something else. He had an unusual spear-thrower's action, the hidden ball appearing late from behind his back, and he could make the ball fly from a good length. Helmets were still in the future. Lillee openly admitted that he aimed to hit the batsman and make them think twice about going on batting. He was only voicing what other fast bowlers felt, but he was the first to put it so graphically. So did Thomson, with an even blunter turn of phrase: 'I thought, stuff that stiff upper lip crap. Let's see how stiff it is when it's split.'

Edrich (twice), Amiss, Luckhurst and Lloyd all broke bones on that tour, and the tail-enders were certainly not exempt – Lillee even gave Willis a beamer. Lloyd had his box 'turned inside out', which makes the eyes water just reading it. During the tour 41-year-old Colin Cowdrey, uncowed and certainly not cowardly, flew out to join the shell-shocked team. He nonplussed Thomson by greeting him at the crease with 'I don't think we've met. My name's Cowdrey.' He was said to be the only batsman to hook Thomson. It's interesting in retrospect, though, that despite this barrage which led to new forms of body protection all over the torso, no one yet tried a helmet: Mike Denness said this was because they didn't want to show they were scared. The pitches were fast and uneven, and England no longer had Snow to retaliate, until Peter Lever hit Greg Chappell on the chin in the last Test. As we've seen Lever went on to inflict a far more serious injury when Ewen Chatfield deflected the ball that fractured his skull in Auckland. A year later, in a gruesome irony, a flatmate of Jeff Thomson died after being hit in the chest by a cricket ball, one propelled at nothing like Thomson's pace.

Commentators called for the Laws to be strengthened and the umpires to get tougher before someone died, but the only thing to be strengthened was the body armour. 'So intense is the competition in World Series Cricket,' said Tony Greig, 'that teams can no longer afford to let tail-enders hang around.' Batsmen put aside their machismo and put on helmets, and Lillee himself led the tail-enders in joining them. By the start of the 1980s few were without them. Richie Richardson was one of the rarities, wearing a wide-brimmed hat – and a watch. The swaggering Viv Richards eschewed a helmet, even at times batting bare-headed. Bowl at my head, he seemed to say, if you dare. Cricket at the end of the 1970s had indeed become a gladiatorial contest. One saving grace was that the leg-side fielding restriction at least avoided a recurrence of bodyline. But it hardly seemed necessary to pack the leg-side with fielders. At Kingston in 1976, in India's second innings against West Indies, only six batsmen got to the crease: two had retired hurt in the first innings when hit on the head, and three had broken fingers, two admittedly from dropping catches. The new West Indies were flexing their muscles.

The new West Indies

The West Indies had just been to Australia to face Lillee and Thomson, the year after England's demise, and suffered the same treatment. They had lost 5–1, despite having Andy Roberts and the young Michael Holding in their team. The batsmen reacted differently from England's, their batsmen perishing through taking the bowlers on. They then hosted India, and lost a Test at Port-of-Spain while themselves playing three spinners: India chased 400 to win. When their pace men destroyed India at Kingston the message was plain: spinners were pointless. It would be another 19 years and nine series before Australia beat West Indies in a series again, and another 24 years and 12 series until England could do it. For the West Indies it became normal to have an attack composed of four top-class fast bowlers bombarding opposing batsmen with bouncers. If you had a batsman who was a reasonable spinner, all well and good, but he wasn't necessary.

By the late 1970s, with helmets almost universally in use, the view among cricketers, if not among commentators, was that bouncers were a legitimate weapon against recognised batsmen, especially if they looked shaky against it. However there continued to be a consensus that recognised tail-enders should be exempt, not least for the practical reason that fast bowlers dishing it out could expect the same in return. In 1976 the ICC agreed an experimental note that 'captains must instruct their players that the fast short-pitched ball should at no time be directed at non-recognised batsmen'. But in 1978 Bob Willis, who had already been warned by umpire Dickie Bird for excessive bouncers, hit Iqbal Qasim of Pakistan in the mouth in the first 1978 Test v Pakistan. Qasim was an obdurate nightwatchman still batting the following morning: did the stricture apply when they batted as nightwatchmen? And who should be 'recognised' as tail-enders anyway? Before the second Test captains Mike Brearley and Wasim Bari did agree a list of tail-enders exempt from bouncers, but the nightwatchman question went unresolved. In the 1980 law revision, the umpires were counselled to 'take the relative skill of the striker into consideration' when deciding if bowling was 'intimidatory'.

In 1976 the ICC had counselled umpires to enforce the intimidation law strictly, but they were still left to make a tricky judgement. The following year they suggested a two-per-over maximum, as an experiment, but some countries – notably and unsurprisingly the West Indies – were reluctant to introduce it. England brought in a maximum of just one per over in county cricket in 1979, but it didn't apply in Tests. In 1983 they tried in vain to persuade the ICC to adopt the legislation, and in consequence withdrew it at home because their Test cricketers felt they were at a disadvantage. That didn't stop England trying though: they kept on nagging away at the ICC until in 1991 they persuaded them to agree to a three-year experimental restriction of one per over to each batsman. In 1994 they switched it to two per over irrespective of the batsman, because bowlers and umpires alike were inclined to lose track. So England got half its loaf, and those were the conditions still in force in 2005.

Thirty years earlier, though, the cricket world was looking forward to something completely new. And fortunately, in view of the previous 12 months, the thrills and spills of the first World Cup would take place without serious injury, despite a West Indies v Australia final. Indeed, Lillee and Thomson would feature with the bat as much as with the ball.

CHAPTER 17

World Cup to Centenary Test

Derek Randall salutes Dennis Lillee during his wonderful 174 in the Centenary Test
at Melbourne, March 1977. England fell 45 short of a target of 462, having been
bowled out for 95 in the first innings.

When Lillee bowled short, Randall ducked, rose, drew himself to his full
five feet eight, doffed his cap and bowed politely. Then, felled by another
bouncer, he gaily performed a reverse roll.

REG HAYTER, Wisden, 1978

It's no good hitting me there mate, there's nothing to damage.

DEREK RANDALL to Denis Lillee, Centenary Test 1977

1975 The first World Cup

Chastening as the winter in Australia had been in 1974–5, there was excitement in the air for English supporters as they welcomed the first World Cup. Positioned midway between the start and end of our 60-year period, it thus divides it neatly in two. Until 1975, Test cricket sedately trod the world cricket stage alone, but from then on it had to move over to accommodate its noisy new rival. Sponsored then by Prudential, the format of the first World Cup was simple. Eight teams, the six Test-playing nations plus Sri Lanka and a team representing East Africa, played against each other in two groups of four. The top two in each group played off in the semi-finals. Each game was of 60 overs a side.

England had what appeared to be the easier group and came through with three comfortable wins after an extraordinary opening game with India. After Amiss's 137 had taken England well over 300, Sunil Gavaskar, seeing no prospect of victory, batted all 60 overs for 36* in a total of 132–3. Thereafter things could only get better, and did. Six years before their promotion to Test status, Sri Lanka put up a promising show against Australia, losing only four wickets in making 276 in a forlorn pursuit of 329, although two men retired hurt when hit by Thomson. The best match in the opening stages came when the West Indies, chasing 267 to beat Pakistan, won off the fourth ball of the last over after Murray and Roberts had added 64 for the last wicket. Australia had already qualified for the semi-finals when they were heavily beaten by the West Indies. Their defeat was sealed when the diminutive Kallicharran struck Lillee for 31 from just eight balls.

SEMI FINALS			
England	93 (36.2)	**Australia**	94–6 (28.4)
New Zealand	158 (52.2)	**West Indies**	159–5 (40.1)
FINAL			
West Indies	291–8 (60)	Australia	274 (58.4)

The first semi-final at Leeds was a sensational match that lasted just 65 overs. The scorecard looked like something from the 19th century: both sides had six wickets down before they had reached 40. The difference was that Doug Walters and Gary Gilmour then added 55 to reach the 94 needed. Gilmour, a burly left-hander with flopping blond hair, had carved through the England top order, swinging and cutting the ball prodigiously in a heavy atmosphere on a damp green pitch to take the first six wickets for 14 in his 12 overs. Old, Snow and Arnold couldn't quite sustain their effort in reply. All but three of the wickets in the match were bowled or lbw.

With West Indies beating New Zealand with ease in the other semi-final, Australia and West Indies came to Lord's for the first World Cup Final on 21 June, a glorious Midsummer Day. Those were the days: the game packed in 119 overs between 11 am and 8.45 pm. The game was turned by Clive Lloyd's arrival at 50–3, with Lillee, Thomson and Gilmour (another 5–48 in this game) in control. His hundred came from 82 balls, fast even by today's standards, but a blistering rate in those days. Australia chased 292, but a series of run-outs, including both Chappells and two direct hits by Kallicharran, left Lillee and Thomson too much to do in a spirited last-wicket stand of 41 that ended – in a run-out – 18 runs short in the penultimate over. This match was the apotheosis of the one-day experiment that had begun so tentatively in England 12 years earlier. The tournament was over in a fortnight of scintillating sunshine, with a brilliant climax between the two best teams in the world. Wisden's rather brief summary of the series ended: 'When the ICC met in London towards the end of June member countries were invited to submit ideas for the next World Cup. India had already said that they were keen to act as hosts, but several members thought it was hard to beat England as the venue. The main view for this reasoning was the longer period of daylight in England in June when 60 overs for each side can be completed in one day.' Oh, days of innocence.

1975 Australia

There had been no plan for a tour that summer, but during the winter Australia had agreed to stay in England and play four Tests. They took place between 10 July and 3 September. In that year, in contrast to 2005, there was always a decent break between the Tests, and the Australians fitted in 11 other first-class matches.

Australia	359	England	101 & 173
England	315 & 436–7d	Australia	268 & 329–3
England	288 & 291	Australia	135 & 220–3
Australia	532–9d & 40–2	England	191 & 538

Although Australia duly won, the series was certainly not as one-sided as the preceding winter's, at least once the first Test was over. This game was another horror story for England. After Denness had put Australia in they made 359, which proved quite enough for an innings win, Lillee, Thomson and Max Walker dismissing England on a nasty wet pitch for 101 and 173. Essex's Graham Gooch made a pair batting at No. 6 in his first Test. Thereafter things improved, and with a little luck England might have squared the series. At Lord's a battling display by the debutant David Steele dragged England up from 49–4 in the company of his new captain Tony Greig. Steele, with his grey hair and steel-rimmed spectacles, looked more like a Northampton accountant. Imagine someone nowadays, without a helmet and wearing glasses, taking on men of the highest pace who delighted in hitting you. But he was a cricketer with an unflappable determination against pace, plucked from the county circuit by Greig, who had canvassed opinion on the most obdurate against fast bowling. Thomson hadn't seen him before – 'Bloody hell, who have we got here, Groucho Marx?' – but he saw quite enough of him during the series. A narrow first innings lead was extended by a big hundred from Edrich, enabling Greig to set Australia 484 in 500 minutes. With an hour's play lost, and the pitch increasingly harmless, Australia saved the game easily.

The third Test at Leeds followed a similar pattern to the end of the fourth day. Steele (73 and 92) top-scored in both innings for England. Although they reached 300 in neither innings, that they were able to leave themselves over 10 hours to bowl Australia out was due to a mesmerising piece of bowling by the tall Middlesex spinner Phil Edmonds in his first Test. He came on at 77–3 and, with Underwood bowling a succession of typically challenging maidens at the other end, took 5–17 in his first 12 overs in Test cricket to reduce a bemused Australia to 107–8. When the fifth day began Australia had battled for 220–3, chasing 445, but no one expected them to survive if the weather held. It actually rained at lunchtime, but that wasn't the point. Overnight the solitary policeman on guard duty had failed to spot a group of impassioned supporters of a friend detained at Her Majesty's Pleasure. They had slipped into the ground during the night, got under the covers, dug holes in the pitch and poured a gallon of crude oil on a good length at the Pavilion End. Unfortunately, they knew their cricket. (Oddly, the prime culprit was called Chappell.) Though Greig and Ian Chappell, according to Wisden, forlornly went through the motions of looking for another suitable strip, that was that. It's hardly likely that the Australians would have agreed in any case to a new pitch at such a critical stage in an Ashes series.

The final Test on a slow pitch at the Oval, even with a sixth day added, gave England no chance of victory. Indeed they followed on over 300 behind, and only stout resistance from Bob Woolmer and others in an innings of 538 ensured a draw. England had lost 1–0, but could take a certain amount of heart from their combined performance against Lillee and Thomson, who after the first Test could only take their wickets at over 30 apiece. Nevertheless Lillee finished with 21 wickets at 21, while no England bowler took more than 11 or averaged under 30. The arrival of Steele and Woolmer, a phlegmatic opening bat from Kent who also bowled medium pace, was the real bright spot. They together with Edrich averaged over 50. Another bonus was the sudden emergence of Phil Edmonds, an eccentric and argumentative Cambridge Blue, brought up in Zimbabwe when it was still Rhodesia, an accurate and aggressive left-arm spinner and fine close fielder.

1976 West Indies

There was no winter tour, but another sizzling summer, the third in four years, brought the West Indies back to follow the Australians. Out of the frying pan into the fire: another tough series in prospect against the World Cup winners, whose previous opposition, India, had finished the last Test in April with five men absent hurt. Tony Greig stayed as England captain and on the eve of the first Test broadcast his infamously bullish comment, 'I intend to make them grovel,' a misjudged remark from a white South African about a black team. Greig had a hard lesson to learn about hubris. He was the one grovelling by the end of the series.

West Indies	494 & 176–5d	England	332 & 156–2
England	250 & 254	West Indies	182 & 241–6
West Indies	211 & 411–5d	England	71 & 126
West Indies	450 & 196	England	387 & 204
West Indies	687–8d & 182–0d	England	435 & 203

The first Test saw the first major innings against England by the great Vivian Richards, his 232 a typical innings of swaggering disdain out of a total of 494. That England saved the game easily was due to two defiant innings by the previous summer's heroes, Steele and Woolmer. Steele reached his first Test hundred against an early instance of the four-man pace attack, in this case Roberts, Julien, Holder and Daniel.

Now to Lord's, and the closest match of the series. Brian Close was recalled, eight years after being stripped of the captaincy, still a tough old bird at the age of 45, for his bloody-minded obduracy against pace. It was an amazing 27 years since Close's first Test, and although he had played only irregularly for England he did so in each of four decades. He didn't let them down, top-scoring in the match with 60 and 46, and adding 84 in the first innings with Mike Brearley, a conjunction of contrasting England captains, one at the start of his career, one at the end. After England's 250, Underwood and Snow took the last six West Indies wickets for 43 to give England the lead. But the complete loss of Saturday through rain meant that England could only set a target of 323 in five hours, and despite a late collapse after Fredericks' frantic 138 there was not enough time. England had fought well here at Lord's, so were more confident that they could make a contest of it, as they went to Old Trafford still 0–0.

On the first morning the Middlesex swing bowler Mike Selvey, playing only because Snow, Old and others were unfit, disposed of Fredericks, Richards and Kallicharran in his first spell in Tests, to make West Indies 26–4. English hopes were high, even when Gordon Greenidge had hit a scintillating 134 in a total of 211. But England capitulated for 71 against Roberts, Holding and Daniel, saw Greenidge and Richards make further hundreds, then collapsed again for 126. This was after a particularly vicious 80-minute evening assault that left even Close so bruised and battered on the body – 'clusters of livid bumps like marbles under the skin', said Pat Pocock, the nervous nightwatchman – that he needed pain-killing injections before he could even lie down, let alone sleep. 'All that Closey,' said his partner Edrich, 'for one not out.' England lost by 425, and none of their batsmen in the match even reached 30.

At Leeds England made five changes, with a completely different trio of fast bowlers – Snow, Willis and Alan Ward of Derbyshire. They were hit to all parts on the first day to the tune of 437–9, a rate of scoring in Tests completely unknown at that time. England slumped to a familiar 80–4, but Greig and Knott fought back with 116 each, and when Willis had run through the West Indies' tail in their second innings England faced a target of 260 in a day and a half on a good wicket. Shortly before the close England stood 140–4 after losing their first three wickets to Roberts for 23. But Peter Willey, playing a second impressive innings in his first Test, was brilliantly caught by the diving Roberts at square leg, a dismissal that turned the game. Next morning Daniel's three quick wickets left Greig to battle alone with the tail, and England lost by 55.

Going to the Oval 2–0 down, any chance England had to recover some self-respect was destroyed by Richards. He scored 200 on a perfect pitch on the first day, and such was his form and the savagery of his strokeplay that year that he might have reached 400 many years before Lara did. But he played on to Greig at 291 shortly after lunch on the second day. Facing 687, England were indebted to a great innings. Dennis Amiss had had two torrid series against Lillee and Thomson, and was now regarded as vulnerable to extreme pace: his heroics in Jamaica in 1974 seemed a distant memory. Bowlers didn't come much faster than Michael Holding at the parched Oval that August, leading the attack with Roberts, Daniel and Holder, even on a slowish pitch. But Amiss made a quite brilliant 203 out of 342 in only five hours 20 minutes, before Holding bowled him round his legs. However, nobody could support Amiss for long, and Holding, gliding in as if on castors and bowling at a great pace and fuller length throughout, followed 8–92 in the first innings with 6–57 in the second to send England to a third successive defeat.

The season's averages were a sorry sight. The West Indies openers Greenidge and Fredericks each scored over 500 runs, while the awesome Richards, the double double-centurion, made 829 in seven innings (1385 in 13 innings in six months in 1976). Steele was England's top scorer with 308 in 10, and that season was to be his last as an England player. Recurrent injuries meant that of the six opening bowlers England used none played more than three Tests. Underwood battled away, but his 17 wickets cost 37, while Holding took 28 at 12, Roberts the same number at 19, and Daniel and Holder a further 28 between them at 24 each.

1976–7 India… and Australia

A winter tour of India was the greatest contrast to a West Indian tour of England imaginable. Technique found wanting against four hostile pace bowlers had now to be adapted to face three top-class spinners who had held a stranglehold over English batsmen in India. It was concern over his ability against spin that led, sadly, to the omission of the courageous Steele. English hopes in India were not high, but the first Test was a revelation, because of an astonishing piece of bowling by a debutant.

England picked John Lever, Essex's left-arm seamer, as much because he seemed less liable to injury than most. Not only did he take 10–70 in the match, but he made a vital 53 in the England innings, more runs than he was to score for Essex in 15 matches in the whole of the following season. After England had lost the first four batsmen to single figures, first Knott, then Lever helped Amiss to make 179 out of

381. Then England, with India comfortable at 43–0, had a stroke of luck when the ball went out of shape and was replaced by one that swung all over the place. Lever took 7–46 in his first Test innings, and India lost by an innings. Bedi complained that Lever's swing was assisted by Vaseline on a sweat-repelling strip across his forehead, but the English denied it and no action was taken.

England	381	India	122 & 234
India	155 & 181	England	321 & 16–0
England	262 & 183–9d	India	164 & 83
India	253 & 259–8d	England	195 & 177
India	338 & 192	England	317 & 152–7

It was Willis's turn at Calcutta for the second Test. His 5–27 bowled out India for 155. Greig, Knott and Roger Tolchard, the reserve wicketkeeper from Leicestershire, gained England a healthy lead, and England won by ten wickets. Then in a low-scoring match in Madras in which only Brearley and Greig reached 50, Lever again did the damage in the first Indian innings, and everyone contributed in the second. It seemed incredible that England could win three out of three on Indian soil, with their fast bowlers doing the bulk of the damage. India hit back in the fourth, batting first on a deteriorating wicket that allowed Bedi and Chandrasekhar full rein, but despite Gavaskar making the only Indian century of the series in the final Test, England, with Amiss and Brearley putting on 146 at the start of their first innings, held on in the second at 152–7 after being set 214 in four hours. It was the only Test of the series that was evenly contested.

England's turn-around in India seemed pretty amazing at the time, and no less so 30 years on. The Indian batting side contained Gavaskar, Viswanath, Patil, Gaekwad, both Amarnaths and Vengsarkar, all with good Test records then or later, and the three spinners Bedi, Chandrasekhar and Prasanna. Yet Amiss and Greig topped the combined batting averages, and four England bowlers led the bowling, with Lever, Willis and Underwood all taking over 20 wickets at well under 20. Underwood out-bowled the Indian spinners throughout the tour, and the success of England's opening attack on Indian wickets was unprecedented. They were helped by brilliant slip catching.

The Centenary Test, March 1977

In March 1977 English and Australian cricketers, past and present, gathered for a single match to mark the 100th anniversary of the first encounter between the two old enemies. To Melbourne came 218 past protagonists, meeting up with the English émigrés now living in Australia, like Larwood, Loader and Lock, Tyson and Knight. It even provided a Compton story, for Denis made it on time despite leaving his passport behind.

Australia	138 & 419–9	England	95 & 417

The game itself was played with a curious mixture of intensity, determination to win and genuine camaraderie. A key figure in all this was the English livewire Derek Randall, whose electrifying cover fielding had won him a place on the tour to India in spite of his somewhat inconsistent batting. After a pair of first innings more redolent of 1877 than 1977 – Australia's sorry 138 followed by England's sorrier 95 – the game became the batsmen's again. Rodney Marsh's hundred gave Australia a seemingly impregnable lead of 462 and nearly two days to bowl England out. But in front of the Queen in her Silver Jubilee year England made a better fist of it second time around.

Lillee had taken 6–26 in the first innings. Randall, without a Test hundred yet to his name, stood up to him and clowned. He muttered to himself continuously. He tennis-smashed a bouncer like a bullet to the mid-wicket fence; ducked another, bowed and doffed his cap; hit by another, he did a backward roll, dusted himself down, grinned at Lillee and started again. Lillee may not have loved it, but the crowd did. At one stage, with Randall past his first Test hundred, England were 279–2 and then 346–4. When Randall was 161 he was given out caught behind but was called back when Marsh intimated he had dropped the ball before securing it – a virtually unprecedented act of generosity fitting the occasion. He went in the end for 174, Lillee took the last three to finish with 11 in the match, and Australia had won by 45 runs, exactly the same margin as 100 years before. Following his earlier 'nothing to damage' comment, man-of-the-match Randall thanked Lillee for bumping him on the head: 'If it had hit me anywhere else it might have hurt.'

A wonderful match, a delightful taster for another Ashes summer, and all seemed well in cricket's garden. But there was something nasty lurking in the woodshed.

CHAPTER 18

Packer, Sponsorship and Money

The *Daily Mirror*'s headline of 9 May 1977, when the news first broke of World Series Cricket. Tony Greig and Greg Chappell are photographed below the headline, Barry Richards, Clive Lloyd, Alan Knott and Viv Richards above.

Cricketers are the only body of British wage earners with no freedom of choice of employer, no representation or negotiation or arbitration, or the protection of independently-framed conditions of employment.

JOHN ARLOTT, 1974

World Series Cricket

On 9 May 1977 the cricket world was stunned to learn that an Australian businessman named Kerry Packer had signed up 35 players to play for a group known as World Series Cricket. Nothing like it had been seen since the mid-19th century, when two rival 'England' XIs of professionals toured the country playing matches against odds. Packer was a blunt man with loads of money, who had previously shown no particular interest in cricket. But the Australian television company he owned, Channel 9, had been thwarted by the decision of the Australian Board of Control (ABC) to deny him point blank the chance to bid for the right to televise cricket in Australia when the broadcasting contract came up for renewal. Stung by the refusal, Packer decided to buy the cricketers, play his own Test series, and televise them himself. Australian cricketers were certainly eager to sign. Their relations with an intransigent ABC over financial compensation – for loss of earnings, as they were all amateurs – had become increasingly sour in the course of the 1970s. Before long the 35 cricketers had become 51. The former Australian captain Richie Benaud, who had become a journalist, was instrumental in the revolution.

Uproar. Commentators realised that the England captain, Tony Greig, had been signing up players on Channel 9's behalf during the intervals in the Centenary Test at Melbourne in March, thus 'sullying' that great sporting and sportsmanlike occasion. The word 'betrayal' was on pursed lips at Lord's. The Australian tourists had arrived but in their bags with their kit were newly-signed contracts with Channel 9. Four Englishmen also had contracts – Greig, Snow, Knott and Underwood (Boycott had declined) – so the TCCB promptly sacked Greig as captain, and called a meeting of the ICC. It decided to delay action until after the current series, for which England would pick players on merit, but then to impose conditions on them. For the England team it meant that they would be banned from playing Test and county cricket if they appeared in an 'unapproved' match, i.e. one that clashed with any match prearranged by the existing authorities.

Tony Greig and players' rights

Greig was not the kind of man to take this lying down. During the summer, still playing for England but now unimpeded by its captaincy, 'Greig and others', in the jargon of legal reportage, mounted a case against 'Insole and others' alleging restraint of trade. Greig's 'others' included John Snow, Mike Procter and later Bob Woolmer. Whatever the TCCB's legal advice, and there were certainly keen legal minds among the MCC membership, the authorities initially seemed unperturbed. True, in 1963 the Newcastle footballer George Eastham had taken the football authorities to court and won the right to end the iniquitous maximum wage, but no similar challenge had been mounted in the cricket world. However, the county cricketer, usually conservative in every sense, had already taken his first tentative steps towards an association designed to protect his rights. In 1966–7 Fred Rumsey had lobbied for such a group, and, from small beginnings under the shrewd and avuncular presidency of John Arlott, the Professional Cricketers Association had grown to the point where it had 100 per cent membership in 1977. The old Warwickshire player Jack Bannister was secretary, there was a group pension scheme and they had representation on disciplinary and registration committees.

£	1900	1950	1977	1986
Earnings for uncapped player	100	95	95	135
Earnings for capped player	100	107	100	171
Earnings for star player	100	114	102	254
Average Benefit	100	86	131	141
Highest Benefit	100	110	96	119
Average skilled earnings	**100**	**114**	**229**	**286**

The need for a pressure group to represent players' rights was growing, in step with inflation. This table comes from Ric Sisson's *The Players*. Professional cricketers' wages in England had remained poor for many years. In 1950 an uncapped player had earned around £3000, increased to £7000 once he was capped. In 1977 these figures had barely moved. While skilled workers had doubled their income in real terms, cricketers' pay had slipped to the point where they were no better off comparatively than they had been in 1900. Between 1973 and 1977 inflation rose by 96 per cent, and yet cricketers' wages increased hardly at all. The fee for a Test appearance by an England cricketer had gone up by just 40 per cent, well below the rate of inflation, despite the money now coming into the game from Test matches, and the fee for an overseas tour was only a fifth of what Packer was offering. Derek Underwood said he could double his income in the tax year 1976–7. Without Packer's contract he could barely save, he had no qualifications: what would he do after he retired? Fair point.

Cricketers were paying for their lack of union representation and their innate conservatism, itself fostered by the knowledge that their employers were hard up (not a factor that put off the industrial unions much at that time) and might simply let them go. And the registration rules meant that they couldn't hop to another county without losing a year's cricket. As John Arlott said in 1974: 'Cricketers are the only body of British wage earners with no freedom of choice of employer, no representation or negotiation or arbitration, or the protection of independently-framed conditions of employment.'

It was against this background that Greig v Insole was brought before Mr Justice Slade in the High Court on 26 September 1977. On 27 October he gave his judgment for the plaintiffs, with the defendants having to pay the substantial costs. He decided conclusively that the ICC action was an unreasonable restraint of trade, as were the TCCB's regulations on qualification and registration.

Sponsorship

Facing a financial crisis, the TCCB was obliged to seek a sponsor for Test cricket. Having secured Schweppes to sponsor the county championship earlier in 1977, they now turned to Cornhill, a largely unknown insurance company, to support Test cricket to the tune of £1 million over five years. Cornhill's 'awareness' index increased from 2 to 17 per cent in consequence. (In the midst of reviling Packer, incidentally, the TCCB had done a deal that brought them £150 000 from his Channel 9 to televise the 1977 Tests.) The TCCB realised that there was a substantial fund of corporate money to be tapped. Its sponsorship income rose from just under £500 000 in 1978 to over £2.3 million in 1985, and kept rising. The casualty was Gillette, who could not match the new going rate. The TCCB secured more for television rights, if by no means as much as the satellite TV revolution was to bring later. To head off further player defections, it then did what it should already have done, and increased Test appearance money fivefold, from £2000 to £10 000. Two years later in 1979 it went up to £12 000 with a £15 000 win bonus, and professional cricketers were granted a minimum wage. Although the county wage bill tripled to £2 million by 1986, it was not doing much more than catching up with inflation. For top cricketers the increase was sevenfold, for they were the ones with the bargaining power, and with it they acquired cars and personal sponsorship. Nevertheless they were still poorly rewarded in comparison with the top players in football, golf and tennis, a situation that still obtains in the 21st century, with the exception of a very few stars, particularly those on the subcontinent, where advertising endorsements are now so lucrative.

And what of the cricket? The World Series Cricket of 1977–8 played to comparatively small but vociferous crowds but to a larger TV audience. Its major innovations, however, were in one-day cricket, where floodlighting, a white ball for day-night games, a 30-yard circle, and coloured clothing all arrived with great haste to add interest to the game for camera and spectator. World Series Cricket was a necessary if distasteful jolt for the cricket authorities. It took a marketing eye to one-day cricket, and decided it had to do something different to attract a new watching clientele. New spectators needed to know who they were watching, so out went the studied anonymity of traditional cricket, in which the aficionados could identify nameless white-clad fielders, but few others could. A name on the back a little earlier would perhaps have prevented the arrival of coloured clothing, but once it had arrived it was irremovable. If this left a sour taste in the mouth of the traditional cricket lover, it certainly appealed to a wider audience, especially in Australia. There season attendances rose from 400 000 to one million between 1977 and the mid-1980s.

The aftermath

What happened next? There were repercussions, some of them undignified. After the 1977–8 WSC series in Australia, England chose not to select its Packer players, who now included Amiss and Woolmer, and Pakistan also took a hard line, thus losing Zaheer, Mushtaq and Asif Iqbal. But the impoverished West Indies Federation felt it couldn't afford to lose so many stars. At the end of the 1977–8 winter they played a legitimate home series against a Packer-weakened Australia side led by their former captain, the 42-year-old Bobby Simpson, whose last Test had been 10 years earlier. The West Indies predictably won the first two Tests, but then Clive Lloyd resigned as captain over the dropping of three players who had just signed for Packer. The next two Tests were shared one each, and the series came to an unsavoury end with a distasteful draw after a riot halted play following Vanburn Holder's dismissal, when West Indies stood nine down with over six overs left.

Back home early in 1978, Kent, with Knott, Underwood and Asif playing in the series, were under no illusions about their side's capability if they didn't play. Kent decided to welcome them back, while depriving Asif of the captaincy (Knott withdrew). They hadn't spoken to the new Professional Cricketers' Association, fearing trouble: the PCA had members on both sides of the divide between Packer and non-Packer men. David Clark, the author of the far-sighted 1966 report, and now both president of the ICC and chairman of the MCC, resigned from the Kent committee in protest. Hampshire, in a similar position, accepted back Barry Richards, Greenidge and Roberts – hardly a surprise. Sussex welcomed back Imran and Le Roux, and would have retained Greig as captain too had he not blotted his copybook for criticising Boycott, then acting England captain in Pakistan, the spokesman for a dressing-room revolt when Pakistan decided to switch tack and let in its own Packer men. The Warwickshire committee, however, prompted by a letter to The Times signed by some of its players, decided to punish Dennis Amiss by withholding a contract for 1979. This led to a furore from the county's members, who called a special general meeting for 26 September. But at the last minute Amiss requested that it be cancelled: the PCA, its secretary Jack Bannister a Warwickshire man, had become involved, and was brokering a deal. Amiss was playing with the county again in 1979.

In the 1978–9 winter, while England were demolishing an Australian side shorn of its Packer players in a series with poor attendances, WSC was mounting a series of floodlit one-day internationals with average crowds of over 8000, copious TV advertisements, free parking and transport. The WSC series that winter was between Australia and West Indies, and it too drew big crowds – and crowd disturbances – and was a financial success. The contrast was galling for the Australian authorities, who had already lost money over the West Indies tour the previous winter. There was no love lost between the two sides. Most ABC members cordially loathed the Packer entourage, and their chairman Bob Parish constantly exhorted the other countries' cricket authorities not to yield an inch.

Sleeping with the enemy

Then in early April 1979 the English were nonplussed when the ABC suddenly announced a deal with Channel 9 that secured them TV rights for three years at a cost of £600 000. The ICC found it had little choice but to agree it. Overnight India's forthcoming Australian tour, not expected to make money for the cash-strapped ABC, was peremptorily cancelled – they wouldn't dare do that now – and England were effectively forced to tour Australia again for a second successive winter. This time it would be against the Australian 1st XI in a three-match series, with one-day internationals interspersed, further confused by its overlapping with one in which the hosts took on the West Indies. The results certainly clarified the world order – West Indies, then Australia, then England a long way behind. But that winter was a financial success, and seemed to justify the ABC in its distasteful volte-face. The six Tests brought 445 000 spectators, and 13 one-day matches were seen by 258 000. A year later the Australia v New Zealand final drew 53 000 spectators. The next year's against the West Indies was seen by 78 000, the following year against the old enemy 84 000 watched, staggering figures. In those days the final was a one-match affair, and only Melbourne was big enough to take the numbers.

The dispute was over. What was its legacy? Some changes that would probably have come anyway were compressed into a painful two-year period. The England authorities had discovered sponsorship, and learnt to demand more from TV rights. The players were now being paid a decent wage – or had at least caught up with inflation. The counties had to pay for it, but they had their share of TCCB money to compensate, and the domestic one-day competitions had not yet become commonplace. The dictates of all that extra money, though, were now beginning to be felt in a big way. This is how the thinking went. One-day internationals are clearly extremely good money-spinners, so let's have more of them. Too many against one team will be boring, so let's have triangular tournaments: we just have to trust that the home side gets through to the final. And while they're here playing one-day internationals, they can play some old-fashioned Test matches too. As a consequence, between July 1979 and February 1980 India played 17 Tests. Between 1974 and 1981 England would play Australia 31 times, an average of four times each year. Wisden's editor in 1981 mused that we were killing the goose that laid the golden egg. But the analogy was wrong. The goose kept on laying, but we were force-feeding her.

Now let's return to the spring of 1977. Australia had won the Centenary Test, and the Ashes holders were back in England for a series played out against a background of controversy and litigation. Could England win back the Ashes? They had a new captain, an exile returning, and a callow youth. They only thing they had in common was that their names began with the letter B.

CHAPTER 19

Brearley and Botham

Mike Brearley and Bob Taylor congratulate Ian Botham after he has dismissed Graeme Wood
lbw at Headingley, July 1981, three days before his series-rescuing 149*.

I called him the sidestep queen. I took him off after three overs and he
got excited at that and wanted to prove me wrong.

MIKE BREARLEY on Ian Botham

He could wind me up in ten seconds.

IAN BOTHAM on Mike Brearley

1977 Australia

England returned from the Indian tour and the Centenary Test more buoyed up than they had been for some while. Could that spirit and the Indian success be repeated in England, when the Australians were over yet again? That Ian Chappell, Lillee and Edwards had declined to tour was encouraging, if puzzling, but it wasn't until the tour was two weeks old that it became clear why, when the news of Kerry Packer's World Series Cricket plans became public. Because he too had a contract, and was indeed implicated in recruiting the English Packer men, Tony Greig was relieved of the captaincy and replaced by Mike Brearley.

Brearley, the Middlesex captain, was a rare beast, an academic sportsman. He'd secured a First at Cambridge and had passed out joint top of the Civil Service exam. Short and trim, with prematurely greying curly hair and his collar turned up, he was intelligent, gifted and tough-minded – no dilettante – yet had never quite fulfilled the early batting promise he displayed when he made 73 (at No.8) and 89 against the 1961 Australians in only his sixth first-class match at the age of 19. That he eventually played 39 Tests yet averaged only 22 with a bat, without a century, would be an indictment were it not for the cool and astute captaincy that kept him his place.

England	216 & 305	Australia	296 & 114–6
Australia	297 & 218	**England**	437 & 82–1
Australia	243 & 309	**England**	364 & 189–3
England	436	Australia	103 & 248
England	214 & 57–2	Australia	385

In the first Test at Lord's, the Jubilee Test, England were indebted to Woolmer, who top-scored with 79 and 120 in their innings of 216 and 305. The unflagging hostility of Willis, 7–78, had held Australia to a lead of 80, and the 216 they eventually needed in 165 minutes was too much to attempt after a bad start. Woolmer was again the batting hero of the second Test at Old Trafford. After Australia had made 297, his 137 steered England to a lead of 140. The second Australian innings centred on a long duel between Greg Chappell and Derek Underwood, who in his 6–66 chiselled out Chappell's partners, none of whom could reach 30 at the other end. Chappell made an exquisite 112 out of 218, but England eased to a nine-wicket win.

At Trent Bridge for the third Test, when the gates were closed for the first time since 1948, England included an old hand and a young one. Boycott returned after three years of self-imposed exile (the selectors hadn't thought to recall the trusty Steele) and he was joined by the 21-year-old Ian Botham, a protégé of Brian Close at Somerset, a young all-rounder who had exhibited some of Close's attributes by winning a cup quarter-final as an 18-year-old, with an epic blood-spattered innings after being smashed in the mouth by Andy Roberts. He started bowling with Australia a comfortable 131–2. The first ball of his second spell was a wide long-hop that a disgusted Chappell dragged onto his stumps, the first of many Botham would take with inviting 'bad' balls. When Australia were all out for 243 he had taken 5–74 in his first Test bowl.

Pascoe and Thomson then set about England. Boycott was grimly defiant, and rode his luck. First, Randall sacrificed himself when Boycott called him for a suicidal run, then, with England 87–5 and his score only 20 after three tense hours, he was dropped by McCosker in the slips. But Knott rallied him and England with a typically jaunty display, and both went on to make hundreds in a stand of 215 that turned the match. McCosker redeemed himself with a century when Australia batted again, but Willis's aggression and Hendrick's parsimony kept them to a lead of 188. The target was by no means easy, but Brearley made light of it in his best innings for England, and England won after he and Boycott had added 154 with bad weather looming.

Two-nil ahead with two to play, England needed only to draw the fourth match to regain the Ashes. In fact they won by an innings. Boycott, whose century at Trent Bridge was his 98th, had scored another at Edgbaston in the intervening game. With the gates of his home ground at Leeds shut well before the game began, and the toss won, it was the perfect setting. His watching fellow Yorkshiremen Len Hutton and Herbert Sutcliffe, had both made 100 hundreds, but he was the first person to reach the landmark in a Test match. He went on and on to 191, once more adding 100 with Alan Knott. A dispirited Australia capitulated first for 103 to Hendrick and Botham, and then again for 248 to Hendrick and Willis. They fared better in the last Test at the Oval, ruined by rain, although Willis managed another five-wicket haul.

The return of the prodigal son gave Boycott 442 runs at an average of 147, but it was Woolmer, averaging 56, who had set up England's dominant position by top scoring in the first three innings of the series. No one else averaged 40. Willis was by some way the best bowler in the series, with 27 wickets at under 20, while Botham and Hendrick took theirs at 20, Underwood his at 27.

1977–8 Pakistan and New Zealand

That winter, because of the Packer shenanigans, England would lose Greig, Underwood, Knott, Amiss and Woolmer. However, the Pakistanis would miss Mushtaq Mohammed, Zaheer Abbas, Imran Khan and Asif Iqbal, their Packer Pakistanis, so things evened up. The series was the first of many around the world in which neither side was at full strength, with preparation disrupted by the coming and going of players contracted to Packer.

Pakistan	407–9d & 106–3	England	288
Pakistan	275 & 259–4d	England	191 & 186–1
England	266 & 222–5	Pakistan	281

The Pakistan series was a laboured affair on slow wickets. In the first Test England were rescued by Derbyshire's off-spinning all-rounder Geoff Miller who, batting with a heavy cold, made 98* when a possible follow-on threatened. In the next Test Pakistan's caution over a second innings declaration left England with only five and a half hours to bat out, during which time Boycott and Brearley added 185. They saw off comfortably the new menace of Abdul Qadir, a compelling figure with a bounding run-up and wristy action, who – as it turned out – was to herald the revival of top class wrist-spin. Except in England, naturally. Only Boycott had played him with any confidence in the first innings, when he took 6–44 as England lost eight wickets for 34.

The final Test nearly didn't happen. Three of Pakistan's Packer squad flew in and were chosen in a party of 23. The England players protested, because they were without theirs. By then they were without their captain too, for Brearley was back in England with a broken arm after a one-day 'friendly'. Boycott led the revolt and the team into the Test, from which the Packer players were omitted at the last minute. In another tedious draw, Phil Edmonds took 7–66 in an admirable long spell.

New Zealand	228 & 123	England	215 & 64
England	418 & 96–4d	New Zealand	235 & 105
New Zealand	315 & 382–8	England	429

Boycott stayed as captain in New Zealand. Such was the state of the pitches in Pakistan that after the first Test England had played three spinners, and therefore, strange as it seems in retrospect, Botham couldn't find a place. He could in New Zealand, in a four-man pace attack, where the wickets were as different as they could be from those in Pakistan. Willis, Hendrick, Old and Botham put England on the way to victory in the first match at windy Wellington, by bowling New Zealand out on an awkward seaming pitch for 228 and 123. England, their first innings glued together by Boycott's battling 77, made with contact lenses that caused him acute pain, needed only 137 to win. But Richard Hadlee hadn't read the script, and took 6–26 as they were catapulted out for 64. It was a delirious moment for New Zealand and their first victory over England, in their 48th Test in their 48th year. Especially so for the Hadlees, as Richard's brother Dayle was in the team too, while the chairman of the New Zealand Cricket Council was their father Walter, captain in England in 1949.

Botham immediately restored England's self-esteem with his first great all-round performance. Supported by Miller, Taylor and Edmonds, his rapid 103 took England from an ominous 26–3 to 418. He took five wickets and Edmonds four to earn a lead of 183, and when he felt Boycott was labouring when quick runs were needed in the second innings, deliberately ran him out before contributing a quick 30. After Willis had broken through early on the last day, Botham held two brilliant catches and took the last three wickets to fall. To Wisden's reporter 'in everything he did Botham was the inspired cricketer'. He was still only 22.

For the last Test an extra day couldn't compensate for a perfect pitch, and England were indebted to a long maiden Test century from Clive Radley, the stocky and steady fair-haired Middlesex batsman, who made a patient 158 in just under 10 hours. It was a return to the funereal pace of Pakistan, and England's first innings lead wasn't enough to force a victory. Thus both series were drawn. While his run-rate got no quicker, Boycott was a rock on this tour, with 495 runs at 56 in total. Botham averaged 53 with the bat and 18 with the ball, while the Surrey batsman and specialist slip-fielder Graham Roope was next with 39. Willis took 21 wickets at 21, Edmonds 19 at 23. Botham, Roope and Edmonds – 22 catches between them in three Tests – led a brilliant close-fielding side. At its heart now was the quietly efficient Derbyshire man Bob Taylor, who seized the chance to exploit Knott's absence with a pretty faultless display behind the stumps.

1978 Pakistan and New Zealand

Such were the mysterious vagaries of the fixture arrangements that a tour of Pakistan and New Zealand was promptly followed by summer visits from... Pakistan and New Zealand. Brearley was fit to lead England again, and so successful was his side, and so comparatively injury-free, that England managed to get through a home series of six Tests without calling on more than 14 players.

Pakistan	164 & 231	**England**	452–8d
England	364	Pakistan	105 & 139
Pakistan	201	England	119–7

The weather was filthy for most of the summer, but so potent was the England attack that they won five of the six Tests. Pakistan were never in the hunt in English conditions without their Packer players. At Edgbaston it was Chris Old with 7–50 who devastated them on the first day. The match was virtually sealed in one over, which went 0 w w nb w w 1, so nearly four in four balls but not even a hat trick. England's 452–8 was founded on Radley's second hundred in successive Test innings and another from Botham, but was notable more for a debut innings. Slim and fair, David Gower had the classic left-hander's languid grace. The new golden boy pulled his first ball in Tests dismissively for four and went on to a sweet 58.

That innings win, marred to some extent by Willis hitting the nightwatchman Iqbal Qasim in the mouth, was followed by another even more comprehensive win at Lord's. Again Gower made 50, as did Graham Gooch, back again after his traumatic Test beginning, and Botham made a third hundred in successive Tests. After England's 364, Willis and Edmonds put out a sorry Pakistan for 105, for Botham to complete the devastation in the second innings with 8–34, using a substitute ball which, like Lever's in India, suddenly swung extravagantly. At the end of that Test the captains agreed that bouncers should not be bowled at recognised tail-enders, although the tail-ender nightwatchman would still remain an issue. Pakistan improved markedly in the last Test, but rain destroyed any chance they had of a comeback.

New Zealand	234 & 182	**England**	279 & 138–3
England	429	New Zealand	120 & 190
New Zealand	339 & 67	**England**	289 & 118–3

Although they had Richard Hadlee available after playing with striking success in the first half of the season for Nottinghamshire, the New Zealanders were severely hampered by the absence of Glenn Turner, who preferred to stay with Worcester throughout his Benefit season. The first Test at the Oval was well fought. Willis brought England into the game with 5–42 after New Zealand had reached 191–3. Gower's 111, his first Test hundred, gave England the edge, but with the fourth day wiped out New Zealand battled for survival on the fifth. They were slowly strangled by Edmonds and Miller, who between them took 6–65 from 69.1 overs, great bowling but grim viewing. England needed 138 against a hostile Hadlee with rain imminent but Gooch batted brilliantly to reach 91* and England won by seven wickets just after the start of the last 20 overs.

Returning from injury, Boycott typically made a hundred in the second Test at Trent Bridge, adding 111 in a new opening stand with Gooch. New Zealand were unlucky with the prevailing rules on covering, which meant that the pitch was left open to the elements, even though only two balls were bowled before the rain set in at the start of day three. Botham took 6–34, then a further three after the follow-on while Edmonds tied up one end – another 4–44 in 33.1 overs. In three successive Test innings his figures were 83–43–85–8. Superb bowling, however supine the batting.

For over half of the final match New Zealand had the edge, securing a lead of 50 after Howarth's hundred and a destructive new-ball burst by Hadlee. But Brearley gave the new ball to Botham, after his 6–101 in the first innings, and he promptly bowled both openers with in-swinging yorkers. He and Willis went on to bowl New Zealand out for 67, exacting some retribution for Wellington. Thus England won by seven wickets the only Test in which it didn't rain, and the light meters given to the umpires for the first time were not tested. While the opposition was pretty poor, and the conditions helped England, this was another great summer for an exciting young side. All of the five-man attack were under 30 – Willis, Old, Botham, Edmonds and Miller (so were Hendrick and Emburey who both played in the last Test) – and it was helped by brilliant fielding. That Botham took 37 wickets at 14, while Edmonds, Old and Willis 57 between them at 16, tells its own story. With the bat Gooch and Gower averaged over 50, Botham 43, and the reliable Radley 38. Moreover the same team won all four one-day internationals.

1978–9 Australia

This England team could now test itself against Australia, in the first Ashes series in which batsmen played with helmets. Unfortunately the opposition was Australia II, then by no means as strong as the heavyweight 2nd XI who would ply their trade for English counties in the first decade of the next century. Australia I was taking on the West Indies and the Rest of the World in a triangular Packer series, and the departure of their whole team was distinctly more debilitating than England's loss of Greig, Amiss, Woolmer, Knott, Snow and Underwood. That had allowed half a new England team to come through, and there were cricketers eager and able to take the chance. The Australians had some, like Alan Border, Kim Hughes, and the opening bowler Rodney Hogg, but they were up against it from the start.

An Ashes win is an Ashes win, and especially with a margin of 5–1. But its true merit would be revealed the following winter. There were no draws, which rightly suggests a series with bowlers on top.

Australia	116 & 339	**England**	286 & 170–3
England	309 & 208	Australia	190 & 161
Australia	258 & 167	England	143 & 179
England	152 & 346	Australia	294 & 111
England	169 & 360	Australia	164 & 160
Australia	198 & 143	**England**	308 & 35–1

Australia's average total was just 192, England's 256, the top score in the series only 309: the pitches were poor. Excellent all-round bowling, led by Willis, enabled England to win the first two Tests with some comfort, but brilliant bowling at Melbourne by Hogg, 10–66 in the match, gave Australia some hope. Ahead with two wickets down on the second day of the Sydney Test, they seemed to be on the way to levelling the series at 2–2. Several English players were ill with a virus and heat exhaustion but Brearley marshalled his depleted resources cleverly. Radley had been displaced by Randall, whose magnificently disciplined innings of 150, in which he cut out the hook, allowed Australia to be set 205 in 265 minutes against an attack deprived of Willis and Botham. They lasted just three and a half hours against the off-spin of Miller and Emburey, making 111 (another instance – why that number's unlucky for England and not Australia is hard to fathom).

The Ashes secured, Miller's value was seen again in Adelaide, when he helped England recover from 27–5 in the first innings with Botham, and 132–6 at a crucial point of the second with Taylor, unlikely as it was for a Derbyshire pair to add 135 for the seventh wicket against Australia. He was there again in the last Test, with Emburey in the second innings spinning out an Australian side manifestly inept against off-spin. Miller deservedly headed the bowling averages with 23 wickets at 15, Hendrick took 19 at 15, Emburey 16 at 19, Willis 20 at 23, Botham 23 at 24. Even Old and Lever, a single Test each, took 9 wickets at 14 between them. Only Randall and Gower – described by Boycott after this tour as the best timer of the ball he had ever seen – scored hundreds, and they averaged 38 and 43 respectively. No one else managed 30, but with contributions down the order and such a strong bowling side, they could afford to have Boycott and Brearley languishing with averages of 21 and 16. The Ashes crown may have been a hollow one, but the scores are there in the book, and England supporters loved it. Brearley had lost every toss but one, but Boycott considered he had done 'a magnificent job on and off the field', lavish praise from one who gave it rarely, but when it was due. He also felt it the best fielding side he had ever played in.

1979   The second World Cup

England took their form back home and to the World Cup, while Australia were once more denied their Packer players. It was again just a fortnight's affair, with two leagues of four teams producing the semi-finalists, and weakened Australia's humiliation was complete when they were comfortably beaten by both England and Pakistan in the qualifying stage. The leadership of that group hinged on the England v Pakistan game, a nail-biter. No England batsman passed 33 in an innings of 165, but Hendrick and Botham sent Pakistan from 27–0 to 34–6. Asif Iqbal led a recovery with the only 50 of the match, and Imran Khan and Wasim Bari inched the score to 145–8, with overs in hand. Brearley then produced an unlikely masterstroke by bringing on Boycott of all people to take the last two wickets, and England won by 14 runs.

The other group was topped by the West Indies as expected, but proved a disaster for India. Not only did they lose comprehensively to both West Indies and New Zealand, but they made a complete mess against the spinning de Silvas of Sri Lanka, still not yet a Test nation. Chasing 230, none of their batsmen reached 40, while three Sri Lankans had done so.

For a long time at the Oval the West Indies v Pakistan semi-final was in the balance, despite West Indies' massive – for those days – 293–6. Majid and Zaheer (back post-Packer) added 166 for the second wicket, and a surprise looked on the cards until Croft and Richards ran through the middle order. Closer still was the Old Trafford semi-final. England made 221, Gooch 71 and with Willis, Botham and Hendrick, all to some degree lame, limping up to bowl, New Zealand had a great chance. But Boycott again bowled a mean spell, nine overs for 24, Randall contributed a trademark run-out, and they could manage only 4 from Botham's final over when 14 were needed.

SEMI-FINAL			
West Indies	293–6 (60)	Pakistan	250 (56.2)
England	221–8 (60)	New Zealand	212–9 (60)
FINAL			
West Indies	286–9 (60)	England	194 (51)

So England had made the final, but had to go in without Willis. To strengthen the batting they chose to play just four front-line bowlers and juggle three part-timers. But Collis King murdered the part-timers with 86 in 70 minutes, after joining Richards at a parlous 99–4. Richards went on to 138* out of 286–9, and the bowling of Boycott, Gooch and Larkins went for 86 between them in 10 overs. When England batted, five of those seven batsmen couldn't get to the crease in time. Well as Boycott and Brearley began the innings with a stand of 129, they weren't natural accelerators, which meant the stroke-makers down the order had to score at seven an over. Against Garner and Croft that was impossible on the day, and England capitulated from 183–2 to 194 all out. While it may have made little difference in the end, England should perhaps have used the aggressive Wayne Larkins to open as usual, rather than bat at No. 7, at which point all was lost.

1979 India

India stayed on after the Cup to play a four-match series. They were on the back foot from the start, but recovered to give the series a memorable finale, and regain some self-respect after their woeful World Cup.

England	633–5d	India	297 & 253
India	96 & 318–4	England	419–9d
England	270	India	223–6
England	305 & 334–8d	India	202 & 429–8

At Edgbaston England passed 600 for only the third time in Tests, with Boycott making 155 and Gower 200* against a depleted attack in which the lanky 20-year-old Kapil Dev took all five wickets to fall. Kapil was the first really exciting pace bowler to emerge for India since the war. Against this formidable total India were bowled out twice for under 300, though Gavaskar and Viswanath both scored fifties in each innings.

In the rain-affected second match India were saved by centuries in the second innings by Vengsarkar and Viswanath. Their first innings paltry 96 was notable for Botham's 100th Test wicket during his 5–35. It had taken him just two years and nine days. England passed 400 in reply, Gower top-scoring again. The weather was even worse at Leeds, where England only managed 80–4 in the first three days. But on Monday morning Botham powered his way to 137 in 165 minutes to give a dead match something to remember it by. So England went to the Oval still 1–0 up.

From the first three and a half days of the final Test you would not have expected it to go to the final over with all three results possible. England led by 103 on first innings, and a Boycott century extended it to 437 at tea on the fourth day. India were 76–0 overnight on a benign pitch, needing a run a minute, and nobody really expected them to get near their target. That they did was due to a magnificent innings by Gavaskar, supported by Chauhan and Vengsarkar, so that when the last 20 overs began India were an astonishing 328–1, needing 110 and with Gavaskar in command. At 365 you felt that England's last chance had gone when Botham uncharacteristically dropped Vengsarkar on the boundary. Characteristically, though, he led the fight back, catching Vengsarkar to make amends and coming back into the attack with eight overs left. Fortified by Brearley's tactical drinks break, and despite figures to that point of 0–80, he first had Gavaskar caught for 221, had Yashpal and Yajuvendra leg before, and ran out Venkat. Willey, who had bowled admirably throughout, bowled the last over with 15 needed, a task too great for two new batsmen. A wonderful last day, and only the most intense of England supporters would have begrudged Gavaskar a remarkable victory.

In this Test Botham reached 1000 runs in Tests to add to his 100 wickets, and he and Gavaskar dominated the series. Botham was a force of nature; Gavaskar gave a master class. The gifted Indian, looking somehow even smaller than his five feet five inches, made over 500 runs, and his only innings less than 50 was 42. Boycott and Gower averaged over 70 for England. Botham, 48 with the bat, averaged 23 with the ball, while Hendrick topped the bowling averages with 12 wickets at 18.

1979–80 Australia... and India

The winter series to which England were subjected in Australia in the winter of 1979–80 was the first of a new era. One-day internationals were now – if only from the viewpoint of money, from which all else stems – just as important as the five-day Tests, and their timing and siting fixed the programme for an awkward two-team tour. The money-strapped Australian Board's forced rapprochement with Packer left the ICC with a *fait accompli*. England and the West Indies would tour jointly, and India, the visitors originally due, would be put back a year. So England played a three-match tour, interspersed with one-day internationals and the West Indies Tests. Thus the same players chopped and changed uneasily between modes. Moreover they were constantly on the move, as their weary manager Alec Bedser complained at the tour's end: in what was only a three-Test series, 31 internal flights and 52 coach trips left them drained.

Australia	244 & 337	England	228 & 215
England	123 & 237	**Australia**	145 & 219–4
England	306 & 273	**Australia**	477 & 103–2

Only Underwood of the Packer players was restored by England, as Brearley put Australia in at the start of the first Test in Perth. Botham's bowling and Hughes's 99 dominated the first day, until Lillee provoked an altercation by emerging with a patented aluminium bat that would cause a hurried rewrite of the Laws. Botham got him in the end on the way to 6–78, but Lillee fought back by dismissing both openers for nought. At 225–7 in Australia's second innings England had a chance, but Botham, another five, and the indefatigable Underwood could not prise out the gutsy left-hander Alan Border, who made his first Test hundred. Despite Boycott's technically rigorous innings England couldn't escape their due defeat, and he was left 99* when the last three wickets fell in a heap.

Sydney began with similar parity. Before the game a violent thunderstorm livened a pitch left exposed to it, and Greg Chappell thankfully put England in while protesting that it was unfit. Two opening innings under 150 attested to that. Just as no one stayed with Boycott at Melbourne, so no one shared Gower's resistance here once the battling nightwatchman Underwood was gone. Again, Willis was unable to stay with a man in his nineties, so Gower was left 98*, a score Greg Chappell matched in taking Australia to victory. England batted better at Melbourne, but it still wasn't enough. Gooch added to the litany of century-missers by running himself out going for his maiden Test hundred on the first day, when Lillee took the first six of 11 in the match. In their second innings England lost six wickets before wiping out Australia's big lead, and only a bravura 119* from Botham enabled them to do even that.

Three-nil was a chastening defeat, but England's batting simply wasn't up to the task against an attack led by Lillee at his peak and the awkward left-armer Dymock, 17 wickets at 15. The tour would have been a complete disaster were it not for a silver lining: a one-off Test in India.

India	242 & 149	**England**	296 & 98–0

England were invited to end their tour by playing a Golden Jubilee Test in Bombay, to mark the 100th anniversary of the Indian Board of Control. This became a sunlit stage for Botham. In an otherwise low-scoring match, in which no other batsman reached 50, he was extraordinary. The pitch was unexpectedly grassy and the weather overcast as he took for 6–58 on the first day. He then dragged England back into the game from 58–5, with a typical century in a partnership of 171 with Taylor. In a gesture that recalled Marsh's reprieve of Randall in the Australian Jubilee match, Viswanath sportingly brought Taylor back when he had been given out caught behind. These two spontaneous instances of camaraderie shine out: such moments would be few and far between for the rest of the century. Finally Botham devastated India, on paper a strong batting side, with another 7–48.

Botham, 114 and 13–106, was the first player to score a hundred and take 10 wickets in a Test, a feat equalled since only by Imran Khan three years later. At this point in his career Botham was a colossus. Utterly fearless, with immense stamina, nerveless in a crisis, a frightening hitter of the ball with a rapidly improving shot selection, a bowler who could swing the bowl both ways at pace when the conditions were right, a brilliant instinctive fielder anywhere who stood two yards closer than anyone else at second slip. English cricket had seen nothing like him since W. G. Grace was a young man. On that four-match tour he averaged 50 with the bat, and took 32 wickets at 14, topping both sets of averages. He won the match in India virtually alone, and without him England would not even have competed in Australia.

1980 West Indies... and Australia

Ian Botham was 24. He had reached such a high point in 1979 that a decline was almost inevitable. It's unfortunate that he was made England captain at the start of a tough West Indies tour which, worse still, coincided with the onset of back problems that made his bowling slower and less potent. In this series, one hampered by the poorest weather in England since 1958, his magic powers were limited to calling the toss correctly each time.

England	263 & 252	**West Indies**	308 & 209–8
England	269 & 133–2	West Indies	518
England	150 & 391–7	West Indies	260
England	370 & 209–9	West Indies	265
England	143 & 227–6	West Indies	245

The opening Test at Trent Bridge was the only one unaffected by the weather, a close-fought match that settled the series. The West Indies' four-man pace battery was matched by four from England, and there were only 11 overs of spin in the entire game – not unusual later, I fear, but a rarity then, deplored by the critics. The game hinged on a spell in the England second innings. Boycott had led a spirited fight back that left them 145–2, 100 ahead, at the start of the fourth day. But Garner, Roberts and Marshall were formidable with the ball moving around, and West Indies were set 208. At the end of that day Richards had propelled them to 109–2, but his dismissal by Botham just before the close gave England hope. Next morning Willis continued to bowl 'with a rhythm and aggression lacking in Australia', and worked his way through the middle order, but Desmond Haynes, natural successor to Conrad Hunte, stood firm, and although run out with three needed, had done enough to see West Indies home.

Rain and the slow over rate meant that the rest of the series rarely ever promised a victory for either side. Although West Indies were clearly superior, England battled away throughout, and deserved the final 1–0 score line. At Lord's Gooch came of age with a dominant 123: it's often forgotten that he had to wait until his 36th Test innings before making a century. For most of the next 14 years his straight-backed guardsman figure, bat raised, would be a reassuring sight for England supporters. Greenidge and Richards both made big hundreds before most of the last two days were wiped out. At Old Trafford, despite a belligerent 70 from the tall Somerset left-hander Brian Rose – his Test captain's county captain, incidentally – England collapsed, and fell behind after Clive Lloyd had made a hundred in front of his home crowd at Old Trafford. England retrieved some face after Boycott's 86 by battling through the last day to save the game, led by the obdurate, obstinate Peter Willey. Like Colin Milburn from Northumberland via Northampton, Willey was a tough competitor with an exaggeratedly two-eyed stance that almost seemed to expect the ball to arrive from mid-wicket, but an utterly fearless player of pace.

Willey was instrumental in saving the fourth Test at the Oval, too, and in an altogether more unlikely fashion. An aggressive 83 from Gooch in an opening stand of 155, batting with a Boycott whose eyes had been blackened by Croft, gave England an early grip. After a blank Saturday, West Indies, minus an injured Lloyd, survived a follow-on scare themselves, then ran through the England batting. At 92–9 they were only 197 ahead with three and a half hours left, but Willey and Willis batted with extraordinary composure. Willis retrieved his winter reputation for leaving batsmen high and dry in the nineties, by sticking at it until Willey had reached a maiden Test hundred. They, and West Indies' 12.3 an hour over rate, kept the series alive. In theory, maybe, but not in practice, for rain blanked out two days of a depressing final Test.

But there was one more Test left that summer.

Australia	385–5d & 189–4d	England	205 & 244–3

Australia and India had had their parties, and England wanted one too. Unfortunately this game did not live up to the other two, and rain was allowed to spoil it. On Saturday, the centrepiece day, once early rain had cleared it was evident to everyone in the sell-out crowd except umpires Bird and Constant, and a reluctant England captain, that the game should restart after lunch. Several hours, five inspections, thousands of angry members, hundreds of thrown cushions, and a scuffle in the Long Room later, it eventually did. For the record Hughes and Wood made hundreds, as did Boycott as England declined to chase 370 in 350 minutes on an extended last day. A damp and depressing end to a damp season. In the six Tests only Boycott of the established players did himself justice, averaging 56; only Rose of the others exceeded 40, and Gower was in such poor form that he played only two Tests. The tall, young, Kent fast bowler Graham Dilley made a promising start, taking 11 at 16, but apart from him only Willis averaged below 30 with the ball. Although a 1–0 defeat stands up against later West Indian horror series, Botham's tough start was emphasised by the reversal in his averages compared to the previous summer – 48/23 with bat and ball had become 17/37.

1980–1 West Indies

Once more the fixtures list threw up a nonsense for the winter – England playing the West Indies in the Caribbean immediately after their tour of England. This time there were just four Tests because the second Test in Georgetown was cancelled. The Guyanese government had refused to allow the England replacement Robin Jackman into the country, one of the effects of the Gleneagles Agreement restricting sporting links with South Africa (though they had actually overlooked the fact that the reserve wicketkeeper David Bairstow had played there).

West Indies	426–9d	England	178 & 169
West Indies	265 & 379–7d	England	122 & 224
England	271 & 234–3	West Indies	468–9d
England	285 & 302–6	West Indies	442

Disappointingly, following their gritty determination the preceding summer, England were outplayed in every Test, and their bowling was particularly ineffective. Their batsmen fired individually but rarely in pairs. None did in the first Test at Port-of-Spain. The 'third' Test, the second to be played after the Guyana fiasco, was over-shadowed by the tragic death from a heart attack of the popular coach Ken Barrington, at the age of 50, which shocked and subdued the team. Gooch's 116 there, bristling with defiance, only delayed the inevitable. He cemented his growing reputation as England's best player of the West Indian pace battery with a brisk 83 out of 144 with Boycott in the second innings in the first ever Test in Viv Richards' Antigua. This was after another remarkable innings by Willey, who had come in at 138–5 in the first innings and made 102* out of the further 133 added. Finally in Kingston England were saved by two magnificent pieces of batting. In the first innings Gooch reached a blistering hundred in only the 40th over, and went on to 153 out of 249. When later England were in danger of defeat at 32–3, Gower pro-duced his best innings for a long while. His 154* was a feat of great concentration, not an attribute regularly granted to him.

A difficult background, certainly, but a poor series for England. Without the injured Willis, and with Botham still horribly out of form (although his 15 wickets were more than anyone else managed) the attack paled in comparison with the West Indies set of Holding, Croft, Garner and Roberts. Meanwhile the batting depended utterly on Gooch, Gower, Willey and Boycott. They averaged between 60 and 40, no one else even reached 15, and Botham averaged 10.

1981 Australia

So England returned home, having taken on successively Australia, West Indies, West Indies again… only to confront Australia once more. Why couldn't England slip in a nice quiet recuperative New Zealand series? For Botham, still only 25 and short of fit-ness, form and confidence, it was a captaincy initiation with no respite from the best in the world. What would happen next?

What happened was a paean to the glorious uncertainty of cricket, and of life itself. By late afternoon of the Monday of the third Test, England, 135–7 in their second innings, were still 92 short of avoiding an innings defeat. Ladbrokes were offering 500–1 against an England win (an offer too good for two gambling Aussies to resist).

They had sacked their young captain, the hero of 1977–9, and brought back a grey-haired old man who was patently unlikely to score many runs. If they lost, as seemed absolutely certain, England would go 2–0 down and have to win each of the last three Tests to regain the Ashes, the state England so nearly reached in 2005. Get out of that.

England	185 & 125	**Australia**	179 & 132–6
England	311 & 265–8d	Australia	345 & 90–4
Australia	401–9d & 111	**England**	174 & 356
England	189 & 219	Australia	258 & 121
England	231 & 404	Australia	130 & 402
Australia	352 & 344–9d	England	314 & 261–7

They did. At Trent Bridge for the first Test both sides played a four-man pace attack, so there was no spin seen at all. With no Thomson on the Australian side, might not Willis, Dilley, Hendrick and Botham outgun Lillee, Hogg, Lawson and the newcomer Alderman? No. The Bedser-built Terry Alderman would have a tremendous series. Here he took nine and Lillee eight as England's batsmen foundered, not least Woolmer, a pair after his post-Packer return. On the first Sunday of Test cricket in England, Australia struggled somewhat to reach what – at this stage of the summer anyway – seemed a modest target, but the third Chappell brother Trevor eventually made the winning hit.

England made a better fist of it at Lord's, where, according to Wisden, the Test followed the 'recent morbid trend... of bad weather, controversy, and abysmal public relations'. Scores in the eighties by Willey and Gower, one in each innings, gave England the edge, but Willis's 28 no-balls out of 55 extras helped Australia to a lead, and in the end they had under three hours to survive. Botham's travails continued with the indignity of a pair, and being cold-shouldered on his return to the pavilion by charmless MCC members, so he chose to take the decision out of the selectors' hands by resigning the England captaincy at the age of 25. In practice, compared with the set of them all, he hadn't been a bad captain on the field (as opposed to off it) but it was his misfortune to follow Brearley, to have no respite from the best opposition, and to see his own form plummet.

Still captaining Middlesex, and averaging 50 for them, Brearley returned to the captaincy at the age of 39. The Australians were cock-a-hoop. England were in disarray, and 'we saw [Brearley] as an advantage to us – that Messiah stuff was bullshit', said Lillee later. At first things appeared no better at Headingley. After Wood and Hughes took Australia past 400, England batted poorly again and were forced to follow on. The only bright spot was Botham's return to form with nothing but his own game to think about. His bowling began sluggishly. 'I called him the sidestep queen,' said Brearley, who took him off after three overs. Stung – 'He could wind me up in 10 seconds' – and advised by Brearley to revert to his original bowling action, Botham found a new bowling gear and took 6–95, then struck a more carefree 50, the only bright spot in another dismal batting performance. England followed on 227 behind and lost Gooch for a duck overnight.

On the Saturday night both teams partied at Botham's house until the early hours, many Englishmen fearing it was their last Test. At 41–4 on Monday morning that seemed a certainty. When in due course Botham came back to the wicket on Monday afternoon England had struggled grimly to 105–5, and soon after that to 135–7. With the tail for company, and the ball still moving around for Lillee and Alderman, Botham was struggling, and it seemed only a matter of time. But Dilley arrived at No. 9 and 'started batting like Sobers', so Botham decided he had nothing to lose by having a clatter.

It's often forgotten that Dilley, a left-hander thundering the ball off the front foot, kept pace with Botham in making 56 out of 117 for the eighth wicket. So did Old, with 29 out of 67. All three rode their luck, while Botham played some stupendous shots in between nerve-racking edges that spiralled out of the reach of the fielders. When Willis arrived they were 91 ahead, not enough, but a last wicket stand of 37 gave a glimmer of hope. Botham finished 149* the next morning, when Willis left immediately. Australia needed 130, and had reached 56–1 when Brearley accepted Willis's 'too old for this' plea to bowl downwind, downhill. Trance-like in his intensity, Willis produced the spell of his life. In the blink of an eye, it seemed, 56–1 had become 75–8, and work stopped in offices all over the country. Hearts stopped too as Bright and Lillee added 35 in four overs, but Gatting scuttled in and tumbled forward at mid-on to catch Lillee, and Willis scattered Bright's stumps at 111 for the most famous comeback victory of them all, by 18 runs. Willis had 8–43, Brearley was nerveless, Botham once more awesome, and a Test side had won after a follow-on for the only time in the 20th century.

Now the pressure was off Botham and on Kim Hughes, a late replacement as Australian captain for the absent Greg Chappell, and unpopular with some of his seniors in the side. So to Edgbaston, at 1–1 with three to play. On a suspect pitch, no batsman reached 50 at all, and for once the spinners had as much success as the pace bowlers. After Australia had taken a crucial first innings lead, it was the black-bearded left-arm spinner Ray Bright who worked his way through England's weak middle order to leave them 115–6, just 46 ahead. Emburey, England's best bowler, engineered some resistance, but Australia still only needed 151. Australia lost three early wickets, but reached 87 before the next fell, 55 short. It was Emburey who removed the determined left-handers Yallop and Border, and it was this latter wicket that persuaded Brearley to ditch a plan to use spin at both ends, and call on Botham for one last fling. He had done little in this match, and seemed hesitant, but, bounding in and bowling fast, straight and full, he took the last five wickets at a cost of a single run, three of them clean bowled, as Australia went from 114–5 to 121 all out and lost by 29 runs. Another crowd went into ecstasy.

England's problem position was number three. So far in this series the various incumbents had made 77 between them in eight innings; in the winter in the West Indies the figure had been 22 from eight. For Old Trafford England chose to recall

Chris Tavaré, the tall, slim, Kent man, trimly moustached as befitted his personality and batting style. That moustache contrasted with some of the facial decoration that then prevailed: five beards adorned the team that won at Edgbaston, a throwback to sepia Victorian team photos. England's batting problems continued here, but at least Tavaré clung on until help arrived at 137−8, whereupon in his first Test the Lancashire opening bowler Paul Allott made a maiden fifty at a crucial moment. Australia then played a series of suicidal strokes on their way to 130 all out in just 30.2 overs. England's second innings approach was completely different, as batting continued to be a hazardous business. The score was 104−5 from 69 painful overs when Botham arrived.

Having failed to score in the first innings, Botham started carefully, but then went mad, thrashing his last 90 off 49 balls. It was by far the best innings of the series. It included six sixes, the most by an Englishman against Australia until the climactic last day of the 2005 series. That kind of batting mayhem had been seen only very occasionally before in Tests, if more often in subsequent years, but coming in that context −25 wickets had fallen for only 465 runs in the match so far, and 29−3 in 28 overs in the morning before he arrived − it was quite extraordinary. Apart from an inside edge for four past the leg stump, the other 12 fours and six sixes in his 118 came off the middle of a supercharged bat. From 18 balls from Lillee he took 45, including three hooks for six in two overs − 'I was sure I'd get him with the bouncer, but the more I fed him with it the further the ball disappeared.' Botham transformed the game to such an extent that Knott and Emburey each added fifties to Tavaré's seven-hour 78 (he batted for nearly 12 hours in the match). Australia, forlornly chasing 506, did at least restore their self-esteem by scoring over 400 on a pitch somehow so much easier to bat on, and Yallop and Border made centuries as the Ashes were prised from their reluctant grip.

The drawn last Test was something of an anti-climax, but a good match nonetheless. Border and the debutant Wellham made centuries for Australia, Boycott one for England; Botham took 10 in the match and Lillee 11. England were in some trouble on the last day at 144−6, but Brearley and Knott, returning to replace Taylor in the last two Tests to stiffen the lower order, made half-centuries − in what would turn out to be their last Tests − and saw England to safety. Brearley, ordinary batsman but master magician, who had thought the Indian Jubilee Test would be his last, left the Test arena to a standing ovation.

That's the story of a remarkable series. The figures underline the fragility of both sides' batting. Alderman and Lillee (42 and 39), and Botham and Willis (34 and 29) took their massive numbers of wickets at between 19 and 23 each. In a tottering team of batsmen, Border's 533 runs at 59 made him the outstanding batsman of the series, for all Botham's heroics. In a six-match series he was the only man to pass even 400 runs, and apart from Tavaré in two Tests no England front-line batsman averaged over 40, and no Australian even 30.

The Brearley era was over, but Botham's would continue, under new captains − many new captains. Cricket had recovered from the Packer upheaval, and its spirit seemed as strong as ever. But was it?

CHAPTER 20

The Spirit of the Game?

Dennis Lillee and Javed Miandad square up at Perth, November 1981.

To set the Cause above renown,
To love the game beyond the prize,
To honour, while you strike him down,
The foe that comes with fearless eyes:
To count the life of battle good,
And dear the land that gave you birth,
And dearer yet the brotherhood
That binds the brave of all the earth.

HENRY NEWBOLT, *Clifton Chapel*

A golden age?

'You do well to love cricket, for it is more free from anything sordid, anything dishonourable, than any game in the world. To play it keenly, honourably, self-sacrificingly is a moral lesson in itself... Protect it from anything that would sully it so that it may grow in favour with all men.'

Lord Harris

This quote is used to preface many a chapter or book, and it's fond to imagine that Lord Harris' time was a golden age when cricketers behaved like angels, similar to the mythic time when Corinthian Casuals footballers would withdraw their goalkeeper if a penalty was awarded against them. There was indeed an ethic that, as C. B. Fry put it, deplored 'the principle that, as there is a penalty for cheating, it is permissible to cheat at the risk of a penalty'. But cricketers had been disputing decisions, abusing umpires and their opponents – if not their equipment – ever since cricket was first played for money or prestige. The betting years of the eighteenth century led to so many notorious incidents that betting was driven out of the game altogether, only to reappear in cricket with a vengeance in the era of the mobile phone. Lord Harris himself was no angel. As a bowler he had run out without warning a batsman backing up too far, a no-no then as now, as long ago as 1870.

In that mythic golden age, bad behaviour extended to: running out in a crucial early Test match a batsman who had been gardening; persuading a batsman to throw the ball back and appealing (successfully) for handled-the-ball; bullying a cowed umpire into giving him not out lbw by pretending to have hit the ball; replacing the bails after the wicket had been broken and continuing an innings. And that was just W. G. Grace, the greatest cricketer of the age. The Great Cricketer was competitive to a fault, and somewhat greedy and graceless: it was the 'expenses' he demanded for his amateur appearances at Lord's and the Oval that led indirectly to a players' strike before the Oval Test of 1896. Gradually, however, an as-yet-unwritten code of conduct began to prevail: there were things cricketers just didn't do.

Although the bodyline series of 1932–3 had severely tested sporting relations between England and Australia, it was something of an aberration, healed by the English voluntarily withdrawing the tactic of a short-pitched attack at the batsman's body with a packed leg-side field. By the 1960s first-class cricketers had established a *modus vivendi*, a consensus about their behaviour on the field that didn't need special rules and arbitration. You didn't question umpires' decisions on the field, although you might shake your head wearily as you trudged off, and let an eager press corps know your views after the event; you didn't bully umpires by excessive appealing; you didn't appeal for things you knew weren't out. Batsmen tended to trust a fielder if he said he'd made a fair catch – I recall Neil Harvey doing that in the great Old Trafford Test of 1961, checking after a slip fielder had scooped the ball up low to the ground, and departing once he had got the fielder's nod. On the next tour Fred Titmus would have been run out by yards after colliding with the bowler Neil Hawke in his follow-through, had not Wally Grout tossed the ball away with a flourish instead of taking the bails off, as he would of course have been fully entitled to do – the runner's job is to keep out of the bowler's way. The crowd applauded the gesture for about 20 seconds, and I discovered to my annoyed surprise that I had tears in my teenage eyes. It's only in the last 20 years that match referees and a written code of conduct have become necessary.

Sledging, sharp practice, barging and intimidation

When did it all begin? Sledging certainly began before the word itself was coined. Simon Rae points out Frank Worrell's distaste at the verbal abuse his batsmen received at the hands of Surrey in 1957, long before Wisden's first mention of the word 'sledging' appeared in its editorial of 1973, referring to the Australian winter of 1971–2. In the summer of 1973, as we've seen, Rohan Kanhai and his team barracked umpire Arthur Fagg continuously after he had given Boycott not out caught behind. The Packer World Series Cricket series of 1977 was determined to woo new watchers by making the games a spectacle. It happened at a time when both Australia and the West Indies had a battery of really fast bowlers, before helmets were de rigueur, and this made its contests and those that followed fiercer and more bloodthirsty than any since 1932–3. After one tour the New Zealand captain Glenn Turner said, 'When you come back from Australia you feel like you've been in Vietnam.' Whether it's true that the 1960s and 1970s led to an increase in contempt for authority, behaviour certainly started to deteriorate on the field and off it. Fewer holds were now barred. Look at what happened in rapid succession: it seemed as though some new cricketing outrage was happening every day.

In 1977–8 in New Zealand the bowler Ewen Chatfield, now recovered from his near-death bouncer experience, ran out Derek Randall without warning as he backed up. The next year, in a tetchy Australia v Pakistan series, first Miandad ran out Rodney Hogg while he was gardening (although Mushtaq Mohammad moved to recall him, the decision stood); then Alan Hurst ran out Sikander Bakht while backing up; and finally, most notoriously of all, Sarfraz appealed for 'handled the ball' when Andrew Hilditch picked it up and handed it to him – an appeal that succeeded (I've always thought that law should be re-framed). Throughout the post-Packer Ashes tour Dennis Lillee gleefully orchestrated the crowd's baiting of Mike Brearley.

In the 1981 Wisden, the new editor John Woodcock complained about the West Indians' behaviour in New Zealand, where they unexpectedly lost a series. Stung by what they saw as biased umpiring – and the New Zealanders did accept that it was poor – they couldn't quite believe that, straight after beating the same Australians who had just trounced Brearley's team, they could lose a series to New Zealand, of all people. Holding kicked over the stumps, Croft deliberately barged the umpire in his run-up, and after tea on the third day of the third and final Test the whole team for a while refused to take the field in a failed attempt to have umpire Goodall replaced. In Australia in a notorious one-day international, Greg Chappell instructed his brother Trevor to bowl the last ball of the match underarm to prevent the New Zealanders hitting the six they need to win the match, and was castigated even by his own supporters. Lillee and Javed Miandad, moustached and fiery, each with a fuse approximately the same length, squared up to each other at Perth. Fed up with being pelted by oranges and worse in Karachi, Sylvester Clarke returned a brick into the crowd and knocked out a leader of one of the student unions (now then, resist your first instincts). Both the England and Pakistan teams were criticised for indiscriminate and excessive appealing after the 1982 series.

All these events happened in a brief period at the turn of the 1980s. The 1980 Wisden carried a notice sent to each of its members' clubs by the New South Wales Cricket Association, advocating that it be pinned up in every dressing room, under the heading:

> **It has to stop!**
> Ridiculous appeals to intimidate umpires.
> Abuse towards umpires.
> Swearing at batsmen to break their concentration.
> Directing a dismissed batsmen to the pavilion with abuse.
> Batsmen disputing decisions and berating the umpire.
> Batsmen abusing fielders in the act of stopping or catching.
> Batsmen swearing and abusing kit when returning to the pavilion.

It didn't stop: it spread. The West Indian commentator Gerry Gomez suggested a system of fines, and ICC members called for independent observers. In 1986 Ian Botham was banned for two months for admitting taking cannabis after he had earlier denied it. Alcohol abuse before and during games had a long tradition, but this was new. (For years opposing cricketers had said that passing the Somerset dressing room presented an acute danger of a secondary ganja high.) In 1990 the umpires at the Victoria v Pakistan game banned Mushtaq Ahmed from bowling for persistently running on the pitch after several warnings: their manager Intikhab Alam ordered his side off the field. The following year in India's Duleep trophy final Raman Lamba and Rashid Patel brawled with bat and stump after Patel had bowled a beamer at Lamba. The crowd rioted and the covers and everything else flammable were burnt. England didn't escape either. In 1997 Robert Croft and Mark Ilott descended to an unseemly barging match late in a crucial one-day semi-final.

A code of conduct

To a member of an earlier generation, the need for a code of conduct seems an admission of defeat, but it undoubtedly proved essential. In due course the ICC introduced such a code, which in its first appearance in the 1996 Wisden contained nine points of 26 lines. In the 2005 version it had expanded to 70 lines, with Wisden listing 35 breaches of the code and their penalties in the previous 12 months' Tests, nine of them by captains. Of course, with so much Test cricket these days, much of it one-day matches with feverish climaxes in front of large crowds, tempers seem increasingly ready to explode, code or no code. Dissent and aggravation almost seem institutionalised, as when England captain Nasser Hussain declared that 'we have to get a bit of nastiness into our game'. The media response to that was not critical. Encouragingly, though, the best response has come from Australia, where in October 2003 their Test team created a Spirit of the Game Pledge. When Andrew Symonds was banned by the Australians after a night on the tiles before the infamous loss to Bangladesh in June 2005, it was his failure to observe the Pledge that his captain cited.

Nastiness was certainly evident in South Africa in 2001–2. You might be excused for imagining that the introduction of a code of conduct and internationally appointed referees for all Tests would at least make it clear where authority stood. But after the second Test, when match referee Mike Denness, the ex-England captain, fined six Indian players, including Tendulkar and the captain Ganguly, and suspended Sehwag for one Test for 'charging towards the umpire', Indian Board president Dalmiya, who had completed an action-packed three-year stint as ICC chairman, 'insisted' that Denness be removed as referee for the third Test at Centurion. Dalmiya claimed he was a racist because he had taken no action against South African sledging. Denness was barred from the ground, but the ICC retaliated by denying the match Test status: today the game is expunged from the record books. Ultimately Sehwag was deemed to have served his sentence by missing that match, and was back for the first Test against England at Mohali later that winter.

Dalmiya wasn't finished – he coerced England into accepting an extra one-day international by threatening to cancel India's participation in the Oval Test the following summer. Ironically, England won the extra match to draw 3–3, and India won that Oval Test to draw 1–1. But it left an unpleasant taste. If the authority of the umpires and the match referee is not respected, the next step is litigation. That step was taken in 2005. In April Ganguly was banned from six one-day matches during the rousing series with Pakistan, for persistently failing to ensure that over rates were maintained – the captain's responsibility. The referee, Chris Broad, a poacher turned gamekeeper, had himself been a frequent miscreant in another era. The Indian management appealed against the ruling, the appeal was rejected by the ICC's appeals commissioner, QC Michael Beloff, the rejection appealed against, and eventually in August the ban was reduced to from six to four matches, by independent QC Albie Sachs. These names are, sadly, becoming as well known as the cricketers'.

As we shall see in Chapter 24, the world order was changing: India was flexing its muscles. And after Botham's Ashes in 1981, he was off to India to see if his and England's renaissance could continue.

CHAPTER 21

The Years of the Great All-rounders

Imran Khan in the delivery stride, left, and Ian Botham hooking Kapil Dev in January 1982, during his 142 in the final Test v India.

1982	Ian Botham	Man of the Series England v India
1982	Imran Khan	Man of the Series England v Pakistan
1983	Kapil Dev	India's World Cup-winning captain[*]
1983	Richard Hadlee	Man of the Series England v New Zealand

[*] And Man of the Tournament, had there been one then

1981-2 India and Sri Lanka

After the heady heroics of the 1981 Ashes series, the tour to India was a sad letdown. The new England leader was Keith Fletcher, a cunning and successful captain of Essex, but someone who hadn't played a Test for five years. The tour very nearly didn't take place, as the Indian Prime Minister Indira Gandhi initially refused to let Boycott and Geoff Cook in the country, because of their playing links with South Africa. Once they had publicly expressed their distaste for apartheid, however, she relented. She might not have done so had she realised what Boycott was actually up to, for, once he had left the tour after the fifth of sixth Tests, citing 'physical and mental tiredness', it was clear that he had been instrumental in recruiting for a rebel South African tour that would have far-reaching effects.

India	179 & 227	England	166 & 102
England	400 & 107–3	India	428
England	476–9d & 68–0	India	487
England	248 & 265–5d	India	208 & 170–3
India	481–4d & 160–3	England	328
England	378–9d	India	377–7

The tempo of the India series was determined by the first Test at Bombay, the only one to take place on a result wicket, and indeed the only one in which more than 28 wickets were taken. Here, after Botham and Dilley had bowled India out for 179 on a wicket of increasingly low bounce, and Boycott and Tavaré had ground their way to 95–1 from 60 overs, England collapsed in both innings, no one else reaching 30. After the match England took the unusual step of complaining officially about the umpiring.

Thereafter the wickets grew deader and the tempo slowed to a crawl. With no sanctions in place to prevent it, Gavaskar, 1–0 ahead, was able to slow the over rate down until it averaged 13 an hour for the entire series: the worst period was an hour when fewer than 10 overs were bowled, with the spinner Dilip Doshi operating. The last five Tests can best be summed up by baldly listing the centuries – Gavaskar 172 in nearly 12 hours in the second, Boycott, Tavaré and Viswanath in the third. Boycott overtook Sobers as the leading run-scorer in Tests – whereupon that 'fatigue' set in and he departed – while Tavaré, under orders, positively scorched to his 149 in 303 balls. In the fourth, in Calcutta, the only game after the first where a win seemed possible, England had a chance on the last day, but smog and Gavaskar soon ended that hope. In the fifth the centuries were from Viswanath, Yashpal Sharma and Gooch, and in the weather-wearied sixth from Botham and Kapil Dev. Those two sound more fun, and they were. Botham made 142 from 214 balls, sedate by 1981 standards but an immaculate innings, while the flamboyant Kapil took only 83 balls to reach his century. But the game and series were long dead.

Sri Lanka	218 & 175	England	223 & 171–3

It was a relief to get to Sri Lanka for their first-ever Test. The Sri Lankans showed they deserved their elevation, recovering from Underwood's 5–28 to concede a first innings lead of just 5, despite Gower's 89. At 113–1 they were getting on top, but Underwood dismissed Dias for 77, and Emburey's 6–33 took them suddenly from 167–3, and winning, to 175 all out and losing. That they lost easily in the end was due to another excellent innings of 85 from Tavaré, rapidly losing his 'strokeless' tag, if only for a while.

At least the pitches resuscitated England's ailing batsmen, with Gower, Botham, Gooch, Boycott, Tavaré and Fletcher all averaging between 55 and 35. The Sri Lanka game helped Underwood and Emburey reduce their bowling averages to below 30, though the most consistently threatening bowler was still Willis. And Willis it was who would be selected as England's next captain.

1982 India and Pakistan

Still the fixture list threw up series against identical opponents. This time it was a twin-tour summer bringing India and Pakistan, so, after a winter in the subcontinent, the subcontinent returned to England. England, though, wore a somewhat different look. Eleven cricketers who had played against Australia or India in the last 12 months had been banned from Tests for three years for taking part in the rebel tour of South Africa. Gooch, Boycott, Amiss, Woolmer, Willey, Larkins, Knott, Old, John Lever, Underwood, Hendrick and Emburey wasn't a bad 12 to select from, but they had gone, and the selectors' problem was even more taxing than in the Packer aftermath. England took a risk with a bowler as captain, Bob Willis, known for his bowling trances. He didn't let them down.

England	433 & 67–3	India	128 & 369
England	425	India	379–8
England	594 & 191–3d	India	410 & 111–3

These were the great days of the heroic fast bowling, big hitting, all-rounder. This series starred Botham and Kapil Dev. After Kapil had taken the first four England wickets to fall, Botham's pugnacious 67 was followed by 126 from a Randall restored to favour, shepherding a sprightly tail to 433. Botham's 5–46 made India follow on, whereupon, after an immaculate 157 from the tall, elegant Vengsarkar, Kapil took centre stage again. He couldn't save the game, but after hitting a murderous 89 from 55 balls, on course to be the then-fastest hundred in a Test, he took the three England second innings to fall. Then, in a rain-ruined second Test at Old Trafford Botham made 128, reaching his hundred with a burst of 32 in 20 balls after being smacked on the toe by a full toss. The runner he summoned simply stood and admired. Miller made 98, Patil 129* and Kapil responded to Botham by again outpacing him. To Botham's 128 off 169 balls he retorted with 65 from 55.

The third Test was a victim of 1–0-up caution. South African adventures created an opportunity for South African émigrés, something of which Allan Lamb, stocky, moustached and happily cavalier in outlook, took full advantage. His first Test hundred paved the way for another Botham onslaught, a majestic 208, in which he reached 200 off 220 balls, probably the fastest English double hundred to date in terms of balls faced. Such was his ferocity that he broke a bone in Gavaskar's shin, a handicap to their iconic captain that didn't cause India to wilt. Once consistent batting had averted the follow-on – Kapil this time made 97 from 93 balls – England had no time or intention to let India in with a chance of levelling the series.

Next came Pakistan, for a desperately close-fought tussle, the first of three cracking home series between the two teams between 1982 and 1992. Botham's opponent in the great all-rounder stakes was now Imran Khan, captaining Pakistan for the first time, a more measured batsman, a dangerous new-ball bowler who swung the new ball in at pace from the edge of the crease, and a proud and inspirational leader.

England	272 & 291	Pakistan	251 & 199
Pakistan	428–8d & 77–0	England	227 & 276
Pakistan	275 & 199	**England**	256 & 219–7

At Edgbaston stupendous bowling from Imran on the opening day, 7–52, kept his country in the game. After England had taken a slender lead, Randall's 105 from his new position as opener held a foundering England together, but Taylor and Willis added 79 from a perilous 212–9. Despite Imran's 65, England won easily. Pakistan's batting had been particularly reckless, but at Lord's they were confronted by a comfortingly paceless England attack in which Jackman, Pringle, and Ian Greig supported Botham. Willis had ricked his neck weaving to avoid an Imran bouncer at Edgbaston. The resulting quartet held no terrors for the opener Mohsin Khan, who made an elegant 200 on what appeared a benign pitch. But England's batting in both innings was supine, tangled up by Abdul Qadir in the first innings, and wafted away on the gentle breeze of Mudassar Nazar's seemingly innocuous in-swingers, bowling like a half-pace, half-size Imran from wide of the crease. Primarily an opening bat, he first disposed of Randall, Lamb and Gower in six balls, and so reduced Tavaré to strokelessness that he batted more than an hour before he scored (on the way to the second-slowest England 50 on record). A last-wicket stand held Pakistan up but they raced to the 76 needed in 13.1 overs before the rain came.

The last Test at Headingley was a thriller dominated by the two great all-rounders. Crucially, Willis returned as captain and opening bowler, while Pakistan lost Taqir Naqqash and Sarfraz Narwaz, who had bowled well in support of Imran. The first two innings were symmetrical. After 119–2, Pakistan needed Imran's 67* to take them to 275. Then, after Botham had made 57 out of 69, batting with Gower, no slouch himself, Imran with 5–49 gave Pakistan a slight edge. That was soon wiped out when Willis disposed of each opener first ball in the opening over. Thereupon Botham chipped away regularly on his way to 5–74, including Imran, last man out for 46 after the stubborn Sikander Bakht had been controversially given out to a batless bat-pad catch off the Somerset off-spinner Vic Marks. England needed 219, and anything could happen after their batting in this series. It certainly did. After a surprisingly confident start, led by a fluent 86 from the young left-handed opener Graeme Fowler in his first Test of the summer, England, at 168–1, were poised for a comfortable win. But Imran and Mudassar, swinging the old ball, cut through the middle order so that the fourth day ended with England 189–6, needing 30 and with a fresh Imran to face next day. They were still 20 short when he dismissed Botham on that tense morning, but Marks and Taylor inched England home.

The Pakistani defeat was a huge disappointment to Imran, who publicly criticised the umpires afterwards. Polite foreign captains were inclined to echo the commonly held view that English umpires were the best in the world; not Imran. As England captains and press consistently criticised Pakistan's umpires, why could he not do the same? This successful summer for England without the South African rebels owed a huge debt to the return to form of Botham, who had been persuaded by his Somerset colleague Viv Richards not to go. In the six Tests he scored 566 runs at 62, and took 27 wickets at 29. The captaincy didn't affect Willis's bowling, 25 wickets at 22, but the loss to the ban of Hendrick, Old and Lever, took out his fast bowling support. Randall, Gower and Tavaré scored over 300 runs, but the batting missed the resilience of two tough nuts on the banned list, Boycott and Willey.

1982–3 Australia

Before Australia entertained England for the next Ashes series, they had gone to Pakistan without Greg Chappell and been beaten badly 3–0, no one quite fathoming Abdul Qadir. That performance encouraged England, who of course had to defend the Ashes without key players.

England	411 & 358	Australia	424–9 & 73–2
England	219 & 309	**Australia**	341 & 190–3
Australia	438 & 83–2	England	216 & 304
England	284 & 294	Australia	287 & 288
Australia	314 & 382	England	237 & 314–7

The first Test at Perth brought stalemate after Tavaré had glued England together on the first day, batting right through for 66 out of 242–4. Randall's second innings 115 staved off potential defeat. However, the game was marred by an injury to Alderman. Goaded into a rugby tackle by a thump on the head from one of a group of boorish England field invaders, he dislocated a shoulder, and missed the rest of the series. The second match was dominated by Australia's own South African import, the phlegmatic left-hander Kepler Wessels who scored 162 in his first Test and gave Australia the critical advantage. Geoff Lawson took 11 wickets in the match, and Thomson proceeded to wipe out the England middle order in the second innings. He had been missing in England in 1981, but returned here because Lillee was injured as well as Alderman: the Australian fast bowling larder was well-stocked. Apart from Gower, whose second innings 114 was his first Test century for 38 attempts, England were unable to cope with Lawson at Adelaide either. His nine here took his tally to 26 in the first three Tests.

Melbourne

Two-nil down with two to play was desperate for England, as they came to Melbourne for one of the closest, most nerve-jarring Tests of all time. The simple statistics, with every innings completed between 284 and 294, made it also the most symmetrical, though it certainly followed no even pattern. On the first day Lamb and the schizophrenic Tavaré took England from 56–3 to 217 in just 32 overs, only for both to depart in the eighties. Similarly Australia recovered from 89–4 to 261–5, before Miller took the last three wickets cheaply. At 160–6 on the third day England were poorly placed but the tail eked out another 134. With unlikely neatness, each of the first three days had seen a complete innings – 284, 287 and 294. What would happen on the fourth, on what was still a pretty good pitch?

Conventional wisdom, then even more than now, dictated that a target of 292 would make the bowling side favourite. Again the bowlers made initial inroads – this time to 71–3 – before a recovery in which this time Hughes and the aggressive left-hander David Hookes added 100 to take Australia to 171–3, needing 121. At this juncture Taylor caught Hughes brilliantly off Miller, and the stage was set for Norman Cowans. Unsuccessful so far this tour, Cowans, the first opening bowler of West Indian origin to play for England, had dismissed Chappell first ball in the first innings, caught at deep square leg in a baited trap, and he had again got him cheaply in the second. Now he took 4–19 in seven inspired overs. Australia were 218–9, and England had the game won.

Only they hadn't. At No. 11 Thomson joined Border. Although Willis gave Border easy singles to get at him, Thomson batted staunchly. The fourth day's close came at 255–9: 37 added, 37 needed. Despite overnight misgivings over the tactics, Willis persisted with his wide-set fields for Border after taking the new ball the following morning. Eighteen thousand people arrived to watch a day that could have ended after one ball. Australia inched towards the target, in disturbingly little trouble. When Botham, with only two wickets in the match hitherto, began the 18th over of the morning to Thomson, only four runs were needed. Just one stroke – was that four a dangerous incitement? No, the opposite: 'I thought I'd push a single and let AB hit the winning runs. Ian Botham bowled a half-tracker which swung away a little bit and I tried to just sort of glide it. I should have played a baseball shot and hit it for four to win the game.' It flew to second slip, where Tavaré could only parry it. Fortunately the ball went up and over his shoulder, not down, fortunately Miller was a couple of yards behind him, fortunately he snatched it inches from the ground. England had won by 3 runs. Events at Edgbaston in 2005 would bring this morning vividly back to mind.

Now the series was back alive. But Australia only needed to draw to regain the Ashes, and they achieved it in comfort. Hughes's 137 in the second innings, coupled with Border's 89 and 83, meant England were always up against it, and they only escaped with a draw thanks to an unlikely hero, the cheerful, amply-proportioned Nottinghamshire off-spinner Eddie Hemmings, who batted most of the last day as nightwatchman for 95, followed by further necessary defiance from Miller and Taylor at the end. So England lost the Ashes but regained some self-respect. Both sides' catching was superb in this series, but apart from Cowans' one burst only Willis could menace as Lawson and Thomson did. Randall, Gower and Lamb averaged in the forties, but Botham's vital importance to England meant that they were missing two players when he was out of sorts, as he was here. When he was on song, they had 12.

1983 The third World Cup

June 1983 was warm and sunny throughout for the third World Cup, again held in England. The home country was drawn with Pakistan, New Zealand and Sri Lanka; West Indies with Australia, India and Zimbabwe, in the days before Zimbabwe had acquired Test status. They did their cause no harm at all by beating Australia in their opening game by 13 runs, a shock that horrified the Australians and enthused every-one else. Their match-winner, with 69[*] and four top wickets for 42, was one Duncan Fletcher, no mean cricketer. With everyone in the group now playing each other twice in a 16-day span, Australia had a chance to recover. But they lost twice to West Indies and once to India, and they were out of the competition. India got through from that half with West Indies, surviving a scare when they were 17–5 against Zimbabwe (one of the more unlikely fixtures Tunbridge Wells had hosted), thanks to a blistering 175[*] by Kapil Dev.

England were efficient, coming top of their group again and losing only once, with Fowler, Lamb and in particular Gower making stacks of runs, the tireless Willis again the pick of the bowlers. Pakistan, who were hampered because Imran could bat but not bowl, sneaked in narrowly on run rate from New Zealand. With England playing India in one semi-final, and West Indies facing Pakistan in the other, experts were predicting an England v West Indies final.

They didn't get it. In the first two World Cups India had been inept and won only against East Africa. This time they had solid but unspectacular batting and, well, solid but unspectacular bowling, with two unexpected master cards in the wobbly medium pacers Roger Binny and Mohinder Amarnath. On a slow pitch at Old

Trafford on 17 June, England stroked smoothly to 69–0 at four an over, then ran into choppy waters. In a total of 213 the top score was only 33. India had the bowlers for the pace of the pitch, and the ball came more readily onto Indian bats as they won by six wickets with more than five overs to spare. At the Oval on the same day Pakistan struggled to 184–9 against the ultimate pace quartet of Roberts, Garner, Marshall and Holding, who all conceded less than three an over and could then put their feet up to watch a typical Richards innings and an eight-wicket win.

SEMI-FINALS			
England	213 (60)	**India**	217–4 (54.4)
Pakistan	184–8 (60)	**West Indies**	188–2 (48.4)
FINAL			
India	183 (54.4)	West Indies	140 (52)

So to Lord's on 25 June. West Indies put India in: once more the pace bowlers conceded fewer than three an over, once more West Indies had a target of under 200. It seemed crucial that India had committed the cardinal sin of not using all their overs, especially as West Indies eased to 50–1, Richards again in ominous form. But the match turned when he mis-hooked Madan Lal to Kapil Dev at square leg, who held on to a brilliant running catch over his shoulder. From that point Madan Lal, Binny, Kapil Dev and Amarnath exerted a stranglehold and it was Amarnath who broke the fight-back stand of Dujon and Marshall by getting them both. India had won by 43 against all the odds, in an unexpected final where the top score all day was only 38. Mohinder Amarnath, an all-rounder notable before only for his extraordinary courage against pace, uniquely won the man of the match award in both semi-final and final. He and Roger Binny – fancy, a cup-winning Indian called Roger – thereupon started a fashion for bits-and-pieces all-rounders that would begin to dog English one-day selection.

1983 New Zealand

New Zealand were the tourists after the World Cup. They had failed to qualify for the semi-finals because they lost to Sri Lanka, so they were expected to be easy opponents again.

England	209 & 444–6d	New Zealand	196 & 270
England	225 & 252	**New Zealand**	377 & 103–5
England	326 & 211	New Zealand	191 & 219
England	420 & 297	New Zealand	207 & 345

For this series Botham's challenger in the battle of the all-rounders was Richard Hadlee. Now 32, and at his peak, Hadlee's 6–53 bowled England out on the first day at the Oval for 209, only Randall passing 50. Hadlee then rescued his side with 84 off 78 balls after Willis had wiped out the top order, until Botham, off whose first over he had taken 16, dismissed both him and the tail. Centuries for Fowler, Tavaré and Lamb set up the England win, duly converted by Edmonds and Marks, bowling in tandem most of the last day.

New Zealand had by now beaten England at home, but never in England. Now was the time. The only oddity was that Hadlee didn't take a single wicket: the damage was done in the first innings at Lord's by Lance Cairns (the older model, who if anything hit the ball even further than his son Chris), who took 7–72, and in the second by Ewen Chatfield. Only Gower, 112* in the second innings, resisted for long and he couldn't conjure enough runs from the tail to set a decent target. Although Willis made 101 look difficult with one of his in-the-zone spells, taking all five wickets to fall, New Zealand had broken their aggravating English duck.

With the series standing at 1–1. Hadlee was back on form at Lord's for the third Test, with five wickets in each innings, but a second successive hundred for Gower took England past 300. When New Zealand were 146–2 it looked as though they would pass it too. But they were stopped in their tracks by someone who hadn't been in the original squad – Nick Cook, the Northants left-arm spinner, only playing because Edmonds had ricked his back getting out of his car. Cook, 'intelligently employing the old-fashioned virtues of flight and spin', nodded Wisden approvingly, emulated the man he replaced by taking five wickets in his debut innings: 26–11–35–5. England clinched victory thereafter with little fuss, Cook taking another three and 8–125 in the match. He took his form into the last Test, too, taking in all 9–150 in 82 overs. On the first day Botham and Randall had added 186 at cracking pace, Botham hitting Bracewell for 31 in two overs, then Hadlee for 28 in his first two when he took the new ball. England didn't enforce the follow-on, and won easily enough despite Hadlee's 92*.

Hadlee had Bothamesque averages of 50 and 26, Botham a more prosaic 35 and 34. Lamb and Gower averaged over 50 with the bat. Willis bowled superbly all summer, his fierce concentration with ball in hand unaffected by the captaincy. He finished with 20 wickets at 13 in the series, to add to his 11 at 19 in the World Cup. Cook's sudden emergence lifted hopes of a classic left-arm spinner of the old school – with Cook and Edmonds, Miller and Marks, Pocock and Hemmings (and Emburey once his ban had ended), England seemed to have the best spin options for many years. Such comparative riches would not last.

1983–4 Pakistan and New Zealand

The tour that winter meant Tests with Pakistan, and New Zealand, once more. Such was the dominance of overseas bowlers in England at this time, and so variable the England bowlers' form, that the bowlers chosen to tour were positioned at 19, 29,

38, 41, 78 and 85 in the national averages. That bowling would be a problem all winter.

New Zealand	219 & 537	England	463
New Zealand	309	England	82 & 93
New Zealand	496–9d & 16–0	England	439.

This tour was dreadful from an England point of view, but it gave New Zealand their first ever series win over England. Looking at the scores, it seems incomprehensible that England could pass 400 in two innings but not reach 100 in the other two. Sandwiched between two high-scoring draws was an utter humiliation. For half the first match Botham dominated, making 138 after he had taken 5–59 on the opening day, but from 165–4 and 335–7 the savvy New Zealand captain Jeremy Coney saved the day with 174*. In a last Test of tedious batting Randall, enjoying a fruitful period, added 104 to his 164 in the first match.

For the notorious second Test at Christchurch, injuries to Dilley and Foster meant a surprise call-up for the Sussex opening bowler, Tony Pigott, who in consequence postponed his wedding. He needn't have bothered: the game was all over in 12 hours. England's bowling matched the pitch for awfulness, allowing Hadlee to make 99 from 81 balls. Their batting was even worse, twice failing even to reach Hadlee's personal mark. His bowling figures in total were 35–15–44–8, extraordinary. England have never played so irredeemably badly (although they got close in the next few years...).

England	182 & 159	**Pakistan**	277 & 66–7
Pakistan	449–8d	England	546–8
England	241 & 341–9d	Pakistan	343 & 217–6

England had no acclimatising match before being plunged into the first Pakistan Test against the tormenting wrist spin of Qadir, and it showed. Apart from two fifties from Gower, battling alone, the only consolation for England in another wretched display was the bowling of Cook. His 6–65 kept the Pakistan first innings within bounds and when they batted again to make just 65, Willis brought him on straight away. Helped by brilliant catches by Botham and Cowans, he took 5–18 but from 40–6 Pakistan recovered their nerve.

At this point in his career Cook had taken 32 wickets at 17 after just six Tests. But he would never be as good again, and ever since Underwood the form of promising England left-arm spinners has come and gone mysteriously. The form of off-spinners has just gone. And of course there aren't any leg-spinners with form to gauge. In the second Test, which reverted to type, the spinners on both sides managed between them just six wickets at 80 apiece. England were hampered by injuries to Willis, Botham and Cowans, but Gower made 152, and Chris Smith, Gatting, Randall, Fowler and Marks all passed 50 without getting out to Qadir – one Test too late.

The captaincy that Willis's injury passed to Gower wasn't affecting his batting, and with Willis still missing for the last Test – Botham and Dilley too – he carried on. This was a much better match. Fowler and Marks rescued England from 83–5 on the first day and Pakistan too were in trouble. Superb bowling by the young Essex opener Neil Foster, tall and lithe, reduced them to 181–8. But Sarfraz helped Zaheer virtually to double the score and it needed a magnificent 173* from Gower to take England to comparative safety. His declaration at the fall of the ninth wicket challenged Pakistan to make 243 in a minimum of 59 overs, but Mohsin and Shoaib added 173 to make a Pakistan victory seem assured. They needed only 70 in more than 14 overs when Shoaib left, but Cowans produced one of his occasional great spells. He took the wickets of Zaheer, Mohsin and Wasim Raja in the 12th over of the last 20, and Pakistan packed it in when they needed 44 from eight. Cowans finished with 5–42.

At least at the end of a debilitating and disappointing tour the young fast bowlers had taken their chance. Willis, 14 wickets at 25 before his injury and Cowans, 12 at 27, headed the bowling by a long distance. Gower recovered from a poor time in New Zealand to make 518 runs at 64, Randall, Botham and the South-African born Chris Smith averaged in the forties, but it was two collective failures of a brittle batting line-up that had led to the two defeats.

1984 West Indies and Sri Lanka

England	191 & 235	**West Indies**	606
England	286 & 300–9d	**West Indies**	245 & 344–1
England	270 & 159	**West Indies**	302 & 131–2
West Indies	500	England	280 & 156
West Indies	190 & 346	England	163 & 202

The year 1984 had an ominous ring to it, and for English cricket it introduced a new word to the vocabulary – 'blackwash'. It was 14 Tests and 10 years since England had beaten the West Indies, so the magnitude of the task facing them was very clear. They did establish some parity by losing the one-day series only 2–1, having lost the first match only after an astounding innings by Richards. He made 189 out of 272–9, bludgeoning his side back into the game from 102–7 – and all of those seven were out in single figures.

Any thought that England could make a serious fight of it seemed to have been dispelled by the end of the opening match at Edgbaston. Within minutes they had lost two batsmen for ducks and a third, Andy Lloyd, in his sole Test on his home ground, to a sickening blow on the side of the head – out of Test cricket for ever despite the helmet. Only the determined Middlesex wicketkeeper Paul Downton provided any hope, with 33 and 56, opening in the second innings after centuries by Richards and the boyish left-hander Larry Gomes.

But by the close of the fourth day of the Lord's Test England seemed the only side likely to win and to level the series. Fowler and a fellow left-hander, Chris Broad, opened with a century stand and Fowler went on to 106. The West Indies innings was notable for Botham's (temporary) return to top bowling form. He took the top six in the order on the way to a tremendous 8–103. Lamb and Botham then put England in control with the bat, but rain on the fourth morning, followed by an odd decision to go off for bad light that evening with Lamb past 100, meant England batted on into the fifth day before setting West Indies 342 in 330 minutes. The consensus was that England had too little time, and so had lost their chance to force a win. No one seriously thought the West Indies would win, but Gordon Greenidge played one of the great last-day Test innings, 214*, one of such dismissive brilliance that they won in a mere 66 overs against a lamentable attack, Willis as ever excepted.

That was the only occasion during the summer when England had the sniff of a win. At Leeds a fighting 100 from Lamb was matched by another from Gomes, following his 92* in attendance on Greenidge on the last day at Lord's. He was becoming an unexpected thorn in England's side – like all the great teams West Indies at that time seemed to conjure up new batsmen and fast bowlers whenever they needed them. He was enabled to reach his hundred by Marshall, batting one-handed at No. 11 with a thumb fractured in two places. With a deficit of just 32, England were confident, especially with Marshall handicapped. But it was his left thumb, and the perpetually menacing Marshall took 7–53, and England were 3–0 down.

Old Trafford witnessed Greenidge's second double hundred of the series, fighting back after Allott's three early wickets. In a curious replica of the previous Test, a batsman was helped to a hundred by a damaged No. 11, this time Hampshire's Paul Terry, his broken arm in a sling, helping Lamb to a third hundred in successive Tests. It was a monumentally gutsy achievement by Lamb against this West Indies team. But he couldn't avert the follow-on, and England capitulated for once to a spinner, Roger Harper, an all-rounder whose fielding was unmatched at the time. Finally, at the Oval, Botham, Allott and the broad-shouldered Kent swing bowler Richard Ellison gave England some hope by bowling West Indies out for under 200 for the first time, but only Botham passed 50 as England's batting capitulated again.

It had been a chastening experience for England to lose all five Tests. With the bat Lamb averaged only 42 despite his three hundreds, Botham 34, no one else over 30. By contrast Greenidge's and Gomes' averages were over 80. Allott took 14 excellent wickets at 20 apiece, Botham 19 at 34, but Garner, Marshall and Holding took 68 between them at under 20.

It had appeared to be in more than one sense men against boys. Not only were the West Indies stronger in every department, they had physically damaged two promising young batsmen who would never play Test cricket again. England's batsmen seemed almost literally broken, whereas Marshall's injury seemed only to elevate him to the Gods. But there was one last Test in 1984 for England to redeem themselves. And the Sri Lankans were surely little men who had neither fierce opening bowlers nor brutal hitters of the ball.

Sri Lanka	491–7d & 294–7	England	370

This was Sri Lanka's first Test in England, a sop at the end of the summer. Their unsung players, led by Wettimuny with 190 and the captain Mendis, 111 and 94, dominated England, whose 370 came at a grim 2.5 an over. Lamb made his fourth hundred of the summer and Broad's 86 gave notice of his temperament, but it was a display typical of a miserable 12 months for England. What next? We were almost afraid to ask. England's batting was broken, and their spinners – well, what had become of them? So promising a year ago, between them they had taken only 13 wickets at over 55 in the six Tests of 1984. In the 1985 season there were only two spinners in the top 20 of the averages, the first one in 15th place. Where had all our spinners gone?

All rounders with 3000 runs and 300 wickets in Tests to September 2005

Player	Test span	No of Tests	Runs	Av.	Wkts	Av.
Ian Botham	1977–92	102	5200	33.54	383	28.40
Richard Hadlee	1973–90	86	3124	27.16	431	22.29
Imran Khan	1971–92	88	3807	37.69	362	22.81
Kapil Dev	1978–94	131	5248	31.05	434	29.64
Sean Pollock	1995–	94	3133	31.33	377	22.09

CHAPTER 22

Where Have all the Spinners Gone?

John Emburey bowling *v* Australia at the Oval, August 1985.

If someone had given me a new back and a fresh pair of legs, I would
have been even better at 50. Slow bowling is a thinker's
game and you never stop learning at it.

RAY ILLINGWORTH

After the war

When England played the final Victory Test against the Dominions at Lord's at the end of August 1945, Doug Wright and Eric Hollies took 15 of the 20 wickets that fell to England bowlers. They were both leg-spinners. Five years later, in the 1950 West Indies series dominated by the young spinners Ramadhin and Valentine, the eight England spinners picked in the four Tests took 36 of the 54 wickets that fell (two-thirds) and 25 of them were to the leg-spinners Hollies, Jenkins and Wright.

These three were born between 1912 and 1918 and learned to bowl under the pre-1935 lbw law in the 1920s and 1930s, at the time when the Kent leg-spinner Tich Freeman dominated the English county game, taking an astonishing 304 first-class wickets in 1928. At that time Australia often played in harness their two great contrasting leg-spinners, Clarrie Grimmett and Tiger O'Reilly, as well as their left-handed equivalent Fleetwood-Smith. England's weren't as good – Freeman, Ian Peebles, Walter Robins – but this was the golden age of the leg-spinner. Wrist spinners like them could turn the ball more than finger spinners and often got more bounce.

In the period immediately after World War 2, when England fast bowling was at a low ebb, spinners dominated county cricket. In the five years from 1946–50 there were usually twice as many spinners in the top 20 of the season's bowling averages as fast or medium-paced bowlers, a statistic that seems extraordinary now. In 1949 the top six were all spinners – Goddard, Kardar, Howorth, Hazell, Young and Laker – and indeed they were the only bowlers with more than 50 wickets who had averages below 20. In fact there were never fewer than 10 spinners in the top 20 between 1946 and 1957. In 1956 once more the top six were spinners – Lock, Illingworth, Hilton, Sam Cook, Laker and Tattersall. Laker was the only one in both lists and he was the first of the new generation of post-war spinners. All, though, were finger spinners: none was a leg-spinner. The decline of the leg-spinner had already begun.

Laker's *annus mirabilis* of 1956 was the last of the great spinners' years, with 14 in the top 20. In 1957 there were 10, and in only one year since have there been as many as that, 1971, when Sainsbury, Wilson, Gibbs, Underwood and Illingworth were all in the top eight. That was a blip, the year when, after two years of full pitch covering, pitches would not be covered once the game had started. In the statistics section at the back of the book, I segment the 60 years into five-year blocks. The table overleaf is extracted from that, and illustrates the sad story of the decline of the English spinner.

Although year-by-year it's more gradual, there appears a sharp divide around 1960. From 1946–60 about half the top 20 were English spinners, from 1961–85 about a quarter. Since then it has averaged little over two. Since 1985 the position has been quite awful. Until 2004, the last year in which more than three Englishmen were in the top 20 was 1983. Emburey, Underwood and Gifford were three of only four bowlers to take 100 wickets that year, and Edmonds was the fourth highest

Five-year period	In top 10	20	English spinners 11–20 in italics
1946–50	8	5	Young Goddard Howorth Hollies Laker Muncer Wardle Wright + *Cook Robinson Jenkins Knott Langridge*
1951–5	3	7	Appleyard Lock Laker + *McConnon Tattersall Hollies Wardle Young Titmus Hilton*
1956–60	5	5	Lock Laker Hilton Wardle Tattersall + *Illingworth Cook Shepherd McConnon Greenhough*
1961–5	1	4	Illingworth + *Gifford Titmus Shepherd Wilson*
1966–70	4	1	Underwood Illingworth Wilson Gifford + *Shepherd*
1971–5	3	1	Underwood Sainsbury Illingworth + *Gifford*
1976–80	1	4	Underwood + *Emburey Miller East Edmonds*
1981–5	3	3	Underwood Emburey Edmonds + *Steele Hemmings Graveney (DA)*
1986–90	0	2	+ *Childs Cook*
1991–5	1	2	Emburey + *Tufnell Such*
1996–2000	0	2	+ *Salisbury Tufnell*
2001–5	0	1	+ *Udal*

wicket-taker with 92. At the time 1983 may not have seemed a high point of English spin bowling, but it certainly looked it 20 years later. The table reveals how complete was Underwood's dominance: the top spinner for 20 years. Only Emburey has made the top 10 in a five-year period since he departed.

Between 1986 and 2004 there were never more than three English spinners in the top 20 in any one year. The late 1990s in particular were terrible for English spinners. Kumble, Muralitharan, Saqlain and Mushtaq all made the top 20 with ease when they played an English county season, but only Giles and Tufnell were in the top 20 in 1996, only Tufnell in 1997, no one in 1998 when no English spinner took even 40 wickets, Salisbury and Michael Davies in 1999, Salisbury and Jason Brown in 2000. Ball of Gloucester scraped in with 34 wickets at 25 in 2001, while again no one managed it in 2002. At least 2003 brought a revival of sorts, with Brown, Batty and Keedy joining Mushtaq, in his great championship-winning year for Sussex. The following year there were seven overall, four of them English, and in 2005 six, with three English, so there have been recent signs of a revival. We must hope it lasts.

The decline was catastrophic. How did England get to this pass? There is no shortage of culprits. Blame has attached variously to pitches, bats, balls, boundaries, fielding restrictions, one-day cricket, batting technique, bowling technique and coaching.

Number one suspect – pitches

In his 1939 Wisden article, Bradman described most pitches of the 1930s as dead and lifeless, no use to bat or ball. Make them fairer, he said – 'fast and true, but amenable to wear so spinners can turn it'. That plaintive cry has been heard ever since. The problem is that it's very hard to achieve this consistently in England. In principle that's what groundsmen have tried to do, apart from in specific games – or even whole summers – when pitches have been doctored to suit the home side. In the 1950s that often meant the spinners. In 1950 Lancashire deliberately under-prepared their wickets – leading as we have seen to a Test pitch on which there was exaggerated turn before lunch on the first day – so that they could have more results. Spinners took 80 per cent of their wickets that season, and they tied for the championship, their sole (semi) success since 1934. In 1956, after England had lost at Lord's on a pitch that helped the Australian pace bowlers Miller and Archer, it's no coincidence that there was no repeat at Headingley, where the pitch broke up on the second day for Lock and Laker. At Old Trafford, where Laker took his 19, the ball was bringing up puffs of dust as early as mid-afternoon on the first day.

Until well after the war, England had traditionally played a game in which the pitch was left open to the elements. With no pitch covering, wet wickets could become spiteful as they dried. Although in theory fast bowlers could be as successful as slow – if not more so – if the run-ups were unprotected only the spinners could operate, and they could reap a rich harvest. Moreover these conditions, often alien to cricketers from overseas (apart from the classic post-downpour 'sticky dog' at Brisbane), tended to help England's cause against the tourists, particularly in the colder, damper first half of the season.

If spectators had still flocked to English cricket regardless of the weather, and if its finances had remained healthy, this state of affairs might have remained unchanged. But as attendances and income declined in the 1950s and 1960s, administrators came to feel that the game could no longer afford long delays after rain. The consequence was a protracted period in which the covering of wickets was endlessly debated. Traditionalists felt, rightly, that full covering would handicap the spinner. Modernisers felt, equally rightly, that spectators would no longer sit in sunshine waiting for a pitch to dry. Moreover, the other Test-playing nations wanted full covering, a level (and dry) playing field across the world. Brisbane in 1950 provided the last Australian Test match 'sticky dog': the MCC agreed to full covering in the Australia series of 1954–5, and thereafter England were always under pressure from other ICC members to introduce covering for Tests in England.

To cover or not to cover

When cricket restarted after the war, pitches in England weren't covered after play had begun, even if the rain pelted down, except for a 12 × 18 foot rectangle at each end to cover the creases. Then Glamorgan, at the end of a very wet season in 1954, in which five of their last six matches had been badly affected when they were pushing for the title, engineered a change that allowed covering during a match after a rain delay 'once the pitch had become saturated'. That was only if the captains agreed, and the pitch was still open to the elements until the saturation point.

In the next 25 years a kind of arm wrestling contest took place between the-game-as-we-know-it-will-die traditionalists and the-spectators-won't-come modernisers. In 1959, when counties were growing seriously concerned about money, and after another foul summer in 1958, full covering was ordained for overnight and as soon as play was called off for the day. By 1963 the legislators had decided spinners were being discouraged, and, just for county cricket, reverted to stipulating the covering of the whole pitch only before the game and at weekends. In 1964, the touring Australians were forced to play the counties on uncovered wickets, not something they were enthusiastic about. By 1969, the pendulum had swung back once more, and we reverted to the 1959 position, with Tests and county matches back in line. But 1971 again brought a swing and we were back to an open-sky policy.

In 1979, the coverers won what seemed a final victory – 'At the wishes of overseas Boards, and in fairness to the paying public, pitches for Tests in England would be fully covered at all times.' This ruling was expected to extend to all county cricket in 1980. The fiasco at the Centenary Test of 1980, when MCC members jostled the umpires and flung their cushions onto the outfield (a very English rebellion) only served to emphasise that the paying public – at that moment anyway – held sway. There was one last stand from the open-skyers, however. E. M. Wellings in the 1986 Wisden lamented the loss of the chance to see the modern equivalent of the Hobbs and Sutcliffe master class at the Oval in 1926, Verity's 14–80 in a day at Lord's in 1934, and Hutton's defiance at Brisbane in 1950. In 1987 wickets were uncovered again, but the run-ups weren't. Only Hemmings of the spinners found his way into the top 20, and the reversion was promptly abandoned. M. J. K. Smith spoke for the pragmatists: 'Seam bowling has proved more versatile than spin. In the old days you would open with a slow bowler on a wet wicket, but seamers have been proved to be more productive in recent years in such conditions.'

	Number of spinners in the top 20.		Covered years in **bold**.	
1958	**59–62**	63–68	**69–70**	71–79	**80–83**
6	**9 7 5 4**	6 6 3 7 6 5	**5 5**	10 5 4 4 8 6 6 6 4	**4 5 6 5**

Almost every old cricketer nowadays attributes the decline of the spinner in England to a large extent to pitch covering. The figures above show the effect. These figures are frankly inconclusive, and, although they certainly don't suggest uncovering in itself made a huge difference, it's important to remember that 'covering' in this transitional period meant 'after abandonment for the day'. From 1980 onwards it meant full covering *once play had been halted*. After 1983 no year had as many as 5 spinners in the top 20 until the 7 in 2004, 3 of whom weren't English.

The old Sussex opening bat Les Lenham, looking back at the end of the 1990s, spoke for most old cricketers when he said: 'It was fun when the spinners bowled on turning pitches. You had great close catchers round the bat, and you had to work the ball through them. I'd love to go back to uncovered pitches.' Spinners, said Trevor Bailey in 1989, are increasingly seen as a luxury rather than a necessity. A vicious circle saw more seamers in county sides, more wickets to suit them, so even fewer spinners. Not only were pitches now covered, there was general agreement that English pitches were distinctly slower in 1981 than they had been 20 years earlier, and spinners couldn't get enough bounce for an edge to carry. In 1987, his last season and the last fling with uncovered wickets, Derek Underwood said he had only three batsmen caught at slip. 'The snick just doesn't carry any more. Slip has become a luxury position.' In 1991 Geoff Cook said the same of his unrelated Northampton team-mate Nick Cook.

Bats, balls, boundaries and leg-side fielders

So the legislators became determined to make pitches as hard and fast as an English summer would allow. In the ideal recipe, such a pitch would wear and take spin as the game progressed, but that still seems very difficult to achieve. It more often happens that the height of bounce starts to vary, and that seems to profit seamers more than spinners. Or perhaps it simply helps the best bowlers, whoever they are. And if spinners have been discouraged, and there are few of them coming through, well...

There is a current view that it's the heaviness of the bats, the hardness of the balls, and the shrinking of the boundaries that militate against the modern spinner. The average bat has increased in weight by about 25 per cent since the war, a topic that I return to in Chapter 26. Pat Pocock said in 1982: 'Players are stronger today, they train harder, they use heavier bats, and they're much better at whacking you'. Meanwhile the ball in use in first-class cricket has got harder, and retains its shine better, aided by lusher outfields. Alec Bedser said that in the post-war years, the ball, then exclusively hand-made, lost its shine after 20 overs, and no amount of rubbing could restore it. What's more the seam would have flattened. Fifty years later in 2005, Ian Salisbury complained that the English ball manufactured by Duke retains its hardness: if it went softer, as do Kookaburra balls abroad, he would get more bowling. Moreover in the years after the war the number of strands that make up the thread of the seam was increased 'at the request of the county clubs', according to Wisden's editor in 1964, thus helping the seamer at the spinner's expense. It wasn't until 1989 that this trend was reversed, when the strands were reduced from 15 to nine, but that seems to have brought swing back rather than spin.

In the early 1950s, when the English spin bowler was still highly successful, the main worry was about defensive batting and defensive bowling. Freddie Brown complained about it in the 1954 Wisden. Compared to before the war, he said, he seldom had to put a deep man straight, so rarely did batsman hit him over the top: only Harold Gimblett and Maurice Tompkin took the aerial route. In the same article he attacked negative bowling at middle-and-leg with a 4/5 or 3/6 leg-side field, at batsmen reluctant to take a risk. In 1957 the legislators tried to remedy the situation by limiting boundaries to 75 yards, and fielders on the leg-side to five, of which only two could be behind square. Although the 75-yard boundary was 'welcomed' said Wisden (by everyone except spinners, perhaps) the leg-side restriction was less popular because it seemed to discriminate against off-spinners, not the defensive medium pacers it was designed to discourage. Bomber Wells called it the biggest single factor to have destroyed the off-spinner's influence. 'It enabled the lesser players to have a slog, so captains simply brought on the medium-paced seamer, who'd bowl short of a length to five on the leg-side.'

One can only imagine what would have happened had one-day cricket *preceded* fielding and boundary restrictions – perhaps batsmen would have attacked, spinners would have been encouraged, and the five-man restriction proved unnecessary. In the event it took eight years for the legislators to react: in 1965 the mandatory boundary restriction was removed – counties could decide – and the five-man leg-side limit was repealed, leaving just the two-behind-square ruling. That year was the one in which wickets were uncovered again. But counties tended to keep their short boundaries. In 1969, when Ray Illingworth arrived at Grace Road to captain Leicestershire, he insisted that the boundaries be extended, and the outfield shaved. When they won the Championship for the first time in 1975 they regularly used four spinners, a luxury they could afford because all of them could bat.

One-day cricket, and batting and bowling techniques

By the time the full leg-side restriction had been removed, one-day matches had arrived at cricket's top level. Although it was taking batsmen some time to adjust, there was soon a marked adaptation of technique. The top batsmen in the years after the war used to play classically straight, and county batsmen tended to copy them. Spinners were more able to keep them quiet. The growth of limited-overs cricket forced batsmen to improvise. Norman Gifford, who began his first-class career just before one-day cricket arrived, said: 'It's much harder bowling at the top players today than when I first started. I might bowl a couple of balls outside the off-stump which are played to my packed offside field, then all of a sudden you can see the batsman has changed his line of attack. I'll bowl the same delivery, he'll play across the line and work me through the on-side, where there aren't so many fielders.'

Batsmen were already adapting their technique to spinners before the one-day game began, especially to leg-spinners. Doug Insole said: 'I'd play wicket to wicket at what I suspected was the googly, shoulder arms to the ball that was missing the off-stump, and just wait for the inevitable bad ball and whack it. During my time, batsmen stopped going down the wicket to leg-spinners.' This reluctance to use the feet hampered one of the leg-spinners' key weapons, turning the ball past the outside edge of a charging batsman, and inevitably meant fewer stumpings. In 1947 there were 320; in 1956 – the year there were 14 spinners in the top 20 – it had already reduced to 209; in 1966 there were 122, representing a percentage per game that has since stayed pretty constant into the new century. Moreover tail-enders changed their attitude. Instead of settling for a short life and a merry one, they would practise assiduously, play down the line, and have to be winkled out. This everyone-must-be-able-to-bat attitude rebounded doubly on the spinners: it denied them cheap wickets at the end of the innings, and it meant that they too, an increasingly endangered species, would have to improve their batting if they were to get the nod over a fourth seamer.

It was variously said at the time that one-day cricket was ruining both batting and bowling. Batsmen began to offend the purists by playing across the line, or by opening the face and running the ball behind square on the offside. Middle-order batsmen, with little time to play themselves in, often didn't, and a series of ugly smears often resulted. Opening the batting was easier: you still had time to build an innings. Bowlers became more defensive-minded. This 1965–80 generation of batsmen was one that had grown up playing in a conservative down-the-line three-day style, and it's small wonder that they found adaptation difficult. They have been replaced by a generation that had to adapt in the other direction: brought up at school on a diet of limited-over cricket, their strokes are there but the patience isn't. Youngsters in England brought into the four-day game are exhorted to 'bat through the session' to try to restrain their instinctive aggression.

Life for bowlers changed in a different way. Without a compelling need to take wickets, seamers tended to 'just put it there' and wait for mistakes. Spinners, even those with confidence and powers of spin and flight, felt obliged to fire it in at leg-stump, playing for figures of 0–35 rather than 3–60. In the 20 years between the great Ashes series of 1961 and 1981, the first-class scene had changed dramatically in England for the poor spinner. In 1961 he would be playing the same cricket, day in, day out. Vic Marks, writing in the 1987 Wisden, pointed out that 'in the 1950s and 1960s the great England bowlers rediscovered their length and line in the nets in April and didn't need to vary it much all season long'. In 1981 he would have a county game on Saturday to Tuesday, with a 40-over Sunday League game intervening. He would be expected to bowl differently on Sunday and revert back for the rest of the week, unless it held a 55- or 60-over Cup game. If you didn't adapt, you didn't play on the Sunday, and your self-confidence inevitably took a knock, and self-belief is crucial to a spinner. Ray East of Essex: 'It's been the bugbear of my career. My action has been spoiled as I pack the leg-side on a Sunday and bowl flat, then try to cope with six fielders on the other side the following day.'

Only the best could do it. For Ray Illingworth, in the England side in 1961 and back captaining Yorkshire in 1982 at the age of 50, spinning is a trade that takes years to learn. Writing before his return, he said: 'If someone had given me a new back and a fresh pair of legs, I would have been even better at 50. Slow bowling is a thinker's game and you never stop learning at it.' He was able to prove it. When Yorkshire won the Sunday League in 1983 he was their best bowler – 20 wickets at 13 apiece at under three and a half runs an over. He was 51.

CHAPTER 23

Blackwash and Ashes

The pivotal moment of the 1985 series, the last day at Edgbaston. Allan Lamb's boot deflects a shot from Wayne Phillips upwards. David Gower, to his left, will in a moment take the disputed catch that triggers an Australian collapse.

England have only three major problems: they can't bat,
they can't bowl and they can't field.

MARTIN JOHNSON, before the winning 1986–7 series

David, the last time we played here I was a nice guy who came last...
This time I thought I had a bloody good chance to win and I was
prepared to be as ruthless as it takes to stuff you.

ALAN BORDER, to David Gower, after winning the 1989 Ashes series

1984–5 India

After their *annus horribilis* of 1984, an England under Gower, and without the injured Botham, went to India fearing a repeat of the grisly tediousness of four years earlier, facing a team that were now world one-day champions. The previous tour had nearly been cancelled by Indira Gandhi. Shockingly, this one was nearly cancelled *because* of her, for, only hours after the team's arrival, she was assassinated by her own Sikh bodyguard in reprisal for the Indian Army's takeover of the sacred Sikh Golden Temple at Amritsar two months before. A few weeks later, the morning after the British High Commissioner had thrown a party for the team at his home, he too was dead, shot in his car on his way to work. The next day's first Test and the series were in the balance, but in the end they went ahead. Fortunately the political turmoil quietened, the pitches livened up, and we had an absorbing series between two well-balanced teams.

England	195 & 317	**India**	465–8d & 51–2
India	307 & 235	**England**	418 & 127–2
India	437–7d	England	276
India	272 & 412	**England**	652–7d & 35–1
India	553–8d & 97–1d	England	417 & 91–0

The series hinged on the final afternoon of the second Test. India had won the first, and if they had drawn the second the tedium of 1981–2 might have been repeated. After that first match at Bombay, English tongues back home had to battle with the six syllables of India's new 18-year-old leg-spinning star, Sivaramakrishnan, diminutive in all but name. He took six wickets in each innings, and only Gatting, in a belligerent 136, batted with any confidence – as he subsequently always did against the spinners, until he met a certain Australian. It was his first Test century in his 54th innings, a statistic that seems extraordinary in view of what followed. At Delhi in the second Test, the calm Nottingham opening bat Tim Robinson, in only his second Test, showed his compatriots how to play the leg-spinner in a fine innings of 160. Siva took another six in only his third Test bowl, but England led by 111. On a slow turner, India reached 207–4 after lunch on the final day, and a draw looked certain. But Pocock and Edmonds, wheeling away beautifully together, suddenly broke through, Kapil threw away his wicket and his place in the next Test, and England had surprisingly squared the series. Were English spinners redeeming themselves?

At Calcutta the customary smog and India's 200-over first innings made a result impossible, so the teams went to Madras still at one-all. Here an inspired piece of swing bowling from Foster, 6–104, put England on top. Equally inspired batting took England past 500 with only two wickets down, Fowler and Gatting becoming the first Englishmen to make double hundreds in the same Test innings. England had ten and a half hours to bowl India out again, and Foster's 5–59 was again responsible for the eventual win, one of epic proportions considering the past 12 months. It only needed a resilient performance in the last Test at Kanpur to secure the series win, and this England managed, despite a mid-innings stutter, after more brilliant batting by the elegant young Muslim newcomer, Mohammad Azharuddin, who thus made a century in each of his first three Tests. Somehow, England had won a series without Botham, their talisman. Gatting's breakthrough gave him 575 runs at 95, while Robinson and Fowler scored more than 400 at over 50. Apart from Foster's 14 wickets at 20, the bowling figures weren't pretty to look at, but the bowlers took wickets when it mattered. England had put out 21 different players in the black summer of 1984; this time they relied on 12, and the difference in morale and fighting spirit was palpable.

1985 Australia

The Australians arrived in 1985 after a series defeat to West Indies, who had actually beaten England and Australia in 11 successive Tests in just eight months of 1984. This at least suggested a more level playing field. A look at the Australian opening attack also encouraged that view, for Lillee had retired, and Alderman, Hogg and Rackemann were self-inflicted victims of another divisive South African adventure. By contrast Gooch and Emburey were now entitled to play again. At first the sides seemed evenly matched, and, after four Tests of a six-match series, the teams were locked at one-all. The crucial shift in fortune took place late on the fifth day of the fifth Test.

Australia	331 & 324	**England**	533 & 123–5
England	290 & 261	**Australia**	425 & 127–6
England	456 & 196–2	Australia	539
Australia	257 & 340–5	England	482–9d
Australia	335 & 142	**England**	595–5d
England	464	Australia	241 & 129

Although Australia had won the one-day series, Gooch had tuned up for his return to Tests with innings of 57, 115 and 117*. At Headingley, though, when the real stuff started, he was overshadowed by Robinson, whose 175 took only 271 balls and included a wide repertoire of strokes. Botham returned from his winter off with 60 off 51 balls and seven wickets, and with Emburey worked through the Australian second innings to give England time to win. At Lord's, as so often, Australia bounced back. Border dominated the match with 196 after the young McDermott had announced himself as the latest fast bowling find with 6–70. England were 91–6 when Botham strode out in the second innings, still 44 behind, and for a while he threatened a 1981-style comeback. But the leg-spinner Holland went round the wicket to use McDermott's rough, Botham when 85 tired of padding the ball away and paid for it, and Border steadied jangling Australian nerves at 65–5 with another captain's innings. It would not be his last that summer.

The wicket was too good for a result at Trent Bridge, Wood and Ritchie replying with big hundreds after Gower's 166. At Old Trafford, after Botham and Edmonds had bowled Australia out on the first day, Gatting's 160 gave England a big lead despite a heroic 8–141 from McDermott. When Australia were 138–4 England were favourites, but Border's implacable defence in a knock of 146, and a final morning lost to rain, ensured that the sides would go to Edgbaston all square.

England's batsmen had been criticised in the past for not making really big hundreds. This summer they made amends. After fine bowling by Richard Ellison of Kent had restricted Australia to 335, made in two days punctuated by rain, England made up for lost time with a brilliant batting display. Robinson (148) and Gower (215) took England into the lead by the end of the third day in a stand of 331, Gatting added an undefeated 100, and Botham's seven-ball 18 on arrival at 572–4 brought the declaration. Ellison's late away swing was unplayable that evening and Australia started the last day desperate at 37–5. But rain delayed play until 2.30 pm and Phillips and Ritchie kept everyone out until the pivotal moment of the series. Phillips thrashed at Edmonds and as Lamb took evasive action at silly point the ball struck him on the instep. The rebound could have gone anywhere, but it popped up to Gower alongside him. Umpire Constant from square leg gave him out, and replays appeared to confirm the decision's correctness, though Border complained that Constant couldn't possibly be sure the ball hadn't bounced before it struck Lamb. Be that as it may, Australia folded in a heap and England were 2–1 up.

Australia now needed to win to get back to 2–2 and retain the Ashes. But Gower, in scintillating form this series, figured in a second successive 300-plus stand. His 157 this time was in company with Gooch (196) and although England lost their last nine wickets for 93 the fight had gone out of Australia. Every England bowler contributed but it was Ellison again, with 5–46, who did the final damage, defied only by Border, visibly agonised by his side's capitulation. His series tally was 597 at 66 and although four of his team-mates scored over 350 runs they were overshadowed by England's top four. Apart from the Lord's Test, England were not bowled out for under 450. Gooch, Robinson, Gower and Gatting scored 2236 runs between them at an average of 72, with Gower's 732 aggregate the highest for England v Australia for over 50 years. They really cashed in: of their eight hundreds, the lowest dismissal came at 148. Moreover England scored at a rate of over 60 runs per 100 balls, unprecedented since the war. For one reason this was especially surprising, because in an amazing season in which he hit 80 sixes, and averaged over 100 at a run a minute for Somerset, Botham's bat wasn't often needed for England. His bowling, though, brought him 31 wickets at 27, back close to his best. With Ellison coming through so devastatingly in the last two Tests, swinging the ball superbly – 75.5–20–185–17 – and Emburey and Edmonds taking 34 wickets between them, England's ultimate superiority was almost total. Only the wholehearted McDermott, 30 wickets at 30, emulated Border's defiance.

1985–6 West Indies

Nothing better characterised the huge differences between the sides in this period than the results of contests between England, Australia and West Indies. In two series each against England and Australia, West Indies won 16 Tests and lost one. In the same time England led 6–4 in three series against Australia. Against other countries West Indies scored 9–2, and only Pakistan achieved any kind of parity with them. It was a dominance rarely ever achieved by one side – they were in the middle of a period of 15 years when they never lost a series. Thus it was that an England side fresh from a series triumph over Australia, with an average innings total of 464, went to the West Indies and averaged 202. In 1984 it had been 227. Here it is in its full horror.

England	159 & 152	**West Indies**	307 & 5–0
England	176 & 315	**West Indies**	399 & 95–3
West Indies	418	England	189 & 199
England	200 & 150	**West Indies**	312 & 39–0
West Indies	474 & 246–2d	England	310 & 170

The toss has rarely been so irrelevant. When West Indies batted first they scored over 400. When England did they never exceeded 200, but even though the pitches were hardly blameless – typically bare at each end and grassy in the middle – they couldn't bowl West Indies out for under 300. It hurts to go through the games, so few are the redeeming features for England. Ellison carried on in the first Test at Kingston where he left off at the Oval, with 5–78 from 33 overs, including Greenidge, Gomes and Richards, all lbw. England had been damaged from the start by another terrible injury. This time it was the loss of Gatting, his nose smeared all over his face by Marshall in the Kingston one-day match. They missed his bloody-minded defiance throughout the series, for when he came back three weeks later he immediately broke his thumb. In the first innings of the next Test, Gower and Lamb made sixties but the rest could scrape together only 30 between them. Emburey took five wickets in an innings in the third Test and Botham five in the fourth, but only Gower ever approached a century, and his seven-hour 90 in the final Test at Antigua was put into context by a murderous 110* off 58 balls by Richards, against a deep-set field as he set up his declaration – in 2006 still the fastest Test hundred of all time.

England were close to the ignominy of having no bowler with an average lower than the top batsman: Emburey's 32 was topped only by Gower's 37. Botham averaged 16 and 48, but the wrong way round. Robinson, hitherto so immaculate and reliable, found his average in single figures. Garner, Marshall, Holding and Patterson were the all-conquering quartet this time – Patterson by common consent now the fastest bowler in the world – and they took 89 wickets between them at less than 20. It was becoming impossible to see how England would ever beat the West Indies again.

1986 India and New Zealand

By the end of the summer of 1986 it was beginning to be impossible to see how England could beat *any* of the Indies.

England	294 & 180	**India**	341 & 136—5
India	272 & 237	England	102 & 128
England	390 & 235	India	390 & 174—5

England had won the last series against India 2–1. Now, if it hadn't been for Gatting's innings in the third Test, not a single England batsman would have averaged even 30. Gooch made 114 in the first innings of the series, but very few more. The graceful Vengsarkar's 126* preceded an England collapse in the second innings of the first Test, enabling India to win at Lord's for the first time. That defeat deprived Gower of the captaincy. Gatting could probably have done without that poisoned chalice at Headingley, when he had to oversee a truly frightful batting performance. True, the pitch deteriorated fast, but Vengsarkar – 61 and 102* in a game when no one else reached 40 – showed it could be mastered. Gatting eventually exhibited his qualities at Edgbaston, with 183* out of 390, a total India were allowed to match. An England middle-order collapse set India 236 in a minimum of 84 overs, but after a bright start they subsided against Edmonds to 126–5 from 55 overs at tea, needing 110 from a minimum of 29 overs. Gallingly for everyone, with an exciting finish in prospect, rain removed 50 minutes and India settled for a draw.

Then came the New Zealanders. Surely England could do better?

England	307 & 295—6d	New Zealand	342 & 41—2
England	256 & 230	**New Zealand**	413 & 77—2
New Zealand	287 & 7—0	England	388—5d

No, they couldn't. And, in a season of firsts for the opposition, New Zealand recorded their first-ever series win in England. They were indebted to their great all-rounder. In the India series Kapil Dev's performances had been muted, while Botham had been suspended for taking dope and for being one. At Lord's Hadlee's 6–80 restricted England to 307 after they had been 196–2, and a century from Martin Crowe gave New Zealand the lead. England stuttered on the final morning but were saved by an innings of 183 from Gooch, one of increasing dominance. The first innings of the second Test at Trent Bridge followed the same pattern, with Hadlee taking another 6-80 in an innings of 256, after England had been 170-3. With New Zealand's first innings at 144—5 the match hung in the balance, but a century by John Bracewell at No. 8 gave New Zealand a commanding lead and emphasised starkly the different abilities of the two sides' middle order. Nevertheless rain that wiped out most of the Monday gave England hope, and Emburey, entering at 104–6, 'jerked and jabbed his way to 75'. But Hadlee took another four wickets to bring his tally to 10, following his innings of 68, and New Zealand had time enough to win.

For England to save the series now they would have to win at the Oval, and they had Botham back after serving a two-month ban. He steamed in to take the two wickets he needed to pass Lillee's 355 as the highest wicket-taker in Tests, but Wright's resolution, and the loss of half the match to rain, made attractive centuries from Gower and Gatting redundant. As was Botham's 50 from 32 balls, which included 24 in an over, equalling Andy Roberts' record... which had been hit off Botham himself. Some frustration had been worked off, anyway.

So, another awful summer for England, and for most of the 24 players who represented them, as the selectors looked this way and that. The three Gs were good enough, with 1300 runs at 45 between them. But the remaining batsmen were pitiful. Of the bowlers, Dilley, still only 27, came back strongly with 19 wickets at 25, and both Edmonds and Derek Pringle of Essex (a Cambridge Blue with an earring – whatever next?) averaged in the twenties. But an England team had been through a six-Test summer, against ordinary sides, with an outside chance of victory in only one Test. With Australia sharpening their claws ready to win back the Ashes, the winter prospects looked pretty bleak, especially as Gooch chose not to tour.

1986–7 Australia, for the wooden spoon

The journalist Martin Johnson summed up the prospects succinctly before the tour began: 'England have only three major problems: they can't bat, they can't bowl and they can't field.' The only consolation in advance for England was that of six Tests against the same opponents the preceding winter, New Zealand and India, Australia had only won one. Indeed New Zealand had won their first ever Test and series in Australia to emphasise how far Australia had sunk. So this was, frankly, a contest for the wooden spoon of world cricket.

England	456 & 77–3	Australia	248 & 282
England	592–8d & 199–8d	Australia	401 & 197–4
Australia	514–5d & 201–3	England	455 & 39–2
Australia	141 & 194	**England**	349
Australia	343 & 251	England	275 & 264

But it was still an Ashes series. Rain halted the first day's play at Brisbane with England 198–2, propelled there by Bill Athey, Gatting and Lamb. Soon after the start next day they were 198–4, and Gower was dropped on the same score. But Botham, relishing his return to the big stage, took control with a typical 138 from 174 balls, including 22 off an over from Merv Hughes, threatening his own record. Dilley bowled well throughout the first Australian innings for 5–68 and in a second crucial phase he and Botham took the last three wickets quickly when Australia looked like averting the follow-on. The painstaking new opener Geoff Marsh held up England with a hundred, but Emburey took the last three wickets to finish with 5–80, and England were one up.

In a high-scoring second Test at Perth, Broad and Athey, a trim and tidy Yorkshireman now at Gloucester, cemented their new opening pairing with a stand of 223, Broad going on to 162, and then both Gower and new wicketkeeper Jack Richards, from Cornwall via Surrey, made hundreds in a rapid stand of 207 for the sixth wicket. Australia's reply was shored up by Border, who this time ensured there was no follow-on after the ninth wicket had fallen with eight more needed, and the game drifted to its draw. At Adelaide the roles were reversed, with Australia passing 500. But Broad made a hundred again in a further century stand with Athey, Gatting made another, and the sides came to Melbourne for the traditional Boxing Day Test with Australia needing to win the last two Tests to get back the Ashes.

The Ashes retained

Australia needed a sporting wicket to ensure a result. They got one, but they were the victims, bowled out by a slower Botham and the admirable Gladstone Small, his strong high shoulders set in a permanent shrug. Small took 5–48, Botham 5–41. Broad then scored his third hundred in successive Tests, and England led by over 200. It seemed inconceivable that Australia could bat as badly again, but they did, slithering to an innings defeat to Edmonds and Emburey, from 153–3 to 194 all out. An Ashes win to savour, and against their supporters' pessimistic expectations. Australia were poor – how long ago it seems – but they were still Australia.

The best Test of the five was the one at Sydney, gripping throughout and deserving of a series decider. It began with the press proclaiming that Australia had picked the wrong Taylor. Mark Taylor was a left-handed opener from New South Wales of whom much more would be heard; Peter Taylor was an off-spinner with only one first-class match that season and six in all. But the selectors got the right one when they chose Peter, whose 6–78 in his first Test bowl gave Australia the edge on first innings after a dominating 184* from Dean Jones, countering another five-wicket haul for Small. Despite a strained groin, Emburey's gutsy 69 kept Australia's lead down to 66, and he posed such problems with the ball in their second innings that they slipped to 145–7. But Taylor helped Steve Waugh to add 98, so that, despite Emburey's 7–78, England needed 320 to win in a day and a bit on a turning wicket. After a decent start, 91–1 became 102–5 when Taylor got Botham first ball, but Gatting took the attack to the spinners in alliance with Richards. When the last 20 overs started England were 230–5, 90 wanted. If Gatting could stay… but he gave Waugh the stand-breaker a return catch when 96. Two wickets fell at 257 in the 11th over, and, though Emburey and Small held out until the 18th, their dismissal gave Australia the kind of dead-match consolation that was all England would be able to scavenge in future Ashes series.

Just as Ellison had been 18 months previously, Small was the late-series bowling find, with 12 wickets at 15, who helped England win the series. Sadly, neither of them would be able to repeat that level of success. Dilley, Edmonds, Emburey and Botham took their wickets at between 30 and 40, but that proved enough. The batting revelation was the left-handed Broad, tall and determined, 487 runs at 69, with Gower continuing his resurgence with 404 at 57, and Gatting 393 at 43. With Richards, Emburey, Athey and Botham all averaging in the thirties, the middle-order support was a lot stiffer than in previous series.

1987 Pakistan

In 1987 England renewed hostilities with Pakistan, granted a full series of their own for the first time for 25 years. They deserved both that and the luck they had with the weather at the start of the season when their talismanic captain Imran Khan was unfit to bowl.

England	447	Pakistan	140–5
England	368		
England	136 & 199	**Pakistan**	353
Pakistan	439 & 205	England	521 & 109–7
Pakistan	708	England	232 & 315–4

Rain cut by half the first Test at Old Trafford, where Robinson temporarily recovered his form at this level with 166, and little more than a day was played at Lord's, where Athey made 123. The contest wasn't fully joined until Headingley in early July. Here England found themselves 31–5 after an hour of high-class bowling from Imran, back at full throttle, and the dangerous new left-arm-over bowler, Wasim Akram. Although David Capel, the Northamptonshire all-rounder, then made 50 on debut, and despite a tremendous effort from Foster, 8–107, England trailed by over 200 on first innings. In the second they were undone by Imran, again devastating, his 7–40 giving him 10 in the match. The fourth Test was the only one closely fought and brought England a chance to square the series. That didn't seem likely when Mudassar Nazar's hundred led Pakistan to a score over 400. But a century opening stand, Gatting's hundred, and the tail's wag, gave England a lead of 82 with an hour left of the fourth day. England had to bowl really well, and they did. After lunch Foster and Botham turned a placid 74–1 into a panicky 116–6, a lead of 34. Imran led a rearguard action, but England needed 124 in 18 overs, quickly reduced by Broad to 87 in 13. However, Imran and Akram kept their nerve, the English big guns didn't fire, there were three run outs, and England fell 15 short with three wickets left. An exciting but ultimately galling final day.

England needed to win the toss at the Oval but they didn't. Miandad's 260, and centuries from Salim Malik and Imran, took Pakistan past 700 and guaranteed them the series. Therafter it was an attritional fight for survival once Qadir had taken 7–96 to force England to bat again, a mere 476 behind. That they drew was due to Gatting's 150*, in company with a dutifully restrained Botham, whose 50 took over four hours. (Had he ever batted as long?) Gatting towered above everyone at the top of the batting averages, with 445 runs at 63. Robinson and Athey faded after their centuries, and no one else could average 40. Foster and Dilley, averaging 22 and 27, did well to match the 21 and 29 of Imran and Akram, but the Pakistan pair saved the day the only time their side's batting had looked vulnerable. Botham's seven wickets cost 47, and Imran won the all-rounder battle with averages of 47 and 21. Off the field a further conflict took place over the umpires, with the TCCB ultimately turning down Imran's objection to Constant and Ken Palmer, a sore festering from 1982. In the end it was of no account, but it kept the tension between the two teams well fuelled. There would be a reckoning…

1987 The fourth World Cup

The World Cup left England for the first time in 1987 and came to India and Pakistan. The shorter daylight hours made it inevitable that there would be fewer overs per side, and the 50 employed here would become the standard. Although the format was the same as in 1983, with two groups of four playing each other twice, the distances involved, and the 21 venues, meant that the tournament took a month to complete, compared to the intensive 16 days of 1983.

It began with a bang and with a string of close finishes. Australia started in Group A by winning by one run off the fifth ball of the last over, after India had lost their collective nerve at the death, chasing 271. The next day in Group B Lamb steered England to a tight two-wicket win over the West Indies. Back in Group A, a day later Houghton's magnificent 141 led a down-and-out Zimbabwe back from the dead, only for New Zealand to win by 3 runs with two balls left. In the next game England lost their last six wickets in 16 balls to go down to Pakistan from a winnable position, and Pakistan became favourites in the group when they beat West Indies by one wicket from the last ball of the match, thanks to Qadir, who hit a straight six off Walsh in a last over which had begun with 14 needed.

This was a heady, hectic start and things inevitably sobered down. In England's group, the second qualifying place was decided when England played West Indies. Batting first, Gooch's 92 received better support than Richardson's 93, once Richards had been bowled by Hemmings, who then threw out Harper with a direct hit – an unlikely reversal – as West Indies crumbled. So England sustained their record of reaching the semi-final in each Cup, and West Indies, missing Marshall, went back to pulverising the opposition in proper Tests.

In the other group, India and Australia were clearly going to finish top. Because India won the return match comfortably, and fetched up with a faster run rate, they came top of the group and avoided having to play the strongly-fancied Pakistan in Lahore. That honour went to Australia. In every game but their defeat by India they had batted first and scored over 230, and here in the semi-final their consistent top-order batting took them to 267–8. Imran followed his 3–36 with 58 but once he had gone Miandad couldn't win the match alone against McDermott, and Australia were through by 18 runs. If that was a surprise, England provided another one next day in Bombay. Led by 115 from Gooch, who attacked the Indian spinners by pulling and sweeping them incessantly, England set India 255. They were always behind the clock, and England's unlikely hero was again Hemmings, who took four key wickets in a spell of six overs.

SEMI–FINALS				
Australia	267–8 (50)		Pakistan	249 (49)
England	254–6 (50)		India	219 (45.3)
FINAL				
Australia	253–5 (50)		England	246–8 (50)

In the final at Calcutta on 8 November, Australia won the toss and batted consistently once more down the order to post 253–5, with a vital 65 from the last six overs. England were as consistent at the outset, with Gooch, Athey, Gatting and Lamb taking them to 170–3, 84 needed at just under seven an over. But in those days the side fielding second always seemed able to exert more pressure on batsmen in the heat of the chase. So it proved here. England fell behind the clock, and needed 19 from the last two overs. Steve Waugh, whose bowling had as usual been as nerveless as his batting, took the wicket of DeFreitas, the only batsman left with the necessary improvising flair, in conceding just two runs from the penultimate over, and England duly lost by seven runs.

So Australia, coming into the Cup as the wooden spoonholders of the major Test-playing nations, resuscitated their spirit under the battling Border, and didn't look back. England got close again, led by the batting of Gooch (471 in eight innings), Gatting, Lamb and Athey, while the bowling was extremely consistent: Foster, DeFreitas, Small, Hemmings and Emburey doesn't sound like the greatest ever England one-day attack, but they rarely bowled badly, and Gooch bowled some tidy spells when he needed to. Gatting led the side well, although he was castigated for getting out to the new-fangled reverse sweep in both the semi-final and final, after he had made 56 and 41 respectively. In the final it was to Border's first ball, which was the crime that enraged his critics. Cheekily clever when it succeeded, it only looked ghastly when it failed. But Gatting was about to run into worse trouble.

1987–8 Pakistan, Australia and New Zealand

A three-match tour to Pakistan followed hard on the heels of the home side's loss in the World Cup semi-final, a defeat that characteristically angered their supporters. After Imran's (first) retirement, Javed Miandad took over the captaincy. A brilliant batsman, a patriotic and incendiary character, he was confronted by England's pugnacious Captain Pugwash, Mike Gatting – solid, four-square, tough-minded. The bickering that had constantly flickered between the two teams was usually about the umpires, with the visiting side deeply suspicious about their neutrality on home soil. The tinder was dry, the petrol at hand, and into the mix came two shaky umpires: Shakeel Khan and Shakoor Rana. Three years earlier Jeremy Coney had led the New Zealanders off in a Test in protest against Shakoor Rana's decision to give Miandad not out caught behind. Rightly or wrongly, it was felt by opposing teams that local umpires would avoid giving Miandad out if at all possible.

At Lahore in the first Test, it was Shakeel Khan who incurred the wrath of the English. After the game they claimed that he had given nine incorrect decisions in favour of Pakistan, and Broad, refusing to go when given out caught at the wicket, had to be persuaded off by Gooch. As Pakistan had done in the summer, England demanded a change of umpire. As England had refused, it was no surprise that Pakistan did too. The Pakistanis' temperature rose further when Broad's manager gave him only a stern reprimand rather than fining him, and Peter Lush took bellows to the flames by criticising the umpires publicly and calling again for them to be neutral. These were the days before neutral umpires, match referees and a code of conduct, and this tour showed exactly why they were needed. Backing Broad to a man, an inflamed England team went to Faisalabad for the second Test, where the Pakistanis did in fact replace Shakeel Khan... with Shakoor Rana.

On the second day Shakoor, standing at square leg, accused Gatting of moving a fielder surreptitiously. Earthy language was exchanged, fingers were wagged in faces, and the flames shot skywards. Next day Shakoor wouldn't umpire if Gatting didn't apologise, and Gatting wouldn't unless Shakoor did too. Shakoor eventually agreed to sign a document drafted by the TCCB chairman Raman Subba Row, but Gatting still refused. A stand-off, and a day's play lost. Eventually Gatting did apologise with the little grace he could muster, and the team issued a written protest. The TCCB recognised that they had been slow to spot the seriousness of the trouble, but a subsequent 'hardship payment' of £1000 a head to the team only led it into more criticism.

So, a sorry mess, and the performance on the field was nearly as bad.

England	175 & 130	Pakistan	392
England	292 & 137–6d	Pakistan	191 & 51–1
England	294 & 258–9	Pakistan	353

The fracas in no way detracts from a brilliant bowling performance from the Pakistani match-winner Abdul Qadir, who bowled exquisitely throughout the series against a side missing Gower and Botham. In the first Test he took 9–56 and 4–45, and he took another 10 in the third, to reach 30 in a three-Test series, one more than all the England bowlers contrived in total.

After their poor batting in the first Test, the irony of the second was that without the row and the loss of a day England might have won. Broad atoned with an excellent 116, to which Gatting added a furious (in every sense) 79 from 81 balls, and Foster, Emburey and Cook earned a lead of 101. But time ran out. In the third Test a decent pitch ensured a draw once Capel and Emburey had extracted England from 85–6, and Emburey's second 70 of the match brought his average to 69, virtually double anyone else's. Winning the one-day series 3–0 was small consolation. As Peter Swan neatly put it in his 'Lament from Lord's':

'Lahore to Karachi – in search of a win
Our cricketers reached their nadir.
For wherever they went on the subcontinent
Was Abdul the spinner, Qadir'.

In the early stages of the subsequent tour of New Zealand, a rather less troubled venue, England flew to Sydney to play a Test to mark the Australian bicentennial.

England	425	Australia	214 & 328–2

Another century for Broad, so reliable abroad, put England on top, but he blotted his copybook again by flattening a stump on dismissal. He had been bowled, so no smidgeon of excuse this time, and he was fined the maximum permitted. After a good all-round bowling performance, capped by a brilliant catch by Foster to ensure the follow-on was enforced, rain and David Boon's patient 184* ensured Australia's escape. Back to New Zealand.

England	319 & 152	New Zealand	168 & 130–4
New Zealand	301 & 350–7	England	323
New Zealand	512–6d	England	183–2

It was Broad again with 114 who gave England the advantage in Christchurch, and Dilley's 6–38 put England well on top. They would almost certainly have won had they not lost most of the fourth day. Hadlee, after recent heroics in Australia, needed just one wicket to overtake Botham at the top of the Test bowling list, but had bowled 18 overs without taking a wicket when a muscle strain sidelined him for the rest of the series. His frustration can only be imagined. Thereafter no result was likely on good wickets unless either side collapsed, which they didn't. The tall watchful Yorkshireman Martyn Moxon took his chance – Gooch missed the New Zealand leg – and was unlucky to miss centuries in the last two Tests, making 99 in Auckland and 81* in Wellington, where rain obliterated the last two days.

1988 West Indies

The West Indies arrived in 1988 having won their last 10 Tests against England. But their recent record gave England cause for hope. After failing to qualify for the World

Cup semi-final, they had drawn one-all in both India and Pakistan. At Madras they had been bowled out by another fleeting leg-spinning success, the studious-looking 19-year-old Narendra Hirwani, who took an amazing 16 wickets in his debut match. Then on the West Indies' own patch in Georgetown, Imran Khan returned in response to an appeal from his country's President, General Zia-ul-Haq, the man trained by Denis Compton in 1945, who would be killed in a suspicious plane crash the following August. Imran bowled the West Indies out twice, and they only just sneaked home to draw the series. So there was some encouragement for England, and that was strengthened after they won the one-day series 3–0.

England	245 & 301–3	West Indies	448–9d
West Indies	209 & 397	England	165 & 307
England	135 & 93	**West Indies**	384–7d
England	201 & 138	**West Indies**	275 & 67–0
England	205 & 202	**West Indies**	183 & 226–2

In the one-day series the West Indian batting had been dominated by excellent bowling by DeFreitas, Small and Pringle. However that superiority disappeared at Trent Bridge. After Gooch and Broad had opened with a century stand, Marshall and the batsmen took control, until Gooch (146) and Gower saved the match with ease. England's seventh draw on the trot interrupted the run of defeats against West Indies. Before the Lord's Test could show whether this was only a blip, however, lurid newspaper accusations about a barmaid and a hotel room deprived England of their captain. Whether allegations of sexual impropriety, which Gatting denied, should have led to his dismissal as captain, is a moot point. But there was certainly a feeling that the TCCB was exasperated with the cumulative effect of events in the winter, and off he went.

At Lord's normal service was resumed. West Indies recovered from 54–5, Dilley's opening burst having disposed of the top four. Facing only 209, England under John Emburey were undone again by Marshall, and only a century from Lamb, another winter absentee, delayed the inevitable after West Indies had added a further 397. At Old Trafford Emburey retained the captaincy as Gatting returned, but the gap in class was even more apparent as England scraped up barely more than 200 in the two innings combined, Marshall this time taking 7–22 in the second.

This was to become the 'Summer of Four Captains'. To the first two were added a third when Chris Cowdrey was plucked from Kent by his godfather, Peter May, who had been a rather more successful captain than he was a chairman of selectors. Cowdrey was one of no fewer than seven replacements. Things looked healthy for England at two points in the game. At 183–4, Lamb and Robin Smith, another forthright batsman of South African origin playing his first Test innings, had added 103. At this point Lamb limped off with a torn calf muscle. The innings ended just 18 runs later. Then at 80–1 in their second innings and with Gooch 50*, England were 6 ahead. But it was a familiar story: the last nine wickets could add only 58, England were 3–0 down, and Gooch got the call-up as captain number four. After Foster's five wickets England took a lead that a grimly determined Gooch extended to 224. In a low-scoring game that figure could have been a defensible target. Indeed it might have been had Gooch caught Greenidge in DeFreitas's first over. But he didn't, it was a no-ball anyway, and the dislocated finger he sustained trying to catch ended his participation. So in truth it became the 'Summer of the Four-and-a-Half Captains'. For the last act Derek Pringle took over, but stemming the flow from the broad bats of Greenidge and Haynes was a thankless task.

England contrived to pick 23 players, and most of them had batting averages too shocking to reveal. They had a chance to rescue them against Sri Lanka, still dismissively regarded by Lord's as apprentices, who were here for another one-match tour. England took the summer's player tally to 27 by picking four debutants, all of whom did well.

Sri Lanka	194 & 331	**England**	429 & 100–3

Of the newcomers, the Worcester seam bowler Phil Newport took seven wickets, while Kim Barnett of Derbyshire made an attractive 64 in the first England innings. But it was the new wicketkeeper who impressed – and surprised. The surprise was his batting. Going in as nightwatchman at the end of the first day, he outscored Gooch in the morning. Had he been able to convert his 94 into a century, he would have been the holder of an unlikely record: a wicketkeeper nightwatchman making his maiden first-class century in his first Test innings. His name was Jack Russell, the Stumper of Gloucester, the neatest and soundest of keepers, and a cussed left-handed bat, hard to get out. Only he of the four debutants here who would have a long Test career in front of him.

In the 1988 summer Gooch made 570 runs, 200 more than anyone else, Lamb averaged 40, Gower 30. Dilley, Foster and Pringle took their wickets at under 30, but Marshall had 35 at 12, and the newcomer Curtly Ambrose 22 at 20. Ambrose would become as mean and menacing as Marshall, and seemed about a foot taller. England had lost 14 of their last 15 Tests against the West Indies, but at least the Sri Lankan win ended a dreadful barren run of 18 Tests without a win. The team was due to tour India, but because the hosts wouldn't allow in the eight team members with South African connections (including Gooch, the appointed captain) the tour was cancelled. So for the first time for 13 years there wasn't a winter tour, which was perhaps as well. The Australians were coming and with the Ashes the only prize in England's possession, they would need to be on top form to retain it.

1989 Australia

Everything went wrong for England at Headingley, before the first Test even began. Gatting and Botham were unfit, they left out their only spinner, and they ignored the groundsman's advice to bat first. It was like Brisbane in 1954–5, but without the happy ending.

In that first Test the new opener Mark Taylor made 136, and Steve Waugh , who – strange to recall – hadn't yet made a Test hundred, scored 177* as Australia passed 600. This was Waugh's 42nd Test innings, and he would make bowlers pay for the wait. Barnett, Lamb (125) and Robin Smith took England past 400 and the declaration gave England 83 overs to hold out. In the event they survived only until the 56th, Alderman, who had missed 1985 but had been playing county cricket, taking five wickets in each innings. This was a disastrous start and Lord's was no better. Waugh made another 152*, nursing the tail to such effect that they virtually doubled the score from 265–6, a point when England were still in the game. Gower and Smith, 106 and 96, held up Australia, for whom Alderman took his tally to 19, but they beat the threatening rain to go two-up.

Australia	601–7d & 230–3d	England	430 & 191
England	286 & 359	**Australia**	528 & 119–4
Australia	424 & 158–2	England	242
England	260 & 264	**Australia**	447 & 81–1
Australia	602–6d	England	255 & 167
Australia	468 & 219–4d	England	285 & 143–5

Rain at Edgbaston helped England, in disarray after Lamb, Gatting, Smith and Foster were forced to withdraw in the run-up to the Test. England's only consolation here was the debut of the hard-grafting Middlesex opening bowler Angus Fraser, who took 4–63 in 33 accurate overs while Dean Jones was making 157. At Old Trafford Smith's aggressive 143 received little support, and more consistent Australian batting left England a deficit of 187. At 59–6 an innings defeat was on the cards, but Russell and Emburey avoided that indignity by adding 142 for the seventh wicket, Russell eventually reaching that maiden century.

On the last day of that Test, with Gower expected to be facing the axe again with his side 3–0 down, the news of Gatting's rebel South African tour broke. That scratched out a few names from the selectors' (long) shortlist for the fifth Test. When they eventually emerged from their conclave they had a side with only Gower, Smith and Russell remaining from the Headingley opener. The outcome in the fifth Test was a big innings defeat, held up only by a belligerently defiant century from Smith: the faster they bowled at him, the faster it went. At the Oval a catalogue of injuries consigned England to a toothless attack of Small, Igglesden, Pringle, Capel and Cook. Small and Cook as batsmen did manage to avert the follow-on, otherwise England would probably have ended the series 5–0 losers, rather than 4–0, which was bad enough.

The statistics of the series are horrendous from an England viewpoint: those of a sensitive disposition look away now. Australian readers, feast your eyes. Robin Smith made 553 runs at 61 each, but no one else averaged 40, and he was topped by four Australians, with Mark Taylor scoring a Bradmanesque 839. Australia's regular four bowlers took 100 wickets at 24 between them, Alderman 41 of them eight years after taking 42 in the 1981 defeat, a tremendous achievement even in two six-match series. No English bowler averaged fewer than 35. Nineteen people bowled for England in the series, seven for Australia. You can look again now.

Cricketers picked for England at home 1984–9

Tests	Players
31–35	Gower
26–30	
21–25	Gooch, Botham, Gatting, Emburey, Lamb
16–20	Downton
11–15	Edmonds, Foster, Dilley, Broad, Pringle, Robinson
6–10	Athey, French, Allott, Smith R. A., Cook N. G. B., Russell, Fowler, Moxon
4–5	Ellison, DeFreitas, Curtis, Barnett, Small, Capel, Jarvis
3	Willis, Pocock, Agnew, Richards, Tavaré, Fraser
2	Miller, Terry, Cowans, Willey, Taylor, Radford, Childs, Atherton, Newport
1	Lloyd T. A., Randall, Sidebottom, Benson, Lever J. K., Slack, Smith C. L., Thomas, Fairbrother, Cowdrey C. S., Bailey, Maynard, Hemmings, Igglesden, Malcolm, Lawrence, Stephenson

Average number of home Tests in six years – 6.2

Thus England ended the 1980s having picked a barely believable 29 players for an Ashes series. Since the Ashes win of 1985 they had lost successive series at home to India, New Zealand, Pakistan, West Indies and Australia (and 4–0 to each), and next winter they had to go to the West Indies. In that time they had lost 12 home Tests out of 23 and drawn all but the sole Sri Lankan match: only Sri Lanka's elevation to Test status prevented England from being bottom of the heap. Since 1987, too, they had been supervised by a full-time coach for the first time, but clearly Micky Stewart was unable to stem the decline. In 1988 Peter May ended his stint as Chairman of Selectors with a heavy defeat, and his successor Ted Dexter – another ex-Cambridge England captain – started his with another. What had happened? England, founder of cricket's international club, had been overtaken by all but its newest member. Originally the game's chief arbiters and legislators, the MCC had, amid rumblings of dissent, been elbowed aside by its creation, the TCCB. Moreover, the centre of gravity of world cricket was starting to shift away from Lord's, towards the East.

CHAPTER 24

Running Cricket in England and the World

Jagu Dalmiya with Malcolm Gray and David Richards at an ICC meeting in 2000.

**International Cricket Council
address up to 2005**

The Clock Tower
Lord's Cricket Ground
London, England

**International Cricket Council
address from 2005**

Al Thuraya Tower
Dubai Media City
United Arab Emirates

In the beginning...

In 1813 the government decided to build the Regent's canal, named in honour of the future King George IV, straight through the middle of Thomas Lord's unpopular second ground at Lisson Grove. With the £4000 he received as compensation, Lord transplanted the original turf to his third ground in St John's Wood, and the Marylebone Cricket Club, teetering on the edge of extinction, was resuscitated. Thereafter the MCC, always a private club since its inception in 1787, contrived to rise to total pre-eminence in cricket in England – and indeed the world – as arbiter of its Laws and its 'spirit'. A century later, in 1909, soon after the South Africans arrived as the third Test-playing nation, the Imperial Cricket Conference (ICC) was formed. To England, Australia and South Africa were added in 1926 the West Indies, India and New Zealand. In 1952 Pakistan arrived, but South Africa departed for 30 years when it left the Commonwealth in 1961. Happily in 1965 the word 'imperial' could be replaced by 'international' without the bother of a change of acronym, and similarly in 1989 'conference' could be replaced by 'council'. This time, however, it wasn't just a change of name.

The MCC and ICC had run cricket together, with only occasional perturbations, into the 1960s. The MCC provided the ICC's secretary, Billy Griffith (1962–74), its headquarters were at Lord's, and an anglocentric view of cricket continued to prevail. Then in 1968, at the end of a troubled decade for English cricket, the Labour government of Harold Wilson fulfilled an election pledge to subsidise sport in this country, through the newly-established Sports Council. The MCC was then, in E. W. Swanton's words 'a private club with a public function – it reigns but does not rule'. The Sports Council could hardly dole out largesse to a private club, and the MCC was certainly not going to open its doors to everyone, so the Cricket Council was formed to administer the government's subsidy, and the Test and County Cricket Board (TCCB) created in place of the then Advisory Cricket Board (ACB) to look after the interests of professional cricket. In its initial incarnation the Cricket Council members were the MCC (five votes), the TCCB (five votes), the pre-existing National Cricket Association (NCA), which administered junior cricket (five votes), the Minor Counties (one vote), Scotland and Ireland (no votes). As for Wales, well for purposes of cricket it had ceded Glamorgan to England, but didn't yet have a team of its own in the Minor Counties championship.

A new order

At the outset the key TCCB personnel were virtually interchangeable with the MCC's. Those responsible for its machinations over the South Africa tours of 1968–70 were MCC men through and through. This incestuous situation began to crack open after 1980. In 1983, those who wanted greater democracy won an internal power struggle, and the Cricket Council committee was reconstituted to give the TCCB chairman eight votes, the NCA five, the MCC three, while the Minor Counties lost their single vote. Eight-all. But its chairman was the TCCB chairman, so if it came to the crunch the TCCB would have the casting vote. This was too much for Gubby Allen, long the torch-bearer of the MCC old guard, who resigned as the MCC representative on the Cricket Council; ultimately for David Clark, who later resigned as treasurer of the MCC; and for Jack Bailey, who retired early as its secretary at the beginning of 1987.

The burden of Allen's message, as editor John Woodcock claimed in the 1983 Wisden, was: 'Beware the small executive subcommittee of businessmen to whom the charm of cricket is little more than a technicality', something of a slander on some of the dedicated ex-cricketers in those positions – the traditionalists always claimed the moral high ground of 'the good of the game'. Between 1946 and 1986 the MCC had had only four secretaries, and until 1976, for all but one year, only two treasurers. They were used to continuity and getting their way, and – despite setting up five inquiries between 1946 and 1968 – arguably were too complacent and conservative in presiding over the decline of English first-class cricket and its finances, until jolted into sanctioning one-day cricket. In due course a group of MCC members rebelled against its committee's compliance in this diminution of its control by voting not to accept the 1986–7 report and accounts, and by calling on its president Colin Cowdrey to resign. A special general meeting had to be called in July 1987 to debate the issue, only for the committee and Cowdrey – absent because he was undergoing open-heart surgery at the time – to prevail by a large majority.

The ICC

So, with that fuss and bother, in England a transfer of effective power took place between the MCC and its offspring the TCCB. As for the ICC, the TCCB chairman was still the ICC chairman, a state of affairs that lasted until 1993. On 2 February that year an acrimonious ICC meeting took place that underlined the nascent shift in power from the anglocentric world, which included the comparatively impoverished West Indies, to the Indian subcontinent. The issue at stake was the location of the 1996 World Cup. The ICC, which had become the International Cricket Council in 1989, had previously agreed that it would be England, but India, Pakistan and Sri Lanka felt they should hold it a second time before England had it a fourth. There followed a series of legal quibbles about ICC rules. India's representatives felt that the destination of the World Cup could be decided by a simple majority, and broke off the meeting to consult India's Chief Justice. The rules of ICC engagement at that time were thus: the nine Test-playing nations had two votes each the (then) 19 'associate' members had one each, but a two-thirds total majority was required for a decision. Furthermore, one of either England or Australia, as founder members, had to vote in favour for a proposal to be carried. You can see how that stuck in the craw of what we might call, with no pejorative intent, the eastern bloc (India and Pakistan tended to vote together despite their governments' mutual antipathy), which remained obdurate in the face of the ICC's own lawyers. The meeting, chaired by the toiling Cowdrey, for whom heart surgery might have been preferable, broke up in disarray.

The doors had been opened to associate members in 1965, and the 19 of them now had clear voting power if they could be persuaded to vote in a particular way: India offered them £100 000 each to back an Asian World Cup, £40 000 more than England. It soon became evident that a clear majority was in favour of the 1996 Cup going east, and England decided to yield 'in the best interests of the game', and settled for the following World Cup. 1996 was a turning point in many ways. Hitherto the Cup had made money for the host nation, but not a vast sum. Now the broadcasting rights were sold for $14 million, with an official sponsor for every product, right down to the gum every modern cricketer seems obliged to chew. Coke and Pepsi, until recently banned in India, bid up to $3.8 million for the soft drinks contract, which Pepsi won. The UK's share of the TV rights was $7.5 million, against just $1 million in 1992. The main sponsor was Wills, an Indian offshoot of British American Tobacco, latest in the long line of cricket's cigarette sponsors, who paid $12 million for the privilege, and the event's profit was a colossal $50 million.

Separation

In July 1993 the ICC ceased to be administered by the MCC and became an entirely separate organisation. In October Sir Clyde Walcott became the first non-English chairman. In 1996 there was a wrangle for the succession, with Jagmohan Dalmiya, India's ICC representative and the driving force behind the country's brash new cricketing self-confidence, competing with two others from South Africa and Australia. Dalmiya needed to exceed a two-thirds majority of full members, but he only had six out of nine, Sri Lanka and Zimbabwe having been the most recent promotions. Of course, if the number had been ten, if – say – Bangladesh had been a full member, then he would have needed only seven... In due course, after a compromise brokered by Sir John Anderson of New Zealand, in June 1997 the ICC was reconstituted with a president and chief executive instead of a chairman, with the presidency going to each member country in rotation. Dalmiya acquired the first presidency, supervising Bangladesh's premature elevation, before handing over in 2000 to Malcolm Gray of Australia, who in turn passed it on to Ehsan Mani of Pakistan. The chief executive has, as it happens, always been an Australian: David Richards from 1993 to 2001, when Malcolm Speed took over.

So, what started as a game administered by a private club in London had become truly international, with money supplanting tradition as the game's driving force. Not that tradition vanished immediately. For a few years more the address of the ICC's chief executive was still, quaintly, The Clock Tower, Lord's Cricket Ground, London NW8 8QN. Late in 2005 it moved temporarily to Dubai Media City. From 2007 it will be in a media block in Dubai Sports City. Thus the world turns.

Don't worry. You won't be tested on all this. You may be thinking that this convoluted story is of distant import for English cricket, but the ICC has become so dominant now in the conduct of the game – presiding over international fixtures, tables, if not the Laws, still MCC's preserve – that it has a crucial effect on the English game.

Only as late as 2005, for instance, did it reluctantly relax its taxing rules that forced each Test team to play the nine others at home and away with punishing frequency. That led to the 2005 arrangement of two Tests with Bangladesh, followed by a two-sided triangular one-day tournament, with the Ashes series beginning only on 21 July, a month after midsummer. Now at least England have 10 years in which to play each country twice.

What of the supervision of English cricket while all this has been going on? In 1997 the Cricket Council, the TCCB, and the NCA were all wound up and subsumed into one body, the ECB, the England and Wales Cricket Board. (So Wales was named at last, but without winning a place in the acronym.) The Management Board of 15 is answerable to the First-Class Forum, which elects five members, and the Recreational Forum, which elects four; their responsibilities are as their names imply. In 2005 it had a chairman and a chief executive, nine directors and eight standing committees. This seems seriously over-complicated and a simplification is in the wind.

Managing the England team

What of running the Test team, a task that became increasingly thankless as the all-conquering 1950s dimmed in the memory? Until the 1980s England's team selection was in the hands of a team of selectors under a distinguished ex-cricketer as chairman, with the captain as part of the committee. Often the chairman would co-opt scouts who would keep an eye on the county game. With eight games running concurrently, and a huge pool of players performing at first-class level, more eyes were necessary. The chairmen since the war have been in turn A. J. Holmes, Bob Wyatt, Norman Yardley, H. S. Altham, Gubby Allen, Walter Robins, Doug Insole, Alec Bedser (1969–81), the first ex-professional chairman, and finally Peter May. In the early days the selectors picked the side and very much left the captain to get on with it on the field, just as they preferred to do, doubtless, in their day. That gradually began to change as more hands-on chairmen appeared, and tensions often emerged between captain and chairman, duly revealed in the more frank autobiographies that began to appear.

In the 1980s the TCCB began a move towards supplementing the chairman's role by appointing a full-time coach. Thus in 1987 Micky Stewart began as a work-ethic coach whose approach chimed with Graham Gooch's but rarely with David Gower's. Ted Dexter, as a player and captain cast more in the Gower mould, replaced May as chairman in 1989 in a new set-up. When Gower, Russell and Salisbury were left out of the Indian tour of 1992–3 there was an unprecedented backlash by MCC members, who called for a vote of no confidence in the selectors. Emotion carried the motion in the hall by 715–412, but lost the overall postal vote by 6135–4600. It's instructive that as late at that point members of the MCC – still a private club, remember – felt they had the power to 'put things right'. In 1993, when Dexter resigned, Matthew Engel in Wisden described him as someone who 'had a powerful vision but didn't let enough people see the picture. He set out to impose a logical system of recognition for young players, and his legacy was a system to identify the best at all levels and give them the best coaches and facilities, age-group squads, and regular A-team tours.' But the consensus was that a more sensible system wasn't yet bringing in more sensible selections. To Engel he 'stood on the parapet with a very English, if slightly batty heroism as shot and shell flew around him'.

Dexter was succeeded by Ray Illingworth, while Stewart's successor Keith Fletcher remained as coach. More strains were evident, and in 1995 Fletcher was sacked, leaving Illingworth to get what he demanded, total control. He was the first to be solely in charge, and the first to learn that sole control meant he would carry the can if things went wrong. They did. His domineering approach didn't endear him to his captains or critics, and he went after England's poor showing in the 1996 World Cup. In 1997, when the TCCB was replaced by the ECB, the new body was headed by Lord McLaurin, the former chief executive of Tesco, with Tim Lamb, ex-Middlesex and Northamptonshire opening bowler, as secretary. McLaurin was determined to 'Raise the Standard' of English cricket, but his blueprint with that neat title was rejected by the counties. David Lloyd, the ex-Lancashire batsman, took over as coach, but another World Cup defeat, this time at home in 1999, saw his departure, and replacement by Duncan Fletcher, a Zimbabwean who had retired from first-class cricket before Zimbabwe acquired Test status. At the time it seemed long odds against his surviving much longer than his predecessors.

But now we must go back to the end of the 1980s, with England in the midst of a terrible run, Ted Dexter and Micky Stewart in charge, and another scary tour of the West Indies to come.

CHAPTER 25

From Splice to Toe

Waqar Younis has just bowled David Gower (not of course Derek Pringle) at the Oval in
August 1992, as England head for defeat. This would be Gower's last Test.

It appeared to swing both ways in the air, turning Pringle both this
way and that before knocking his stumps flat... Pringle confirmed
it was the best he ever received and that neither he nor anyone
could have kept it out.

MICHAEL ATHERTON on Derek Pringle's dismissal v Pakistan 1992

1989–90 West Indies

What a prospect it was for England. They had been slaughtered in their last three series against the West Indies. Not only had they lost 14 matches to them out of 15, they had won only one of their last 25 Tests against all opposition; they had lost 15 players with Test experience to Gatting's ill-conceived and ill-fated rebel tour of South Africa; they had lost Botham and Gower to time and the press box; they had lost the Ashes; and they had lost their self-respect.

West Indies	164 & 240	**England**	364 & 41–1
West Indies	199 & 239	England	288 & 120–5
West Indies	446 & 267–8d	England	358 & 191
England	260 & 154	**West Indies**	446

To everyone's surprise, it turned out to be an engrossing tour, a series that England would have squared with more luck. They started with a bang, the first game going England's way from the moment Devon Malcolm ran out Greenidge from long leg at 62–0. West Indies made only 102 more. Lamb (132), Larkins and Smith batted England into a commanding lead, which was turned into a stunning victory by the opening bowlers. Somehow Small, Malcolm, Fraser and Capel had out-bowled Patterson, Bishop, Marshall and Walsh. The muscular and tireless Malcolm twice got Richards, whose brooding features grew even grimmer at the unaccustomed indignity. The West Indies were used to dishing it out, not receiving it from one of their own, a man born in Kingston Town.

Between the first Test and the next, the Guyana Test was completely washed out, and England lost three one-day internationals and their momentum. So it was at Port-of-Spain in Trinidad a full month later that they awaited the expected backlash. England won a helpful toss and, with Richards missing, West Indies crashed to 29–5 before Logie's 98 took them to 199. Gooch and Larkins responded with an opening stand of 112, and the rest battled away to earn a lead of 89. It was soon knocked off by the openers, but explosive bowling from Malcolm, who took three wickets in four balls and showed great stamina in bowling 24 overs on the fourth day, meant that England would need 151 on the last day in a minimum of 83 overs. A theoretical minimum, that is, because although a side was 'obliged' to bowl 90 overs a day, there was no method of enforcement and, with neither side playing a spinner, in no day of the series was that number completed.

In fact in one hour only eight overs were bowled. Against Bishop, Ambrose and Walsh, 151 would be a tough target at the best of times but it was the less well known Ezra Moseley who struck the blow that almost certainly determined the series' outcome. It was a literal blow too, for he broke Gooch's hand with the score 37–1. Although Alec Stewart and Lamb doubled the score to get halfway there, the rain came for two hours, and when it ceased England needed 78 from 30 overs in ever worsening conditions against a side in a hurry neither to bowl nor to take prisoners. A Gooch might have steered England through, but an hour after the scheduled close, with England 120–5 from 33 overs, they called it a day as the Caribbean night descended and injury seemed more likely than victory.

With luck England would have been 2–0 up, and had they had Gooch, and the constantly-threatening Fraser, who was out with strained ribs, they might well have lost only one of the last two Tests, instead of both. Without them at Bridgetown Lamb surprised everyone by putting West Indies in, shown up as a mistake by 164 from the local hero Clyde Best. Lamb did his best to make amends with 119 in another battling stand with Smith, his sixth century against the most formidable bowling attack in the world. A Haynes hundred on the fourth day, his own delaying tactics in Trinidad replicated by Lamb here, left England with a day and a bit to bat. They were 15–3 overnight, Rob Bailey being given out caught behind off his hip, as Richards charged the umpire in an appeal – indeed a demand – of theatrical physicality. A moment later, according to Stewart, the non-striker, the umpire asked him if he thought it was out. Action like Richards' in later code-of-conduct years would probably have led to an outright ban. That England lasted into the last hour was due to courageous batting initially from Stewart and Russell, the professional nightwatchman, who stayed until the second new ball was taken after tea, and finally by Smith, but no one else could resist Ambrose for long, and his tremendous 8–45 squared the series.

In Antigua England finally gave best to the favourites, and were outplayed for the only time in the series. They were quite literally battered. Lamb played with a chipped elbow, the young Nasser Hussain made 35 and 34 in his second Test with a broken wrist, and Smith had a finger broken in what seemed – to Wisden's correspondent at least – to be a deliberate physical assault, unchecked by the umpires. No England batsman reached 50, and once Greenidge and Haynes had added 298 that was that. In the series Lamb was the only England batsman to score over 200 runs, reaching 390 runs at 55, better than any batsman on either side. Smith averaged 37, but the next best was 25. In the circumstances, though, the brave batting of Alec Stewart and Hussain was a bonus to bring back to England. Stewart may have been the manager's son, but nepotism played no part in his arrival. A cheerful, neat, crisp stroke-maker, whose self-confidence had been given a hard edge by his winters in Perth, he was also an improving wicketkeeper, though still not in the Russell class. The aggressive, driven Hussain, born in Madras of an English mother and an intensely supportive Indian Muslim father, himself a fiercely enthusiastic cricketer, was the first of a crop of young Asians to play for England. Most impressively of all, Fraser, Small and Malcolm took 47 wickets between them at an average of 26, the best performance by an England fast-bowling trio since 1981.

1990 New Zealand and India

With the unexpected encouragement of that tour, England took on New Zealand and India in the summer of 1990. They had learnt the previous year's lesson and played just 16 cricketers all summer, a mere 12 of them against India, a selection consistency that paid dividends. Gooch was restored to fitness, to captaincy and to imperious form.

New Zealand	208 & 59–2	England	345–9d
England	334 & 272–4	New Zealand	462–9d
England	435 & 158	New Zealand	249 & 230

Rain ruined the Trent Bridge Test. Hadlee bade farewell to his erstwhile county ground by dismissing Gooch with the first ball of the England innings, and took two more early wickets, but he was kept at bay by the young fresh-faced Michael Atherton, the Cambridge and Lancashire prodigy who had played the last two Tests the previous summer after completing university. Concentrating fiercely, he made 151 in his first Test innings as an opener. At Lord's, where a day-and-a-half's rain and a placid pitch ensured an otherwise featureless draw, England were for the first time faced by a knight on the cricket field. Sir Richard Hadlee had received the honour in the Queen's birthday honours list. It would have been fitting had he made a hundred, but, after a typically swashbuckling bombardment in which he reached 50 from 42 balls, he left to rapturous applause for 86.

The series was decided at Edgbaston, where New Zealand were to rue putting England in. Gooch and Atherton put on 170, Gooch going on to 154, and the tail wagged for once. After Malcolm's early burst, Hemmings, with 6–58, took his first five-wicket haul in a Test at the age of 41, his cheerful enthusiasm undiminished. Hadlee signed off with 5–53 as England pressed for runs, and New Zealand had eight and a half hours to survive. That they didn't was due to more fine bowling by Malcolm, 5–46, and England had won their first home series for five long years. Malcolm had come a long way since Dexter had thought he was called Malcolm Devon.

Next were India, and they brought hot dry weather with them, which made it a batsman's series. England were only once bowled out for under 500, India only once under 400. Again, one result would settle it.

England	653–4d & 272–4d	India	454 & 224
England	519 & 320–4d	India	432 & 343–6
India	606–9d	England	340 & 477–4

At Lord's, a few days after his 37th birthday, Graham Gooch was disappointed to lose the toss in what seemed perfect batting conditions. At the end of the second day he was looking rather more pleased, contemplating his innings of 333 and a total of 653–4, assisted by centuries from Lamb and Smith. The Indian manager Bishen Bedi had not been thrilled, to say the least, by Azharuddin's decision to put England in, but along with everyone else there he must have been entranced by his captain's batting on the Lord's Saturday when, after Shastri's hundred, he produced 'a rare exhibition of audacious, wristy stroke-play' that took him to a hundred from 88 balls, and India to 376–6. A collapse to Fraser next morning, though, left Kapil Dev with 24 to save the follow-on and Hirwani at the other end, a certified rabbit. There followed a wonderful cameo, surpassing even Botham's seven-ball innings in 1985. He blocked the first two balls from Hemmings, then drove each of the next four for huge sixes, unprecedented in a Test, to clear the deficit. Magnificent stuff, not least because the rabbit was shot out next ball. Although a draw seemed probable, Gooch rattled up another 123 from 113 balls, and England had seven hours to force a win. They didn't need them because India, infected by the intoxicating spirit of Azharuddin and Kapil Dev, batted as though they could win, and England needed only 62 overs to prove them wrong.

That Test produced 1603 runs at 4.7 an over. The second brought 1614. Gooch and Atherton both scored hundreds in their second successive opening stand of over 200, and Smith made another. Once again the Saturday was illuminated by Azharuddin's pyrotechnics, his 179 including 100 between lunch and tea, and the pace of the Indian innings again allowed England to try to force a win, Lamb the centurion this time. India had 92 overs to make 420, not out of the question given their batting, but rash strokes from his seniors left a 5ft 5in Bombay student to try to save the match. He was badly dropped from a caught and bowled chance to Hemmings when 10, but he knuckled down in company with Prabhakar, and saved the day from 183–6. In so doing, and wearing the old pads of his mentor Gavaskar, Sachin Tendulkar made his first Test century at the age of 17 years 112 days.

The third Test gave India their only real chance of a win, and for a while it looked possible. Shastri's 187 and Kapil Dev's typically forthright 110 took them past 600, and by lunch on the fourth day England had followed on. But Gooch and Atherton added 176 before both were out in the eighties, and Gower exhibited 'sublime stroke-play, unwavering determination and considerable stamina throughout the final day' in scoring 157* to put the game out of India's reach and win the series. Gower, still only 33, had been restored for the India series, and this innings cemented his hitherto uncertain place for Australia.

Batsmen gorged themselves in a gorgeous sunny series, with 4620 runs at an average of 57 runs per wicket. The summer as a whole continued the winter's revival, and became a genuine Indian Summer for Gooch, whose 1058 runs in 11 innings is still a Test record for an English season, despite his starting with a first ball duck in the opening game. The English batsmen gloried in the conditions, making 10 centuries as well as Gooch's triple – still the only time a batsman has made a triple and a single century in the same game. Atherton made 753 at 68 in his first full season, Smith 513 at 73, Gower 291 at 72, and Lamb 493 at 49. Malcolm and Fraser took 38 wickets between them at just under 30, and the ageless Hemmings, stout of heart and girth, 21 at 31. Russell's wicketkeeping continued to be immaculate.

1990–1 Australia

How would England's improved side measure up to the born-again Australians? At Brisbane they would have to try to do it without Gooch, who had a poisoned finger, and it led to a bad start from which they never recovered.

222

England	194 & 114	**Australia**	152 & 157–0
England	352 & 150	**Australia**	306 & 197–2
Australia	518 & 205	England	469–8d & 113–4
Australia	386 & 314–6d	England	229 & 335–5
England	244 & 182	**Australia**	307 & 120–1

In each of the first two Tests England led on first innings and capitulated in the second. In the first match on a damp and difficult pitch they caught brilliantly to secure a lead of 42, which might have been crucial in such a low-scoring game. When that lead had doubled with one wicket down on the second evening things were looking promising, but two wickets that night, and a grisly morning against Alderman, left Australia to coast home on a wicket growing easier by the minute. At Melbourne they again held a strong position on the fourth afternoon, when they led by 149 with only one wicket down, but once again the chance was squandered by a sudden collapse. Gower's hundred, and fifties from Larkins and Stewart, had taken England to 352, and Fraser's magnificent spell with the second new ball – he took 6–34 in 26 overs – abruptly ended Australia's hopes for a lead. With Gooch the disciplined Larkins scored another fifty. but no one else reached 10. The last six wickets fell for three runs in 12 overs, poor batting against superb bowling from the awkward 6ft 8in left-armer Bruce Reid. At 28–2 overnight, it appeared Australia would have their work cut out on the final day, but Geoff Marsh and David Boon batted serenely to victory.

Two-nil down seemed an irrecoverable position, but England put up an unexpectedly tough fight at Sydney after Australia had compiled 518. In reply Gooch cracked off with 59, Atherton made a long slow 105, but Gower an exquisite 123 – to Atherton at the other end 'it looked as though an ugly shot would have been an impossibility'. He and Stewart, who made 91, picked up the pace, and with the ball starting to turn Gooch made an enterprising declaration late on the fourth day. Hemmings and the talented but anarchic young left-armer Phil Tufnell, 17 years his junior, then spun Australia into some danger. The seventh wicket fell at 166, and had England wrapped up the last three wickets quickly they would have had about 50 overs to make, say, 230. The way Gooch and Gower charged off at seven an over at a target of 255 in 28 overs meant they would have tried, and Australia's spinners were decidedly worse than England's, but it wasn't to be.

At Adelaide a superlative first Test innings by Mark Waugh, displacing his elder twin – to whom he was alike in little but cricketing prowess – took Australia to 386. England's reply foundered after Gooch and Smith had added 126, and Border eventually set England 472 in a day and 45 minutes. Unexpectedly Gooch decided, lunching on the final day at 115–0, that the wicket was good enough to give it a go. He and Atherton raced past 200, Lamb added 50 at more than a run a minute, and Border started to get alarmed, declining to attack when England lost three quick wickets. So, after two Tests thrown away following a first innings lead, two Tests had been saved by gutsy recoveries. If England could just win the last Test… but no. From the heights of 191–2 before tea on the opening day, (Lamb 91), hostile bowling by McDermott (8–97) cut England down. Australia started poorly but took a lead of 63, then brought England back to reality by bowling them out more cheaply still the second time.

It had been a disheartening tour, emphasising, for all England's recovery after the 1989 defeat, that a substantial gulf had opened up between them and their opponents. Border, deliberately turning himself into Mr Nasty, had welded Australia into a much more smoothly functioning machine. Wisden asked whether England had lost the sense of national pride that Australia had regained. Gooch and Gower had made over 400 runs, at averages of 53 and 45, but the support was lacking, only Atherton of the others above 30. The batting was indeed deemed so weak that Russell, who in Stewart's view and that of most other judges was the best keeper in the world at the time – his leg-side stumping of Jones while standing up to Gladstone Small's pace in the third Test was astonishing – was sacrificed to strengthen it. Fraser took his 11 wickets at 28, and at little more than two runs an over, so his accuracy was missed when he was injured for two Tests. DeFreitas and Malcolm were the only others to take more than 10 wickets, at 31 and 41 respectively.

1991 West Indies

Viv Richards brought another strong West Indies team to England in 1991, with the customary phalanx of four fast bowlers. Would they batter England into submission again, or could the life that had flickered back into England's game in the West Indies be rekindled here? After the Australian defeat in the winter no one was optimistic.

England	198 & 252	West Indies	173 & 162
West Indies	419 & 12–2	England	354
England	300 & 211	**West Indies**	397 & 115–1
England	188 & 255	**West Indies**	292 & 157–3
England	419 & 146–5	West Indies	176 & 385

The first Test at Headingley was the hundredth between the sides. The game was played in damp, cold, overcast conditions, and Richards had no hesitation in putting England in. Thus two young batsmen were thrust in at the deep end straight away – Graeme Hick, the prolific broad-shouldered Zimbabwean who had waited patiently to become qualified, while piling up the runs at Worcester, and the boyishly immaculate Mark Ramprakash, who had made a fifty on his Middlesex debut when only 16. Hick failed, but Ramprakash impressed with two defiant innings and brilliant fielding. Batsmen struggled throughout. England's 198 was followed by West Indies' 173, but they slipped to 38–3 on a rain-affected third day. However Gooch, batting with an unwavering intensity of purpose and concentration in a innings that umpire Shepherd said was the best he had seen by an Englishman in Tests, found support from first Ramprakash, and then Pringle, to carry his bat for a monumental 154, an innings in which, by his own admission, the ball rarely hit the middle of the bat. In both innings West Indies batted with less discipline than England, and a three-wicket burst at 77–2 from the Glamorgan debutant seamer Steve Watkin made defeat inevitable. DeFreitas, Watkin and Pringle took 17–238 between them.

That unexpected win brought the series alive, and stung the West Indies into realising they had a fight on their hands. From the moment they finished the first day at Lord's at 317–3, they held the initiative throughout each of the next three Tests. England were saved there by the weather and Robin Smith, whose ability against top-class fast bowling was never better exemplified than in the 148* with which he rescued England from 84–5. He wasn't out in the first innings at Trent Bridge either, but in retrospect it seems odd that someone so accomplished against pace should be batting at No. 6. This time the tail didn't stay with him for long enough, and he was left 64*. Consistent batting gave West Indies a lead of 97, and only late resistance from 110–8, organised by DeFreitas, delayed the inevitable. Unfortunately Smith was absent injured at Edgbaston, where the game followed the same pattern. England batted poorly, West Indies took a lead of 104 despite six wickets for the talented but unreliable all-rounder Chris Lewis, then England slumped to 144–8. That seemed to be that, but Pringle and Lewis added 92, West Indies needed 152, and DeFreitas had three men out for 24. But Richards marched to the crease to join Hooper, and there was no reprieve for England.

Two-one down with the Oval game left, England brought back Smith, now recovered, Tufnell, Stewart for his first game as wicketkeeper, and Botham the grizzled old hero, now 35 but bowling well for Worcester. This time England's batting fired properly. Gooch and the Glamorgan left-hander Hugh Morris opened with 112, Smith made 109, and Stewart, Botham and Lewis added breezy contributions, Botham's innings ending with the bizarre 'leg-over' hit-wicket dismissal that caused such paroxysms of hilarity in the commentary box. Late on the third morning West Indies were sailing serenely on at 158–3, held together by Haynes. But Haynes could only watch in disbelief from the far end as the last seven batsmen went for 18, six to Tufnell for 3 runs in an inspired spell of 33 balls, in which he tossed the ball up and induced a form of mass suicide by grown men, three of them caught by Botham, who had lost none of his alertness at slip. In the follow-on West Indies fared better, with Richie Richardson leading the way with his second century of the summer. At 305–4 he and Richards had taken West Indies 62 ahead with nearly eight hours left, and England supporters were starting to twitch. But the hard-toiling David Lawrence, physically similar to the boxer of Frank Bruno, but as a bowler cast in the Malcolm mould, dismissed both of them on his way to 5–106, and England wanted 143. They wobbled at 80–4, but Stewart batted with reassuring verve, and Botham fittingly hit his only ball for four. This was Botham's first win over the West Indies at his 20th attempt, a measure of their total dominance during his career.

England	282 & 364–3d	Sri Lanka	224 & 285

The summer ended with another one-Test tour by the Sri Lankans. Stewart, playing again as a batsman only, made his first Test hundred to shore up England's jittery first innings, and DeFreitas' outstanding 7–70 gave England a lead. Gooch extended it to over 400 with a rapid 174, and Tufnell worked his way through stubborn Sri Lankan resistance on the last afternoon. The performance in 1991 of DeFreitas, lean and wiry, was a real bonus for England, his stamina and accuracy crucial in the prolonged absence of Fraser. He took 30 wickets at 19 in the six Tests, Tufnell 12 at 24 in his two, Pringle and Lawrence 12 and 14. With Malcolm misfiring, Lawrence seemed the natural replacement. With the bat Gooch and Smith were totally dominant. Gooch made 692 runs at 69, only once out for less than 29, his consistency and application deeply reassuring. Smith made 483 at 80, and looked top class against any bowler of pace. But until Stewart arrived there was a huge gap. Lamb, Atherton and Hick failed completely, averaging only 10 between them in 23 innings. At least Ramprakash, scoring between 19 and 27 in eight of his nine innings against the West Indies, showed admirable concentration, but he couldn't help conveying the impression of somehow still being a boy pitted against men. Ambrose led those men with 28 wickets at 20, Marshall 20 at 22.

1991–2 New Zealand

England arrived in New Zealand before the fifth World Cup down under, anxious to expunge a poor record against what used to be the weakest Test-playing country – they hadn't won a single Test against them in their last three series.

England	580–9d	New Zealand	312 & 264
England	203 & 321	New Zealand	142 & 214
England	305 & 359–7d	New Zealand	432–9d & 43–3

Gooch won the toss in all three games and the first at Christchurch provided a wonderful climax, a fascinating test of nerve between Tufnell and Martin Crowe. England's first innings dominance was begun by a second Stewart hundred, carried on by Lamb and Smith, two of four batsmen in the match to be out in the nineties, and completed by Dermot Reeve and Lewis. Tufnell then took four early wickets as New Zealand slipped to 91–5. Rescued by the belligerence of Patel (run out 99) and Cairns, they nevertheless had to follow-on 268 behind, with over eight hours left. Tufnell spun away, a strong breeze his ally, but New Zealand seemed safe at 211–3 soon after tea on the final day. The breakthrough came when Wright (another 99) charged the aggravating Tufnell and was stumped. Crowe then watched while Tufnell wreaked damage at the other end. The climax was an extraordinary moment. With the last pair together, exactly 10 minutes left and four runs to make England bat again – but no time for them to bat – Tufnell had everyone in to save the single. He tossed the ball up invitingly into the wind, Crowe saw the chance to end the torture and save the match with one stroke, came down the pitch, but only skied a catch to Pringle at mid-off. Victory by an innings and those four runs, ecstasy for England and Tufnell, whose figures were 46.1–25–47–7 of masterly left-arm spin.

A low-scoring match on a difficult pitch at Auckland was settled by the only two innings of real command. England recovered from 9–3 and 91–6 to 203 on the opening day. New Zealand got to 91–2 but superbly sustained hostility from Lewis (5–31) bowled them out for 142. England effectively won the match with aggressive batting on the third afternoon, Lamb ignoring the pitch's vagaries to belt a 33-ball fifty, outscoring even Gooch, who was on his way to 114. England's seamers there-after never lost their grip. Wellington produced a slow, low turner for the last Test. Hundreds by Stewart in the first innings and Lamb in the second were matched by Wright and Jones, but New Zealand couldn't score quickly enough against Tufnell and Hick, a presentable but occasional off-spinner, who bowled 140 overs between them, conceding fewer than two an over. Unfortunately the last hour of a dying game was notable only for the cry of agony as Lawrence crumpled in his run-up as if he had been shot: the sound, though, was the snap of his kneecap. It was a horribly freakish injury that would end the promising Test career of a genial and whole-hearted character.

Stewart and Lamb, restored to form, had been the pick of the batsmen, with aver-ages in the sixties, and there was much better middle-order support for them than in the West Indian summer. Tufnell's contribution was immense and Lewis looked like becoming a world-class all-rounder, not least because of his tigerish fielding. England won the one-day series 3–0 too, so seemed to have the right ingredients for the World Cup.

1991–2 The fifth World Cup

This was the first World Cup to take place in the southern hemisphere, the first in which each team played each other once in the preliminary phase, the first where white balls were used and coloured clothing worn, and the first – ironically, as the first three had all been in England – to be seriously and controversially disrupted by rain. The nonsensical rules that then applied when rain curtailed the innings of the side batting second led directly to Duckworth and Lewis. Those who scorn that method's complexity should recall what happened in this event.

Each side would play eight matches. England began by beating India by 9 runs in a day-night game in Perth, while four hours and over 3000 miles away in Auckland, New Zealand were beating Australia, confused by Crowe opening the bowling with his off–spinner Patel. In impressive form, England went on to beat West Indies, Australia, Sri Lanka and South Africa to qualify early with New Zealand, as well as bowling Pakistan out for 74 in a rain-ruined game without a result; Pakistan at this point were pitiful. Australia were slaughtered by eight wickets, led by a gleeful Botham with 4–31 and 53. The champions Australia were in deep trouble, having been beaten just as easily by South Africa by nine wickets. The last two places lay between them, South Africa and Pakistan. South Africa chased six an over in a 30-over game to beat India and qualify. Pakistan, who had started abysmally by beating only Zimbabwe in their first five matches, had to win their last three matches to get to the semi-finals. They did, and, by beating Australia on the way, displaced their chastened hosts.

The semi-final line-up was New Zealand v Pakistan in Auckland, followed by England v South Africa in Sydney. New Zealand had headed the qualifying table, and were expected to win here. Crowe's 91 took them to 262–7 but his innings ended with a pulled hamstring and he had to watch from the sidelines. Pakistan struggled to 140–4, needing an unlikely 123 in 15 overs. But the tall, young Inzamam-ul-Haq, cherub-faced and unperturbed by the crisis, strode in and struck 60 from 37 balls, and Pakistan had won with an over to spare.

The distances to be travelled, across the vastness of Australia and the Tasman Sea, brought the decision not to have over-flow days in case of rain. This had put the rain-revision rules under severe strain in the preliminary stage. They had bent for Pakistan, when in one match a target of 212 from 50 became 193 from 36. They bent further for England, when a target of 237 from 50 became 226 from 41. In each of these cases the beneficiaries were South Africa, though England did reach their total with a ball to spare. But in this semi-final the rules shattered completely, and it was South Africa who were broken. Wessels had put England in and after Hick's fine 83, and 18 from Donald's last over, the innings ended at 252–6 after only 45 of the 50 overs because South Africa had bowled far too slowly. South Africa were behind the clock, but stuck at it, and the target was 22 from 13 balls when the rain came – not once, but twice. The outcome? A target of 22 from one ball. The South Africans and the Sydney crowd – on their side since the Australians had been eliminated – were livid, England delighted but embarrassed. The floodlights were on, why couldn't the game continue? (This floodlight issue would give those in South Africa in 2004–5 a sense of déjà-vu.)

SEMI–FINALS			
New Zealand	262–7 (50)	**Pakistan**	264–6 (49)
England	252–6 (45)	South Africa	232–6 (43)
FINAL			
Pakistan	249–6 (50)	England	227 (49.2)

So on to Melbourne for the final, England's third and Pakistan's first. Imran, now 39, won the toss, batted and top-scored with 72 as Pakistan recovered from a poor start against the probing Pringle, 3–22 in his 10 overs, to reach 249–6. England suffered their own stuttering start, losing four for 69, but Fairbrother and Lamb added 72. However, with the target now 109 in 15 overs, Wasim Akram settled the match.

228

From round the wicket he first removed Lamb's off-bail with a ball that swung away extraordinarily, then comprehensively bowled Lewis first ball with one that did the exact opposite. Astonishing bowling with an old ball. Thereafter the tail could only scuff their way to 227. Pakistan had been inspired by Imran, the force of his personality driving on a young team. They had the best opening bowler in the tournament in Wasim Akram, and the best spinner in Mushtaq Ahmed, only 21, and they did it even without the injured Waqar Younis. The great irony was that, had it not rained after England had bowled Pakistan out in their qualifying game, the winners would probably not even have reached the final stage.

After England had qualified, they somehow lost impetus, losing dead matches to New Zealand and even to Zimbabwe, and looked increasingly jaded. Although disappointed at losing their third final, they had nevertheless beaten in the tournament every former winner. Their batting depended increasingly on the neat and nimble Lancastrian left-hander Neal Fairbrother. A rapid accumulator in the middle-order, he was the first of the one-day specialists. He averaged 57 and Alec Stewart 38. Stewart might with hindsight have opened, because Gooch lost his form and Botham only succeeded in that position twice. Botham, however, slower at the age of 36 but just as clever, was by far the most successful England bowler with 16 wickets at 19.

1992 Pakistan

A glowing Pakistan team arrived in England soon after winning the World Cup, for their first full tour here for 30 years. Without their great captain, who really had retired for the last time, they were at least strengthened by the return of Waqar Younis, back to restore his new ball pairing with Wasim Akram. It was an enthralling series.

Pakistan	446–4d	England	459–7
England	255 & 175	**Pakistan**	293 & 141–8
Pakistan	505–9d & 239–5	England	390
Pakistan	197 & 221	**England**	320 & 99–4
England	207 & 174	**Pakistan**	380 & 5–0

Apart from the first and third Tests, where the bat dominated, this was a series full of fine fast bowling, collapses and recoveries, and again one tinged with controversy. The first at Edgbaston turned into a first innings contest over three days, after rain had wiped out the first two. Javed Miandad and Salim Malik added 322, Stewart and Smith 237. Stewart showed he had the self-discipline as well as the strokes in making 190 from the opening position in under six hours. At Lord's though the conditions were very different, and moreover Wasim had returned from an injury that had kept him out at Edgbaston. Injuries past and present figured crucially at Lord's – the recovery of Waqar and Wasim, and the breakdown of Botham and DeFreitas.

At Lord's Gooch and Stewart cruised to 123 in conditions helpful to the bowlers. Not for the first time, though, Waqar and Wasim bowled better with the old ball than the new, and by the end of the series we would be grappling with the mystery of reverse swing. This time Waqar scythed through the middle order, and England stumbled to 255. At 225–3 Pakistan looked set for a big lead, but three key wickets in 13 balls by Malcolm turned it only into a useful one, of 38. England cleared the arrears on the second evening before losing Gooch, and next morning Stewart again played immaculately. However a worrying collapse to Mushtaq was turned into a horrific one by Wasim, who took the last three wickets in four balls. Pakistan needed only 141, and England were down to just three bowlers – Malcolm, Lewis and the young Sussex leg-spinner Ian Salisbury, the first to play for England for 21 long years. But a startling collapse ensued, three wickets to Lewis, three to Salisbury, certainly not over-awed, and Pakistan were 95–8 when Waqar joined Wasim. For all their formidable bowling that summer, it was their stand with the bat on the Sunday evening at Lord's that turned the series. With neither DeFreitas' accuracy nor Botham's inspiration to turn to, Gooch had to rely on a tiring trio, and they couldn't make the breakthrough that would have brought in No. 11, whose season's batting average was 2. 'Rarely,' said Wisden, 'can a Test crowd have been through so many emotions in a single day's play.'

At Old Trafford an excellent wicket and a day lost to rain ensured no result once England averted the follow-on. Aamir Sohail's 205 was responsible for Pakistan passing 500; Gooch and Gower, Lewis and Salisbury for saving the follow-on. Gower marked his return, and his 115th Test, a record for England, with a typically charming 73. Unfortunately the inconsequential latter stages were marred by a dispute between Aqib Javed, Miandad and umpire Roy Palmer, who had warned Aqib for intimidatory bowling at No. 11, Malcolm, a rabbit's rabbit. (It could actually have been construed as wise advice – Aqib bowled Malcolm next over with a slow yorker.) At Headingley, on a wicket that suited them, England's faster bowlers got in the groove, led by a debutant, Neil Mallender from Somerset. Only Salim Malik stayed any time on the first day, and he finished with 82* out of 197. At the end of the second day England had passed it with just one wicket down, Atherton for 76, and Gooch leading them on to 270–1 in an innings of 135. England's last nine wickets fell for 50. Again Salim held Pakistan together with 84*, but Mallender took his debut match tally to eight with 5–50, and England hobbled to victory against a background of more umpiring aggravation, the Pakistanis complaining among other things that Gooch should have been given run out by umpire Ken Palmer (no relation to Roy). The replay confirmed their view.

England's victory set up an enticing finale at the Oval with the series 1–1. England's hopes were dashed on the first day in the all-too-familiar fashion, when 182–3 became 207 all out, five of them to Wasim Akram. Malcolm tried his best on his latest return, but Pakistan batted right down the order to secure a big lead. That lead proved enough after Waqar had wiped out the top four, leaving Smith to wage a lone battle with 84*. Pakistan had won 2–1. A fortnight later, a notorious ball change in the fourth Texaco Cup match led to the ball-tampering allegations that emerged in the press, and led to the train of events that wasn't halted until the Sarfraz v Lamb trial described in Chapter 26.

Reverse swing

Irrespective of whether their ascendancy was achieved with any sleight of hand (or nail or bottle top), Waqar and Wasim, as Imran before them, had become absolute masters of the new reverse swing phenomenon, in which an old ball can be somehow made to swing in the opposite direction to that taken by a new ball, when held in the same orientation. It was mystifying, but it's one thing to get that unnatural swing, quite another to propel it at high speed at a length full enough to destroy a batsman's stumps or toes. Batsmen when set had a chance, but not new arrivals at the wicket. Atherton described one ball to Pringle that seemed to swing both ways in the air, the batsman adamant that no one could have played it. In the series Wasim and Waqar took 43 wickets between them at 24 apiece, 25 of them bowled or lbw. For England Stewart averaged 56, Gooch 48 and Smith 44, but the support was virtually non-existent. No England bowler took more than 13 wickets. Mallender was best, with 10 at 21, but he was of that sad group of England bowlers who flare into prominence in their first Test but then disappear – he didn't play another.

So England, after years of developing their technique to deal with a fusillade of short-pitched bowling, had been undone by bowlers propelling the ball to a full length, and scarcely bowling bouncers at all. Most pundits were enthralled to be watching a series in which the ball wasn't constantly pitching halfway down the wicket, but were puzzled. How had they managed to swing an old ball so much? It's time to look at the tools of the cricketer's trade, those implements of pleasure and pain.

CHAPTER 26

Implements of
Pleasure and Pain

Body language study No. 1. A thunderous Greg Chappell with Dennis Lillee's experimental aluminium bat, to which Mike Brearley has successfully objected, Perth, December 1979.

This thing here, which looks like a wooden club, is actually several pieces of particular wood cunningly put together in a certain way so that the whole thing is sprung, like a dance floor. It's for hitting cricket balls with. If you get it right, the cricket ball will travel 200 yards in four seconds, and all you've done is to give it a knock like knocking the top off a bottle of stout, and it makes a noise like a trout taking a fly.

TOM STOPPARD, *The Real Thing*

At the core of a complex game is the meeting of bat and ball. One of cricket's great pleasures is that its implements are so beautiful. The smell of a lightly-oiled bat is heavenly. So is that of a ball once it has lost its factory lacquer, as is the feel of both bat and ball in the hands, which seems to have a direct link to the memory of pleasure. The composition of both had essentially been settled by the time Test cricket had begun. But the beauty of bat and ball, like that of nature, disguises a Darwinian struggle for supremacy.

The bat

The business part of the bat is cut from the wood of the cricket bat willow, *Salix Alba Caerulea*, which is ideally harvested after 15–20 years. A 52-inch circumference willow should yield 30–36 blades, cut to shape, shaved, and pressed to remove moisture and harden them. Spectators huddling together in the gloom, whether at Old Trafford or New Milton, have often puzzled as to how the game could conceivably come to have been invented in the dank English climate. The willow stands of Essex perhaps give one answer – nowhere else but in England, and at Great Leighs in particular, grows the perfect cricket bat tree. The right willow may not quite propel the ball Stoppard's 200 yards, but nothing else gives it that trout-taking sound, nor the sweet sensation in the hands as the ball leaves the middle of the perfect bat.

Since the 1850s, into that blade has been spliced a handle made of flexible Manau cane, originally from the jungles of Sumatra before Indonesia introduced an export ban in the 1980s, with three rubber strips inserted to provide greater shock absorption. One or more rubber grips are rolled onto the handle, and in principle rubber is the only material other than wood in the bat. In fact, until recently, all the components of the bat came from trees. Not that the early lawmakers felt a need to specify that, nor did anyone until the moment Denis Lillee was inspired by the sight of a metal staircase balustrade to construct one made of aluminium. His notorious entry onto the field at Perth with the 'ComBat' in the England v Australia Test at Perth in late 1979 led to a hasty revision of the Laws. Now 'the blade of the bat shall be made of wood', though it can be covered with material that is no thicker than one 16th of an inch for 'strengthening, protection or repair'. The components of this material are not constrained by the Laws as they now stand, so the graphite film that coats the back of Ricky Ponting's bat is in theory allowable. The bat shall be not more than four and a quarter inches wide, nor shall the whole bat be longer than 38 inches; most are around 33. From the 19th century until recently no one has tried to exceed the width limit of four and a quarter inches, set hurriedly in 1771 after 'Shock' White played with a bat that was wicket-wide. Interestingly, though, questions were raised over the width of some bats after the 2003 World Cup.

Once in the hands of an expert, there's not a lot you can do to improve a cricket bat, if it's well balanced and the willow is top grade. The bats used now would be instantly recognisable to anyone playing immediately after World War 2. They would be heavier, ranging now from 2 lb 8 oz to a little over 3 lb, whereas Bradman and

Compton typically used bats of around 2 lb 4 oz. This weight increase has been a trend that began in the 1970s, and only Azharuddin of top Test batsmen since then has used a really light bat. Glenn Turner used a bat of 3 lb 5 oz, arguing that its weight ensured he brought it down straight – provided the pick-up was straight, of course. Guardsman Gooch used a bat of similar weight, augmented in his case by the weight of extra rubber grips, and took no risks with the pick-up by standing with the bat ready-raised. This bat-aloft approach had been pioneered in the modern era by Tony Greig, a very tall man vulnerable to yorkers early on. He and Gooch ignored the frowns of their contemporary critics: actually the bat-raised stance seems to have been common a century earlier. Of modern batsmen Sachin Tendulkar, small of stature but immensely strong, also uses a bat weighing around 3 lb.

Handles are marginally different, now shaped to form an oval at the bottom to steady the bottom hand's grip. Weight distribution has been altered in recent years by various means since the 1970s – sloping shoulders, thicker edges, oval depressions scooped out of the back, even holes drilled through – but most bats have settled back into the familiar pattern, with really only the thicker edges and sharper 'V' of the back to distinguish them from Hutton's and Compton's. The only major difference at top level is that many top cricketers have blades that have been much more lightly pressed: it's claimed that the ball goes more sweetly, but the blades don't last – not an issue for sponsored players. There is no weight limitation in the Laws: a proposal to limit it to 2lb 12oz in 1988 was rejected by the ICC. A recent innovation that caused concern was that of removing some of the blade's wood and replacing it with cork, itself of course wood bark, to offset the weight of a heavier blade. That was specifically banned by an ICC cricket committee meeting in May 2005, which ordained:

1 that the dimensions of the bat should remain the same;
2 that the bat should have a conventional shape;
3 that the splice and handle be clearly defined;
4 that the blade of the bat should be made of a single piece of solid wood;
5 that the practice of injecting substances such as cork is to be illegal;
6 that any cover should be used to protect, strengthen and repair the bat and not improve the striking power of the bat;
7 that the bat should remain the colour of natural wood.

The ball

> 'Take worsted and corke scolded in water; take one inch square of the hardest corke dry, then thin squares one eighth inch thick wound round with four cords worsted, then weges – thin corke to make the round, fasen off and hammer now.'

Little had changed in ball-making, when the ball-maker Thomas Twort jotted this summary in his notebook in or before 1853, since the Duke family and others regularised ball manufacture in the previous century. Little has changed since. The ball is still made of cork layers, usually interleaved with quilted wool, wound round a central cork block, covered with leather and dyed red (now with a white variant, of course). Its two hemispheres are stitched together with a seam of six stitches, the outer two pairs thicker than the inner pair, made up of strands of flax, waxed and twisted together. The ball has changed even less than the bat in the last 200 years. It does have a weight limitation, between $5\frac{1}{2}$ and $5\frac{3}{4}$ oz, as well as a size constraint, within $8\frac{13}{16}$ and 9 oz (no metric intrusion here). The inherent variation in these figures seems sufficiently small to have never been an issue.

Apart from the recent one of colour, the prime variation in the ball's natural state comes from the seam – the number of stitches composing it, and how much it stands out from the ball's leather surface. The more stitches in the seam, and the prouder it stands, the more help it provides to seam bowlers. There has never been legislation about the seam. As the Wisden editor Norman Preston discovered in 1964, counties had 'recently been asking for more threads in the seam'. In 1989, concerned that a 15-strand seam, standing 0.9 mm from the ball's surface, was giving too much help to humdrum medium-pace bowlers, the TCCB decided to reduce the strands to nine and the seam's height to 0.7 mm. This immediately shifted the balance of advantage between bat and ball. In 1989 the total bonus points awarded in the county championship were 828 for batting, 1141 for bowling. In 1990 – admittedly a dry summer – the balance shifted to 1048/909 in favour of batting, and there were more centuries than in any previous season. Spinners as a consequence bowled more than 30 per cent more overs in 1990 than they had in 1989. This was at a time when four bonus points were available for both batting and bowling. That temporary shift to the spinners was not maintained, sadly.

The ball in use in first-class cricket in England in 2005 was manufactured by Dukes, a long-standing family firm, now taken over but still based in Kent, whose progenitor was a 17th-century bailiff to Lord Lisle at Penshurst. Its ball now differs from the majority by being harder, a recent development achieved by omitting the quilting between the layers of cork. There is no doubt that more batsmen hit the ball further than was the case after the war. In those more decorous days the ball stayed largely on the floor and – as old players would say – you still only got four if you hit it a mile. But the prevalence now for lofted shots has led to demand for heavier bats that can carry hits and mishits alike further. Heavier bats led to a demand for balls that don't lose their hardness, which has led to more finger injuries among fielders and fewer overs from the spinners captains would employ when the ball softened.

Changing the state of the ball

In the battle with the bat and its wielder, a bowler can spin the ball from the turf and, since swing was mastered in the early years of the twentieth century, change its direction through the air. Until the 1980s swing was achieved by polishing one side so it was shinier than the other, and delivering the ball with the shiny side facing away from the desired direction of swing. For this you need a newer ball, for once the bat has been at it the ball is less easy to swing. (The white ball, incidentally, is reputed to swing earlier but get grubbier sooner.) The shine can be maintained by manipulating the ball's surface with sweat and spit, but using Vaseline, sun cream, or hair oil – Cardus's 'unguents' – is not allowed. Bishen Bedi accused John Lever of using Vaseline from a gauze strip, stuck on his forehead to prevent sweat running into his eyes, in the 1976–7 series.

That was to help natural swing. But the phenomenon of reverse swing was perfected at the end of that decade by the Pakistani fast bowlers, who were able to swing an old ball in the opposite direction, sometimes prodigiously. To do this, you need a ball heavier on one side of the seam than the other, a weight difference achieved by wetting one side only. The effect can be exaggerated illegally by roughing up the other side: gouging the ball to break up its surface and picking apart the quarter seam. The two quarter seams, set a quarter rotation apart on opposite sides of the ball, are barely visible when it's new, but can open up on a battered old ball – especially with human help. Lifting the main seam, practised covertly since the game began, is illegal too, of course. Imran Khan, the chief exponent of reverse swing, somewhat implausibly admitted illegal tampering only once, in 1981, but Don Oslear was convinced he had done it more often: notably in an astounding spell of 6–6 in a Sussex game in 1983 with a ball 'scratched and torn, with pieces of leather ripped out… and a triangle of leather pulled up… by which the ball could be suspended'.

The hard-fought Pakistan v England series in 1992 was made especially enthralling by a series of sudden collapses, largely by English batsmen, from positions of strength. Typically Wasim Akram or Waqar Younis, or both, would reverse swing the old ball at a full length to such a startling extent that incoming batsmen were bowled or lbw before they had got their sea legs. What was particularly crippling – sometimes literally – was the pace at which it swung, and the fact that it did so in the last few yards. Normally exaggerated swing could only be achieved by a newer ball and at a lesser pace. Wasim and Waqar were brilliant exponents of this, both with a lower arm than the textbook recommended, and with Waqar by holding the ball in his palm like a baseball pitcher. They achieved their deadly delayed swing because the heavy-side bias comes into effect only as the ball slows below a critical speed in its last moments – and a batsman has perhaps just a 10th of a second to adjust, heavy bat and all. By the 2005 series English bowlers too had become expert, as slow-motion examples and explanations of the phenomenon abounded.

The aftermath of the 1992 series

Cricketers have always been suspicious of something that others can do to perfection and they can't. So it was in 1992. After the Test series, which Pakistan won 2–1, the one-day series resumed. In the rain-delayed fourth match at Lord's, Allan Lamb noticed while batting that one side of the ball was unusually damaged. He pointed it out to umpires John Hampshire and Ken Palmer, who changed the ball during the lunch interval. So far so good, but what happened next enraged the English, notably Lamb and Botham. The match referee Deryck Murray insisted on changing the wording of the announcement so that instead of the change taking place under the then Law 42 (5), Changing the Condition of the Ball, it was because it 'went out of shape'. Botham leaked this wording change to the press, and Lamb spilt the beans to the Daily Mirror, which published it with relish.

The upshot was that Lamb was upbraided by the TCCB – fair enough, for his contract with them didn't allow him to write without permission – and eventually fined the substantial sum of £5000. Later that day a sub-committee of the TCCB, which had admittedly got itself into an administrative tangle, gave Surrey a suspended fine of just £1000 for ball-tampering in the previous year in four separate matches, in three of which Waqar had been playing. Surrey had actually been warned in 1991 of the 'severe consequences' if they transgressed again. To the layman, the disparity of sentence between the whistle-blower and the offender seemed entirely against natural justice. What message did it give to umpires and players?

The accusation that the TCCB was intent on covering up what really happened was strengthened later when Sarfraz Narwaz took Lamb to court for libel. Lamb had said that Sarfraz once told his Nottinghamshire team-mates how to damage one side of the ball to accentuate reverse swing. As the case neared, Lamb's lawyers attempted to subpoena the TCCB to release the ball in question and the umpires' report. This they refused to do, and the case went ahead without them. Nevertheless enough damning evidence emerged, notably in over 50 filmed instances of ball manipulation by the Pakistanis in Tests, that Sarfraz dropped the case. Despite – perhaps because of – the TCCB's stalling, more information about ball-tampering emerged during the court case than had ever done before. Such is often the way with cover-ups.

Although many old cricketers had been aware of puzzling occasional instances of reverse swing, until it was (re)discovered and perfected in Pakistan it was little understood. Their opening bowlers – first Sarfraz and Imran to Northamptonshire and Sussex, then Waqar and Wasim to Surrey and Lancashire – brought the idea with them. It's no coincidence that Surrey and Lancashire were the counties most often accused of ball-tampering at the beginning of the 1990s, and Surrey indeed forfeited eight points in the championship in 2005 in a more recent recurrence. The misdemeanour persists, so great can be the benefit (although suitably in Surrey's case the eight points docked were greater than the margin by which they were eventually relegated). But the Laws state that the umpires shall take possession of the ball at the fall of each wicket, so if they're observant any transgression seems certain to be discovered. Cupidity and stupidity can be a fatal combination.

Protection

If the implements are inherently attractive, the accoutrements are not. When cricket started again post-war its batsmen wore pads, gloves and abdominal protector – the so-called 'box', a word whose origins in this context remain elusive. Even thigh pads were not universally used when cricket restarted in 1946. In England a peaked cap, more rarely a floppy hat, protected cricketers from the sun. That's all. But the bouncer bombardments of the 1970s brought a sober reassessment of risk. Although Patsy Hendren's wife had fashioned a home-made helmet for him to use against Larwood and Voce in the 1930s, it wasn't until Mike Brearley adopted a curious reinforced skullcap under his cap in the 1970s that the helmet was seen again on the cricket field. The Australians scoffed until they found themselves in the firing line. In 1978 Dennis Amiss pioneered the use of a fibreglass helmet in England.

At that time, predictably, many old batsmen and commentators scorned the use of the helmet. John Woodcock, editor of the 1981 Wisden, loathed them: 'They reduce the batsmen… to wretched anonymity. I find it sartorially and aesthetically an objectionable trend… an unsightly adjunct to an increasingly dangerous game.' In their selective memory, once the Bodyline tour of 1932–3 was over, few batsmen had been hit, and certainly not the best. It wasn't quite so: Len Hutton had been felled in South Africa in 1938, Compton and Crapp as we've seen in 1948, Jim Laker in 1953–4, Peter Richardson in 1956, and this is just a selection of those reported in Wisden. Lindwall and Miller didn't spare the bouncer, nor did Hall and Griffith and their West Indian successors. If Nari Contractor had died after Griffith had fractured his skull in 1962, as he so nearly did, perhaps the helmet would have come sooner. But Packer's viciously competitive World Series, which led to such a fusillade of bouncers, forced batsmen to start wearing helmets, and their design swiftly improved. The writing was on the wall when Ian Botham, the most macho of English batsmen, decided to wear a helmet, even though Viv Richards still loftily disdained one. And of course, once helmets were *de rigueur*, batsmen were more inclined to be hit because they felt safer when hooking.

The use of helmets naturally spread to close fielders. Billy Griffith in recodifying the Laws considered banning them for fielders, but legal concerns prevailed. In 1984 Chris Tavaré wore a forearm guard while batting for the first time, so in the present day batsmen usually have chest, arm, hands, crotch and legs protected. The coloured clothing effectively imposed on England after the Packer revolution began has at least brought with it numbers and names, something that might have been tried earlier to help the spectator: Woodcock's 'wretched anonymity' had applied to those in white too, to the watching majority if not to aficionados.

So a time-travelling spectator, plucked from 1946 to watch a day-night one-day match in 2005, would at first happen on a strange scene. While the grass is still green, the familiar colours have been transformed like some negative image. Dark clad umpires walk out onto a field where the pitch, still – blessed relief – 22 yards, is book-ended by black stumps, framed by black sightscreens, and surrounded by a circle of white dots. Fielders arrive in coloured clothing with names and numbers on their backs, followed by helmeted and multiply-padded batsmen. The bowlers use a white ball, gratifyingly more easy to see than the old dark red. The bowling at least is familiar: despite the comparative paucity of spinners, each side will usually play one or two slower bowlers, even though none is a wrist-spinner. The batting is audacious, the ball aloft more often than it ever used to be. The fielding – diving, sliding, stopping, catching, throwing – is breathtaking. With luck, the same sun shines, but it's augmented by floodlights even in mid-afternoon.

But at the heart of it all, where poor players still strut and fret, bat and ball still meet with the sound of a trout taking a fly.

CHAPTER 27

County Cricket –
Life Support

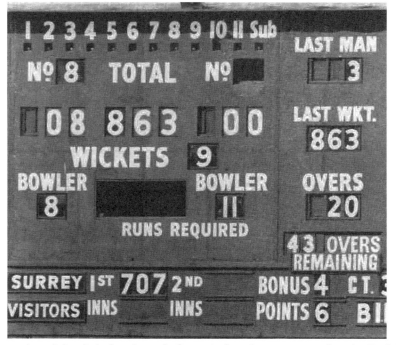

The scoreboard shortly before the end of an early four-day county match at the Oval, May 1990. Neil Fairbrother had made 366 for Lancashire after Ian Greig's 291 for Surrey.

Cricket, to maintain its hold on the national character, must be eager, quick and full of action. Today it is the reverse… Fifty per cent of the matches are drawn, and the game itself, becoming listless and dull, is bound to suffer.

A. G. STEEL, Wisden, 1900

The 1992 season of Waqar and Wasim was the last in which three-day county cricket was played. Depending on your viewpoint, argued over by E. W. Swanton and Alan Lee in the pages of the 1993 Wisden, it was either a necessary change, to fit potential England players better for the different timing and rigours of five-day Tests, or another capitulation to Mammon that would end the charm of county cricket as we knew it. Or both. We left county cricket in Chapter 11 in the 1970s, thriving again after a dangerously rocky period, due to an injection of one-day cricket, foreign imports and a still small but increasing quantity of money from Tests.

Financing county cricket

That Test money would be increasingly crucial to counties' survival. In 1950 their income from members' subscriptions and match days was typically around 90 per cent of the total, very much as it had been in 1930. In 1960 it was down to about 80 per cent as county attendances declined and Test match income (including television money) went up. That Test effect continued to increase in the 1960s and by 1970 its proportion had slipped further to around 65 per cent, despite the Sunday League's arrival in 1969, which gave a temporary boost to gate receipts. At that point three- and one-day income was neck-and-neck. But it was the 1970s that brought the most marked shift. By the end of the decade, one-day cricket provided two to three times as much income as three-day, depending on whether a county had enjoyed a Cup run, but even that was now being dwarfed by soaring TCCB, corporate hospitality and advertising revenue. By 1980 membership and match income had declined to about 25 per cent of a county's total. By 1990 it was down to 20 per cent; by 2000 it had sunk to 10 per cent.

Of that 10 per cent in 2000, gate money accounted for just 3 per cent – is it even worth charging and manning for admission to county games? Moreover, one-day cricket had lost its initial appeal. Unless a side had a run in either of the Cups, attendances had halved for one-day cricket as well as for three-day in the 30 years since the one-day league's first flush, a time when Old Trafford saw the ground packed and gates shut for a crucial Sunday League game. A new century was ready for a new format, and cricket found it in Twenty20, building on the attraction of day-night matches. Whether it, too, will lose the appeal that saw 20 000 sell-outs at Lord's and the Oval in 2004 and 2005 will be discussed in the final chapter.

Meanwhile, Test and one-day international cricket maintained and even increased its support in England. Whereas from the 1930s to the 1970s Test match income fluctuated wildly with the varied degree of attraction of the touring team, that effect gradually reduced. As the originally weaker countries gained strength at England's expense, support for a poorer performing Test side might have been expected to fall away, whereas in fact it has strengthened. In 1983, Wisden's editor despaired of the future of Test cricket, imagining that one-day internationals would 'drive [it] out as the grey squirrel did the red'. But despite wall-to-wall television coverage, Test and one-day international attendances have become consistently strong – except for the clearly weaker countries in the early 2000s, Bangladesh and Zimbabwe. Corporate hospitality, sustained by a time of strong economic performance, has had a lot to do with it, and contributed to extra income from price increases. Typically in 1980 for a Test match, across five days 60 000 spectators would pay on average just under £5 each; in 1990 the same number would pay £10, in 2000 £20, and in 2005 – admittedly a crucial Ashes summer – it peaked at over £50, increases way above the rate of inflation. For one-day internationals, supposedly becoming too frequent and boring, the increase has been just as sharp, with no sign of a fall-off in sales of England matches.

Thus the money coming into the game to buttress the ailing counties has continued to increase. For years, the opacity of the TCCB made it difficult to analyse its financial position, but the ECB that replaced it was more open. In the 2000 Wisden, Stephen Fay was able to analyse its first year of operation, 1998. Its annual turnover was £50 million, and of cricket as whole in England £88 million. That was very much the same as Manchester United's: a salutary reminder of cricket's position in relation to football. Cricket equates to just a single club, albeit the biggest one, of the 20-strong Premier League, itself just the visible part of professional soccer's iceberg. Of the ECB's revenue 40 per cent came from broadcasting, 26 per cent from ticket sales, 21 per cent from sponsorship. Of the ECB's £50 million, £28 million was circulated to subsidise the 18 first-class counties, the MCC and the Minor Counties, an increase in 1998 of 15 per cent for the third successive year, largely courtesy of BSkyB, cricket's major paymaster in the new era of satellite television. The average county's share was £1.2 million, which for 10 counties was more than half of their income.

The distribution of largesse is often, and rightly, described as propping up a county cricket system that would otherwise collapse completely. But it has had one important effect, the relevance of which is notable when cricket is compared with football, its unutterably richer rival. Since the onset of the 20-strong Premier League, that game at top level has been skewed to such an extent that only perhaps four clubs at the start of the 2005–6 season have a realistic chance of the championship. In 2004–5 the top three clubs reached 95, 83 and 77 points respectively, the fourth 61. Thus 17 of 20 teams scored less than two-thirds of Chelsea's winning tally. The feather-bedding of county cricket, which doesn't allow the rich clubs – principally those with the Test grounds – to pull away into an elite, has in practice led to a much more competitive season. At the midway point of the 2005 summer, in the first division of the four-day championship the points for a single win covered the top seven sides of nine, and yet one of those (in 2005, if not in 2006) would be relegated. An amazing contrast to football. Moreover, a relegated team still stood a good chance both of promotion next season and of staying up. Twenty years ago only half a dozen sides had something to play for in mid-season, whereas in 2005 – even without relegation from division two – 17 sides out of 18 did.

More bonus points, fewer results

This continuing competitiveness is perhaps one of the reasons why county championship cricket has been able to retain a following. Its death has been foretold many times since the 1950s, and increasingly frequent tinkering with the format has resulted. From 1946 to 1968 the number of matches in a season fluctuated from 26 to 28–32, dropping to 24 when the Sunday League began. Thereafter it oscillated between 20 and 24 until 1993. When cricket began again in 1946 there were just 12 points for a win, plus four for a first innings lead in a lost or drawn game. Until 1968, when bonus points for runs and wickets in the first 85 overs of the first innings came in, wins were almost everything. Only five times in this 23-year period did the side winning the championship not have more wins than anybody else (and then they had the same number as the side finishing second). Most of a county's points came from wins, and roughly 60 per cent of games came to a decision. However, the chart below shows what happened after bonus points came in.

Period	% matches won	% points from wins	Scoring
1946–50	64	80	win 12, 1st inns lead 4 if not won
1951–6	59		
1957–60	62		1st inns lead 2, + 2 if scored faster
1961–7	55		
1968–73	48	30	win 10 + bonus pts in 1st 85 overs
1974–6	60	35	bonus pts in 1st 100 overs, max 8 200 over limit on 1st 2 inns
1977–80	46	36	win 12
1981–4	49	40	win 16 + overs limit ends in 1982
1985–7	43	40	
1988–92	53	45	hybrid of 16 three- and 6 four-day
1993–5	74	52	4-day throughout
1996–8	65	44	win 16 draw 3
1999	67	32	win 12 draw 4
2000–2	58	34	2 divisions
2003–5	58	36	win 14 draw 4

Bonus points arrived in 1968, the same year that instant qualification for one foreign player was first allowed, to attempt to enliven county cricket. An immediate effect was that fewer than half the matches came to a decision, and the points gained from a win plummeted to only 30 per cent of the total. This had a big skewing effect. In its first year Kent had 120 points from 12 wins, plus 136 bonus points, only to be beaten by 14 points (more than one win) by Yorkshire, who had only 11 wins, 110 points, but a massive 160 bonus points to go with them – nearly 60 per cent of their total. As we saw in Chapter 11, from 1952–67 only four sides won the championship in 16 years. Bonus points contributed to the levelling process brought about by foreign imports, and a different county won the championship each year and the tournament became much more exciting as a result. In 1977 the championship went to its last day with three sides contesting the title, and it ended in a tie. All three had nine wins, and more bonus points than points for wins. This levelling certainly increased interest: whether bonus points in themselves made more exciting watching is much more questionable.

The table on the previous page shows that bonus points exacted a further price: fewer results in county cricket. From 1946–67, around 60 per cent of county matches ended in a result. In 1968–73, this figure had dropped to below half. Bonus points made winning less crucial. Before 1967, around 80 per cent of a county's points came from wins. Afterwards this fell dramatically to just 30 per cent, although increasing the points for a win inched it upwards. In 1974, in an attempt to produce more results, a 100-over first innings limit was brought in, but despite increasing percentage results to 60 per cent it was disliked and dropped in 1981.

In 1983 there were the first discussions of four-day cricket in Wisden's editorials, and two divisions were discussed in 1984. In 1987 its editor, wanting to encourage attacking bowling, suggested bonus points for bowling only. This would probably only have encouraged sides to create even more 'result' wickets, which is what hit the headlines next. Essex notoriously lost the title to Worcestershire in 1988, despite winning more matches, because they were deducted a swingeing 25 points for a poor pitch at Southend, a ground theoretically outside their control. Worcestershire had been lucky to escape such a fine themselves.

County cricket was increasingly caricatured as a one-innings match for bonus points over the first two days, followed by a one-day thrash with relaxed bowling in the third innings – getting the poor spinners on to raise the over rate and avoid a fine – on the last. In 1987 the Palmer report proposed a championship consisting of 16 three-day matches and 8 of four days; the counties agreed to 16 and 6. It brought immediate dividends in terms of results. In the last three years in which there was just three-day cricket, 1985–7, 43 per cent of matches brought results. In the mixed 16/6 period, the average shot up to over half. That was despite 1990, when a dry summer coincided with the abandonment of the Reader ball, whose 15-strand seam had encouraged seamers to the expense of swing and spin purveyors.

The pressure for a complete move to four-day matches started to become overwhelming. As well as generating more results, ran the argument, it would give English batsmen more time at the crease to build an innings and so compete more effectively with their overseas counterparts, reared on longer games, at a time when the Test side was in a poor state. For E. W. Swanton, in the 1993 Wisden debate, it would encourage 'workaday grimness', and slower, duller cricket. He feared that of the 66 county grounds played on in 1992 at least 20 would disappear. (In fact the run rate per 100 balls has gone up from 52 in the last days of solely three-day cricket to over 58 in 2002–4, although over rates have deteriorated; 20 grounds have certainly gone.) Swanton was supported by Wisden's then editor, Matthew Engel, who called the four-day game 'much admired by those who sit in offices, much disliked by those who still go and watch it'.

Four-day cricket, more results…

In the first three years of four-day cricket, the proportion of results leapt to 74 per cent. Compared with 42 per cent before the mixed experiment this was thus a resounding success. The proportion of points due to wins was over half for the first time since bonus points began. But by 1997 a feeling had grown up that sides that were losing heavily capitulated because they had no incentive to draw, so in that year there were 16 points for a win and 3 for a draw. The ECB was not satisfied with the effect, so that became 12/4 in 1998, redressed slightly to 14/4 in 2002. Because losing sides were now more difficult to winkle out, on increasingly good batting wickets and with even fewer real rabbits than hitherto, there was a sharp reduction in results.

…until points for draws

The moment there were points for draws, the number of wins dropped once more. When in 2000 the championship split into two divisions of nine, in theory creating fewer one-sided contests, in its first six years the result percentage slipped to below 60 per cent, while the percentage of points from wins fell back again to little more than a third. Hence the average side got roughly double its points from bonuses, combined with avoiding defeat, than it did from winning matches. In 2004, when Warwickshire won the first division title with just five wins out of 16, two fewer than Kent in second place, only 70 of their 222 points came from winning matches, less than a third. In their 16 matches, only four times did their first innings fail to produce 400. Win the toss, bat for the best part of two days, and if you get maximum bonus points and a draw, that's 12 in the bag, and only 10 more if you convert it into a win. In 1993 the respective figures had been 8 and 16, hence much more incentive then to go for a win.

County v country

County championship cricket is still followed avidly by a large and loyal following in the country, fed with a continuous scoreboard via Ceefax and the Internet. But with county cricket in its longer form watched by few actual spectators, providing a derisory income, what is it for? Is it, as Patrick Collins wrote in the 2000 Wisden, 'like Monty Python's Norwegian Blue – nailed to its perch and dreaming of the fjords, but still a dead parrot'? If it is just a feeding ground for the England team, and if little more than half the matches are finished over four days, does it matter? Actually, four-day State matches in Australia are also played in virtually empty grounds, but no one worries while their Test team is winning. If you want excitement, watch a one-day match or a feverish Twenty20. In the 1994 Wisden the sceptical Matthew Engel had reluctantly acknowledged the success of four-day cricket, but argued that it 'was better than three-day cricket *had become* on the dead wickets of modern England'. There had always been conflict between 'best for the counties' and 'best for England', but it had been pretty low-key. In the early 1990s, the TCCB's anxiety about the Test team's performance led to a determination to create the right conditions for Test players. Hence the drive to prepare better, long-lasting covered wickets, which would ideally start to take spin late in the game, something still notoriously difficult to manage. That has contributed to the increase in the number of draws, even allowed four days.

The TCCB line was that better pitches and four-day county cricket would produce a Test team more readily equipped for a world of increasingly tough competition. That eventually came to involve a full-time coaching staff and centrally-contracted squads, based on the increasingly successful overseas model. The money was there for it, and it didn't come from the counties, so they had to grin and bear it. The counties brought up-and-coming players into the game, but the moment they reached the England side they were snatched away to a central England contract, and let out when the England coach permitted. There is little doubt that this has helped in the recovery of English fortunes in this new century, but it has left the counties feeling bereft. In the year 1999, the year before he broke into the England Test team, Michael Vaughan played in all 17 of Yorkshire's championship games. In 2000, when he played four Tests, he took part in nine of Yorkshire's 16 championship games. Thereafter central contracts came in – and he has played only seven such matches for them in five years since.

It's a self-fulfilling prophecy. Test players are no longer on the county circuit. If Yorkshiremen can't see their England captain in the flesh then they will watch him on television and not at a county ground. But that was all ahead of us. Let's turn back to the England team after the last summer of three-day cricket in 1992, and follow their fortunes on a tour of India and Sri Lanka in the winter of 1992–3, once more under Ted Dexter and Keith Fletcher. They would be judged on this winter and the following summer's visit from Australia.

CHAPTER 28

Under New Management

Body language study No. 2. Ray Illingworth and Michael Atherton at a press conference following the dirt-in-the-pocket affair, July 1994.

During the match [Illingworth] removed the Rev. Andrew Wingfield Digby, the team's chaplain and spiritual adviser for the last three years… 'If any of the players need a shoulder to cry on, they're not the men to go out and stuff the Aussies next winter'.

WISDEN, 1995

1992–3 India and Sri Lanka

England's performances since the Ashes defeat two years earlier had been full of character, even though they hadn't been able to resist the Pakistani opening bowlers at the end of 1992. But things would change, starting with a hapless tour to India and Sri Lanka in the new year of 1992–3. India had just been on the first tour of South Africa after the ending of apartheid, and their defeated players had returned with their tails between their legs. They were wagging furiously after this series. They were helped by England's selection. Gatting had returned along with Emburey, unexpectedly reprieved half-way through their ban. Apartheid had ended peacefully, to everyone's surprise and delight, but Gatting's return led to the omission of Gower, a successful captain in India and an excellent player of spin. To compound the felony, the best wicketkeeper, Russell, was also omitted, a decision that would rebound when the selectors had to play Yorkshire's Blakey, who as both batsman and wicketkeeper was nowhere near his equal.

India	371 & 82–2	England	163 & 286
India	560–6d	England	286 & 252
England	347 & 229	India	591

The England team was out-played from the moment Azharuddin arrived at the wicket at Calcutta. He played a brilliant innings of 182 out of 269, depositing England's ill-conceived four-man pace attack to all parts. The follow-on mark was only 172 but England fell 9 runs short, and only Gatting batted with any authority in the second knock. At Madras England were battered for centuries by Sidhu and Tendulkar, who was still not yet 20. After a good start from Stewart and Hick, Fairbrother glued a flimsy tail together with 83 but England again couldn't reach the follow-on point, and the obsequies were enlivened only by a dashing 117 made out of 153 by Lewis, the only man to take on the tall, accurate, quickish leg-spinner Anil Kumble. England would have followed on, too, at Bombay, had they not batted first. Their 347 emerged from a grim start of 118–6 thanks to the first Test innings by the Real Hick. After reaching 99 overnight with eight wickets down, he went on to 178 in the company of Tufnell, who made just 2 of a last-wicket stand of 68. That should have made England competitive, but along came another young Indian batsman, this time the 21-year-old Vinod Kambli, to make 224 in his first Test innings. England crumbled once Smith and Gatting had gone, and lost by an innings again. Gooch went back to England and Stewart, the new captain, was left to preside over England's first defeat by Sri Lanka.

England	380 & 228	Sri Lanka	469 & 142–5

England started so well in this Test that defeat was all the more disappointing. Smith's 128 as opener and sixties from Hick and Stewart took them to 316–3, but they collapsed to the two Sri Lankan off-spinners, Warnaweera and a certain Muttiah Muralitharan, about both of whose bowling actions there were already murmurings. Going in again with a deficit of 89, England slumped once more. If England had batted with more discipline in that innings, Sri Lanka might have been tested, for they lost four for 61 to Emburey and Tufnell on their way to 142. The only plus from the tour for England was the emergence of Graeme Hick. He topped not only the batting averages against India, but the bowling averages as well with his off-spin. That says it all about England's mainline bowlers, none of whom could average less than 40.

1993 Australia

It's intriguing to reflect, half-way through the first decade of a new century, that in 1993 the top seven Test bowlers of all time, in terms of wickets taken, were all opening bowlers. All had played between 1970 and 1992 – Hadlee, Kapil Dev, Botham, Marshall, Imran Khan, Lillee, Willis – and they included four of the greatest all-rounders who ever lived. In 1993, in successive Tests, England met for the first time two bowlers who would change all that: Muttiah Muralitharan and Shane Warne, who at the end of the 2005 season headed the all-time list by a very long way. The ball England's batsmen had faced had just gone from splice to toe – now it would be fizzing off the pitch. In 1993 for the first time England faced the stocky, rumbustious, leg-spinner Warne, and he exploded into the English psyche that summer.

Australia	289 & 432–5d	England	210 & 332
Australia	632–4d	England	205 & 365
England	321 & 422–6d	Australia	373 & 202–6
Australia	653–4d	England	200 & 305
England	276 & 251	Australia	408 & 120–2
England	380 & 313	Australia	303 & 229

Ironically, when the first innings of the first Test was over, it was an English debutant spinner who was being lauded. Peter Such of Essex bowled so beautifully on the first day of the series that, after Australia had begun with 183–1, he took the wickets of Taylor, after an innings of 124, Boon and Steve Waugh. He followed it next morning by getting the captain Border stumped, on his way to 6–67 at precisely two an over. Such a wonderful debut might have been something to shout about had we not been deafened by the roar from Australia that greeted the defining ball of the series, and of the next dozen years, Warne's first against England. It dipped – almost swerved – late in flight, pitched outside the leg stump and hit the top of the off of a bewildered Gatting, who dragged himself from the scene as if traumatised by something completely outside his experience. And he had battled against Abdul Qadir. Only Gooch thereafter played Warne with any certainty, and after taking a lead of 79 Australia extended it remorselessly to 511. With a day and a half to bat, England felt that they could save it as long as Gooch was there. But, after batting superbly for 133, he gloved a lifter from Hughes. As it fell towards his stumps he unthinkingly brushed it away with his glove, and so became the fifth batsman to be out in Tests for handling the ball. Although the tail battled on into the last hour, the persevering Hughes took the last two wickets, thanks to brilliant catches by Warne and Border.

At Lord's the first three Australian batsmen made centuries, the next 99, the fifth 77. In reply only Atherton with 80 stood out for long against Hughes and Warne, a battle he continued into the follow-on, only to be grievously denied a century when he slipped when attempting a third run to take him there, and was run out 99. A third successive disaster was averted at Trent Bridge by a side transformed by wholesale changes. Nasser Hussain made 71 and 47* in his first Test since his challenging Caribbean debut four years earlier. Encouragingly, the Surrey left-hander Graham Thorpe showed his promise with a cool century in the second innings on his debut, and with Gooch making another from No. 5 they led England to safety. A raw attack of McCague, Caddick, Ilott and Such – two who had grown up down under and two Essex men – did well to restrict Australia to 373 after a Boon hundred, and even better to reduce Australia to 115–6 when England left them 77 overs to make 371, but they couldn't force a win.

Gooch and Dexter depart

Any hope that this would signal a revival was ended at Headingley, whose seaming pitch had been dug up and replaced by something altogether more agreeable to batsmen. England went in without a spinner, although Such had been their best bowler in the series by far. Facing only four seamers, with just five previous Tests between them, it was no wonder Australia rattled up another 600. Border and Steve Waugh added an unbeaten 332, more than England managed in either innings, despite Warne taking only a single wicket. With the Ashes went Gooch, who resigned the captaincy, as he had promised, at the end of a Test in which he turned 40. At the age of 25, Atherton took over for Edgbaston. With McDermott and Hughes labouring with injury, he asked for a pacy pitch, but got one that was white and 'snuff-dry'. When Tim May spun his first ball on it he turned to Atherton and said 'Jeez, mate, this is better than playing in India', and he and Warne went on to share all 10 wickets in the second innings. England's batsmen failed again, shown up by Mark Waugh's vivid stroke-play in innings of 137 and 62*. Carrying the can was Dexter, who resigned as chairman of selectors, though Keith Fletcher soldiered on.

A second set of wholesale changes was made for the final Test on a faster pitch at the Oval, taking England's representatives for the summer to 24 in all. The whole seam attack was replaced by Malcolm, Fraser and Watkin. Fraser had only just returned from a debilitating and poorly diagnosed hip injury that had kept him out of Tests since 1990–1; Watkin had not played since bowling so well against the West Indies in 1991, and his performance here prompted the question why. Hick and Ramprakash returned from the wilderness too. Fifties from Gooch, Atherton, Hick and Stewart took England to 380 on a pacy pitch, and consistent bowling by all the seamers gave them a lead of 77. After a mid-order collapse Ramprakash coaxed precious runs from the tail, and England bowled Australia out on the last day with the help of some debatable decisions.

It was their first win over Australia for 18 Tests, but it couldn't disguise another awful series for England. Australia made mincemeat of England's attack. They scored their runs at an average of 51 per wicket, and not only did five of their batsmen exceed that mark, but six scored more than 400 runs. With the bat Gooch and Atherton stood out for England, with 673 at 56 and 553 at 46 respectively, but England suffered from the decision to bat Gooch down the order. Forty or not, he remained a tower of strength, and the start of the innings missed his authority: six times out of eight when he and Atherton opened they added 60 or more. As for the bowling... Such, with 16, was the only bowler to take more than 10 wickets, and the averages were headed by the three who returned for the last Test – Fraser, Watkin and Malcolm – who took all 20 wickets there between them. The other 12 bowlers contrived 33 wickets at an average of 76. Watkin didn't play another Test. In the three he played he took 11 wickets at 27, England beat the West Indies and Australia and drew the other. A future Galactic cricket historian will look at the records of Watkin, Mallender and Such, shake his head in puzzlement, sigh, and move on to the cases of Butler, Jackson and Bicknell.

1993–4 West Indies

Next to the West Indies. Gooch didn't come, and so England toured without a single member of the batting backbone of Gooch, Gatting and Gower in their ranks for the first time since 1977. Thus it was an inexperienced team, with no one who had played a Test before 1988. After much criticism of his absence, Russell returned as wicketkeeper, with Stewart opening the batting untrammelled by extra duties.

England	234 & 267	**West Indies**	407 & 95–2
England	322 & 190	**West Indies**	556
West Indies	252 & 269	England	328 & 46
England	355 & 394–7d	West Indies	304 & 237
West Indies	593–5d & 43–0	England	593

At Kingston an attack led by Walsh and Ambrose, with a pair of Benjamins following them, bowled England out for 234 after Atherton and Stewart had opened with 121. After a poor start, three of the new generation of West Indian batsmen took control – Brian Lara, Keith Arthurton and Jimmy Adams, all left-handers (and all with uncharacteristically dull first names). England faced a deficit of 173. They lost six wickets clearing it and, although Hick (96) batted better than he had ever done against pace in another of his intermittently encouraging innings, England lost by eight wickets. The ultimate frustration – why couldn't Hick bat like that more often?

At Georgetown England recovered from a calamitous start with a stand of 171 between Atherton and Smith, and were looking good until Ambrose struck in mid-innings. England were then subjected to a brilliant piece of batting by Lara, whose 167 came in only four and a quarter hours, and a more pedestrian 137 from Adams. With Laker and Lock turning in their graves, a spin attack of Salisbury, Hick and Ramprakash bowled 72 overs between them in an innings of 556, and England lost by an innings. By contrast, at Port-of-Spain for the third Test the contest was grippingly even for three days. Fraser and Lewis bowled out West Indies for 252 after they had been 158–1. Thorpe defied Ambrose to steer England to a lead of 76, and an excellent spell of 6–65 by Andy Caddick, despite missed catches, left England a target of 194 late on the fourth day. Caddick, a tall, moody, pitch-hitter who needed sympathetic handling, of English parentage but brought up in New Zealand, was often a better bowler in the second innings than the first.

Could England chase 194 to keep the series alive and come back to 2–1? Fifteen overs later at the day's end England had been ambushed by Ambrose, and lay in ruins at an abject 40–8. The final 46 was England's lowest Test score since 1896. So England went to Bridgetown 3–0 down. Their spirited response to the Trinidad debacle was led by an opening stand of 171 by Atherton and Stewart and a total of 355. Then came a stupendous spell of bowling by Fraser, who took 8–75 in an innings of 304, the best figures ever by an English bowler against West Indies. Stewart continued his impressive form of the first innings with 143, the first English batsman to score two centuries in a match against West Indies, who were set 446 in four sessions. On the last day Caddick took another second innings five, and he and Tufnell had won the match for England by tea time. A well-merited consolation victory, and a deep sigh of relief following their destruction by Ambrose, who here went for an unlikely three and a half an over, underlining the spirit of the recovery, typified by Stewart, never daunted.

Brian Lara – 375

The last Test was Lara's. A 24-year-old from Trinidad, small of stature but with quick eyes, feet and hands, in this series he laid claim to being the best batsman in the world. During the next dozen years he would have challengers, but he stayed at the top for years until the team fell apart around him. Here in Antigua he rescued West Indies from 12–2 to 274–3 on the first day, which he ended on 164; on to 502–4 at the end of the second, when he had reached 320; and to 593–5 by the time he was out with his score 375, 10 more than the previous record, held by the great Sobers, who was there to applaud and greet him. Less than half of Lara's runs had come in boundaries, not the least impressive statistic as it attested to the sluggish nature of the outfield. The pitch remained perfect for English batting too, and Atherton with 135, Smith with 175, and Russell and Lewis with fifties, allowed England to chug precisely level as the game petered out.

Again it was the opening pair that led England's batting, Atherton and Stewart averaging over 50, no one else managing 40. Four young left-handers headed them for West Indies: Lara, Adams and Arthurton were joined by the imperturbable Shivnarine Chanderpaul, reminiscent of Kallicharran in build and origin, who made fifties in each of his first four Tests. Fraser, Caddick and Lewis took 48 wickets between them, and each bowled well at times, but they rarely fired together. Ambrose, Walsh and the Benjamins took 79, a familiar story. Although the last two Tests were a recovery from the black day in Trinidad, England still had a long way to go. Since beating New Zealand in 1991–2 they had lost a series to each of the top four Test-playing nations. New Zealand would return in 1994, followed by the first appearance of the new South Africa.

1994 New Zealand and South Africa

England replaced Keith Fletcher as manager with Ray Illingworth, who demanded, and eventually got, total autonomy. He removed the team's chaplain and spiritual adviser, the engagingly eccentric Andrew Wingfield Digby, who had once instructed his minor county's bowlers to bowl wides to bring the opposition's receding target into view again, and won: 'If any of the players need a shoulder to cry on, they're not the men to go out and stuff the Aussies next winter,' quoth Yorkshire man. For the first Test, with Caddick and Lewis injured, and Tufnell up before the Bench for his domestic troubles, he picked only five of the team that played the final West Indies Test. In his first team was one of Yorkshire's traditional wicketkeeping exports, Steve Rhodes of Worcester, and Yorkshire's Australian import but, crucially, born in Yorkshire – the all-rounder Craig White. There was no place for Thorpe, Ramprakash or Hussain.

New Zealand	251 & 226	**England**	567–8d
New Zealand	476 & 211–5d	England	281 & 254–8
England	382	New Zealand	151 & 308–7

Two of the old faces did rather well at Trent Bridge. Gooch belied his age by making 210 in dominating a stand of 263 with Atherton. DeFreitas took the first three New Zealand wickets on the first morning, and finished with nine in the match. England won by an innings, while a few miles away at Edgbaston in a dead game Brian Lara was becoming the first batsman to pass 500 in a first-class innings. He had now broken both individual scoring records in a seven-week period. At Lord's the New Zealanders fought back, and very nearly levelled the series. After they had amassed 476 (Crowe 142) it needed a gutsy three-and-a-half hour innings by Rhodes to inch England past the follow-on mark after Dion Nash had taken England's top four. Had England been forced to bat again, it's unlikely that they would have survived. As it was they had to battle to save the match. Nash again dismissed the top four, but not Stewart until he had made 119. When he was out at 217–5, Rhodes again led England's struggle for survival, and achieved it as the sky darkened. The poor light prevented Nash from bowling the last few overs, but he still took 11 wickets in the match, and made a bright 56 at No. 9 for good measure.

At Old Trafford it was England's turn for frustration, as rain prevented much play on either of the last two days. Atherton's patient 111, an innings that took until the second day, seemed to have gone to waste at 235–7, but DeFreitas and the fresh-faced, engagingly uncomplicated debutant Darren Gough added a sprightly 130 before they combined to bowl New Zealand out for 151. Crowe had made 70 of those, and he had to effect a rescue again when four wickets fell for 73 after the follow-on. At the end of the third day they were 205–5, still behind, but the paucity of play thereafter meant they had reached 308–7 when the match was finally washed out, a lead of only 77 and Crowe gone.

This series was followed by the historic first post-apartheid South African series. It had a controversial beginning, and an amazing end. The last series between the countries in 1965 had ended 1–0 to South Africa, and until the third afternoon a 2–0 win for them seemed highly probable. But one retaliatory bouncer too many provoked a historic reaction.

South Africa	357 & 278–8d	England	180 & 99
England	477–9d & 267–5d	South Africa	447 & 116–3
South Africa	332 & 175	**England**	304 & 205–2

At Lord's a century by the South African captain Kepler Wessels, an oddity in the modern era as someone who played Tests for two countries, took South Africa to 357. England batted poorly first time against Donald and de Villiers, and worse against everybody the second time, to lose by 356 runs. For South Africa it was a triumphant return, for Atherton a setback compounded by the fracas over the use of dirt in his pocket to dry the ball and help Gough's reverse swing. Caught on camera, fined by Illingworth in a swift pre-emptive move, and admonished by referee Burge, he clung on to the captaincy with TCCB support and in the face of calls for his resignation, notably from the pundits Jonathan Agnew and Geoffrey Boycott. Atherton came out at Headingley, though, with a fighting 99, to which Thorpe, Stewart and Rhodes added brisk fifties. Facing 477, South Africa were at one stage 105–5, but their tail got them to within 30. Hick's first century in England, the pressure off, enabled South Africa to be set 297 in 60 overs, but there was never any real chance of a result.

So to the Oval, one down, and the fastest pitch of all. Surrey had a third Benjamin, Joey. On his debut on his home pitch he took 4–42 on the opening day, during which McMillan and Richardson led a recovery, after Jonty Rhodes had ducked into a low bouncer from Malcolm and gone to hospital with concussion. But Malcolm had bowled poorly, and his captain told him so. Facing 332, Thorpe and Stewart batted fluently, but nine were down for 293 when Malcolm, a natural No. 11 of the old school, came out to face his first ball. Rhodes himself hadn't at all blamed Malcolm for his injury, but de Villiers clearly thought retribution due, so he clattered Malcolm between the eyes with a bouncer first ball. Malcolm's response of 'You guys are history' may be apocryphal, but is now itself part of history. Half an hour later he was tearing in at top speed and disposing of the two Kirstens and Cronje for one run. He came back to get Wessels at 73. Daryl Cullinan led a recovery, so that at one stage South Africa stood 137–4, a healthy 165 ahead. But Malcolm disposed of McMillan, Richardson and Matthews, and Rhodes came in at No. 9 to try to stem the bleeding. For a while he did, but 175–7 became 175 all out when Cullinan was caught off Gough, the only wicket to be taken by anyone else, and Malcolm cleared out de Villiers and Donald, the latter to a suitably fulminating yorker. Malcolm had 9–57 in 16.3 overs of high-class fast bowling. Needing 205, England reached it in flamboyant fashion. Following a cameo from Gooch, Atherton made 63 and Hick 81* at a run a ball. Donald's bowling was so inferior to Malcolm's that his 12 overs cost 96.

England's summer was thus restored by Malcolm's bowling, though it would need all of the faster bowlers to fire in the winter if England were to compete with Australia. England's most consistent bowler by far in the six Tests was DeFreitas, with 30 wickets at 26. Malcolm's Oval burst gave him 12 at 18, while Gough and Fraser took theirs in the thirties. Caddick, partly because of injury, hadn't played a single Test. Thorpe returned belatedly to head the batting averages, with the wicketkeeper Rhodes next with some obdurate performances. Stewart, Atherton and Hick scored over 400 runs and averaged close to 50. They too would all need to keep that form in Australia.

1994–5 Australia

England started the tour of Australia with 16 players and ended it with 16, but such was the toll of injuries and illness sustained by the touring party that only 10 of the original contingent remained at the end. The two old campaigners, Gooch and Gatting, 41 and 37 and with over 200 Tests between them, did actually stay fit, but their form deserted them and this was one last tour too many for the old stagers. Border, of the same generation, had called it a day after scoring more Test runs than anyone in more Tests, and made way for Mark Taylor. Taylor was even more tactically aware than his predecessor, but had suffered a reverse in his first series as captain, in Pakistan, where an epic one-wicket victory for their hosts had suggested that Australia weren't entirely infallible.

Australia	426 & 248–8d	England	167 & 323
Australia	279 & 320–7d	England	212 & 92
England	309 & 255–2d	Australia	116 & 344–7
England	353 & 328	Australia	419 & 156
Australia	402 & 345–8d	England	295 & 123

With the Oval hero Malcolm going down with chicken pox three days before the first Test, England lost their latest talisman. On a perfect pitch Slater and Mark Waugh made big hundreds. England batted abysmally against McDermott, Taylor chose not to enforce the follow-on, and Warne took advantage of a last-innings pitch to take 8–71 after better resistance from Hick, Thorpe and Gooch. Although the scores were lower at Melbourne, the pattern was the same. After Australia's 279, Warne took another six as England finished 67 behind after Stewart had broken a finger and ended his tour. Boon extended the advantage, and England performed pitifully against McDermott and Warne, who took his 20th wicket of the series so far – his dominance at this point was total. England had been Warned.

Two-nil down, England at last showed some spirit at Sydney. Atherton, with his fellow Lancastrian John Crawley, repaired the first innings damage of 20–3 with a stand of 174. After another collapse, Gough, 51 off 56 balls, and Malcolm, an unlikely 29 from 18, took England past 300. They then showed that their batting had taken nothing out of them by taking the first four Australian wickets between them for 38. This time there was no recovery, as an exuberant Gough tore through the tail to finish with 6–49. Atherton, Hick and Thorpe pressed home the advantage, and Atherton was able to declare – with an unhappy Hick on 98 – and leave Australia a target of 449 in what would be 122 overs. If England had turned this into victory as Australia had done in a similar position in the first two Tests, the Ashes would still have been alive. But Slater and Taylor replied to such effect that they added 208, forcing Atherton onto the defensive, and the stand was only broken by a brilliant catch by Tufnell, his fielding much improved after it had been remorselessly heckled on his first tour down under. That led to an unexpected avalanche of wickets from Fraser, but, with a delay for rain, the last hour didn't begin until 6.25. Australia had seven wickets down, but it was getting so dark that Atherton had to take the quicker bowlers off, and Warne and May survived against their spinning opposite numbers.

A win at last

That last innings chase clearly favoured the fielding side. It was followed at Adelaide by one that didn't, but led to a surprising win against the odds. A depleted England had lost Hick, Gough and Stewart, who had all flown home. There were only five fit batsmen, but the old warrior Gatting, whose form had been wretched, summoned up all his reserves of concentration to make a seven-hour 117 that held England together after Atherton had gone for 80 at 175–1. Two century partnerships gave Australia the edge. Slater and Taylor produced the first, before Healy helped Greg Blewett make a hundred in his first Test innings. At 396–5 Australia led by 43, but Malcolm and Fraser cleaned up the tail. Despite a brilliant 83 from Thorpe, England struggled against the occasional off-spin of Mark Waugh, and were 181–6, only 117 ahead, when DeFreitas joined Crawley. DeFreitas proceeded to play the dashing innings he had always threatened, taking 22 off one McDermott over on his way to 88 from 95 balls. Setting out to make 263 from 67 overs, on a pitch that still looked good, Australia were immediately in trouble against Malcolm, while Lewis, who had been hastily summoned from club cricket in Melbourne, disposed of the middle order. The game already looked won at 83–8, but Healy and Fleming threatened to thwart England again, until they were separated after two hours defiance, and England won with six overs left.

Two-one was better, and England had competed strongly in the last two Tests. But Australia in this era were always stung by defeat into a steely determination not to be beaten again. So it happened at Perth. Slater and the Waughs took Australia past 400, a score England might have challenged had they not lost their last six wickets for 60 after Thorpe and Ramprakash, the latest replacement, had added 158. Blewett made his second century in his second Test when Australia batted again, and England plummeted to 27–6 and defeat to McDermott and McGrath. The two Macs, old and new, here met at the crossover of two generations of Australian fast bowlers.

England had lost again too easily, despite their mid-series resurgence. Thorpe, Hick and Atherton had batting averages in the forties, but the support was minimal. At least the confident Gough had arrived to lead the attack, and his *joie de vivre* kept the team spirit going in adversity. But the only other bowlers to take 10 wickets at under 30 were Lewis and Fraser, neither originally chosen for the tour (Atherton said he had McCague 'foisted' on him by the selectors instead of Fraser). Add to these three Malcolm, DeFreitas and Caddick, and you had six opening bowlers all capable of excellent spells, but never consistently together, and all liable to injury. There was a seventh, though, waiting in England to be uncorked.

1995 West Indies

England returned to face the West Indies, led by Richie Richardson, for whom Lara was expected to be the lynchpin. How England's bowlers would deal with him, and their fragile batting face up to the usual high-class four-man pace attack, would determine whether England could wrest the initiative back after so long. Until this year, West Indies still hadn't lost any series since March 1980, but a 2–1 defeat to Australia at home confirmed their new vulnerability, and the shift in the balance of power. Could England capitalise on it?

England	199 & 208	**West Indies**	282 & 129–1
England	283 & 336	West Indies	324 & 223
England	147 & 89	**West Indies**	300
West Indies	216 & 314	**England**	437 & 94–4
England	440 & 269–9d	West Indies	417 & 42–2
England	454 & 223–4	West Indies	692–8d

Not at Headingley, where the series began with the old familiar story: two England batting breakdowns against a hostile attack. Atherton resisted in the first innings and Thorpe in the second, and England's bowlers kept some order in the first innings after Lara's early fireworks, but he and Hooper eventually romped to victory at virtually seven an over.

Lord's provided the best game of the series by far: thrills and spills and a startling debut. Thorpe and Smith added 109 on the first day, but England then suffered the usual subsidence to finish on 283, to which West Indies, harried by the accurate Fraser, replied with 324. England lost two early wickets, together with Thorpe, sent to hospital by a beamer from Walsh, but the battling Hick and Smith, supported on his return by Thorpe, took England to a position where they left West Indies to make 296 in just over seven hours. England were slight favourites, but everyone was reminded of Greenidge by the way Lara began on the Sunday night. He went past 50 next morning before being brilliantly caught at 99 by Stewart, restored to keep wicket after Illingworth had overturned the selectors' (and Atherton's) original choice. Could the rest stay with Campbell, the adhesive opener? Enter the fifth bowler to be tried, the exuberant debutant from Derbyshire, Dominic Cork. Bowling with, in Wisden's words, 'a fierce and demonstrable will', on top of a perfect out-swinger, he got Adams, Richardson and Arthurton, the last two for ducks, Campbell for 93, and the tail, to finish with a return of 19.3–5–43–7, the best figures ever by an Englishman in his first Test. England had squared the series.

With some dressing-room disharmony emerging from the West Indies camp, and a humiliating innings defeat by Sussex behind them, England's supporters hoped their team could capitalise on fragile Caribbean team spirit in the third Test. What they got was another English nightmare. It was like 1993 over again, an Edgbaston pitch tailor-made for the opposition. There was fevered debate about who exactly was responsible for a pitch that was shaved at the ends, grassy in the middle, and of uneven bounce, but it was exactly what the West Indian quicks ordered. After the first ball, said Atherton, Ambrose 'stood in the middle of the wicket for an age, his eyes bulging, and grinning from ear to ear'. He was soon off injured, but it scarcely mattered: Walsh and Bishop had a heyday, taking 15–146 between them. England ended the match with no batsman reaching 50, and four with hand injuries – Stewart, Thorpe, Gallian and Richard Illingworth. Only Atherton, Smith, Thorpe, Cork and Fraser survived for Old Trafford, as England tried to fashion yet another comeback.

Cork's hat-trick

On the opening day only Lara with 87 reached 30 as Fraser and Cork bowled intelligently, helped by first-class catching. On the second day Thorpe's 94 took England to 347–7, and Cork's first Test fifty extended it to 437. It was in this innings that he blithely replaced a bail he'd dislodged in completing his stroke, after an all-run four, noticed only by the cameras. The match, as so many during this summer, seemed to depend on Lara, and he was still there when the fourth day ended with West Indies 159–3. The kernel of the match was the first 10 minutes of the fifth morning – anyone arriving late missed it. Cork first bowled Richardson, then had Murray and Hooper lbw with successive balls, to take the first hat trick for England since 1957. Although Lara batted brilliantly afterwards for 145, England needed only 94. Though they lost four quick wickets and Smith to a broken cheekbone, Russell batted coolly and England won on the fourth afternoon to square the series.

So now it was 2–2. This was a six–Test series, so England had two more Tests to try to win their first West Indian series since 1969, back when Ray Illingworth himself had been captain. With Hooper, Adams and Ambrose unfit at Trent Bridge, and Ambrose replaced – we rubbed our eyes – by the leg-spinner Dhanraj, England sensed their opportunity, but the pitch was too benign. Atherton and Nick Knight were still there at tea on the opening day, and Atherton and Hick went on to score centuries as England totalled 440 towards the end of the second day. Lara responded with a masterclass, 152 from 182 balls, and England began again on the fourth afternoon with a draw probable. But after being 111–2 overnight they limped to 189–9. At that point Mike Watkinson gave a simple chance to mid-wicket that would have given the West Indies a tasty target of 214 at five an over, and the chance of a thrilling finish. But, after his reprieve, Watkinson, the Lancashire captain playing in his second Test, made 82* in adding an unbeaten 80 with a bandaged Richard Illingworth, and that opportunity was gone. At the Oval another good pitch enabled England to top 400 again, with Hick and Russell reaching the nineties. But West Indies galloped towards 700 at more than four an over, with Lara on song again, 179 from 206 balls, and four other batsmen passed 80. England had to bat for seven hours, but Atherton led them out of trouble with another innings in the nineties, and the series was shared.

Despite the last two Tests, it was an excellent series and a fair outcome. No one on either side batted like Lara, who made 765 runs at 85, and always at speed. From his batting no one would suspect he was bickering with his management throughout the tour. Overall England's batting was more solid than in recent series, with Hick, Smith, Thorpe and Atherton averaging between 40 and 50, and Russell ironically out-scoring Stewart after replacing him. The irrepressible Cork, man of the match in both victories, took 26 wickets at 25, as well as scoring 197 runs at nearly 30 and adding zest to the fielding. Only Fraser of the rest took more than 10 wickets: despite Cork's arrival, the opening bowlers could still rarely bowl well together – or be fit together.

1995–6 South Africa

Before the 1996 World Cup, England undertook their first official visit to South Africa since the cancellation of the 1969 tour. It was close, but it was surprisingly wet – disappointing for all but the many farmers who welcomed the end of a drought – and the weather lost the teams nearly eight days of cricket out of 25. That meant the series went to the final match still without a win for either side.

England	381–9	South Africa	
South Africa	332 & 346–9d	England	200 & 351–5
South Africa	225	England	152–5
South Africa	428 & 162–9d	England	263 & 189–3
England	153 & 157	**South Africa**	244 & 70–0

Put in to bat by Hanse Cronje at Centurion, England had batted themselves to safety after a poor start, Hick making 141 to follow 118* and 96 in his last two Test innings. He was becoming established at last, it seemed. At Johannesburg things went wrong for England as Atherton tried to justify his selection of four fast bowlers by putting South Africa in. Only Cork bowled well until he and Malcolm got it right with the second new ball. Thereafter a poor batting display by England and consistent batting by South Africa put them 428 ahead at the end of the third day. They pottered on inconsequentially for another hour and a half on the fourth, which would look a bad mistake by the end of the fifth, not least because it deprived Donald and Pollock of a decent final fling with a third new ball. England would have to bat for over 10 hours in search of a theoretical 479. With 82 at the start of the last day out of 169–4, Atherton lost Smith at 232, but he and Russell – already a hero for catching 11 in the match to break Bob Taylor's world record – batted out the last four and a half hours. Russell finished 26*, while Atherton made 182* in over 10 hours of ruthless application through 165 overs. He had atoned for his mistake with the toss with one of the great defensive innings, in a situation made for his strengths.

More rain at Durban ended a match without a fifty or five wickets for anyone. At Port Elizabeth for the penultimate Test, South Africa scored consistently to post 428. England proceeded with caution against Paul Adams, South Africa's new 18-year-old unorthodox left-arm bowler. He was unorthodox in every possible sense: in his extraordinary action, in which his gaze was fixed skywards as he delivered the ball, and in his wrist spin, mixing chinamen and googlies. England made 263 in little over two an over in their first innings, and faced another uphill slog in the second. Their target was 320 in 99 overs, but on a slow pitch neither side exhibited enough urgency. Stewart held the innings together, and a game that might have had an exciting climax petered out lamely.

So to the last Test at Cape Town, and it seemed only a dramatic batting collapse from either team would prevent the series ending 0–0. Actually, there were three, but two of them were by England. Dismissed for a paltry 153 by Donald on the opening day, England had hit back to such an extent that when last man Adams joined wicketkeeper Richardson South Africa were 171–9. They added a crucial 73. Thorpe led a recovery from a bad start to take England to 138–4. If they could add another 100 it might be enough in a low-scoring game. Then Hudson hit the stumps direct as Thorpe went for a quick single. Umpire Orchard gave him not out, but had forgotten he now had a TV replay facility available. Those in the hospitality boxes immediately saw the replay, and started a call for the umpire to check it. Cronje harangued the umpire, the replay was reviewed, and Thorpe had to go. He was rapidly followed by the other five, Pollock doing the damage this time, and South Africa coasted to a 1–0 victory inside three days.

Once again in the 1990s England took a step back as soon as they had taken one forward. It was a galling end for England after Atherton's heroics had kept them in the series. He averaged 55, Hick 48, Smith 36, but no one else more than 30 against the penetrating double spearhead of Donald and Pollock. Of the England bowlers Cork, 19 at 25, received little support until the steady Lancastrian Peter Martin played in the last two Tests, taking 11 wickets at under 20 each, and moreover at two runs per over. After the Tests England went on to lose a protracted one-day series 6–1, hardly encouraging preparation for the next World Cup, which took place in India, Pakistan and Sri Lanka. Three weeks after leaving South Africa, England were in action in Ahmedabad.

1996 The sixth World Cup

The event got off to a troubled start because of recent events in Sri Lanka. The Tamil Tigers had taken their armed struggle into Colombo itself, and a bomb blast in the city persuaded Australia and West Indies to decline to play there. The organisers refused to budge, and both sides forfeited to Sri Lanka the points they might have won. That this didn't prevent either of them from getting through the qualifying stage, was due to the organisers' decision that a final set of seven games would be much more lucrative than one of just three, so they inserted a quarter-final phase. With 12 sides in two groups of six – the eight first Test-playing nations, Zimbabwe and three no-hopers – it was clear that unless any of the top eight made a complete mess of it they would all go through. That made the first three weeks of the tournament largely academic, though neutrals were delighted by the success of Kenya in defeating the West Indies, bowling them out for 93.

But West Indies and all the other big teams did indeed get through. England looked rather jaded and old-fashioned in their approach. Having only a week off before the tournament was hardly ideal. Moreover England's one-day cricket was out of kilter with the rest of the world. Domestic tournaments of 60, 55 and 40 overs with red balls, white clothing and no fielding restrictions, were hardly ideal preparation for a 50-over, white ball, fielding-restricted World Cup. But they made it to the quarter-finals despite losing to all the Test-playing nations in their group. Defeat by New Zealand by 11 runs was certain once Hick, batting with a hamstring strain, was run out for 85. He made a century against The Netherlands, which England only won by 49. But he lost form as they lost heavily to South Africa and Pakistan, leaving them in poor shape as they took on Sri Lanka in their quarter-final.

Despite the prevailing view that they were playing too much one-day cricket, England were beginners compared with Sri Lanka. Six of their players had passed 100 one-day caps, compared with one for England, DeFreitas. In the event England batted on winning the toss at Faisalabad, and made 235–8, DeFreitas hitting 67 from 64 balls. That didn't seem likely to be enough against a side that had developed a policy of thrashing furiously in the first 15 overs, to which scores of 90–2, 117–1 and 123–2 in their qualifying matches attested. Here they took only 13 overs to reach 113–1 when Jayasuriya was out, having plundered 82 off 44 balls, including 22 from DeFreitas' second over. After that it was a formality, and for the first time England had failed to reach a World Cup semi-final.

The other quarter-finals threw up three potentially and politically juicy rivalries – India v Pakistan, Australia v New Zealand, South Africa v West Indies. That India reached 293 in the first was due to Sidhu's 93 and a late onslaught that took 40 off Waqar Younis's last two overs: they won by 49. New Zealand too put together a big score, with Germon making 89 and Harris 130, but Mark Waugh's 110 in pursuit of 286 got Australia home with 11 balls to spare. South Africa were favourites in the fourth, but West Indies were revived after the Kenyan debacle by Lara's 111 in an innings of 264–8. Their surprising match-winners were the spinners Harper and Jimmy Adams as South Africa went down by 19.

That gave us all four semi-finalists from one group: Australia v West Indies and India v Sri Lanka. Both matches were extraordinary, if for different reasons. Australia were 15–4 before Law and Bevan added 138, then slithered to 207–8. Chanderpaul steered West Indies to 165–2, needing just 43 from the last nine overs, but a horrendous slump ensued. Warne took 3–6 in three overs, belying received wisdom about spinners bowling at the death, and Richardson, not out 45, needed 10 off the last over from Fleming. He hit the first ball for four, but ran a daft single, running out Ambrose and, in so doing, losing the strike and the match. Meanwhile India were playing Sri Lanka in an exuberant and emotional Calcutta. That emotion hit the heights during the match's first over, in which Srinath had both openers caught at third man, off strokes epitomising their approach. Did Sri Lanka retrench? Oh no. Aravinda de Silva clattered 66 before he was out at 85 in the 15th over, and they eventually reached 251–8. Would it be enough? India's batting line-up was strong, and Tendulkar dominated its early stages with 65. But he was second out at 98, and India collapsed in a heap to 120–8 at the start of the 35th over. We can only speculate about what might have happened next, because a riot began that effectively ended the game, officially awarded to Sri Lanka by default. The hosts India were thus doubly humiliated.

SEMI–FINALS			
Sri Lanka	251–8 (50)	India	120–8 (34.1)
Australia	207–8 (50)	West Indies	202 (49.3)
FINAL			
Australia	241–7 (50)	**Sri Lanka**	245–3 (46.2)

That brought together for the final in Lahore the gnarled old hands Australia, and exciting and excitable youngsters Sri Lanka. After passing 100 in fewer than 20 overs,

Australia were strangled by the lack of pace of the four Sri Lankan spinners and could finish only 241–7. Once the openers had again gone cheaply, Aravinda de Silva began more circumspectly this time, but tucked into Warne when he came on and finished 107* as Sri Lanka won, to great enthusiasm from the neutrals, by seven wickets with 22 balls to spare. Sri Lanka had defied history by putting Australia in, because all the other World Cup finals had been won by the side batting first.

Sri Lanka had risen above its national troubles and lifted the Cup for the first time, in its own part of the world. They deserved it for rewriting the rulebooks of the one-day game. Cricket enthusiasts all over the Indian subcontinent were thrilled for them once they had got over their own parochial disappointments: they listened, they watched, they discussed, they gambled... The centre of gravity of world cricket was indeed changing. But that wasn't the only thing that this shift was bringing to the game. There was something rotten in the state of cricket, and no one knew it.

Records of England's post-war Test captains to September 2005

Captain Dates		p	w	l	d	%age wd–won
Vaughan	2003–2005	31	19	5	7	73–61
Brearley	1977–1981	31	18	4	9	73–58
Hutton	1952–1955	23	11	4	8	65–48
May	1955–1961	41	20	10	11	61–49
Illingworth	1969–1973	31	12	5	14	61–39
Cowdrey M. C.	1959–1969	27	8	4	15	57–30
Smith M. J. K.	1964–1966	25	5	3	17	54–20
Willis	1982–1984	18	7	5	6	56–39
Dexter	1961–1964	30	9	7	14	53–30
Denness	1974–1975	19	6	5	8	53–32
Hussain	1999–2003	45	17	15	13	52–38
Brown F. R.	1949–1951	15	5	6	4	47–33
Gooch	1988–1993	34	10	12	12	47–29
Atherton	1993–1998	54	13	21	20	43–24
Gatting	1986–1988	23	2	5	16	43–09
Greig A. W.	1975–1977	14	3	5	6	43–21
Yardley	1946–1950	14	4	7	3	39–29
Stewart A. J.	1998–2000	15	4	8	3	37–27
Botham	1980–1981	12	0	4	8	33–00
Gower	1982–1989	32	5	18	9	30–16

England had 15 men who captained on fewer than 10 occasions. The most successful was Close (6–0–1). England had 10 captains in all in the 1980s. Botham led only against Australia and West Indies, drawing eight out of 12. Only Gatting drew a higher percentage of matches. Brearley never captained against West Indies, though 14 of his 31 were against Australia. Vaughan's period goes up to September 2005.

Note: the percentage pair give a 2–for–a–win + 1–for–a–draw rating, followed by a straight win percentage.

CHAPTER 29

Something Rotten in the State of Cricket

South Africa's former captain Hansie Cronje testifies to the
King Commission investigating match-fixing, June 2000.

It was 19th March which is my mother's birthday, and Hansie... said to
me that... they were prepared to offer... US$15 000 if I made less
than 20. I knew that... I would have to look after my mom for
the rest of her life... And that is why I said yes.

HERSCHELLE GIBBS, Testimony to the King Commission

Behaviour on the field had been bad enough as the 20th century drew to a close, but events off the field took an ugly and unexpected turn in 1996. Two hundred years ago aristocratic patrons with money to burn and a passion for gambling became enthusiastic for cricket. Naturally, they gambled on the games they played in. Naturally, a betting demi-monde trailed in their wake. Naturally, in an era before professionals, the players they hired to play were often labourers or semi-skilled workmen with few pennies to rub together. It wasn't long before bribes were being offered to throw a match. And as the rewards on offer were often much greater than the rewards for winning, or loyalty to the team or its master, those bribes were happily accepted. So notorious did the issue eventually become that the MCC cracked down, even banning from Lord's the best batsman in England, William Lambert, in 1817. Betting and bribery had been removed from the game by the time county cricket began in the second half of the nineteenth century.

Since then until the 1990s instances of betting on matches by players were few and far between and comparatively harmless. England supporters regarded the Lillee/Marsh bets of 1981 as something of a joke, rather enjoying the way it under-lined how close England seemed to be to losing until Botham and Willis effected their miracle. And Australian supporters recognised that no true Aussie could pos-sibly pass up a bet at 500–1 on a two-horse race. No one seriously thought that the betting pair actively tried to lose. 'Lillee and Marsh would bet on a game of marbles, but they wouldn't throw it,' as an Australian journalist said. Anyway, no one believed a cricketer would actually throw a match. No one that is, until the evidence hit them in the face.

A game in a flutter

The roots of the trouble lay in the fanatical enthusiasm for betting on cricket, in the subcontinent in general, but in India and the Persian Gulf in particular, and in the ever-increasing number of one-day international matches, many of them in tournaments the results of which mattered comparatively little. Huge sums of money were being placed on matches that the players themselves were not particularly desperate to win. Although it came as something of a surprise to innocents like me at the time, in retrospect it looks inevitable. The only puzzling thing to the layman was that, with 11 players on the field, it would seem virtually impossible for a single man to influence the result more than marginally. If he misses a yorker in the first over, he has team-mates able and willing to make a hundred; if he bowls a series of long-hops his captain will probably banish him from the attack. If he tries to suborn his team-mates, the likelihood is that someone will leak the truth sooner or later. Of course, if a lot of money is at stake, any tipping of the odds may bring a reward to the bookmaker in the long run, but there is clearly some double dealing at work. A player might pocket the money with no intention of playing badly. If his team loses anyway, so much the better; if not, well, I tried my best but… However, such was the sophistication of the betting, with things like spread betting on a batsman's score –

for example that he will be out for between 25 and 35 – that it became apparent that there were things a corrupt player could do of his own accord without anyone being any the wiser.

Australians in Pakistan

It was early in 1995 that Shane Warne, Mark Waugh and Tim May alleged that on the fourth evening of the first 1994–5 Test at Karachi – where Pakistan had never yet lost – they had received the offer of a bribe (reputedly $200 000) from the Pakistan captain Salim Malik to bowl badly on the last day. They refused it, although amazingly Pakistan actually won by one wicket after a last wicket stand of 57 – the bribe wasn't needed. The Pakistan Board set up an internal inquiry under Justice Ebrahim, but their Australian counterpart would not let the players go to Pakistan to testify. They recorded their testimony from Antigua, but nevertheless Salim Malik was cleared. If it was true, one wondered, who gave Salim the money? There would surely be others keen for an acquittal. The Pakistan Board was noticeably reluctant to clear the matter up, but rumours persisted and in 1998 the government stepped in and set up an inquiry under Justice Qayyum.

What wasn't known until October 1998, when they were conveniently touring Pakistan again, was that Waugh and Warne had admitted to their Board three years earlier that they had accepted money from an Indian bookmaker on the 1994–5 tour, to provide apparently innocuous information about the pitch and weather for a one-day international. The Australian Board sat on the information and their hands, other than telling the ICC, who did likewise. Moreover the Pakistan Board chose not to release Qayyum's report. Since then Javed Burki, chairman of the committee running Pakistan cricket at the time, has said he was sure that match-fixing and betting was going on in the Pakistan dressing-room at the time. In India, too, reports of match-fixing began to surface about this time. In 1997 Manoj Prabhakar alleged that he had been offered money in 1994 to swing a match in Pakistan's favour. Indian Board secretary Dalmiya, soon to be ICC president, followed the hear-no-evil line by affirming, 'I don't think the players are involved at all, and if it is proved it will be the shock of my life.' He would get his shock all right.

Cricket doesn't reward players in the same way as tennis, for example, does. In 1997 there were 110 one-day internationals played across the world, and India alone played 48 in 1997–8. There is only one World Cup, every four years, the rest are played for national pride, and sometimes barely even that. In December 1977 England went to Sharjah under Adam Hollioake and won an unimportant one-day competition. Who would normally care who won it? (Well, England supporters did, because their team didn't win one-day tournaments.) The winning team shared just £25 000. A pair of tennis players arriving in a new town for a minor tournament can expect at least that for the winner, and substantial sums for getting as far as the last eight. It would be simple, and untraceable, for the two finalists to agree amiably to share first- and second-prize money. Cricket doesn't have such easy money, and with heavy betting syndicates operating the temptations are obvious. It's almost axiomatic that unregulated betting leads to corruption, as it did in baseball in the USA after World War 1.

Hansie Cronje – the naming and shaming

The gambling seems to have begun around 1984 when an Indian bank clerk, Makesh Kumar Gupta, saw people placing small sums on the outcomes of cricket matches, and decided to expand his horizons. That was at the beginning of the rapid spread of one-day internationals, some to hitherto non-cricketing venues like Sharjah and Singapore. Singapore was typical in giving Indian businessmen living and working there access to the home market. Within 10 years betting on cricket was seriously big business. When they found out what was going on, the reaction of the ICC, as of most cricket authorities in general throughout history, was to do too little, too late. The problem continued to fester, untreated, until April 2000. That month a Delhi detective, investigating complaints by Indian businessmen about extortion with menaces, was listening to a tape of phone taps when the name of the South African captain Hansie Cronje came up, and Cronje's voice was subsequently heard debating match-fixing. When the news came out Cronje, an avowed Christian – the WWJD on his bracelet standing for 'What Would Jesus Do?' – initially denied the accusations, but admitted them four days later. He also revealed, somewhat to England's chagrin, that his noble gesture in proposing a dual-forfeiture in the rain-affected dead match in the 1998 series against England – which England won in an unexpected and exciting run-chase – was so that a gambling acquaintance could then back both sides to win at long odds. As a result Cronje acquired £5000 and a leather jacket. The subsequent King Commission banned Cronje for life, and the two most vulnerable members of the team, Herschelle Gibbs and Henry Williams, were given temporary bans for agreeing to fix a one-day international with India

It became clear that Cronje had been taking Gupta's money for a long time, but was not delivering the results Gupta wanted with any regularity. That included a one-day international for Mohinder Amarnath's benefit, when the whole South African team was drawn into it but declined to participate. The Indian captain Mohammad Azharuddin had been another of Gupta's targets. In October 2000 he admitted involvement in fixing one-day internationals. As a consequence Azharuddin and Ajay Sharma received life bans, Ajay Jadeja and Manoj Prabhakar – blowing the whistle and getting caught himself – each had five-year bans.

Gupta alleged that other players had accepted his money for information or to under-perform, and he named them. Predictably, the accusations met a barrage of denials. On the one hand, why should anyone believe him? On the other, why should he bother to impugn innocent cricketers, unless piqued by their refusals? Among the accused were Crowe, Ranatunga, Lara, de Silva, Salim Malik, Mark Waugh and the only Englishman, Alec Stewart. All were top-class cricketers. They couldn't have been involved, could they? If they weren't, this was grossly unfair, slur by association.

These revelations forced the Pakistan Board to release the 1999 Qayyum report, revealing that he had proposed a life ban on Salim Malik, and censured other members of the team for 'failing to cooperate', a euphemism for a cover-up, following a retraction of evidence against Wasim Akram by one of the team, Ata-ur-Rehman.

Alec Stewart protested his innocence. England hitherto seemed to have escaped involvement, although in 1999 Chris Lewis reported that he had been approached by an Indian to under-perform in the Old Trafford Test against New Zealand – odd, since he wasn't selected – and to request others to, as had the New Zealand captain Stephen Fleming before the same match. Subsequent investigation by Sir Paul Condon, ex-chief of the London Metropolitan Police, cleared Stewart in 2001, and in the end named no names. But he was suitably scathing about the international Boards' collective reluctance, first to admit the seriousness of the gambling scandal, then to clear up the problem, and challenged each Board to put its house in order. Since then no new prosecutions have taken place. However, serious doubts remain about the probity of some members of some Boards in this period, doubts that are never likely to be resolved.

CHAPTER 30

Sinking to the Bottom

Position	Team	p	w	d	l	pts	average
1	Australia	14	11	2	1	24	1.71
2	West Indies	14	7	4	3	18	1.29
3	South Africa	15	9	1	5	19	1.27
4	Pakistan	14	6	3	5	15	1.07
5	India	15	5	3	7	13	0.87
6	Sri Lanka	16	4	5	7	13	0.81
7	Zimbabwe	10	2	3	5	7	0.70
8	New Zealand	16	4	3	9	11	0.69
9	**England**	14	3	2	9	8	0.57

The Wisden World Championship Table – 22 August 1999

The unofficial Wisden world championship table, forerunner of the current ICC table, in August 1999 after defeat by New Zealand had sent England to the bottom, at the end of Nasser Hussain's first series as captain.

The English game is stuck in the mud of the past. Its Little Englander insularity, the refusal to accept that we have been left behind, has bred a generation of players who, with a few rare exceptions, have neither the technique nor the mental toughness to compete with even the weakest of the other eight Test-playing nations.

PETER JOHNSON, *Daily Mail*

1996 India and Pakistan

After Sri Lanka's subcontinent World Cup win, 1996 was a subcontinent twin-tour summer, with Pakistan following India, and another chance for restitution after the bleak midwinter. A disgruntled Illingworth resigned the manager's job, and tossed it across the Pennines to David Lloyd, an engaging blunt-speaking eccentric who got on well with the players and especially Atherton, a fellow-Lancastrian. Illingworth stayed as Chairman of Selectors, growing increasingly grumpy over the summer as a dispute played out with his employers, the TCCB. India had their own problem, with the growing unpopularity of their captain Azharuddin, who was accompanied by the Bollywood starlet who had supplanted his wife.

India	214 & 219	**England**	313 & 121–2
England	344 & 279–9	India	429
India	521 & 211	England	564

At Edgbaston England picked the Indian-born Nasser Hussain, restored after successfully captaining England A in Pakistan, and three debutants, one of whom was the Kent spinner Min Patel. (Odd to see an Indian side without a Patel play an England side with one.) Fine bowling by Cork, Lewis and Alan Mullally, Leicester's left-arm pace bowler, English-born but Australian-bred, dismissed India for 214 on day one. England's reply was glued together by Hussain, helped to his first Test century by 98 for the last two wickets. Tendulkar did a similar job for India, but no one could stay with him against Lewis, 5–72, and England won comfortably by eight wickets. India had four debutants for that Test, only one of whom would become a long-term success, but they found two more for Lord's who both would. The slim left-handed Sourav Ganguly and the tall, correct Rahul Dravid made 131 and 95 respectively in their first Test innings. Azharuddin had put England in on a seamer's pitch, and England were 107–6 when Russell joined Thorpe in pulling England up to 344. Russell's 126 was his second Test century, and he continued his cussed obstinacy when England were in trouble at 168–6 second time around, before becoming Dickie Bird's last victim as a Test umpire.

At Trent Bridge a bland pitch allowed India no chance to level the series. Another 136 from Ganguly and 84 from Dravid, in support of Tendulkar's 177, took India past 500, giving notice of the future strength of Indian batting. Atherton and Hussain replied with centuries of their own to ensure the series victory. Hussain, though, broke a finger, which would keep him out of the first Test of the Pakistan series. Pakistan's World Cup defeat had upset their supporters and the press, who had turned on Wasim Akram in particular.

Pakistan	340 & 352–5d	England	285 & 243
Pakistan	448 & 242–7	England	501
England	326 & 242	**Pakistan**	521–8d & 48–1

On the first day at Lord's, Inzamam's 148 put Pakistan in control, and England stuttered to 285, 55 behind. Their bowlers could make no impression in the Pakistan second innings, and England were set 408 in four sessions. They were 168–1 early in the third, with Atherton and Stewart going well, but the leg-spinner Mushtaq Ahmed dismissed both, then three more, Waqar another three, and eight wickets had fallen for 40 to send England to defeat. The pitch at Headingley was too good for a result in the second game. Ijaz and Moin scored centuries for Pakistan, Stewart (opening) and Knight (at No. 6) for England. The pitch for the last Test should have been too good for a result too, but England couldn't capitalise on Crawley's 106 on the opening day. With Saeed Anwar making 176, Pakistan were able to declare virtually 200 ahead and exert pressure on England on the final day. Although they started it at 74–0, that pressure told on England, whose top order batsmen folded to Mushtaq just as they had at Lord's.

With Mushtaq and Kumble joining Warne and Muralitharan at the top of the spinners' tree, England were being exposed by top-class wrist-spin, after years when they had largely had to contend with pace alone. The batsmen who could deal with it best were Stewart, who in the six Tests made 532 at 66, Hussain 429 at 61, Atherton 424 at 47, Thorpe 352 at 39. But England's batting folded too often against Pakistan, and their bowling wasn't good enough after the first Indian Test to bowl sides out twice. No bowler managed an average lower than 30. Mullally's consistent and miserly performances gave him 22 wickets at 31, Cork took his 22 at 36, Lewis 16 at 37. Assorted spinners took just six wickets at over 100 each. No spinner had taken a five-wicket haul for England since Peter Such on the first day of the 1993 series. But at least Tufnell and the Glamorgan off-spinner Robert Croft were picked for the winter tour to Zimbabwe and New Zealand.

1996–7 Zimbabwe and New Zealand

Zimbabwe had achieved Test status in 1992, an elevation England had voted against, and this winter tour was the first time the two teams had played since then. England were not entirely popular tourists, and if they expected an easy time they were mistaken. Having lost two one-day games and one of first-class, England were not in good form as they approached the first Test in Bulawayo.

| Zimbabwe | 376 & 234 | England | 406 & 204–6 |
| England | 156 & 155–3 | Zimbabwe | 215 |

Zimbabwe's home Tests had been played on slow pitches, and results had been hard to come by unless Zimbabwe were overwhelmed – with a solid batting line-up they were hard to bowl out twice. But the first Test, a slow burner, finished with a bang. England bowled badly on the first day, and a century from their prolific wicket-keeper-batsman Andy Flower the next day took Zimbabwe to 376. Centuries for Hussain and Crawley gave England a narrow lead. Zimbabwe started the last day 107–5, but clung on until England needed 205 from 37 overs. It was now effectively a one-day game, which suited Knight and Stewart, but one without the fielding circles, which suited Zimbabwe. The two took the score to 154–1, whereupon Stewart was out with 51 needed from eight overs. A clatter of wickets brought England to the last over still needing 13 to win. Knight picked up the third ball for six over square leg, leaving five needed in three balls. The first of them, like many earlier, might well have been called a wide (Streak said so himself, only to be fined for his honesty). Knight scored two off the fifth and – needing three to win and a six for a well-merited 100 – two off the last, only for Gough to be run out going for a third. So this became the first Test to be drawn with the scores level.

In his intense frustration, the England coach David Lloyd didn't endear himself to his hosts with his notorious 'We flippin' murdered 'em' comment, and for much of the second Test in Harare it was England who were the more likely murder victims. Only Crawley batted with any patience on a slow pitch and slower out-field, as England struggled lamely to 137–9 on the opening day. Zimbabwe laboured to 215 between the showers, but at the end of the fourth day England had taken the initiative through Stewart's undefeated century, his first while keeping wicket. But it rained all the last day before England could push for victory. Within a few days they had lost all three one-day internationals, so were relieved to get off to New Zealand for a series that was to give them two enthralling denouements.

New Zealand	390 & 248–9	England	521
New Zealand	124 & 191	**England**	383
New Zealand	346 & 186	**England**	228 & 307–6

Since the New Zealand tour five years earlier, England hadn't won a single overseas series. They made a bad start in Auckland with wayward bowling after Atherton had asked the opposition to bat. (Interviewer: 'Did the damp, green pitch give your bowlers the help you expected?' Atherton: 'We'll never know.') Fleming's hundred took New Zealand to 390, which looked unassailable, but Atherton and Stewart added 182. Stewart went on to 173, and Thorpe added another hundred in a century stand with Cork. A lead of 131 was enough to exert some pressure, and New Zealand started the last day at 56–3. Tufnell and Mullally soon made that 105–8, and it was 142–9, a lead of 11, when last man Danny Morrison joined Nathan Astle. There were nearly three and a half hours left, and essentially the runs/time equation was such that England had about two and a half hours to take the last wicket. In a state of mounting desperation, they failed. Astle made a hundred, but Morrison's perform-ance for an avowed No. 11 was amazing.

Morrison was dropped for Wellington, but his new-found defensive skills would only have prolonged the inevitable. A rainy first day delayed the start till after tea, but Caddick and Gough bowled so well that New Zealand were soon 23–5, and next day all out for 124. Thorpe made a second successive century in reply as England built a big lead. Then rain and the New Zealand openers prevented them from taking a wicket until the close of the fourth day, leaving them to get all 10 on a day of dark clouds, more than they had managed in Auckland. But this time Croft broke through, the rain came but not for too long, and the new ball gave England a deserved innings victory. Gough had 9–92 in the match, Caddick 6–85.

England were unchanged for the first time for 33 Tests at Christchurch. As at Auckland Atherton put the opposition in, and with the same result. New Zealand, with a new young captain, 23-year-old Stephen Fleming, made 346 despite intelli-gent off-spin from Croft, who had five wickets in a Test innings for the first time. When England batted, Atherton stood alone amid a flurry of rash strokes at the other end, and carried his bat for 94. Ahead by 118, New Zealand sought to press home their advantage, but Tufnell and Croft had them 95–6 at the end of the third day. Next day Gough ended a partial recovery by Cairns and Vettori, playing his second Test within three weeks of his 18th birthday, and England needed 305 in nine hours. Vettori showed his class, bowling left-arm spin over the wicket into the rough, but the game was evenly poised when England ended the fourth day 110–2, Atherton 65. Atherton continued to bat better than everyone else, until he was fourth out with victory in sight. But two quick wickets for the accurate Vettori – 4–97 in 57 overs from someone barely out of school – left England 231–6, needing 74. Cork wasn't renowned for his self-discipline, but he hung on to it, and he and Crawley gradually wrenched the game away from New Zealand, and won in the eighth over of the last 20.

So, largely through his own guts and determination, Atherton had turned a pos-sible 1–1 series draw into a 2–0 win, and England's supporters could forget the Zimbabwe leg. After hardly making a run in Zimbabwe, Atherton finished with 359 runs at 51, below both Crawley's 55, and Stewart's excellent 71 for an aggregate of 498. Gough came through with 26 wickets at 20. Support for him was sporadic, but at least for once England bowled two spinners in tandem, and Croft and Tufnell did well to take 32 wickets between them at 30. New Zealand weren't the opposition that Australia would prove to be, of course, but it was a start. Another one.

1997 Australia

If England supporters were looking for portents, Australia had lost a one-off Test in India in the winter, and then only beaten South Africa 2–1. So they were beatable. England's abiding problem against the best sides was that their batting capitulated too often in the second innings of games they should be saving, and their last five batsmen never seemed able to summon the dogged resistance that the last five of other sides did. Time for another try.

Australia	118 & 477	**England**	478–9d & 119–1
England	77 & 277–4	Australia	213–7d
Australia	235 & 395–8d	England	162 & 200
England	172 & 268	**Australia**	501–9d
Australia	427 & 336	England	313 & 186
England	180 & 163	Australia	220 & 104

England began the summer by unexpectedly winning all three one-day internationals, on all three occasions chasing a target to win. This was the Hollioake spring (which, in folk lore, usually portends an awful summer). Adam made two aggressive not-out fifties, and his 19-year-old brother Ben made a carefree 63 from 48 balls, batting at No. 3 in the last game, to bring a target of 270 to one of more manageable proportions. Sons of English parents, their Australian upbringing showed in their energetic and self-confident approach. The English player most like them, Cork, was injured and would miss the whole series, a serious blow.

The first Test at Edgbaston was an even greater surprise, and its start was sensational. Taylor won the toss and batted. With 25 minutes still to go before lunch he was staring in disbelief at a scoreboard that read 54–8. Malcolm (2–25) and Gough (3–43) began it, and Caddick (5–50) finished it. A flurry from Warne took the score to 118 in the 32nd over. England lost three for 50, and home supporters feared the worst, but Hussain and Thorpe batted with such fluency and authority that they had taken the score to 200–3 at the close, reducing even Warne to impotence. The next day they took their partnership to 288, the lead already over 200, when Thorpe left for 138. Warne (1–110) got Hussain in the end, but not before he had made 207 in 337 balls. (Stewart to Hussain: 'I didn't know you could bat so well.' Hussain to Stewart: 'Neither did I.') The declaration came on the third morning. Taylor, who had not reached 50 in any of his last 21 Test innings, knew the Australian press hounds were after him, and responded with the appropriate determination and stamina. He added 133 with Elliott and 194 with Blewett, so that at 327–1 before lunch on the fourth day they were just 33 behind. If this continued there was a strong chance of Headingley 1981 in reverse. But Croft dismissed both, Gough got the Waughs and Bevan, and the Kent all-rounder Mark Ealham proved his worth by disposing of the tail. Needing 118 to win, Atherton and Stewart batted with such aggression and confidence that they won the game on the fourth evening in the 22nd over, and the crowd and its joy overflowed.

So what were these Australians made of? We discovered at Lord's. Rain took most of the first two days. When it stopped, the tall, menacing, relentlessly accurate Glenn McGrath, now bowling the fuller length required by English pitches, took 8–38 in 20.3 overs to bowl England out for a miserable 77. Elliott's rapid hundred enabled Australia to get at England again after more rain, but they were thwarted by an opening stand of 162 by Atherton and the busy Surrey left-hander Mark Butcher. A draw, but England had been warned. Only Steve Waugh prevented another major opening-day collapse at Old Trafford, a stoic 108 against good bowling from Gough and the Kent opening bowler Dean Headley, grandson of the great West Indian George Headley, a third generation playing Test cricket. Australia's 235 didn't seem many, but after Warne had got weaving it became respectable. Warne disposed of Stewart, Hussain, Thorpe and Crawley on his way to 6–48, and a lead of 73. Steve Waugh's second hundred of the game put Australia out of reach, and only Crawley delayed the end, with a defiant 83 out of 122 until he trod on his wicket.

Level at 1–1, Australia were back in the groove. At Headingley it was the lean and piratical Jason Gillespie who took six of the last seven to fall, and caught the other, as 154–4 became 172 all out. Gough and Headley had Australia 50–4, and Thorpe dropped Elliott, a sitter from the left-armer Mike Smith, whose only Test it was. But Elliott got away to 199, Ricky Ponting made his first Test century, and Australia were out of sight. In England's second innings Hussain and Crawley resisted till the end of the fourth day, but after Hussain had gone for 101 the last five wickets tumbled again, the beneficiary this time Paul Reiffel, who had been parachuted in to off-set injuries. At Trent Bridge England brought in the Hollioakes together for their first Tests in the hope of inspiration, but the Australian machine was now uprooting everything in its path. Each of the top five Australians made 50 in an innings of 427. Stewart made a brisk 87 in 107 balls, and two more Surrey players added 112 for the fifth wicket, Thorpe and Adam Hollioake, but the deficit was 114. A day later England were setting out to bat for eight hours, and lasted fewer than four, in an inept batting display that only Thorpe's 82* relieved. At the subsequent Press conference Atherton 'resolutely resisted the journalists' invitations to resign at once'.

After the promise of the season's opening, grim reality had struck back, and there seemed nothing to stop Australia making it four wins in a row when England were bowled out for 180 by McGrath, before tea on the first day at the Oval. Tufnell, playing his first Test of the summer after being omitted from the final selection in each of the first five games – enough to exasperate anybody – took the two wickets that fell overnight. The next day, the pitch, dry but seemingly unexceptional, began taking a little spin, and Tufnell put in one of those immaculate, teasing spells he produced from time to time. He took seven of the first eight wickets to fall, and Australia's lead was restricted to 40. England lost three wickets seeing off the arrears, and the fourth soon after, but with Warne hampered by a groin strain, Thorpe and Ramprakash fashioned a partnership of 79. It didn't last: Michael Kasprowicz became the third player in the match, and the third Australian fast bowler in the series, to achieve a seven-wicket haul, and Australia needed a mere 124. Atherton lost no time in getting Caddick and Tufnell bowling together, and 36–1 suddenly became 54–5. Ponting and Healy took the score to 88, 36 needed, but Tufnell had Ponting lbw and Caddick juggled heart-stoppingly before catching Healy off his own bowling. Warne, the danger man, holed out off Tufnell, and a few minutes later England had won by 19. Caddick had 5–42, Tufnell 4–27 and 11–93 in the match.

England had fought back at the end of the summer, but after such joyous early promise the three successive defeats were a bitter disappointment. Their batting had let them down. Thorpe was consistent and averaged 50, but Hussain slipped below 40 despite his swaggering double century opener. Crawley, Butcher, Stewart and Atherton averaged from 30 down to 23. The bowling did well enough – Caddick took 24 wickets at 26, Headley and Gough took 16 each at 27 and 31 respectively – but one wonders what would have happened had Tufnell played sooner. He took 11 in his only Test, Croft just eight in the other five. McGrath with 36 wickets was the bowler of the series. Despite the setback, England went to the West Indies hoping that the tide that had turned in 1995 would sweep them to victory.

1997–8 West Indies

Buoyed by the Oval win, Atherton held on to the captaincy, but suffered an early blow when Gough was injured and withdrew from the tour. The series started and stopped in Jamaica. The Kingston pitch was so appalling, on a hastily re-laid square made worse by a wonky roller, that it lasted for 61 lethal balls from Ambrose and Walsh before the captains, umpires and referee agreed it was too dangerous. The teams flew gratefully to Trinidad where an extra Test could be inserted.

England	17–3	West Indies	
England	214 & 258	**West Indies**	191 & 282–7
West Indies	159 & 210	**England**	145 & 225–7
West Indies	352 & 197	England	179 & 137
England	403 & 233–3d	West Indies	262 & 112–2
England	127 & 321	**West Indies**	500–7d

England could easily have left there two up. As it was they had to settle for 1–1. In the first of them, nagging line-and-length bowling from Fraser, restored from injury in his first Test bowl for two years, brought him a magnificent 8–53. A second fifty by Stewart on an awkward pitch left West Indies 282 to win, by far the highest score of the match. They shouldn't have got there. That they achieved it from the depths of 124–5 was due to a stand of 129 from the brilliant Carl Hooper and the keeper David Williams. With 102 still needed, and Ambrose next in at the head of a long tail, Williams was dropped from a caught-and-bowled chance to Fraser from the first ball of the last day. Anguish for England, and especially for Fraser, 11–110 in the match.

The return match the following week was played on a slow, low pitch, which brought some slow, low batting. It was like the first match in reverse. Caddick and Fraser took five each on the first day. Ambrose matched them, and eventually Atherton and Stewart set out to make 225 to win. Their gritty opening stand of 129 won England the match, despite some typical late-innings palpitations. Stewart top-scored in each innings, and Fraser took his Trinidad tally to 20–190 to emphasise how much he'd been missed. So, to Guyana at 1–1, which could have been 2–0 either way. This game, played in the midst of a drought, decided the series. The toss was crucial: Lara and Chanderpaul added 159 on the opening day, whereupon the pitch deteriorated. Only Ramprakash for England passed 30, and England lost heavily. In Barbados a fortnight later in the fifth Test he did even better. Coming to the wicket at 53–4, and promptly losing Thorpe to a back spasm, he made his first Test hundred, 154 and a 'masterpiece' according to Wisden. Thorpe's back recovered to allow him too to reach three figures, and England topped 400. On the fourth afternoon they were able to set a target of 375 on a turning pitch, but rain on the last day left them rueing their luck.

England might have been 3–1 up going into the final Test in Antigua, but were 2–1 down instead. After a rain-affected first day the match seemed virtually over by the end of the second – England 127, West Indies 126–0, clattered by Wallace and Lambert in just 27 overs. But Stewart, Hussain and Thorpe led a revival on the last two days, until Hussain's run out at 4 pm on the last afternoon turned 295–3 into 321 all out. The threatening rain held off, compounding England's misery, and they had somehow lost the series 3–1. The surprising man of the match was the leg spinner Dinanath Ramnarine (a trivia question in years to come), and he and Hooper actually took 24 wickets in the series between them for just 21 each. England's experienced spinners couldn't match them: Tufnell took only seven wickets all series, and Croft six in just a single Test, reversing the summer's position. After his magnificent start Fraser took only seven more wickets, but finished with 27 at 18, supported by Headley and Caddick with 19 and 13. Ramprakash led the batting averages with 66, Stewart and Thorpe weighed in at over 40, Hussain's was 32, but no one else reached 20. It was the batting again. Atherton averaged just 18, and resigned the captaincy.

1998 South Africa and Sri Lanka

South Africa arrived in 1998 for their first full series in England since 1960. In the winter they had won one in Pakistan and lost a close one to Australia 1–0, so they were clearly resilient tourists. Indeed, on the fourth morning of the third Test they seemed to have the series won.

England	462 & 170–8	South Africa	343
South Africa	360 & 15–0	England	110 & 264
South Africa	552–5d	England	183 & 369–8
South Africa	374 & 208	**England**	336 & 247–2
England	230 & 240	South Africa	252 & 195

Stewart took over the captaincy, and began at Edgbaston by watching Atherton make a battling redemptive hundred, in an opening stand of 179 with Butcher.

England's 462 took the first two days, so a result would depend on whether South Africa could avert the follow-on. Thanks to Jonty Rhodes they did, despite nine wickets for Fraser and Cork. Cork was again on form at Lord's, taking the first four wickets, but so was Rhodes. His 117 in a big stand with Cronje was decisive, for England capitulated to Donald and Pollock. Hussain led them to 222–3 after following on, but six wickets fell for 11 and that was that.

So to Old Trafford, which was a long uphill battle for England. Early on the fourth day England were 11–2 after again suffering the indignity of following on, this time 369 behind after Kirsten's 210, made in 10 minutes under 11 hours. In prospect was another ignominious defeat, but Atherton and Stewart added a round 200 undefeated by the close. Atherton went for 89 next morning, and Stewart advanced to 164, but there were nearly two hours left when Gough joined Croft at 329–8. They gutsed it out until Gough left with 19 balls remaining. Croft brought the scores level, which took two overs out of the equation, and Fraser saw out Donald's last over – just – to complete another Great Escape against South Africa. If England had lost then they would have been 2–0 down with two to play.

As so often, if not with Australia in 2005, a long rearguard action to save a probable lost game can leave the weaker side with an unexpected psychological ascendancy. With a football World Cup dominating the screens, and crowds staying away, England desperately needed a win at Trent Bridge. Stewart put South Africa in, only to see Cronje dominate the first day, notably in a calculatedly brutal attack on the leg-spin of Salisbury. Butcher and Atherton replied to the eventual 374 with a stand of 145, but England couldn't capitalise. After a bad start Cronje again put South Africa in a strong position, but Cork and Fraser (who took nine in the match) worked through the middle order to give England a target of 247. It's hard to believe, now, that England hadn't chased that many and won at home since Jessop's match in 1902, but Atherton took them to 82–1 before he gloved Donald to Boucher. Notoriously, he stood his ground and was given not out. In truth it was just one of several debatable decisions in the match, but it was the one we all remember. It led to a furiously hostile spell from Donald, but Atherton and Hussain weathered it, Stewart played a crisp cameo to finish the game, and England had won by eight wickets with Atherton 98[*].

All-square going to Headingley, and the crowds returned. England made a mess of the first day, losing their last six wickets for 34 after Butcher's aggressive 116. But South Africa fared little better against Fraser and Gough, and led by only 22. At the end of the third day England stood well at 206–4 after Hussain's emotionally intense 94, but they again lost their last six wickets for 34. This fourth day became a roller-coaster. After 15 overs Gough and Fraser had South Africa 42–5, but the 219 target began to look closer and closer as Rhodes and McMillan took the score to 144. The game then twisted again as both were out, Cork breaking the stand and Rhodes giving Gough his 100th Test wicket. Then crucially, at 183–8, with England's three seamers close to exhaustion and Pollock well set, Stewart's quick wits and a South African communication failure led to their failing to claim the final half-hour. The next morning Gough and Fraser were fresh, and England won by 23.

So by the skin of their teeth England won a series 2–1 that could have been lost 3–1. The summer had turned out well after all. There was just the little matter of one Test against Sri Lanka, still to their chagrin unable to secure a proper tour. Ranatunga put England in at the Oval, and when, late on the second day, England were all out for 445, their supporters felt it was a matter of win-or-draw. How wrong they were.

England	445 & 181	**Sri Lanka**	591 & 37–0

A solid century by Hick gave England control on the first day, but it was a beautiful innings of 156* by Crawley, mastering Muralitharan, that brought them what seemed total command on the second. Fraser helped him add 91 for the last wicket against a tiring Murali, who finished with 7–155. By the close Jayasuriya had raced ominously to 59, and next day he thrashed his way to 213 out of 328. Aravinda de Silva took over with 152, and Sri Lanka reached 591. Thereafter it was all Murali. He might have taken all 10 had Stewart not been run out, but 9–65 from 54.2 overs gave him 16 for 220 in the match, and England had been bowled out for 181 in 130 overs – shades of Ram and Val's iron grip in 1950. During this, his 42nd Test, Muralitharan reached 200 wickets, the same number that Shane Warne had needed: their great rivalry was under way. While there were constant rumblings about his action – England manager David Lloyd's dark mutterings on the subject brought him a reprimand – it was still a marvellous piece of bowling.

Taking the summer as a whole, England's batting was headed at 55 by an Atherton freed from the captaincy, Stewart and Butcher at 45, with Hussain and Ramprakash in the mid-thirties. Fraser, Gough and Cork took 66 wickets, but the support was threadbare, with the spinners taking just 2–550. Caddick took 105 wickets for Somerset, but was neither required during the summer nor invited to Australia. It seemed the Australian batsmen would make hay unless something turned up, but Warne's absence through injury for most of the series gave hope of a better English batting performance.

1998–9 Australia

Australia	485 & 237–3d	England	375 & 179–6
England	112 & 191	**Australia**	240 & 64–3
Australia	391 & 278–5d	England	227 & 237
England	270 & 244	Australia	340 & 162
Australia	322 & 184	England	220 & 188

After Australia's first innings at Brisbane, the bowlers acquitted themselves well. After England's first innings there the batsmen acquitted themselves poorly, and never reached 300 thereafter. Hundreds from Steve Waugh and Healy at Brisbane helped Australia add over 300 for the last five wickets. Butcher's 116 led England's reply, and Slater's typically jaunty innings left England a day and a bit to hold out. A classic Brisbane thunderstorm probably saved them when it ended proceedings after tea. A classic lightning pitch at Perth was England's undoing in the second Test. Bowled out for 112 in just 39 overs, England hit back through the debutant Alex Tudor on day two. Tudor, with a boxer's physique but without a boxer's mentality, was one of the great might-have-beens. Although Hick counter-attacked with 68 from 73 balls, it was all over on the third afternoon. England needed at least a draw at Adelaide to stay in the hunt. Australia's 391 was founded on Langer's 179*, and at 187–3, with Hussain and Ramprakash both past 50, England threatened to match it. But the last seven wickets fell for 40, and when they batted again they never looked like saving it. The Ashes were gone.

England and 58 000 spectators watched the rain come down on Boxing Day in Melbourne. A hundred from Stewart next day, opening again, took England to 200–3, but again they subsided. Gough took five in reply, but Steve Waugh produced a typical 122* to chisel out a lead of 70. England's second innings disappointed despite three fifties, and Australia needed a mere 175 to win. At 103–2 they were coasting, but Ramprakash pulled off a stupendous catch to dismiss Langer, and at 130 Headley removed the dangerous Mark Waugh. That began an inspired spell in which he took three wickets with the score 140. Steve Waugh inched them past 150, 25 short. It was past 7.30 pm, England had been on the field continuously for nearly four hours, and Stewart this time failed to prevent Waugh claiming the last half-hour. Tiring, Headley and Gough ploughed on, and Headley got his sixth wicket and the eighth at 161, 14 needed. Unaccountably, Steve Waugh took a single off the first ball of the next over, and Gough seized the chance to get MacGill and McGrath in the next three balls. Australia had again folded chasing a moderate total, and England won by 12 runs.

Now 2–1 down, England could draw the series at Sydney, especially as, after the Waugh twins had added a brilliant 190, Gough brought the innings to an abrupt end with the first hat trick in an Ashes Test for 100 years. But England batted poorly against MacGill on the second day, Slater hit a rumbustious 123 out of 184 on the third, remarkably over two-thirds of the innings total, after escaping a run-out when the bowler obscured the poorly-positioned camera. Technology was here, as the next chapter explains, but it was hardly perfected yet. England eventually lost again, despite Warne taking only two wickets on his return. Another leg-spinner, Stuart MacGill, took his match analysis to 12–107. That Australia had a ready-made match-winning replacement for Warne was too galling for England. Of their batsmen Ramprakash and Hussain averaged in the forties, but only Stewart of the others over 30. Without Thorpe, who had left after the first Test with a back problem (though Atherton stuck it out with his) the batsmen let the bowlers down. Headley headed the bowling with 19 wickets at 22, Gough's 21 cost 32, while Such and Mullally reached double figures. The wholehearted Headley, not yet 30, could have been a key figure for England in the new century, but a (further) bad back injury forced his retirement, soon after he became one of the first to be awarded a central contract in 2000.

1999 The seventh World Cup

Back to England for the seventh World Cup, which began encouragingly in mid-May with a comfortable England win over the holders Sri Lanka. From that high point England crashed spectacularly. They duly beat Kenya and Zimbabwe, but were bowled out for 103 by South Africa. England turned up to play India at Edgbaston on 29 May needing a win to be sure of proceeding to the Super Six stage. However if the unbeaten group leaders South Africa defeated Zimbabwe as expected the same day, England would be through irrespective of the India result. When rain brought a premature end to the first day, England were 73–3 chasing 232, needing another 160 at 5.4 an over on a slow pitch. That was bad enough, but the news from Chelmsford was worse, for South Africa, chasing 234, had lost their first six wickets for 40. Though they rallied, they lost to Zimbabwe for the first time in any form of cricket. Next day England stumbled to 168 and out of the tournament on run-rate to Zimbabwe, who were in contention only because Henry Olonga had taken three wickets in an amazing last over to beat India by three runs. Sharing England's ignominy were Sri Lanka, the holders.

The Super Six format had partly been devised to maximise the number of games and the tournament's income, partly to ensure that the best teams all played each other. The 12 teams were split into two groups of 15 games each. In the other group Pakistan won their first four matches, then, with qualification secure, lost a dead match to Bangladesh that soon fuelled suspicions of match-fixing. Australia struggled, losing to Pakistan and New Zealand, but together with New Zealand squeezed through on run-rate at West Indies' expense.

Teams took their two results against other qualifying teams, together with their net run-rate, into the Super Six stage. This suited Pakistan and Zimbabwe, who brought two wins with them, but not Australia and India, who had none. With each team now playing three games against the sides from the other group, the scoring was sensible enough. So Australia, with a poor run-rate, would almost certainly have to win all three to reach the semi-final. They beat India and Zimbabwe comfortably enough, but then had to beat South Africa, who had already qualified after a gripping win over Pakistan. Australia v South Africa was the first of two tremendous matches. Herschelle Gibbs's 100 set Australia 272, but his dropping of a sitter from Steve Waugh at a crucial stage arguably lost his team the Cup, as Waugh famously told him at the time. Waugh had rescued Australia from 48–3, and was 120* when they won with two balls to spare.

Although Pakistan had slipped in the second stage, they only had to beat Zimbabwe to qualify, and in so doing met New Zealand in the first semi-final at Old Trafford. New Zealand had only managed to qualify on run-rate from Zimbabwe, and were no match for Pakistan, losing by nine wickets after a Saeed Anwar century. The next day Australia and South Africa met again at Edgbaston in a match whose switchback excitement and nerve-racking finish probably made it the most gripping World Cup match ever. A stand of 90 by Steve Waugh and Bevan held Australia together from 58–4, but the last four wickets fell in a heap to Pollock and Donald, who took nine wickets between them. South Africa stuttered against Warne (4–29), recovered through Kallis and Rhodes, fell behind the clock, then were resuscitated when Klusener clubbed 31 from 12 balls. That brought the scores level with four balls left. A tie would put Australia through because their run-rate was superior over the whole tournament – unsatisfactory, but what alternative was there? With every-one up for the single, Fleming pitched the ball up twice, and Klusener drove the second to mid-on and charged down the wicket like the bull he resembled. Donald hesitated, dropped his bat, set off too late, and was efficiently run out. Anguish.

SEMI-FINALS			
New Zealand	241–7 (50)	Pakistan	242–1 (47.3)
Australia	213 (49.2)	South Africa	213 (49.4)
FINAL			
Pakistan	132 (39)	**Australia**	133–1 (20.1)

As anti-climaxes go, the final was a corker. Pakistan batted appallingly and Warne bowled beautifully for another 4–33, emulating Amarnath in becoming man of the match in both semi-final and final. Top-class spinners are match winners whatever the class of cricket. Australia won in the 21st over, untroubled by the threat of Shoaib Akhtar, who had uprooted stumps throughout the competition. His four overs went for 37, and Gilchrist's dismissive 50 came from 33 balls.

1999 New Zealand

The resignation of David Lloyd left England without a coach – the replacement, Duncan Fletcher, would see out his term at Glamorgan – and with a new captain. Alec Stewart stood down in favour of Nasser Hussain. This was an important series for England, if not an obvious attractant for the spectators, for whom the New Zealanders were small beer after the World Cup. It all started well enough.

New Zealand	226 & 107	**England**	126 & 211–3
England	186 & 229	**New Zealand**	358 & 60–1
England	199 & 181–2	New Zealand	496–9d
New Zealand	236 & 162	England	153 & 162

With the ball swinging at Edgbaston, batting looked difficult from the off. This was a most peculiar match. New Zealand recovered from 73–4 until Tufnell diddled out the tail. The second day centred on two extraordinary collapses. England plunged to 45–7 before Caddick and Tudor added 70. New Zealand's reply began as badly, Caddick and Mullally reducing them to 52–8 before Doull doubled the score with a rapid 46. He was last out when 20-year-old Chris Read stumped him off Tufnell, his sixth dismissal of the second innings of a promising first Test. England had time to lose Stewart for a duck before the close. In retrospect that was a good thing, because it brought Alex Tudor to the crease overnight. Next morning he batted with growing freedom with Butcher and Hussain, and was nearing 100 when his Surrey colleague Thorpe appeared to deny him the chance to be the first Englishman to score a century as nightwatchman. He won the match with a top-edged hook for four but could only finish 99[*].

Hussain had begun with a win, but wasn't so fortunate at Lord's. Last out after glueing England together in a first innings dominated by Chris Cairns (not least by the threat of the outrageous slower ball that bowled his county colleague Read as he ducked), Hussain broke a finger in the field as New Zealand took a healthy lead. He had to watch as another grim batting display, marked by poor shot selection, consigned England to defeat. He had entrusted the captaincy to Thorpe, but the selectors gave it to Butcher for the third Test. He in turn presided over an innings that limped to 199 at under two an over, then over a big New Zealand total. Stewart anchored a better display second time round, and might have saved the game anyway had not rain saved him the trouble.

So to the last Test at the Oval, 1–1. Butcher lost his place and the captaincy as Hussain returned, but it made little difference, England ceding a first innings lead of 83. Hope flared when Caddick and the debutant Sussex seamer Ed Giddins plunged New Zealand to 39–6, but Cairns restored the advantage and turned the match with a belligerent 80. England needed 246 and got half-way with two wickets down, but it was no surprise when the house of cards folded for another 39, and England lost the series 2–1. Their batting in 1999 had been found out by two seamers, Nash and Cairns, certainly competent but hardly life-threatening, who took 36 wickets between them at 19 apiece. Caddick matched them for England with 20 at 20, and Tufnell played in every match for once to take 14 at 22. But the batting was truly awful. The top average was 35, and the 10 batsmen chosen could average only 23 between them.

England's first foreign coach arrived to take over for the winter tour in South Africa. That Duncan Fletcher was a Zimbabwean led some people to scoff, but in the summer Zimbabwe had even overtaken England in the new Test rankings, condemning them to ninth out of nine for several months. England had sunk to the bottom. It was 15 Tests since England had led on first innings, a horribly revealing statistic. Fortunately there was no relegation, and Bangladesh's elevation was just a year away.

CHAPTER 31

Decisions, Decisions...

Mike Gatting, in an attitude of despair rather than prayer, after being given out lbw to Abdul Qadir by Shakeel Khan in the first Test v Pakistan at Lahore, November 1987. The non-striker is Chris Broad, later to go even more reluctantly when given out.

It sowed the first harmless-looking seed of something that could grow to being thoroughly pernicious.

MATTHEW ENGEL, Wisden, 1993, *on the first third-umpire decision in a Test*

The ICC's view is that we want humans to umpire the game, not robots. It is essential that the umpires are in control and not simply glorified coat stands.

MALCOLM SPEED, 2005

Cricket umpires have always had a difficult job to do. When cricket began again after the war, their function had barely changed since Victorian times. Stand, concentrate, adjudicate impartially, slip away at the end of the day. In England they were exclusively old professional cricketers, underpaid but glad to retain contact with the game that had been their way of life. The advantage was that they were under little scrutiny or interference from the authorities. Players, on the other hand, were not necessarily sympathetic but certainly understood how hard umpiring was. Playing day in, day out, they reckoned that luck and umpiring error evened out over time. They tended to help umpires rather than hinder. Moreover, in the tightly-knit world of English professional cricket, cheats – those who appealed for a catch that they knew wasn't out, for example – would soon be known and marked out on the circuit, if they hadn't already received a stinging rebuke from their captain.

The end of innocence

By the 1970s that was changing. David Constant wrote that at the start of his umpiring career, in the late 1960s, 90 per cent of batsmen gave themselves out when caught behind. Twenty years later 90 per cent did not, which meant much more opportunity for contention (though, to be frank, many batsmen walked when it suited them, and not for a faint edge at a crucial moment in their career). As late as 1982, Surrey captain Roger Knight was telling the young Alec Stewart: 'Walk when you've nicked it – otherwise you'll get a reputation and the umpires will do you.' Stewart said he walked 90 per cent of the time – not 100 per cent, note – until he went to Australia that winter. That cured him of walking at all. David Shepherd wrote that 'Players used to help umpires make the decisions, now it's not the case. Everyone's trying it on. The chorus of appeals make my head hurt.' Behaviour towards umpires deteriorated rapidly. Club players, initially largely in Australia, aped and often exceeded what was going on at the top, which they could see for themselves in the no-holds-barred Packer contests. As we've seen in Chapter 19, the New South Wales 'It has to stop!' edict from 1980 implied that 'ridiculous appeals towards umpires; abuse towards umpires; and disputing decisions and berating umpires' had become commonplace.

When the television boom of the late 1950s began, and Tests were watched by a wider community with access to replays, umpiring errors became more visible, noted and remembered, even if commentators, largely old cricketers, were initially reticent in their public criticism. Moreover they generally subscribed to the view that English umpires, with masses of experience and four months of each year devoted to non-stop umpiring, were the best in the world. This was doubtless true in general, and overseas cricketers tended to feel they were more fairly treated on an England tour than elsewhere. But it didn't stop them complaining if they felt hard done by. In 1953 Lindsay Hassett objected to the legendary and hitherto almost spotless Frank

Chester after two bad mistakes that went England's way at Headingley, and he was removed from the crucial final Test. Moreover one can imagine the furore that would have attended the constant refusal of lbw appeals by Ramadhin at Edgbaston in 1957 had they occurred in the West Indies.

Backing into the limelight

Until the late 1970s, umpires in England were pretty much ignored by legislators. As ex-professional cricketers, in a game largely run by an 'upstairs' MCC hierarchy of former public school and Oxbridge cricketers, they were very much 'downstairs'. They were seen and not heard, and rarely consulted. They didn't write books. The first significant mention of them in the MCC, TCCB and ICC meeting summaries printed in each year's Wisden comes in 1976, following the Lillee/Thomson bouncer barrage in 1974–5, when umpires were assured of support 'up to the hilt' in dealing with intimidatory bowling. You'll recall Dennis Amiss saying that early in that series Thomson ignored warnings for persistent short-pitched bowling, got away with it, and the umpires wilted. They remained reluctant to tackle it, until practically forced to do so: at Old Trafford in 1976 Close and Edrich were battered by continuous and venomous short-pitched bowling by the West Indies, in the 80 minutes before the close. Only in the last few minutes did umpire Alley remonstrate with the bowlers.

Nor did umpires achieve any mention in Wisden editorials until 1981, when the then editor, John Woodcock, in a piece headed 'Who would be an Umpire?', lamented that with the game becoming more fiercely competitive, and with 'every decision subjected to a slow-motion television replay', the umpire's job was becoming increasingly difficult. But he felt that neutral umpires would be a mistake because 'England will never again have the benefit of playing under those who by common consent are the best of all umpires'. Rightly or wrongly, an anglocentric view prevailed in Wisden and at Lord's.

That 'common consent' did not extend to Imran Khan, who severely criticised the English umpires at the end of the hard-fought 1982 series. The TCCB's refusal to replace the umpires at Pakistan's request in 1987 was supported by the next Wisden editor, Graeme Wright, who went on to add, 'Pakistan is a young, aggressive state fired by a fierce nationalism and a strict fundamentalist religion', reflecting a common viewpoint at the time. That air of Western superiority cannot have assuaged a sense of injustice. The following winter's series in Pakistan brought the Shakoor/Gatting fracas. Most observers began to feel that neutral umpires were bound to come, but the prime movers in the end came from two of the countries whose umpires were most often criticised. Imran, like his Indian opposite number Sunil Gavaskar, was a campaigner for their introduction, and indeed it was Pakistan who first employed them, umpires Ramaswamy and Reporter of India standing in their series versus West Indies in 1986–7, an important gesture considering the long-term rivalry, cricketing, religious and political, between India and Pakistan.

Neutral umpires

The idea of neutral umpires had been voiced intermittently every time England ran into what they considered to be poor umpiring abroad. The charge was sometimes bias, sometimes lack of experience, the fear of a buckling under local pressure, and occasionally sheer incompetence. In 1976 the TCCB decided to invite foreign umpires to England to give them experience. Umpires Brooks and Sang Hue came, but the experiment was limply abandoned in 1978, despite foreign umpires' eagerness to test themselves through an English summer. It wasn't until 1990 that the ICC came up with a combined plan for neutral umpires, match referees and a code of conduct, a process that was implemented patchily. It needed money, which in today's world meant sponsorship. At the end of 1993 the ICC appointed an international panel of 20 umpires, one of whom would stand in each Test together with an umpire from the host country. This worked up to a point, but it didn't ensure the best umpires were in charge of the top matches.

Eventually a sponsor was found to fund an elite panel – the Emirates airline, an apparently odd choice but certainly a neutral one. In March 2002 the ICC appointed an élite panel of eight umpires: Bucknor, de Silva, Harper, Koertzen, Orchard, Shepherd, Tiffin and Venkat. Peter Willey declined because of the travelling involved – over 200 days a year away from home. That May they were augmented by a panel of second-tier international umpires. Initially there were 18 of these, later increased to 30 (three from each of 10 Test-playing nations). Tests in 2005 were umpired either by two elite panel members, or by one elite member and one from the aspiring international panel. Neither could be from either of the countries playing, except in one-day internationals, which had one local umpire from the panel (although continued calls for two neutral umpires in one-day matches suggest that this may not last).

That eight-strong elite panel has changed number and composition since. In January 2003 there was widespread criticism of their standard, which led to changes in personnel and better monitoring and feedback. By 2005, as well as post-match assessments by captains and match referees, an ICC assessor was monitoring every appeal and sending umpires a detailed DVD of their key decisions in the match. As a consequence, in the year to May 2005 elite panel members were being rated at a 94 per cent accuracy rate, a rate matching that achieved in major league baseball. That's 16 right decisions for every wrong one. Umpires can no longer be accused of bias or gross incompetence, but their every decision is minutely observed, and they know there are 30 others waiting for their place on the panel. That's pressure.

Technology

The pressure on umpires, once television replays led inevitably to such scrutiny, ratcheted up inexorably. The flaw in the system was manifest: if an observer 100 yards away has better tools and more time at his disposal than an umpire, who in the heat of the action has an instant decision to make, the umpire is on a hiding to nothing. The use of technology to assist him was mooted in the 1970s, and notably by Bradman, ahead of his time again, who was reported in the 1984 Wisden as being in favour of it for run outs, stumpings and disputed catches. A bad run-out decision, in the first over of the crucial final Test of the 1982–3 Ashes series, had helped to change conservative English views originally hardened against its adoption. That year the ICC studied a Sri Lankan report on electronic aids, and the TCCB asked scientists to investigate. But it was innovative television technology, largely ignored by a complacent BBC in its long monopoly of English TV coverage, that paved the way for a fundamental and final break with the umpire-as-sole-arbiter tradition.

It took the best part of another decade, though, before technology available to TV commentators and viewers was provided to umpires. It was in the first ever Test between South Africa and India in November 1992 at Durban that, appropriately enough, Jonty Rhodes was adjudged to have run out the 19-year-old Sachin Tendulkar with the aid of a camera at square leg. Wisden's latest editor, Matthew Engel, disapproved: 'It... sowed the first harmless-looking seed of something that could grow to be thoroughly pernicious.' The following year saw him record its spread 'to engulf the cricketing world'. He remained 'utterly convinced that this is a disaster'.

At first many experienced umpires were forthright in their antipathy to the new aids, Dickie Bird among them. 'What worries me is the thought that all this could undermine the confidence of umpires in making their own decisions. Too much authority – responsibility, too, if you like – is being taken away from them.' More recently Simon Taufel too feared becoming a coat stand: 'Technology is all about replacing the skills of the umpire and I'd like to think I've worked my way up this far to employ those skills. Why de-skill that part of the game just for the sake of an extra two or three correct decisions per game?' (Ask the players concerned...) The problem, of course, is that the technology cannot be uninvented, and if it's there for the viewer, and sufficiently accurate, it simply has to be available – eventually – for the umpire. David Shepherd, suspicious at first, came round to the view that there was 'an unchallengeable logic to their use'. Daryl Harper thought that 'in many ways the increased use of technology eases the pressure for the on-field umpires'.

Electronic aids are here to stay. The problem areas remain those in which it has not been perfected, and may never be: where viewers can form a view that itself may be wrong. Leg before wicket, with its multiple issues of height, direction, pitching point, interception point and bat avoidance, remains complex. Hawk-Eye has been available for some years, with its superimposed stump-marking lines, but is it foolproof? An idea for painting actual lines on the pitch was proposed in 2003 but shelved. Would it give the batsman too much help? It wasn't until the ICC Champions Trophy in 2004 that experiments were made with the third umpire assisting with lbw decisions. Harper changed his mind on just one lbw decision when told by Rudy Koertzen that the ball had pitched in line with leg stump and not outside. He for one is happy with this experimentation, though Billy Bowden is not so sure: 'Are we going to use the Hawk-Eye? If we do there won't be any more four- or five-day Test matches, they'd be one or two-day Test matches.' This interesting if extreme observation by inference attacks the technology for being too authoritative when there's still doubt. Harper said that he was surprised how often Hawk-Eye showed a ball clipping leg-stump that he thought might miss; equally the frequency with which the ball went over the stumps gave him pause for thought. Height has always been particularly difficult for the bowler's umpire in assessing leg before.

The technology can certainly deal with adjudicating no-balls better than the umpire can, and third umpire intervention seems inevitable here. It would save the heart-searching David Shepherd went through when missing those no-balls that gave Saqlain Mushtaq wickets on the last day at Old Trafford in 2001. Low catches in the field remain a thorny issue, though. The super-slow motion approach seems to lead to real confusion, as Mark Nicholas has pointed out, citing an occasion when two expert commentators continued to differ radically after over a dozen viewings. I have always felt when playing that the fielder (a wicketkeeper possibly excepted because the gloves dampen finger sensitivity) almost always knows instinctively whether he has made the catch cleanly or the ball has pitched just in front of him; Bowden for one would like to see a players' agreement, as it used to be, accepting the fielder's instinct, but he may be hoping too much of human nature. Vaughan and Ponting expressed different views on this at the start of the 2005 Ashes series.

Snicks too remain a bone of contention. An umpire has to contend with a variety of sources of sound – ball on bat, pad or glove (or even stump), bat on pad or ground. He has to integrate hearing and vision and come up with a virtually instantaneous conclusion. The bat-pad catch, and the inside edge onto pad, are particularly vulnerable to misinterpretation. Occasionally he's shown to be wrong by the 'snick-ometer', itself not an infallible guide, particularly to the source of soft sounds. In 2004 experiments were made with the umpire's earpiece picking up sounds from the stump cam; whether it will help, or the third umpire come into play, remains to be seen. In 2005 Malcolm Speed, the ICC's chief executive, said:

> 'At the ICC we will continue to have an open mind to technology... but we will only incorporate those innovations that benefit our sport without changing the fabric of the game we hold in trust for future generations. Technology will only be used in decision making if it: can provide conclusive answers; is practically feasible to introduce for all international cricket; will not have the effect of changing the essence of the way the game is played (the technique of batting or bowling); and will not compromise the role of the on-field umpire.'

In a fast-moving field like umpiring technology, any book is likely to be out of date soon after publication. For speculation on the possibilities ahead, on this and other thorny matters, see Chapter 38. Meanwhile we return to South Africa in 1999, and the last Tests of the 20th century, with England languishing at the foot of the Test table. 1899 had seen the end of an era, W. G. Grace's last Test. Could England in 1999 bring an end to a less happy era now, under a new manager, Duncan Fletcher?

CHAPTER 32

The Turn of the Tide

Graham Thorpe and Nasser Hussain in near-darkness at Karachi in December 2000,
celebrating England's unexpected first win in Pakistan since 1961.

By now I couldn't see a thing. As I ran back for a second run I realised
quite how dark it was because I looked back at the pavilion and…
it was pitch black apart from our dressing room. These are
the moments I played the game for.

NASSER HUSSAIN

1999–2000 South Africa

Nasser Hussain had experienced a torrid start to his stint as England captain, breaking a finger and seeing England go down 2–1 after leading in a four-Test series against New Zealand. The coach-in-waiting, Duncan Fletcher, arrived for the tour of South Africa, and his baptism was also one of fire.

England	122 & 260	**South Africa**	403–9d
South Africa	450 & 224–4d	England	373 & 153–6
England	366–9d	South Africa	156 & 572–7
England	258 & 126	**South Africa**	421
South Africa	248–8d & forfeit	**England**	0–0d & 251–8

It began horribly. England's debutants Michael Vaughan and Chris Adams met after 15 minutes in Johannesburg with the score 2–4. Welcome to Test cricket. The experienced Butcher, Atherton, Hussain and Stewart had been despatched by Donald and Pollock on a seaming pitch under a glowering sky. Donald restarted his feud with Atherton by uprooting his off-stump. Although Vaughan's coolness impressed, and Stewart made a forthright 86 in the second innings, England were outclassed, losing by an innings to South Africa for the first time for nearly 100 years – Donald 11–127, Pollock 8–80.

Cullinan and Gibbs had led South Africa past 400 in the first Test, and at Port Elizabeth it was a typical thumping 174 from Lance Klusener at No. 7 that enabled them to pass it again. This time England didn't lie down, Hussain leading from the front with 86 – begun with a thrilling 4, 6, 6 in his first five balls from Pollock – and Atherton, extracting some revenge on Donald with four fours in an over on his way to 108. With a lead of 77, South Africa still had time to force a win, but so slowly did they bat that Cronje couldn't declare until the last morning, and Hussain steered his side to safety. At Durban he continued batting with bloody-minded obstinacy, as England took all the first day and 85 overs to make just 135–2. He went on to 146* in ten and a half hours next day, and Stewart enlivened things with a bright 95. On the third day Caddick bowled a spell of immense stamina and hostility in the heat and humidity, 7–46 in 16 overs, to enable England to enforce the follow-on. But any optimism England had was snuffed out by Kirsten, who batted for the rest of the match, over 200 overs, to make a monumental 275.

Recuperation from more than two broiling days in the field needed more than just two days' recovery time, of which the first was Millennium Eve. What would the millennium bring for England? A century opening stand from Butcher and Atherton, but then a familiar story unfolded against Donald, 5–47 and 3–42. Chris Silverwood took five, but couldn't prevent centuries from Kallis and Cullinan bringing South Africa another innings victory and the series. Not a happy start for the inscrutable Fletcher, who had put down a style marker by refusing any comment on six highly questionable decisions that had gone against England in the second Test. At this stage there was one neutral and one home umpire standing, and the third had some but not all of the technology available.

So to Centurion to perform the damp obsequies over a forgettable series for England. Or so it seemed when the last day started. South Africa had been inserted and reached 155–6 on a truncated first day. There followed three blank days. At the time, everyone was delighted by Cronje's imaginative offer to Hussain to make a game of it. Long-suffering spectators would get some cricket. They got a thrilling finish after Hussain, seeing the last-day pitch easing up, had rescinded his initial refusal of the offer. 'How about us chasing 250? Fine, said Cronje. I couldn't believe it. No haggling. No banter. No bartering. No mention of how many overs we would face.' The double innings forfeiture that ensued was strictly illegal in a Test first innings, which is why the England scorecard reads 0–0 declared although the openers never took the field. When they did, needing 249 in 76 overs – more than generous in Donald's absence – England lost four wickets for 102 and seemed unlikely to try to win. But Stewart made 73, Vaughan emerged from his first-series shell with a fluent 69, and, after a flurry of late wickets, England won from the first ball of the last over.

Hussain was an imaginative captain, and his batting seemed to thrive on the added responsibility. But England's series averages starkly illustrated the problems he and Fletcher had to grapple with. Hussain's own average was in the sixties, Stewart's in the forties, but no one else topped 30. Caddick and Gough took 30 wickets between them at a combined average of over 30, but Donald and Pollock had 42 at 20, and no other England bowler reached double figures. Moreover, by the end of the 2000 summer Stewart would be 37, and Atherton, Hussain, Caddick, Gough and Tufnell already in their thirties. So too would be Hick, Ramprakash and Thorpe, all left behind in England but destined to play a part next summer. New blood was needed, and soon.

2000 Zimbabwe and West Indies

The first summer of the new millennium brought a new approach to Test cricket in England. For the first time the ECB awarded central contracts to 12 players, and they were essentially under the control of the England coach: it would be up to him to decide whether they played outside the Tests. In particular he could keep his fast bowlers fresh and ensure they weren't over-bowled by their counties, as Andy Caddick, for example, often was. That summer's tourists were Zimbabwe and West Indies. England had beaten neither in their last series, and indeed only India of the Test nations had been last beaten by England. Zimbabwe should indeed have won their first Test against the West Indies in March, but were bowled out for 63 when chasing just 99. That emphasised that they were no pushover, and that Ambrose and Walsh were still menacing.

| Zimbabwe | 83 & 123 | **England** | 415 |
| England | 374 & 147 | Zimbabwe | 285–4d & 25–1 |

As it turned out, Zimbabwe were pulverised at Lord's. Hussain put them in on a greenish pitch under overcast skies. In the two innings Gough took 6–93, Caddick 7–66, and Giddins, swinging the ball both ways, 7–42. Centuries for Hick and Stewart emphasised the disparity between the sides, but that margin wasn't evident at Trent Bridge. Once Atherton's 136 had given England the edge, after a blank second day Murray Goodwin scored a rapid 148* to restore Zimbabwe's self-esteem, further buttressed when they bowled England out cheaply on a dead last day. So it was a mixed outcome for England, who would have to sharpen up for the summer's main course. While West Indies' recent away form had been awful, no one was quite prepared for what happened, and how.

England	179 & 125	**West Indies**	397
West Indies	267 & 54	**England**	134 & 191–8
West Indies	157 & 438–7d	England	303 & 80–1
West Indies	172 & 61	**England**	272
England	281 & 287	West Indies	125 & 215

In the middle of the second afternoon of the second Test at Lord's, West Indies began their second innings 133 ahead and looking certain to go 2–0 up. England had suffered a horrible first Test defeat at Edgbaston. Swept away by Walsh in the first innings, and by all four pace-men in the second, no batsmen reached 35. That score was exceeded by five West Indians as they romped along to 397, on a helpful pitch, against an attack that seemed toothless by comparison. It looked little better in the first innings at Lord's, where Stewart, restored as captain when Hussain again broke one of his notoriously fragile fingers, put West Indies in. Campbell and Hinds had cruised to an unruffled 162–1 by mid-afternoon, but Cork turned the game by dismissing them both. He and Gough took four each, but so did Ambrose and Walsh, and it looked all over when West Indies went out to bat again.

The pitch was bouncier and more uneven. An unlikely tumbling catch by Gough at third man started the rout, then Caddick, Gough and Cork destroyed West Indies for 54. Caddick extracted steep bounce, bowling unchanged to take 5–16 in 13 overs. Ramprakash took three sharp catches at short leg as the batsmen's techniques were exposed by the short ball. The atmosphere was electric as the England openers played out the final over, on the Day of Four Innings that had begun with Walsh lbw to Caddick to the first ball of the day. But England needed 188, and their supporters could imagine what Ambrose and Walsh could do on this track. Atherton records that at the start of Saturday's play Ambrose 'stared intently... at the area to which he intended to bowl. Then he looked up at me with a huge grin.' Atherton was still not off the mark 27 balls later, and the patch Ambrose had fixed on was a cluster of red marks. But Atherton and Vaughan, constantly playing and missing, added 92 in an atmosphere of grim intensity until both were out in the forties. Ambrose bowled the dot balls, Walsh took the wickets, and England slipped to 160–8, 28 needed. But

Cork, bowing to no occasion, pulled, drove, and stole sharp singles, and with Gough firm at the other end he rattled off the runs for a famous two-wicket victory.

Had England lost and gone on to lose the series, Hussain's job might have been on the line. As it was he resumed the captaincy at Old Trafford. The England seamers prospered again to bowl West Indies out cheaply, and Alec Stewart illuminated his hundredth Test with 105, adding 179 with the phlegmatic left-handed debutant, Marcus Trescothick from Somerset, after the first three wickets had gone for 17 (including Atherton, also appearing in his 100th Test). But Stewart's innings was matched by Lara's, West Indies rediscovered how to bat, and the game petered out. To Headingley at 1–1, and a damp and uneven surface, where a Yorkshireman took five wickets on the opening day. Not Gough, but Craig White, England-born but Australia-bred, who had suddenly discovered reverse swing at a surprising pace from a short run-up. At the end of an all-action first day, England had stumbled to 105–5 in reply to West Indies' 172, and the series was still in the balance. The following morning Vaughan and Hick batted assuredly on a difficult pitch to add 98 and give England a crucial lead of 100. Crucial, but not, we thought, conclusive. But Gough took the first four wickets, Caddick the last five when switched to Gough's end, including four in one exhilarating over – one lbw, then three bowled – and, amazingly, West Indies had been blown away again, for 61. The game was over in 158 overs in two days.

Now to the Oval. If England could avoid defeat they would win a West Indies series for the first time since 1969, 14 series and over 30 years earlier, when Hussain was only a year old – no wonder he'd never even heard of the Wisden Trophy. Atherton and Trescothick gave them a tremendous start with a stand of 159. Although England were pegged back to 281 on a rain-reduced second day, more fine bowling from White left West Indies 156 in arrears. Atherton then produced a master class in his last encounter with Ambrose and Walsh, last out for 108, a century acknowledged as generously by the Surrey crowd as Stewart's had been by Lancastrians a month earlier. On the Monday the first sell-out crowd for a last day at the Oval since 1953 watched England duly win, and touching guards of honour were improvised by Hussain for Ambrose and Walsh as they came out to face the inevitable. Hospitality boxes were flung open and enjoyed by real cricket supporters. Hussain sank to his knees at the end of a vivid game of emotional final encounters, ending in unforgettable fashion an unforgettable era in West Indies cricket.

It was a heady moment, a triumph for the fast bowlers. Over the summer Cork took 20 wickets at 12, Caddick 30 at 19, Gough 34 at 20, and White chipped in with 13 at 18, nearly 100 wickets in all at well under 20. The arrival of Trescothick to open, an average of 47 in three West Indies Tests, was a real boon, and, although Vaughan only averaged 28, he came of age as a Test cricketer at Lord's and Headingley. Atherton, back problems and all, had a late flowering, scoring 536 at 44 over the summer. Stewart averaged 34, but no one else touched 30 and Hussain had a wretched summer with the bat, averaging 10. But his bowlers had done enough, and his place was in no jeopardy for the winter tour to Pakistan and Sri Lanka.

2000–1 Pakistan and Sri Lanka

England undertook two tours that winter, separated by Christmas and a two-month break. Both were expected to be hard work. England had only ever won one in Pakistan, in 1961–2, and 15 of the 18 matches there had been drawn. And Sri Lanka, as they had shown in 1999, had a string of aggressive batsmen, and the spinning prodigy Muttiah Muralitharan. This would be a good test of England's resuscitation under Fletcher and Hussain. Was the epic West Indies win a flash in the pan?

England	480–8d & 77–4d	Pakistan	401
Pakistan	316 & 269–3d	England	342 & 125–5
Pakistan	405 & 158	**England**	388 & 176–4

Lahore's first Test was the first time England had played in Pakistan since they had been tortured by Abdul Qadir during the ill-fated Gatting tour. The match soon fell into the typical Pakistan attritional two-innings grind once Atherton and Trescothick had continued their prospering alliance with a stand of 134. After a stutter, Thorpe and White – No. 7 and now a genuine Test all-rounder – added 166 for the sixth wicket. Saqlain Mushtaq took all eight wickets to fall but it took him 74 overs, because of the interminable patience of Thorpe, his Surrey colleague, who had hit only a single boundary when he reached 100. The tall Warwickshire slow left-armer Ashley Giles then bowled 59 overs for 4–113 in his first long Test bowl, and the game died its predictable death. The game at Faisalabad followed a similar pattern. Giles took another five, Thorpe again top-scored, and Atherton steered England to safety after they'd been set 244 in 62 overs.

So to Karachi, where Pakistan had never been beaten in 34 Tests. For four days there seemed little chance of that record going, or of a result. Inzamam and Yousuf Youhana scored brisk centuries on the first day, and Atherton replied with 125 in nine and a half hours, a testament to his concentration and endurance in the heat. By the last few minutes of the fourth day Pakistan were 88 ahead at 71–2, but Giles bowled Inzamam with a beauty, and he, Gough and White bowled so well next day that England needed 176 in 44 overs. Pakistan's captain Moin Khan was warned by the match referee at tea for a funereal over rate of 12, mostly bowled by spinners. From 65–3 Thorpe and Hick put on 91, and though Waqar bowled Hick in the gloom, and Moin appealed against the light three times, the courageous and principled umpire Steve Bucknor would have none of it, and Hussain gleefully helped Thorpe home in virtual darkness.

So, after breaking the West Indies hoodoo, England had cracked the Pakistan equivalent as well. Could they now go to Sri Lanka and avoid entrapment in Murali's web? It didn't look like it after the searing heat of Galle.

Sri Lanka	470–5d	England	253 & 189
Sri Lanka	297 & 250	**England**	387 & 161–7
Sri Lanka	241 & 81	**England**	249 & 74–6

Marvan Atapattu batted over 11 hours, and England out of the game, for his double century. Although Atherton and Trescothick opened with 83 and 101, and Trescothick went on to a massively impressive first Test hundred, no other batsman could cope with Muralitharan and the blander slow left arm of Jayasuriya, and England were soundly beaten. England felt the questionable umpiring decisions had gone against them in this Test, but the balance was redressed in the next, at Kandy. After Jayawardene's fluent hundred had taken Sri Lanka to 297 on the first day, Hussain – who had been contemplating resigning the captaincy before the match – got his first break, and his first runs, since his hundred in Durban 12 Tests before. His 109, together with fifties from Thorpe and Stewart, gave England a lead of 90. By the close of the third day excellent all-round bowling had left Sri Lanka 98–6, only just ahead, but a brilliant counter-attack from Sangakkara left England a tricky 161 to win. The openers went for 25, and though Thorpe made 46, half the side were out for 97. But White batted coolly, Thorpe was Murali's only wicket in 27 overs, and England edged home by three wickets.

At Colombo it all happened on the third day. An increasingly effective Croft took four in Sri Lanka's 241, to which England had replied with 175–4 by the end of the second day. Thorpe reached a century on the third morning, but Chaminda Vaas restricted England to a lead of just 8. In the second innings Gough and Caddick made early inroads, Giles took 4–11, and when the dust settled England had bowled a side out in double figures for the fourth time in under a year. An extraordinary turnaround. The drama wasn't over. England needed only 74, but they lost four for 43 before Thorpe calmly shepherded them home once again. For the third Test out of four an England team had chased a tricky target against world-class spinners and got there. They were exhibiting some real steel: England had won four series in a row for the first time for over 20 years.

Thorpe was instrumental in England's success in this tour: determined, concentrating intensely, able now to switch his game as events dictated. He made 553 runs at 61. Atherton averaged 42, Trescothick and White in the thirties, though no one else managed 25. But it was enough. Crucial to the batsmen's success was Fletcher's recruitment of young local spinners to bowl at them (in flip-flops) on deliberately roughed-up nets. (They too could spin the ball the other way with an off-spinner's action. Why can't ours? thought Hussain.) The attack's spearhead was Gough, with 24 wickets at 22, while Giles's arrival was a huge bonus. He relished the wickets he found in Pakistan, and although he was less successful in Sri Lanka he finished with 24 wickets at 29. With Croft compensating by bowling well there, and White an effective third seamer, the side wore a nicely balanced look. The tail was short, but more runs were needed further up the order. And the Australians were coming.

2001 Pakistan and Australia

Hussain and Fletcher had forged a good working relationship, and the England setup looked more confident and settled than it had for some time. The real test, though, would be an Ashes summer, but before that were two Tests against Pakistan, over for the triangular series. They arrived in apparent disarray after the publication of Justice Qayyum's report fining five of them. Wasim Akram was only there because of the casting vote of the Pakistan Board chairman, playing under Waqar Younis as the Pakistan captaincy continued on its usual merry-go-round.

England	391	Pakistan	203 & 179
Pakistan	403 & 323	England	357 & 261

Neither side played a spinner at Lord's, where the bitterly cold first day was lost to rain. England batted consistently, Thorpe top-scoring again with 80, but Hussain's 64 was ended by his third broken digit in three years, this time his right thumb. Pakistan then folded twice against the same attack that had destroyed West Indies the previous year – Caddick eight wickets, Gough eight and Cork four – and England had again won a match in less than three days of playing time. The Old Trafford Test, though, played before big Pakistan-supporting crowds against a background of racial tension in deprived Lancashire towns, lasted the distance. England's bowling supremacy vanished on the first day, when the majestically statuesque Inzamam led them to a (then) remarkable 370–8. Vaughan and Thorpe replied with a forthright stand of 267 – Vaughan's first Test hundred, and the fifth England innings running that Thorpe had top-scored – but the last eight wickets fell for 75. Pakistan again rattled on at more than four an over, and England were set 370 in 112 overs. Atherton and Trescothick added 87 overnight – the target now an intriguing 285 from 90 – and Trescothick went on past 100. But so slowly did England bat, strangled by Saqlain, that by tea, 196–2, they had added only 109 in 58 overs. Only 32 more overs didn't seem enough to make a further 174, but it was enough for Pakistan to take eight wickets. England unaccountably collapsed. There was controversy over umpiring errors at both ends that gave Wasim and Saqlain wickets with no-balls, the camera evidence leading a shocked David Shepherd to contemplate giving up umpiring altogether.

In a single session England, without Hussain at the helm, had plummeted from the pinnacle they had so resolutely climbed in the last year. They followed by failing to reach the triangular one-day final, so all the old doubts returned as they faced an Australian team stung by an amazing and unexpected 2–1 defeat in March in India, their first Test defeats after 16 straight wins. Like England in Sri Lanka, India had overturned a 1–0 deficit, through the heroics of Harbhajan Singh, Laxman and Dravid. Perhaps a better point of comparison was that Australia had destroyed West Indies 5–0 earlier in the winter.

For England the first three Tests make all-too-familiar upsetting reading. A poor start at Edgbaston was redeemed by a last-wicket stand of 103 from Stewart and Caddick. Rapid centuries from Steve Waugh and Damien Martyn profited from poor slip-fielding. Then, after Butcher's wobbly seamers had taken an unlikely 4–5, Adam Gilchrist capped a crushing 152 from 143 balls by hitting him for 22 in an over during a last-wicket stand of 63, of which McGrath made just a single. Hussain broke yet another finger as England went from 142–2 to 164 all out, and the tone was set for the series. At Lord's Atherton took over, Thorpe this time broke a finger, Caddick took five, Butcher made 83 but no one else reached 50. A relaid pitch meant a low-scoring third Test at Trent Bridge, over in three days. McGrath and Warne did the damage in successive innings, Alex Tudor came back with 5–44, but Australia had no difficulty in the fourth innings.

England	294 & 164	**Australia**	576
England	187 & 227	**Australia**	401 & 14–2
England	185 & 162	**Australia**	190 & 158–3
Australia	447 & 176–4d	**England**	309 & 315–4
Australia	641–4d	England	432 & 184

Because Australia were determined to try to win the series 5–0, they only won it 4–1. At the end of the third day at Headingley they led by 207 with nine wickets in hand. Ordinarily England might have been chasing 450 in eight hours. As it was, rain restricted Sunday's play to 25 overs and Gilchrist, standing in as captain because Steve Waugh had a calf strain, set England 314 in 110 overs. More bad weather reduced it to 311 in 90 on the last day. That England not only didn't slide to an expected fourth defeat, but won by six wickets with over 16 overs to spare, was due to a quite brilliant innings from Butcher. Helped by Hussain, restored to action but very much second fiddle in a stand of 181, he despatched the vaunted Australian attack to all parts in making 173* from 227 balls.

Order was restored at the Oval, where Langer and the Waugh twins made hundreds – superhuman Steve 157* despite his injured leg – in 600-plus scored at more than four an over. With Sunday's play again limited by rain, England might have saved the game had Ramprakash not been dismissed for a confident 133 within sight of the follow-on mark, which was missed by 10. Warne's 7–165 in that innings was then followed by four more in the second and five for McGrath, and Australia had regained their utter dominance.

In 1997 McGrath and Warne had taken 60 wickets; this summer they took 63 between them at less than 18 apiece. In contrast Gough and Caddick's 32 cost 44, though success in the two Pakistan Tests brought their tally up to 60 at 33, while in the seven Tests no other bowler took more than seven wickets. So in command were Australia's batsmen that four averaged over 60. In the seven Tests as a whole only Butcher and Vaughan averaged 50, and Vaughan's knee didn't allow him back against Australia. Hussain, Ramprakash, Stewart and Trescothick averaged in the high thirties, but they were outgunned. Despite the new set-up, England called on 24 players in all, an indication of disarray. Back to the drawing board.

2001–2 India and New Zealand

The winter split tours to India and New Zealand followed the pattern now current of having a long break over Christmas. The break could easily have been longer still, for political tension in the area put the India leg in doubt. Moreover there was an unseemly wrangle between the ICC's chief executive Malcolm Speed and ex-ICC president Dalmiya, now Indian Board president, over referee Denness's banning of Virender Sehwag for his excessive appealing in South Africa. Sehwag would miss the first Test. More serious were the English losses. In the wake of the 9/11 terrorist attacks in New York and Washington, security concerns kept Caddick and Croft away. Stewart and Gough preferred to rest injuries, while Thorpe returned to a domestic crisis after the first Test.

England	238 & 235	**India**	469 & 5–0
England	407 & 257	India	291 & 198–3
England	336 & 33–0	India	238

England lost the series on the first afternoon at Mohali. A bright start from Trescothick and Hussain had been undone by Harbhajan Singh, the young Sikh off-spinner who had taken 31 wickets in three Tests the previous winter against Australia while still only 21. Here his 5–51, the wicketkeeper Dasgupta's maiden Test hundred against a novice bowling attack, and Kumble's 6–81 in the second, consigned England to a 10-wicket defeat. At Ahmedabad Kumble took another seven, but Trescothick made 99 and White 121 from No. 7 for his maiden Test hundred. Giles, beset by foot problems that kept him out of the first Test, 'trundled up to the crease like an old wheelie bin' in the notorious description in Wisden that would have had the Pardons and Prestons turning in their graves. But the trundler took 5–67 in over 40 immaculate overs, against Tendulkar in top form. Hussain didn't declare after Butcher's gritty, stomach-bugged 92, and the last day drifted to a somnolent end.

After three days of the last Test at Bangalore, India 218–7 in reply to England's 336, there was a chance of a result, but it evaporated in the filthy weather. The game was marked by Hussain's decision, made with Jardinesque logic, to starve Tendulkar of runs by getting Giles to bowl a foot outside the leg stump to him, and he was stumped for 90 in frustration as a result. The pitch was perfect but the bowler's rough certainly wasn't. As Hussain was to say, with impeccable logic, why is it deemed unworthy for a left-arm spinner to bowl over the wicket to right-handers, when off-spinners do it to left-handers without a murmur of complaint? Soon after-wards umpires were empowered to end deliberate negative bowling by calling it wide.

England	228 & 468–6d	New Zealand	147 & 451
England	283 & 293–4d	New Zealand	218 & 158–4
New Zealand	202 & 269–9d	England	160 & 233

 A quite astonishing Test at Christchurch began the New Zealand series in March. The drop-in pitch prepared for the game reversed the normal rule – it was difficult early on and benign later. A masterly 106 from Hussain prevented total collapse on the first day. On the second the bustlingly workmanlike Matthew Hoggard, another Yorkshireman in Gough's place, got his out-swinger working and took 7–63. On the third England had slumped to 106–5 when Thorpe and Flintoff gave the game a complete makeover. The England selectors had persevered with Andrew Flintoff, whose performance hadn't matched his promise, and for the first time he fulfilled it. His bludgeoning 137 in a stand of 281 inspired Thorpe, characteristically a neat accumulator, to let go to the extent that he reached 200^* in 231 balls, then the second fastest Test double hundred (of those measurable by balls received) after Gilchrist's in South Africa a month earlier. Gilchrist hit eight sixes in that innings, but both marks would be surpassed on an amazing fourth day.

Behind by 550 runs, New Zealand were languishing at 333–9 when the injured Cairns emerged to join Nathan Astle, who had just reached a century in 114 balls. That was rapid enough, but he now went berserk, going to 200 in just 39 more balls, 59 fewer than Gilchrist's record, and ending with 222 from 168, with 11 sixes. In 93.3 overs New Zealand had reached 451, the highest fourth innings in Tests apart from the Timeless aberration of 1938–9. Another hour of that and New Zealand would have won with a last wicket stand of 200, and Astle over 300. Unlikely as it may seem now, it didn't seem so at the time.

Nothing in the series could match that. At Wellington rain prevented play on most of the first two days, and neither side could force a win, although Flintoff sparked the game to life with 74 from 44 balls to set up a declaration. Flintoff was now truly a Freddie, a name seemingly reserved for larger-than-life characters like Brown and Trueman. During that match the players learnt of the death of Ben Hollioake in a car crash, and they took a sombre mood to the last game, on another drop-in pitch at Auckland. Only four days between the Tests made it impractical for the whole team to go to Perth for the funeral (although Hussain made the journey), so Butcher organised a moving memorial service to coincide with it. Rain at Auckland meant that the game didn't really fire until the fourth day, which England began at 12–3. Once the tall Daryl Tuffey had given them a lead of 42 on a green top, New Zealand were indebted to the rugby floodlights, which extended the day until 8 pm – something that changed regulations would not allow for much longer in a Test. England needed to bat the last day or make 312 on a capricious pitch, but, although Hussain battled on to 82, he couldn't prevent a dispiriting defeat.

So the winter began and ended badly for a weakened England. Over the six Tests Thorpe again led the averages with 59. Hussain came back to form with 471 runs at 47, followed by White, the now-established Trescothick, Butcher and Vaughan, promoted to open the batting. Without his 137 and 75, the carefree, careless Flintoff would have averaged a mere 6, but his bowling was improving gradually. It brought him 15 wickets in support of Caddick and Hoggard, 19 and 26 respectively. With Caddick and Gough now well past 30, new pace bowlers were a priority, and

Hoggard was making his claim, especially in bowling sapping long spells in India. And a settled wicketkeeper was needed to replace Alec Stewart, when he eventually hung up his gloves. Not that he was finished yet.

2002 Sri Lanka and India

Sri Lanka were seriously hampered by the absence of Muralitharan at the start of the tour: he had dislocated a shoulder in a pointless one-day game in Sharjah. That didn't prevent Sri Lanka from taking charge in the first Test at Lord's.

Sri Lanka	555–8d	England	275 & 529–5d
Sri Lanka	162 & 272	**England**	545
England	512 & 50–0	Sri Lanka	253 & 308

A spinner-less England were kept in the field for most of the first two days by another long innings from Atapattu. England batted sloppily, and were in again before the end of day three. Far more application in the second innings brought centuries for Vaughan and Butcher, and no one was out for less than 50 as the game meandered away. At Edgbaston Hussain was rewarded for the rarity of winning the toss when Sri Lanka fared badly in good bowling conditions. On a flat pitch Trescothick led the way in reply with an ebullient 161; Thorpe made a hundred and Butcher just missed one. Muralitharan took five wickets but he needed 64 overs. Hoggard's 5–92 then saw England home in comfort, a recovery for him after a bad game at Lord's. At Old Trafford England passed 500 for the third time running, unheard of in recent years. Trescothick again batted with confident aggression, while Butcher and Stewart each hit 123. Rain had held England up, and a draw seemed probable when Sri Lanka were 130–1 at the end of the third day. But, with Caddick nursing injury, Hoggard and Tudor engineered a late innings collapse. England would need another one on the final afternoon if Sri Lanka, 253–4 at tea, were not to earn a draw. But again they stumbled, Giles finished the innings with two wickets in successive balls, and England had 50 to win in six overs. A triumphant Trescothick and Vaughan did it in five.

England	487 & 301–6d	India	221 & 397
India	357 & 424–8	England	617
India	628–8d	England	273 & 309
England	515 & 114–0	India	508

India arrived after an unexpected defeat in the West Indies – the world order hadn't completely changed yet. England took their buoyant form into the first Test at Lord's, where they were in charge until the last two hours. Hussain dominated the first day, and went on to 155, followed by fifties from Flintoff and White, a rather useful pair to come in at 7 and 8. After Virender Sehwag, batting as usual as if in a one-day match, had opened with a typical swashbuckling 84 from 96 balls, India folded unexpectedly. Hussain chose not to enforce the follow-on, watched Vaughan and Crawley each make 100, and won with something to spare despite Agarkar's disconcerting late flurry on the last morning. Three successive wins, and a fourth looked on the cards after England had battered their way to 617 at Trent Bridge. Despite losing a day's worth of cricket on the first two days, they were put on top by a scintillating innings of 197 (made within the day, from 258 balls) from Vaughan, breathtaking in its simple run-plundering orthodoxy. Shades of Bradman, even, in that every bad ball went for four. But a still perfect pitch meant Dravid, Tendulkar and Ganguly could save the game in comfort.

England's dominance was unexpectedly shattered at Headingley. Batting first on a typical grey Headingley morning, India were indebted to their stopgap bit-part opener Sanjay Bangar, whose 68 paved the way for superb hundreds from Dravid, Ganguly and Tendulkar, who made 193. Missing Trescothick, England then made a mess of it against a disciplined attack including two spinners, and lost easily despite Hussain's 110 at the last. One-all to the Oval, and a long hard slog on a wicket that was just too good. A second innings of 190-plus by Vaughan – how many will he make if he ever gets past 200? – put England in control, but his command this summer had been matched by Dravid, whose long, patient 217, and a last day lost to rain, ensured stalemate and an unsatisfactory end to a series England felt they should have won.

As the summer progressed, England's bowlers grew steadily less effective. Hoggard took 28 wickets in the seven Tests, but they cost him 35, and no one else managed more than Caddick's 14. Injuries to several bowlers didn't help, and Gough's recovery would certainly be essential in Australia. The batting of course was a different matter, with Vaughan scoring 900 runs in all – only Gooch had made more in an English summer. He and Trescothick averaged 90, an opening pair to challenge Australia at last, while Stewart, Butcher, Crawley, Hussain and Thorpe averaged between 60 and 40. The batting now looked stronger than it had for years, but Australia lay in wait, the ultimate test. By a ludicrous statistical quirk, they had been headed at the top of the international table by South Africa, but no one believed that for a minute. England had fought their way back up from bottom to fifth, with a suitably middling score of 1.00. Could England now bridge the gap with Australia?

2002–3 Australia

No. England surrendered the initiative at the moment Hussain put Australia in at Brisbane. That Waugh too would have bowled had he won the toss was no consolation. Hayden made 197 and Ponting 123 as Australia sailed to 364–2 on the first day. Doing well to restrict Australia to 487, England reached 158–1 at the close of the second, and were still well placed at 268–4. But first a routine collapse, then a really horrible one after a second Hayden hundred, left England defeated by 384 runs. At Adelaide Vaughan's superb innings of 177 lit up the first day. England were within six balls of going in at 295–3, but Vaughan couldn't last out the final over, the tail folded, and another century for Ponting took apart a seriously weakened attack. Gough had come and gone, not fully recovered, Simon Jones had suffered an agonising ligament injury during the first Test, Harmison had broken Giles's wrist in the nets, and Flintoff was missing with a nagging hernia problem aggravated at the end of the Indian summer. Another 500-plus score by Australia, another second innings collapse by England.

Australia	492 & 296–4d	England	325 & 79
England	342 & 159	Australia	552–9d
England	185 & 223	Australia	456
Australia	552–6d	England	270 & 387
England	362 & 452–9d	Australia	363 & 226

At Perth on a lightning-fast wicket England managed to collapse in both innings. Silverwood became the next injured bowler after just four overs as Australia reached 456. Their total team ethic was illustrated by the fact that no batsman made more than 71, and only one bowler took as many as three wickets in either England innings. England had lost the series and the Ashes on 1 December, indecently early. At Melbourne Langer led Australia past 500 again with 250. From 118–6 England recovered through White, 85* in the city where he'd been brought up, but couldn't avoid the follow-on. Vaughan played another exquisite innings to at least make Australia bat again, and reach 1481 runs in 2002 in the process.

If only England could play in the first four Tests of Ashes series like they did in the last. They were helped in Sydney at New Year by the absence through injury of McGrath and Warne, and Butcher's 124 gave them a decent start. Caddick now took three early wickets, as he had done in the truncated second innings at Melbourne, but England ran into a Steve Waugh determined to equal Bradman's 29 Test hundreds, after a poor series for him. Although second fiddle to a crackling 133 from Gilchrist, he reached it in dramatic fashion from the last ball of the day, to rapturous applause. Vaughan, though, played his third immaculate big hundred of the series, 183, and Caddick stormed through Australian batting unaccustomed and disinclined to play for a draw, 7–94 in 22 overs telling its own story.

That Vaughan should be made man of the series in a badly beaten side was a real accolade. (Australians may not have liked it, but they didn't have their own bowling to face.) He made 633 runs at 63 to follow his 900 in the previous summer, despite a troublesome knee injury. The other batsmen were strung out behind him – Stewart, Hussain, Butcher, on down to Trescothick at 26, his off-stump frailty inexorably exploited. Caddick took 20 wickets at 34, White 14 at 38, while the rest can be too easily imagined. Equally predictably, six Australian batsmen shared nearly 2300 runs at 50 runs apiece, and six bowlers took more than 10 wickets. Was this the best Test side ever? Only the batsman at No. 6 varied, but, with Gilchrist at No. 7 averaging over 50 at nearly a run a ball, it hardly mattered.

Australia had lost their first Test at home for four years, but they were still a class above England and everyone else. That they had managed to win 16 games on the trot, before their Indian slip-up, was due to an intensity and self-belief that took the attack to their opponents whether with bat or ball. In 13 series between November 1999 and July 2003, apart from winning 36 Tests and losing six, in only one of the series was there ever a draw. In 2002–3 against England they scored at a rate of 3.95 an over, unprecedented in an Ashes series, and took each wicket on average in fewer than 10 overs. Test cricket was no longer turgid – they were redefining its rules. The name of the new game was Speed.

The transformation – England's Test record 1992–3 to 2005

Period	England innings		Opposition innings		Diff.	Matches won/lost	Wins minus defeats
	400+	200–	200–	400+			
1992/3–1995/6	8	14	4	18	−20	7/18	−11
1996–1999	8	23	13	12	−14	10/15	−5
1999/2000–2002/3	12	16	14	23	−11	15/16	−1
2003–2005 (Sept)	20	8	14	9	+17	22/5	+17

The Diff. column measures the difference between the number of scores above 400 and below 200 by England and their opponents.

CHAPTER 33

On Speed – and Entertainment

The climax of the World Cup semi-final at Lord's 1999. With the scores level, Alan Donald has been run out off the fourth ball of the final over, and Australia are through to the World Cup final.

Waugh's wars have been about the most efficient means of despatching the enemy… Fast scoring is done first to undermine the opposing bowlers, and with them the rest of the fielding side. And then it gives Australia extra time in the quest for 20 wickets: a free session for your bowlers every innings.

SIMON BARNES, Wisden, 2003

C ricket is a team game, but one built around a brief flaring of action lasting only a moment, when just two of its 22 combatants are involved, bowler against batsman. It's a leisurely game: its staccato nature allows time for reflection or distraction for spectator and player alike – unlike most games, the performer sits on the sidelines for under half the time, where he can glow, glower or forget. It can have rapid bursts of excitement that punctuate long somnolent periods of equilibrium, a diet that does not satisfy every palate. To some, only the longer game, when spectators can indulge, say, in a long philosophical discussion while a handful of runs is scored, is real cricket. At Bath in 2005, while the score ticked over gently, I spent a happy hour in a rickety stand in a one-off conversation with a nuclear engineer, a hospital nurse and a professor of mathematics, none of whom I would meet again. To others, to watch a day's sport and not see a result, only a shifting of the balance to and fro on the way to a distant conclusion, is anathema.

Cricket, cracket and crashet

Readers who have stuck with me so far will construe that I'm a devotee of the long game, but one who gets pleasure – of a very different kind – from a good contest of any length. How, I wonder, has the appeal of cricket changed since World War 2? Nowadays the game must cater for every taste. As we've seen, first-class cricket in England began to be unsustainable in the early 1960s, so had to be propped up by a version begun and ended in one day. By the early years of the 21st century, the game's administrators had force-fed the golden goose so much that it was seriously bloated. Its international administrators decided in their wisdom that it needed refinements (or short-lived gimmicks) such as substitutes and variable periods of field restrictions. Were they becoming even more bored than the spectators? Had the new Twenty20, a version of the game which allows virtually no time for breath-catching for participant or viewer, made it seem sluggish by comparison?

The three current versions of cricket – four- or five-day, 50-over or 20-over – have aptly been called 'cricket, cracket and crashet'. They move at approximately three, five and eight runs an over. In a day of 90 overs, you might see 300 for seven wickets in cricket, or 500–15 in a 50-over match. In 20-over cricket you'd see perhaps 300–15 in two and a half hours. On a three-match Twenty20 finals day you'd get perhaps 900–45, a rate that should sate any glutton – or leave him desperate for the *ancienne cuisine* of a Test match. Soon Twenty20 will give us the first 1000-run day…

Lies, damned lies, and run rate

So how has cricket's appeal changed since the war? To compare like with like, we must look at the longer game, county and Test matches: real cricket. One of the most common shorthand indicators of entertainment value has been runs-per-over, now more often expressed in tables of statistics as runs-per-100-balls, even though that's not as instinctively understandable (and is moreover an irritating construct because 100 isn't divisible by six). The usual measure of a satisfactory scoring rate used to be three runs an over, and that equates to 50 runs per 100 balls. On that measure Test and county cricket proceeded with very little change from 1946 to 1969 – in Test cricket about 40, in county cricket about 45, resolutely below that 50 mark. In the 1970s, perhaps under the influence of one-day cricket and generally better wickets, it rose steadily in county cricket, reaching 50 for the first time in 1980. It stayed around there for 20 years, but shot up in the new millennium to around 58. Test cricket stayed at 40 until about 1980, for the next 30 years moved up and settled between 45 and 50, then again there was a rapid rise, also to 58, in 2000. This yields some surprises: in the golden year of 1947, for example, the scoring rate in the Tests was 45 runs per 100 balls. Hence 100 overs of the average Test in 1947 would have yielded 270 runs. In 1955 it would have produced less than 220, Compton and May notwithstanding. Fifty years later, in 2005, that figure was nudging 400. (If you're already muttering about over rates, never fear, we'll get there in a minute.)

But how good is run rate alone as a measure of entertainment value? It's hardly entertaining if unchallenged batsmen are milking undemanding bowling on good wickets. Spectators want to see runs *and* wickets. Often low-scoring matches are more compelling, as long as they don't induce just grim defence from the batsmen. It's no surprise to discover that the run rate began to increase as batsmen became relatively more successful. From 1946–69 the runs-per-wicket in an English county season ranged between 21 and 27, averaging just 25. Bowling was strong, batting more cautious than now. Pitches were not particularly good, and sometimes rain-affected. In 1959 Wisden's editor said that 'sporting pitches have been the vogue in this country since the war', and urged improvement, as did Brian Statham, among many others, who in 1965 said that all but two English county pitches had deteriorated, some to 'an astonishing degree'. As pitches improved for batsmen in the 1970s, so the runs-per-wicket started to ramp up until it reached a plateau at just over 30 from 1981 to 2000. Pitches continued to get better (for batsmen), and in the period 2001–5 the run-per-wicket increased again to nearly 34. So the run rate certainly should have risen.

A better measure?

We need a better measure than the simple run-rate. Ask an experienced cricket-watcher what makes a four- or five-day game exciting and he will come up with a mixture of runs, wickets, challenge, variety, attack when needed, defence when unavoidable – a good contest. Figures cannot combine all that, but the best approximation is a measure that takes both runs and wickets into account. So I've constructed an 'action rate' that takes both into account. It's derived by adding 20 for each wicket per 100 balls to the runs scored in the same period (yes – it's arbitrary, but it works, and it gives 100 as an ideal target). So 50–2 in 100 balls rates 90 (50 + 2×20). The best days of Test cricket – to the neutral anyway – are when a bat/ball

Action rate per 100 balls

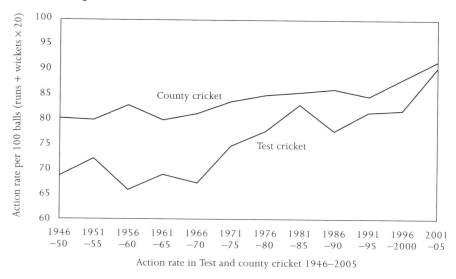

Action rate in Test and county cricket 1946–2005

balance is reflected by a score of, say, 340 all out in 90 overs, an action rate of exactly 100. (For those who want the maths, that's 340 + 10×20, divided by 5.4, the number of 100-ball blocks in 90 overs. It would be neater if they had 100 overs in a day, which they should of course.) Until the last five years that's about as good as you could get. More frequent would have been something like 280–6, rating 74. Averaged over a series or a season this gives a better overall impression than the simple run rate. The graph above makes the trend clear.

The graph shows the change since the war for Test and county cricket. As you can see, the action rate for Test cricket stays doggedly down in the range 65–70 in the first half of the period. It then climbs steadily to top 80 in the first half of the 1980s, drops back in the second half, stays there throughout the 1990s, then takes off after 2000, where it rockets above 90 despite a bad year in 2002. This recent trend can be attributed principally to the gear change in approach to Test cricket by successive recent Australian captains, who, leading very strong sides, reckoned that a game moving at a higher tempo would reward their superiority with more victories. Inferior sides couldn't escape with draws. If the first Ashes Test of 2005 had moved at the rate of those in 1953 or 1956, England would have wriggled away with a draw because of the rain that would have shortened the last two days. As it was they lost late on the fourth.

This trend is reflected in the county scene in England. In county cricket the action rate stays very steady between 78 and 81 from 1946–80, before increasing to a new plateau of around 85 in 1981. It stays there for another 15 years, then moves up to 87 in 1995, before topping 90 for the first time in 2002. It has averaged 92 since. What does that prove? Has county cricket improved by around 15 per cent since the war?

Old cricketers would hardly agree: 'People don't bowl line and length any more; pitches are better and batsmen have it easier.' Did the increased tempo of one-day cricket spread to the longer game? If so, it was a long-delayed effect. Did the arrival of four-day county cricket have an impact when it began in 1994, for good or ill? Doomsayers foretold a kind of Parkinson's Law effect, with the work expanding to fill the time available. Actually, the rate improved about that time, but the water is muddied by the ECB's tinkering with wides and no-balls. In 1997 they ordained that wides and no-balls in the championship should count two, and though that was rescinded for wides in 2003, and the overall effect is in fact rather small, it does make comparisons tricky.

But now stir in over rates...

Now, what is the effect of the decline in over rates? In the first five years after the war, when Tests were sometimes of three or four days' duration, and England's side had no pace men and two or three spinners, Tests in England provided about 130 overs per day. That slipped to below 110 in the next two decades, before dropping irrevocably under 100 for the first time in 1972. Since 1975 it has averaged below 90. Of course, to some extent it's a matter of taste whether you prefer to see 300 all out scored in a day of 90 overs or one of 120. Are you more bored by the wait between balls – the field-tinkering, the field-placing debates, the bowler's amble back to the mark – or by the extra 30 overs of dot balls? If you feel short-changed by the reduction of overs bowled in a day, then this chart is for you. It shows the action rate modified to account for the over rate shift – a kind of action-per-day rating. Now a reasonable target figure would be about 500.

Action per day in Tests

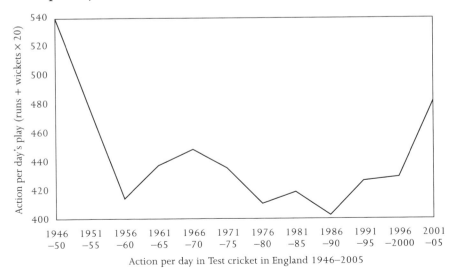

Action per day in Test cricket in England 1946–2005

This graph is pretty dramatic. It certainly supports those who were watching Test cricket after the war, and feel nostalgically that things were so much better then. They certainly saw more action in a day. Of course the 1946 and 1949 Tests were of three days, and that of 1947 of four days, so the players had to get on with it if they wanted a result. A better benchmark is perhaps 1951–5, when all the Tests were of five days' duration. With an average of 114 overs a day, there was an action score of 485. From then it plummeted, never rising above 445 before 2000, and reaching a nadir of 394 in 1986–90. In 2001–5 it began to climb spectacularly, averaging 486 in that period – but only the same as 1951–5, note – climaxing at 550 in the Ashes summer of 2005. Thus the figures clearly reflect that Test cricket in the years after 2000 has been decidedly more engrossing than it had been for the best part of 50 years, helped in part no doubt by England's improved performance.

From the 1950s onwards commentators complained about the infiltration of cricket by prevailing utilitarian attitudes. For every Compton and Miller, there were half a dozen Barringtons and McKays. Has Test cricket now changed spectacularly for good in the last five years, or is this just a passing phase? Or will weaker sides in reaction deliberately set out to defend, stall, slow down and otherwise frustrate the stronger, returning us to an Age of Grind? In the past five years Australia's aggressive attitude has rubbed off on their opponents. The England team were towed along in Australia's wake during their latest traumatic Ashes defeat of 2002–3. (While they didn't match their opponents' galloping 4.1 runs an over, they did contribute to an action-per-day figure of 542.) But at least they had at last secured a stirring victory after four successive defeats. How would they fare in South Africa for the 2003 World Cup? Only vaguely aware of political rumblings in the region, the team arrived in Cape Town to find themselves in the midst of a political row that was coming rapidly to the boil.

CHAPTER 34

A New Dawn

The England Test team huddle after their surprising last-day victory at Johannesburg in January 2005.

I had run out the local hero at a crucial moment… I thought God, I can't go now. If we don't win this game I'll be the villain of Lord's and will always be remembered as such if it's my last game.

NASSER HUSSAIN, *on his last Test and Andrew Strauss's first*

Look, you miserable git, stop behaving like a pork chop. Let's win this game.

GRAHAM THORPE, *on joining him*

The Zimbabwe affair

After the latest Ashes debacle, the massive disparity between Australia and England showed no signs of narrowing during the 2003 World Cup in South Africa — or rather Southern Africa. It was the laudable determination of the organiser, Ali Bacher, the doctor who was captain of South Africa when they had been banned, to ensure that Kenya and Zimbabwe should host some of the matches. But both had domestic problems that led to serious political and security concerns. New Zealand and Sri Lanka were due to play Kenya in Nairobi; England and Australia to play Zimbabwe in Harare. England's political relationship with Zimbabwe had deteriorated to breaking point because of the repressive Mugabe government. The England players arrived in the midst of conflicting messages: from the UK government (We think you shouldn't go, but can't stop you), the ICC (You can refuse to play on security grounds, but it's OK, we've checked), the ECB (You decide, we're right behind you... Oh, but we'll be fined a crippling amount if you pull out), and the public back home, where opinion was split, but friends and family wanted them to pull out. Duncan Fletcher, their Zimbabwean coach, felt they would be safe, but said the public in his home country were split, too, and he made it clear he would not pressure the players either way. He was becoming a master at keeping his counsel.

Holed up in the Cullinan Hotel in Cape Town, the players were increasingly bewildered. Nasser Hussain had warned them that they had to 'start taking some serious growing-up pills and take the issue very seriously indeed'. Back in Australia, some had seen a damning documentary on Zimbabwe, alleging the torture and murder of Mugabe's political opponents. They had been sent dossiers by an opposition group elaborating the reasons why they shouldn't go, in particular that it would give tacit support to the regime. Mass demonstrations were predicted, and precedent suggested they would be brutally repressed. The team asked for the match to be switched to South Africa. In a brief meeting Malcolm Speed, the ICC chief executive, bluntly dismissed their objections, and walked into a tirade from a fired-up Hussain. It's a moot point whether the captain was more wound up by Speed, or by the apology for his outburst that he later discovered Tim Lamb of the ECB had made to Speed. South African security experts then tried unconvincingly to assure the team they would be safe in Zimbabwe, hardly helping by their disturbing assertion that 'if anything goes wrong, we've got the South African SAS to pick you up and take you out'. They dismissed as a hoax a letter sent to the team from a group called The Sons and Daughters of Zimbabwe, which included the words: 'Come to Zimbabwe and you will go back to Britain in wooden coffins.'

Despite the fact that for some of the team this was the only chance of a World Cup appearance, at this point they voted 15–0 not to go. After an inspirational opening ceremony, though, some were having second thoughts, but at a further team meeting they were told that the letter containing the death threat had been discovered to be genuine after all. That clinched it for everyone. The ECB now appeared confident they could have the games switched on security grounds — they were anxious the team should use that construct rather than the moral reasons some had been citing so they could avoid the swingeing fine – but failed to budge an obdurate ICC. (Morality? No place for it.) The players were portrayed elsewhere as typical whingeing Poms, a view accentuated by the decision of Australia, under no such acute pressure and determined to prove they were the best team in the world at all forms of the game, to play there regardless. It was barely noticed at the time in England that New Zealand refused to go to Kenya. Henry Olonga and Andy Flower, the ex-Zimbabwe captain and a friend of Hussain at Essex, chose to wear black armbands for Zimbabwe's first game, and issued a 'death of democracy' statement. Olonga as a consequence played no more games and was promptly expelled by his local club. As an example of what might have happened had they gone, four demonstrators outside the Zimbabwe v Australia game were arrested, tortured and raped. Neither the ICC nor the ECB came out of the affair with much credit. The ECB, twisting and turning between a rock and a hard place, in the end had to forfeit $3.5 million from its share of the massive World Cup revenue.

2002–3 The eighth World Cup

Back to the cricket. Money seemed ever the spur: 14 teams played 54 matches in 43 days. Of the 42 games in the pool stage only five could be described as at all close. From two initial pools of seven, three countries would go through to the intermediate Super Six stage that had been inaugurated in 1999. England were competing with Zimbabwe, to whom they had to forfeit the points, with two minor teams, and with Australia, India and Pakistan. In effect they would have to beat two of these last three, a daunting prospect with Australia so dominant. After winning against the lesser lights, games in which the raw young Lancastrian James Anderson came encouragingly to the fore, England played superbly to beat Pakistan. Shepherded to 246–8 by Paul Collingwood of Durham, they were bowled to victory by Anderson's 4–29, which sent Pakistan crashing to 80–9 and 134 all out. That match demonstrated the advantage of batting first in a day-night game, although England suffered in turn when they collapsed to Ashish Nehra, batting second to lose to India.

So England would have to beat Australia to be sure of qualifying. It was a topsy-turvy, heart-stopping match on a poor pitch. Trescothick and Knight thumped an improbable 66 off nine overs from McGrath and Lee, but five quick wickets from the unsung Andy Bichel left them 87–5. Stewart and Flintoff added 90, but Bichel returned to post an astonishing 7–20 from 10 overs, the best World Cup figures ever between top-line nations. Chasing an uncomfortable 205 to win on that pitch, Australia promptly lost their first four wickets to Caddick for 48. Lehmann and Bevan added 63, but three more fell quickly to make them 114–7, and seemingly down and out. When Bichel joined Bevan they stood 135–8 with only McGrath to come. They needed 70 in 74 balls, but these two, not part of the Test team, brought them to the point where they needed 14 from the last two overs. That they might have won anyway didn't prevent the opprobrium heaped on Hussain for preferring Anderson

(0–54) for the penultimate over, to Caddick (4–35), whose previous over had been unthreatening. (Had Gough been playing, no one could have wrenched the ball from him.) Anderson's over went for 12, and Australia won with two balls to spare. England still might have qualified had Pakistan beaten Zimbabwe in Bulawayo, as expected, but that game was rained off and Zimbabwe were through at England's expense. So Zimbabwe probably advanced because their country's regime was so repulsive that England refused to tour. Exasperating on every level.

Australia's win meant they were unbeaten, and India were the third team through from group A. The other group was South Africa's. The opening match of the tournament was one of the best, Lara's hundred just enough to beat by 3 runs another late Klusener surge. Despite losing twice thereafter, West Indies would have gone through had they not been rained off against Bangladesh – there was no second day overflow in this tournament, so another top team disappeared because of the weather. The surprise beneficiaries were Kenya, whose leg-spinner Collins Obuya had bowled Sri Lanka to comprehensive defeat, and whose win over Bangladesh put them through.

The final place would go to the winners of South Africa v Sri Lanka on 3 March. South Africa had suffered from rain before, in the notorious 1992 semi-final defeat by England that led to the Duckworth-Lewis method. A far better system, it nevertheless depended on the batsmen realising the position when rain was about. Here, after Atapattu's uncharacteristically brilliant 124 had taken Sri Lanka to 268, the match was finely balanced as rain fell steadily. Would the 45th over be the last? It was. Boucher's six off the fifth ball brought the score to 229. Thinking that was the Duckworth-Lewis target to win, Boucher made no attempt to run off the last ball, only for his horrified team to realise that 229 was the target to tie, and the hosts were out of the tournament. There's a whole sheaf of what-ifs here. Had South Africa made their 230, both they and Sri Lanka would have gone through on run rate. Had West Indies not been rained off and beaten Bangladesh, five teams would have tied on points, from which the run rate differential would have had to extract three. As it was, Kenya went through as the second African nation, instead of South Africa, who had beaten them by 10 wickets. Not easy stuff for the South African cricket supporter, desperate to replicate their rugby players' World Cup success on their own soil.

The Super Six stage began, again with teams carrying some points with them. The complexities of this left Australia on top as the stage began, with Kenya second. Australia carried all before them, though Bevan and Bichel had to do a repeat rescue job against New Zealand, whose promising young pace bowler Shane Bond had almost equalled Bichel with 6–23. Kenya beat with remarkable ease their third Test-playing nation, Zimbabwe, as well as giving India a scare, and against all the odds they qualified third for the semi-finals behind India, for whom the sublime Tendulkar had been transcendent. Sri Lanka squeezed in fourth. Of the nine Super Six matches, none was remotely close, and the same went for the semi-finals and final.

In the first semi-final Australia stuttered at first against Sri Lanka, but were rescued by Andrew Symonds' disciplined 91*. Sri Lanka's batting failed, and they needed 90 at 123–7 when rain set in, and the Duckworth-Lewis chart decided emphatically that they couldn't win from there (although Australia had of course against England). Against Kenya, Ganguly and Tendulkar rattled up 270–5, and the underdogs subsided gracefully to bring their day in the sun to an end. (Unfortunately their exuberant but disciplined cricket was not to be rewarded, as decline and corruption would prevent a push for Test status.) Fortunately the best two teams in the tournament reached the final. Unfortunately the final proved nearly as one-sided as 1999's had been. Ganguly paid for putting Australia in, first blitzed by Gilchrist and Hayden, 107 in the first 14 overs, then destroyed by Ponting and Martyn, who added 234 in 30 overs and one ball. India needed Tendulkar to fire. He didn't, and though Sehwag blazed 82 in 81 balls, there was only ever going to be one winner.

SEMI-FINALS				
Australia	212–7 (50)		Sri Lanka	123–7 (38.1)
India	270–4 (50)		Kenya	179 (46.2)
FINAL				
Australia	359–2 (50)		India	234 (39.2)

Australia were utterly dominant in winning all 11 games, and clearly now the best at all forms of cricket. England, the only side that looked like beating them, and who should have done so, were off home early, unable to negotiate the Zimbabwean minefield. Their team spirit, though shaken, seemed somehow tightened rather than loosened by the experience, even though Hussain resigned the one-day captaincy.

2003 Zimbabwe and South Africa

Although there was a Stop the Tour campaign to try to prevent the Zimbabwe Tests, unlike its 1970 counterpart it fizzled out quickly, not least because the country's beleaguered opposition party wanted it to go ahead. Nevertheless Zimbabwe, minus Andy Flower and Olonga, were a shadow of the team that had proved so tough to beat in the last two series. It was a good opportunity for England debutants.

England	472	Zimbabwe	147 & 233
England	416	Zimbabwe	94 & 253

The matches followed the same pattern throughout. Butcher's 137 put England on top at Lord's. Thereafter Anthony McGrath of Yorkshire made 69 on his unexpected Test debut, the stripy-haired Anderson took 5–73 on his, and England won on the third day. In England's first Test in Chester-le-Street McGrath added another 81, Richard Johnson of Somerset took 6–33 on his debut, and again the game was over on the third day. As preparation for South Africa it was mildly useful but hardly sufficiently taxing. England went on to win the triangular one-day series under Vaughan, who had a different approach that the press were ready to admire, then reverted to Hussain for the Tests. South Africa, too, had a new captain, the mature 22-year-old Graeme Smith, already a natural leader. Not a bad batsman either.

South Africa	594–5d & 134–4d	England	408 & 110–1
England	173 & 417	**South Africa**	682–6d
England	445 & 118	South Africa	362 & 131
South Africa	342 & 365	England	307 & 209
South Africa	484 & 229	**England**	604–9d & 110–1

A tall, powerful, lantern-jawed left-hander with intense concentration, Smith had technical flaws, but England took three Tests to spot them, by which time he had made 277, 85 and 259. It's a good job they did, otherwise he would have been way over 1000 by the end of the series. This was the most astonishing start to a series since Bradman. The England bowlers, criticised for their belated adjustment from one-day to five-day disciplines, were made to look completely innocuous. At Edgbaston Gibbs opened with 179 in a stand of 338 with Smith, but after a day of rain the follow-on was averted by Vaughan's cultured 156, and by Giles's urgent 41 on the fourth morning, and with it any risk of defeat. That defeat came at Lord's. There had been only two days for England to get used to a new leader. Hussain, recognising a new reality and determined to be in charge of his own destiny, chose to resign the Test captaincy to Vaughan as well. This time Smith put England in, Makhaya Ntini bowled out a 'gormless' England, in Wisden's words, and Smith's second big double (after being dropped at 8 by a chastened Hussain fielding uncharacteristically at cover) gave South Africa a lead of over 500. When England lost three wickets at 208 before lunch on the fourth day, the game was all but wrapped up, but at last they had something from Flintoff to savour in a home Test. He batted immaculately to reach 100 from 112 balls, until, with the last man in, he bludgeoned 29 from seven consecutive balls from Hall and Pollock before being last out for 142. In a losing cause, his celebration was muted. Ntini's was not: the untiring and popular bowler took 10 wickets in the match and kissed the Lord's turf to celebrate.

It took a poor pitch to get England back into the series at Trent Bridge, where the toss proved all-important. Butcher and Hussain made hundreds, Ed Smith of Kent (on his debut) and Stewart fifties, in an innings of 445. With the pitch deteriorating, South Africa recovered from 132–5 to just 83 behind, and by bowling England out for 118 left themselves just 201 to win. But 'just' is the wrong word for that strip, and James Kirtley of Sussex on his belated debut, swinging the ball both ways, took advantage of the variable bounce to take 6–34 and get England back into the series. By mid-afternoon on the first day at Headingley it looked as though England were poised to go 2–1 up. Yet more new seamers, Kabir Ali of Worcestershire for his first Test and Martin Bicknell of Surrey for his second, 10 years after his first, had reduced

South Africa first to 21–4, then to 142–7. But England bowled increasingly badly on a helpful wicket, and the debutant opening bowler Zondeki, replacing Pollock who had flown home for the birth of his first child, managed to help the unflappable Kirsten add a priceless 150 for the eighth wicket. In reply, England were in full flow when they misguidedly went off for bad light on the second afternoon. South Africa regrouped, and their bowlers wrenched the game away from England. After falling short on first innings, they allowed Andrew Hall to chisel out 133 for the last three South African wickets, and finally slid to defeat against Kallis, who had missed the first two Tests to be with his dying father. Butcher and Flintoff both made their second half-centuries of the match, but they couldn't stop the rot.

England came to the Oval 2–1 down and facing a full South African side for the first time in the series. When the opposition were 345–2 shortly before the end of the first day it looked like curtains for England, even when Gibbs went for 183. Next day Pollock took them to 484, and England faced a mountain. Enter Trescothick. He had had a poor series thus far, averaging under 25, but he and Thorpe gradually wrested back the initiative in a superb stand of 268. Trescothick eventually went on to 219, but couldn't last till the third day's close, and England were in danger of losing the advantage until Flintoff thundered 95, Harmison hanging on to make 6* of a stand of 99. A lead of 120 was significant but not conclusive on a pitch still reasonable for batting. But the seamers made early inroads – Bicknell getting Smith lbw cheaply for the second time in two Tests, and his swing and Harmison's bounce yielded them four wickets each. Needing just 110 to win, Trescothick took his match aggregate to 288, and England had squared the series against the odds.

This rescued series was a tough and unexpected baptism for Vaughan, whose batting suffered – he made only 140 runs from eight innings as captain. Over the summer Trescothick, Butcher and Flintoff averaged over 50 for England, but the support was flaky: Hussain averaged in the thirties and Stewart in his last series in the twenties (although his wicketkeeping remained of a high standard). The fifth batting position still remained open. There were at least plenty of competent seamers around, and injuries made them essential. Kirtley took 13 wickets in his two Tests, Bicknell 10 in his, Anderson and Harmison took 26 and 18 respectively at just over 30, but Flintoff and Giles found wickets hard to come by. Now clearly into the post-Gough/Caddick era, England needed to settle its fast bowling combination. It was a recovery from Australia, certainly, but there was a lot yet to be done for the new Fletcher/Vaughan team.

2003–4 Bangladesh and Sri Lanka

Such was cricket's international merry-go-round now that there were three series confronting England in the winter of 2003–4. England's first two Tests against Bangladesh would be in October, followed by three in Sri Lanka in December. Plenty of practice against spin, then, before a complete contrast in March and April in the West Indies. Although the previous month they had come desperately close against

Pakistan, losing to the magisterial Inzamam by one wicket, Bangladesh had still not yet won a Test match, and indeed had lost 23 out of 24, most by substantial margins. Expected to win easily, England were thus on a hiding to nothing.

Bangladesh	203 & 255	**England**	295 & 164–3
England	326 & 293–5d	Bangladesh	152 & 138

Although there was very little play on the first day of the first match, England were well on top by the end of the second, 111–0 after Harmison had topped and tailed the Bangladesh innings with 5–35. On the third, some undistinguished cricket after Trescothick's 113 led to Bangladesh going ahead with only one wicket down. Although Hoggard and Harmison took the last four wickets for 7, England needed a potentially tricky 164 to win, more than they had bargained for. Vaughan eased them home with 81*, but it was a wake-up call. The Chittagong Test brought a more convincing performance. Another century opening stand, followed by one from Hussain and Surrey's Rikki Clarke, gave a platform for Johnson, in for the injured Harmison, and he took five again in only his second Test bowl. In the second innings he took a further four, one to a stupendous catch at deep fine leg from Kent's Martin Saggers, another new seamer on debut, after Hussain had again top-scored. It was just about satisfactory in the end. In Sri Lanka, though, England were up against it from the start. An ill-timed one-day series was wrecked by the monsoon, and England lost the only match played in it by ten wickets even before the first 15 Sri Lankan overs were up.

Sri Lanka	331 & 226	England	235 & 210–9
Sri Lanka	382 & 279–7d	England	294 & 285–7
England	265 & 148	**Sri Lanka**	628–8d

The first two Tests followed an identical pattern. Sri Lanka took a first innings lead of nearly 100, and left themselves over a day to bowl England out. Muralitharan was a constant threat, so was the fast left-armer Chaminda Vaas, and well though Giles bowled, the England attack was no match for Sri Lanka's. However England held out, in the first through a combined backs-to-the-wall effort that left Hoggard to face only one over from Murali before bad light came to the rescue, in the second through a cool and psychologically important 100 from Vaughan, his first as captain, and more defiance from the lower orders. Sri Lankan frustration was evident, but they won a comprehensive victory in Colombo after a massive polysyllabic partnership from Samaraweera and Jayawardene that took them to 400–2 against a team wilting in the field, followed by more exquisite bowling by Murali. The England players were convinced that he threw his new *doosra*, which spun from leg, and which allowed him to be, in Hussain's words, Murali and Warne in the same over. Ensnared by his control and powers of spin – 26 wickets at 15 apiece at less than 1.3 an over – England had been forced in this series into a siege mentality, and their supporters wondered whether the bold recovery in the South Africa series had been just another false dawn.

2003–4 West Indies

When England arrived in the West Indies in March 2004 neither side had had a good winter. West Indies seemed in a permanent reconstruction phase, and had just lost badly in South Africa. But England hadn't won a series here for 36 years, so it wasn't easy to call, particularly after the first three days of the first Test in Jamaica. On the fourth morning, though, a hurricane struck from a clear blue Caribbean sky.

West Indies	311 & 47	**England**	339 & 20–0
West Indies	208 & 209	**England**	319 & 99–3
West Indies	224 & 94	**England**	226 & 93–2
West Indies	751–5d	England	285 & 422–5

England had suffered a disappointing first day, allowing the inexperienced Devon Smith and Ryan Hinds to pull West Indies round on a fast and bouncy pitch after their best four batsmen had gone for 101. On two rain-affected days, England then battled towards a lead they achieved narrowly thanks to their top-scorer – Extras – with 60. On that fourth morning belated good weather brought a long-awaited Harmison breakthrough. He had seemed on the verge of one for some time, with his threatening pace and bounce, but had been maddeningly inconsistent. He had been successful enough against the weak Zimbabwe and Bangladesh batting, but against South Africa and Australia in the last two series he had gone for an average of 50. Before Christmas back problems had sent him home early (moreover he confessed to homesickness on tour) for a spell of rest and recuperation, work on fitness and stamina, and sessions with Newcastle United. But would he ever really make it?

Yes, and how. On the fourth morning he bowled a fuller length than in the first innings, and everything slotted into place. It was a stunning spell: he bowled unchanged for figures of 12.3–8–12–7. At the end he had a cordon of eight fielders in an arc from wicketkeeper to gully, with ex-captain Hussain under the helmet at short leg. At Port-of-Spain he did it again on a slower pitch, if not with quite so much devastation, to turn the match. He had not bowled well initially, while West Indies had sprayed boundaries on their way to 100–0 in the 25th over, but from the other end he got both openers and Lara – fending off a bouncer – in eight balls, and went on to finish with 6–61. After a bad start, Butcher and Hussain made their second century stand in succession, and 90 from the gutsy Thorpe, hit by both beamer and bouncer, ensured a healthy lead. Simon Jones, restored at last after that terrible leg injury in Australia 16 months earlier, took the first three wickets in West Indies' second innings, and although Jacobs and Chanderpaul moved them ahead, England had too much firepower and won by seven wickets.

Unprecedentedly 2–0 up with two to play, England went to the old West Indian fortress of Barbados with two to play, and Vaughan decided to put the opposition in on a pacy pitch while his opening bowlers still had the ascendancy. It worked in the end, after dropped catches had helped West Indies past 150–3 in the late afternoon, and this time it was Flintoff who took five. Now England's four-man pace attack was matched by West Indies' line-up, all from Barbados, all sporting a rich variety of first names in the true West Indian cricketing tradition. Fidel Henderson Edwards and Pedro Tyrone Collins were half-brothers, supported by Tino la Bertram Best and Corey Dalanelo Collymore. Hussain reckoned them as fast as anything he'd faced before in the Caribbean, and in this innings their bowling did recall their illustrious forebears. Only one Englishman reached 20, but he made a priceless 119*. It was Thorpe, again, and he gave an exhibition of cool courage to chivvy England to a two-run lead in the company of Harmison, who stayed while 39 were added against the new ball, the longest stand of the innings. This was still West Indies' chance to come back into the series, but England's fourth man emerged to join the fun, and conjured up a hat-trick as his party piece. With the ball swinging for him in ideal conditions, Hoggard took the wickets of Sarwan, Chanderpaul and Ryan Hinds with successive balls, and West Indies plummeted to another double-figure total and defeat.

In the context of a run of ghastly West Indian collapses against England, the boot now snug on the other foot, the last Test at Antigua was astonishing. Certainly it was a perfect pitch – ironically it was prepared by the legendary Antiguan fast bowler Andy Roberts, who would hardly have liked to bowl on it – but Lara was facing the same four England pace bowlers who had limited him to 100 in six innings. Batting into the third morning, to predictable criticism from Australians who had seen Hayden's new record 380 against Zimbabwe last only six months, he declared on being the first Test batsman to reach 400. (With a combination of rapid modern scoring, and a wide divergence in teams' ability, he seems likely to be joined before long. Considering the bowling, this was a decidedly more worthy record than Hayden's.) With 240 overs at their disposal to bowl England out twice, West Indies got half-way there in 99, despite dropping Flintoff three times on the way to a maturely restrained 102*. But, without a spinner, they couldn't dislodge Trescothick and Vaughan until they had added 182. Vaughan went on to reach 140, Butcher scored his second fifty of the match, and England never looked in danger of defeat.

There had been nine Tests in England's winter, which ended in another rain-sodden one-day series on 5 May. By the time they had returned home, the New Zealand tourists had played their first match, and the fourth round of championship matches was under way. In the nine Tests in the winter campaign a settled England side had begun to emerge. Six batsmen had averaged between 50 and 30 – Thorpe, Vaughan, Butcher, Flintoff, Trescothick and Hussain. For the first time for years England bowlers were sharing the wickets around. Harmison (36 at just 12), Hoggard, and Giles, all took over 30 wickets at less than 30 apiece, as did Flintoff with 20, while Johnson and Jones made a fifth between them on the two tours. Only Stewart's successor as wicketkeeper was now in doubt, with Chris Read in possession until being usurped by Geraint Jones, of Welsh parentage, Papua New Guinea birth, and Australian upbringing, for the last West Indies Test, a switch that rankled with Rod Marsh, the Academy director back home.

2004 New Zealand

England had nudged ahead of New Zealand in the world rankings, in that cluster of teams in the middle, way behind Australia. Australia had just beaten them comprehensively in a two-Test series, revenge for the indignity of a tight three-draw series of 2001–2, but they had a canny captain in Stephen Fleming. His opposite number at Lord's would be – Marcus Trescothick? Three days before the Test began, Michael Vaughan twisted his knee sweeping a net bowler. This set in train an unexpected and dramatic sequence of events. Andrew Strauss, the 27-year-old Middlesex captain, was drafted in to the Test squad and made his debut as Trescothick's opening partner. Just nine months later he had made 1246 runs for England in 12 Tests at an average of 56, with five centuries.

New Zealand	386 & 336	**England**	441 & 282–3
New Zealand	409 & 161	**England**	526 & 45–1
New Zealand	384 & 218	**England**	319 & 284–6

It's a measure of how the pace of Test cricket had changed that Wisden's correspondent could describe the first day's play as 'stodgy' when New Zealand scored at 3.2 an over. Admittedly, Mark Richardson's 93 had taken over six hours, but Astle and Oram had made brisk fifties. Next day the journalist got his money's worth. In the morning a fantastic display of hitting from Chris Cairns brought 82 from 47 balls, including four sixes in 10 balls, and no one would have begrudged him Viv Richards' fastest hundred record had he beaten it. The rest of the day belonged to Trescothick and Strauss, who added 190 as the compact left-hander Strauss calmly moved to a Test century on his home Lord's ground on debut. Richardson, again, and McCullum pushed New Zealand comfortably ahead, and Richardson had batted another seven hours when a delayed new ball removed him. Set 282 to win in a day and five overs, England were struggling at 35–2 on the final morning. Only a few years earlier, a target of 250-plus in the fourth innings would have strongly favoured the bowling side, especially for England in England. This summer changed all that. Hussain helped the amazingly mature Strauss take the score to 143, but with 83 and a second hundred beckoning – never achieved by an England batsman on debut – he sacrificed himself and was run out when Hussain made a bad call.

After Strauss's first innings hundred Hussain had already figured that his place would be in jeopardy after Vaughan's return, and to avoid being dropped was contemplating retiring straight away. Now he was beside himself. 'I had run out the local hero at a crucial moment… I thought God, I can't go now. If we don't win this game

I'll be the villain of Lord's and will always be remembered as such if it's my last game.' He said Thorpe was the right person to straighten him out: 'Look, you miserable git, stop behaving like a pork chop. Let's win this game.' The celestial scriptwriter took his cue. Thorpe manoeuvred him towards his hundred – 'I've been crucified for five years for not letting Alex Tudor get a hundred like this at Edgbaston. I'm not going to do that again' – and Hussain duly reached it with successive fours. With that, he strode off into the sunset: it would be his last first-class innings. Nothing became him in cricket more than his manner of leaving it.

Vaughan returned at Headingley, as captain but not opening bat. After losing most of the first day to rain, New Zealand must have felt reasonably secure with 409. But Trescothick and Strauss put on another 153, Trescothick the centurion this time. In trickier conditions on the fourth day Flintoff and Geraint Jones had a second century partnership in successive Tests, Jones going on to a maiden Test hundred. New Zealand stumbled against Harmison and Hoggard, and England had won in surprising comfort. The next Test followed a similar initial pattern, New Zealand winning the toss and running up a score that should have made them safe, with centuries for Fleming and Styris. But this time Cairns and the left-armer James Franklin, called up from the Lancashire League, bowled better in helpful conditions, and earned a lead of 65. When they'd reached 185–4 it had stretched to 250, but late wickets for Giles made the England target 284. As in the first Test, England lost early wickets, and 46–3 might have been terminal had New Zealand not lost two of their pace bowlers to injury (Vettori was already missing, so they had no spinner). Butcher defied a broken finger, Thorpe – a wonderfully cool player in this situation – took charge, and Giles capped a fine all-round display by helping him add 70 undefeated for the seventh wicket to seal victory. New Zealand were desperately unlucky to go down 3–0 – no one more so than Cairns in his last Test, who had had to bowl 25 overs in the last innings – but the luck was with England, and their batsmen were now showing cooler nerves in a crisis than they had for many years.

2004 West Indies

England	568 & 325–5d	West Indies	416 & 267
England	566–9d & 248	West Indies	336 & 222
West Indies	395–9d & 165	England	330 & 231–3
England	470 & 4–0	West Indies	152 & 318

Before the Lord's match Butcher suffered a whiplash injury in a minor car crash, and his place went to the chunky Robert Key, blooded on the tough Australia tour and scoring heavily for Kent – indeed he had reached 1000 first-class runs on 2 June, earlier in the year than anyone since 1988. While the West Indian pace bowling was undoubtedly a shadow of their predecessors', his 221 in seven hours, full of crisp driving and robust pulls, was a magnificent first Test hundred. He added 291 with

Strauss and 165 with Vaughan, who each made centuries. Held together by Chanderpaul, West Indies averted the follow-on with some ease. Vaughan's second hundred of the match set up a target of 478 in over eight hours. The key wicket was Lara's, beautifully deceived by Giles for his 100th Test wicket, and although Chanderpaul played another exemplary innings, England won with time to spare.

With nine wickets in the match, Giles was unexpectedly England's most successful bowler, and at Edgbaston he repeated the feat. A Trescothick hundred led England off, then Flintoff went to town. Adding 170 with Geraint Jones, an increasingly prolific pairing, he powered his way to 167, three of his seven sixes coming in one over. Sarwan and Lara responded with an *élan* of their own, motoring to 184–2, on a day when 437 runs were scored. However, Flintoff got them both next morning, Giles took four of the next six, Trescothick made another hundred as Vaughan declined to enforce the follow-on, and Giles emphasised his grip as West Indies subsided in just two of the five sessions remaining.

Already 2–0 down, at Old Trafford West Indies batted first for the only time in the series, and consistent and disciplined batting for once gave them a score that seemed healthy enough, especially as the second day was wiped out. Batting on the third afternoon, England lost three early wickets, and were indebted to a 177 stand from Thorpe and Strauss, the old cool head and his young counterpart. Thorpe crept past 100, despite having a finger broken at 91 during a lightning spell from Edwards, but only Hoggard of the rest passed 20, and England trailed by 65 (the same deficit they'd won from against New Zealand). Starting well enough, West Indies then fell apart once more, and England wanted 231 to win on the last day on a far from easy wicket, with rain clouds threatening. With both openers out early, and the fourth-innings talisman Thorpe nursing his finger, it took a fine innings of 91* from Robert Key, arguably more important than his double at Lord's, to steer England home, in Flintoff's massively reassuring company, as the Manchester rain gods for once smiled on England.

West Indies were flagging, 3–0 down, as they came to the Oval. Thorpe's absence brought in Warwickshire's Ian Bell, just 22 but like Key averaging 70 for his county, and rapping on the door. Coming in at 64–3, and reminiscent of Atherton, he responded with a mature 70 to some short-pitched stuff from Edwards. From 321–7, Giles, Hoggard and Harmison led a rare England tail-wag. England's domination was illustrated by the way West Indies folded first around Lara against Harmison, 6–46, then again around Gayle. The languid opener relieved his frustration by hitting every ball of Hoggard's second over in the second innings spectacularly for four, on his way to a century in 80 balls, but it was all over by the third afternoon. England had beaten West Indies seven times out of eight inside six months, calling on just 15 players. They had gone some way towards avenging all those 5–0 defeats. West Indian gloom was lifted somewhat when a ninth wicket stand of 81 from the hitherto unknown Browne and Bradshaw – their Bevan and Bichel – rescued West Indies from imminent defeat by England in the final of the one-day Champions Trophy late in September. This was a 15-match appendage to the season, and England weren't desperately disappointed. Their minds were already running on to the Ashes the following summer, and they had beaten Australia by seven wickets in the semi-final. That the Australians were not match-hardened mattered not a jot. England needed every psychological boost they could gather.

England had won all seven Test matches of the summer. To do that they had to have the rub of the green and luck with the weather, and they did. Neither of their opponents was in great shape, and they wilted under England's pressure. England's batsmen scored at close to 60 runs per 100 balls to set up winning positions, and three times they chased over 200 to win. The opposition made over 300 eight times in 14 innings, but the bowlers took wickets when they needed to. Thorpe, Key and Flintoff averaged over 60 with the bat, Trescothick in the fifties, Vaughan and Strauss in the forties, Geraint Jones and Giles (numbers 7 and 8) in the thirties. Harmison, Flintoff and Giles took their wickets in the mid-twenties – Harmison and the unjustly maligned Giles over 30 of them – Hoggard his at 35. The batting looked so settled that there wasn't even room for Bell in the South Africa party, while Anderson and Simon Jones contested the fifth bowling place.

2004–5 South Africa

The South Africa series was to prove a proper test of England's readiness to tackle Australia. It began after more Zimbabwean uncertainty, a two-Test series abandoned but a limp one-day series going ahead. England won it 4–0, but as practice it benefited only those not in the Test party – Bell, Pietersen, Solanki, Gough and Wharf – until Vaughan and Geraint Jones added 150 in the last match. Vaughan was the only batsman to pass 50 in the sole first-class game before the series, too, which England lost ignominiously.

South Africa	337 & 229	**England**	425 & 145–3
England	139 & 570–7d	South Africa	332 & 290–8
South Africa	441 & 222–8d	England	163 & 304
England	411–8d & 332–9d	South Africa	419 & 247
South Africa	247 & 296–6d	England	359 & 73–4

England came to Port Elizabeth for the first Test of five in 40 days looking severely undercooked. Fortunately South Africa came up with a strange team selection that they would rue. After Rudolph and Dippenaar had given South Africa the edge on the first day, England fought back on the second, Strauss with another calm century leading them to 227–1. But he and Butcher left early next morning, and South Africa had come back to parity as the fourth day began. At 152–2, though, a brilliant diving catch at long leg by Simon Jones dismissed Smith, and a pumped-up Jones continued by taking four of the last six wickets that tumbled for 28. Set only 142, Strauss ignored an early stumble in helpful bowling conditions, and powered England home with 94*. His trademark shots were square with the wicket, and he once more exhibited his inherent ability to hit bad balls for four.

On Boxing Day in Durban South Africa put England in and bowled them out before tea for 139. When the following morning South Africa were 118–6 it looked as though the game could be over in three days. But this was a classic game of two halves. Kallis found allies in every subsequent batsman, and had accelerated to 162 when he was last out with the lead close to 200. Trescothick and Strauss spectacularly wiped that out, each making hundreds in a stand of 273. Thorpe fashioned a third in century stands with both Flintoff and Geraint Jones, allowing Vaughan to set South Africa 378 in a day and nine overs. A wonderful comeback win looked probable when their opponents stood at 183–7 with on paper over 40 overs left, but de Villiers hung on, Pollock at No. 9 repeated his first innings display, and finally, after Simon Jones had run him out with a direct hit, bad light intervened with 15 overs still due. 'Bad light' needs some explanation, because there were floodlights on. England knew the score – the captains had agreed at the outset that play would continue as long as floodlights were augmenting natural light. Once it was replacing it, defined by the moment the players cast four shadows instead of one, the batsmen – and fielders – could be offered the light. (This, of course, was a red ball issue. How long would red balls survive in Test cricket?)

England had come through the calendar year 2004 unbeaten in 13 Tests. The only days intervening before they started 2005, though, were New Year's Eve and New Year's Day. Back-to-back Tests are universally condemned by players, press and public alike, but continue; no need to wonder why. While it was draining for both teams, here at Cape Town England were on the rack. The rock-like Kallis again made them suffer on the opening day, making 149, and Boje's cheery 76 rubbed salt in the wound. After an opening stand of 52, England collapsed against Ntini and the debutant Charl Langeveldt, who had been largely responsible for England's defeat before the first Test but had unaccountably not been picked for it. Forced to field again, England were batting again before lunch on the fourth day with a deficit of 500. That Harmison top scored with 42 in an innings of over 300 says enough. A pretty abject defeat, a tired side, and a captain who hadn't yet passed 20. Shades of Peter May in 1956–7.

Johannesburg

The first day at Johannesburg belonged to Strauss. Having reached 1000 Test runs in Durban in just his 10th Test, he made another 147 here, adding 182 with Key. Three wickets before the close, and a slump on a rain-limited second day, threatened to undo their good work, but a studiously disciplined Vaughan had worked his way out of his bad patch with 82* when the fielders came off for bad light. The regulations allowed them to do so, but it seemed somewhat absurd, and Vaughan's mild but public remonstration lost him his match fee. Well as Hoggard bowled after a wayward start, both Harmison and Anderson (oddly brought in for Simon Jones) mislaid their radar, and the third day belonged to the immaculate Gibbs. South Africa's robust tail inched them ahead, before England, coasting at one point at 175–2, wobbled to finish the fourth day 197–5, Trescothick a measured 101*. Next morning, as he continued in that placid vein, a draw seemed most probable, with South Africa more likely to win if anyone did. Twenty overs in, England were still not safe at 274–8, but when Harmison joined him Trescothick switched abruptly into his murderous one-day mode, and made the last 52 of his 180 in 32 balls, while Harmison made 3. Harmison's batting, alternating between obstinate defence and gigantic hitting, was becoming surprisingly crucial.

This onslaught allowed Vaughan to make an imaginative and tantalising declaration, setting South Africa 325 in a maximum – the light question made that an issue – of 68 overs. That didn't seem enough for an England win: Anderson was out of form, Harmison had damaged his calf and his confidence, and Giles (like Geraint Jones, who in the first innings had dropped two catches in successive overs) had a damaged thumb. As Flintoff was ignoring a nagging ankle injury, that left only Hoggard fully fit, and it could all go horribly wrong. But the ball was swinging for him, and by the ninth over he had taken the first three wickets, including the key one of Kallis, first ball. Hoggard went on to take the first six, whereupon the normal opening partnership was reconstituted, the defiant Gibbs joined by his cussedly courageous captain, who had been concussed when hit during fielding practice, and came out at No. 8 against doctor's advice. They looked ominously secure until Gibbs fell lbw to Giles for 98. Smith did his best to marshal the tail, usually so obdurate, but was left high and dry when Flintoff got Pollock and Ntini, and Hoggard returned to get Steyn in his 19th over and the 60th of the innings. The magnificent Hoggard had 7–61 and 12 in the match.

So to Centurion 2–1 up. After a blank first day, Flintoff and a returning Simon Jones took four each as South Africa were bowled out for 247. England started badly on a truncated third day, but an unusually cautious partnership from Thorpe and Flintoff took them ahead. Centuries from de Villiers and Kallis allowed a bold Smith to set a tasty last-day target of 185 in 44 overs, but England evinced no interest after losing three for 20, and grimly ground out the last overs. So, a tough tour was won in effect on the final afternoon in Johannesburg. Hoggard and Flintoff carried the attack, their 26 and 28 wickets at mid-20 averages matching Pollock and Ntini. But England's support was better, Simon Jones in four Tests finishing with 19 wickets, and Giles taking 13. The worry was that Harmison's 11 cost 70. In 2004 he had plundered 61 wickets at 21 each, so getting him back to that form for the Ashes series was vital. Strauss dominated the batting with three centuries and a 94* in his 656 runs at 72, and though Trescothick averaged 44, down the order things weren't so pretty. Thorpe averaged 35, a triumph of fierce will over fading form, Vaughan got his up to 30 but had failed too often, and Flintoff and Jones too frequently gave their wickets away. There was space waiting in the middle order, and one applicant made his claim – in triplicate – in the subsequent one-day series, lost by England 4–1 with one tied. With an English mother, Kevin Pietersen had been born and brought up in South

Africa, but, thwarted as he saw it by their quota system, had thrown in his lot with England. The predictable barracking clearly proved a spur, for he made 108 in 96 balls, 100* in 69, and 116 in 110. Flamboyant in every sense, could he translate that form to the Test arena in 2005, against his new county captain at Hampshire, Shane Warne?

Pietersen and Warne, for different reasons, were outsiders in the English county system. Pietersen had come from South Africa, and Warne was one of an increasing number of Australians who had gone from disparaging the English county system to using it. They had joined that body of county cricketers whose lives in many ways were similar to those of their post-war counterparts. They toured the country incessantly, now in cars paid for by sponsors. They were better off. Their training was better organised, but was it better training? They enjoyed the camaraderie still, but just as often feared for their futures at the summer's end. Some hoped for Test cricket, but since the recent development of the ECB Academy to fast-track promising youngsters to the national side, fewer and fewer would have that opportunity. How had these changes come about?

England's fourth innings chases 1946–2005

Target	w	d	l	%	Years of successful chases of 225+
125–149	11		1	92	
150–174	7	2	1	80	
175–199	3	1	4	44	
200–224	7	2	1	80	
225–249	5	2	2	67	1962–3, 1970, 1997–8, 1999–2000, 2004
250–274			2		
275–299	3	3	2	56	1970, 2004, 2004
300–324	2	5	4	41	1996–7, 2001
325–349		6	2	38	
350–374		4	6	20	
375–399		3	3	25	
400–424		2	14	6	
425–449		1	3	12	
450–474		2	7	11	
475–499		1	6	7	
500+		1	3	12	

This tabulates every England run chase where there was a reasonable chance of victory or defeat. The percentage column is calculated on the basis of 2–for–a–win, 1–for–a–draw. Of the (only) 10 successful chases over 224, eight took place after 1996. That of 1970 was in the Rest of the World series, thus usually omitted. Note the statistical quirk that appears to make just under 200 a dangerous target to attempt, as in Pakistan in November 2005. Observe too how many captains declare as soon as the lead tops 400, with an apparently predictable psychological effect.

CHAPTER 35

Playing the Game

Len Hutton, Alec Bedser and Denis Compton on the ship
taking them to South Africa, October 1948.

Be grateful to God that he has given you health and strength to go
through the great fatigue and dangers of your professional career,
and that it hath pleased him to suffer you to return to the bosom
of your families after six months' laborious avocation, and that
you bring back to your homes the good name that the foul
slander of your enemies would take from you.

NICHOLAS WANOSTRACHT, known as FELIX, 1851

Getting there

F elix, quoted at the start of this chapter, was speaking to the players of the All England XI, of which he was President, at a dinner after they had toured the country in 1851. His address would have been just as apt for the England team returning from Australia in 1933 by sea after the Bodyline tour. In 1950 they travelled the same way, via the Suez Canal and Colombo. On 14 September that year they left for Australia on the Stratheden. (On that date in 2005 there were two rounds of the county championship left to play.) With the 17 players went two joint managers and a scorer who doubled as baggage-master. They played their first game in Australia on 14 October, after a month at sea. It was not until six weeks later that they played their first Test, having crossed the country, as Alec Bedser recalled, in a sapping two-day journey across the Nullarbor Plain, 1700 miles in a train with no air-conditioning. The tourists didn't arrive home until late April, when today two championship matches would already have been played. Not until 1964–5 did the touring team fly to their winter destination. Then, with memories of Manchester United's crash at Munich airport still vivid, the team flew to South Africa in two separate parties.

Thirty years after his trek across the Nullarbor Plain, Bedser's views as manager of the first post-Packer series in 1979–80 were barely printable. In 12 weeks the team had undertaken 18 internal flights, five times flying into and out of Sydney. No two successive matches were played at the same venue. Those were the days when the one-day internationals were dotted about between the Tests. At least that practice was soon abandoned. Nevertheless in 2002–3 there were still 17 internal flights, and another five stops at Sydney. Vic Marks summed it up in the 1987 Wisden:

> 'The commercial wizards planning a tour of Australia now insist that the intervals between Test matches are spent, not with missionary visits to the outback, but in a series of lucrative one-day games. A modern international cricketer, when asked his impression of Australia, is scarcely able to give anything more than a vivid description of the airport lounges of Sydney, Melbourne and Perth.'

In 2002–3 the tourists were in Australia for three months; 50 years earlier it had been seven. Back then just three people looked after the 17 original players, plus Statham and Tattersall who, daringly and scarily for them, later became the first cricketers to fly out to Australia. In 2002–3 there were 31 players in all, including the one-day additions and a stream of injury replacements. Wisden lists eight looking after them (plus another two replacements for the one-day series): coach, operations manager, assistant coach, team analyst, physiotherapist, physiologist and – a further sign of the times – two media relations managers. By 2004–5 there were two more, a bowling coach and a masseuse.

Back in England

Travel has always been a necessary part of the professional cricketer's life. At home in England in the 21st century, because they now play so few county games, Test cricketers are spared the journeys their predecessors undertook. Back in England at the end of April in 1951, Len Hutton found himself successively at Lord's, Oxford, Bradford, Hull, Manchester, Cambridge and Chesterfield in the first three weeks of the season. No dipping out of the university games in those days, and just Sundays off, with no time to get home to see the family he had been away from since the end of the previous season, unless Yorkshire were at home. Hutton would have played on 27 days out of the first 31 had the rain and Yorkshire's bowlers not given him some respite by ending games early.

There were no motorways in those days either, no Severn Bridge, and some of the journeys were frightful – it's amazing that more cricketers weren't killed on the roads. Nor did everyone have a car. Stephen Chalke's delightful book *Caught in the Memory* vividly recalls that time. Peter Walker of Glamorgan remembers an eight-hour journey from Glamorgan to Sheffield, including a two-hour wait at the Aust ferry. One year, leaving Middlesbrough at six o'clock after a game, the team arrived at Llanelli 40 minutes before the start next morning after four changes of train. At least they won the toss, so three men padded up and the rest went to sleep. For Robin Hobbs of Essex, who drove the kit van with Paddy Phelan, Clacton to Cardiff was the worst journey: 'You knew you wouldn't get there till two in the morning.' Professional cricketers in England were always obliged to have, as Vic Marks said in the 1987 Wisden, 'a reliable car, an understanding wife, and a thick skin'. He described the season as 'one prolonged, frenetic, dash around the highways and byways of the country', and the job as a 'precarious, cut-throat way to earn a living'.

At least when the Sunday league began, and teams sometimes had to break a Saturday to Tuesday county game to travel somewhere else on a Sunday, the country's motorway building programme was under way. It was still a test of stamina, as Marks's Somerset captain Peter Roebuck asserted in *It Never Rains*. From 27 April to 15 September he was required on 121 days out of 147, while on 10 of the remainder he would be turning out to support a beneficiary. He described it as akin to trench warfare – you needed graft and endurance to survive. Some enthusiasts who would have loved the opportunity to play first-class cricket might point to the 31 weeks he wasn't on the road, but few cricketers could afford not to work in the winter, and a job for seven months of the year could not construct an alternative career for the man discarded in his late thirties. Ray Illingworth, whose ability eventually made him luckier than most, still spent 17 winters selling Christmas cards and fireworks on commission in Scotland.

Preparing to play

Until comparatively recently, county sides had no manager. Players arrived for early season nets in April, and until one-day cricketers began in earnest, bowlers in particular could get into the pattern they would maintain throughout the season. As Alan Oakman reflected 30 years later, of his playing days in the 1960s: 'I don't envy the young players now. We had one style of batting and bowling, and we were broken into it.' Team meetings were a rarity. As Tom Graveney later said: 'Far from there being no tactical team meetings, there were non-stop meetings in the bar each night about the game.' Don Wilson, writing in the 1988 Wisden, said that after a Yorkshire v Middlesex game, in the 1950s, 'both teams would go together for a drink on the first night of the match. It was compulsory... As a youngster, I squeezed in between Denis Compton and Bill Edrich... and simply listened as Bill and Denis chatted about the game to Johnny Wardle, say, or Bob Appleyard... They were intensely interested in techniques... It was fascinating for us young players; it was part of our cricket education.' Then, cricketers constantly learnt from each other.

Players still learn that way, but it seems to be only a subsidiary part of a much more formal tutelage. Sometimes it starts at a county, sometimes at the ECB Academy, begun in 2001. For the majority of English cricketers the bulk of their training takes place at a county with a full-time coaching staff. Ed Smith, in his absorbing *On and off the Field*, describes in a diary the 2003 season, not realising at the outset that he was destined to join the England set-up later in the summer. It's an instructive depiction of the modern English game, inside and outside the increasingly exclusive Test fold. He describes how his Kent season starts with a fitness test on 18 March, followed by three days of 'team bonding', at somewhere he describes as like 'an open prison without the openness'. In his diary for 19 March he asks:

> 'Will historians be able to tell us when it all began? And who started it? Team bonding, team building, team values, core covenants, buying in, signing off, shared commitments, norming-performing-storming...'

Perhaps it had its roots in the 1970s, when the overseas cricketers were making such an impact. Tony Borrington remembers the effect the South Africans had, particularly Eddie Barlow at Derby, a county then as now in a bad run. In the dressing room there had been an automatic, perhaps unconscious, tendency to talk up opponents. Think you're a batsman? Wait till you've faced John Snow bowling down the hill at Hove. Barlow banned all such negativity, and wouldn't allow any praise of the opposition. Of Procter, who had been terrorising opponents, he would say: 'Watch me bounce him, he doesn't like it any more than you do.' Borrington recalls their first tracksuits, the pre-game warm-ups that everyone does now, the jeers from Yorkshire supporters as they ran round the ground at Hull.

For Ed Smith in 2003, nets began on 24 March, then practice games until the Cambridge match on 18 April and the start of the championship season on 24 April, a week later than most counties. By then, he was practised out: 'No one, least of all you, is much interested in how well you can hit the ball in practice.' After a bad start, a century against Middlesex, a brilliant 99 against Surrey in a one-day match, and his season was away in perfect weather. Four successive centuries, including a superb 203 televised by Sky, catapulted him into contention and on 9 August he got the call.

From county to country

At the pre-match press conference the questioners asked why he was a 'late developer' and whether he saw himself as a 'representative' of county cricket: he had just missed being part of the academy when it began. Five years earlier these questions wouldn't have been asked: he was virtually the same age as Alec Stewart, the man who had played most Tests for England, had been on debut, and four years younger than Herbert Sutcliffe, the man with the best batting average. But so great had the divide become, in the three years since central contracts began, that the gulf between county cricket and Tests was increasingly difficult to bridge. After a calmly assured 64 against South Africa on a tricky Trent Bridge pitch in his first Test innings, he failed to secure a place in the winter's touring team. At the end of 2005 he still had just three caps. James Kirtley of Sussex, England's match-winner at Trent Bridge with 6–34, had four. In the last two Test matches Martin Bicknell returned to Test cricket 10 years after his only previous Test, and his bowling contributed to England's series-squaring win before he too left the scene. All were back in county cricket with just a rosy memory to arm them against regret. Geoff Cook, another player who lasted just a few Tests, wrote in 1991 that: 'To become fully integrated into the Test system... requires a period as long as 18 months. It is hardly surprising then that so few Test players ever fulfil their promise'.

Until the late 1990s, the process of running the Test team had been no more professional than running a county, in some ways less so. It started to change with full-time coaches. Malcolm Ashton recalled in the 2005 Wisden how, after a meeting with Duncan Fletcher at Chandigarh in 2001, he was transformed from the same scorer-cum-baggage-master his predecessors had been into something completely different. In Australia Fletcher had seen the use the Australian coach John Buchanan had made of computers. He wanted Ashton to become the team logger, analysing the previous Test and creating a DVD for the management and players to use. 'I sat down at the computer with special software that allowed me to get a picture from the TV output on to my laptop. I'd start at the beginning of the run-up and stop it when the ball went dead. Before the next delivery I would then have to input the length of the ball (bouncer, short-pitched...), the direction, the type of shot played, where the ball went and how many runs.' A cricket anorak's dream job.

The rewards

While the rewards for English professional cricketers, except for those few at the very top, remain small compared with their counterparts in football, tennis and golf, they have at least improved in the last 30 years, since the welcome spin-off from the Packer revolution in 1977. There are no comparable published current figures to those on page 148, but most cricketers would accept that with a sponsored car they are now reasonably well off, so much so that they are criticised for complacency, for being content in their county's safe embrace. Ed Smith talks of the 'straw man set up by angry sports columnists to explain the failings of English county cricket (who) lacks ambition, preferring to sit in his sponsored car counting his £50 000 salary', perhaps a third of a successful Test cricketer's earnings. But their professional cricketing will still end when they are between 35 and 40, and they must find a second career. The lucky ones will have a tax-free Benefit to act as a bridge to that uncertain future.

The Benefit system, which has a somewhat feudal ring, was devised to reward long-service professionals, and was usually granted after about 10 years as a capped player, although it was by no means secure at a hard-up county. Because salaries were so low, a tax-free Benefit was crucial, so, combined with the threat of a year away from the game if a disaffected player wanted to move, it had the incidental effect of tying a cricketer to his county. Moreover, if you were capped at, say, 25, you would still need to be performing at first team level at 35 to be sure of receiving one. While in later years you could insure to some extent against the weather, rain or fortune could wipe you out. In 1953, Bertie Buse's Benefit match on a terrible new-laid pitch at Bath, Somerset v Lancashire, was over in a single day. At the other end of the scale, Lancashire allowed Cyril Washbrook to use the 1948 Lancashire match v Australia, and his £14 000 takings remained a record until well after 1970s' inflation should have left it far behind. Washbrook was perhaps the first to organise his benefit professionally, extending it to many games throughout the county. That subsequently became a routine, exhausting and to some rather demeaning business. Though many, like Jack Simmons, also of Lancashire, had the outgoing personality to enjoy the year, others did not. Nasser Hussain expressed it with apologetic frankness:

> 'Basically I had to ring people up and say to them: I don't know you. I've probably never met you. Probably, being the way I am, I have walked past you sometimes at Chelmsford…You have probably tried to say hello to me or just exchange a few pleasantries with an England cricketer, and I've told you to piss off or completely ignored you. Now I'm ringing you up because it's my Benefit year and I'm asking you for money even though I've probably already got more than you.'

The system may change eventually, however, as Hussain says: 'It would take a brave man to come along and stop Benefits, because, whenever you abolished them, there would always be some very worthy cricketers just about to be awarded them'.

The divide between county and Test cricketers would be emphasised again in 2005, when only 12 players would be picked for the Ashes series. Whatever happened on the field, it looked certain to be rewarding for the Test players, who would produce a joint book of the series, have massive marketing spin-offs, and big extra paydays for those chosen for the Rest of the World team to play Australia in October. Would Australia still be world champions? Could England knock them off their perch at last?

CHAPTER 36

A New Jerusalem?

After England's 2 run victory at Edgbaston in August 2005, Andrew Flintoff stops to console
Brett Lee after the courageous fight back that so nearly took Australia to a 2–0 lead.

For the moment, an Australian gives thanks. For years my countrymen
have publicly pined for a 'competitive Ashes series' without perhaps
something quite so competitive in mind, but no ground for complaint
exists. A sporting rivalry is only a rivalry if there is a danger of defeat;
England have not only won the Ashes, but reflated the whole currency
of Anglo-Australian cricket.

GIDEON HAIGH

The year 2005 was to be an Ashes summer. But we would have to wait for it – the first Test did not begin until 21 July, a month after the longest day of the year. Moreover we would have to endure a first tour for Bangladesh to England, a triangular one-day series – a triangle that looked to have two long sides and one very short one – and then another one-day series with just Australia, before the real stuff could begin. That would be over 100 days after the start of the first-class season, MCC v Warwickshire at Lord's on 8 April, when – guess what – it snowed. In 1948 the Australian tourists were still on the southern ocean on that date, and Bradman would make his obligatory century against Worcester three weeks later. The first Test in 2005 coincided with the fourth Test back then.

2005 Bangladesh and Australia

Observing Australia's increasingly triumphant march over the previous 12 months (1–0 v Sri Lanka, 2–1 in India, clearing up that festering sore, 2–0 v New Zealand, 3–0 v Pakistan) England were under no illusions. In that time the top six Australian batsmen averaged over 1000 runs each at 54, and the four main bowlers 57 wickets at 23. Far from being over the hill, McGrath and Warne, both 35 and back from injury and suspension, each took over 60 wickets. While the talk in England was of Ashes regained, optimism-scarred realists would venture only that at least the series would still be alive in August. For now, there were two batting places to settle.

Bangladesh	108 & 159	**England**	528–3d
Bangladesh	104 & 316	**England**	447–3d

After much speculation England chose to pick Thorpe and Bell over Key and Pietersen for the two open places. Fears about Bangladesh's ability to compete were shown to be a complete underestimate. Their bowling was slaughtered by Trescothick, 191 in six hours and 151 in barely three. Vaughan made a hundred at Lord's, and Bell 162*, while Thorpe played himself into form. Bangladesh's batting was pitiful until the second innings at Chester-le-Street, which at least took Durham's inaugural Test into a third day. Hoggard had been the most consistent bowler, but everyone except Giles had some practice. Allowed out to play for Warwickshire, where he made an excellent start, he had damaged a hip and rested it. That was the new dilemma for the central contract era – wrap them in cotton wool or give them match practice.

That was the first of the sideshows. The second was a one-off Twenty20 match. Although irrelevant in the summer's context, the sight of an Australian team going from 23–0 to 31–7 had English supporters pinching themselves. So did their inability to defend 343 in 50 overs against Somerset, although there was no West Country burr from their openers, Jayasuriya and Graeme Smith. Worst of all was their last-over defeat in the first one-day international by the Bangladesh team that England had swept aside. When that was followed by a hammering from Pietersen, 91[*] in 65 balls, to lose a game they should have won, Australia had lost four games in a row in a week. Amazing. They had begun to restore normality by the time the Tests began, though, first tying the triangular series final in a roller-coaster match that would set the tone for the summer, then beating England in the NatWest final with a pulverising century from Gilchrist. That was their first moment of real ascendancy over England in 2005. The second would take place at Lord's on 21 July.

Australia	190 & 384	England	155 & 180
England	407 & 182	Australia	308 & 279
England	444 & 280–6d	Australia	302 & 371–9
England	477 & 129–7	Australia	218 & 387
England	373 & 335	Australia	367 & 4–0

The first day's play was frenetic, and it set a pace and produced an excitement that would continue throughout the series. Sparks flew from the moment Harmison hit Langer on the arm with the second ball of the match, and he had taken 5–43 by the time Australia were all out for a panicky 190 in just 40.2 enthralling overs. But England's batsmen in turn were held in thrall by McGrath. An exquisite spell of 5–7 left them 21–5, and they staggered on to finish the day on 92–7. Although his performances had in truth been patchy, the promise exhibited by Pietersen in the one-day series had given him the nod over Thorpe, and next morning he passed 50 on his debut until dismissed by an extraordinary boundary catch by Martyn. Australia were more disciplined second time around – scoring at under four an over, a mere 3.84 – and fifties from Martyn, Clarke and Katich meant England had to make 420 to win. More realistically, with rain forecast, they had to bat for a long time. While Trescothick and Strauss added 80 that seemed a possibility, but another collapse left them 156–5 at the close. When play eventually got under way late on the fourth afternoon, England supporters hoped for some determination to keep the game alive until the last day. What they got was a dismally familiar story in which only Pietersen, two fifties in his first Test, made any runs at all – watching from the other end as Geraint Jones give his wicket away with a poor shot, and the rest succumb for ducks like, well, ducks in a shooting gallery. Desolation for England supporters. Pietersen was the only faint silver lining. Flintoff, playing his 48th Test, but somehow his first against Australia, had made 0 and 3, and his four wickets had cost 173 at over four an over. One journalist summed up the national mood: 'It is only one match, but to all intents the Ashes cannot be regained by England this summer.' Were they going to go up in a puff of smoke yet again?

The ball that turned the series was neither bowled nor hit, it was trodden on. McGrath's ankle turned on it on the morning of the Edgbaston Test, in the touch-rugby warm-up beloved by modern cricketers, and he was out. For the second successive Test the opening day produced fewer than 80 overs, rain preventing England bowling five overs at the end, but no one asked for their money back. Ponting surprised most people by sticking to his plan of inviting England to bat, despite the loss of McGrath. Trescothick and Strauss responded by batting with much more aggression, setting the tone by adding 112 in only 25 overs. They were parted only by a monstrous Warne leg break, and Trescothick's 90 took only 102 balls. The partnership all England had been relishing, Pietersen and Flintoff, raced to a century stand at six an over, Flintoff hitting five of the day's 10 sixes, and a breathless day ended with England 407 all out. While an amazing display, to some that seemed a waste of a good start, but Australia couldn't capitalise on a brilliant fifty from Ponting and a more measured one from Langer. Their 262–5 became 308 all out, and England were in again on the second evening. But first Lee and then Warne exhibited England's frailties and they tottered to 131–9, only 230 ahead. As it turned out, every run in this game would prove vital, and Flintoff and Simon Jones made 51 of them in a crucial last-wicket stand. Flintoff hit Kasprowicz and Lee for two sixes each, making nine in the match in all out of 141 from 160 balls. Warne took six wickets, making 10 in the match, Lee the other four to recover well from a wayward first innings that yielded 111 from 17 overs.

Australia needed 282, and no one was betting against them when the openers were adding 47. At this point Flintoff, who had finished the first innings with two wickets in two balls, made it three in four when he bowled Langer in his first over, and for good measure had Ponting caught behind from the last ball of a rip-roaring over. That started a sequence of wickets that continued unchecked to the close. A key component was the dismissal of Katich and Gilchrist in quick succession by the once-more-maligned Giles. Delirium for England supporters at the close, Australia 175–8, 107 behind. That Australia could win from here seemed far-fetched, but it wasn't long before memories of the Border/Thomson last-wicket stand of 1982–3 started to surface. Lee and Warne had begun with ominous ease, adding 45 before Warne trod on his stumps at 220. Surely Lee and Kasprowicz couldn't add over 50 for the last wicket? They could, bowling along at over five an over. Vaughan had relied on Flintoff, Harmison and Giles – had the run rate been slower he would have been able to try someone else, but now wouldn't risk it. With 14 needed Simon Jones missed a difficult chance at third man, next ball was a no-ball that went for four leg-byes, and England supporters were despairing. But with only three needed Harmison found Kasprowicz's glove, Geraint Jones plunged to take a leg-side catch, and England had levelled the series.

If the last ball had been a foot further to Jones's left they would have been 2–0 down, as they probably would too had the umpire spotted that the batsman's hand had left the bat fractionally before the ball brushed it. But no one remonstrated. On his knees, a distraught Lee, who had batted with great bravery and had been hit more than once, was consoled by Flintoff in one of the summer's most enduring images. Australia had been virtually dead and buried but nearly clambered out of the coffin. The flesh was showing signs of weakness but the spirit fought on, as it did at Old Trafford, where the teams reassembled after only two days' break, again victims of modern scheduling.

England's worry was plainly the batting, the more so as McGrath managed to be fit in time. Three times out of four they had failed to reach 200, Strauss and Vaughan hadn't reached 50, and Bell's place was in some danger. In the third Test, though, all three came good on the opening day. Vaughan took part in century stands with Strauss and Bell, stroking the ball with increasing freedom to make 166 in under five hours of a first day total of 341–5. Facing 444, Australia's top-line batsmen again let them down, losing three early wickets to Giles, and they finished the day 214–7. On a rain-ruined third day, Warne gave the follow-on short shrift, this time with Gillespie helping to show up the top order. Next morning Warne failed by 10 to make the maiden Test hundred his batting and chutzpah deserved, Simon Jones taking the last three wickets to finish with 6–53. Strauss's 106 and Bell's pleasing second fifty of the match gave Vaughan the acceleration he needed, and he set Australia 423 in 108 overs. They hadn't lasted 100 overs yet, could they do it now? Wickets fell regularly, and when Gilchrist was fifth out at 182 there were 50 overs left. But Ponting had been constructing a captain's innings, with the determination to be last to leave the ship before it sank, and as the coiled-spring tension wound up he found able partners first in the injured Clarke, and then once more in Warne and Lee. There were just four overs to go when the captain was forced to abandon his ship, gloving a Harmison bouncer, leaving Lee and McGrath – instructed to bat a yard out of his ground – to see out the last 24 balls. They did, and it stayed at 1–1.

To Trent Bridge at 1–1

Although Australia could point to a match saved against the odds, England felt they now held a clear psychological edge, feeling that only rain had prevented them going ahead. That advantage was increased when McGrath was again unfit, this time an elbow, and was replaced by the raw but exciting Shaun Tait. England made a measured start on a first day reduced to 60 overs. Trescothick and Strauss started with 105, Vaughan passed 50, then next day Flintoff and Geraint Jones took the score past 400 before Warne chopped off the tail as usual. At this point Hoggard, anonymous for most of the summer, found his swing and line, and with Australia 99–5 at the end of the day England seemed to have the game as good as won. Despite Lee's brief pyrotechnics next morning, Simon Jones's reverse swing accounted for four of the wickets. Flintoff took the other, a flying Strauss plucking at full stretch a rocketing edge from Gilchrist, out of form but as dangerous as ever, and Vaughan had the option of enforcing the follow-on.

None of the commentators had any doubt that he would do so. My instant reaction was that England should bat again, convinced that Australia would not bat as badly a second time and fearing Warne on a wearing pitch. Moreover, the weather was set fair and Australia would have had 11 hours to bat. But no one in the England camp recalled or cared about Benaud in 1961, and doubtless felt the force was with them. Simon Jones wasn't though, limping off after four overs. Despite the brilliant run out of Ponting when he was going well, by the substitute Gary Pratt, prompting an outburst at England's use of substitutes – inside the Law but against its spirit, he felt – a more disciplined effort took Australia to 222–4 at the close of the third day, just 37 behind. Next morning, as England's nerves began to jangle, Clarke and Katich nudged ahead, adding 100 from an old-fashioned 48 overs before they were parted. Katich got a rough decision, but Warne laid into Giles before being deliciously deceived and stumped. When Tait unaccountably left all three stumps open to Harmison, England had only 129 to win.

Only 129. They began at a dash, Trescothick making 27 from 22 balls, until Ponting brought Warne on for the sixth over and caught him at bat-pad first ball. Vaughan played a leg glance at a waspish leg-break and was bemused to find himself caught at slip, and England were soon 57–4. Was this to be revenge for Headingley '81? Pietersen and Flintoff added 46 in 10 overs to ease the palpitations before the heroic Lee, bowling flat out, had Pietersen caught behind and bowled Flintoff with a vicious break-back. Geraint Jones charged Warne and holed out irresponsibly at long-off, and then it was 116–7, 13 needed, the palpitations back. Giles and Hoggard were at the crease, Harmison and the injured Simon Jones to come, all four of them Warne's bunnies this series. At the other end Lee was steaming in at over 90 mph, but Hoggard drove him for two and four as he over-pitched, striving for the yorker. Both Hoggard and Giles seemed imperturbable, and Giles won the match with a push through mid-wicket. The two bowlers whose places had been at risk, the no-nonsense get-on-with-it boys, had done the job. A collective sigh of relief echoed round the country.

To the Oval

The sides went to the Oval on 8 September with England 2–1 up, and the good weather breaking. They could as easily have been 3–1 up or 3–1 down, such were the permutations possible from three desperately close finishes in succession. Australia needed to win to retain the Ashes with a 2–2 draw, so their approach certainly wouldn't change. England, though, were unable to select the same XI that had played all four games, unprecedented in modern times, because Simon Jones hadn't recovered. Instead they played a seventh batsman, the in-form Collingwood, who could bowl well enough to provide respite for the main bowlers, as he had with effect in the one-day matches. Objective observers felt that McGrath's return and Jones's absence brought the teams back to parity. As the side batting first had won (or deserved to) every game, the toss would perhaps prove crucial.

The crowd's roar when England won it and batted told its own story. Trescothick and Strauss began with an untroubled 82 in quick time, but that only brought Warne on early, and he struck four times either side of lunch, luring Vaughan and Pietersen into poor shots. Strauss and Flintoff added an increasingly commanding 143 at over five an over, but three late wickets, the last Strauss to Warne for 126 in the last over before the new ball was due, left England 319–7 at the close. Out for 374 next morning, England toiled as Langer and Hayden, the latter with exaggerated care after a poor series for him, added 112 before the weather closed in. It interfered on Saturday too, irritatingly for Australia, who closed at 277–2, Langer and Hayden redeemed with centuries. Still, if they could post a healthy lead, England would have a hard task in the third innings to save the game against Warne. But Sunday began and finished just as gloomily, and, obliged to bat on a dour morning in poor light, Australia were bowled out six behind by Flintoff – bowling unchanged for 14 overs – and Hoggard.

At least it dawned fine on the last day, which England began at 34–1, 40 ahead, with 98 overs left. They would need to bat for well over 60 of them to make the game safe. For a while all went well, but a brilliant diving catch by Gilchrist – not at his best this series – disposed of the confident Vaughan, Bell went for a pair next ball, and the hat-trick ball was caught at slip off Pietersen's shoulder after narrowly missing his glove. Pietersen might have gone then, or next over from Warne when an edge cannoned between Gilchrist and Hayden and down, or at 89 when Warne at slip dropped a head-high chance he would have caught eight times out of 10. At that point 16, Pietersen somehow survived, but with Warne disposing of Trescothick and Flintoff, England lunched at 127–5, still 72 overs left. An Australian charge for 200 to win from 50 overs, say, was well on the cards at this point. It all depended on Pietersen, with his blond streaked hair, sparkling ear stud, big ego – and big match temperament.

After all the promise of his one-day heroics, and three fifties in his first three Test innings, Pietersen had frankly disappointed. Since then he had made only 109 from five innings, after reaching 20 in four of them, and for such an athletic fielder to have dropped all the six catches that had come his way seemed an extraordinary aberration. Was it a concentration problem? Had he failed that day at the Oval, the jury would still have been out. But his priceless asset was his self-confidence. Encouraged during the lunch interval to play his natural game, afterwards he took the attack to Lee, belting 33 from 13 balls, including two hooked sixes. By the 56th over he had reached 90, but now seven were down for 199. With England 203 ahead and 55 overs left, there was still time for Australia. But Giles brought out with him his abundant good sense, and his stand of 109 with Pietersen snuffed out Australia's last chance, and allowed a nervous populace to creep out from behind their sofas. Both made their highest Test scores – Pietersen 158, and Giles 59 – before Warne bowled Giles round his legs with a huge leg break to show what might have been. So England had regained the Ashes due to a debut hundred, in which a batsman had hit seven sixes, a record for England against Australia, six of which were hit while the game was still in the balance. Nothing better exemplified the transformation of Test cricket than that.

Apart from the four successive nail-biting finishes, what made it such a wonderful series – for Richie Benaud it shaded 1981 as the best Ashes series since the war – was both the balance between the two teams and that between bat and ball. Pietersen's innings leapfrogged him to top the batting averages with 52, but only he, Trescothick and Flintoff on either side scored more than 400 runs and averaged over 40. Strauss averaged 39 and Vaughan 32, although the worry was that more than half the captain's runs came from one innings. Bell made fifties in two innings, but only

47 in the other eight: his position was still open. Five England bowlers took 10 wickets: Simon Jones, Flintoff, Hoggard and Harmison shared 75 at between 18 and 32. Giles's figures looked ordinary, but his reassuring presence was anything but, figuring as he did in a crucial partnership in each of the last two Tests, and he represented the team ethic on which England's revival was so clearly based. For once that strength prevailed, while Australia's stars shone more fitfully.

Two stars, though, shone over the series. Andrew Flintoff made 402 runs at 40 each and took 24 wickets at 27. Shane Warne scored 249 runs at 27 and took 40 wickets at under 20. But figures alone only told the half of it. Flintoff bowled 194 overs and was the man Vaughan turned to when he needed something to happen: the Australians would belittle him no more. And for a faltering Australia, it seemed that only Warne stood between them and defeat, time after time. An extraordinary cricketer, 36 the day after the series ended, he twice took 10 wickets in the match, and became the first Australian to take 40 wickets in a five-match Ashes series. If the fates had conspired differently, he would have caught Pietersen, run through the tail, and made the winning runs in the last over to save the Ashes.

Had the fates been *really* treacherous and altered the last hours of the second, third and fourth Tests by just a little, England could even have lost 4–0. The teams were that close, for all the talk of England revival and Australian slump. Vaughan's captaincy, far from being lauded, might have been under close scrutiny.

But the fates relented. England halted a run against Australia in which they had lost 28 and won seven in eight successive series. Their average age was 27 to Australia's 31, and 10 of the 13 Australians who played in the series would be 35 or over the next time they toured England in 2009; only two of the England side would. Could Australia find new blood as quickly as usual? Could England, wanting only one batsman and some young spinners, compete as successfully on the subcontinent in 2005–6, and go to the top of the international table for the first time since its inception? And defend the Ashes in 2006–7? Hopes were high, but a tour of the subcontinent is never easy, as this history has reminded us…

CHAPTER 37

The Game We Live Now

Andrew Flintoff pulls Brett Lee during an Australia v Rest of the World one-dayer in October
2005, played on a drop-in pitch in front of a sparse crowd at the covered Telstra Dome.

We can all remember what happened in the Test matches, but,
my dear old thing, who on earth can remember what went on
in all those one-dayers?

HENRY BLOFELD, quoted by Frances Edmonds

Ashes to Ashes – 1953–2005

In the summer of 1953 England regained the Ashes at the Oval after a gap of 19 years and six series. In 2005 the gap was 16 years – but nine series. In 1953 England won 1–0 after two nerve-racking narrow escapes, in an atmosphere of grim defiance, against a side that had dominated them for years. In 2005 England won 2–1, this time after two nerve-racking narrow victories, in an atmosphere of aggressive bowling and buccaneering batting, once more against a side that had dominated them for years. In 1953, after Lord's, or Headingley, or the Oval, if you had told a spectator that, 50 years on, a batsman would save the game in a last-day crisis by hitting a maiden Test century, one that included more sixes than an Englishman had ever hit in an Ashes innings, he would have questioned your sanity. Through the 1953 series he would have seen England grind out the runs at a rate of 2.1 an over; in 2005 you saw them bat at just under 3.9 an over. He saw England hit three sixes all series, you saw 34. And that was against an attack that included two bowlers, still at the height of their powers, who during the summer took respectively their 600th and 500th Test wickets.

Freddie Brown, you should be alive today! Then chairman of the selectors, it was he, recalled for the Oval Test in 1953, who in the following Spring's Wisden inveighed against safety-first batting in his article entitled 'Batsmen Must Be Bold'. Well, they are certainly bold today, and that's one of the many changes that we have seen in the last 60 summers. In this chapter I want to go back to the question I posed in the Preface, and examine the cricket of today. While at its batsman-to-bowler core it is virtually the same now as it was then, it has changed in many ways to a remarkable degree, for good or ill. Most of us like some of the changes and dislike others.

Batting

In an article for the 2003 Wisden entitled 'The 21st Century Coaching Book', Simon Briggs referred to the MCC Coaching Manual of 1952, the one I was given for my eighth birthday. He describes as its central tenet the conviction that 'every shot is really an adaptation of either the forward or back defence'. Indeed, we were taught defence first, attack second: only if you have a rock-solid defensive technique can you be trusted to play run-making strokes. The epitome was Geoffrey Boycott's style, for his attacking strokes all seemed to emerge from an instinctive, mistrustful, defensive posture. The coaching manual 'proceeds to list five major species – drives, cuts, pulls, hooks and leg-glances – with all the fussiness of a lepidopterist'. One minor species, the sweep, remains undescribed, despite its joyous deployment by Denis Compton, as though it was a dangerous mutation not for the eyes of children.

Briggs goes on to explain the explosion of new strokes that have evolved in response to new cricketing micro-environments. The bouncer bombardment of the English by Lillee and Thomson in 1974–5 brought forth the 'uppercut' from Tony Greig and Alan Knott, probably first used seriously by the South African Eddie

Barlow in the previous decade. With the ball rarely pitched in the batsman's half, the deliberate stroke over the slips profited from one of the few areas in which it was possible to score. The new fielding position of 'fly slip', a fine short third man, was the response. How many batsmen did bowlers have caught at third man in 1953, I wonder? In the 1996 World Cup the stroke was enthusiastically adopted by the flailing Sanath Jayasuriya, and both Sri Lankan openers were caught at third man in the first over of the semi-final. Fast bowlers dozing down at third man in the 1950s would have been aghast. More recently Tendulkar and Sehwag, Gilchrist and Hayden, are among its leading exponents. Gilchrist typically sways back to a bouncer and flips the ball delicately fine over the slips with the face of the bat.

Yes, it's dangerous, but so is the hook, and one-day cricket demands that the most is made from every scoring opportunity. The same goes for the reverse sweep, a stroke designed for those strangulation periods fielding captains hope to impose in one-day matches after the 15-over fielding limitation has ended, often with a 3–6 predominantly leg-side field, and without a man behind square on the off-side. Prince Ranjitsinhji is credited with inventing the 'heathen' leg glance when he was at Cambridge in the 1890s, though it's more likely that he simply played an existing stroke more audaciously from straight balls. It was his nephew Duleepsinhji, another adopted Indian who batted for England, who first played the reverse sweep in the 1920s, amid appeals for unfair play that the umpire rejected. It's certainly perplexing for the bowler to see a batsman switch his stance, and sometimes his hands, when the ball is in flight, and 'sweep' the ball to the untenanted third man area rather than to fine leg. Although it's only usually employable against slow bowling, Jonty Rhodes has been quick enough to use a 'reverse pull' against quicker bowlers.

The article goes on to define other shots, even more risky, and potentially physically dangerous too. Neil Carter of Warwickshire memorably emulated his 19th-century Australian namesake Hanson Carter, who 'lifted the ball over his left shoulder just as a labourer shovels the dirt out of a drain he is digging', by doing the same to the only ball he faced, the last ball of the one-day semi-final in 2002. Needing two to win, he reached forward and 'scooped' a full length ball over his shoulder for four. Dougie Marillier of Zimbabwe had recently done the same to, of all people, Glenn McGrath, and nearly scored the 15 needed to win in the last over of a one-day international, taking fours with it from the first and third balls. The scariest shot of all has been called the 'ramp', employed by the Australian Ryan Campbell. Down on both knees, almost in the *hara-kiri* position, and with the bat's toe facing the bowler, the batsman plays it back over his own and the wicketkeeper's head.

These are shots increasingly deployed in one-day cricket, and Twenty20, whose arrival may spawn stroke mutations stranger yet. Players in Twenty20 matches are now sometimes taught to settle on an untenanted area of the field before the ball is bowled, and fashion a shot to get it there. And while such strokes are still comparatively rare in Test cricket, there is no doubt that batsmen whose minds have been freed up by an apprenticeship in one-day cricket are able to score faster in all forms of the game. The art is to have a mind strong enough to stay focused on the batting style and shot selection required for the occasion. The 180 by Marcus Trescothick that set up England's win in Johannesburg in 2004–5 was notable for containing two entirely distinct components: the mature Test century, continued on the sober fifth morning, followed after Harmison's arrival at No. 11 by an abrupt switch – indeed just as if he'd thrown a switch in his head – into the devastating one-day mode of which he's an expert exponent. Others have been less able to discriminate, exemplified by the worrying over-use of 'open-face' off-side shots in Tests, learnt for picking up singles in the one-day game. Some, like Flintoff and Pietersen, seem to have an all-purpose block-or-hit style, in which the difference in Test cricket is just that they block (slightly) more often.

Bowling

It is often said by old cricketers that bowling has deteriorated, that bowlers seem unable to bowl the basic repetitive line-and-length of their counterparts in the 1950s and 1960s – they don't have the patience. They will tell you that they were all like McGrath in those days: they gave you nothing. There's no doubt that bowling has deteriorated relative to batting. Equally, a batsman now is less likely to let a bowler settle into his groove, and is quicker at taking advantage of minor variations of length and direction. He lets fewer pass outside the off-stump, and is much more adept at working good-length straight balls on true pitches to the leg-side. Above all, he hits in the air more. Bats are heavier and pitches are better, breeding confidence that the ball won't misbehave, allowing a batsman to dominate. Impossible, but fascinating, would be to pit England's batsmen today against the Lindwall-and-Miller-led Australians of 1953 on 1953 pitches; or Hutton, Compton, May and Bailey against the Australian attack of 2005 on today's pitches.

We can conclude only with certainty that the bat v ball balance has shifted sharply in favour of the bat. That's despite three particular trends. One is that the average fielder is clearly fitter, faster and more skilful than his 1953 counterpart, and often better positioned in the field. The demands of one-day cricket bred it, and the rise of Twenty20 will demand it even more. A second is the growth of faster and more aggressive pace bowling, from the West Indian quartets, through Thomson and Lillee, to England's four-man hunting pack of 2005. The third is the invention and increasing perfection of balls that belie logic and go the wrong way: weapons like reverse swing and the *doosra*, Urdu for 'the second one', the leg-break bowled with an off-break action.

Pace

In 1948 Norman Yardley would have given his eye-teeth for just one of England's 2005 quartet to partner the labouring Alec Bedser. While their Australian opponents had in Lindwall and Miller a classic pair of fast bowlers who could stand in comparison for skill and hostility – and bouncers – with any pairing since, Yardley had to make do with 'pea-shooters against bren guns', and juggle himself and his spinners to give a rest to Bedser and whoever happened to be his opening partner. Ever since Trueman and Statham arrived in the 1950s, supplemented by Tyson, the typhoon that seemed to blow itself out as mysteriously as it arrived, England have sought lethal new-ball pairings. After the brief heyday in the same period of Laker and Lock, Wardle and Appleyard, England relied on pace, as all the opposition bar India have. England's batsmen were pulverised by West Indies fast bowlers from the moment Hall and Griffith arrived in 1963, with the briefest interlude before Roberts and Holding, Marshall, Ambrose and Walsh, continued the terror until 2000. England batsmen's technique against intimidatory bowling at top pace was found wanting. As they were battered into submission in the 1970s, a desperate England recalled the over-forties, Cowdrey at 42 against Lillee and Thomson in 1974–5, Close at 45 against Roberts and Holding in 1976. That's as if Atherton and Hussain were to be asked to come out of retirement to face Brett Lee's successors in the Ashes summer of 2013, if they were still playing county cricket.

By the end of the 1980s England supporters were inured to the sight of their batsmen weaving, ducking and fending off short-pitched bowling, with little variation. In 1992 they were watching them hopping about trying to keep out swinging yorkers from Wasim Akram and Waqar Younis. The reverse swing phenomenon, hotly disputed at first as some kind of illicit black art, has since become legitimised in English eyes by its mastery first by Darren Gough, and most recently by Simon Jones and Andrew Flintoff. Batsmen used to be able to rely on weathering the early effect of the new ball, and settle down to a period when, in the rare event of the ball being pitched up, it would swing only fitfully. By the summer of 2005 it was clear that, like Lock and Laker in the 1950s, England bowlers were impatient for the ball to go dull as fast as possible. Batsmen had to remain wary throughout the life of the ball. Four pace bowlers are still the ideal, with a mixture of new-ball and old-ball swing, Hoggard, Jones and Flintoff, and in-the-ribs hostility from Harmison and Flintoff. Thus England in 2005 effectively had five bowlers, as long as they didn't overbowl Flintoff into injury. Spin was little more than a helpful variation, a giver of respite to keep the pace men's daily over ration below 20.

Spin

We have seen that England's green and pleasant land, once full of spinners of all varieties in the aftermath of the war, was soon covered by dark satanic fast bowlers. Like most other commentators, we have speculated on the reasons for their disappearance. That absence used to be replicated around the world. Who were the spinners who joined the ranks of top wicket-takers in Tests between the 1960s and early 1990s? For England, despite the number of Tests now played, only Derek Underwood is in the top 10, with 297 wickets. Emburey, Edmonds, Allen, Illingworth and Tufnell are among the 40 with more than 100 wickets, but none took more than 150, and they all averaged over 30. Elsewhere, away from the Indian subcontinent, the picture is even worse. Since Lance Gibbs took 309 wickets in 79 Tests, only Carl Hooper has taken 100 for the West Indies, and they cost him 49 each. For Australia, between Richie Benaud and the arrival of Shane Warne and Stuart MacGill, only Ashley Mallett and Bruce Yardley took 100 wickets in Tests. For New Zealand no one achieved it. This contrasts with India and Pakistan, who have eight and four spinners in their top 10 respectively. Admittedly their pitches have always been slower and more conducive to spin, or simply less helpful to bowling of any kind, but they have always had role models for youngsters to copy, and a tradition that spinners can be attacking bowlers, and not primarily of a defensive cast.

But the world has changed dramatically. When Warne took his 300th Test wicket at the beginning of 1998, the spinner with the most wickets in Tests was Lance Gibbs, who had played his last Test in 1975, and he was only in ninth place. At the end of 2005, Warne and Muralitharan were first and second, and Kumble fifth. Daniel Vettori was on the point of becoming New Zealand's second highest wicket taker. He and Harbhajan Singh had taken over 200 Test wickets and neither was then older than 26. Saqlain Mushtaq, arguably the first to master the *doosra*, passed 200 when he was 26 too, but loss of form and injury stopped him in his tracks. Even South Africa, pretty unsympathetic to spin, had Paul Adams in sixth place despite his never making the side consistently. Only West Indies continues to be a hopeless case. It's telling, too, that Kumble, Warne and Muralitharan all began in Test cricket between 1990 and 1992, and were still playing at their peak in 2005. What you get with spinners is longevity: good spin bowlers are an ideal long-term investment, compared with the speed merchants, many of whom burn out after a few years.

Although Ashley Giles consolidated his place by the sheer determination of his all-round cricket, the prospect of England finding a spinner with anything like the variations and/or power of spin of their counterparts in the opposition seemed slim in 2005. Moreover, the more formidable their pace attack grows, the more likely the opposition are to prepare slow, turning pitches. Nasser Hussain's constant refrain was to stress that England couldn't compete on equal terms around the world without a class spinner who really turned the ball. At the time when, as Hussain said, every net bowler they employed in Pakistan in 2000–1 seemed to be able to turn it both ways, there seemed no coaches in England concentrating on other than traditional right- or left-hand finger spin, plus the one that goes 'on with the arm'.

It's encouraging, though, that an unexpected phenomenon emerged in Twenty20 matches after 2003. Sides began to play two spinners, sometimes even three. They were successful: of the 40 bowlers who took eight wickets or more in 2005, 15 were spinners, and 10 of those English, led by Nyan Doshi of Surrey with 17, another English-born spinner of Indian origin. Three or four overs in a Twenty20 match is a far cry from bowling a long spell in a championship game at a key juncture. But, when spinners are usually brought on when batsmen are set on a perfect wicket, or simply to avoid an over-rate fine, it is at least an encouraging straw in the wind. And we have stumpings back. It may take a while for Warne's highly public success in England in 2005, when he was the leading wicket-taker both in the Tests and in all cricket, to inspire young wrist-spinners. But at least some finger-spinners have at last begun to learn oriental tricks, notably Alex Loudon, experimenting with the *doosra*.

Throwing

The throwing issue of the late 1950s was brought forcefully back into the limelight when Muttiah Muralitharan was controversially no-balled for throwing by the Australian umpire Darrell Hair in the Boxing Day Test of 1995, and from the bowler's end at that. Since that moment Murali's bowling action has divided the cricketing world. Contrary to popular belief, it has divided Australians too. Here is the view of Don Bradman, the ageing oracle: 'Clearly Murali does not throw the ball. No effort in that direction is made or implied by him. His every effort is to direct the ball unto the batsman. Murali wants to bamboozle, to trick through flight and change of pace.' Bradman was as delighted by Murali's ability as he was by Warne's. Nothing however better illustrates Bradman's own assertion after the 1958–9 rumpus that throwing is a subject that 'is so involved that two men of goodwill and sincerity can hold opposite views'. Could we ever break free from that bind? Especially when the two men are umpiring in the same game.

The throwing law was last modified in 2000 to say that a delivery is fair if 'once the bowler's arm has reached the level of the shoulder in the delivery swing, the elbow joint is not straightened partially or completely from that point until the ball has left the hand'. An umpire is required to call no-ball if he thinks a delivery has been thrown. Some umpires thought Murali threw, some didn't, some couldn't tell, which makes enforcing the law really hit-and-miss. In his autobiography Hair called his action 'diabolical' – hence literally devilish – and his compatriot Ross Emerson, who called him one notorious day in 1999, clearly agreed. By that year his action had been cleared by biomechanics experts in university labs, who said that his permanently bent arm, a genetic trait shared by his brothers, created an optical illusion of throwing. The ICC asked the experts to try to set a maximum elbow flexion level. At first they proposed flexion limits of 10 degrees for a fast bowler, 7.5 degrees for a medium-pacer, 5 degrees for a spinner. Why should they be different, one asked? Subsequently, when Murali had perfected his *doosra*, after the match referee Chris Broad reported his delivery, the ICC decided to request a standard maximum for all bowlers. The experts at the University of Western Australia came up with a flexion figure of 15 degrees, announced in March 2005.

15 degrees

To the untutored layman, 15 degrees seems a considerable degree of latitude, and conspiracy theorists – not least Geoffrey Boycott – promptly assumed that the figure was arrived at to allow Murali to pass muster. The experts however are adamant that 15 degrees is correct, not least because analysis made it clear that many current fast bowlers, clearly regarded by their peers as legitimate, had flexion levels over

10 degrees. Why should they be allowed that and spinners not? Angus Fraser, on the ICC throwing panel, said: 'While we watched the likes of McGrath, Pollock, Harmison and Donald, we quickly realised that the levels of tolerance are far too low. All these bowlers possessed actions any youngster would be wise to copy, yet their bowling arms were nowhere near as straight as we anticipated.'

Dr Paul Hurrion stressed that the lab uses at least four cameras firing at 200–250 frames a second. 'I would challenge anyone who criticises the 15 degrees rule to come and have a look at the high-speed camera, the footage and the angles. The camera doesn't lie and the computer data doesn't lie. That's basically what biomechanics is. It can analyse any movement.' The human brain, he says, effectively operates at around 15 frames a second, and fills in the gaps, just as it does for those old paper-flicking tricks where successive slightly different images convey to the brain the impression of movement. Coincidentally 15 degrees is roughly the angle at which people think they can recognise a throw with the naked eye. Hurrion said that old film taken at 50 frames a second raises questions not only about Charlie Griffith, but also about Harold Larwood, whom no one appears to have doubted at the time, as Bradman had discovered to his surprise 45 years before.

As long as lab conditions can adequately replicate what a bowler does in the middle, an important caveat, there seems no alternative to the use of technology here. It's now recognised at last that the umpire's 15-frames-a-second eyes cannot be expected to be sure about all but the most blatant throwers. The rules of engagement in internationals now require an umpire to consult with the match referee. That can lead to the bowler being reported – as has happened with Shoaib Akhtar, with his 'hyper-extensive elbow', Shabbir Ahmed, Shoaib Malik and James Kirtley – and banned from bowling until he has undergone remedial treatment in the lab. Also referred were the *doosras* of both Harbhajan Singh and Murali, who continues to confound his critics by passing the lab tests. Murali subjected himself to bowling in a rigid elbow brace, and could still produce everything in his armoury. Apart from the permanently bent elbow, the film revealed a remarkable rotation of both wrist and shoulder. He is unique.

The domestic game – the county championship

For over 50 years after the war every England player was employed by his county. In the 1953 Ashes series Hutton, Compton, Bailey, Graveney, Evans and Bedser played in all five Tests. Nevertheless they still played in more than half their county's championship games, and all appeared both for their counties and for festival teams against the Australians. Even as late as 1998, none of the 18 players called up by England against South Africa played fewer than half their county's games unless they were injured. That included all those who played in every Test, including Alec Stewart the England captain, apart from the injured Hussain. By contrast, in 2005 the 10 players who played in all five Tests, plus Simon Jones, who missed only the last, played just 41 county games between them. Nearly half of those appearances were by

Pietersen and Bell, not certain of their places at the start of the season, and Hoggard, omitted from the one-day series.

In 1953 there were 190 cricketers who played at least half of their county's championship games. Of these, 10 were overseas players, leaving 180 qualified for England, 120 of them either born in the county or a nearby minor county. (Of those that weren't, Yorkshire émigrés accounted for 19. Yorkshire had enough for two county teams then.) In 1979, half-way between 1953 and 2005, and a decade after the first major influx of overseas cricketers, the equivalent figures are 191, 32 overseas, and 95 local, almost exactly half. The ruling allowing two overseas players per county was much criticised at the time. In 2005, the figures were 183, 42 overseas, and 43 local, less than a quarter. So in that year, of those who played at least half a county's games, as many came from overseas as were born within its borders or in a neighbouring minor county. Because of the reduction in matches, English cricketers are playing in fewer than half the first-class matches that their counterparts were 50 years ago. Old cricketers tend to see this as a shame, but a hardening current view is that there is too still too much cricket to allow cricketers to maintain form and fitness. That's the principle behind the England Test management's approach.

Kolpak and after

Until recently we used to shake our heads at Premier League football, where sides often had only one or two players qualified for England, and were grateful that cricket had not been reduced to that extreme. Not any more. The so-called Kolpak ruling effectively meant that no longer could the ECB restrict the number of overseas players in the championship. Kolpak, the name of a Slovakian handball player, derives from a European Court of Justice ruling in May 2004. If someone with a valid UK work permit comes from a country that has an 'association agreement' with the EU, he can be available to play in domestic county cricket, without any residential qualification period. For our purposes, that means principally South Africa and some of the Caribbean islands.

This has created the situation where players can be parachuted in and out of a county to replace overseas cricketers required to play for their home country. In 2005 it was worse than football, which has a 31 August pre-season transfer deadline, followed by a mid-season window of a month in January. The effect can be seen by examining the last two rounds of championship matches in 2005, when titles, promotion and relegation were at stake. The 18 counties played 55 overseas cricketers in these games. Lancashire, for whom Murali had taken 36 wickets at 15 each in six earlier matches, flew in the aptly named spinner Murali Kartik from India, who took 16 wickets in the last two games, which were instrumental in securing them the second division title. Glamorgan were the only county who played no foreigners at the end of the season – commendably they played eight born in Wales – but only because they had already been relegated. Hampshire played five in their late assault on the title, and the Durham v Northamptonshire game had five each, so there were 10 in the match. In all, 88 overseas players appeared in the championship in 2005, so assiduous were the counties in finding temporary substitutes, and most of them played in fewer than half their county's games. Moreover they switch county from year to year: the Australian Mike Hussey has played for three. At least from 2006 the legal loophole that allows them to come in on visas as holiday-makers (yes, really) will be closed, and new ECB restrictions will be introduced. It remains to be seen how effective that will be.

All this means that nowadays we don't so much have a County Championship, as a championship played between teams based at the grounds where first-class cricket originated. These days, once a cricketer has reached Test level, he is effectively gone until his Test career is over – and how many in future will want to continue in the county game once the central contract is gone? The championship is still the only breeding ground for the Test team, but once a cricketer has emerged from his county chrysalis, the butterfly will rarely return to his home patch.

As I pointed out in Chapter 27, the relationship between win, draw and bonus points has exacerbated a tendency for toss-winning sides on good pitches to bat on and on, then hope to bowl the other side out twice. This has given us far fewer close matches than we had in the three-day era. The result of having two divisions with promotion and relegation, though, is to make more matches really matter. It bears repeating that half-way through the 2005 season any one of seven of the nine sides in the first division could have won the title, and any one of eight could have gone down. There were still four sides that could have won it with two games to go, and we would have been granted a splendid last-week climax had Kent not witlessly connived with Nottinghamshire in agreeing a virtually impossible last-day target, and promptly capitulated. Nottinghamshire were thus fortunate to wrap it up a match early, denying spectators the tantalising prospect of a showdown at the Rose Bowl, Warne v Fleming, with Hampshire needing to win to overtake them. In the event Hampshire exacted a hollow revenge in the final match, reaching 700 only moments after lunch on the second day and winning by an innings, small consolation for their feisty captain.

As well as six Tests, Warne had played 11 championship games for Hampshire, far more than any England player had done for his county. For Warne, the best practice for bowling is, as Alec Bedser famously averred, bowling, and in the middle at that. Meanwhile, in the battle to stay in the first division, were it not for one side-effect of bonus points, Surrey would have needed simply to beat Middlesex to send their London rivals down instead of themselves. But by declaring at 400–5 to deny Surrey further bowling points, Middlesex condemned their opponents to having to avoid losing three wickets in the first 130 overs, and then go on to win. Some may enjoy such subplots, but it's hardly what the bonus point inventors intended, and meant the game was dead by the second morning. It's no surprise that the last round of county games saw three teams score over 680, despite the rain. The sole consolation of that last round was the unlikely fact that two English-born spinners, Brown and Panesar, took all 20 Yorkshire wickets for Northamptonshire.

Nurseries

County cricket is a decidedly stubborn form of life. In 2003 the unofficial Cricket Reform Group, including Bob Willis and Mike Atherton, published a plan suggesting that the counties should be replaced by six elite regional teams playing 10 games each. The idea was not popular: as they say, turkeys don't vote for Christmas. Early in 2005, Stephen Baddely, director of sport for Sport England, concerned that government money for cricket doesn't seep down to the grassroots – 96 per cent goes to the counties – warned that £11 million over three years might be withheld if the ECB did not commit to reform. The amount that the recreational, non-professional game gets in England is less than a quarter of the 20 per cent distributed to it in Australia. Decryers of the current system ask if the counties are the real nursery of future Test players, or more of a finishing school. Was Marcus Trescothick produced by Keynsham CC or Somerset, Steve Harmison by Ashington or Durham? Over 30 per cent of English county cricketers come from independent schools, which only 7 per cent of the population attends. In 2005 Gloucestershire had only one locally-born player who was from a non-fee-paying school. Fifty years ago they all were. Cotham Grammar School produced three Test players – now it doesn't even have its own ground. However there are some hopeful initiatives. The Chance to Shine is a scheme designed to link 800 clubs with state schools, providing coaching each summer term and holidays. It aims to have reached a third of state schools in 10 years, and received great interest after the 2005 Ashes win.

The paradox of the current situation is that the Test side creates the income that goes to the counties, who then use it to buy in cricketers from abroad. That they qualify for England after a four-year residence is hardly an ideal way to find future England cricketers, for all the success of the South African-born Allan Lamb, Robin Smith and Kevin Pietersen.

Test cricket

Undoubtedly the introduction of central contracts has been popular with the England players and management. In their biographies both Mike Atherton and Nasser Hussain were forthright about the benefits. It cannot be a coincidence that all 11 England players stayed fit for the first four Tests of 2005, until Simon Jones was injured in the fourth. To outside observers, if not to the team management, there does though seem a price to pay. The compression of Test series, and the reluctance to allow players to play competitively between Tests (even when there is time), means that lost form cannot be recaptured in the middle. This is perhaps less important for pace bowlers than for batsmen and spinners. Moreover tour arrangements allow little time for acclimatising matches. In South Africa in 2004–5 England played only one three-day match before the Tests began, so had to play the intended Test side, only one of whom passed 50. They went into the first Test looking unprepared, but won thanks to a strange South African selection and to Andrew Strauss. When

Key replaced the injured Butcher, he hadn't played a first-class innings for over three months. At least in Pakistan in the autumn there were two three-day warm-up matches, but the three Tests were all back-to-back.

Between 2000–1 and 2005 England played 56 Tests against nine different opponents. Fifty years earlier, from 1950–1 to 1955, they played 47 against six. Superficially that's not a huge difference, but of course in the latter period England played over 60 competitive one-day internationals as well. Fifty years ago the top players went on only three tours, although sea travel forced them to be protracted; in the five most recent winters they went on nine separate tours and a World Cup. Back then, three of their opponents were pretty weak – New Zealand, India and Pakistan. In 2005 two of their opponents were abysmally weak, and so, because the ICC has a programme requiring each side to play all the others twice in a 10-year period, over a third of all the Test series now played are extremely one-sided. Within 12 hours of the end of the epic Ashes series we had the bathos of two totally one-sided Test series involving Bangladesh and Zimbabwe, in only one match of which did the weaker side not lose by an innings (it lost that by 10 wickets), or extend the opposition beyond a third day.

As we have seen, Test cricket in England went through a poorly-supported period in the 1970s and 1980s, but came back to popularity well before England's fortunes recovered so strongly. This seems likely to continue unless ticket prices rising above £50 deter paying customers, prices that have much to do with increased corporate interest. However the enforced fixtures against weaker teams, and proliferation of one-day internationals, have at least allowed the ECB to explore new Test grounds such as Chester-le-Street and Southampton's new Rose Bowl, and thus to fire warning shots across the gates of some of the more tired traditional venues.

One-day cricket

In the late 1970s, heady heyday of one-day cricket in England, typically 10–12 days of one-day cricket drew twice as many spectators to a county's ground as 36–39 days of first-class cricket. The same ratio prevailed at the turn of the millennium, but spectator numbers had halved in each form. The one-day game that had filled some grounds to bursting point in its early days now only does so for a Lord's final. Spectators have suffered from over-exposure, not least because of the quantity (not quality) of one-day cricket on satellite television now. A potential spectator who has already paid his 'price of admission' to Sky television for the season can sit back and watch the televised game rather than one he might have gone to see, particularly if the weather looks uncertain, and especially if his county contains unfamiliar foreign names that may be gone next week. While the Twenty20 format has been outstandingly successful in its first four years in England, a 5–8 pm game ideal for someone who can leave work a shade early and still get back home in time for a meal, there is bound to be a risk of it going the same way. The attendance at Twenty20 games in 2005 was 545 000, 80 per cent higher than 2004, with an average crowd of nearly

7 000. This figure is slightly higher than the attendance at *all* county championship games in the whole of 2003, the latest year for which figures are available.

For 2006 the ECB again altered the domestic one-day structure. In the 1970s we settled to two knockout cups, one a straight knockout, the other begun by a four-match league phase, plus a 16-match season-long league. Like the FA Cup, the knock-outs yielded an opportunity for giant-killing, allowing separate minor counties and a combined Oxbridge team to play, together at times with Scotland, Ireland, Holland and Denmark. This added spice. The combined university side produced several upsets in the days Hussain and Atherton played for them, failing by three runs to reach a cup semi-final in 1989. And although the amateur minor counties have beaten their professional betters only 32 times in over 40 years, the pleasure such a win affords all but the shamefaced county was worth its rarity. That Surrey, one-day league and Twenty20 cup holders, were knocked out by Ireland in 2004, for exam-ple, afforded huge pleasure for supporters of 17 other counties. But such incidental enjoyment is now even rarer. There is no proper knockout any more. The cup will transmogrify into two leagues of 10, designated North and South, with Scotland and Ireland included but the minor counties gone. The final will simply be between the two league winners, a guaranteed flat cap v southern toff affair, though at least we are spared a Super Six stage. While leagues guarantee the counties more games, the whole point of a knockout – lose and we're out – is lost. Every game in a knockout is life-or-death. A one-winner league of 10 ensures simply that after half the games half the teams are playing on with little further interest in the outcome. There continues to be a two-division national league, back to 40 overs after a spell at 45. So for 2006 there will be over 160 one-day league matches and only one of them is a knockout match. (No, two, because there is now a third-place play-off in the 40-over league to settle a third promotion and relegation spot.)

The spirit of the game

I wrote in Chapter 20 about the way the attitude to the game had deteriorated on the field. Just as helmets seemed to legitimise intimidatory bowling, and led ironically to more players being hit, so the ICC code of conduct seems to have led to poorer behav-iour becoming almost routine. The 2005 Wisden cites 35 instances of breaches in a year, with 28 resulting in fines of up to the whole of the player's match fee. Two brought match bans, one of which was overturned on appeal. Since then, as we have seen, the banning of the Indian captain Sourav Ganguly, for constantly failing to reach the over rate standard, was subject to a protracted legal wrangle that left him with a lesser ban. Because they rightly carry the can, captains are more liable to be fined. Nine of the offences were by captains. Of those 35 offences, 32 were breaches of the spirit of the game in one form or another. Dissent at decisions, obscene lan-guage or gestures, plus conduct 'contrary to the spirit of the game' or 'bringing the game into disrepute', which cover a multitude of sins. Of these two each were by Australians, two by Englishmen.

However, after many years of pioneering offensive language, the Australians have moved to rescue their reputation with their Spirit of the Game Pledge. This is clearly a welcome move in the right direction, though not surprisingly the pressure of the threat to the Ashes in the fourth Test in 2005 led to fines for Ricky Ponting and Simon Katich. There are other encouraging signs too. The long suspicion of Muralitharan in Australian minds, aggravated by his rivalry with Warne at the top of the world spinning tree, began to soften with their rapprochement in the wake of the tsunami on Boxing Day 2004, and the Tsunami games themselves generated much obvious fellow feeling among the top players. The 2005 Ashes summer, which had begun with some needling and aggravation in one-day matches, created welcome and genuine warmth between the teams. Generally, rather than railing at cheating opponents or crucial decisions – which in a series of so many tantalising twists of fortune were bound to be legion – the players seem to have been swept up in the general euphoria at the magnificence of the contests. That Andrew Flintoff took time off from England's exhilaration to console Brett Lee after his courageous back-from-the-dead innings in the second Test was testament to it, and it seemed to set the subsequent tone. What was less remarked at the time is that the Australians did not complain at all when the slow-motion replay showed that Mike Kasprowicz's gloved hand had detached from the bat milliseconds before the ball brushed it. It was clear, too, that the praise given by the two captains and key players to the opposition was genuine and not formulaic. Warne was particularly generous in this regard, and by the end of the series had endeared himself to the home crowds, who sang 'We wish you were English' as well as the more usual banter. In fact the turn-round in the players' behaviour and attitude only served to emphasise the unpleasant nature of some of the crowds. While England's crowds still come second to Australia's, it was distasteful to be among them at times. Perhaps we need a Spirit of the Crowd Pledge.

What next?

The most dangerous way to end is to attempt a prediction. Many cricket books have finished with a list of young hopefuls the author has noticed, who within a short time have largely disappeared from sight. Moreover, some cricketing changes are completely unexpected: witness the arrival of reverse swing, the rise of the great spinners, the invention of the *doosra*, Twenty20, and the sudden change of tempo in Test cricket in the last 10 years. Why should I be so foolhardy as to attempt it? I'm going to take a different tack. In the final chapter I don't want so much to predict the state of the game in the year 2020, as to follow some of the historical trends that have emerged, and see what might happen. I am not proposing them – some I like, some make me recoil, and doubtless you will feel the same.

CHAPTER 38

2020 Foresight

The Father Time weathervane at Lord's, damaged after a
battering by a storm. The arrow points defiantly onwards and
upwards. The wind comes from the east.

Prediction is very difficult, especially if it's about the future.

NILS BOHR

Test cricket

After the premature promotion of Bangladesh, it seemed that the ICC were determined to introduce countries to Test status as soon as they could demonstrate a strong record in the ICC Trophy, which is designed for the lesser teams. But Bangladesh have not reduced the gulf in ability, Zimbabwe have plummeted to their level, and Kenya, after their 2003 World Cup heroics, have been enmeshed in corruption charges. Combined with this, the desire to move from a 10- to a 12-year Test championship cycle, with all playing all home and away twice, has lessened the risk of the premature birth of an eleventh Test nation.

However, other countries will continue to clamour for a place at the top table. What would happen if a new side – one of Bermuda, Canada, Holland, Denmark, Scotland, Ireland, Namibia, the UAE, as well as Kenya – began to beat Bangladesh or Zimbabwe regularly in one-day internationals? After reaching the World Cup semi-final in 2003, Kenya were granted one-day international status, but their game descended to such a level that during the period ending July 2005 they played only two top-level games and were dropped from the rankings. Five years earlier they had looked set to be the next nation promoted; now any one of that group of nine could produce a challenge.

It is tempting for old hands to conclude that the number of Test sides should reduce to eight, thus freeing up the fixture list, and removing embarrassingly one-sided series like England v Bangladesh 2005. The existing arrangements lead to so many one-sided games that records become demeaned. Soon I suspect a captain will allow a gluttonous batsman to gorge himself on weak bowling, pass 400 and go on even to 500. Moreover, if the poorest sides do not improve, and the ICC take no action, the second division nations might reasonably take umbrage if they legitimately feel stronger than a side in the first division. That could well lead to a form of promotion and relegation. For example, every two years the side at the bottom of the ranking table could be challenged by the winners of the 12-team ICC Intercontinental Cup, a tournament of three-day matches between the second division countries that in 2005 was won by Ireland, defeating Kenya in the final. That somehow seems more sensible, more fair, and caters for the weakest Test side spiralling downwards.

Test match ratings have certainly added interest, although the requirement to play every other team home and away twice in a 10-year cycle – the original plan for a yet shorter cycle deservedly collapsed – has led inexorably to more short tours with little playing opportunity outside the Tests, wearying back-to-back matches, and tiresomely uneven triangular one-day tournaments. The outcome we have is a curiosity, a timeless league. The quirks of the system led to South Africa being top briefly when they had not even won a series against Australia, then virtually unbeatable. It takes some time, too, for trends to work themselves through. A side patently slipping from their pedestal – I make no predictions about Australia – will cling on to top spot when clearly no longer the best. It's artificial, clearly, but is it the best we have?

Far more satisfactory, it seems to many, would be to augment it with a World Test Cup, which could be played every four years, two years out of phase with the current one-day World Cup. In the simple form I describe below, it would take just under eight weeks, a similar length of time to the 2007 World Cup in the West Indies. It would comprise the top eight teams in the rating table, split into two groups of four. Each team would play the other three in the group in a five-day Test, with draws possible, and the top two in each group would go through to semi-finals and final, which would be (only theoretically) timeless. It would pan out like this:

Week 1	4	first round
Week 2	4	second round
Week 3	4	third round
Week 4	2	5th–8th semi-finals
Week 5	2	semi-finals
Week 6	2	5th–8th place matches
Week 7	2	final and 3rd place play-off

There would be 20 games in all, and each side would play five matches, a neat symmetry. The first three games would have a three-day gap, which the ICC have at last ordained as the minimum. There would be longer gaps before the games in the last three weeks. The group scoring would be simple: one point for a win. (Sides with the same number of wins could be separated by net run-rate, or – say – by a single innings play-off match of 150 overs each.) The first three matches are back-to-back, exactly as England's were in Pakistan at the end of 2005, but the gaps between them could be extended by adding a week. To every enthusiast who loves Test cricket, it seems wrong that only the one-day game has a great winner-takes-all climax.

At this point, the sceptic may mutter the single word 'rain', and it's true that severely prolonged bad weather remains as much a problem as it ever did, though not enough to ruin a tournament designed like this. That brings in the question of covered arenas and drop-in pitches. Though it might seem anathema to the traditionalist, the pressure from television to avoid long periods of replays while the rain lashes down might well create more covered venues. In Melbourne in October 2005 the Australia v The World matches were played on imported pitches at the Telstra Dome, a stadium designed for Australian Rules football. Such drop-in pitches were used in New Zealand in 2001–2 and one can imagine their use extending, especially if more such arenas are built. England seems to cry out for one. Indeed, making over the ill-starred Millennium Dome was a fleeting fantasy for a few cricket-lovers. It would need an unlikely level of entrepreneurship and cooperation between sports to build a covered stadium in England, but stranger things have happened. In fact, it was just before Christmas 2005 that the idea emerged to turn over the new 80 000-seater Olympic stadium at Stratford to cricket. Will it take root? If it did, then perhaps there would be a drop-in pitch industry – the flat, the bouncy, the turner, the death by low bounce – to suit the home team's bowlers of the time. Let's hope not, but these things can develop a momentum of their own.

Limited overs cricket

When one-day cricket was first thriving in England, the three-day game began to look sleepy and slow to many, if not to its traditional supporters. Spectators left it for the one-day game, and Test gates suffered too. But it wasn't long before gates began to dip, as surfeit led to the novelty wearing off. (The same reaction will doubtless be felt eventually in Twenty20.) The proliferation of one-day internationals, many meaningless, that led to the betting boom and to match-fixing, has given many games a tired, formulaic look. A brisk start to an innings while the 15-over fielding limitations are in place, a flat 25-over consolidating middle period against defensive bowling, and a 10-over thrash at the end.

Soon one-day cricket may seem to some like Twenty20 with a dull phase in the middle, and it's no wonder the ICC have begun tinkering with ideas to spice up the 50-over game. However the introduction of substitutes in 2005, and variable periods of fielding limitation, seem set to confuse spectators and captains alike. Captains are better, now, at juggling five bowlers to ensure they bowl 10 overs each, than they were in those wryly amusing days when a bemused captain would discover he had to give a new bowler one key over at the end because he had fouled up his calculations. But give them a threatening sky, reduced overs in total and for each bowler, and a looming Duckworth-Lewis moment, and there will be nervous breakdowns and flummoxed crowds. That kind of tinkering seems a sure sign that there is something inherently wrong, like any complex solution to a simple problem. Is there a real problem with the game, or is it simply a surfeit of unappetising food that provides no real nourishment?

One relieving feature for the traditional cricket watcher is that innovations from the one-day game have largely not yet spread to Test cricket. Its continued popularity has been its bulwark. There is no reason to believe that innovation will end in the one-day game, however. Increased income will probably remain the spur: when the number of matches approaches spectator saturation, legislators will continue to look at variations of diet to keep the golden goose a-laying. If they do, what's happening at any moment needs to be obvious to the spectator. By the year 2020 I can imagine a host of format changes, accelerated by the financial success of Twenty20. I think we should steel ourselves. Like it or loathe it, what other innovations might be tried between 2005 and 2020?

Batting restrictions Ever since one-day cricket began, everyone has taken for granted that bowlers should be restricted but not batsmen. Why? Bowlers complained at first, but soon gave up. If legislators feel that more interest should be added by more personnel changes on the field, then a rule restricting each batsmen to an initial 50 or 60 balls would have that effect. They could return if every other batsman was dismissed. Indeed, you could envisage a successful pair of openers returning after a later collapse. The scoreboard could keep everyone up to date.

Boundaries One aspect of the game that has remained virtually untouched since the 19th century is the scoring for boundaries. I can foresee that, after the first flush of enthusiasm for Twenty20 games fades, and crowds begin to drift away, some innovations will be sought to jazz it up. One, tried lamely when cricket has been played indoors at smaller venues, is to add the super-boundary. Imagine a strip of two rows of seating around the ground, painted a distinctive colour and unoccupied, 10 to 20 yards in from the boundary. Any six that landed above that strip would count 10. Whether or not you recoil in revulsion at the prospect, imagine a last over with desperate batsmen chasing a forlorn target. Nine to win off the last ball…

Domestic cricket

It would take a brave man to forecast the future of the county game. There are pressures mounting for a complete overhaul, which could lead to the end of county cricket as we know it. Equally, most cricket traditionalists would be appalled at the sweeping away of so much history, and of their team. The proposal by the self-appointed Reform Group in 2003 had at its core the belief that we have too many ordinary professionals playing for too many teams. Look at what happens elsewhere. Australia has six state teams playing 10 games each. South Africa has 11, split into two groups, and the top six qualify for an all-play-all Super Six. India has 15 teams but a six-team zonal tournament that takes the best players. West Indies has six island teams which it augments each year with one or two others. Sri Lanka has 16 teams, but its best players compete in a five-team provincial tournament. Pakistan is constantly chopping and changing to find the right mix of teams, regional and sponsored.

Australia has never had anything between its fiercely-contested weekend club cricket, and its state tournament, and it clearly works well. Some arch-reformers in England hanker after the same model, at the cost of the county set-up. Can England come up with an alternative that saves it? The format that has most sense elsewhere is clearly the hybrid, with long-standing traditional teams – their equivalent of counties – in one tournament, and their best players taking part in a regional contest. There seems no reason why such a hybrid should not work in England, built on the existing county system, diluting but not abandoning it. Here's how it could work. The aim would be to provide tougher competition for the best English players, yet to reduce the overall quantity of cricket.

Divide the 18 counties into six regions based on three county teams each. Introduce a rule that only cricketers qualified for England may play in an early-season tournament in which every region plays each other once. Everyone will have his own preference for the regional make-up. Mine is north (Yorkshire, Lancashire, Durham), London (Surrey, Middlesex, Essex), south (Kent, Sussex, Hampshire), south west (Somerset, Gloucestershire, Glamorgan), north Midlands (Derbyshire, Nottinghamshire, Leicestershire) and south Midlands (Worcestershire, Warwickshire, Northamptonshire).

Take 2005 as a model: that was a summer of two Test series, split 2/5 with a triangular series in between. Start the summer with a regional tournament of five weeks in which the six regions play each other once. In 2005 that would have taken

359

place instead of the first five rounds of county fixtures, and thus would have run from 13 April to 21 May. The beauty of this is that the Test team could play in at least part of this series, getting themselves back into English form by pitting themselves against the best of the rest, who would all be striving for the England management's attention. In 2005 the contracted players were allowed up to four early county games for just that reason, and this would provide tougher competition.

During May, as in 2005, the Test squad would disappear back to international duty. The two Bangladesh Tests ran from 26 May to 7 June . Between then and the five-Test Australia series was a 10-match triangular one-day tournament, followed by three more games between England and Australia. Were that unwelcome latter series to have been omitted, the Test series could have started on 14 and not 21 July and none of the subsequent Tests would have needed to be back-to-back. The later matches would have begun on 28 July, 11 and 25 August, and 8 September. A beneficial spin-off of the regional tournament now becomes clear, because the six regions could each play the tourists, before the first Test and between each one. This gives the tourists the tougher opposition they would prefer, and allows new England claimants a tilt at them, and injured Test players a chance to measure their regained fitness. This method works for a two-tourist summer split 3/4 just as well as 2/5, like 2006.

This seems a far better way of bridging the gap between the county game and the Test team. How would it affect the counties? The first thing to say is that, with Twenty20 arriving, there is simply not enough time in the summer for this rapidly-growing cuckoo to join the nest without heaving something else over the side. In order of crowd-pull per day the formats rank: Twenty20 (c. 6900), limited-over (c. 2600), county championship (c. 1000). Yet in 2005 the number of games in each was 8, 16, 16, while the number of scheduled days of cricket was 8, 16 and 64 respectively. Even without adding a regional tournament, the financial success that has fed the growth of Twenty20, which for reasons of day length has to take place in midsummer, will force a change. Logic suggests that sooner or later, like it or not, the county championship will have to shrink to eight games rather than 16. The number of matches would now be 10, 16, 8, with counties in the three Twenty20 groups playing each other twice.

	April	May	June	July	Aug	Sept
Regional	− − − − − −					
1st Tests × 2		− − + +				
One Day Tests			+ +			
2nd Tests × 5				− − + − + − + − + − +	
Twenty20			− − − − − −			
Championship					− − − − − − − −	
One-day leagues	− −					

The tourists would play regional teams before and between the Tests. The number is flexible, but this schedule allows for up to six such matches in a five-Test series.

How would the county season look? This is one option. Until late May, 15 of the 18 counties would host a midweek four-day regional game (the others would host one against a touring team later). The one-day tournaments would start as usual: they would be unaffected. To make up for the lack of four-day county cricket in this period, the three counties in each group would play each other. Local derbies could take place, containing cricketers not needed for the regional squad. Thus every year there could be a Roses match after all: the two-division split made that fixture annoyingly variable. A Twenty20 tournament expanded from 72 games to 90 would take place from early June to mid-July (the longest day is 21 June). A nine-week county championship would not be split by Twenty20, as it was in 2005, but follow it, starting on 20 July and ending on 17 September, a week earlier than in 2005. The earlier attendance figures are from a 2005 study of county cricket, which analysed the variables that affected attendances. Briefly, the County Championship does better later in the summer and when played at out-grounds. (E. W. Swanton would have a wry smile.) Limited-over matches do better later in the season, too, and far better when floodlit.

The counties desperately fear an overhaul of the English game that jettisons their structure, support and history. But if they try to dig their heels in too far they may find themselves uprooted whether they like it or not. In 2009 the current lucrative broadcasting contract with Sky will end. One of the reasons the ECB courted criticism by accepting their bid was that it could secure English cricket's finances better than a terrestrial contract would. That gravy train may not be running in 2009 – or at the next renewal, or the next – and the counties, who as we have seen are utterly dependent on Test and broadcasting income, may have little choice. This approach provides a measure of reform without destroying them. Crucially, it creates an early-season testing ground for the best 66 players qualified for England.

Technology and umpiring

Extending the degree of technological support for umpires remained a contentious issue in 2005. Its further adoption tends to split cricket enthusiasts sharply. It seems unlikely to stop with stumpings, run-outs, boundaries and some disputed catches. This is particularly so when the view seen instantly, at several angles and speeds, by several million spectators in Mumbai or Melbourne, is not available to an umpire 22 yards from the batsman. Only a short while ago Wisden editors and other commentators were bewailing the prospect of a third umpire, and the consequent irritating hold-ups. But, as in rugby union, the effect has been to add suspense among the crowd without detracting too much from the flow of the game. And now we have big-screen replays. The watching experience at Tests has been transformed from the days when, after a wicket had suddenly fallen, the spectator at deep extra cover was obliged to mentally replay a single image received in (sometimes literally) the blink of an eye. Attuned to seeing the television replay at home, we feel cheated if we can't see it at the ground too.

Now, although top umpires achieve a 94 per cent rating according to the ICC, that relates of course to the number of appeals and their quality. If two-thirds of the appeals are spurious, and easily turned down, that figure reduces to 82 per cent. With cricketing livelihoods at stake, to continue with a situation when an umpire's mistake is revealed instantly but not corrected seems untenable. So what can we expect to see by 2020? It depends partly on whether new sensing technology, certainly available, is adapted for cricket. We can expect that on-field umpires in Tests will be in continuous radio contact with a third umpire. Here, like it or not, is a set of possibilities that emerge.

LBW Hawk-Eye uses six cameras capturing images every $1/100$th of a second, and generates a prediction that can be with a third umpire within two seconds. While extraordinarily accurate in pinpointing the ball's flight, it cannot ever be 100 per cent so in predicting it. So if used it needs a benefit-of-the-doubt extension to the stumps in its software – making them appear, say, an inch wider and higher – to maintain centuries of custom and practice enshrined in the Laws. Hence a ball that Hawk-Eye estimates to be just clipping the stumps or bails would be ruled not out. This technology is clearly the most mature, and as lbw has always been one of the toughest decisions for the umpire to assess, I would be most surprised if this is not in place well before 2020, and mandatory.

Bat and glove contact The snickometer attempts to distinguish the sound of bat, glove, pad and ground on the ball. This is notoriously tricky for an umpire to assess, and to some it is surprising how often umpires fail to notice thick edges in lbw decisions. It is easier to understand why faint glove contact is hard to spot. While the technology does still seem fallible at times, this is an area where umpires fail most often. I can envisage a long series of experiments, leading initially to a third umpire providing advice when requested when he is unsure about contact. However, unless the entirely feasible development of cricket balls with embedded electronic transmitters takes place (don't blanch) it seems unlikely to become mandatory.

No-balls Umpires tend to miss no-balls occasionally, and cameras make it crystal clear when a call should have been made. While a no-ball call transmitted by a third umpire would cause a delay, and prevent the batsman profiting, it's clearly better than a wicket falling by mistake. A variant of Cyclops, the automated line-judge system used in tennis, seems feasible, although it would need some redevelopment to use boundary cameras. Whether by a beep or a third umpire's voice in his earpiece, some form of no-ball call assistance seems certain well before 2020 for the on-field umpire. He calls the clear-cut cases early, the technology calls the ones he misses.

The greatest game?

A pre-war cricketer returning today might be dismayed by the paraphernalia that surrounds Test cricket, but he would recognise it as soon as he reached the middle. Only for an lbw law change would he have to adapt his approach, for balls pitching outside off-stump. A batsman would find more opponents bowling faster, and more often at his head, and he would probably not stay superior about helmets for long. He would find fewer spinners, but with new tricks up their sleeves. He would soon adapt, though, as he would to reverse swing. A pre-war bowler returning today would find fewer batsmen content to wait for the bad ball. He would find himself hit on the up more often, in the air more often, and see his straight good-length balls worked away on the leg-side. But he too would soon adapt, and the great bowlers then would be the great bowlers now.

Apart from more spinners bowling more *doosras*, more fast bowlers mastering reverse swing, and more batsmen adapting eccentric strokes for the longer game, I think we will see a game little changed at its core in 2020. Whatever happens to its tournaments, its government, and its umpiring, at its heart cricket is still resilient, a game of ebb and flow that can be played over three hours or five days. Between 2000 and 2005 English cricket recovered from a long period of depression. The speed and intensity of Test cricket in these years has become electrifying. The spirit of the game, dragged down by steadily worsening behaviour and match-fixing scandals, appears to be recovering. Tsunami matches have reminded cricketers to respect each other and the game itself. The palpitating Ashes series of 2005 was played in front of intent crowds, to crowded sofas and packed bars, with the perfect mixture of passionate fervour and mutual admiration. Will we look back in 2020 with nostalgia at that series as a high-water mark, before the players slid back into backbiting, and Test cricket retreated into tedium? No, no. Will we recall it as the moment cricket reclaimed its position as the best, the oldest, the greatest game? Yes, yes, we will. The Romantic and the Realist in me collide.

Anorak's Almanack

Odds impossible for two Australians to resist. Headingley, the afternoon of 20 July 1981.
Australia 401–9d, England 174 and 135–7.

N o cricket history would be complete without a statistical appendix. But what form should it take? I wanted something that would enable the reader to observe the way the English game has changed over the years through the figures. In the text, the Test narrative breaks off at suitable intervals to explore certain themes more or less as they occur. However, matching the statistics to these periods would not allow sensible comparisons, so I've split the period into 12 blocks of five years each, starting with 1946–50 and ending with 2001–5. As you will see, each period fits on a page, so you can examine 10 years at once.

Each of the first 12 pages summarises the five summers that each period covers, and the Tests England play, at home and away. For the domestic season you have the top 20 batsmen and bowlers who meet the qualifying conditions. These criteria vary depending on how much first-class cricket is played. So for the first 25 years, before one-day cricket led to a reduction in the county first-class programme, the qualification is 5000 runs or 250 wickets in three or more seasons. Through the second half, the qualification threshold drops in stages until it reaches 3000 runs and 150 wickets in our four-day era. As well as the best batsmen and bowlers, I give those all-rounders who meet the qualifying criteria, and whose batting average exceeds their bowling average. Note the heyday of the English all-rounder, 1961–5, before one-day cricket made the summer too taxing: 11 players met the all-rounder criteria, more than double any other period, though I have room only for the top six.

For the Test side I chose a representative team for each period, the best-balanced set of 11 players who appeared in at least a quarter of the Tests England played in each five-year span, in at least three series. This decision was usually tricky, as you can imagine. Where there are choices I explain them, and you can see whether you agree. It's often a juggling act that takes into account the number of Tests cricketers have played, and their averages. This can often leave an unbalanced side, and you simply have to compromise, as selectors always do. At times the five-year boundary cuts across a player's career, so he risks being left out. When this happens I have occasionally included him, where there are reasonable grounds for doing so. Thus, in the 1966–70 section, Brian Luckhurst at the start of his career displaces Colin Cowdrey towards the end of his. Because there was no 1945–6 tour, I include those winter tours that come between periods within the preceding section. Thus the Ashes victory of 1970–1 goes with 1966–70.

I court criticism by including the 1970 Rest of the World series. Wisden's editors at the time gave it Test status, for two reasons. First, the team was billed unequivocally as England, and players awarded Test caps. Second, the side they were playing was chosen from virtually all the best players in the world, so was quite clearly of Test standard. The series contained brilliant and challenging cricket. By denying it Test status you remove Peter Lever's amazing 7–83 debut, dismissing Barlow, Graeme Pollock, Mushtaq, Sobers, Clive Lloyd and Procter; you deny Alan Jones his only Test appearance; and you ignore Brian Luckhurst's match-winning century in his second Test as England chased 284 to win. After many years of stubborn resistance Wisden finally caved in – but I don't have to. The series was far more deserving of Test status than the Australia v Rest of the World match in October 2005.

There are heroes, some unsung. Ten cricketers appear in the top 20 in four periods: Les Jackson, Tom Graveney, Brian Statham, Fred Trueman, Colin Cowdrey, Derek Shackleton, M. J. K. Smith, Ray Illingworth, Derek Underwood and, remarkably in the modern era, Martin Bicknell. Colin Cowdrey's longevity is such that he does it in four periods out of five, and he misses out in 1966–70 because he lost almost the whole of 1969 to an achilles tendon injury. He would have come 11th then had he made just a few more runs. It's the misfortune of Jackson and Shackleton that their careers should coincide with those of Trueman and Statham. Of the four-timers, Graveney, Statham and Underwood always appear in the top 10. So outstanding and consistent was Statham that he's always in the top two. Underwood is particularly remarkable in that, as English spinners decline, he is always the top spinner and twice the top Englishman. Pride of place however, must go to Geoffrey Boycott. He comes in the top five batsmen in each of five periods from 1961–85, and twice he's top, in 1971–5 over 25 runs ahead of the nearest Englishman. Only Peter May has also been top twice. Moreover Boycott does it in the period when overseas cricketers are beginning to dominate.

Perhaps the toughest task of all is to maintain top-level all-round ability across a 10-year span. Ten have done that: Vic Jackson, Ray Illingworth, Bill Alley, Fred Titmus, Martin Horton, Mushtaq Mohammad, Mike Procter, (uniquely, with a batting average more than double his bowling across 10 years) Ian Botham, Mark Ealham and Dougie Brown. These last three are outstanding in achieving it in the modern era, with Brown the only one never to have played in a Test, but at the top of the tree is Trevor Bailey, the only person to do it in three periods.

This composite table illustrates: first the influx of overseas players, second the decline of the spinner, and third the shifting balance between bat and ball.

Domestic Season Top 20 summary, 1946–2005

	1946 −50	1951 −55	1956 −60	1961 −65	1966 −70	1971 −75	1976 −80	1981 −85	1986 −90	1991 −95	1996 −2000	2001 −05
1 Overseas												
Batsmen	0	1	2	3	3	9	13	10	2	4	6	12
Bowlers	1	1	1	0	0	6	7	8	5	7	2	6
2 Spinners												
All	14	11	11	5	5	6	5	6	2	4	3	4
English	13	10	10	5	5	4	5	6	2	3	2	1
3 Batsmen/Bowlers with averages:												
50+	5	2	1	1	2	5	8	10	5	8	6	15
20−	6	16	18	12	11	2	4	3	2	1	2	0

You can see, first, that overseas players dominated the domestic game between 1971 and 1985. There were six overseas batsmen in the top 10 in 1971–5, eight in 1976–80; Boycott standing alone at the top in both periods. In 1981–5 it was seven. That the 1980s was a poor period for English bowling is shown dramatically. In 1981–5 the top five bowlers were all foreign pace men, while in 1986–90 five of the top six were, with no Englishman even able to top a *Dane*. Greater balance was achieved between 1991–5, but more recently players on the fringes of the Australian team have invaded English cricket. In 1996–2000 the top five batsmen were all Australian; in 2001–5 six of the top seven were. Indeed only six of the most recent top 20 are English-born. There can be no better illustration of two recent trends – the utter domination of Australian batsmanship, and the sharp reduction in the domestic cricket played by the England Test squad. In 2001–5, for instance, Marcus Trescothick scored nearly 1000 more runs in Tests for England abroad than he did for his county at home.

The second section illustrates the decline of the spinner in England, discussed in Chapter 22. From 10 in the top 12 in 1946–5, they decline catastophically to just one in 19th place in 2001–5. The third depicts starkly the period of almost total bowling dominance between 1951 and 1970, and its rapid end. Now, in 2001–5, for the first time over 10 batsmen have averages above 50, four of them English-born joined by a fifth, Kevin Pietersen, in 2005. No bowler has an average below 20, Warne heading the list at 22.07 with no one else even below 25. By contrast, the 20th bowler in 1956–60 and 1961–5 had an average under 21. The leading English spinner in 2001–5 was 19th with an average of 27.74. Thus the world turns, as do old spinners in their graves.

On the Test scene, there is of course more variation. The most striking continuity is the wicketkeepers. There, six – Godfrey Evans, Jim Parks, Alan Knott, Bob Taylor, Jack Russell and Alec Stewart – are the only keepers to feature, and only Parks fails to appear twice. Evans does so three times. Just two batsmen, Geoff Boycott and Graham Gooch, are there for a solid 20-year span, despite largely self-inflicted absences. Batsmen who appear three times are Tom Graveney, Ken Barrington, John Edrich, David Gower, Graham Thorpe and Alec Stewart with Colin Cowdrey narrowly missing out. Graveney is present three times in the 20-year span 1951–70. Brian Statham is the only opening bowler to appear three times and Derek Underwood the only spinner, although Trevor Bailey remarkably does it three times too: of the all-rounders even Ian Botham only manages it twice.

The final two pages summarise 60 years of Test, domestic and one-day cricket. The post-war Test batting averages are headed by Ken Barrington, and the bowling, surprisingly perhaps, by Johnny Wardle. Both in a way benefit from avoiding the deterioration of declining years: Barrington retired abruptly with a heart condition, and Wardle equally unexpectedly after an outburst at the end of the 1958 season. Nick Knight, still playing at the end of 2005 but not in the England one-day Test side, is nevertheless the only one-day international with a batting average over 40. Otherwise Andrew Flintoff is the only one-day Test all-rounder to feature, as is Ian Botham in domestic one-day cricket. Finally, first-class domestic cricket is so dominated by players from before the one-day era that it's a mark of Graeme Hick's longevity and consistency – if, alas, only at county level – that he comes third in both first-class and one-day batting averages, and as high as seventh and third in the catching. An outstanding achievement in the modern era.

1946–50

Batsman	Runs	Av	Bowler	Wkts	Av	County Champions	
Qual – 5000 runs in 3+ seasons			250 wickets in 3+ seasons				
Washbrook	10188	63.67	Young	661	18.77	1946	Yorkshire
Compton	12157	62.66	Goddard	837	18.77	1947	Middlesex
Hutton	12348	61.74	Gladwin	565	18.88	1948	Glamorgan
Hardstaff	8519	53.24	Howorth	570	19.46	1949	Yorkshire
Edrich W. J.	11870	52.06	Hollies	757	19.47		+ Middlesex
Ames	9098	46.66	Laker	479	19.75	1950	Lancashire
Brookes	10538	45.42	Wardle	513	20.20		+ Surrey
Simpson	8622	44.91	Muncer	475	20.23		
Fagg	8704	44.87	Coxon	463	20.56		
Fishlock	10383	44.37	Wright D. V. P	659	21.10		
Robertson	11577	43.36	Cook C.	636	21.42		
Keeton	8014	41.63	Robinson E. P.	457	21.49		
Oldfield	5368	41.61	Jackson H. L.	278	21.79		
Crapp	8392	41.54	Bedser	605	22.36		
Gimblett	9255	41.32	Pollard	442	22.66		
Langridge John	10250	41.00	Jenkins	516	23.20		
Place	8140	39.51	Walsh (A)	717	23.52		
Ikin	7082	39.34	Knott C. J.	467	23.76		
Dollery	8888	39.33	Butler	418	23.86		
Cox	9282	38.67	Langridge Jas	339	24.35		
All-rounders	7146	37.41	Langridge Jas	339	24.35		
	6580	28.36	Jackson V. E. (A)	429	26.00		

Test Team   A quarter of the Tests in 3 series

No. Player	Runs	Av	Wkts	Av	Year	Result	Opp
38 Hutton	3423	56.11			1946	1–0	Ind
34 Washbrook	2448	43.71			1946–7	0–3	Aus
22 Edrich W. J.	1793	49.81	35	40.00		0–0	NZ
35 Compton	2879	52.35	19	56.00	1947	3–0	SA
13 Simpson	788	35.82			1947–8	0–2	WI
12 Bailey T. E.	567	47.25	40	25.75	1948	0–4	Aus
19 Yardley	805	25.97	21	33.66	1948–9	2–0	SA
37 Evans	1146	23.39			1949	0–0	NZ
33 Bedser	547	13.35	132	29.97	1950	1–3	WI
25 Wright D. V. P.	184	9.20	81	37.75	1950–1	1–4	Aus
10 Hollies	29	4.83	34	32.79		1–0	NZ

		w	l	d	
This team picks itself, as only 11 played 10 Tests.					
Fortunately it's well balanced – Bailey arrived at	**Series**	4	5	2	45%
the end of the period to partner Bedser.	**Tests**	9	16	18	42%

1951–55

Batsman	Runs	Av	Bowler	Wkts	Av	County Champions	
Qual – 5000 runs in 3+ seasons			250 wickets in 3+ seasons				
May	10995	56.38	Appleyard	440	14.05	1951	Warwickshire
Hutton	8619	52.55	Statham	508	15.67	1952	Surrey
Sheppard	8671	49.55	Lock	677	16.50	1953	Surrey
Livingston (A)	8747	47.03	Bedser	711	16.65	1954	Surrey
Compton	8465	45.76	Jackson H. L.	485	16.65	1955	Surrey
Graveney T. W.	10240	45.71	Loader	313	17.14		
Kenyon	12005	43.18	Laker	652	17.28		
Watson	7614	42.07	Gladwin	709	17.67		
Washbrook	7315	39.97	Trueman	482	17.93		
Insole	9789	39.96	Dooland (A)	518	18.07		
Dollery	8560	39.27	Shackleton	678	18.11		
Ikin	6693	39.14	McConnon	405	18.18		
Wilson J. V.	8877	38.76	Tattersall	672	18.56		
Simpson	9412	38.73	Hollies	590	18.78		
Edrich W. J.	10349	38.33	Wardle	800	18.88		
Subba Row	5144	38.10	Young	630	19.82		
Cowdrey M. C.	7112	38.03	Titmus	423	20.06		
Lowson	7758	36.94	Watkins	422	20.67		
Brookes	8782	36.90	Cannings	507	20.96		
Robertson	10022	36.85	Hilton	433	21.18		
All-rounders	6791	32.65	Watkins	422	20.67		
	6659	35.23	Bailey T. E.	470	24.50		
	6740	29.05	Jackson V. E. (A)	446	21.90		

Test Team   A quarter of the Tests in 3 series

No. Player	Runs	Av	Wkts	Av	Year	Result	Opp
28 Hutton	2203	52.45					
14 Simpson	613	30.65					
29 May	2000	43.48			1951	3–1	SA
29 Compton	2089	50.95			1951–2	1–1	Ind
31 Graveney T. W.	1590	36.98			1952	3–0	Ind
27 Bailey T. E.	1103	31.53	44	39.59	1953	1–0	Aus
29 Evans	685	19.03			1953–4	2–2	WI
20 Wardle	514	23.36	72	20.78	1954	1–1	Pak
10 Tyson	125	10.42	58	17.03	1954–5	3–1	Aus
18 Bedser	167	12.85	104	18.46		2–0	NZ
27 Statham	231	8.88	89	23.96	1955	3–2	SA

There was no settled opening partner for Hutton.
Watson made 678 at 29.78 but didn't normally open.
Laker took 54 wickets at 22.24 in 15 Tests.

		w	l	d	
If he played, he would replace Wardle or Statham.	**Series**	6	0	3	83%
Trueman took 44 wickets at 22.91 in 9 Tests.	**Tests**	19	8	13	64%

1956–60

Batsman	Runs	Av	Bowler	Wkts	Av	County Champions	
Qual – 5000 runs in 3+ seasons			250 wickets in 3+ seasons				
May	6872	52.86	Statham	625	13.83	1956	Surrey
Subba Row	5631	46.92	Lock	787	15.10	1957	Surrey
Smith M. J. K.	11210	45.20	Jackson H. L.	707	15.11	1958	Surrey
Watson	8181	42.83	Laker	452	16.37	1959	Yorkshire
Cowdrey M. C.	8149	42.66	Trueman	615	16.71	1960	Yorkshire
Graveney T. W.	8904	42.40	Moss	509	17.00		
Parks J. M.	9392	41.37	Hilton	336	17.17		
Barrington	8489	40.04	Wardle	358	17.22		
Dexter	8181	39.52	Shackleton	738	17.28		
Bailey T. E.	7062	37.97	Tattersall	366	17.37		
Insole	8247	37.15	Illingworth	520	17.68		
Pullar	7482	36.86	Gladwin	337	17.94		
Milton	6877	36.78	Cook C.	526	18.11		
Wight (WI)	8810	36.71	Loader	550	18.11		
Marshall (WI)	10228	36.40	Shepherd D. J.	633	18.60		
Horton H.	8584	35.77	Thomson	593	19.32		
Wharton	8238	34.91	*Tribe (A)*	508	19.65		
Smith D. V.	7762	34.81	Bailey T. E.	512	19.97		
Stott	6222	34.76	McConnon	342	20.02		
Parkhouse	8190	34.27	Greenhough	397	20.27		
All-rounders	7062	37.97	Bailey T. E.	512	19.97		
	5343	27.54	Illingworth	520	17.68		
	5488	27.30	*Alley (A)*	258	22.12		
	7602	32.09	Horton M. J.	344	27.19		
	5435	23.84	Titmus	519	21.13		

Test Team   A quarter of the Tests in 3 series

No. Player	Runs	Av	Wkts	Av		Year	Result	Opp
41 Cowdrey M. C.	2809	44.59				1958	4–0	NZ
25 Richardson	1623	40.57				1956–7	2–2	SA
33 May	2265	51.48				1957	3–0	WI
17 Graveney T. W.	1000	43.48				1958	4–0	NZ
14 Barrington	1004	47.81	10	35.70		1958–9	0–4	Aus
22 Bailey T. E.	620	20.67	48	22.58			1–0	NZ
25 Evans	608	18.42				1959	5–0	Ind
32 Trueman	513	15.55	130	21.03		1959–60	1–0	WI
19 Lock	243	12.79	84	15.25		1960	3–0	SA
22 Laker	184	9.20	107	15.93				
27 Statham	292	14.60	107	22.26				

Pullar made 920 runs in 11 Tests at 51.11 from 1959.

*Dexter replaced Bailey from 1959 in 17 Tests making
1037 runs at 38.41 and taking 16 wickets at 27.94.*

	w	l	d	
Series	7	1	1	83%
Tests	21	7	14	67%

1961–65

Batsman	Runs	Av	Bowler	Wkts	Av	County Champions	
Qual – 5000 runs in 3+ seasons			250 wickets in 3+ seasons				
Cowdrey M. C.	7854	53.43	Trueman	664	17.59	1961	Hampshire
Barrington	8759	49.21	Statham	566	17.86	1962	Yorkshire
Graveney T. W.	8244	48.49	Illingworth	525	17.92	1963	Yorkshire
Edrich J. H.	10377	44.54	Coldwell	491	18.08	1964	Worcestershire
Boycott	5335	43.02	Cartwright	525	18.15	1965	Worcestershire
Parfitt	9005	41.69	Flavell	592	18.23		
Smith M. J. K.	9358	40.69	Rumsey	320	18.48	**Gillette Cup**	
Dexter	7578	39.88	Shackleton	762	18.56	1963	Sussex
Marshall (WI)	9606	37.52	Larter	482	18.79	1964	Sussex
Russell W. E.	9593	37.33	Sydenham	423	18.96	1965	Yorkshire
Leary (SA)	6501	36.32	Palmer K. E.	488	19.28		
Alley (A)	8203	36.14	Rhodes H. J.	417	19.61		
Pullar	7687	36.09	Wheatley	517	20.01		
Stewart M. J.	8176	35.86	Gifford	474	20.05		
Richardson	8579	35.30	Titmus	605	20.13		
Pressdee	8061	35.05	Shepherd D. J.	574	20.13		
Stewart W. J.	6583	35.02	Jackson H. L.	260	20.18		
Horton H.	8862	34.75	Wilson D.	405	20.30		
Atkinson	8588	33.94	Moss	271	20.39		
Brearley	6165	33.87	Thomson	566	20.41		
All-rounders	8203	36.14	*Alley (A)*	353	21.37		
(top six)	8061	35.05	Pressdee	290	21.25		
	5658	29.16	Illingworth	525	17.92		
	6400	31.84	Bailey T. E.	504	22.33		
	5125	29.12	Titmus	605	20.13		
	7543	32.80	Close	252	25.39		

Test Team A quarter of the Tests in 3 series

No. Player	Runs	Av	Wkts	Av	Year	Result	Opp
					1961	1–2	Aus
					1961–2	0–2	Ind
20 Boycott	1134	39.10				1–0	Pak
18 Edrich J. H.	1072	44.67			1962	4–0	Pak
43 Dexter	3368	53.46	50	36.62	1962–3	1–1	Aus
37 Cowdrey M. C.	2810	55.10				3–0	NZ
50 Barrington	4483	64.04	10	54.10	1963	1–3	WI
33 Parfitt	1722	44.15	12	46.33	1963–4	0–0	Ind
32 Parks	1420	37.37			1964	0–1	Aus
40 Titmus	1095	25.47	130	30.63	1964–5	1–0	SA
31 Allen	683	25.30	107	29.50	1965	3–0	NZ
26 Trueman	395	11.97	133	21.68		0–1	SA
15 Statham	143	11.92	56	31.20	1965–6	1–1	Aus
						0–0	NZ

This omits Knight (610 at 27.73 and 49 at 32.80 in 21 Tests)
and Barber (1323 at 37.80 and 32 at 46.31 in 24 Tests).

Series	5	5	4	50%
Tests	16	11	33	54%

Larter took 37 at 25.43 in 10 Tests.

1966–70

Batsman	Runs	Av	Bowler	Wkts	Av	County Champions
Qual – 5000 runs in 3+ seasons			250 wickets in 3+ seasons			
						1966 Yorkshire
Sobers (WI)	5754	53.28	Underwood	606	15.31	1967 Yorkshire
Richards B. A. (SA)	5502	51.91	Statham	263	15.92	1968 Yorkshire
Edrich J. H.	9888	49.69	Rhodes	343	17.18	1969 Glamorgan
Boycott	8585	48.78	Shackleton	347	17.27	1970 Kent
Graveney T. W.	6854	46.00	Illingworth	441	17.28	
Smith M. J. K.	5424	43.05	Cartwright	512	17.31	**Gillette Cup**
Luckhurst	7924	40.22	Wilson D.	446	17.84	1966 Warwickshire
Prideaux	8559	39.81	Gifford	427	18.27	1967 Kent
Bolus	8877	38.93	Graham	323	18.39	1968 Warwickshire
Amiss	8133	38.91	Higgs	365	18.45	1969 Yorkshire
						1970 Lancashire
D'Oliveira	6608	38.42	Nicholson	422	19.49	
Jones A.	8594	37.04	Trueman	254	20.15	
Mushtaq M. (P)	8263	36.40	White D. W.	427	20.15	**John Player League**
Fletcher	8253	36.36	Arnold	307	20.24	
Parfitt	7735	35.81	Shepherd D. J.	484	20.33	1969 Lancashire
Harris	6315	35.28	Cottam	480	20.56	1970 Lancashire
Russell W. E.	7244	35.00	Shuttleworth	277	20.86	
Milton	6704	34.38	Snow	447	21.41	
Denness	7311	33.53	Price	367	21.84	
Stewart M. J.	5889	33.08	Brown D. J.	377	22.80	
All-rounders	5754	53.28	Sobers (WI)	273	22.90	
	8263	36.40	Mushtaq M. (P)	322	23.14	

Test Team A quarter of the Tests in 3 series

No. Player	Runs	Av	Wkts	Av	Year	Result	Opp
					1966	1–3	WI
28 Boycott	2392	55.63			1967	3–0	Ind
12 Luckhurst	931	46.55				2–0	Pak
32 Edrich J. H.	2422	46.58			1967–8	1–0	WI
16 Barrington	1267	57.59	9	44.67	1968	1–1	Aus
24 Graveney T. W.	1775	49.31			1968–9	0–0	Pak
37 D'Oliveira	2230	42.88	40	42.90	1969	2–0	WI
28 Illingworth	1219	29.73	76	27.16		2–0	NZ
30 Knott	1295	33.82			1970	1–4	RW
34 Snow	524	16.38	141	27.57	1970–1	2–0	Aus
20 Brown D. J.	323	14.68	57	29.74		1–0	NZ
26 Underwood	230	12.11	107	19.96			

	w	l	d	
Cowdrey made 1356 at 38.74 in 22 Tests and could				
displace Luckhurst, whose 12 Tests include the Rest of the World **Series**	7	2	2	73%
series. Higgs took 44 wickets at 24.34 in 10 Tests. **Tests**	16	8	19	59%

1971–75

Batsman	Runs	Av	Bowler	Wkts	Av
Qual – 4000 runs in 3+ seasons			200 wickets in 3+ seasons		
Boycott	8958	73.43	Cartwright	318	17.83
Kanhai (WI)	6274	59.19	Procter (SA)	209	18.70
Turner G. M. (NZ)	8000	55.94	Arnold	322	20.00
Richards B. A. (SA)	7842	51.93	Underwood	354	20.41
Lloyd C. H. (WI)	6299	50.39	Sainsbury	296	20.55
Amiss	7221	48.46	Hendrick	278	20.68
Sobers (WI)	4032	46.34	Old	278	21.49
Fletcher	6246	45.93	Illingworth	239	21.63
Majid K. (P)	7913	45.22	Cottam	292	21.66
Edrich J. H.	7070	45.03	Holder V. A. (WI)	319	21.79
Procter (SA)	5733	43.76	Lever P.	248	21.87
Zaheer A. (P)	5533	43.57	Nicholson	240	21.93
Harris	7826	42.30	Bedi (I)	435	22.12
Steele	7375	41.20	Boyce (WI)	312	22.33
Davison (Z)	6757	41.20	Lee	335	22.83
Luckhurst	6955	41.15	Gibbs (WI)	212	22.83
Asif I. (P)	5329	40.99	McKenzie (A)	307	22.98
Smith M. J. K.	6308	40.96	Gifford	321	22.99
Roope	6249	40.84	Jackman	391	23.25
Cowdrey M. C.	4722	40.36	Willis	202	23.68
All-rounders	5733	43.76	Procter (SA)	209	18.70
	7328	39.61	Mushtaq M. (P)	239	23.96
	5362	34.15	Greig A. W.	267	30.22

County Champions
1971 Surrey
1972 Warwickshire
1973 Hampshire
1974 Worcestershire
1975 Leicestershire

Gillette Cup
1971 Lancashire
1972 Lancashire
1973 Gloucestershire
1974 Kent
1975 Lancashire

John Player League
1971 Worcestershire
1972 Kent
1973 Kent
1974 Leicestershire
1975 Hampshire

Benson and Hedges Cup
1972 Leicestershire
1973 Kent
1974 Surrey
1975 Leicestershire

Test Team A quarter of the Tests in 3 series

No. Player	Runs	Av	Wkts	Av	Year	Result	Opp
					1971	1–0	Pak
17 Boycott	1313	46.89				0–1	Ind
36 Amiss	2730	48.75			1972	2–2	Aus
29 Edrich J. H.	1595	37.09			1972–3	1–2	Ind
36 Fletcher	2421	49.41				0–0	Pak
27 Denness	1610	39.27			1973	2–0	NZ
42 Greig A. W.	2729	42.64	117	30.83		0–2	WI
48 Knott	2240	32.94			1973–4	1–1	WI
24 Old	460	15.86	74	30.28	1974	3–0	Ind
15 Snow	304	11.69	57	26.88		0–0	Pak
31 Arnold	347	10.84	107	28.76	1974–5	1–4	Aus
35 Underwood	432	12.70	102	31.28		1–0	NZ
					1975	0–1	Aus

			w	l	d	
This team is one of the few to pick itself.						
No other batsman makes 800 runs, and		**Series**	4	5	4	46%
no other bowler takes 35 wickets.		**Tests**	12	13	23	49%

1976–80

Batsman	Runs	Av	Bowler	Wkts	Av
Qual – 4000 runs in 3+ seasons			200 wickets in 3+ seasons		
Boycott	7024	65.64	Daniel (WI)	322	18.87
Lamb (SA/Q))	4427	61.49	Hendrick	270	18.99
Richards I.V.A.(WI)	7703	54.63	Underwood	401	19.01
Turner G.M.(NZ)	8329	52.38	Jackman	444	19.84
Wessels (SA)	4329	52.16	Imran K.(P)	266	20.76
Amiss	9011	52.09	Lever J.K.	400	20.90
Greenidge (WI)	7642	51.99	Procter (SA)	378	21.13
Zaheer A.(P)	8273	51.71	Old	220	21.31
Lloyd C.H.(WI)	4144	48.75	Arnold	219	22.02
Rice (SA)	7354	46.84	Rice (SA)	236	22.03
McEwan (SA)	7809	46.21	Emburey	309	22.10
Davison (Z)	7092	44.60	Selvey	362	22.14
Hampshire	5545	44.36	Sarfraz N.(P)	276	22.20
Javed M.(P)	4322	44.12	Miller G.	294	22.87
Roope	5520	43.12	Clift (Z)	275	23.07
Kirsten P.(SA)	4176	43.05	Willis	225	23.12
Fletcher	6401	42.39	East	314	23.14
Woolmer	6562	41.53	Edmonds	306	23.51
Rose B.C.	6481	41.28	Moseley H.(WI)	212	23.73
Kallichar'n (WI)	5036	40.96	Turner S.	312	23.92
All-rounders	7354	46.84	Rice (SA)	236	22.03
	4271	38.13	Imran K.(P)	266	20.76
	6043	37.30	Procter (SA)	378	21.13
	4178	34.82	Botham	340	24.14
	4271	38.13	Willey	202	30.63

County Champions

1976	Middlesex
1977	Middlesex/Kent
1978	Kent
1979	Essex
1980	Middlesex

Gillette Cup

1976	Northamptonshire
1977	Middlesex
1978	Sussex
1979	Somerset
1980	Middlesex

John Player League

1976	Kent
1977	Leicestershire
1978	Hampshire
1979	Somerset
1980	Warwickshire

Benson and Hedges Cup

1976	Kent
1977	Gloucestershire
1978	Kent
1979	Essex
1980	Northamptonshire

Test Team A quarter of the Tests in 3 series

No. Player	Runs	Av	Wkts	Av	Year	Result	Opp
					1976	0–3	WI
35 Boycott	2536	52.83			1976–7	3–1	Ind
28 Gooch	1824	39.65				0–1	Aus
35 Brearley	1301	23.65			1977	3–0	Aus
26 Gower	1792	45.95			1977–8	0–0	Pak
27 Randall	1125	27.44				1–1	NZ
35 Botham	1578	31.56	168	21.33	1978	2–0	Pak
25 Miller G.	828	27.19	43	28.88		3–0	NZ
25 Taylor R.W.	616	21.24			1978–9	5–1	Aus
21 Underwood	266	9.17	77	27.23	1979	1–0	Ind
41 Willis	334	11.13	151	23.34	1979–80	0–3	Aus
20 Hendrick	102	6.00	57	24.72		1–0	Ind
					1980	0–1	WI
						0–0	Aus
					1980–1	0–2	WI

This is the Packer-divided period. The selection is for balance: Old (64 at 25.06) or Lever J.K. (60 at 26.35) could replace a pace bowler. Edmonds (43 at 23.88) could replace Miller, but the batting weakens. Knott (886 at 27.69) played 20 Tests to Taylor's 25.

	w	l	d	
Series	7	5	3	57%
Tests	19	13	20	56%

1981–5

Batsman	Runs	Av	Bowler	Wkts	Av	County Champions	
Qual – 4000 runs in 3+ seasons			200 wickets in 3+ seasons			1981	Nottinghamshire
						1982	Middlesex
Gatting	8544	61.03	Hadlee (NZ)	391	15.83	1983	Essex
Zaheer A. (P)	5424	59.60	Marshall (WI)	417	16.98	1984	Essex
Javed M. (P)	5521	59.37	Garner (WI)	226	17.71	1985	Middlesex
Richards I.V.A. (WI)	6707	59.35	Clarke (WI)	291	20.24		
Boycott	8087	58.18	Le Roux (SA)	301	21.66	**Nat West Trophy**	
Younis A. (P)	5719	53.45	Underwood	406	21.91	1981	Derbyshire
Greenidge (WI)	6711	52.84	Lever J. K.	451	22.18	1982	Surrey
Gooch	9225	52.71	Daniel (WI)	319	23.26	1983	Somerset
Kallichar'n (WI)	8033	51.49	Emburey	384	23.77	1984	Middlesex
Wright J.G. (NZ)	5690	51.26	Edmonds	398	24.11	1985	Essex
Lamb	6695	49.23	Allott	296	24.11	**John Player League**	
Slack	7436	46.47	Sidebottom A.	237	24.16	1981	Essex
Gower	6677	46.37	Clift (Z)	229	25.05	1982	Sussex
Rice (SA)	6530	45.35	Philip (WI)	242	25.33	1983	Yorkshire
Botham	5345	45.30	Foster	204	25.80	1984	Essex
McEwan (SA)	8065	44.81	Steele	245	26.22	1985	Essex
Randall	6918	44.35	Botham	258	26.72		
Amiss	8641	44.09	Hemmings	362	27.05	**Benson and Hedges Cup**	
Smith C. L.	5720	43.66	Greig I. A.	248	27.08	1981	Somerset
Davison (Z)	5399	42.85	Graveney D. A.	224	27.30	1982	Somerset
						1983	Middlesex
All-rounders	5345	45.30	Botham	258	26.72	1984	Lancashire
	5924	35.26	Ontong (SA)	307	30.66	1985	Leicestershire

Test Team   A quarter of the Tests in 3 series

No. Player	Runs	Av	Wkts	Av	Year	Result	Opp
					1981	3–1	Aus
23 Gooch	1442	36.05			1981–2	0–1	Ind
15 Robinson R. T.	1006	43.74				1–0	SL
55 Gower	3963	44.53			1982	1–0	Ind
34 Gatting	2014	41.10				2–1	Pak
43 Lamb	2435	35.81			1982–3	1–2	Aus
49 Botham	2999	36.57	186	32.24	1983	3–1	NZ
31 Taylor R. W.	536	13.07			1983–4	0–1	NZ
18 Edmonds	411	19.57	42	44.64		0–1	Pak
18 Emburey	332	16.60	57	29.84	1984	0–5	WI
33 Willis	328	10.58	127	24.78	1984–5	0–0	SL
19 Cowans	175	7.95	51	39.27	1985	2–1	Ind
						3–1	Aus
					1985–6	0–5	WI

This period includes the first South Africa ban.
Four other pace bowlers (Ellison, Foster, Allott, Dilley)
played 9–13 Tests. Tavaré made 1688 at 34.45,
Fowler 1307 at 35.32, Randall 1345 at 40.76. Downton
made 609 at 21.00 in 23 Tests. Tricky selection!

	w	l	d	
Series	7	6	1	54%
Tests	16	20	20	46%

1986–90

Batsman	Runs	Av	Bowler	Wkts	Av
Qual – 4000 runs in 3+ seasons			200 wickets in 3+ seasons		
Hick (Z/Q)	10767	67.29	*Marshall (WI)*	354	17.00
Gooch	8908	55.68	*Alderman (A)*	243	19.29
Gatting	7413	54.91	*Mortensen (D)*	213	20.15
Haynes (WI)	4912	54.58	Cowans	281	22.05
Lamb	5833	51.17	*Stephenson (WI)*	271	22.56
Smith R. A.	6493	49.56	*Walsh (WI)*	352	22.93
Curtis	7597	46.90	Foster	450	23.11
Atherton	5179	46.66	Pringle	296	23.80
Smith C. L.	7132	46.01	Allott	228	23.84
Fairbrother	6563	45.26	Fraser	283	24.10
Bailey R. J.	7961	44.47	Sidebottom A.	203	24.70
Roebuck	5474	44.15	Jarvis	291	25.05
Athey	6014	43.90	Dilley	231	25.13
Benson	6883	43.02	Small	278	25.33
Whitaker	7125	42.92	Radford	354	25.78
Morris J. E.	7383	42.68	Childs	282	26.13
Barnett	7488	42.31	DeFreitas	322	26.19
Robinson R. T.	7105	42.29	Bicknell	251	26.50
Mendis	7035	41.88	Newport	324	26.95
Stewart A. J.	6511	41.47	Cook N. G. B	287	27.15
All-rounder	4935	33.80	Capel	239	30.52

County Champions

1986	Essex
1987	Nottinghamshire
1988	Worcestershire
1989	Worcestershire
1990	Middlesex

Nat West Trophy

1986	Sussex
1987	Nottinghamshire
1988	Middlesex
1989	Warwickshire
1990	Lancashire

One-day League

1986	Hampshire
1987	Worcestershire
1988	Worcestershire
1989	Lancashire
1990	Derbyshire

Benson and Hedges Cup

1986	Middlesex
1987	Yorkshire
1988	Hampshire
1989	Nottinghamshire
1990	Lancashire

Test Team A quarter of the Tests in 3 series

No. Player	Runs	Av	Wkts	Av	Year	Result	Opp
					1986	0–2	Ind
						0–1	NZ
32 Gooch	3033	50.55			1986–7	2–1	Aus
20 Broad	1380	41.82			1987	0–1	Pak
26 Gatting	1608	39.22			1987–8	0–1	Pak
33 Gower	2326	42.29				0–0	NZ
27 Lamb	1741	37.85				0–0	Aus
23 Smith R. A.	1635	48.09			1988	0–4	WI
20 Russell R. C.	767	30.68				1–0	SL
16 Foster	308	14.67	54	28.28	1989	0–4	Aus
23 Dilley	191	10.05	88	28.55	1989–90	1–2	WI
17 Small	263	15.47	55	34.02	1990	1–0	NZ
11 Fraser	88	6.77	47	26.70		1–0	Ind
					1990–1	0–3	Aus

A side without a spinner, but the only one with
enough Tests, Embury, took his 49 at 49.33.
No wonder it was such a depressing period.
DeFreitas had 48 at 42.31. Atherton in 13 Tests
made 1087 at 45.29.

	w	l	d	
Series	4	8	2	36%
Tests	6	19	25	37%

1991–5

Batsman	Runs	Av	Bowler	Wkts	Av	County Champions
Qual – 3500 runs in 3+ seasons			175 wickets in 3+ seasons			1991 Essex
						1992 Essex
Gatting	7999	65.03	*Wasim A.* (P)	305	19.55	1993 Middlesex
Waugh M. E. (A)	4067	64.56	*Ambrose* (WI)	262	20.00	1994 Warwickshire
Gooch	9200	63.45	*Donald* (SA)	301	20.92	1995 Warwickshire
Salim M. (P)	4073	60.79	*Walsh* (WI)	313	20.96	
Hooper (WI)	6776	57.42	Emburey	353	25.08	**Nat West Trophy**
Moody (A)	5371	53.18	Munton	280	25.10	1991 Hampshire
Moxon	6974	52.04	Bicknell	253	25.20	1992 Northamptonshire
Robinson R. T.	7376	50.87	Cork	269	25.43	1993 Warwickshire
Wells A. P.	7114	49.40	*Mushtaq A.* (P)	291	25.46	1994 Worcestershire
Ramprakash	6784	49.16	McCague	207	25.80	1995 Warwickshire
Hick	6709	48.27	Tufnell	308	26.13	**One-day League**
Crawley	6445	47.74	Caddick	214	26.38	1991 Nottinghamshire
Lamb	5578	47.36	Millns	257	26.30	1992 Middlesex
Hussain	6600	46.81	*Stephenson* (WI)	261	26.81	1993 Glamorgan
Smith R. A.	5980	46.72	Newport	316	27.12	1994 Warwickshire
Taylor N.	5463	46.30	Igglesden	195	27.30	1995 Kent
Barnett	5990	46.08	Watkin	354	27.86	
Brown A. D.	4225	45.43	Such	284	27.88	**Benson and Hedges Cup**
Bowler	6790	44.97	Curran (Z)	233	28.06	1991 Worcestershire
Maynard	6965	44.94	DeFreitas	292	28.13	1992 Hampshire
						1993 Derbyshire
All-rounder	4006	34.53	Curran (Z)	233	28.06	1994 Warwickshire
						1995 Lancashire

Test Team A quarter of the Tests in 3 series

No. Player	Runs	Av	Wkts	Av	Year	Result	Opp
					1991	2–2	WI
						1–0	SL
33 Gooch	2564	43.46			1991–2	2–0	NZ
43 Atherton	3115	39.94			1992	1–2	Pak
41 Stewart A. J.	2862	42.72			1992–3	0–3	Ind
42 Hick	2629	38.25	21	54.95		0–1	SL
39 Smith R. A.	2601	41.29			1993	1–4	Aus
26 Thorpe	1842	40.93			1993–4	1–3	WI
24 Russell R. C.	827	26.68			1994	1–0	NZ
23 Lewis C. C.	939	25.38	65	36.98		1–1	SA
24 DeFreitas	556	16.35	92	29.01	1994–5	1–3	Aus
20 Malcolm	134	5.83	64	36.38	1995	2–2	WI
18 Tufnell	49	3.77	59	39.42	1995–6	0–1	SA

				w	l	d	
Cork (45 at 25.47) & Gough (43 at 31.58)							
played too few Tests. Fraser (72 at 34.08)							
could replace Malcolm. Stewart only kept		**Series**		3	7	3	35%
wicket in seven Tests in this period.		**Tests**		13	22	16	41%

1996–2000

Batsman	Runs	Av	Bowler	Wkts	Av
Qual – 3000 runs in 3+ seasons			150 wickets in 3+ seasons		
Lehmann (A)	4021	63.83	Saqlain M. (P)	248	15.60
Langer (A)	4280	59.44	Walsh (WI)	231	16.12
Bevan (A)	3747	58.55	Smith A. M.	298	21.17
Law (A)	7227	57.82	Bicknell	306	21.39
Hayden (A)	3461	55.82	Martin	230	21.99
Crawley	5915	51.89	Dean	174	22.05
James	6967	49.76	Caddick	405	22.26
Ramprakash	6112	48.13	Gough	219	22.92
Hick	5909	47.65	Mullally	244	23.80
Moody (A)	3572	46.39	Watkin	261	23.99
Thorpe	4127	46.37	Giddins	213	24.25
Maynard	4957	45.48	Ormond	159	24.35
Smith B. F.	4525	44.36	Millns	208	24.37
Habib A.	4234	43.65	Brown S. J. E.	272	24.61
Barnett	5107	43.28	Munton	159	24.66
Brown A. D.	4501	43.28	Salisbury	231	24.67
Knight N. V.	4266	43.09	Lewry	212	24.76
Fairbrother	4040	42.98	White C. L.	169	24.94
Lloyd G. D.	4772	42.23	Tufnell	285	25.41
Butcher M. A.	5664	41.34	Silverwood	238	25.47
All-rounders	5150	39.02	Irani	199	27.63
	3012	33.47	Ealham	175	25.77
	4217	31.01	Alleyne	170	29.21
	3154	27.67	Brown D. R.	221	27.61

County Champions

1996	Leicestershire
1997	Glamorgan
1998	Leicestershire
1999	Surrey
2000	Surrey

Nat West Trophy

1996	Lancashire
1997	Essex
1998	Lancashire
1999	Gloucestershire
2000	Gloucestershire

One-day League

1996	Surrey
1997	Warwickshire
1998	Lancashire
1999	Lancashire
2000	Gloucestershire

Benson and Hedges Cup

1996	Lancashire
1997	Surrey
1998	Essex
1999	Gloucestershire
2000	Gloucestershire

Test Team   A quarter of the Tests in 3 series

No. Player	Runs	Av	Wkts	Av	Year	Result	Opp
					1996	1–0	Ind
						0–2	Pak
52 Atherton	3207	35.63			1996–7	0–0	Zim
55 Stewart A. J.	3681	40.45				2–0	NZ
52 Hussain	3010	35.83			1997	2–3	Aus
40 Thorpe	2406	40.10			1997–8	1–3	WI
23 Ramprakash	1263	35.08			1998	2–1	SA
20 Crawley	999	37.00				0–1	SL
21 Cork	458	16.36	73	29.73	1998–9	1–3	Aus
20 Croft	418	17.42	48	37.81	1999	1–2	NZ
35 Caddick	462	10.04	129	25.60	1999–0	1–2	SA
37 Gough	377	8.98	154	25.93	2000	1–0	Zim
14 Fraser	123	7.69	58	22.88		3–1	WI
					2000–1	1–0	Pak
						2–1	SL

Butcher (1253 at 25.06) is the only batting
option. Headley (60 at 27.85) and Mullally
(56 at 30.59) were the other pace bowlers,
Tufnell (52 at 32.98) the other spinner. But
look at the tail we have already . . .

	w	l	d	
Series	7	7	1	50%
Tests	18	19	19	49%

2001–5

Batsman	Runs	Av	Bowler	Wkts	Av	County Champions	
Qual – 3000 runs in 3+ seasons			150 wickets in 3+ seasons			2001	Yorkshire
						2002	Surrey
Hussey M. (A)	6710	72.93	Warne (A)	180	22.07	2003	Sussex
Lehmann (A)	3144	71.45	Sidebottom R. J.	183	25.14	2004	Warwickshire
Ramprakash	6864	64.15	Mascarenhas	207	25.56	2005	Nottinghamshire
Love (A)	4457	61.90	Saggers	248	25.60		
Jaques (A)	3886	60.72	Mushtaq A. (P)	289	25.87	C & G Trophy	
Law (A)	6072	59.53	Kirtley	290	25.94	2001	Somerset
Knight N. V.	5837	54.55	Smith G. J. (SA)	239	26.08	2002	Yorkshire
Hodge (A)	3717	53.87	Kabir Ali	231	26.25	2003	Gloucestershire
Pietersen (Q)	5633	53.14	Cork	207	26.34	2004	Gloucestershire
Key	6742	52.67	Saqlain M. (P)	184	26.66	2005	Hampshire
Flower A. (Z)	4865	51.76	Tremlett	168	26.73	One-day League	
DiVenuto (A)	5333	51.28	Mason (A)	180	26.81	2001	Kent
Goodwin (Z)	6633	51.02	Anderson	177	26.85	2002	Glamorgan
Trescothick	3661	50.85	Ealham	173	26.92	2003	Surrey
Shah	6394	50.35	Bicknell	228	26.94	2004	Glamorgan
Thorpe	3199	49.98	Kasprowicz (A)	161	27.03	2005	Essex
Joyce (Ire/Q)	5247	49.97	Harmison	197	27.27		
Blackwell	4998	49.49	Lewry	209	27.68	Benson and Hedges Cup	
Symonds (A)	3209	49.37	Udal	235	27.74	2001	Surrey
Vaughan	3402	49.30	Lewis J.	241	27.89	2002	Warwickshire
All-rounders	3159	35.49	Ealham	173	26.92	Twenty20 Cup	
	3938	37.15	Brown D. R.	220	32.30	2003	Surrey
						2004	Leicestershire
						2005	Somerset

Test Team A quarter of the Tests in 3 series

No. Player	Runs	Av	Wkts	Av	Year	Result	Opp
					2001	1–1	Pak
						1–4	Aus
57 Trescothick	4619	46.66			2001–2	0–1	Ind
53 Vaughan	4106	46.66				1–1	NZ
44 Butcher M. A.	3035	41.01	12	31.00	2002	2–0	SL
37 Hussain	2470	41.17				1–1	Ind
34 Thorpe	2496	54.26			2002–3	1–4	Aus
25 Stewart A. J.	1379	40.56			2003	2–0	Zim
43 Flintoff	2408	37.05	136	31.15		2–2	SA
43 Giles	1190	21.64	112	39.93	2003–4	2–0	Ban
19 Caddick	229	9.16	82	32.49		0–1	SL
44 Hoggard	307	8.30	173	29.35		3–0	WI
35 Harmison	347	10.84	138	28.49	2004	3–0	NZ
						4–0	WI
					2004–5	2–1	SA
					2005	2–0	Ban
						2–1	Aus

For the first time there are six batsmen with averages
of 40+ and four bowlers with 100+ wickets. S. P. Jones
(59 at 28.24) could replace Caddick. To bring Strauss
in (1716 at 50.47 in 19 Tests) would mean leaving out…?
G. O. Jones played 19 Tests to Stewart's 25.

	w	l	d	
Series	9	4	4	65%
Tests	29	17	14	60%

Test Cricket 1946–2005

Batsman	3000+ runs Runs	Av	Bowlers	100+ wickets Wkts	Av	Wicketkeeper	100+ dismissals ct	st
Barrington	6806	58.67	Wardle	102	20.39	Stewart A. J.	263–14	
Hutton	5626	54.62	Laker	193	21.24	Knott A. P. E.	250–19	
Compton	5339	49.90	Trueman	307	21.57	Evans	173–46	
Dexter	4502	47.89	Statham	252	24.84	Taylor R. W.	167–7	
Boycott	8114	47.72	Bedser	236	24.89	Russell R. C.	153–12	
May	4537	46.77	Willis	325	25.20	Parks J. M.	153–11	
Amiss	3612	46.30	Lock	174	25.58			
Trescothick	5206	45.27	Underwood	297	25.83			
Thorpe	6744	44.66	Snow	202	26.66	**Fielders 1+ catch per match**		
Graveney T. W.	4882	44.38	Fraser	177	27.31	**Fielder**	ct	matches
Gower	8231	44.25	Old	143	28.11	Botham	120	102
Cowdrey M. C.	7624	44.06	Arnold	115	28.29	Cowdrey M. C.	120	104
Vaughan	4513	43.81	Gough	229	28.39	Thorpe	105	100
Smith R. A.	4236	43.67	Botham	383	28.40	Hick	90	65
Edrich J. H.	5138	43.54	**Harmison**	134	28.59	Greig A. W.	87	58
Gooch	8900	42.58	Bailey T. E.	132	29.21	Graveney T. W.	80	79
Greig A. W.	3599	40.43	**Hoggard**	173	29.63	**Trescothick**	76	66
Fletcher	3272	39.90	Dilley	138	29.76	Lock	59	49
Stewart A. J.	8463	39.54	Cork	131	29.81	Smith M. J. K.	53	50
Atherton	7728	37.69	Caddick	234	29.91	Brearley	52	39
All-rounders	3599	40.43	Greig A. W.	141	32.20			
	5200	33.54	Botham	383	28.40			

One-day International Cricket 1972–2005

Batsman	2000+ runs Runs	Av	Bowlers	50+ wickets Wkts	Av	Wicketkeeper	40+ dismissals ct	st
Knight N. V.	3617	40.11	**Flintoff**	95	23.21	Stewart A. J.	159–15	
Fairbrother	2092	39.47	Willis	80	24.60	**Jones G. O.**	53–2	
Lamb	4010	39.31	**Anderson**	59	25.49	Russell R. C.	41–6	
Smith R. A.	2419	39.01	**Gough**	234	25.99	Taylor R. W.	36–6	
Trescothick	3848	37.72	Mullally	63	27.42			
Hick	3846	37.33	Caddick	69	28.47	**Fielders**		
Thorpe	2380	37.18	Botham	145	28.54	Hick	64	
Gooch	4290	36.98	**Harmison**	50	28.70	Gooch	45	
Flintoff	2212	34.56	Lewis C. C.	66	29.42	Knight N. V.	44	
Stewart A. J.	4677	31.60	Emburey	76	30.86	Gower	44	
						Trescothick	44	
All-rounders	2212	34.56	**Flintoff**	95	23.21			

First-class Domestic Cricket 1946–2005

Batsman	Runs	Av	Bowlers	Wkts	Av	Wicketkeeper	ct	st
Hutton	27300	56.99	Statham	2260	16.37	Taylor R. W.	1473–176	
Boycott	48426	56.83	Jackson H. L.	1733	17.36	Murray	1270–257	
Hick	38437	52.79	Tattersall	1369	18.04	Knott	1211–133	
Compton	30316	52.27	Trueman	2304	18.29	Taylor B.	1083–211	
May	27592	51.00	Laker	1944	18.41	Rhodes S. J.	1139–124	
Gatting	36549	49.40	Shackleton	2857	18.65	Parks J. M.	1088–93	
Ramprakash	26355	49.26	Wardle	1846	18.97	Booth R.	948–178	
Gooch	44846	49.01	Cartwright	1536	19.11	Bairstow	961–138	
Crawley	21034	46.74	Lock	2844	19.23	Stephenson H.	748–334	
Barrington	31714	45.63	Hilton	1006	19.41	Binks	895–176	
						Evans	816–250	
Edrich J. H.	39790	45.47	Young	1341	19.60	Long	922–124	
Thorpe	21937	45.04	Hollies	1582	19.66	Tolchard	912–125	
Washbrook	25006	44.97	Illingworth	2072	20.28			
Graveney T. W.	47793	44.91	Underwood	2465	20.28			
Cowdrey M. C.	42719	42.89	Bedser	1924	20.81	**Fielders**		
Amiss	43423	42.86	Cook C.	1782	20.52	Lock	830	
Moxon	21161	42.83	Wheatley	1099	20.84	Close	813	
Robinson R. T.	27571	42.15	Cottam	1010	20.91	Milton	758	
Hussain	20698	42.06	Coldwell	1076	21.18	Walker	697	
Smith M. J. K.	39832	41.84	Shepherd D. J.	2118	21.32	Cowdrey M. C.	638	
						Stewart M. J.	635	
All-rounders	28641	33.42	Bailey T. E.	2082	23.13	**Hick**	632	
	24134	28.06	Illingworth	2072	20.28	Sharpe	618	
	34994	33.26	Close	1171	26.42	Roope	602	
	19399	33.97	Botham	1172	27.22			
	20176	26.86	Sainsbury	1316	24.14			
	21588	23.11	Titmus	2830	22.37			

One-day Domestic Cricket 1968–2005

Batsman	Runs	Av	Bowlers	Wkts	Av	Wicketkeeper	ct	st
Fairbrother	14761	41.69	Underwood	572	19.43	Rhodes S. J.	532–129	
Smith R. A.	26155	41.51	Lever J. K.	674	19.70	Russell R. C.	465–98	
Hick	20806	41.11	Willis	421	20.18	Hegg	466–61	
Adams C. J.	10608	40.80	Old	418	20.86	Stewart A. J.	443–48	
Gooch	22211	40.16	Jackman	439	21.10			
Curtis	10280	39.69	Martin	353	22.19	**Fielders**		
Thorpe	10871	39.67	Radford	484	23.28			
Lamb	15658	39.14	Jarvis	399	24.22	Hick	269	
Boycott	10095	39.12	Gough	539	24.25	Gooch	261	
Bailey R. J.	12076	38.82	Botham	612	24.94	Botham	196	
						Maynard	183	
All-rounder	10474	29.50	Botham	612	24.94	Emburey	181	

Bibliography

Agnew, Jonathan, *Eight Days a Week*, Ringpress Books, 1988; Allen, D. Rayvern, *Arlott*, Harper Collins, 1994; Allen, D. Rayvern (ed.) (with Hubert Doggart), *A Breathless Hush*, Methuen, 2004; Amiss, Dennis, *In Search of Runs*, Stanley Paul, 1976; Arlott, John, *Arlott on Cricket*, Willow Books, 1984; Atherton, Michael, *Opening Up*, Hodder and Stoughton, 2002

Bailey, Jack, *Conflicts in Cricket*, Kingswood Press, 1989; Bailey, Trevor, *The Greatest of my Time*, Eyre and Spottiswoode, 1968; Bailey, Trevor, *Championship Cricket*, Sportsman's Book Club, 1962; Bailey, Trevor, *The Greatest Since my Time*, Hodder and Stoughton, 1989; Baldwin, Mark, *The History of the Cricket World Cup*, Sanctuary, 2003; Barker, Ralph, *The Cricketing Family Edrich*, Pelham Books, 1976; Barnes, Simon, *A la Recherche du Cricket Perdu*, MacMillan, 1989; Barrington, Ken, *Running into Hundreds*, Stanley Paul, 1963; Barrington, Ken, *Playing it Straight*, Stanley Paul, 1968; Barty-King, Hugh, *Quilt Winders and Pod Shavers*, Macdonald and Jane's, 1979; Bedser, Alec, *Twin Ambitions*, Stanley Paul, 1986; Bedser, Alec and Eric, *Our Cricket Story*, Evans Brothers, 1950; Bedser, Alec and Eric, *Following On*, Evans Brothers, 1954; Benaud, Richie, *Willow Patterns*, Hodder and Stoughton, 1969; Benaud, Richie, *On Reflection*, Hodder and Stoughton, 1984; Benaud, Richie, *Anything But…An Autobiography*, Hodder and Stoughton, 1999; Berry, Scyld, *A Cricket Odyssey*, Pavilion, 1988; Birley, Derek, *The Social History of Cricket*, Aurum, 1999; Blofed, Henry, *The Packer Affair*, Collins, 1978; Botham, Ian, *Botham*, Collins Willow, 1994; Botham, Ian, *The Botham Report*, Collins Willow, 1997; Boycott, Geoffrey, *Put to the Test*, Arthur Barker, 1979; Boycott, Geoffrey, *Opening Up*, Arthur Barker, 1980; Bradman, Sir Donald, *The Art of Cricket*, Hodder and Stoughton, 1958; Brearley, Mike, *Phoenix from the Ashes*, Hodder and Stoughton, 1981; Brearley, Mike, *The Art of Captaincy*, Hodder and Stoughton, 1985; Brooke, Robert, *A History of the County Cricket Championship*, Guinness, 1991

Cardus, Sir Neville, *The Playfair Cardus*, Dickens Press, 1963; Cardus, Sir Neville, *Cardus in the Covers*, Souvenir Press, 1978; Chalke, Stephen, *Runs in the Memory*, Fairfield Books, 1997; Chalke, Stephen, *Caught in the Memory*, Fairfield Books, 1999; Close, Brian, *Close on Cricket*, Sportsman's Book Club, 1966; Compton, Denis, *Testing Time for England*, Stanley Paul, 1947; Compton, Denis, *Playing for England*, Sampson Low, Marston and Co., Ltd, 1948; Compton, Denis, *End of an Innings*, Oldbourne, 1958; Compton, Denis and Edrich, Bill, *Cricket and All That*, Pelham Books, 1978; Cook, Geoff and Scott, Neville, *The Narrow Line*, Kingswood Press, 1991; Constantine, Learie, *Cricket in the Sun*, Stanley Paul, 1946; Constantine, Learie, *Colour Bar*, Stanley Paul, 1954; Cowdrey, Colin, M.C.C., *The Autobiography of a Cricketer*, Hodder and Stoughton, 1976; Crace, John, *Wasim and Waqar*, Boxtree, 1992

Denness, Mike, *I Declare*, Arthur Barker, 1977; Dexter, Ted, *Ted Dexter Declares*, Stanley Paul, 1966; D'Oliveira, Basil, *The D'Oliveira Affair*, Collins, 1969

Edmonds, Frances, *Cricket XXXX Cricket*, The Kingswood Press, 1987; Edrich, John, *Runs in the Family*, Stanley Paul, 1969; Edrich, W. J., *Cricket Heritage*, Stanley Paul, 1948; Edrich, W. J., *Cricketing Days*, Stanley Paul, 1950; Emburey, John, *Spinning in a Fast World*, Robson Books, 1989; Evans, Godfrey, *Action in Cricket*, Sportsman's Book Club, 1957; Evans, Godfrey, *The Gloves are Off*, Hodder and Stoughton, 1960

Fingleton, Jack, *Brightly Fades the Don*, Collins, 1949; Fingleton, Jack, *Brown and Company*, Collins, 1951; Foot, David, *Wally Hammond*, Robson Books, 1996; Frith, David, *The Fast Men*, VNR, 1975; Frith, David, *The Slow Men*, George Allen and Unwin, 1984

Gatting, Mike, *Leading from the Front*, Guild Publishing, 1988; Giller, Norman, *Denis Compton*, Andre Deutsch, 1997; Gooch, Graham and Keating, Frank, *Gooch*, Collins Willow, 1995; Gough, Darren, *Dazzler*, Michael Joseph, 1991; Gower, David, *Gower, The Autobiography*, Collins Willow, 1992; Graveney, Tom, *Tom Graveney on Cricket*, Frederick Muller, 1965

Haigh, Gideon, *Mystery Spinner,* Aurum, 1999; Harte, Chris, *A History of Australian Cricket,* Andre Deutsch, 1993; Hill, Alan, *Bill Edrich,* Andre Deutsch, 1994; Hill, Alan, *Peter May,* Andre Deutsch, 1996; Hill, Alan, *Jim Laker,* Andre Deutsch, 1998; Hill, Alan, *The Bedsers,* Mainstream Publishing, 2001; Hill, Alan, *Johnny Wardle, Cricket Conjuror,* David and Charles, 1988; Hollowood, Bernard, *Cricket on the Brain,* Eyre and Spottiswoode, 1970; Howat, Gerald, *Len Hutton,* Heinemann Kingswood, 1988; Hughes, Simon, *A Lot of Hard Yakka,* Headline, 1997; Hussain, Nasser, *Playing with Fire,* Michael Joseph, 2004; Hutton, Len, *Just my Story,* Hutchinson, 1956; Hutton, Len, *Fifty Years in Cricket,* Stanley Paul, 1984

Illingworth, Ray, *Yorkshire and Back,* Queen Anne Press, 1980; Illingworth, Ray and Bannister, Jack, *One-Man Committee,* Headline, 1996; Insole, Doug, *Cricket from the Middle,* Heinemann, 1960

James, C. L. R., *Cricket,* Allison and Busby, 1986; James, Steve, *Third Man to Fatty's Leg,* First Stone, 2004

Khan, Imran, *All Round View,* Chatto and Windus, 1988; Knott, Alan, *Stumper's View,* Stanley Paul, 1972

Laker, Jim, *Spinning Round the World,* Frederick Muller, 1957; Laker, Jim, *Over to Me,* Frederick Muller, 1960; Lewis, Tony, *Playing days,* Stanley Paul, 1985; Lillee, Dennis, *Menace,* Headline, 2003; Lock, Tony, *For Surrey and England,* Hodder and Stoughton, 1957; Lodge, Derek, *Figures on the Green,* George Allen and Unwin, 1982

McKinstrey, Leo, *Boycs,* Partridge, 1988; McLean, Teresa, *The Men in White Coats,* Stanley Paul, 1987; May, Peter, *A Game Enjoyed,* Stanley Paul, 1985; Midwinter, Eric, *The Lost Seasons,* Methuen, 1987; Murphy, Patrick, *The Spinner's Turn,* Dent, 1982

The Nawab of Pataudi, *Tiger's Tale,* Stanley Paul, 1969

Oborne, Peter, *Basil D'Oliveira,* Little, Brown, 2004; Oslear, Don, *Wisden, The Laws of Cricket,* Ebury Press, 2000; Oslear, Don and Bannister, Jack, *Tampering with Cricket,* Collins Willow, 1996

Parks, Jim, *Runs in the Sun,* Stanley Paul, 1961; Paton, David, and Cooke, Andy, *Attendance at County Cricket: an Economic Analysis,* Journal of Sports Economics, 2004

Rae, Simon, *It's Not Cricket,* Faber and Faber, 2001; Randall, Derek, *The Sun Has Got His Hat On,* Willow Books, 1984; Roebuck, Peter, *It Never Rains,* George Allen and Unwin, 1984; Sheppard, David, *Parson's Pitch,* Hodder and Stoughton, 1964; Rose, E. M., *How to Win at Cricket,* Hodder and Stoughton, 1988; Russell, Jack, *Jack Russell Unleashed,* Collins Willow, 1997

Sandford, Christopher, *Tom Graveney,* H. F. and G. Witherby, 1992; Shepherd, David, *Shep,* Orion, 2002; Sisson, Ric, *The Players,* Kingswood Press, 1988; Smith, Ed, *On and Off the Field,* Viking, 2004; Smith, Tom, *Cricket Umpiring and Scoring,* Weidenfeld and Nicolson, 2001; Snow, John, *Cricket Rebel,* Hamlyn, 1976; Statham, Brian, *A Spell at the Top,* Souvenir Press, 1969; Stevenson, Mike, *Illingworth,* Ward Lock, 1978; Stewart, Alec, *Playing for Keeps,* BBC Books, 2003; Swanton E. W., *As I Said at the Time,* Willow Books, 1983; Swanton, E. W., *Gubby Allen, Man of Cricket,* Hutchinson/Stanley Paul, 1985

Taylor, Bob, *Standing Up, Standing Back,* Willow Books, 1985; Trueman, Fred, *Ball of Fire,* J. M. Dent and Sons, 1976; Tyson, Frank, *A Typhoon called Tyson,* Heinemann, 1961; Tyson, Frank, *In the Eye of the Typhoon,* Parrs Wood Press, 2004

Underwood, Derek, *Beating the Bat,* Stanley Paul, 1975

Vaughan, Michael, *Calling the Shots,* Hodder and Stoughton, 2005

Walker, Peter, *Cricket Conversations,* Pelham Books, 1978; Watson, Willie, *Double International,* Sportsman's Book Club, 1964; Wilde, Simon, *Letting Rip,* H. F. and G. Witherby, 1994; Willis, Bob, *Lasting the Pace,* Willow Books, 1985; Woolmer, Bob, *Woolmer on Cricket,* Virgin, 2000; Wright, Graeme, *Betrayal,* H. F. and G. Witherby, 1993

And, of course, *Wisden Cricketer's Almanack* 1934–40 and 1946–2005, to whose editors and contributors I and all cricket-lovers are deeply indebted. All unattributed quotes in the book come from Wisden.

Index of Names

Index of Major Topics

Illustrations and Acknowledgements

The author would like to thank the following for permission to reproduce photographs and copyright material. Every effort has been made to trace the copyright holders of images and text used in this book. The author would be grateful for any information enabling omissions to be rectified in a future edition.

Picture acknowledgements

Adrian Murrell p. 364; AFP p. 212; Allsport p. 304; Cricketer International pp. 80, 94; Daily Mirror p. 146; Getty Images, back cover (Denis Compton scores the winning runs at the Oval, August 1953) and pp. 56, 94, 100, 120, 169, 174, 246, 263, 289, 327, 333 and 341; Ken Kelly pp. 64, 108, 187 and 195; Patrick Eagar, front cover (Andrew Strauss's catch at Nottingham, August 2005); back cover (Kevin Pietersen on reaching 150 at the Oval, September 2005) and pp. 124, 133, 138, 152, 218 and 310; Roger Mann Collection pp. vi, 1, 31 and 74; Willy Vanderson, front cover (Frank Tyson bowling at Sydney, December 1954); Wisden Cricket Monthly p. 35

Bernard Hollowood cartoon (front cover) reproduced with permission of Punch Ltd, www.punch.co.uk.

Text permissions

Aurum Press p. 333; Collins p. 31; The Cricketer p. 208; The Daily Mail p. 268; Faber & Faber p. 232; Frederick Muller p. 47; HarperCollins Publishers Ltd © David Gower 1992 p. 195; HarperCollins Publishers Ltd © David Rayvern Allen 1994 p. 94; Heinemann (Kingswood Press) p. 341; Hodder Headline pp. 218, 348; Hutchinson p. 105; The Lutterworth Press p. 64; Eric Midwinter pp. 10, 13; Nelson Thornes Ltd p. 169; Penguin Group UK pp. 289, 310, 320, 330; Random House (Stanley Paul) pp. 1, 35, 45, 51; Souvenir Press Ltd pp. 13, 19; Weidenfeld and Nicholson pp. 187, 193, 194; All Wisden quotations are reproduced by kind permission of John Wisden & Co Ltd.